Policing Shanghai 1927–1937

A

Philip E. Lilienthal

■ ■ ■

B O O K

The Philip E. Lilienthal imprint honors
special books in commemoration of a
man whose work at the University of
California Press from 1954 to 1979 was
marked by dedication to young authors
and to high standards in the field of
Asian Studies. Friends, family, authors,
and foundations have together endowed
the Lilienthal Fund, which enables the
Press to publish under this imprint
selected books in a way that reflects the
taste and judgment of a great and
beloved editor.

Policing Shanghai 1927–1937

FREDERIC WAKEMAN, JR.

University of California Press

BERKELEY   LOS ANGELES   LONDON

University of California Press
Berkeley and Los Angeles, California

University of California Press, Ltd.
London, England

© 1995 by
The Regents of the University of California

First Paperback Printing 1996

Library of Congress Cataloging-in-Publication Data

Wakeman, Frederic E.
    Policing Shanghai 1927–1937 / Frederic Wakeman, Jr.
        p.   cm.
    Includes bibliographical references and index.
    ISBN 0-520-20761-0
    1. Shanghai (China)—Social conditions. 2. China—History—1928–
1937. 3. Police—China—Shanghai. I. Title.
DS796.S2W4 1995
951'.132—dc20   93-42415

Printed in the United States of America
9 8 7 6 5 4 3 2 1

To Sarah and Matthew Wakeman

owing page 194

If protection rackets represent organized crime at its smoothest then warmaking and statemaking—quintessential protection rackets with advantage of legitimacy—qualify as our largest examples of organized crime.

Charles Tilly,
"Warmaking and Statemaking as Organized Crime"

Police systems exhibit an enormous inertial strength over time; their forms endure even across the divides of war, violent revolution, and shattering economic and social change. The fact is that people seem to become habituated to certain procedures and organizational patterns; they do not know what else to do even when given the chance.

David Bayley,
"The Police and Political Development in Europe"

If such a posture of retreat from actual control endures for an appreciable length of time, it may actually become customary practice.

Benjamin Schwartz,
"The Primacy of the Political Order in East Asian Societies"

Contents

Author's Note

Currency Values in Shanghai, ca. 1930

Chinese yuan	Taels	U.S. dollars	Pound sterling
Ch. $18.00*	Tls. 15	US $5.00	£ 1.00

Shanghai Areal Measures, ca. 1930

Shanghai *mu*	Square meters	Acres
1 *mu*	674 meters square	0.1667 acre

*Unless identified as "US $" or "Ch. $," the dollars quoted in the text are Mexican silver dollars, roughly equivalent to Chinese yuan.

Acknowledgments

Support for the research that resulted in this book was provided by the Center for Chinese Studies, the Committee on Research, the Institute of East Asian Studies, and the Walter and Elise Haas Chair endowment at Berkeley; by the Committee on Scholarly Communication with the People's Republic of China, by the National Endowment for the Humanities, and by the United States Information Agency.

I would like to express my sincere gratitude to the many archivists, librarians, and scholars who helped gain access to materials for me at the Beijing National Library, the Beijing University Library, the Bancroft Library (Berkeley), the British Library, the Bureau of Investigation Archives (Taiwan), the Cambridge University Library, the Center for Chinese Studies Library (Berkeley), the East Asian Library (Columbia), the East Asiatic Library (Berkeley), the Government Documents Library (Berkeley), the Harvard-Yenching Institute, the Hoover Institution and Archives, the Library of Congress, the Military Reference Division of the U.S. National Archives, the Modern History Research Institute Library of the Chinese Academy of Social Sciences, the New York Public Library, the Public Record Office, the Second National Archives (Nanjing), the Shanghai Academy of Social Sciences, the Shanghai Municipal Archives, the Shanghai Municipal Library, the Wason Collection (Cornell), and the Yale University Library.

Especially helpful in this regard were Cai Shaoqing, Annie K. Chang, C. P. Chen, Ch'iu Jung-hua, Chou Han-ch'in, Feng Shoucai, Suzanne Gold, Han Weizhi, Hu Sheng, Huang Miaozhen, Richard C. Kagan, the late Li Zongyi, Bih-jaw Lin, Ma Changlin, Ni Mengxiong, Shi Meiding, Sun Jiang, Wang Dehua, Wang Qingcheng, Martin Wilbur, Wu Tiqian,

Xu Youfang, Zhang Zhongli, Zheng Zu'an, Zhu Hong, Zhu Qingzuo, and Zhu Weizheng.

Research assistance was provided by a number of Chinese history graduate students at Berkeley. These include Douglas Fix, David Fraser, Blaine Gaustad, Shang Quan, Jeffrey Wasserstrom, Timothy Weston, Xu Guomin, and Yu Maochun. I owe a very great debt to my two professional research assistants: Susan Stone, who helped copyedit an earlier version of this book, and Elinor Levine, who provided assistance with tables, charts, appendixes, miscellaneous research, collation, and final compilation of the manuscript.

Scholarly recommendations and suggestions were provided by colleagues such as Sherman Cochran, Sue Farquhar, Bryna Goodman, Thomas Grunfeld, Brian Martin, Marcia Ristaino, and Carolyn Wakeman. Members of the Berkeley Shanghai Seminar, supported by the Luce Foundation, also contributed to the revision of the book, especially to the section on crime and social control. I am particularly grateful to my father, Frederic Wakeman, Sr., and to Professors Christian Henriot, Emily Honig, Nicholas Riasanovsky, and Irwin Scheiner for their close and careful reading of the manuscript. Sandy Freitag, the developmental editor, did a superb job of catching superfluities and tightening the narrative. Finally, I wish to thank Professor Wen-hsin Yeh for her valuable insights and comments about many of the topics analyzed in this study, and for her encouragement to study materials on the Chinese police in the first place.

Contents

Photographs following page 194

If protection rackets represent organized crime at its smoothest then warmaking and statemaking—quintessential protection rackets with advantage of legitimacy—qualify as our largest examples of organized crime.

Charles Tilly,
"Warmaking and Statemaking as Organized Crime"

Police systems exhibit an enormous inertial strength over time; their forms endure even across the divides of war, violent revolution, and shattering economic and social change. The fact is that people seem to become habituated to certain procedures and organizational patterns; they do not know what else to do even when given the chance.

David Bayley,
"The Police and Political Development in Europe"

If such a posture of retreat from actual control endures for an appreciable length of time, it may actually become customary practice.

Benjamin Schwartz,
"The Primacy of the Political Order in East Asian Societies"

Introduction

China has so far experienced three revolutions in the twentieth century. The first was in 1911 when the Manchus' Qing dynasty was overthrown and the warlord-republic was instituted under the presidency of Yuan Shi-kai. The second was in 1927 when the Nationalists conquered South China, broke with the Communists, and established a party-republic under the chairmanship of Chiang Kai-shek. The third revolution took place in 1949 when the Communists defeated the Nationalists and unified all of mainland China under a people's republic ruled by Mao Zedong.

This book is about the second revolution and the ten years of Nationalist (Guomindang) rule between 1927 and 1937, when war finally broke out with Japan. During that decade the central government in Nanjing was dominated by Chiang Kai-shek, who tried to carry out the program of national construction left unfulfilled by Sun Yat-sen at the time of his death in 1925. A central feature of that program was the establishment of a special Chinese municipality in Shanghai, which was by the second quarter of the century China's only real metropolis. Shanghai was also partly under foreign rule, and Chiang Kai-shek's determination to create an effective Nationalist urban government there was partly to prove to the world that the Chinese deserved to recover their sovereignty over the treaty ports and rule themselves.

The Chinese Special Municipality of Shanghai thus became something of a test case for the Guomindang régime. Could the Nationalists actually set up and administer a modern municipal administration that would come to grips with such a turbulent, unruly, and crime-ridden city as Shanghai? In the eyes of Chiang Kai-shek and the Shanghai mayors he appointed, the key to the problem was the Chinese police force, which was only one among several law enforcement agencies that sought to bring law and order to the city in its various concessions, zones, and districts. Could the Nationalists constitute a modern police force, modeled on the best law enforcement agencies in the world, that would cope efficiently with Shanghai's public health, housing, traffic, commercial licensing, entertainment, labor union, kidnapping, censorship, indigence, narcotics, prostitution, and racketeering problems, while simultaneously pursuing a program of recovering national sovereignty over the concessions and controlling popular disorder and unrest within the Chinese sectors of the city?

By the Nanjing régime's own reckoning, the police agents of the Public Security Bureau were to be the Nationalists' primary instrument for imposing their new revolutionary political order upon China's largest urban conglomerate, long the imperialists' key outpost and a center of comprador capitalism on the one hand, and a stronghold of the Communist labor movement on the other. By focusing on the efforts of the Chinese police to transform Shanghai into a Guomindang showplace during their decade of rule, this study hopes to clarify other aspects of the Nationalist régime, including the relationship between the central party-state and Republican local elites, the role of clandestine organizations and criminal syndicates in delegitimating national political structures, the balance between police and civilian power in an urban setting, and the evolution of municipal political organizations under the extraordinary stress of military invasion and occupation.

For, as we shall see, any effort to read revolutionary intentionality back into the ten years of Nationalist rule instantly runs athwart the Japanese-shaped outcome of this critical decade. Because we know that the Manchurian Railway and Marco Polo Bridge Incidents loom ahead, it is extremely difficult for the historian to perceive 1927 without anticipating the military debacle that the Nationalists were to suffer in 1937 when 250,000 Chinese troops were lost during the Battle of Shanghai. But if we can for awhile look at this decade without preordaining its end, we can begin to appreciate how the Nationalists acted upon Shanghai's complex society, and how their régime, even at the national level, was in turn influenced and changed by the city itself. We will see, in effect, the Republican bureaucratization of certain aspects of urban society, and a corresponding and deeply consequential social transformation of the régime by which it was ruled. We will understand, I hope, why the second revolution in the end was bound to fail.

Twentieth-century China's political history has been construed in many different ways by Western historians, but four themes have prevailed: the disintegration of an imperial order followed by military chaos and disunity; the quest for a new political order under Nationalist rule that was aborted by the Japanese invasion of 1937; the building of a populist revolutionary movement led by the Communists in the countryside; and the search for a new national identity punctuated by the failure of democratic movements in the cities. Each of those four historical readings, faithful to the uncertainties of the 1990s, emphasizes discontinuity and incompleteness.

In contrast, this book is about connections and continuities—the affiliations that link the late Qing reforms with Guomindang integration and socialist consolidation; the networks that enmesh racketeers and revolutionaries together; the affinities that tether policemen to criminals; the bonds that develop between secret agents on opposite sides of the fence; and the processes that tie together the Tianjin police of 1910 with the Shanghai Public Security Bureau of 1931 and the Beijing Committee on State Security of 1989. Above all this study is about the lamentable durability of governmentalized autocracy, whether Nationalist or Communist: it suggests the staying power of bureaucratic instruments of control and coercion that are institutionalized in the modern police state.

1

THE CONTEXT

1   Law and Order

The criminal is naturally demoralized. He is attracted to a place not so much by the opportunities he finds to commit crime as by the attractions the place offers to him to lead a life that appeals to his distorted mind—women, gambling, and other forms of depraved amusement. . . . It is certain that Shanghai will continue to be highly criminal till such time as it is thoroughly cleansed of its worst evils: (1) illicit trade in opium, (2) gambling, (3) general looseness in forms of life, all of which not only attract and hold criminals to the place, but put in the hands of the principals enough money to maintain hordes of loafers in their pay and to defeat justice.

Shanghai Municipal Police Commissioner F. W. Gerrard,
October 30, 1930

In 1933 several writers were asked to describe their visions of Shanghai in the future. Three of these visions suggest the activities in Shanghai that competed for priority in the decades we will examine. Invoking a popular image of a "heaven" built on top of a "hell," Ming San responded satirically. In the future—he imagined—Shanghai would have movie houses equipped with hot and cold running water; in addition to showing movies of "fragrant and voluptuous sensuality," the theaters would feature international dance troupes demonstrating the latest fox-trot steps in the nude. In each public park there would be a special office to teach the practice of kissing to young men and women who had not yet attained their majority. In addition to theaters there would be a host of circuses, athletic stadiums, horse tracks, greyhound racing tracks, bull fight rings, and cock fighting arenas. The courts would handle five hundred divorce cases a day. "There is no doubt that the future Shanghai will be a heaven on top of a heaven."[1]

Liu Mengfei—another writer speculating on Shanghai's future—was probably not amused by Ming San's erotic tongue-in-cheek fantasy. "Shanghai," he sternly wrote, "is a vise compressing the exploited classes. It is a powder keg filled with contradictions." For Liu the fundamental contrast in Shanghai was between "upper class Chinese" (*gaoteng Huaren*) and the shriveled "beggars of the street" (*malu biesan*); the elementary confrontation was between the bourgeoisie and the proletariat—

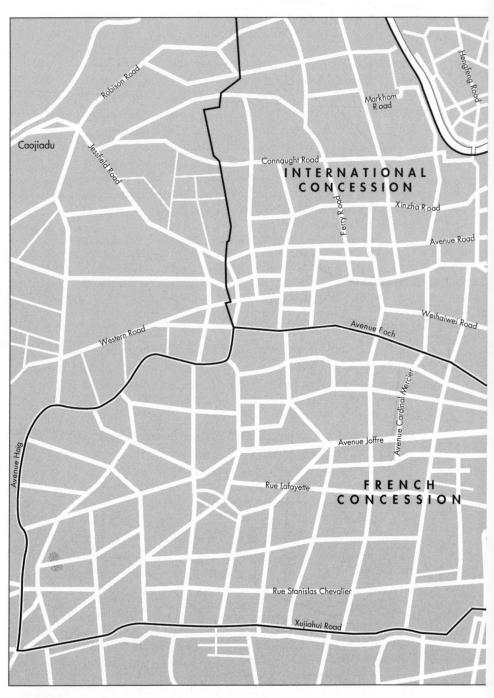

Central Shanghai, 1937

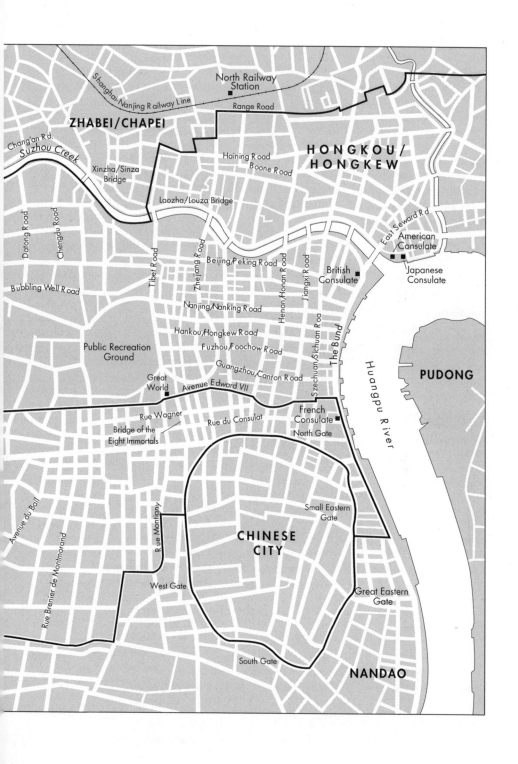

those "black insects" crouching beside the machinery in the mills of their ironhanded masters. The imperialists would redouble their tyrannical efforts and the warlords would continue to put the country on the auction block, but the time was soon to arrive for an end to the old Shanghai and the rise of a new city when the dawn would come and the "black insects" would shout victoriously, "Long live the New China."[2]

Wang Xiuhe's futuristic vision of the New China was much less apocalyptic and much more concerned with the construction of an orderly municipal environment by the Chinese themselves. He saw two possibilities for the Shanghai of the future: complete westernization or independent nationalization. In the first scenario the International Settlement grows to engulf the entire municipality, where the native Shanghainese turn into a spiritless, listless group only to be pitied by their foreign masters. In the second scenario, the municipal authorities of the Chinese government implement Sun Yat-sen's plan for national reconstruction. Gradually the International Settlement declines into a cold and deserted area, and eventually the foreigners return the concessions to the Chinese in order to maintain their trading relations with the country as a whole. Which of these two roads will Shanghai take? According to Wang Xiuhe, the outcome would depend upon the vigor with which the Chinese residents of Shanghai exerted themselves to control their own destiny and create a new civic culture free of vice and crime.[3]

Perceiving Crime and Disorder

Yet Chinese residents faced formidable obstacles to this third vision. For instance, Shanghai crime rates soared in the early 1920s. In 1922 there were 47 armed robberies reported in the International Settlement. Two years later the number had increased more than fourfold to 204 armed robberies, and by 1926 there were 448 instances of this felony—an increase of more than 950 percent within five years.[4] The number of robbers arrested during this period also increased nearly threefold, which was not nearly at the same rate as the number of armed robberies committed. (See Figure 1.) By 1927, official reports spoke of a "crime epidemic" in the Lake Tai area just outside of Shanghai, where "armed marauders" robbed, kidnapped, and murdered the inhabitants.[5] Within the Settlement there was a striking rise in the number of ax slayings both in crimes of domestic passion and in more public deaths related to robbery or revenge.[6] And in parts of the Chinese section of the city known as Zhabei (Chapei), robberies were so severe that certain precincts felt their forces inadequate to cope with the crime wave.[7] (See Figure 2.)

The causes of this statistically confirmed disorder and criminality (the

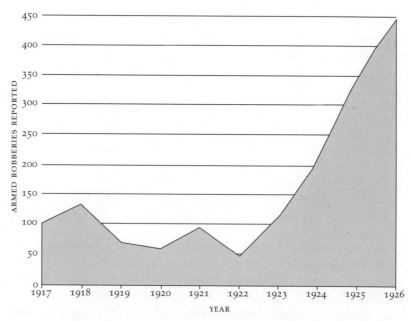

FIGURE 1. Reports of armed robberies, Shanghai International Settlement. Source: *CWR*, 11 May 1927, 226.

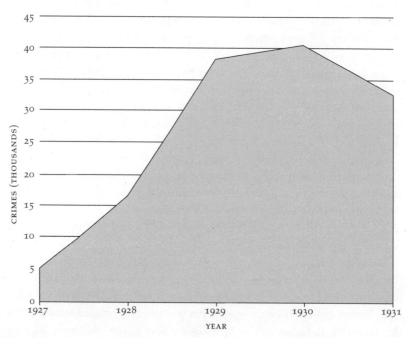

FIGURE 2. Crimes recorded, Greater Shanghai. Source: *China Yearbook 1934*.

two were often confused, especially by Chinese law enforcement officials) were multifarious.[8] Western journalists—who took a certain hard-boiled pride in the opinion that "Shanghai has become the crime center of the Orient"—usually attributed it to the prevalence of warlordism in China.[9]

> The army is the finest school of training in crime. Nobody in
> China joins the army unless he is of the semi-criminal, loafer class,
> unable to earn an honest living. In the army he learns the use of
> firearms, and that knowledge he turns to his own account. Instead
> of any patriotic activity, he leaves the army and preys on his fel-
> low men, using his army training to get a living at the point of
> a gun.[10]

The leading foreign businessmen (or "taipans") of Shanghai, on the other hand, simplistically associated criminality with the wave of radical strike activity and revolutionary mobilization that occurred before, during, and after the May Thirtieth Movement of 1925, when the populace tried in vain to push back foreign privileges in China.[11] The foreign "griffins" believed that "Bolshevik propaganda" aroused "the greed and covetousness of the proletarian classes" in order to destroy all respect "for property and the rights of others," a belief shared by the International Settlement police (Shanghai Municipal Police or SMP).[12] In that sense, revolutionary political activities were treated as a form of urban crime.[13]

In contrast to Shanghai's foreign businessmen, Chinese Nationalist officials had a more complex appreciation of the city's lawlessness, commonly identifying crime either with a general lack of social order (*zhixu*) associated with urban commerce and industry, or with Shanghai's position as a semi-colonial treaty port.[14] Eight reasons were usually given for the difficulty of "keeping the peace" (*baoan*) in Shanghai: (1) the city's position as a great entrepôt;[15] (2) its openness of communications; (3) the complexity of human affairs in the city; (4) industrial expansion; (5) labor agitation; (6) the presence of the International Settlement spread across the middle of the city; (7) the presence of Communists; and (8) the existence of "reactionary elements" (*fandongfenzi*) living within the asylum of the foreign concessions.[16]

Precisely because of its status as the country's major treaty port, Shanghai had by 1927 become a symbol to the new Nationalist régime of the westernized world of international commerce that now occupied China's shores. Shanghai's crime problems seemingly stemmed from its victimization by the imperialists. The lawlessness of the city, after all, was directly related to the extraterritoriality of the foreign concessions, where criminals could flee from arrest by the Chinese authorities for crimes committed in the native parts of the city.[17] But it was also related to the sheer size and relative affluence of the metropolitan population, living in five different major zones under four different sets of rulers. In that respect crime and disorder, which were not clearly distinguished by the new Chinese revolutionary régime after 1927, were linked concurrently to Shanghai's metamorphosis into a city with modern utilities and an entertainment industry (movies, cabarets, brothels, amusement centers) that transformed popular culture in the protective shelter of the foreign concessions.

Issues of urban control emerged clearly from these twin influences of metropolitan growth and foreign concessions. Shanghai's growth was unmistakable. The population of the city almost tripled between 1910 and 1930. By October 1930, the registered inhabitants of the city totaled 2,980,650. Of these, 971,397 Chinese and 36,471 foreigners lived in the International Settlement, 434,885 Chinese and 12,335 foreigners in the French Concession, and 1,516,092 Chinese and 9,470 foreigners in the Chinese Municipality.[18] During those three decades of human growth the city underwent a profound physical transformation.

> It might be said that reinforced concrete and the Electricity Department have made a new Shanghai. From the fluttering little experiment for which the rate payers voted Taels 80,000 in 1893, the Electricity Department has become a giant which outrivals Glasgow and Manchester, lights and heats a city of a million and a half people, drives their trams and runs a hundred mills.[19] Meanwhile, reinforced concrete has given the builders an easy and expeditious medium with which to satisfy the house famine. . . . But already some owners are tearing down houses not ten years old to replace them with huge blocks of flats. With land even three or four miles from the Bund [the street running along the Shanghai riverfront] selling for eight or ten thousand taels a mow [7,620 square feet], it is necessary to economize in space.[20]

The International Settlement was incandescent at night, "a vast crucible of electric flame," its new twenty-story skyscrapers anchored to rafts of concrete that floated on long pilings in the alluvial mud below.[21] The red neon lights along Nanking Road illuminated a new urban landscape of grand hotels and huge commercial palaces (the Hong Kong and Shanghai Bank building on the Bund was the second largest bank house in the world at the time) that altered the cultural lives of its inhabitants.[22] A long-time foreign resident wrote in 1926 that

> Even twenty years ago . . . life was spacious and slow-moving; at the spring races we took up our carpets for the summer and at the autumn races we put them down for the winter; dinner parties broke up at 11:00, except on the rare occasions of a ball; there were no supper rooms, no night life, and the visit of a third-rate theatrical company was almost as much an event as would be the appearance of a dodo.[23]

Crime and Entertainment

During the civil wars of the early 1920s, a new form of night life appeared under the curfew imposed by the warlords' police forces: "Cabarets, night-clubs, Chinese sing-song houses [where story-telling prostitutes entertained], Japanese geisha houses, gambling houses and brothels were packed with polyglot pleasure-seekers who, locked in by the curfew, caroused all night and struggled home at dawn, when the ban lifted."[24]

Other Chinese entertainment patterns changed, too. In 1923 the Victrola was introduced; Shanghai gentry began renting gramophones from individuals who would come to their houses and operate them for a fee.[25] And as early as 1903 moving picture shows started to play a big part in the life of Shanghai people.[26] That year a Spaniard named A. Ramos began to show silent films, hiring an Indian to stand in front of the Shengping Teahouse on Fuzhou Road and play cymbals and a horn while the title of the day's showing was shouted out to the assembled crowds.

Five years later, Ramos built Shanghai's first movie house, the 250-seat Hongkew (Hongkou) Theater, at the intersection of Haining and Zhapu Roads.[27] Ramos steadily expanded his cinematic domain; between 1927 and 1932 there was a tremendous growth of second-run theaters as well. In 1930 there were thirty-three to thirty-six movie houses, while the illustrated newspaper *Dianying huabao* (*Movies Illustrated*) claimed to have a circulation of over one million readers.[28] By 1933 the Da Guangming Theater, which was refurbished for $1 million and seated 1,951, and the Da Shanghai, which was bought for $800,000 and seated 1,629, were absolutely central to the entertainment life of the city.[29] Together they provided an utterly engaging arena for lovers young and old, who could find romance on the silver screen above while courting in the darkened seats below. As one observer commented, "The real salvation of the Shanghai suitor [given the lack of room for privacy] is the moving picture theater."[30] They also served as palaces of high-society culture—at least for the foreign community. "Shanghai did not offer much along the line of sophisticated entertainment. There was still no opera, no lectures to speak of, no Western stage. The first showing of a Hollywood movie under these circumstances assumed the proportions of a major event on the social calendar with all the consuls and taipans attending in full evening dress."[31]

It is difficult to exaggerate the centrality of the cinema to Shanghai's mass culture. Movie actors and actresses were national celebrities and popular idols. Ruan Lingyu (1910–35), one of Shanghai's great silent film actresses who was often called "China's Garbo," impressed one quintessential image after another on the public's mind in her twenty-nine film appearances: writer, factory worker, wealthy society woman, social butterfly, flower girl, prostitute, nun, and beggar. Gossip about her divorce ultimately drove Ruan to take her own life, when, it was said, all of Shanghai wept.[32]

Western theater, Hollywood movies, and "modern" Chinese films were also readily taken as signs of degeneration. Movies like *Shanghai hua* (*Three Shanghai Girls*, 1926) seemed deliberately designed to promote the sales of modern products and to advertise the love mores of their westernized characters.[33] They were thus despised by cultural conservatives as seductive media that drew provincial girls into the sordid life of the big city, as Ding Ling's first published short story, "Meng Ke," depicted in 1927.[34] Qian Zhongshu's satirical masterpiece, *Wei cheng*, portrayed the influence of movies in cosmetic terms, like the foreign rouge plastered on the face of a teenage girl riding a Shanghai trolley car: "The girl's book covers were all decorated with pictures of movie stars. Though she was no more than 16 or 17, her face was made up like a mask, kneaded out of gobs of rouge and powder."[35]

If Shanghai had been transformed into a sexual marketplace as a result of overthrowing the old order, then why had there been a political revolution in the first place? Mao Dun captured a young progressive's dismay over the vulgarity of this change in an ambivalent, angry story about a political prisoner released after the Northern Expedition of 1926–28, when the Nationalists attempted to unify China:

> The world had certainly changed. The girls had cut their hair and developed protruding pairs of breasts. Their faces were smeared with red or white, while their arms and legs were quite bare. Motion picture theaters had increased in number. They displayed wordy advertisements: "New drama of mystery and heroism." What lay beyond all this [the former political prisoner] did not know. One thing was certain. There had been a revolution, but the revolution had already proceeded beyond the wildest reaches of his imagination. He stood stupidly at a tram station on the street corner. All around him were perfumed women with gleaming arms

and legs, the rumble of vehicles, the noise of people, the arresting green and red electric signs. An indescribable disgust arose in him.[36]

Westernization, in this extreme form, represented the debasement of Shanghai's Chinese population, which was assailed on all sides by the temptations of gambling, narcotics, and prostitution,[37] now vices for the masses.[38]

During the early twentieth century, for example, prostitution in Shanghai became a mass industry in which lower-class commercial whoring came to overshadow high-class courtesanship. By 1915 there was probably one prostitute among every sixteen females in the foreign settlements.[39] Edna Lee Booker provides a vivid description of Northern Sichuan Road in the 1920s:

> Narrow alleyways dimly lighted by red lights hanging over the doorways of low, tenement-like buildings stretched into the darkness. It was lurid. Figures slump along: Chinese girls with painted cheeks; Japanese women with calcimined faces of the Yoshiwara, Tokyo type; faded hags of almost any nationality. . . . Jazz notes from half a dozen brightly lit cabarets and bars . . . broke through the night. . . . Russian girls from Harbin, whose stock phrase was "my Prince, ples, you buy little Sonya small bottle vine" were there. American girls from the old Barbary Coast and women from the dives of Marseilles acted as hostesses.[40]

Whereas cabarets in the foreign concessions closed at 2:00 A.M. (except for Saturday nights, when they stayed open until dawn), the Chinese teahouses (*chalou*) virtually never shut down. And in the massage parlors along Avenue Joffre and Range Road, where Chinese masseuses had begun to displace the White Russian women who introduced these sexual services in the first place, conditions were "simply scandalous."[41]

Shanghai's range of erotic attractions may have entranced short-term visitors like the German film director Josef von Sternberg, who perceived the amusement resort Great World (Da·shijie), located at the corner of Thibet Road and Avenue Edward VII, as a monument of exotic, if somewhat sinister, spectacles. "The establishment had six floors to provide distraction for the milling crowd, six floors that seethed with life and all the commotion and noise that go with it, studded with every variety of entertainment Chinese ingenuity had contrived."[42] But long-time residents such as the American newspaper editor John B. Powell were deeply offended by gangster-run amusement resorts like the Great World, where free beer was given away to all visitors—including children under ten years of age—on Sunday afternoons. "The shows inside were not fit for words, and yet they were open to children." Such "obscene entertainments" were "polluting the public mind."[43]

Chinese criminology experts also blamed the big "exhibition halls" (*youyi chang*) such as the Great World or the World of Blessed Immortals (Fuxian shijie) for offering the middle and lower classes unhealthy amusements that fostered criminal behavior. Noting the lack of routine public intercourse between the many different classes of Shanghai's "extraordinarily complex" society, sociologists also remarked upon the way in which people clustered into small groups that became their own points of reference, encouraging criminal behavior and lacking a broader and more communal moral sense.[44] Moreover, interviews with convicted criminals demonstrated how intimately felony was connected with the numerous "amusements" that Shanghai had to offer. Time and again it was shown that white-collar crime such as embezzlement was linked to houses of ill fame, where young clerks and apprentices often fell in love with the prostitutes and borrowed or stole to spend time together with them or try to persuade them to run away.[45]

Crime and Extraterritoriality

But to most Chinese living in Shanghai, these sociological explanations for the city's terrible crime waves, and especially for its robberies and murders, were probably far less compelling than the extraterritorial issue.[46] The Nationalists firmly believed that the enormous narcotics, gambling, and prostitution industries of the city all depended upon the protection of the consular system of extraterritoriality set up under the "unequal treaties" of the nineteenth century.[47] And while these forms of vice might be tolerated as necessary diversions for the city's sophisticated populace, even the most jaded urbanite had to be dismayed by the underworld's more violent manifestations in the form of kidnapping, robbery, and homicide committed by criminals who based themselves in the French Concession or International Settlement.[48]

The French Concession was particularly visible in this regard, especially when it came to vices that the more prudish authorities of the International Settlement had difficulty tolerating. "The tendency at the present time is that when anything socially unsound is discovered in the International Settlement," wrote one observer, "it is immediately removed to the French Concession, where it can comfortably settle down

and therefore the French Concession in Shanghai today has become, mor-
ally speaking, the dirtiest spot in the Orient." Indeed, the French Concession had the largest opium dens, the fanciest casinos, the biggest brothels,
and the most brazen prostitutes.[49]

> When one takes a stroll along the Rue Montigny shortly after 7:00
> in the afternoon, one will find a long row of girls ranging from the
> Great World amusement ground to as far as Nan-yang ch'iao. The
> French Concession police are doing nothing whatever to stop this
> immoral traffic. . . . [By contrast,] in the International Settlement,
> whenever such girls see policemen, they try to run away.

Most of this laxity was attributed to French attitudes about all their
colonies: "let the 'natives' go to degradation and demoralization; their fate
is no concern of the French nation."[50] But it was also seen as a result of
the foreigners' special privileges under the unequal treaties system. As
one of Shanghai's Chinese police chiefs put it, the greatest "obstacle" to
law and order in Shanghai was the system of *tebie qu* (special zones, i.e.,
the concessions).[51] "Every person who performs criminal or treasonable
acts makes the special zones his base area." All that a criminal had to do
was to step over the concession border to slip from sight before arrest was
possible.[52] In the end the only way to get rid of these "evils" would be to
abolish extraterritoriality altogether.[53]

As the Nationalists reasoned, the most persuasive argument for abolishing extraterritoriality would be a demonstration of effective law enforcement within the Chinese sectors of the divided city. Consequently, a
top priority of the new Special Municipality of Shanghai that the Nationalists established on July 7, 1927, was to engender and guarantee "public
safety" (*gongan*).[54] This would not only bring "peace" (*anning*) and "order" (*zhixu*) to the native inhabitants of the city, protecting their lives
and property from criminal harm; it would also prove to the world that
the Chinese deserved to recover control over the foreign settlements for
themselves.[55]

The Public Security Bureau, established in Shanghai on July 22, 1927,
was thus intended to be one of the primary instruments of the Nationalists' new order. As an agent of revolutionary modernization, it would
help build a strong and honest municipal administration, create a healthy
and orderly urban environment, and educate a twentieth-century citizenry to assume proper civic responsibilities.[56] As a force representing the
Chinese people and the new national government, it would also strive to
recover long-lost sovereign rights by establishing the authority of the

Chinese state over those parts of the city it ruled. Its efforts to bring law and order to Republican Shanghai were thereby viewed as a crucial test of the overall effectiveness of the new régime. In the Nationalists' eyes, a prime critical index of the Guomindang revolution itself would be the success or failure of their own Public Security Bureau, Shanghai's Chinese police.[57]

2 From Constabulary to Police

Our patrol bureau has received a legal commission to manage
patrolling and local control matters within the city and outside
in the suburbs. We have hitherto heard that there are various
notorious villains and rowdies (*pigun*). . . . Four or five form a
group, and they gather in tea houses and wine shops, calling
themselves *chijiangcha* (drink-and-talk tea). They form groups
that gather together to swindle, behaving perversely and
illegally, bringing calamity upon the locale. . . . We ought
immediately to seize those aforenamed and take serious steps,
being indulgent toward the ignorant and unforgiving toward
the intractable, who will be executed.

> A late Qing Patrol Bureau announcement,
> *Shanghai yanjiu ziliao*

Shanghai's original Chinese constabulary, the Green Standard, dated
back to the 1860s, when the city's population swelled with refugees from
the Taiping occupation of eastern Jiangsu.[1] While a small force of about
two hundred regular garrison guards (*yingxun* or *chengxun*) defended the
seven city gates under a chiliarch (*qianzong*) and occasionally arrested
known robbers, it was felt that a special law enforcement squad was
needed to maintain order and cope with the immigrants who had recently
flocked into Shanghai.[2] Consequently, the Qing circuit intendant (daotai)
established in 1860 a Patrol Preventive Baojia Bureau (Xunfang baojia ju)
under a chief patrol officer (*zongxun*) whose office was located in the
Ever-Normal Granary (Changping cang) next to the district yamen in
Nanshi (South Market, or Nandao). This bureau and its substations were
manned by regular soldiers (*bingding*) transferred from the provincial
governor's garrison, but now under the separate command of the chief
patrol officer.[3]

The mandate of the Patrol Bureau from the outset was quite clear—
and not that different from one of the central tasks of the later Public
Security Bureau: to establish order in a burgeoning entrepôt attractive to
liumang (vagabonds) who clustered together in criminal gangs. Although
the functional distinction between this new constabulary and the regular Green Standard garrison forces blurred, the Shanghai Patrol Bureau

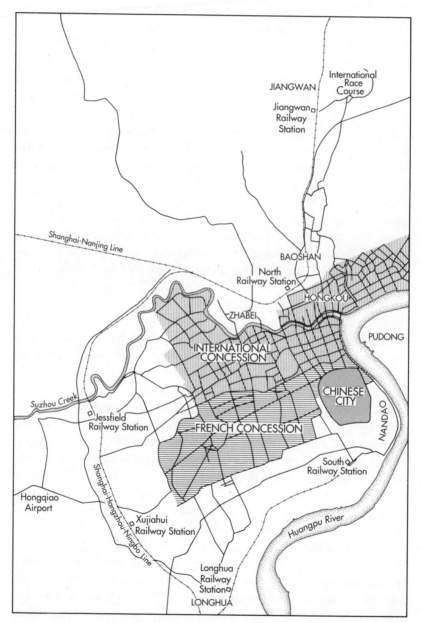

Shanghai Greater Metropolitan Area, 1937

effectively worked against conventional robbers located around the periphery of the city during the 1880s and early 1890s.[4]

Early Reform Efforts

The transformation from a government constabulary to a modern metropolitan force commenced in 1898 and stemmed from two different impulses: a top-down bureaucratic initiative to replace the old *baojia* mutual
responsibility system with regular police patrolmen or *xunbu* ("patrol and
arrest," a term used by the Qing government to describe the military
police who were supposed to keep public order on the country's highways);[5] and a parallel bottom-up gentry-led campaign to develop, in step
with urban expansion and road construction, a police force clearly influenced by the police systems in the foreign concessions.[6] In each case, the
policing organ was under the management of a board of works (*gongbu*)
that supervised the building and patrolling of the expanding system of
roads throughout the International Settlement, French Concession, and
Chinese municipalities.[7] Thus, down to the Second World War, the name
of the International Settlement's Shanghai Municipal Police force in Chinese was *Gongbu ju xunbu fang* (Patrol and Arrest Office of the Bureau
of the Board of Works).[8]

Gentry-led police initiatives preceded bureaucratic reforms. The creation of a Chinese counterpart to the International Settlement's Board of
Works in the late nineteenth century accompanied the formation of new
municipal institutions like fire brigades, which were closely connected
with merchant guilds.[9] Guild leadership in turn was channeled through
local bureaus (*ju*) specially created to collect taxes, administer military
installations, and oversee telegraph and postal facilities. This network of
local elite-managed institutions, which historians have identified as a new
"public order" (*gong*), led to the first independent Chinese municipal organizations in Shanghai when Magistrate Huang Chengxuan in 1894 ordered the building of roads along the Huangpu River south of the French
Concession.[10] In December 1895 a South Market Road Works Bureau
(Nanshi malu gongcheng ju) was opened in the old Chinese portion of
Shanghai to take charge of the maintenance of the new roads.[11]

That bureau in turn opened up a Patrol and Arrest Office (Xunbu fang)
that for the first time had its own policemen, quite apart from the army
recruits transferred over from the provincial garrison. According to the
regulations employed to "recruit police" (*zhaobu*) in 1898, candidates had
to be in good health, about thirty years old, familiar with the local dialect,
of good moral character and habits (no smoking, drinking or gambling),
and guaranteed by a local respectable shop or household. Sixty constables

were ultimately selected to patrol, clean, and light Shanghai's streets, as well as to collect taxes on boats, vehicles, and shops in the South Market area.[12]

Meanwhile, the first top-down effort was initiated in 1898, during the Hundred Days of Reform, by the Shanghai circuit intendant, Cai Junjian, who asked the Japanese consul general to recommend an expert on Meiji police reform. A Tokyo police officer named Nagatani Ryūchū reported to Cai shortly afterward, and proceeded to set up a police post in Yang-shupu where he trained 150 soldiers from the circuit intendant's yamen in police procedures. However, Cai Junjian was dismissed after the first Qing reform movement failed in September 1898, and the following year Nagatani packed up and left.[13] Bureaucratic initiative resumed during the second Qing reform movement after April 1901. Orders were issued by the imperial court in July 1901 to governors and viceroys to establish "police brigades" (*xunjingying*) in each province.[14] The fiat was largely ignored by all but the viceroys of Hu-Guang, Liang-Guang, and Zhili.[15]

Viceroy Yuan Shikai in particular quickly saw that modern police forces on the Western or Japanese model provided a new and more effective way of counterbalancing the power of local elites, and especially of the local gentry, who were arrogating judicial and taxation privileges unto themselves.[16] A modern police system, in his view, also provided a means of formally centralizing or integrating the political system, bypassing locally entrenched officials to connect directly with the vast, scattered, rural population of China.[17] In 1902 Yuan established a five-hundred-man police force in the city of Baoding, southwest of Beijing. Equipped with its own training academy, the Baoding police department was soon overshadowed by the Tianjin police bureau, which was set up by Yuan late in the fall of 1902 after he recovered control over the city from the Allied Forces that had defeated the Boxers.[18] The Tianjin police then became a model for the entire province of Zhili, where local police forces were established under the control of a new Ministry of Police, founded in 1905.[19]

In Beijing itself, police reforms were carried out in the spirit of the Meiji Restoration in Japan, where a system of town constables had given way to a metropolitan police force in Tokyo in 1871.[20] Indeed, the Chinese got their modern word for "police" (*jingcha*) from the Japanese *keisatsu*. The Japanese inspiration for the development of the modern Chinese police, however, was not unalloyed; it carried with it a distinct German strain. Prussian police officials strongly influenced the curriculum of the Tokyo Police Academy, which graduated over a thousand sergeants and inspectors during the six years just before and after the revision of treaties with Japan in 1899 that allowed foreigners the privilege of residing in the interior of Japan.[21] Part of the Japanese police officer training program, which included the teaching of English to special officers assigned as interpreters to local police stations, had been intended to prevent antiforeign incidents from occurring once the foreigners and the Japanese began to commingle.[22]

The best known of the Japanese experts brought to advise the Qing was a "continental adventurer" (*tairiku rōnin*) named Kawashima Naniwa, who had qualified as an interpreter of Chinese in the Koakai (Rise Asia Society) language school. After the Boxer Uprising he became head of the police in Beijing's Japanese section, and then assumed directorship of a school to train Chinese in Japanese police methods, working closely with the Manchu Prince Su, who became head of the national Police Bureau during the late Qing reforms in 1910.[23] The impulse to establish a centralized national police administration thus stemmed from the strong statist impulses of establishment reformers who believed that the Japanese Meiji régime was the best model to follow either to preserve the dynasty or to save the country.

Meanwhile, in Shanghai the two processes—bureaucrat-led and gentry-led police reforms—had begun to converge after 1904.[24] The bureaucratic process complied with the central government's decision in 1904 to create a new Board of Police (Xunjing bu), while it also represented an official reaction to Western expansionists in Shanghai who justified the extension of Settlement police authority beyond the agreed-upon boundaries of the foreign concessions by claiming that the Chinese government was failing to police these zones.[25] The gentry reform impulse, on the other hand, was expressed the following year, 1905, in a petition from a group of Shanghai notables proposing that the circuit intendant appoint a board of local gentry and merchants to oversee a general office of works (*chengxiang neiwai zong gongcheng ju*) modeled on that of the International Settlement.[26]

The circuit intendant, Yuan Shuxun, granted the petition, transferring 560 men from the Shanghai garrison to serve as patrolmen (*xunjing*) at the new police station in the Temple of the City God (Chengmiao).[27] At the same time, he extended a ward patrol system to the Chinese portions of the city and replaced the old South Market *baojia* bureaus with a modern Japanese-style police force (*jingcha*).[28] Yuan invited Liu Jingyi, who had graduated from a Japanese police academy, to take over the Qiuzhi Academy, just inside the South Gate of South Market, and turn it into a police academy (*jingcha xuetang*).[29] A group of 216 soldiers and officers from the Hu Army's garrison troops was culled for its strongest members, who then received three months of training and were assigned that winter to local police posts modeled after the Japanese *kōban* or police boxes.[30]

While the police commander (*jingcha zongxun*) was the former head of the *baojia* bureaus, the director of the entire operation was the local magistrate, who controlled an annual budget of Ch. $25,000 drawn from Hu garrison military rations, the city's *baojia* funds, and additional subsidies provided by the circuit intendant. At the same time there was a committee of five gentry managers (*shendong*).[31] The police force—now renamed the Police Headquarters Bureau (Jingcha zongxun ju)—thus had a mixed nature, being drawn from the military, trained by a professional police graduate, commanded by the highest civil authority, and supervised by a committee of local gentrymen.[32]

It is important to recognize that this first attempt at police modernization around the turn of the century was very different in nature from the modernization program that was undertaken twenty-five years later by the Nationalist régime.[33] The Nationalists' efforts were not only inspired by contemporary examples of police professionalization and technocratic crime fighting in England, France, Germany, and the United States; they were also directed toward creating an efficient arm of the state, respecting of but not responsive to local elites.[34] According to a widely used Nationalist police handbook, local and municipal police forces had to consider themselves part of a nationwide police system; they were an instrument of "national ruling power" (*guojia tongzhi quan*) whose duty was to maintain "order" (*zhixu*) and "check selfish individuals' freedom and coercive power."[35] They were, in effect, the state, at least as far as governing the street and neighborhood were concerned.[36] As Chiang Kai-shek put it in his presidential address to the graduating class of 1937 of the Central Police Academy:

> There are two great forces in our country; the army and the police; one is for national defense, and the other is for maintenance of peace. Like a plane, it takes two wings to fly; but because of the complexity of modern police duties and because they are the only public functionaries that are in constant contact with the people, the position of the police is even more important in our society.[37]

The late Qing reformers, by contrast, had certainly wished to emulate the police powers of the Meiji state, but they were much more interested in mobilizing core-area elites to transform local government.[38] Police municipal responsibilities were thus quite broadly framed throughout China during the early 1900s. They included regulation of business, censorship of newspapers, inspection of buildings, oversight of drugstores, issuance of doctor's certificates, and conduct of children's asylums. Police were also responsible for food inspection, sanitation, fire prevention, welfare, education, and the census operation.[39]

The Issue of Gentry Control

At the same time, however, the "committee supervision" (*huiban*) of the Police Headquarters Bureau by the Shanghai gentry linked the South Market police reforms to the local self-government movement of the early 1900s, which was an endogenous form of gentry home rule designed by influential local notables to create a kind of municipal plutocracy.[40] One instrument of this plutocracy was to be an armed Merchants Corps (Shangtuan), which was organized in 1907 on the model of the International Settlement's self-vaunting Volunteer Corps, an urban militia that could be mobilized to protect foreign lives and property.[41]

By 1906 the new Shanghai police system on balance was dominated by the gentry-merchant coalition that had established the original Police Headquarters Bureau. The viceroy of Jiangsu and Zhejiang, Zhou Fu, continued to divert regular government funds to train an additional five hundred *xunjing* under bureaucratic control.[42] But Mu Xiangyao, the actual head of the bureau that dispensed those funds, was an "urban gentryman" (*yishen*); and his purview was extended into Zhabei where a North Market General Roadworks and Patrol Bureau (Beishi malu gongxun zongju) was soon organized to take charge of street construction and police patrols.[43] In short order, therefore, Shanghai's urban gentry and upper-class merchants had managed to gain control of the central headquarters, southern bureau, and northern offices of the new police. Shanghai's local elites clearly won the competition between top-down and community-controlled police systems.

However, the outcome was not to be free of foreign influence. Shanghai's consular authorities balked at seeing a unified Chinese city administration forming under gentry home rule, and the provincial viceroy, Duan Fang, was persuaded to put the Zhabei *xunjing* under the jurisdiction of the imperial administration. In 1907 the Zhabei bureau was folded into the Shanghai General Patrol Bureau (Shanghai xunjing zongju), which reported directly to Circuit Intendant Wang Ruikai.[44] The Chinese saw that decision explicitly as a defense against foreign imperialism.[45]

This did not by any means put an end to gentry efforts to set up their own militia-manned police stations. Simultaneously, a South Market General Works Bureau (Nanshi zong gongcheng ju) was opened under local gentry managers, who established their own police academy and four local precincts.[46] These merchant militiamen played a decisive role in the Revolution of 1911 when Chen Qimei attacked the imperial garrison in Shanghai, and the reward earned by the local notability as a result of the revolutionaries' victory in November 1911 included the amalgamation of all of the city's police bureaus under an "office of local government" (*zizhi gongsuo*) that was renamed the Municipal Government of Zhabei (Zhabei shizheng ting) and given responsibility for administering North and South Markets by the new republican régime.[47]

Although the gentry's militia survived as a relatively autonomous organization, its municipal police powers were short-lived.[48] In 1913, at the time of the "Second Revolution," when Yuan Shikai extended his domination over Central China, the Shanghai Chinese police force was placed under provincial control. A new Songhu Police Prefecture (Songhu jingcha ting) was created directly under the governor's office.[49] It in turn supervised two subprefectures (*fenting*): one for South Market called Hunan, and one for North Market called Zhabei. The two subprefectures, separated geographically by the International Settlement and French Concession, were linked by the office of the Commissioner for the Songhu Water and Land Police (Songhu shuilu jingcha duban). In 1914, just as Yuan Shikai was reducing the gentry organizations in Shanghai to the role of dike maintenance agencies devoid of authority over local police posts, the office of the Commissioner was abolished, and the northern and southern subprefectures were combined into a single prefecture.[50]

The reunified Songhu Police Prefecture was a powerful organ by presidential intention. Emerging victorious from the Second Revolution, Yuan Shikai believed that the two divided subprefectures were too weak, and that a combined force was required to deal with the Shanghai area and its ambitious local elites.[51] The united police prefecture therefore contained a roster of more than three thousand policemen divided into one Peace Preservation Police Brigade (Baoan jingcha dui), four Patrol Police Brigades (Youxun jingcha dui), one River Police Brigade (Shuixun jingcha dui), and one Criminal Investigation Brigade (Zhenjidui).[52] These brigades were scattered among all the precincts of South Market, Zhabei, and Pudong.[53]

In addition to unifying all of the Shanghai police under a single authority, Yuan Shikai attempted to replace its personnel—which came mainly from the Zhejiang-Jiangsu region—with northerners. Yuan appointed as Commissioner for the Songhu Water and Land Police Sa Zhenbing, who brought with him more than a hundred police officers from the Beijing-Tianjin area.[54] From this time on, the Shanghai police force was strongly imbued with the Beiyang warlords' military culture—a flavor which eventually succumbed to local culture in the 1930s despite militarizing efforts by later police chiefs such as General Cai Jingjun.[55]

The presence of these northerners was not at first so evident to Shanghai residents, for whom the Songhu Police Prefecture had a malodorous reputation precisely because most of the patrolmen seemed to be natives of the region. Behind their backs the police were contemptuously called "local dogs" (*ben quan*)—"dogs," because they patrolled like dogs guarding a household; "local," because they were natives of the area and it was considered part of their corvée duties to provide this kind of manpower to the provincial government.[56]

Songhu Prefecture detectives (*zhentan*) were also notorious for extorting money from the innocent, raping young girls, and falsely accusing people of belonging to gangs.[57] According to popular lore from "behind the black screen," their activities were especially noisome during the Yuan Shikai period, when district officials literally got away with murder, covering up their crimes of passion by pressuring local detectives into conniving with *baojia* heads in order to frame the innocent for false rewards.[58]

The image of the Songhu police under Sun Chuanfang's warlord régime was further darkened by their role as strikebreakers and sidewalk executioners.

> [During the winter of 1926–27] an executioner with a two-handed sword paraded the streets. He was accompanied by an officer and a squad of soldiers, and woe betide any Chinaman who causes trouble or commits a crime, for he would be seized and forced down on his knees and in a couple of minutes his head would be rolling in the dust. Cases were tried on the spot and witnesses listened to, and a man might be tried and executed in less than half an hour.[59]

When the Nationalists finally arrived in Shanghai in March 1927, after defeating Sun's forces, "even the Chinese police were so anxious to greet their new masters as plain, peaceful civilians that they tore their uniforms off as fast as they could and threw them into the dark waters of Suzhou Creek."[60]

3   Foul Elements

Police, customs, local government officers, pseudo-reform
citizens, even diplomats, could not resist getting their fingers
covered with the sticky brown poppy juice in get-rich-quick
grabs, and some ended in disgrace, in jail, or in the Whangpoo
River. Crusading newspapermen who dared expose the trade's
machinations were smartly disposed of by professional
removers attached to the merciless underworld organizations
then fighting an underground war for supreme control over
this vast illicit business with customers counted by the scores
of millions.

John Pal, *Shanghai Saga*

By 1920 Shanghai's underworld consisted of an estimated 100,000 hoodlums (*liumang*).[1] This enormous criminal population lived in part off the
illegal trade in opium, which had soared in value after being banned in
1917.[2] Virtually all of these underworld elements belonged to small bands
of gangsters called *bang* or *hui* that were ruled over by a massive criminal
confederation and secret society, originally organized by Yangzi River
boatmen, called the Green Gang (Qingbang).[3]

Organizing Crime

Very little that was illegal—ranging from the organization of beggar
gangs to the procuring of prostitutes and the management of opium parlors—went on without the Green Gang's permission.[4] Criminals who
tried to ignore its hegemony or who flouted its rules ended up with the
Shanghai equivalent of "knee-capping": having every visible tendon severed with a fruit knife before being left to die on the city pavement.[5]
Businessmen who tried to operate without paying off the gang risked being kidnapped or shot, or having their houses bombed and burned. Like
the modern Mafia, the Green Gang was initially the underworld's enforcer.[6] And because it guaranteed access to the illicit receipts of "black
society" and kept the criminal world of Shanghai in a certain state of
order, the gang was more or less tolerated by the International Settlement, French, and Chinese police forces.[7]

Historians agree that the Green Gang's early membership was drawn
mainly from boatmen in the Ming-Qing grain tribute system along the

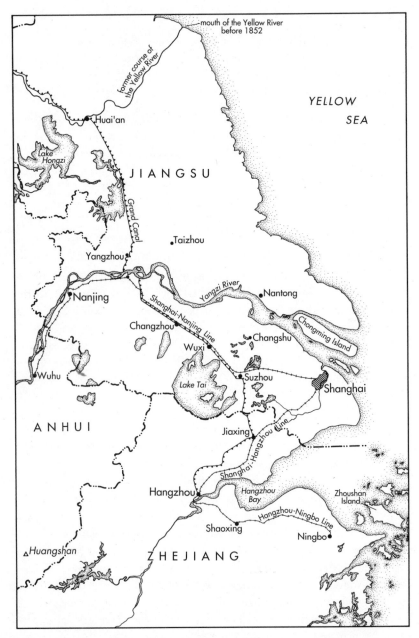

Jiangnan in the early twentieth century

Grand Canal. There is some evidence that the Qingbang evolved directly from the "altar community" (*shetuan*) that was established around 1698 as the boatmen's branch of the Hongmen (Great Gate) society, which in turn was supposed to have been an offshoot of the Hanliu (Descendants of the Han) Ming loyalist network set up by Zheng Chenggong (Coxinga).[8]

The Qingbang's own account of its origins claims that the Green Gang (which was then called the Qingmen) was founded during the 1450s by Jin Bifeng, a Ming official in charge of grain transport. The internal structure of the organization, supposedly created by "three patriarchs" (*san zu*) during the seventeenth and eighteenth centuries, followed the model of the imperial grain tribute system. The seventy-two lodges conformed to the seventy-two piers along the Yangzi River and the seventy-two locks along the Grand Canal. Members were grouped into 148 "fleets" (*bang*), which in turn formed "six greater fleets" (*liu da bang*) with the highest-ranking being the Jiang-Huai-Si River Fleet.[9]

The formation of the "six greater fleets" may have corresponded with the organization of a new tribute fleet during the Yongzheng period (1723–35), when several Qingmen disciples led by Pan Qing responded to the government's request for transport vessels by organizing the boatmen of the Huai River area into what came to be called the Anqingbang (Pacify the Qing Fleet). Each member of the Anqingbang—which was the formal name of the Green Gang down into the twentieth century—belonged to a generation junior to that of the "master" who had sponsored him for membership in the gang. There were said to be twenty-four word-generations since the Green Gang had been founded.[10] The last four of these, in descending order of seniority, were *da* (big), *tong* (comprehensive), *wu* (consciousness), and *xue* (study).[11]

Because Green Gang members served in the dynasty's grain transport system, anti-Qing societies like the Triads or the Hong (Vast) society were reluctant to accept them into their own organization. A Hong saying went: "To be first Qing and afterwards Hong is like a carp jumping the Yellow River gorges. To be first Hong and then later Qing is like pulling out the sinews and flaying off the flesh."[12] Pro-dynastic feelings began to shift, however, when many Anqingbang members became unemployed after the China Steam Merchants Navigation Company was granted a monopoly by the Qing government to carry tax grain north by sea. Unemployed boatmen among Green Gang members subsequently began to move into other lines of work that were mostly against the law: smuggling salt, trading in opium, opening brothels, managing gambling parlors, and so on.[13] Some, however, retained a kind of semi-official status as "grain runners" (*liang chai*), like the yamen lictors and magistrate's runners who served the old bureaucracy as county policemen and constables. Many of these made their way to Shanghai and quickly found employment in the "police stations" (*bufang*) of the International Settlement as "patrolmen" (*xunbu*).[14] From the very beginning of their arrival in the treaty port, then, Green Gang members were affiliated with the police.[15]

Like the Triads, the Shanghai Qingbang was a confederation of individual gangs, which were constantly in conflict during the early 1900s over Shanghai's riches.[16] Before and during the Revolution of 1911, their rivalry with the Hongbang (Red Gang) was partially superseded by an alliance within Sun Yat-sen's Revive China Society (Xingzhonghui) and Revolutionary League (Tongmenghui). On July 1, 1912, Chen Qimei—who led the revolutionary forces in Shanghai and was Chiang Kai-shek's patron—momentarily joined together the Qingbang and Hongbang to form the China Mutual Progress Association (Zhonghua guomin gongjinhui) with headquarters in the French Concession.[17] However, members of that association either sold out to Yuan Shikai and became involved in the assassination of Song Jiaoren, or were betrayed to Yuan by Chen Qimei who was seeking a compromise with the dictator before dying himself.[18]

After the failure of the "Second Revolution" in 1913, Qingbang members in Shanghai momentarily relinquished political conspiracies and directed their attention to economic expansion.[19] As membership grew to as many as twenty thousand people throughout the city, Green Gang leaders discovered that there was a natural symbiosis for them with the "contract labor" (*baogong*) system that prevailed in many of the city's industries.[20] The *bangtou* (gang head) became, in effect, the *baotou* (contract foreman): "invariably the foremen and inspectors at factories were 'old men' in the Qingbang. They did the hiring, firing, and labor contracting; and it was through them that management tacitly worked to keep the workers subdued."[21]

Later in the early 1920s, when the Chinese Communist Party (CCP) began trying to lead strike movements at the British-American Tobacco Company or the French Tramway Company, they found it very difficult to break the hold of the Green Gang's foremen over the workers.

> The authorities of the foreign concessions and the capitalists had all along utilized the influences of the secret societies in exercising their rule. . . . All had leaders of the Qingbang occupying important positions, including detectives, inspectors, investigators, superintendents of work, squad leaders, and foremen.[22]

Under these circumstances, the CCP's strategy was to try to win over the rank-and-file, and especially younger leaders who were unhappy with the senior foremen and inspectors.[23] In some cases, this "on the waterfront" plan worked. During the August 1921 strike at the Pudong factory of the British-American Tobacco Company (BAT), for example, CCP activists turned younger workers against the *lao touzi* (boss) who served as the plant's chief inspector and scab.

> While the chief inspector was still making a show of himself by the main gate of the factory, one of his disciples, a leader of the factory workers, silently approached him from behind carrying a huge watermelon. The melon was filled with nightsoil. Suddenly, as if putting a hat on him, the worker tipped it upside-down on the 'old man's' head. As nightsoil covered the face and body of the overbearing great man, the watching workers, all of them his disciples, burst out laughing. The chief inspector, who had always had his own way, had irreparably lost face, and he had also lost all power over the workers, just as a religious idol cast into a dung pit loses its potency.[24]

The August 1921 BAT strike was a big victory for the Communist labor organizers, but in the long run the Green Gang never lost control of the Shanghai labor movement. Later, the Qingbang and especially its overlord Du Yuesheng exercised a dominant influence in Shanghai labor unions, which fell under their hegemony after Chiang Kai-shek's April 1927 purge of the left wing.[25]

Still, the major key to the Green Gang's power in Shanghai was its members' close affiliation with the city's police forces—an affiliation strengthened by the French Concession and International Settlement authorities' "long-standing policy of deliberately recruiting gangsters into their Chinese detective squads."[26] After 1911, in fact, the chief of the Shanghai Municipal Police (SMP) detective squad, Shen Xingshan, was a Qingbang boss who headed the Eight-Legged or Big Eight Mob (Bagudang) that dominated Shanghai opium smuggling until 1923, and who maintained a close relationship with the River Police's Anti-Smuggling Squad (Jisi ying) and Red and Green Gang members in the French and Chinese police forces.[27] There was even a loose association of all the major Chinese detectives working for the foreign authorities; it was called the "One Hundred and Eight Warriors," and it provided an effective channel of communication between the French, International Settlement, and Chinese police forces, which were not directly linked by telephone before 1925.[28]

The French Garde Municipale was especially dependent upon Chinese police personnel, whose position vis-à-vis their European superiors was analogous to a comprador's relationship with foreign businessmen.[29] The

French authorities, regarding their Shanghai Concession as the single most important center of French influence in the Far East, worried that they did not have enough soldiers or policemen to defend themselves. This insecurity strongly increased the French sense of reliance upon allies among the Shanghainese, whether they be the "Gentry-Councillor Clique" of influential Roman Catholic Chinese businessmen or the Green Gang members who dominated the police force.[30]

There were such close connections between the detectives and the gangs, in fact, that special courses were given in some of the police training programs, instructing Public Security Bureau agents—policemen and policewomen alike—how to become gang (*banghui*) members themselves.[31] For, even if a detective were not a gang member, then he at least had to consort with underworld informants in order to solve crimes.[32] Before 1927, a detective's salary consisted mainly of bonuses for successful investigations.[33] His "rice bowl," in effect, was the very "foul elements" (*ezhuo fenzi*) who provided him with the information he needed to make arrests and recover stolen property.[34]

Huang Jinrong, Criminal Boss and Police Chief

The most notorious racketeer-policeman in the 1920s was the head of the French Concession Chinese detective squad: Huang Jinrong, the gangland "celebrity" or *wenren* who dominated all the other criminal bosses. In later life, long after he had ceased to be the chief of chiefs, Huang Jinrong still possessed a sinister aura. A portrait of him in 1944 showed a bald or nearly shaved head with wide-spaced eyes, tight-lidded and piercing, over bags of loose skin surrounding a squarish nose. This was the face of a man one would hesitate to affront—a man accustomed to the vicious deployment of power, yet one who wished to be thought of as a "master" (*xiansheng*) famed for his aristocratic benevolence and fraternal righteousness. A hagiography of him read: "In his affections he is openhearted, his natural disposition is magnanimous, he has a zeal for public welfare and is devoted to righteousness, and he has the air of an ancient knight."[35] Like the other two gangster "celebrities" of his time, Zhang Xiaolin and Du Yuesheng, Huang tended to think of himself as a hero out of a medieval romance; and in the eyes of the public, the *sange wenren* (three celebrities) or the *san daheng* (three bigshots) were often compared to the three heroes who took the Peach Garden oath together in *The Tale of the Three Kingdoms*.[36]

Although people sometimes claimed that he was from Nantong, Huang Jinrong said that he had been born in Suzhou in 1868. His father had been head of the constables (*bukuai*) in the Suzhou yamen before migrating into Shanghai to open a little teahouse in South Market. As a boy, Jinrong had spent some time as a monk in the temple at Wenmiao Road and had worked as an apprentice in the painting mounting shop run by the Temple to the City God. Somewhere along the way he had contracted a bad case of smallpox, and while his future disciples were to address him as Huang Laotaiye (Grand Master Huang), behind his back everyone referred to him as Mapi Jinrong (Pock-Marked Jinrong).[37] Eventually, Jinrong went to work as a waiter in his father's teahouse, which wasn't very far from the Zhengjia Bridge at the North Gate, next to the French Concession. By the 1890s both ends of Zhengjia Bridge sheltered a large population of "loafers" (*liumang*) and "petty hustlers" (*xiao biesan*) whose bosses were paid protection money by the local merchants. Huang Jinrong, a quintessential "hustler" (*biesan*) himself, quickly formed sworn-brother relations with two of the strongest of these neighborhood bosses: a martial arts expert named Ding Shunhua, and a darkly complexioned strong-arm enforcer named Cheng Ziqing (also known as *Hei pizi qing*, "Black-skin lord").[38] With their help, Huang began to organize the "loafers" of South Market and the French Concession into a gang of followers who later became his sworn disciples.[39]

Meanwhile, thanks to his father's contacts among the constabulary, Huang Jinrong was able to "test" his way into the French Concession police force or Garde Municipale in 1892 at the age of twenty-four.[40] Because he was strong and brash and capable, he did very well on the police force, becoming a detective (*zhentan* or *tanmu*) in the Criminal Justice Section (Xingsheke or Police Judiciaire) with badge number thirteen as his shield.[41] He soon arranged to bring into the French police his two lieutenants, Ding and Cheng, who helped him use his Zhengjia Bridge "runners" to solve a number of major cases.[42] In fact he was so good at detective work that when he retired briefly to return to Suzhou after a quarrel with his French superior, the then-chief detective followed him and hired him back as an inspector (*duchayuan*) on the strength of his record as a sleuth.[43]

With the exception of that brief period away in Suzhou, Huang Jinrong served in the Police Judiciaire continuously for two decades until his retirement in 1925 after several major scandals shook the department.[44] Although Huang was always closely associated with gangs such as the Big Eight Mob, his public identity was with the police rather than the Green Gang, which he did not formally join until 1927. Huang benefitted from French military needs in Europe during the First World War. When many French police officers returned to Europe for military service, the French consul general reorganized the Concession police, conferring greater responsibilities on Chinese members of the force. At that time, Huang Jinrong was promoted to chief superintendent (*duchazhang*); and he promptly repaid his French superiors by helping them break the Chinese shopkeepers' strike of 1919, and by assisting successive chiefs of the French detective squad (Sûreté) in periodic "clean-ups" that led to the arrest of 124 major mobsters in thirteen separate gangs during 1922 alone.[45]

To the French police authorities, hiring gangsters as detectives set a thief to catch a thief. Conversely, having gangsters control the gambling and narcotics rackets in the late 1920s seemed merely a matter of convenience to the chief of the French Concession Police, Etienne Fiori, who otherwise had only a handful of French officials at his side to control a native population of nearly one million Chinese.[46] If a particularly brutal robbery was committed or a major theft performed, all that Captain Fiori had to do was to ask his Chinese detectives to look into the matter.[47]

A gangster such as Huang spent every morning after 10:00 in the Cornucopia Teahouse on Rue du Consulat holding court. One of his disciples stayed at his side to receive the payments for favors and fixes from well-wishers and petitioners, while Huang decided whether or not the felon should be turned over to the police, and had his gangsters recover a portion of the stolen property.[48] Criminals in turn could request special favors from Huang vis-à-vis the police, getting charges dropped, or helping to arrange for a police raid on a competitor's gaming establishment.[49]

But Huang Jinrong was more than just a particularly capable secret society *touzi* (capo or boss) who managed to slip into the French police force. For one, he was a master at manipulating vast and complicated social networks of hundreds, and then thousands, of disciples. These were often grouped under subchiefs and would-be rivals such as the Jiangbei (northern Jiangsu) community leaders, Jin Jiulin and Gu Zhuxuan (alias Gu Si), who were directors of the native place association for Subei sojourners in Shanghai. Jin, who was a member of the *tong* "word-generation" (*zibei*) of the Green Gang, had five thousand Jiangbei disciples of his own in the *wu* generation.[50] On his part, Gu, originally a patrolman in the SMP, had twice that many *mentu* (disciples). Among Gu's ten thousand followers were numerous rickshaw company owners and an important group of plainclothes detectives who carried out his bidding as much in fear as in respect. A cold-blooded killer who had personally murdered at least seven local notables (including two lawyers), Gu Zhuxuan long escaped punishment through the protection of his friendship with Yu Xiaqing, the prominent business leader who had negotiated the April 12 coup with Chiang Kai-shek; and by his kinship ties to Guomindang leader Gu Zhutong, his nephew. Eventually, the French police brought him to trial for complicity in the murder of Tang Jiapeng, the manager of Huang Jinrong's Great World amusement center who was felled in a fusillade of bullets at the center's entrance just after midnight on June 18, 1933.[51]

In addition to keeping such sinister figures in line, Huang set up ancillary businesses in emulation of his father. While ostensibly working full time on the police force, he opened up a teahouse on the side in the Dongxin Bridge quarter and called it the "Cornucopia" (Jubao).[52] The Cornucopia became the center of his intrigues—the place where he brought together his contacts in the underworld to further his performance as a policeman. This form of entrepreneurship was a second reason for his eventual promotion to the top of the Chinese detective squad, and it was also the source of much of Huang's wealth. By the time he formally retired in 1925, Huang Jinrong had already branched out into the entertainment business by becoming the owner of a number of theaters, amusement centers (including the Great World), and other pleasure palaces in the French Concession, and he was also a major figure in the drug, gambling, and prostitution rackets.[53]

Finally, a third talent accounted for his success. Huang Jinrong skillfully cultivated foreign patrons through intermediaries like Zhang Yishu, who had studied for a time in France. Zhang brought him into close contact with Chief Fiori and with the head of the Municipal Office (Gongdongju), M. Verdier. Their sponsorship was probably crucial in the decision to appoint him chief superintendent of the entire Chinese detective squad. And later, when he was forced to resign from the squad because the Chinese manager of the Municipal Office and the leader of the Gentry-Councillor Clique, Wei Tingrong, denounced him to the Quai d'Orsay as a racketeer, Huang Jinrong was instantly invited by Chief Fiori to remain a high-level adviser to the French Concession Police.[54]

Although comparisons are often made between Chinese gangsters like Huang Jinrong and American racketeers like Al Capone, there are significant contrasts. Al Capone began and ended as a criminal, bribing policemen and putting them on his payroll. Huang Jinrong combined both police and criminal careers from the very beginning. Like many other gang leaders in Shanghai, he used contacts in both sets of networks to enhance his public and private interests. Before 1927, even minor Green Gang leaders often controlled their bailiwicks through the local police force.[55] And major racketeers like Huang or, later, Du Yuesheng, made a special point of creating venues where they could bring police officers together in order to create a camaraderie to link their enterprises.[56]

These activities were not so different from gangster behavior in other cities around the world. What made Shanghai special, and more like Chicago than Calcutta, was the Chinese equivalent of bootlegging during Prohibition.[57] That is, Chinese gangsters refined and sold narcotics during a period when the national government, with the cooperation of the League of Nations, ostensibly attempted to suppress opium addiction throughout China and above all in Shanghai.[58]

Opium and Criminality

Modern Shanghai was literally built on the opium trade. Before the 1850s Shanghai served as the terminal port for the coastal opium traffic, which was carried on in a semi-public way.[59] Shanghai was opened to foreign trade on November 11, 1843, and soon afterward Jardine's, the biggest British company operating in China, set up a branch there and began hiring compradors, one of whom was solely employed in supervising the payment and delivery of opium.[60] By 1845, according to Jardine's agent in Shanghai, Shanghai outstripped Chusan (Zhoushan, Dinghai) as a center of opium trade, which rose from 16,500 chests in 1847 to 37,000 chests in 1858, constituting nearly half of the total opium imported to China. By 1860, two years after the opium trade was legalized, Shanghai's share of the trade came to 60 percent of the total.[61] Indeed opium, and opium orders, actually functioned as money in Shanghai to pay advances to foreign firms' compradors for up-country purchases of tea and silk.[62] Around 1850, Yungkee, a Cantonese merchant at Shanghai who was then the comprador for Dent, Beale & Co., devised the "Soochow System." Chinese merchants brought opium from Shanghai to Suzhou where they exchanged it for silk. The "Soochow System" was dominated by Dent's, but Jardine's, Lindsay & Co., and Russell & Co. also sent opium to Suzhou on a regular basis.

The human cost of this "commercial revolution" may be measured in staggering rates of drug addiction. In 1880 nearly thirteen million pounds of opium came into China, mainly from India. By 1900 imports declined because China was producing an average of forty-five million pounds a year. Shanxi had 150,000 acres under poppy cultivation and sixteen wholesale houses, each with a capital equivalent to US $1 million. Sichuan province alone annually produced twenty-six million pounds of the drug, and in Chengdu there was one opium den for every 67 of its 300,000 inhabitants. At least fifteen million Chinese were confirmed addicts.[63]

In Shanghai, where some of the foreign missionaries who resided in South Market complained that their homes were completely surrounded by opium dens behind conspicuous bamboo fences, "the very air seemed to be flavored with the faint smell of burning opium."[64] In the early part of the twentieth century, $40 million worth of opium came into the port of Shanghai every year. The city had over eighty shops where the crude drug was sold openly, and there were over 1,500 opium houses—many of which catered to a clientele of coolies who could only afford 10 cents apiece for Tye, a mixture of opium and the residue of opium smoked by more fortunate individuals. James Lee was led to such a place up a narrow passageway littered with refuse.

> When my eyes became accustomed to the dim light of the place, I saw that we were in a large room entirely bare of furniture. On the boards of the floor were stretched, alongside of each other, about a dozen grass mats, and on most of them there was a Chinese coolie. Some of them were already lying insensible like dead bodies, while others were still smoking opium. Some were filthy and in rags, and I noticed that some were quite young boys, although there were old men too.[65]

The owners of these dens bought their supplies of the drug from three major opium businesses in the International Settlement: the Zhengxia ji, Guoyu ji, and Liwei ji. All three were owned by Swatow (Chaozhou) merchants who constituted their own guild which in turn, around 1906, bought the Persian and Indian opium from four foreign merchant houses: David Sassoon & Co., E. D. Sassoon, S. J. David, and Edward Ezra.[66]

On November 21, 1906, the Qing government issued a decree providing for the gradual prohibition of opium over a ten-year period. Britain agreed in December 1907 to reduce the importation of Indian opium from 61,900 chests a year to zero over ten annual installments, beginning in 1908. In 1909 the International Opium Commission was created at the suggestion of President Theodore Roosevelt, and it met in Shanghai to work out details of the plan.[67] The other foreign powers supported this policy of progressively abolishing foreign opium imports into China at the Hague Conference of 1911–12. Under this new international pressure, the Shanghai Municipal Council temporarily closed down the opium houses in the International Settlement.[68]

The foreign opium merchants—who were at this point mainly Indians from Calcutta and Jewish merchants from Baghdad operating with licenses sold to them by the Shanghai Municipal Council—responded to the cessation of legal opium imports with a triple strategy. First, they sought to corner the available supply of Indian opium and keep the price high by forming the Shanghai Opium Merchants Combine in 1913 and by signing an agreement with the Swatow opium merchants binding the latter exclusively to buy their Indian and Persian opium.[69] Second, they made an arrangement with the Municipal Council to enlist the services of the SMP so that only the combine's opium could be sold or smoked in the International Settlement.[70] And third, they reached an agreement with Yuan Shikai's government in May 1915 to keep Jiangsu, Jiangxi, and Guangdong open for opium sales until March 31, 1917 (when the legal traffic ceased completely), in return for payments of $3,500 per chest outside the regular duty.[71]

Because of the Opium Combine's success in cornering Indian opium, which was of much higher quality than domestic Chinese opium, the price of the drug rose appreciably in Shanghai.[72] From 1912 to 1916, a chest of Bengal opium increased in price sixfold, Malwa fivefold.[73] The foreign merchants prospered, and even when the end was in sight, they managed to negotiate an agreement with the Chinese government of warlord Feng Guozhang to sell the combine's remaining opium stocks of 1,578 chests at 6,200 taels each, which brought them a total of $13,397,940 payable in government bonds at 40 percent of face value. Most of these opium stocks were destroyed in January 1919.[74]

Once the legal trade ended, the Swatow clique had to find other means of maintaining its monopoly, which had depended upon the clique's comprador-like brokerage for the foreign opium merchants and on the merchants' ability, in turn, to use their Municipal Council contacts to keep retailers from competing in the Shanghai market. The Swatow wholesalers now had to try to establish an unofficial and illegal monopoly over contraband opium with the help of the Anfu warlords and members of the Green Gang. While the militarists provided protection outside the city, inside Shanghai the Big Eight Mob kept hijackers from attacking the opium convoys as the chests were unloaded from lighters along the Bund for conveyance to hidden warehouses.[75]

This new opium monopoly system was initiated by Lu Yongxiang late in 1919 after he had been appointed military governor of Zhejiang by President Duan Qirui, head of the Anfu clique. Together with his lieutenants, He Fenglin (who succeeded him as defense commissioner of Shanghai and Songjiang) and Xu Guoliang (Su-Song-Shanghai police commissioner), paunchy and amiable Lu arranged with Swatow opium merchants Su Jiashan and Fan Huichun to establish a new opium monopoly under the cover of a real estate company called the Jufeng maoyi gongsi (Joint Prosperity Trading Corporation) capitalized at $10 million.[76] The company imported and sold opium, paying Lu Yongxiang and his lieutenants a fee of approximately two Mexican silver dollars per ounce of drug landed, in exchange for military protection of the opium in transit. In practice, this worked out to a fee schedule of $600, $1,000, and $1,400 for each chest respectively of Chinese, Turkish, and Indian opium that the wholesalers brought into Shanghai.[77]

As the narcotics business flourished in Shanghai, however, it became increasingly difficult for the Anfu warlords to control it by themselves.[78] In 1923 He Fenglin tried to ensure that only "protected" opium circulated in the city by establishing the Wusong-Shanghai Investigation Bureau of All Prohibited Articles. But the bureau only had five inspectors and six constables, all of whom were military officers and soldiers operating out of the barracks of the Sixth Mixed Brigade near the Jiangnan arsenal.[79] It was impossible for so small a force to interdict the hundreds of freelance operators who smuggled opium into Shanghai along the numerous roads, creeks, rivers, and canals. Indeed, so large a "free" trade invited hijacking, and what was then to keep the hijackers from robbing "protected" dealers as well?

Opium and Rule

At just this same time in 1923, the SMP created a special anti-narcotics squad commanded by Assistant Commissioner M. O. Springfield. The squad enlisted informers, patrolled areas used by the traffickers, and raided storage depots. For two years "staggering blows" were dealt to the contraband dealers in the International Settlement: massive warehouses belonging to the Swatow monopolists and "protected" by the Big Eight Gang were discovered and raided, and it quickly became clear to the opium syndicate leaders that they needed to abandon the International Settlement for the greater lenience of the French Concession.[80] Precisely because they needed the help of the Green Gang in the French Concession, He Fenglin and the Swatow opium merchants turned to chief detective Huang Jinrong, inviting him to become a full partner of the Joint Prosperity Trading Corporation. He accepted, and under his protection, the opium monopoly's profits soared, netting over Ch. $50 million during that next year. Huang himself received a special gift of Ch. $2 million for his part in the operation.[81]

This was not to say, however, that the arrangement was completely stable. For one, the hijackings continued. The most notorious example was the Ezra opium case. A group of opium dealers with Middle Eastern connections pooled their money and bought heavily on the Turkish drug market. A multimillion-dollar cargo of high-grade Turkish opium was shipped by a Japanese vessel in January 1924 from Constantinople to Vladivostok, where it was to be transshipped and fed back into the China market. The captain of the ship, the *Kamagata Maru*, made a separate deal of his own with rival opium smugglers, and on February 26, 1924, he hove his freighter to off the coast near Shanghai where he unloaded fifty chests of opium into a waiting junk and pocketed the profits. The Chinese smugglers brought the drug back into Shanghai and stored it in one of the many underground warehouses dealers had constructed in the French Concession and International Settlement.[82]

Somehow news of the existence of this cache at 51 Canton Road reached a member of the original syndicate, Alexander Ezra, who informed the SMP.[83] The International Settlement police discovered nothing at the original address, but by tapping the ground and probing with crowbars several hundred feet away, they broke into an elaborate storage depot for opium, complete with false walls, secret doors, and a warren of tunnels.[84] In the hearing that followed, revelations of the magnitude and extent of this Persian-Turkish opium syndicate shocked the world and led to a recommendation by the League of Nations that all ships heading for the Far East be searched at the Suez Canal.[85] Japan refused to support this measure and the scheme was never adopted.[86]

In addition to the risk of hijacking, the Lu Yongxiang opium monopoly arrangement was also vulnerable to military conflict. The Shanghai drug traffic was estimated to bring in $6 million per month to whoever controlled the city.[87] Once the Anfu warlords were drawn into this contraband trade, the opium monopoly became an irresistible lure to other militarists. The warlords in the provinces already knew that planting arable land with poppies was a way of guaranteeing payments for their troops.[88] In Guangxi, for instance, at least one-third of the provincial government's revenue came from taxing opium that was shipped from Yunnan and Guizhou down into Guangdong.[89] As Chinese domestic production soared, the militarists looked more and more to Shanghai's illicit narcotics profits for their own survival.[90]

Survival was very much the issue by 1924 for Zhejiang governor Lu Yongxiang. The Zhili faction was by now on the verge of unifying all of China under its confederated rule, and Lu himself—the last great Anfu hold-out—was looking to the Northeast to help him protect his Zhejiang-Shanghai fiefdom against the pincers of antagonists to the north and the south.

Meanwhile, in Jiangsu proper the provincial government was under the control of a member of the Zhili clique, Governor Qi Xieyuan, who ignored his personal ties with Baoding Military Academy classmate Lu Yongxiang to cast envious eyes upon the opium revenues of Shanghai.[91] The war that broke out on September 3, 1924, between the Jiangsu and Zhejiang governors thus mainly fought for control of the city's narcotics traffic.[92] At the time, in fact, a number of people referred to the conflict, which involved 120,000 men on both sides, as the "opium war" (*yapian zhi zheng*).[93]

In truth, however, there was a considerable difference between the first Opium War of 1839–42 and this twentieth-century namesake—if only in terms of the drug traffic itself. The sheer volume of the trade by now, and the appearance of refined drugs like heroin and morphine, had changed the political economy of the traffic and its protectors.[94] Warlords and chemists had together helped crystallize a modern narcotics industry that would eventually become a major stake in the new Nationalist régime's interest in Shanghai.

2

NEW POLICING
CONCEPTUALIZATIONS

4   Policing the New Civic Order

The Shanghai Special Municipality cannot be compared to an
ordinary city. The Shanghai Special Municipality is East Asia's
premier municipality. Whether it be China's military affairs,
economy, or communications problems, every single one has
the Shanghai Special Municipality as its base. If the Shanghai
Special Municipality cannot be regulated (*zhengli*), then
China's military, economic and communications [systems] will
be in a hopeless tangle.

Chiang Kai-shek, July 8, 1927

Creating a new civic order in Shanghai involved both a reordering of
administrative structures and a modernization of the police. Indeed, the
two were seen as inseparable by participants at the time and by analysts
in retrospect. The classical attributes of political modernization in the
modern literature on development include the differentiation of political
roles and institutions, the specification of political goals and orientations,
the centralization of the polity, the weakening of traditional elites, and
the extension of central legal and administrative activities into all spheres
of society.[1] Modern political control, in Michel Foucault's sense of "governmentality," implies the direct and indirect management of a population in all of its extents and details.[2] One of the primary agents of that
population management is a modernized police force, whose primary
characteristic is professionalization.

> Professionalization is a modern attribute of police more clearly
> than either publicness or specialization. It is also a more complex at-
> tribute. Professionalization connotes explicit attention given to the
> achievement of quality in performance. Minimal indicators of a pro-
> fessional police are recruitment according to specified standards, re-
> muneration sufficiently high to create a career service, formal train-
> ing, and systematic supervision by superior officers.[3]

This was precisely the sort of modern police force that Shanghai's Public Security Bureau (PSB) was meant to be. Its success, however, was
linked directly to the achievement of a new civic order, as well as a modernization of police standards and training.

Creating a New Civic Order

The image of a new civic order for the Chinese-administered portions of Shanghai was unveiled at 10:00 A.M. on July 7, 1927, when General Huang Fu was formally installed as mayor of the Special Municipal Government.[4] The inauguration ceremony of General Huang—who was a sworn follower of Sun Yat-sen and one of the oldest members of the Revolutionary League (Tongmenghui)—was held in the downstairs audience hall of the former yamen of the Shanghai daotai (circuit intendant).[5] Sun Yat-sen's portrait, inscribed with revolutionary parallel phrases and placed under a banner declaring "All Under Heaven for the Public" (*Tianxia wei gong*), appropriately dominated the hall, which was guarded by troops from the garrison command, the peace preservation patrol, and the police prefecture.[6]

The ceremony opened with martial music played by the Shanghai and Wusong police band as the officials took their positions. The conveners included Shen Yulin, the new Songhu police prefect; Huang Boqiao, head of public utilities; Xu Dingnian, in charge of the bureau of finances; and Zhu Jingnong, director of the education bureau.[7] After bowing three times to the national flag, Huang Fu read aloud the last will and testament of Sun Yat-sen. When he finished he was given his mayoral seal and swore an oath of office, standing in white tie and tails in front of Sun's portrait.[8]

The array of speakers underscored the investment the state was making in this new civic order. Gu Yingfen, the first speaker, represented the Nationalist Party.[9] Gu reminisced about Huang Fu's role as the chief of Chen Qimei's staff in Shanghai during the 1911 Revolution[10] and lamented that, since then, Shanghai's history had stagnated, even in the face of Sun Yat-sen's special plans for the city.[11]

> When the former *zongli* was in Shanghai, after Yuan Shikai had died, [Sun Yat-sen] spoke of two things: as for the Shanghai concessions, in twelve years the treaties would have expired and they would surely be able to recover them. . . . How ought we to think of a way first to recover a portion of the concessions? Now, Shanghai Municipality will be under the control of Mr. Huang Fu, and there is no doubt that we will be able to develop [the city], although there are three particularly vexing problems: a large population not easy to manage, extraterritoriality, and crime control.[12]

Chiang Kai-shek, representing the national government, spoke next, invoking Sun Yat-sen's program of national construction and linking it to the recovery of the concessions.[13] If the orderly governance of Shanghai would help China recover control of the foreign concessions, then in Chiang's opinion no better person could have been asked to assume this responsibility than Huang Fu. Chiang Kai-shek hoped that Mayor Huang would not only turn Shanghai into a model, but make the city a "base area" for initiating Sun's plan for national construction. The creation of this paradigm—where public law and order would totally justify restoring the foreign concessions to the Chinese—could not be Mayor Huang's work alone. It also had to be the national government's responsibility, and Chiang himself promised to provide that help in any way he could.[14]

Huang Fu's inaugural address also emphasized the importance of creating a modern municipal government in Shanghai "so as to pave the way for the eventual restoration of the foreign settlements."[15] Speaking with a strong Hangzhou accent in a dramatic cadence that stirred his listeners, General Huang declared that the imperialist powers had shown by the very failure of their colonial administration in the International Settlement and French Concession that foreign domination, and especially extraterritoriality that gave haven to Chinese criminals fleeing the central government's justice, only aided and abetted crime.[16] Under foreign rule, Shanghai had become a cesspit of corruption.[17] But now that the Nationalists had taken power, this corruption would be cleansed—at least in the portions of the city under Chinese dominion.[18] Invoking the stable rule of Governor Chen Qimei over Shanghai after the Revolution of 1911, Huang Fu concluded that the obstacle of the warlords to urban progress and to "the maintenance of order" (*zhixu weichi*) had now been removed. With the help of the party and the city's people (*shimin*), the newly appointed municipal administration would demonstrate the way in which "our Chinese people are spiritually capable of reconstruction."[19]

The swearing-in ceremony at the daotai's yamen, which partook of the authority of the central state, was now over. In deference to the recent tradition of municipal self-rule in Shanghai, the new administration held a second ceremony, as well, at the General Chamber of Commerce. Chiang Kai-shek in military uniform and cape accompanied Huang Fu on horseback to this purely civic fete attended by more than five hundred representatives of the county chamber of commerce, the Zhabei chamber of commerce, the banking and coin shop associations, the merchants' association, and the united street associations. The Chamber's auditorium was set for a banquet under banners that read: "The Revolution has yet to be accomplished," and "Welcome to Commander-in-Chief Chiang."[20]

Mayor Huang Fu emphasized even more strongly in this second speech the fact that a revolutionary municipal administration would "cause the foreigners to lose their excuses for monopolizing power." To this audience

he added an additional motif, reflecting the determination of the Nationalist authorities in Nanjing to supervise all municipal affairs and to decide upon the appointment of top urban officials.[21] According to Mayor
Huang, the model for this new revolutionary municipal administration
was to be Canton, which was the first Chinese city under the Nationalists
to be given an urban government inspired by the West.[22] It was also a
city with an appointed mayor and an only partly elected municipal council—and that was precisely what Huang Fu planned to put in place in
Shanghai, despite the vitality municipal self-rule had demonstrated, even
under Lu Yongxiang and Sun Chuanfang's warlord régimes.[23] That is, by
invoking the example of Canton, Huang Fu was leaning toward centralized authority under state and party direction rather than the "gentry
democracy" represented by the Chamber of Commerce or the more populist rule characteristic of the street associations.[24] The new mayor concluded by calling for "three great movements" (*san da yundong*) to bring
about the modernization of Shanghai—public health, production increases, and public order. These constituted the critical elements in the
new civic order. If in three years the Chinese city was still as polluted as
at present, then the foreigners would certainly continue to have an excuse
to keep their concessions. Furthermore, to increase the productive capacity
of the workers was absolutely necessary if they were going to overthrow
imperialism and flourish economically. Third, "the movement collectively
to preserve public order [*zhixu*]" was essential to counter a deep sense of
deficiency between lawlessness in the Chinese sections of the city and
obedience in the concessions.[25]

Civic culture, then, was to begin with the maintenance of *zhixu*. It is
important to note, quite immediately, that order maintenance is a different mission than law enforcement, except for the special case of riots or
demonstrations. "Law enforcement situations, once the intervention has
occurred, can often be handled by rule; order maintenance situations usually cannot." Because they fear ambiguity, police administrators prefer to
define their mission as law enforcement, although "the patrolman's role
is defined more by his responsibility for *maintaining order* than by his
responsibility for enforcing the law."[26] Shanghai police officials were thus
placed from the outset under greater tension than their colleagues in most
other world cities. Nonetheless, they themselves repeatedly emphasized
their mission to bring order to the unruly and chaotic life of the city, and
that task remained the dominant justification for considering the city's
policemen its basic cadres and Shanghai's basic cadre of lowest-level public
officials throughout the entire period of Nationalist rule.[27] That is why
the establishment of a modern police force to enforce that order, a Public

Security Bureau (Gonganju), was envisaged even before the new mayor took his oath of office.[28]

Reorganizing the Police Administration

By their own account, the Nationalist police in Shanghai initially acted as an arm of the National People's Revolutionary Army in helping to settle the city. At least in their own rhetoric, the revolutionaries saw Shanghai as a den of sino-foreign iniquity, "a place where the Chinese and the foreign are mixed up, the good and the bad growing together."[29] The mission of the police, once the Northern Expedition was completed and a period of political tutelage initiated, was to implement the Guomindang's Greater Shanghai Plan (Da Shanghai jihua) and carry out urban reform so as to lay the groundwork for recovering China's treaty rights.[30]

A series of reorganization moves initiated the new civic order. On July 22, 1927, three weeks after the founding of the Greater Municipality of Shanghai, a Shanghai Special Municipality Public Security Bureau (Shanghai tebie shi gonganju) was created, in accordance with points eleven and twenty-one of the new "temporary regulations" (zanxing tiaoli).[31] This new Public Security Bureau—which was the first of the "cadre organs" (ganbu jiguan) set up by the administration—absorbed the Songhu Police Prefecture. Nearly all of the three thousand policemen under the Songhu office were kept on in the new organization. The first three offices or ke (general affairs, administration, and judicature) of the former police prefecture were renamed; and the public health section merged with the regular Public Health Department. The River Police and Criminal Investigation Police were joined into a single department.[32] These units were supposed to be staffed with graduates from the first class of what was to be the new police academy, designed both to prepare erstwhile soldiers for urban policing and to disengage former civilians from their previous life patterns.[33] Although a Police Affairs Committee (Jingwu huiyi) was set up immediately to carry out political reform, it was obvious that for the moment the new PSB would have to remedy the old police force's deficiencies piecemeal while training a new cadre to replace the old.[34]

Organization of a new PSB thus partly meant absorbing former police forces, including both the former Roadworks and Patrol Bureaus, as well as the militia forces.[35] On November 9, for instance, the Songhu Garrison Command ordered the PSB to assume responsibility for the Songhu Defense Militia (Songhu baoweituan). The ostensible purpose of this decision was to "improve the police system and to enlarge and extend police power" (gaishan jingzhi, kuochong jingli).[36] The real goal was to increase,

at the expense of the local militia, the responsibilities of the new Nationalist PSB—which was being lectured to, unit by unit, on Guomindang political principles by Party Secretary Liu Kaizhong.[37]

The office to administer the militia was set up within PSB headquarters, whose members were appointed to serve as secretary, assistant secretary, and so forth of the militia units (baoweituan). The latter were reorganized from being neighborhood units into twenty-eight corps (tuan)
under new, centrally appointed commanders. Meantime, all of the weapons, uniforms, and accounts registers, including the names of the militiamen (tuandingren) were collected together and put under the control of
the police.[38] Physical facilities for this new organization, however, were
woefully inadequate. Precinct offices, especially administration bureaus,
were dilapidated and decrepit, badly in need of repair and lacking vital
equipment. Modest building funds were provided, and within the year a
Western-style central police headquarters with an imposing yamen gate
flanked by large lampposts was built. But many of the local offices continued to be temporarily housed in temples and guild halls.[39]

Similarly, weapons—even for the regular police—were in very short
supply. When the PSB took over the Songhu prefectural organization, the
Nationalist police found less than 10 percent of the supposed quota of
weapons actually to be in the armory of the ting (subprefecture),[40] and
these few were mainly rusted and useless. One of the top priorities of
the new PSB was therefore to acquire rifles and semi-automatic pistols.[41]
Weapons seizures helped, for the criminal population of Shanghai was
one of the best armed in the world. "Scarcely a day passes without a
robbery, kidnapping case, or even murder being chronicled in the newspapers, and in each case, the central fact is that the criminal or criminals are
well armed with modern automatics, such as a criminal in any Western
country is likely to possess."[42] For example, when the Shanghai River
Police seized eighty-four rifles and pistols in a 1927–28 raid on a smugglers' den, these were distributed to precinct forces with the permission
of the municipal government.[43]

This source of weapons, however, was clearly too intermittent and
unreliable, and recourse had to be had to public funds. During the first
year of its existence, the PSB received Ch. $48,000 in "patriotic contribu-
tion" (aiguo juan) funds levied on real estate rents precisely for this purpose.[44] The moneys were transferred to the municipal Office of Finance,
which represented the police force in purchasing repeating rifles and semi-
automatic pistols. By the end of its first year, the Chinese police force had
in hand a total of 1,500 guns, each inscribed with the characters "Hu
Gonganju" (Shanghai Public Security Bureau) on barrel and stock. And

by the end of its second year, eight out of every ten policemen had been given guns.[45]

At the same time, the composition of the police force changed significantly. Although the new police department co-opted and absorbed a number of local militiamen, most regular policemen during the first four years of the PSB's existence came from North China.[46] These were not, initially at least, entire contingents of policemen transferred from the North like the Beijing brigade in 1925, but rather individual officers and patrolmen who had served or been recruited there. Many of the higher-ranking police officials appointed to the new Public Security Bureau during 1927–28 were typically graduates of the Baoding Military Academy who had been trained in Japanese police schools, and broken in by duty as military police adjutants in the Northeast.[47] They preferred to recruit their men from provinces like Hebei and Shandong, continuing to believe that the farmboys from that region were bigger, stronger, and more honest than southerners.[48] In 1928, 71 percent of Shanghai's Chinese police force came from Hebei, Henan, and Shandong, with local agents only representing 18 percent of the bureau's total manpower.[49] And in 1931 the same ratios roughly prevailed: 1,545 from Hebei, 1,295 from Shandong, 839 from Jiangsu, 517 from Anhui, 247 from Henan, 127 from Zhejiang, 60 from Hunan, and so on.[50]

The major reason for the prevalence of northerners was their superior height and physical strength, as well as their lack of complicity in local crime. Shanghai policemen had to be at least 5 *chi* 2 *cun* (6 English feet, 1.86 metres) tall, in addition to having an elementary school education and guarantors in the area.[51] The former standard favored northerners, the latter southerners.[52] However, another virtue of northerners was their supposed integrity, which was somehow equated with a more considerate, slower and less devious mode of thought than the thinking deemed characteristic of the "slippery" (*huatou*) and more dubious inhabitants of the Jiang-Zhe region.[53] Fearing the corruption of the South, the Beiyang military officers who commanded the Public Security Bureau realized that their constables' integrity was accompanied by unfamiliarity with local conditions. That is, outsiders were less likely to resort to corrupt practices than insiders familiar with all the ins-and-outs of Shanghai lowlife.[54] In their Beiyang commanders' eyes, the Shanghainese who dominated the detective squads were too smart for their own good.[55] Furthermore, linguistic incompetence in the Shanghai dialect was a kind of shield against the corruption that everyone knew infested the former Shanghai police forces.[56] In that regard, the policemen that these officers brought in were more like an army of occupation than a domestically recruited constabu-

lary. Special missions were even sent off to Beiping to recruit volunteers
either from among the former capital's police force or from among young
men—many of them of Manchu banner descent—seeking decent employment.[57]

As far as reform was concerned, a group of "sincere and honest"
(*laoshi*) patrolmen from the North would be a far more reliable cadre than
would local officers. They might have trouble communicating with local
inhabitants speaking the Shanghai dialect, but northern patrolmen would
certainly be able to man the Japanese-style police-box system, which had
been at the heart of the new law enforcement system in Baoding and
Tianjin.[58] Police boxes, linked by telephone to precinct headquarters, depended upon the visible presence of a uniformed policeman to prevent
crime in the making, rather than on the forensic skills of a plainclothes
detective sent out to catch criminals after the felony had been committed.[59]

Civic Funding of Reform

One obvious consequence of this policy of recruiting northerners, therefore, was greater dependence upon regular public salaries. Although these
salaries were relatively low for policemen, in the aggregate they constituted a major burden on the city's budget. Two months after the PSB
was established, patrolmen (*xunjing*) were paid Ch. $10–13 per month,
sergeants (*xunzhang*) earned Ch. $16–18, and officers (*xunguan*) received
Ch. $30–40, handed out under the supervision of the inspectorate (*ducha-
chu*) at each precinct station. These salary levels were Ch. $1–2 higher
than Songhu Police Prefecture rates, but even though they were raised
again in 1929 by Ch. $3, 4, and 10 per month respectively, they were still
relatively low compared to police salaries in the private sector.[60] Nevertheless, the increasing numbers of policemen on the roster meant that
the Songhu Police Prefecture budget, originally provided by the Shanghai
Political Committee and meant to pay for the original 1914 quota of three
thousand policemen, amounted to Ch. $58,600 per month.[61]

To pay the salary increases mentioned, the monthly budget was elevated to Ch. $67,700, which was provided by the provincial and municipal
bureaus of finance (*caizheng ting* and *caizheng ju* respectively). However,
this was more than the two bureaus could sustain, and in early October
1927 the total went down to Ch. $65,354 per month. The raises in salaries
the following year, plus the purchase of weapons and other equipment,
continued to drive up costs. At the same time manpower increased as
well.[62] Obviously, this personnel represented a tremendous drain on the
municipality's financial resources, although the public works and educa-

tion budgets increased at roughly the same rate. Yet, just as clearly, the police force had to proceed with its program of modernization lest it fail to live up to its assigned mission of urban reform.[63]

The mission—however vague the contours of municipal modernization in Nationalist leaders' minds—was important because of the visible connection between urban reform and national sovereignty. In his speech at Huang Fu's inauguration, Chiang Kai-shek had said that:

> All eyes, Chinese and foreign, are focused on the Shanghai Special Municipality. There simply has to be a successful completion of its construction. If all is managed according to the way described by the *zongli*, then it will be even more perfect than in the foreign concessions . . . [and] the foreigners will not have any way to obstruct the recovery of the concessions.[64]

In order to implement Sun Yat-sen's plan for the new civic order, however, the Shanghai police were assigned diametric tasks. They were to be, on the one hand, instruments of central government integration and the maintenance of social order; and, on the other, agents of local municipal autonomy and the enforcement of legal authority. The attention devoted to the external forms, of what successive public security commissioners took to be the obvious attributes of a modern police force, simply diverted their energies from confronting that crucial contradiction along with its deeper implications.

For these reasons, the new police force's leaders were determined to push ahead with police modernization regardless of the budgetary toll. In the summer of 1928, when "special municipalities" (*tebie shi*) were placed under the direct authority of the central government, the PSB planned to reform the administrative system by ensuring accurate personnel titles, by clearly demarcating police precincts' jurisdictions, by continuing to supplement weapons and ammunition, by increasing the number of police from 3,582 to 6,000 regulars, by setting up model police districts, by constructing precinct stations, and by raising policemen's salaries.[65]

Their determination to reform notwithstanding, the leading cadres of the Public Security Bureau found that their ability to implement municipal modernization was severely hampered by excessive bureaucratic segregation and hasty executive replacement. The bureaus themselves enjoyed very little horizontal communication. Each was—in the words of one historian—"a fief jealously guarded by its director who kept absolute control over its personnel."[66] At the same time, however, the director was changed frequently in such "strategic" offices as the municipal Secretariat, and the Bureaus of Education, Finances, and Public Security. During the period 1927–31, the average tenure of the chief of the PSB was twelve months; each new director, invariably an active military man, brought "a cloud of officers and soldiers" with him.[67]

This frequent change of top leadership in the PSB exacerbated the corruption problem because underlings had little to worry about when it came to discipline. Of course, some managerial officials stayed on through successive police chiefs, but the only person who did so for the entire Nanjing decade was Yu Hongrun, who also happened to be the brother of the secretary-general of the municipal government, Yu Hongjun.[68]

Professionalizing the New Police

Occupations whose members exercise wide discretion on their own, as do the police or physicians, are usually "professions." Police professionalization in modern times usually means emphasizing knowledge acquired in academies and not just on the job, the founding of serious professional societies, and the producing "in systematic written form [of] new knowledge about their craft."[69] The Nationalist Shanghai police force vigorously pursued all these policies of modernization, especially seeking to improve the educational level of Public Security Bureau cadres. Huang Zhenxing supported police officer training courses just as energetically in 1929 as Chief Yuan Liang did in 1930, when the latter proclaimed that "education is the mother of a profession (shiye)," and pleaded with the Ministry of the Interior for more training funds:

> Police work is a specialized profession. It therefore requires that academic knowledge and experience be linked together. Above all, academic knowledge is the source of progress (gaijin). Without academic knowledge and relying [solely] on experience, the police will not truly progress. There is a need for more well-trained police. We cannot impose limitations because of the budget. In any modern country police costs are a large portion of the budget of the country. The numbers of police trained should be determined by need, and not by the available budget.[70]

Police in their own manuals repeatedly stressed the importance of education, emphasizing the duty of the patrolman to "guide and advise" the masses. At the time of the formation of the Shanghai PSB, for example, it was felt that a combination of general and specialized courses was necessary for all those who had not received police training in the past. Officers would be enrolled in a Police Officers School (Jingguan xuexiao), designed to provide men with military backgrounds specialized knowledge in police affairs. Next, several short-course programs were set up for the rank and

file, the hope being that all of the 3,500 policemen currently on the force
would be reprocessed through this new Shanghai Municipal Police Training Institute (Shanghai shi jingwu jiaoliansuo). However, it was clear by
1928 that these short courses were not enough, especially since the initial
educational level of the recruits was so low. Although the higher-ranking
officers of the new PSB were often educated at the college or university
level, medium-grade officers were usually only middle school graduates,
and the rank and file were in the main illiterate.[71] Plans were therefore
made to enlarge the training centers and to recruit more students and
outsiders (especially in Beiping) for longer training periods during the
first year of service.[72]

The size of the training class of police cadets was limited by the extent
of their facilities. In 1927 the police academy had been moved from Longhua township to the Qianjiang guildhall in Zhabei. The guildhall could
only accommodate 140 cadets for each four-month session, however,
which meant that even with attrition it would take more than six years
just to train the current roster.[73] Moreover extra courses in fingerprinting, police dog handling, and advanced criminal investigation were out of
the question.[74] A plan to move the Shanghai police training group to the
former municipal government hall (*zhengting*) on Gonghe Road in Zhabei
was delayed because the building was occupied by an army brigade. Finally, the police moved their own men in on March 4, 1931, but by then
only about one-fifth of the existing police force had received any training
whatsoever. With the opening of the new building, room could be set
aside both for a sergeants' training class and for an enlarged policemen's
class that included provisions for training policewomen.[75] The sergeants'
class enrolled ninety policemen every six months, with the top thirty students being sent out to serve as precinct sergeants upon graduation.[76]

Police training included a fair amount of instruction in Chinese boxing,
the "national art" (*guoshu*), which was seen as a way both of strengthening police ability to defend public order as well as converting "foreign
ridicule" (*waiwu*) of Chinese physical weakness into admiration for their
martial prowess. Although physical education had been associated with
national salvation since the introduction of Prussian *Türnen*, this interest
in *guoshu* may have had a lot to do with the fact that so many Chinese
military and police officers had studied in Japan, where national martial
arts forms (and especially judo) were seen to be linked with the nativist
vigor of the Meiji Restoration and where "the greatest experts in these
arts were to be found among police officials."[77] According to the Shanghai
police gazetteer, national martial arts were "related to the strength of the
race," (*minzu*) being a way of "disciplining the body's strength in a

forge."[78] The PSB ordered its officers and patrolmen to study the principles of *guoshu*, and established a research society to study methods of teaching China's national self-defense tradition.[79]

Although the PSB training course was intended to familiarize men of army backgrounds with civilian law enforcement, the police cadets' manner was quite military in appearance. Military garb helped insulate the police from the civilian population, and in that guise the uniformed police represented a distinctly differentiated element by comparison with the plainclothes detectives who were immersed in, similar to, and contaminated by ordinary Shanghai society.[80] The class photograph of the second group of graduates from the Shanghai Municipal Police Training Institute shows a group of instructors in military uniforms with Sam Browne belts together with cadets in regular army puttees.[81] Policemen themselves dressed in khaki uniforms, some with kneeboots, all with army-style Sam Browne belts and epaulets.[82]

Policemen and soldiers who shared the common "military spirit" were cautioned against fighting among themselves. When one of the PSB precinct captains complained to Yuan Liang that his men were having trouble with soldiers gambling in teahouses, the chief of police (a former military officer himself) told the officer that army and police "are one family." In the case of disputes like this—he added—one should always go to a higher officer in both chains of command and report the problem there.[83]

Creating "Modern," Rationalized Structures

Although certain aspects of the administrative organization of the PSB resembled traditional Chinese bureaucracy, the chain of command was theoretically modeled on modern rational procedures and rules.[84] The inclusiveness of the PSB, however, mitigated against a strictly functional division of labor. In addition to supervising the police department's internal affairs, the new PSB Inspectorate was also supposed to collect patriotic contributions, maintain connections with "mass movements," lead antismoking campaigns, regulate price controls over goods like kerosene, oversee the distribution of rations, provide postal inspectors, recruit new policemen, and supervise public health work.[85]

Structures to provide a rational flow of information, however, began with the police chief (*juzhang*), who was routed information by the Receiving and Dispatching Office (Shoufachu) of Section One (the headquarters section containing the Inspectorate and the General Affairs Office). The original report was sent to the chief and copies were filed with each of the other sections.[86] If the matter were routine, the chief had the appropriate section draft a response, which was then screened by his Confidential Department (Jiyaochu) and submitted for approval. Once endorsed the document was routed back to the Receiving and Dispatching Office where it was printed and distributed to the appropriate section of the bureau. Secret documents were treated in precisely the same way except that they were entirely handled by the Confidential Department—much the way secret palace memorials were sent through the Grand Council in the Qing imperial bureaucracy.[87]

An investigation was strictly administered from the highest command post by the chief himself through a series of checks and balances within the bureaucracy he supposedly controlled. After Section One's Confidential Department or Receiving and Dispatching Office had sent the relevant documents on, the chief placed the investigation in the hands of two officials: an officer from the section in question and the inspector in charge of the Inspectorate, which was a bureau carried over from the old subprefecture system and modeled on the traditional censorate, and which maintained liaison with the Shanghai Garrison Command. The two officials investigated separately, with their work confirmed by specially appointed assistants within each organization, and they eventually handed in their reports side-by-side. At that point their commanding officer, the chief of police himself, decided on the outcome of the case and issued orders correspondingly.[88]

Military forms of command called for army-like discipline. Policemen not only were supposed to look and act like well-trained soldiers; they were also expected to relinquish their personal liberty to brigades that controlled their physical presence during duty hours. Police regulations stipulated that patrolmen were not allowed to abandon their official posts for more than two nights a week, when they could sleep out of their regular police dormitories and take furlough to attend to their personal affairs at home.[89] And policemen who slipped away from the canteen, where they were supposed to consume official rations prepared by PSB cooks, to eat at home with their families and friends, were also strictly reprimanded and punished.[90]

These kinds of regulations formed part of the ordinary bureaucratic rationalization that accompanied the professionalization of the Shanghai police.[91] New rules were set for sick leaves, for individual retirement, for creating police cemeteries.[92] Police handbooks were edited; a new professional journal (*Gongan yuekan* or *Public Security Monthly*) was founded; a special forensic museum was set up in the central police station.[93] Efforts were made to secure uniform weaponry (by 1930 the PSB had a total of 4,184 guns in their armory), while patrolmen were taught how to use and display the traffic policeman's baton cut to standard weight and length.[94]

Above all, the importance of proper clothing was emphasized, the police-men's uniform being a device to "express the individual spirit" of the force and to attract the favorable attention of the public, including the many foreigners who came to Shanghai.[95]

In that same spirit of rationalization, the policeman's duties were mi-nutely detailed in organizational charts and lists prepared by the PSB's clerical staff.[96] According to the 1928 annual summary of police affairs, the activities of the Shanghai police consisted of four categories, labeled inner duties (*neiqin*), outer duties (*waiqin*), course of studies (*xueke*), and course of techniques (*shuke*).[97] The fundamental distinction in these "duties" (*qinwu*) was between inner (*nei*) and outer (*wai*) work. "Inner duties" consisted of receiving and filing reports, accepting petitions, man-aging household registration records, sorting documents, compiling statis-tics, fingerprinting prisoners, storing stolen property, and cleaning up the station.[98] Although a great deal of attention was paid to making sure that policemen carried out these tasks promptly and politely, station-house work clearly was subordinate to "outer duties." According to a widely read Chinese police manual, foreign police experts all agreed that patrol work was the number one duty of a policeman, and the inner service was meant to support the man on the beat.[99] This stance was not easily ac-cepted. Police supervisors had to combat the appeal of the precinct station to patrolmen both as a haven from the disorder of the city outside and as a kind of mini-yamen where police scribes could adopt the status of a traditional magistrate's clerks. Of course, the status of a traditional yamen-runner was also very low in the eyes of genteel society, and police-men found it difficult to avoid being stigmatized as lictors living off "squeeze" and illegal fees, and consorting with criminals.[100] The very in-tensity of the effort to get policemen to stop gambling, avoid getting drunk on the job, and refrain from hanging around with gamblers and whores, was an indication of the prevalence of these habits.

Detectives especially departed from police standards. In the literature on police work the point is often made that detectives operate according to their own schedule and frequently spend a lot of their time working without supervision. This creates a very independent sort of individual who is difficult to control. Obviously the same sort of freewheeling qual-ity characterized the detective force of the Shanghai police, which was given the duty of arresting criminals and was supposedly sent out to each precinct according to temporary need. Faulted for not reporting in on a daily basis and for spending too much time at the precinct itself, these detectives often lost touch with central headquarters.[101] In the face of se-vere penalties, individual detectives sent to each precinct still tended to attach themselves to that local station, no doubt because their own private sources of revenue were to be found there.[102]

Reformers struggled, then, to get the detective or patrolman away from his yamen on a regular, formal, and rational basis. Foreign-trained police officers such as Yu Xiuhao thus found it necessary to enhance the patrolman's respect for street work by casting it in an official and quasi-judicial role. "Out on the pavement," Yu said, quoting the New York chief of police, "the patrolman is no less than the street's judge."[103] Only the patrolman could make certain that business premises were permanently lighted or protected with burglar alarms. He could also check on pawnshops; supervise dance halls, low-class hostels, movie houses, coffee houses, and garages; search persons carrying parcels at night; and confirm the credentials of unsavory characters hanging around banks, bus stops, docks, theaters, and trucks carrying luxury goods.[104]

The American praise of the beat cop overlay the Japanese emphasis on the local neighborhood police-box system perfected during the Meiji period. At the heart of both systems lay the precinct station. After the 1927 reorganization, the Shanghai PSB had seven districts with twenty precincts (*suo*). Under these in turn were seven subprecincts (*fenzhusuo*) and seventy police boxes (*paichusuo*).[105] More subprecincts and police boxes were added during the next three years.[106] The precincts themselves, which kept in touch with Section One and the chief through Wednesday-afternoon weekly discussion meetings, formed the apex of a system of police telephones and beat patrolmen who were supposed to bring law and order to unruly Shanghai.[107]

According to Chinese police science, "outside duty" meant venturing out in all sorts of weather, and required special training (marksmanship, martial arts, first aid, driving a car), special information (reading headquarters bulletins and newly promulgated laws), and special equipment (baton, whistle, and flashlight).[108] Policemen on patrol were counseled not to talk too much, but to watch their wards instead. Police manuals advised them: Never let your guard down or become overconfident. Keep an eye on strangers in the neighborhood. Watch out for cars with motors running in front of banks.[109] If you see people at night rushing along with goods, then take them back to the precinct station for a more detailed investigation. If you detect a robbery in progress, call for help and keep calm so that you do not alarm the felons and they flee. Be careful when answering a fire alarm because it may be a ruse to "get the tiger away from the mountain."[110]

Police boxes were also important, but not emphasized as frequently as the patrol system.[111] New style "report boxes" (*baojingting*) were supposed to have a telephone linkage to headquarters, and the PSB requested a total of Ch. $1,400 from the municipal government and the Public Works Bureau to set up fourteen of these boxes around the Chinese sections of the city.[112] The municipal government eventually provided more than thrice that amount to create a police telephone network.[113] In the meantime, the older Japanese-modeled police box or *paichusuo* continued to be very effective because of its control over the household registers (*hukou*) based upon the *baojia* mutual responsibility system.[114]

Modernizing for Mastery

Police modernization along the lines described above—professional training, rationalized lines of command, modern military discipline, the latest armament, advanced patrol methods based upon Western and Japanese models, telephone and wireless communication systems—visibly enhanced the ability of the new Nationalist régime to compete with Western and Japanese imperialists for mastery of the city. During the first year of its existence, the Shanghai Public Security Bureau displayed a strong sense of revolutionary mission, both to recover national sovereignty and to prove that the Chinese could begin to organize a unit comparable to the most efficient and advanced police forces in the world.[115] Through stringent law enforcement, the PSB sought to convey an image to Westerners of a stern and even harsh régime that would not hesitate to punish its enemies.

The effort was successful in part because of the 1927 purges, in which the police summarily executed criminals and radicals in order to awe and intimidate the populace.[116] These executions were carried out under martial law, which was imposed to "maintain law and order" (*wei zhi an*) against the "reactionary elements" (*fandongfenzi*) waiting to ambush the new régime.[117] When martial law lapsed after the civil and military authorities thwarted Communist plans for an insurrection in Shanghai in November 1927, the government passed a special emergency law for the suppression of crimes against the safety of the republic.[118] The Emergency Law of March 7, 1928, listed as punishable by death such crimes as "disturbing peace and order," "instigating another person to disturb peace and order or to associate with rebels," and "conducting a campaign of propaganda against the state."[119] Persons who "organized associations or unions, or spread doctrines incompatible with the Three Principles of the People" would be sentenced to as many as fifteen years in prison.[120]

To some extent, these draconian PSB efforts to create a new civic society on the basis of a modernized police force succeeded in the eyes of the foreigners with whom they competed precisely because of their harshness.

Reading between the lines of numerous Criminal Investigation Department (CID) reports, one senses that the International Settlement's Municipal Police warily admired the PSB's tough, no-nonsense approach to malfeasance and political subversion. However, its British authorities also associated such hardheadedness with the ultranationalist and anti-foreign passions of the Shanghai populace in the wake of the Nanking Road massacre that had precipitated the anti-imperialist May Thirtieth Movement in 1925.[121] To the SMP and its masters in the Municipal Council and Consular Corps these passions were recklessly inflammatory, threatening to ignite relatively minor disputes over extraterritoriality and police jurisdiction into major political and diplomatic conflicts.[122] Ultimately, the problem revolved not around the successful reform of the Special Municipality's Public Security Bureau, but around the claims to sovereignty the Chinese police would make in the name of the Nationalist revolution. Inevitably, the conflict focused on contesting claims to the regulation of public spaces and to the condition of civic society in Shanghai itself.

5   Asserting Sovereignty through Policing

There is an increase in the number of deliberate attempts of Chinese officials to prevent efficient functioning by the Settlement. . . . These interferences can be construed only to mean a fixed determination to occupy the Settlement by fair means or foul, thus rendering more difficult than ever the preservation of that law and order which is absolutely necessary to protect life and property in the Settlement. Notable instances of official Chinese interference along this line [include] attempts to establish branches of the Nationalist government within the Settlement such as the propaganda bureau and the flour tax bureau, the protest in regard to the laying of water mains on extra-settlement roads, the demand that Chinese permits be obtained for the erection of houses on these roads, the attempt to take a census of all nationals residing on such roads, the protest against continuance of barbed wire in the Settlement, the protest against erection of a watchtower on North Zhejiang Road, and other instances.
Dispatch from the Beijing Legation, U.S. Department of State,
August 24, 1928

The Shanghai Public Security Bureau's ideological raison d'être was the reassertion of Chinese sovereignty over the treaty port. The new Chinese police were not only going to demonstrate that they could impose law and order in order to justify their reclamation of sovereign rights in the city; they were also going to pursue vigorously and aggressively every opportunity they could to supplant the jurisdiction of the International Settlement and French Concession police with their own *jingquan* (police sovereignty). We see this most clearly in the dispute over patrolling the extra-settlement roads that is examined later in this chapter. But it is also visible through the threat to foreign police officers—including leading members of the Criminal Investigation Department's Special Branch— posed by the Nationalist revolutionaries after the Guomindang took over the municipal government in 1927 and before it came to an accommodation with the Shanghai Municipal Police (SMP) and French police in 1931.

Indeed, the relationship between the new Chinese police system and the policing exerted by the European powers was a complex one, given the tendency of the International Settlement law enforcement authorities (the British-led SMP) and the French Concession Police to confuse anti-imperialist political activity, including any attack whatsoever upon the extraterritoriality of the foreign settlements, with criminal motives and behavior.

It is important to remember that "before the Nationalists came into power in this area, it used to be the custom of the local police department to 'frame' cases against members of the [Guomindang] who resided within the International Settlement."[1] Supposedly, when a northern militarist informed the Shanghai Municipal Police of the identity of a suspected Guomindang (GMD) member, the latter would be accused of an alleged crime and turned over to the warlord for execution. Continuing this approach in his annual report to the Municipal Council in 1926, Commissioner E. I. N. Barrett explicitly charged the "political element" of the revolutionists—by which he indiscriminately meant both Guomindang and Communist Party members—with being the cause of much of the criminality in the foreign concessions of Shanghai.[2]

The new Chinese municipal government meanwhile appeared to many colonial diehards as a diabolical force intent upon arousing the Shanghai "mob" against the foreigners. A few days before the inauguration of the Special Municipality in July 1927, the *North China Herald* in typical high dudgeon decried the Nationalists' program to recover national sovereignty as simply more of the same old May Thirtieth Movement xenophobic propaganda:

> Having laid their plans, they declared war upon the Settlement by reviving and intensifying anti-foreign feeling, plastering the environs of the Settlement with gruesome posters, stimulating meetings at which the mobs were inflamed by the usual grotesque lies, and filling the daily papers, including those published in the Settlement, with the most outrageous slanders upon the foreign community in Shanghai.[3]

Policing by the Shanghai Municipal Police

The SMP, in turn, felt quite justified in applying sanctions of its own against the daily newspapers in question, seizing their premises without warrants and turning off their electrical power if they supported, for instance, the Chinese ratepayers' struggle against taxation without representation.[4] This high-handed and illegal police behavior did not go unobserved even within the International Settlement. The Shanghai Municipal Police's most vociferous critics were the American editors of the *China*

Weekly Review, who challenged Commissioner Barrett's assertion that Communism was a major cause of Shanghai's armed robberies and kidnappings—kidnappings which in fact were part of a concerted campaign by Chiang Kai-shek to raise money for the military expenses of the new anti-Communist régime.[5] The *China Weekly Review* charged instead that the SMP was top-heavy with foreigners, most of them British; that the SMP had become a self-serving bureaucracy, which had forgotten that the police were public servants; that politics, social considerations, and favoritism influenced the selection of men for the top posts; that the police had semi-public bars and canteens, which caused its men to be publicly intoxicated; and that the police department employed a large number of White Russian refugees, many of whom were counterrevolutionary political agitators.[6] Moreover, "many of the activities of the Shanghai police department are concerned with espionage work and propaganda activities connected with European politics or British empire politics, with which Shanghai as an international community on Chinese soil has little interest and which is detrimental to the best interests of the community."[7]

Citing the report of Judge E. Finley Johnson (chief justice of the Philippines Supreme Court), who had conducted the investigation of the May Thirtieth Nanking Road massacre and who had called attention to the SMP's inefficient police methods, the *China Weekly Review* linked the administrative inabilities of the force with the failure of the municipal government to modernize itself.[8] Except for the discharge of certain officials who were paid handsome retirement allowances, practically nothing had been done to ameliorate conditions within the SMP. "The fundamental trouble still exists and apparently will continue to exist until something serious happens which may force the Powers, particularly Japan and America, to step in and drastically compel the adoption of reforms and modernization of this important branch of the municipal government."[9] What the *China Weekly Review* wished to address as "fundamental trouble" related to three activities of the International Settlement Police: the manipulation of public information about affairs in the Chinese community; the surveillance and harassment of foreigners suspected of being radicals or progressives; and the recruitment and formation of a White Russian mercenary force of police reserves.

The manipulation of public information actually began with the foreign press itself. In 1928 not a single foreign newspaper in Shanghai had a staff of Chinese reporters and translators, yet the newspapers pretended to publish accurate reports of what was happening in the Chinese community. How could this be? The answer—a "state secret" known to most foreign journalists—was that they depended upon the so-called "police reports." Any time a public meeting was held by Chinese in Shanghai, the SMP would send its Chinese detectives to attend.[10]

> These Chinese detectives in the employ of the police department then make out reports in English which are supplied to the foreign press, but always with instructions to the reporters to vary the text [so] that the source of the "news" cannot be discovered. . . . These reports . . . compiled by the police department . . . constitute the chief if not only source of news supply regarding Chinese affairs that appear in the local foreign press. . . . Still worse, they also constitute the chief source of information regarding Chinese affairs for the various foreign consulates in Shanghai, copies being supplied daily. . . . The situation naturally is a vicious one because these reports often are inaccurate and worse are of a propaganda character, tending to mislead the public.[11]

This helped to explain why the collapse of Sun Chuanfang's régime and the Nationalist victory had been such a startling surprise to the Western residents of Shanghai.

> Foreign newspapers in Shanghai kept publishing reports tending to create the impression of the impregnability of Marshal Sun Chuanfang, the northern militarist who controlled this area. Day after day the foreign newspapers, particularly the *North China Daily News*, the official British organ here, published reports of Marshal Sun's "victories" and the collapse of the Nationalist advance. Practically all of these reports originated in the so-called "intelligence" reports of the Shanghai police department, and naturally they did a tremendous amount of damage, for many of the foreign newspaper correspondents then in Shanghai telegraphed them to their newspapers abroad.[12]

In return, as controllers of the news, the SMP Special Branch political police were especially sensitive to the activities of foreign journalists and visitors who might report unfavorably on the situation in Shanghai.[13] Negative newspaper reports were often attributed to suspect foreign journalists such as Agnes Smedley.[14] The Special Branch of the Criminal Investigation Department (CID) repeatedly claimed to have secret information that such-and-such a reporter was actually an ex-IWW agitator in the pay of the Comintern. This news would be "whispered" around Shanghai by police agents, until the journalist was discredited. American writers coming from Europe via the Trans-Siberian Railway were automatically labeled as Bolsheviks, and this information was then sometimes fed out of Shanghai to other Far Eastern cities. When the well-known English writer Arthur Ransome wrote several articles offensive to the police, for instance, a whisper campaign claimed that he had been in Russia and had a Russian wife. The most egregious example of this flat-footed police slander involved Eugene O'Neill, who came to Shanghai in December 1928. Someone apparently "tipped off" the CID that a radical American writer was in town, and thereafter "Mr O'Neill and his party were subjected to the usual surveillance to which all American newspaper men and writers are subjected who visit this part of the world." O'Neill left Shanghai shortly afterward, having sent a letter to his doctor in which he said that Shanghai had "more snoops and gossips to the square inch" than in a New England village of a thousand people.[15]

Despite these comical aspects of CID meddlesomeness, the Special Branch's secret agents cast something of a pall over public political life in the Settlement. When a Chinese scholar lectured to a YMCA audience on the special status of Shanghai, criticizing the authorities' racial discrimination, the Special Branch felt it necessary to warn the YMCA's foreign directors that "political meetings are not usually allowed."[16] Special Branch was also quite capable of attempting to destroy the reputation of top Chinese officials by spreading rumors of their personal or political unreliability.[17] The *China Weekly Review* therefore welcomed rumors in December 1928 that there would be an investigation of the SMP that might extend to the CID. "If this is true, there is hope that the investigators will go thoroughly into the 'CID' and once and for all put an end to its so-called 'political' investigation and propaganda activities."[18]

One of the most troubling aspects of SMP activities was the employment of White Russian "volunteers"—most of whom were said to be remnants of the Tsarist Army and some of whom had served as mercenaries under the brutal Shandong warlord Zhang Zongchang.[19] The situation came to a head for the *China Weekly Review* on November 7, 1927, when a crowd of White Russians attempted to raid the Consulate General of the USSR in Shanghai during the tenth commemoration of the Bolshevik régime. Weeks prior to the event, there had been articles in the press (including an editorial in the *North China Daily News*) that called for an incident; anti-Soviet handbills had been posted; and at a meeting of the Shanghai Fascist Organization speakers had suggested that the Soviet Consulate be "closed and cleaned out."[20] White Russians wearing Tsarist armbands began to gather on the evening of November 7 opposite the consulate,[21] and SMP patrolmen and armed White Russian volunteers in British uniforms did nothing to interfere when the crowd began to throw bricks at the building. Finally, when the mob forced open the door of the consulate and were fired on by the Soviet diplomats within, police whistles blew and Sikh and Chinese patrolmen rushed onto the scene from adjoining streets, followed by riot police who brought the situation under control.[22] The arrival of the riot police, an hour after the affair began, seemed suspiciously late to critics of the SMP. "Had these posters and effigies been put up by the Chinese attacking the British," the *China Weekly Review* argued, "they wouldn't have been permitted to remain up an hour and there would have been wholesale arrests, but the police did not interfere in this instance." The newspaper concluded that the November 7th incident had been encouraged by the very elements supposed to detect criminality among the Russian residents of the Settlement.[23]

Moreover, less than a year later, the *Shanghai Times* announced the Shanghai Municipal Council's plan in September 1927 to increase the size of the White Russian Volunteer Corps from 120 to 250. The proposed purpose was to provide further protection against robbers and kidnappers, but to the *China Weekly Review* the real intention was to defend "the Republic of Shanghai" against the Chinese.[24] Instead of relying upon these mercenaries to preserve order during times of political trouble, the *China Weekly Review* urged that the SMC "work out some form of cooperation with the Chinese military and police authorities in the Chinese-administered areas about the International Settlement, for this undoubtedly was and is what the Powers have in mind in the gradual relinquishment of the local foreign administration to Chinese control."[25] That cooperation was indeed forthcoming, but not in terms of turning over foreign administration to the Chinese authorities—as illustrated by the outcome of the struggle between the Shanghai Municipal Police and the Public Security Bureau over control of the extra-settlement roads.

Controlling the Extra-Settlement Roads

One of the most heated issues between the International Settlement's Municipal Council and the Chinese police had to do with sovereignty over the so-called extra-settlement roads (*yuejie zhu lu*). The Public Security Bureau's efforts to recover "police sovereignty" (*jingquan*) over the extra-settlement roads was clearly regarded by the municipal government of Greater Shanghai as an issue of "national sovereignty" (*guoquan*).[26] It also seemed to the Chinese public security authorities themselves to be part of a general effort to assert their control over autonomous sectors of the city, whether hitherto in the hands of foreigners or Chinese.[27]

Extra-settlement roads had been built by the SMC outside of the regular boundaries of the foreign concessions during the previous twenty-five years.[28] These roads also led out to the posh new suburbs west and south of the city, where the wealthy erected large villas or—like Victor Sassoon—replicas of English country houses.[29] The Chinese haute bourgeoisie built their houses along the extra-settlement roads as well.[30] Nonetheless, this land grabbing was aptly viewed by the Chinese authorities as ill-disguised attempts by the imperialists to extend their police control and extraterritorial jurisdictions beyond the old treaty port area.[31] Indeed, once a road was built by the Municipal Council, Westerners claimed the need to have it patrolled by their own International Settlement police force, whose authority was supposed to extend not only over the roads as such, but over the properties facing onto the road as well.[32] This new penetration into Chinese territory was supposedly legitimated by the 1866 and 1898 revisions of the Land Regulations of the Settlement, and condoned (if not altogether approved) by the consular corps.[33] The American consul general invoked the authority of the latter by quoting a letter from the senior consul in 1905, which stated that: "All police measures having for their object to insure peace and good order are valid in the International Settlement as well as on the roads constructed by the Shanghai Municipal Council (SMC) outside the Settlement, provided they are approved by the consular body."[34]

These extra-settlement roads represented a considerable piece of Shanghai real estate, where land values increased by 973 percent between 1906 and 1936.[35] By December 31, 1926, the SMC had built more than 45.5 miles of streets and highways, which included an area of 1,589,500 *mu* (about 265,000 acres) outside the Settlement boundaries, with an estimated value of more than 15 million taels (that is, gold $10 million).[36] Although Qing authorities had objected to SMP patrols on the extra-settlement roads since 1905, this land grab went largely unchallenged until the May Thirtieth Movement erupted in 1925.[37] Responding to nationalistic demands for the recovery of national sovereignty, the régime of Sun Chuanfang dispatched Chinese police to patrol the extra-settlement roads in March 1926.[38] The SMC complained vigorously, and American Consul General Cunningham protested to the Shanghai Bureau of Foreign Affairs, which soon capitulated.[39]

For his part, Consul General Cunningham earnestly believed that the roads should be patrolled instead by SMP constables, because of the proprietary need to protect public utilities provided by contract to residents on municipal roads outside the Settlement.[40] The matter was temporarily settled at the end of December 1926, in an exchange concerning the Mixed Court Rendition Agreement, which provided for the appointment of a new Provisional Court.[41] According to this compromise, "the Chinese authorities conceded the right of the municipality to police roads outside the settlement."[42]

Less than ten months later the new Nationalist Public Security Bureau aggressively challenged that agreement.[43] On October 13, 1927, "with the help of the masses," the Chinese recovered "police sovereignty" over Hongqiao Road in the western suburbs by transferring an officer and twenty-two regular policemen from the Peace Preservation Corps to garrison the area under the jurisdiction of the first *suo* of the sixth district.[44] And a little over two weeks later, on October 30, just as the Shanghai street associations were sending a protest to the foreign consuls against the extension of imperialist rule over the outskirts of Shanghai, the PSB began to actually patrol the length of Hongqiao Road in spite of running into resistance from foreign soldiers and police.[45] Nevertheless, the Shanghai Municipal Council's Board of Works continued to buy land and make plans for further road extension outside the Settlement.[46]

Both the Chinese Ratepayers Association and the Chamber of Commerce expressed dismay at such blatant imperialist expansion, and sought to involve the new Chinese municipal administration in the matter. On March 19, 1928, the Chinese Ratepayers Association wrote to the Special Municipality of Greater Shanghai, requesting that the mayor devise a way to recover land parcels in his jurisdiction that had already been sold to the International Settlement's Board of Works in preparation for road building.[47] On July 28 Secretary-General Yu Hongjun appeared before the Chamber of Commerce, and it was agreed that the Special Municipality would work out a joint plan with the Jiangsu Foreign Affairs Bureau, which was enjoined to consult with the foreign consuls (who were known to be much more reasonable about the roads issue than the land-grabbing Shanghai Municipal Council).[48] On March 15, 1929, the Foreign Affairs Bureau reported back to the mayor's office that, although it seemed clear the SMC's Board of Works would continue to extend the roads unless otherwise impeded, the foreign consuls offered some hope of resolving the matter.

The problem now was to think of a "concrete way" of responding to the question of "road sovereignty" (*luquan*).[49] Consequently, after a series of discussions in March and April with the Foreign Affairs Bureau, the mayor's office convened a meeting on June 5 that decided: first, there was no legal basis in the treaties for extra-settlement roads; second, the roads' infringement of Chinese sovereignty should be widely "propagandized"; and third, the International Settlement's Board of Works should be made "to experience difficulty" by "any means possible to block the construction of extra-settlement roads."[50] On September 26, 1929, the Shanghai Land Bureau (Tudi ju) forbade selling land to the SMC for any purpose whatsoever, and threatened to confiscate the property of anyone who attempted to do so.[51] Meanwhile, the mayor's office also increased the Public Security Bureau's budget so that Chief Yuan Liang could assign more men and equipment to guard against the extension of the roads.[52] The PSB was particularly exercised by signs that the Shanghai Municipal Council planned to convert relatively temporary cinder roads into more permanent macadam or gravel highways.[53] Since the Chinese police were already able to gain access to about an eighth of the extra-settlement roads area thanks to the construction of a road by the Special Chinese Municipality across the western midsection in 1928, they were already able to station their own men and members of the military police there. Several clashes between the Chinese police and the International Settlement police had resulted when the former tried to impede SMC road repair crews crossing Chinese-patrolled areas. Soon, the PSB began arresting employees of Shanghai utilities companies extending or repairing equipment outside of the concessions.[54]

These measures were effective, though few publicly recognized it at the time. On January 15, 1930, Commissioner of Public Works J. E. Needham told the Shanghai Municipal Council that there was the possibility of a clash with the Zhabei authorities over an SMC-owned lot on North Sichuan Road. "In order to avoid any trouble I suggest that all work be suspended."[55] And the following day, Director-General Fessenden and Commissioner Needham agreed privately not to buy any more lots for extra-settlement roads.[56]

Reclaiming Sovereignty on the Roads and in the Courts

The political authority for the area around the city temple constituted a related issue of sovereignty. Authority had been placed in the hands of a committee organized by that quarter's local civic leaders; and after getting a letter of authorization from the Bureau of Finance, PSB officials from the Second District met together with officers of the association on January 5, 1928, and established their police sovereignty over Yuyuan and the City God's Temple. Police sovereignty was also imposed on the Pudong godowns of the China Steam Merchants Navigation Company, which had been patrolled by the Pudong Self-Defense League (Pudong baoweituan) until it relinquished its authority to the Second District and dissolved itself on April 1, 1928.[57]

The attempt to assert police sovereignty also formed part of a conscious effort to bring tangible physical order to the city by opening up alleys blocked by peddlers or vendors, and by establishing a system of signal lights to regulate the flow of traffic dominated by foreign automobiles, which first appeared in the city in 1901.[58] Although it may seem far-fetched now, the connection then between traffic control and the issue of police sovereignty appeared obvious to foreigners whose movement outside the home and place of business centered on the motorcar.

During the 1920s Shanghai's city streets had become dangerous thoroughfares. Motorcars abounded, being much more important social distancing devices for the upper classes (and especially the foreign upper classes) sealed behind their thick glass windows than automobiles in many Western cities.[59] It was also socially de rigueur even for the middle classes to have access to a motorcar.[60] There may have been a functional purpose to this fashion: it was safer to be inside a vehicle than in its path.[61] Traffic regulations were inadequate and hardly observed by pedestrians who did not know how to stay on the sidewalk.[62] During the single month of June 1929, the International Settlement's police counted 803 street accidents in which 10 persons were killed and 252 injured; the following month, there was an average of 27 traffic accidents every twenty-four hours in the foreign concessions.[63] "Besides kidnappings and armed robberies," one observer wrote, "life in the Settlement is endangered by another growing menace in the form of traffic accidents."[64]

The Chinese Public Security Bureau determined to bring order to this deadly chaos. Realizing that the public would simply fail to understand why regulations were suddenly being enforced, and that their resentments might readily harden into anti-police feelings, the PSB decided to proceed slowly but firmly. Over the last six months of 1927 twenty traffic regulations were promulgated after consultation with other municipal offices. Six major roads (Zhonghua, Minguo, Guangfu, Datong, Gonghe, and Hengfeng) running north and south were taken as major pedestrian thoroughfares, and their streets were cleared of stalls and peddlers' stands. During the first six months of 1928 the regulations were gradually enforced. A total of thirty-eight traffic cases were prosecuted; and another forty-four cases involving road impediments, speeding trolley cars, and boats blocking river traffic were formally logged.[65] Foreigners were involved in a number of these incidents. Not only did the PSB stop and detain automobiles that entered the Chinese-controlled districts of Shanghai without proper licenses;[66] they also frequently complained to the English and French authorities about the behavior of unruly drivers who held concession licenses but who repeatedly infringed the PSB's traffic rules.[67]

These efforts at traffic law enforcement appeared to the foreign community, however, to be part of a sinister campaign by the new Nationalist government of Shanghai to humiliate Westerners and drive them out of the concessions altogether.[68] The Chinese police force's aggressive and seemingly xenophobic participation in a rights recovery movement thus gave the imperialists in the International Settlement a corresponding pretext to increase their own police department budgets.[69] The SMP cost the ratepayers of the Shanghai Municipal Council about 3 million taels per year. Despite this heavy fiscal burden, Commissioner Barrett asked in March 1929 that the manpower of the SMP be substantially increased. He made no bones about the strategy behind his wish to hire more policemen. "One of the principal aims which the Shanghai municipality hopes to accomplish in operating a large Police Force is to perfect an organization which shall make it as difficult as possible for the Chinese community to regain possession of the Settlement."[70]

The competition for police sovereignty moved beyond budgets and traffic lights; it also linked directly to the Nationalist authorities' long-fought campaign to bring the Shanghai concessions' court system under their partial legal jurisdiction.[71] The original Mixed Court of the International Settlement was established on May 1, 1864, to try Chinese and foreigners without consular representation. It met every day at the British Consulate with a Chinese judge appointed by the Qing circuit intendant, and a British vice consul sitting as an assessor. According to rules drawn up in 1869, if the litigants were both Chinese, then the Chinese magistrate could sit alone and adjudicate independently. If foreign interests were involved, or if the peace and order of the International Settlement were affected, then the foreign assessor's concurrence was necessary.[72] In 1910, the Qing government tried to abolish the Mixed Court, but when revolution broke out the following year the consular body in Shanghai took over control altogether and unilaterally instructed the Chinese magistrates of the Mixed Court to act under the guidance of, and in concert with, the assessors appointed by the consuls themselves. The result was complete independence of the Mixed Court from the Chinese judicial system along with foreign superintendence of purely Chinese civil suits.[73]

In the summer of 1926 negotiations began between representatives of the Jiangsu provincial government and the consular body. The result of these negotiations was an agreement for a Provisional Court. The judges of this new court and the court of appeal were appointed and paid by the Jiangsu provincial government. They sat alone in purely Chinese civil cases. In civil cases where foreign interest was involved, or in criminal cases where a foreigner with extraterritorial rights was the complainant, the consul concerned or the senior consul had the right to appoint a deputy to sit jointly with the Chinese judge. The deputy could record objections, but his concurrence was not necessary to validate the judgments rendered by the Chinese magistrate. However, the dictates of the court, and control of its houses of detention and prison within the International Settlement, were to be enforced and supervised by the Shanghai Municipal Police. This new Provisional Court formally replaced the Mixed Court on January 1, 1927, and it was expected to remain in existence for the next three years.[74]

Although the police force of the International Settlement was under foreign governance, the Nationalists' growing control over the Provisional Court allowed them to veto legal actions taken by Settlement authorities against the Chinese. Moreover, the new government also tried to use the court to collect so-called rent-taxes from Chinese landlords in the International Settlement.[75] On June 20, 1927, the central government issued a special tax schedule. All Chinese landlords in the International Settlement were supposed to pay to Nanjing the equivalent of two months' rent on their properties.[76] Of course, the Nationalist government had no direct power to enforce this tax, but it could—and did—announce that the Provisional Court would turn away all cases brought by landlords for payment of rent by tenants or for issuing eviction notices, until such landlords paid the rent-tax.[77]

The issue of tax collection inside and outside the International Settlement continued to plague SMP-PSB relations for several years. Often the dispute, which was of course a controversy about police sovereignty as well, focused on the extra-settlement roads, where the foreigners could claim that they had paid for permanent municipal utilities and where the Chinese could insist that tax collection was their sovereign right.[78] But, as the Jiangsu Foreign Affairs Bureau had pointed out to the Special Municipality, the consular body was far less aggressive than the Settlement's Municipal Council in this regard. By 1929 the foreign consuls had come to agree that the extra-settlement roads question would have to be settled by agreement in order to avoid any risk of friction due to "double control." The U.S. consul general wrote that

> the policing of the extra-settlement roads, on which front numerous foreign-owned properties, should be continued, if possible, under an agreement by the [International Settlement] municipal police even if it is necessary for the Municipal Council to collect taxes as agents of the Chinese municipality and turn them over to the Chinese authorities. It does seem in view of the very large investments and the establishment of public utilities at a time when the Chinese were unable, even if willing, to do so, that the Municipal Council should receive compensation before the roads are turned over to the Chinese.[79]

The belief that the Chinese were unwilling or unable to carry out certain necessary public administrative tasks for themselves was at the heart of traditional Western imperialism. It had, after all, motivated the creation of the Imperial Maritime Customs in Shanghai in the first place, less than eighty years earlier. And in both cases, of course, the supposed altruism was quite self-serving. But times had most certainly changed, especially since the May Thirtieth Movement, and the question of legal jurisdiction was being viewed by the foreign powers in a new light altogether.

Within the year, for instance, the fate of the Provisional Court would be determined by a conference of Chinese and foreign delegates that met twenty-eight times over two months in Nanjing.[80] At a final meeting held on January 21, 1930, agreement was reached on a proposal, good for three years, that abolished the deputy judge system, placed the power of appointment and dismissal of foreign secretaries of the court in the hands of the Chinese government, used civil codes promulgated by the Nationalist authorities, and created out of the old Provisional Court two new courts—a district court that was directly under the Judicial Yuan, and an appeal court, with final appeal to be brought to the highest court in Nanjing.[81] Eventually, in August 1931, the Chinese Ministry of Judicial Administration replaced the 1902 rules defining jurisdictions of the former mixed courts with the Chinese civil and criminal codes.[82] Moreover, the foreign powers' representatives conceded to Chinese police sovereignty concerns to the extent that they agreed that members of the new courts' police force would be appointed by the Chinese themselves.[83]

On January 1, 1930, the Nanjing government also issued a decree abolishing extraterritoriality.[84] But on this imperialistically sacrosanct point—which was widely acknowledged to rest at the very foundation of the concessions' separate commercial and political existence—the foreign powers would not yield. The USSR did acknowledge the decree, but England, France, and the United States simply ignored the announcement and continued to behave as though extraterritoriality were a permanent condition of their nationals' presence in China.[85]

A Reformed Public Security Bureau to Rule Everyone

Needless to say, the Chinese Public Security Bureau deeply resented the insinuation, which lay behind most Settlement foreigners' concern about their own extraterritoriality vis-à-vis the Provisional Court and Nationalist police powers, that they would not receive fair treatment under Chinese law. From its very inception the Shanghai PSB had sought to be intensely scrupulous about cases involving foreigners within their jurisdiction, and bureau members were proud of the protection they had extended to foreign tourists and residents—including Japanese residents threatened with mob violence.[86] Moreover, the Public Security Bureau itself was simultaneously trying to implement a new set of reforms in order to make the case for recovering police sovereignty all the stronger. Yuan Liang had succeeded Huang Zhenxing as police chief in May 1929. When he was appointed he had been given a mandate to reform the Public Security Bureau by Zhang Qun, the new mayor of Shanghai (March 28, 1929, to December 10, 1931), who had also been a police chief.[87]

Yuan Liang certainly seemed to have the qualifications to carry out such a program.[88] Born in 1883 in Hangzhou and educated at Waseda University in Japan, Colonel Yuan had actually fought on the side of the Japanese during the Russo-Japanese War—an accomplishment that earned him merit in Viceroy Zhao Erxun's eyes and resulted in his being appointed a police circuit intendant (*xunjingdao*) in the Northeast during the late Qing. After several subsequent positions, he ended up as a representative of the Chinese government in Japan and director of the second department of the Ministry of Foreign Affairs in Nanjing. At the time of his directorship of the PSB he was forty-eight years old.[89] During the next seven months Yuan raised police salaries, expanded the River Police, trained women inspectors, renovated some of the weapons, and increased the number of telephones in precinct stations. New statistical methods were introduced, and police rules were refined.[90] A police bulletin was published every ten days. New fingerprint techniques were introduced, and a household census was completed.[91] By Colonel Yuan's own reckoning, more than one hundred cases involving Communists and "reactionaries" were investigated;[92] several hundred thieves and robbers were arrested; more than a hundred weapons and several hundred thousand rounds of ammunition were seized; and tens of thousands of ounces of narcotics were confiscated.[93]

In his estimation, nonetheless, much remained to be done. In a speech on January 13, 1930, Colonel Yuan Liang called for a reorganization of the First Section into two divisions and the reapportionment of precincts according to population. Because of his Japanese training and his service in North China, he was absolutely convinced that the police box (*paichu-suo*) was the key to effective law enforcement, and even though putting police boxes in each district and precinct meant paying for at least one thousand more policemen, he insisted that this was necessary. At the same time he called for the recruitment of more "specialized talent" by raising salaries. A section chief (*kezhang*) only earned Ch. $60–80 per month, which was not a decent wage for someone with college-level education given the current cost of living in Shanghai. "High-level police" were needed, like the foreign police officials in Shanghai who were specially recruited for service among the Chinese[94]—Chinese who for their part did not understand the importance of recruiting superior police talents and paying them commensurately.[95] Also, ordinary patrolmen's salaries needed to be elevated. SMP constables had just had their wages raised from Ch. $18 to 25, and the PSB needed to follow suit.[96]

Education levels also had to be elevated across the board, though police training was certainly not a novelty in Nationalist China. At a meeting on internal affairs held in Nanjing on December 23, 1928, it was resolved that police officers' training institutes be established in each of the provinces; and by 1930, the Central Police Academy alone had already graduated 3,200 cadets. If you added to that number the students sent abroad and graduates of local police academies, then throughout China there were 6–7,000 who had received high-level police instruction, and another 15–16,000 who had been given basic training.[97] Yet of the 4,000 policemen in the Shanghai PSB, less than 20 percent had received any education whatsoever. At the present rate of training (140 students for each three-month course—or 60 less than the 200 policemen who would have left the force during that same time), it would take at least six years to retrain the entire Shanghai Public Security Bureau roster. Yuan Liang planned therefore to imitate the Beiping "police recruit classes" (*mujing jiangxi suo*), in which every new recruit took a short course before being sent out on duty. Colonel Yuan also hoped to get the help of the central government to carry out police reforms along the lines of American law enforcement leaders, whose training methods he much admired.[98]

Yuan Liang's admiration for American police reform was unusual, if not exceptional.[99] As we have seen, the Japanese police system had been a model for the Chinese since the late Qing. After 1928, German police advisers came to play an important role in shaping the central government's perceptions of structure and deployment.[100] The Americans, on the other hand, appeared to be masters of professional organization and training.[101] Their most prominent spokesman for the "professional method of policing" was August Vollmer, the Berkeley town marshal who was elected head of the International Association of Chiefs of Police and who was the University of California's first Professor of Criminology. Chief Vollmer's emphasis upon elevating the educational level of patrolmen and attracting college graduates into the Berkeley Police Department was known throughout the world.[102] During Yuan Liang's own tenure as Shanghai's police chief, Vollmer's deputy, Captain Arthur G.

Wood, former head of the Berkeley detective squad, was serving as a police adviser to the Nanjing Ministry of the Interior.[103] Colonel Yuan consequently looked to the central government for advice and aid.[104]

On January 15, 1930, the Ministry of the Interior convened a meeting of police department personnel, and Colonel Yuan Liang submitted several special requests, all of which had to do with standardizing police practices, increasing the power of the police, and enhancing police budgets. He suggested, for example, that all over the country police forces simply be called *jingcha ju*.[105] A uniform national fingerprinting system should be established, and all local police should be given the authority to hand drug addicts over to courts for sentencing.[106] A distinction should be drawn between the army and the police, and for the latter special uniforms should be designed with gold and silver stars of rank. Most important of all, police forces not directly under the Ministry of the Interior should be given supplemental funds directly from the national treasury amounting to 30 percent of their regular budget.[107] This would permit the Chinese police throughout the country to raise salaries and counter foreign imperialists like the Japanese who openly opposed the modernization of China's law enforcement agencies.[108]

And that was, after all, precisely the point. Foreign imperialists preferred to see a poorly policed Chinese municipality of Shanghai the better to hold on to their extraterritoriality and other special privileges, including the right to have their own police forces hold sway over the concessions. This was all the more reason for the Chinese police to feel intensely humiliated by jurisdictional exclusion, which persisted even though (or perhaps because) the chief of the PSB had insisted, after January 28, 1928, that the International Settlement and French Concession were thereafter merely to be known as "special districts."[109]

This nominal rectification notwithstanding, the Chinese pretension of control over the International Settlement was belied whenever the PSB wanted to exercise a formal presence there.[110] For example, if they wanted to familiarize their police cadets with the layout of downtown Shanghai by giving them a tour of Avenue Edward VII, the customs jetty, major companies and emporia, and so on, they had to request special permission from the SMP in order to enter the Settlement as a uniformed group.[111]

Members of the foreign Shanghai Municipal Police, in contrast, often seemed to move in and out of the PSB's jurisdiction with impunity.[112] The SMP even sent secret agents into Chinese-administered areas posing as reporters to gather information on Guomindang activities, and when these spies were arrested, their foreign case officers boldly presented themselves to the Chinese police and demanded their agents' release. On September 8, 1929, for example, agent no. 4 of the Intelligence Section of the SMP—one Ni Zimeng—was arrested by a Guomindang party member for pretending to be a *Minguo bao* reporter in order to attend labor union and GMD party branch meetings. Deputy Superintendent Papp, himself an intelligence specialist and undercover operator, and a Chinese inspector together went to the PSB to ask Colonel Yuan Liang to agree to his release. Since Yuan Liang was having his own personal difficulties with the local *dangbu* (party headquarters) at this time, he had the fifth precinct station in Zhabei refer the matter to Guomindang authorities.[113] SMP agent no. 4 was released reluctantly with GMD consent only after Inspector Papp gave a written guarantee that the agent would no longer use *Minguo bao* cover—an activity that was also condemned by the newspaper's editor, Chen Dezheng.[114]

The result was a widely shared feeling by many Chinese policemen that they could no longer "express a spirit of mutual aid" toward colleagues from the SMP and French Concession Police, even though Chief Yuan Liang reported to his section heads on August 18, 1930, that he had gotten the head of the SMC to agree that International Settlement police would phone ahead when they planned to visit a Chinese police station.[115]

The key question, after all, remained the issue of police sovereignty, which to Chinese police officers was still the single major impediment to effective law enforcement on both sides of the Settlement boundary.[116] On December 9, 1930, Chief Yuan Liang ordered each precinct commander to be especially alert to the issue of extra-settlement roads and the "question of police sovereignty."[117] And the following month he told a newspaper reporter that

> So long as police rights are not settled, criminals, after committing a crime in the Settlement, receive refuge in Chinese territory. For the sake of peace and good order in Chinese territory, there is urgent necessity for the restoration of police rights. Moreover, the number of cases of armed abductions in Chinese territory represent but 8–9% of the number of such cases in the Settlement. The inefficiency of the Settlement authorities to preserve peace and good order justifies the demand for restoration of these police rights. The rendition of the settlements is desired by the National Government. The administrative and judicial rights in the special district [i.e., the International Settlement] are being gradually taken back by Chinese.[118]

The police chief concluded by declaring that "the efforts of the government to secure the restoration of police rights will be supported by all

Chinese."[119] Insofar as the Shanghainese continued to identify the new police with just law and order and with legitimate social control, and insofar as well-informed Chinese of every political hue believed in the importance of recovering national sovereignty over the foreign concessions of Shanghai, Yuan Liang was absolutely right.[120]

6   Crime and Social Control

Any time we come across a *youmin* (refugee) who is
unemployed, has no dependents, and is behaving incorrectly,
then we will seize him and send him to the reformatory. In
that way we can get close to his nature and transform it so
that he can be broken like a wild horse into a tractable person,
who will no longer be a threat to local peace and order.

Shanghai shi gonganju yewu baogao
[Shanghai Municipality Public
Security Bureau report of affairs] (1931–32)

In the contemporary West, law enforcement and order maintenance are
regarded as two related but quite separate sets of goals of modern police
forces. In Shanghai during the Republican period the two sets of activities,
"judicial police work" (*sifa jingcha*) and "administrative police work"
(*xingzheng jingcha*), were considered by the Chinese Public Security Bureau to be integral parts of a unified system of social control that should
not be divided. The two together constituted an executive mission that
made the policeman on the street at once both judge and teacher—two
roles that combined to reflect the Legalist-Confucianist legacy (discipline,
instruction) of late imperial county administration. Such a conjoined objective, however, could only be attained if the policeman were able to play
both roles effectively. In Shanghai this would prove to be nearly impossible for two reasons. First, order maintenance resulted in a kind of legalistic
fussiness over minor social misdemeanors that constituted four-fifths of
the PSB's hopelessly clogged docket. Second, the challenge to law enforcement posed by an enormous urban underclass was amplified by a crime
rate that grew dramatically in the late 1920s, even as new felonies—
"vices" such as casino gambling and mass prostitution—proliferated. To
understand the impact of these changes in the scale of criminality in
Shanghai, we need to see how attempts simultaneously to maintain order
and enforce the law were predicated on certain assumptions about the
nature of crime and the best way to control it. This chapter provides the
context for the more extended examinations of particular kinds of crime
that follow.

Perceptions of Crime

Crime certainly did flourish in Republican Shanghai, where the Chinese police claimed to hold a "heavenly mandate" to protect the good and punish the bad.[1] "When one turns to the local news column," one Chinese commentator noted in 1929, "he will find it full of cases of kidnapping, robberies and murders."[2] On a typical fall day the year before, twenty-four articles about various kinds of crime appeared in one issue of the *China Weekly Review:* "Police Shoot Two Desperadoes in Alleyway"; "For the Execution Ground—Twenty-Seven People Including a Woman to Be Handed Over for Capital Punishment"; "The Sun Sun Jewel Robbery"; "Chauffeur Robbed by Bandit Trio in Uniform"; "Robber Wounded in Battle with Police"; "Foreign Woman Shot: Wounded by Bag Snatcher in Settlement"; "Hired Assassin Killed: Two Aides Taken by Police"; and so on.[3]

Although homicide was decried most commonly, crimes against property were taken with the utmost seriousness in Shanghai. It is true, of course, that most crimes result in damage both to persons and to property, but the basis of the modern criminal code rested on the division between criminal attacks upon personal and material objects.[4] And in China in general during this period, "economic crimes" were distinctly prominent. In 1930s Beiping, for example, economic crimes amounted to about 80 percent of all felonies.[5] And in Shanghai at the same time, theft was for many otherwise unemployed part-time laborers a form of business.[6]

The Chinese police were keenly conscious of the linkage between damage to property and person. Larcenies were usually reported in Shanghai under the name of the person robbed, rather than the apprehended felon, and after March 1928 the criterion for deciding whether or not police precincts were doing their job well was the number of robbery cases solved.[7] The most severe and frightening form of larceny, in effect, was robbery and seizure of a person, who was after all treated as a form of property by kidnappers during this period.[8]

Kidnapping, classified by the Chinese police as a crime in-between robbery and extortion, had been the bane of Shanghai for more than twenty years.[9] In 1912, in fact, an Anti-Kidnapping Society had been created to engage a corps of ten detectives who carefully watched incoming and outgoing trains and ships in order to detect criminals and their hapless victims.[10] During the second decade of the twentieth century through the early 1920s, most of the victims were young girls, who were abducted by gangs with elaborate networks of safe houses and middlemen to sell the victims—whose bodies were now regarded as property to be traded—to brothels.[11] By the late 1920s, however, the most visible targets of kidnappers were wealthy businessmen and their progeny.[12]

> In 1928 the practice of kidnapping—abducting for ransom—flourished in China. The result was that every Chinese of any means had his own personal guards. Often these were just simple unemployed roustabouts who were armed and were really no more than bandits. There was also the danger of getting a bodyguard who was actually in the enemy's pay. The wealthy, therefore, sought beefy native mountaineers, or, even better, Russian ex-officers. These latter—countryless Whites at loose ends—got up in British colonel uniforms and with their revolvers drawn gave their masters "much face."[13]

"Face" or not, bodyguards offered some protection against a crime that by 1929 was rapidly becoming commonplace: "Shanghai among all its distinctions is especially distinguished for its kidnappings. . . . In Shanghai kidnappings are practically a daily occurrence and the municipal authorities do not take them as a serious matter."[14] In a typical kidnapping, the victim was blindfolded and carried away in an automobile to a prearranged house. In many cases, the servants of the victim were accomplices of the gang. Usually the ransom was paid after the kidnappers informed the victim's family of the dire consequences of reporting the crime to the police. The victim, who was generally treated courteously by his captors, would then be released and if necessary fabricate a story of escaping from imprisonment. There seemed to be a rule—or at least the Chinese newspapers claimed so—that once a person had been kidnapped he would not be seized again.[15]

All of this helps explain why, during the year July 1930 to June 1931, only ten cases of abduction were actually reported to the Public Security Bureau.[16] The press, on the other hand, was filled with hair-raising accounts of kidnapping. During a dozen weeks from late March through mid-June 1929, when the Guomindang was putting enormous pressure on the Shanghai General Chamber of Commerce to raise money for the renewed Northern Expedition, there were at least fifteen cases of attempted or successful abduction in Shanghai.[17] On March 23, Xu Shengzhang, the thirty-seven-year-old son of a prominent factory owner in Xujiahui, barely managed to escape a gang of kidnappers, one of whom was seized by the Peace Preservation Corps.[18] Five days later, the manager of the Huada Bank was almost set upon by abductors, who were captured by alert French police *tanmu* (detectives).[19] Hu Siyi, chief of the Jiangxi Provincial Finance Department, was less fortunate on the night of April 1, when he was kidnapped shortly after 9:00.[20] Two days later the head of the Chinese staff of the Shanghai Tug and Lighter Company was seized in the French Concession.[21] On April 4, at six in the evening, the second son of Chen Bingqian, director of the Nanyang Brothers Tobacco Company and comprador of A. R. Burkill and Son, was abducted by four men who disabled his chauffeur and drove the boy off in the family's car.[22] On the night of April 7, Li Shengchun, a retired Henanese military officer, fought off a gang of armed kidnappers who assailed him and his wife as they were returning from the Empire movie theater in a rickshaw.[23] The next morning at 8:00, Li Jiumei—the fifty-eight-year-old Ningbo comprador for the Defeng Trading Firm—was forced at pistolpoint into a Ford motorcar by three kidnappers who sped off, leaving Li's rickshaw puller behind to report the crime to the French Concession Police.[24] Less than two hours later exactly the same thing happened to Wu Zhicheng, twenty-seven-year-old son of financier Wu Shengyuan, who worked as a comprador for David Sassoon.[25] On April 11, thugs also tried to kidnap Zhu Baosan, the donor of entire tracts of land to the International Settlement and French Concession, killing one of the Russian bodyguards who drove them off.[26] One week later, Suzhou merchant Wu Meisheng was about to step into his gray Austin, having just enjoyed a stop at the public baths, when four men with pistols pushed him into the back seat, threw out his chauffeur, and sped off into the night. Thirteen days later, an executive of a Chinese insurance company was shot and killed in his automobile during an attempted kidnapping; and less than three weeks after that the son and nephew of Zhu Jing'an, the well-known oil press factory owner, were seized by abductors and driven off in the family car.[27] Finally, sometime between June 13 and 15, Zhang Junmai, the famous political figure (later head of the Third Force confederation of democratic parties opposed to both Communists and Nationalists) and philosopher, was seized and held for three weeks before being ransomed by his younger brother through the intercession of racketeer Du Yuesheng.[28]

The use of the telephone and special reporting procedures did speed the apprehension of kidnappers, and in several dramatic cases (the kidnapping of the *Shibao* manager, Huang Bohui, in August 1930, and of Wang Guilin a year later) the victims were saved and the kidnappers quickly arrested and imprisoned by the Chinese police.[29] Convicted kidnappers were also frequently sentenced to death.[30] But these deterrents did not work. On December 28, 1930 the Chinese Bankers Association complained to the SMC that

> The crime wave, especially as relates to kidnapping in the International Settlement of Shanghai, has increased in recent years by leaps and bounds, and the local police have succeeded in bringing

some of the outlaws to book and dealt with them very severely. Criminal gangs are as active as ever. . . . The kidnappers have become so bold as to carry off their victims and they have resorted to the use of arms in broad daylight in the so-called strongly policed International Settlement. So it may well be concluded that the Settlement police are held in contempt by criminal gangs.[31]

The subtexts of this popular indictment were twofold. One was the suspicion that elements within the Shanghai Municipal Police—not the French Concession Police nor the Public Security Bureau—were working in cahoots with the kidnapping gangs.[32] This suspicion was later confirmed by the sentencing to death of Detective Sergeant Liang Cheng-yu, of the central police station of the SMP, on two counts of kidnapping.[33] The second was the growing complaint on the part of the Chinese Ratepayers Association that their high municipal taxes did not pay for sufficient police protection. In 1926 the SMP budget had cost the ratepayers 2,580,000 taels. By 1931 this amount had climbed to 6,850,000 taels.[34] In the face of the city's current crime wave, the Chinese ratepayers found these costs intolerable: "The lives and properties of citizens are in danger. This Association therefore questions the ability of the Municipal Council to maintain law and order. Chinese ratepayers do not desire to pay millions in revenue in a locality where they cannot be assured of protection for their lives and property."[35] Commissioner F. W. Gerrard could challenge the notion that the incidence of crime in Shanghai was high. He could claim that the statistics in his annual police report for 1930 "showed that Shanghai does not deserve its popular reputation of vying with the most criminal cities of America in criminality." He could argue that the enormous trade in arms and the conditions that "tend to attract the crime element" were factors beyond the Settlement's control. But this did not dispel the populace's opinion that the Shanghai Municipal Police was failing in its mission to prevent crime from getting out of hand.[36]

The Public Security Bureau and Crime Control

In contrast, the Public Security Bureau, which had promulgated a tough new set of regulations against kidnapping on November 21, 1928, seemed to be doing a better job.[37] However, the wide-ranging civic and nationalistic goals of the PSB sometimes appeared to conflict with a more narrowly focused and presumably more effective approach to crime control—another instance of order maintenance impinging upon law enforcement.[38] Samples of police events from the PSB blotter for the period July 1, 1929, to June 30, 1930, included an order by local precincts to the Chinese municipal council to stop tearing down properties along the boundary with the International Settlement (4 July 1929); the banning of pictures that affront public decency, including "peep shows" (*xiyangjing*) (21–22 July); the seizure by the River Police of a large shipment of opium on the waterfront (7 Sept.); a request to the Japanese consul to punish a Japanese who created a drunken scene (9 Feb. 1930); a prohibition of young girls singing in tea and wine shops (12 Apr.); and the ordering of precincts to devote more attention to preventing the Communists from convening a party congress in Shanghai (16 Apr.).[39] But are we right to assume that the narrower definition of police work would have been a better, more efficient way to deal with Shanghai's "crime element" than a combination of law enforcement and order maintenance? Certainly not if one took a holistic view of social order, that is, if one believed that crime prevention and social control were intimately related. The PSB, after all, contended that the police had the most important role of all agencies in the administration of internal affairs. "Outside of subduing the violent and soothing the good, its primary goal is the preservation of public peace and order, restricting individuals' easy-going ways that break the law, taking precautions against what has not yet happened, and investigating what has already taken place."[40]

So wide a mandate justified preemptive social intervention in the name of public order. During 1927–28, for instance, the Chinese police saw themselves as Shanghai's defenders of the peace against the "labor tide" (*gong chao*).[41] During the first six months of its existence, the PSB recorded 256 instances of controlling the "formation of associations" (*jieshe jihui*). Readily conceding that public association belonged to the "realm of freedom" (*ziyouran*), the police simultaneously insisted that freedom itself depended upon the maintenance of public order. In other words, treading a line between the Nanjing government's distrust of mass movements and the local Guomindang branch's support of the workers, the PSB declared itself ready to protect the right of workers to strike while insisting that the strikes be conducted in an orderly way.[42] In practice this meant, during this period, that the police protected six "legal" (*hefa*) labor actions and "preserved the peace" (*baoan*) in forty more labor disputes by arresting Communist agitators and warning workers that they were not permitted to strike under martial law conditions. In addition, repeatedly stressing the importance of mediating between capitalists and workers, they helped resolve thirty other labor disputes.[43] Later, as the government's conservatism won out over the local GMD branch's policies of mass mobilization, the police increasingly identified with owners and management, and even acted as guards for the textile mill dormitories where women contract laborers were kept.[44] But they also attempted to intervene paternalistically in labor relations, trying to prevent the victimization of longshoremen by foremen who were hoodlums or thugs.[45]

These efforts notwithstanding, Chinese and concessions police together were viewed by the left as instruments of capitalist domination over the workers, and there was certainly evidence enough to make this claim plausible.[46] In 1930, for instance, there was a strike at the American-owned China General Edison Company, which was located in the Chinese-administered portion of the city. After being called in by the factory owners to break the strike, the Chinese police fired point-blank into the workers' ranks, wounding five workers including a fourteen-year-old girl who may have died later in the Chinese Red Cross Hospital. Needing reinforcements at this point, the PSB turned to the SMP, which readily sent its iron-helmeted riot squad to disperse the strikers.[47]

In addition to labor and riot control, the Public Security Bureau's self-defined, and to a certain extent self-assigned, responsibilities included public health. The original Shanghai Bureau of Public Health (Weisheng-ju) was founded in 1926.[48] After the Nationalists took over the city, there were repeated misunderstandings and conflicts between the health bureau's seventeen inspectors and PSB men.[49] The police eventually requested and received a special set of regulations to govern the activities of the health inspectors. These measures included distribution of a notice that public health inspectors now operated under the authority of the police, whose uniformed officers would henceforth be attending public health movement rallies in Zhabei and Nanshi.[50]

Fear of infection was rampant in Shanghai—the great nemesis being the "white scourge," tuberculosis—and the police routinely took responsibility for seeing to the burial of corpses left to putrefy on the streets or in the Huangpu River.[51] After cold winter nights as many as four hundred bodies would be found dead in the morning, and during the 1920s the police annually disposed of about twenty thousand corpses decomposing in the streets and alleys of Shanghai.[52] By 1930, in the third year of the North China famine, more than thirty-six thousand dead bodies were picked up in the streets of the International Settlement, French Concession, and Chinese city altogether.[53]

In addition to disposing of the city's dead as a public health measure, the Chinese police were charged as well with repairing garbage cans, building public toilets, and keeping public swimming pools and baths from becoming sources of infection.[54] After December 1930 the PSB also assumed responsibility for keeping the streets clean—a task given to them by the municipal council after the Public Health Bureau failed to mobilize sufficient labor brigades to do the task properly.[55]

But these sanitation tasks were also metaphorical. The Public Security Bureau's larger social mission was sometimes cast in medical terms, as though the police were white-smocked doctors warding off pathological infections.[56] Opium and gambling were frequently described as "contagions" (*ran*) emanating from the International Settlement and transmitted to the masses via the commercial classes. The job of the police was to "ban and prohibit opium and gambling" from entering their jurisdiction, much as they tried to quarantine infectious disease in their capacity as public health officials.[57]

Chief Yuan Liang thus often spoke of the body politic, and compared social elements to the blood cells that carried energy throughout the system. The police were supposed to guarantee that the system worked, whether through prevention ("administrative police work") or through criminal investigation ("judicial police work").[58] The image of the former was prophylactic: "a good doctor cures an illness before it appears, which is not as costly as curing one that has already broken out." The metaphor for the second task was epidemiological, with policemen guaranteeing quarantine by "expelling those who threaten the maintenance of public security."[59]

The key to the latter was population control by means of the household registration system.[60] The system inherited by the new Public Security Bureau had not been kept up to date.[61] Household registration had been a responsibility of the police force in Shanghai since the establishment of the Songhu Police Prefecture in 1913, but there had been only one such census taken during the entire period up to 1926. Then, at the time of the turmoil of transition, many of the records of household population investigation (*hukou diaocha*) were destroyed or scattered. The PSB reorganization plan in 1928 therefore contained twelve chapters of seventy-six regulations that called for the continual recording of births, deaths, and changes in marriage status, and that was designed to keep track of persons moving in and out of households.[62]

In addition, at the urging of editorial writers alarmed by the crime wave in 1929, hotels and lodging houses were obliged to report guest registration.[63] This was part of a larger effort, decreed by law on May 20, 1930, to take a census of Shanghai, which was to be divided (like every other city in China) into *qu* (districts), *fang* (wards), *lu* (streets), and *lin* (neighborhoods).[64] Authority for the census and for the registration of *qu* members was assigned to the Public Security Bureau.[65]

This was an enormous task, especially during 1930 and 1931 when hundreds of thousands of civil war and flood refugees fled to the city.[66] During the single year from July 1930[67] to June 1931 alone, 136,760 newcomers were registered as members of an additional 29,629 households, bringing the legal residents of Shanghai's Chinese-administered quarters to a total of 1,807,582 persons (*kou*) registered in 384,785 households (*hu*).[68] Of that total population, in which there were roughly three men for every two women, 76.1 percent lived in residences, 12.4 percent in shops, 7.2 percent in sheds or hovels, and 4.3 percent in hotels.[69] That same registered population had increased by 64,240 persons six months later in January 1932.[70] By then, about 27 percent of the registered population was identified as industrial workers or manual laborers, 21 percent as working in the home, 10 percent as being in commerce, 10 percent as peasants, and 18 percent as unemployed (see Table 1).[71]

Refugees (*youmin*) and vagabonds (*liumang*) were a continuing challenge to the household control system of the Shanghai police.[72] Both elements were a threat to public order.[73] The *youmin* lived off of others, whether as non-productive beggars who "eat but don't till, wear but don't weave," or as threatening predators who "frequently link up together and make the good people their fish and meat."[74] Seen through Western eyes, the beggars of Shanghai were a deliberately loathsome lot of professional, well-organized swindlers who intentionally mutilated their children and deformed themselves to arouse the pity of others.[75]

> Horribly disfigured people would stretch their rotting limbs toward you. Half-starved mothers would hold up their half-starved babies, miserable crying little bundles. Groups of three or four filthy children would descend upon you demanding their kumshah. Old men would follow you for two or three blocks, murmuring please in the first block, obscenities in the second, curses in the third. And you were wise to drop your dragon coppers into their hollow hands. You did not know, of course, that in the fourth block they were likely to transfer some of their lice to your coat. You did not know that begging, as every other racket in this wide open town, was organized as a monopoly. You did not know that those half-grown children were working for an unseen overlord; and that the half-starved mother had driven a pin into her half-starved baby to make it cry when you were passing her. You had not heard of His Heinous Majesty, the King of Beggars, who was ruling this mendicant army from behind the scenes.[76]

Contrary to this fear of a single clandestine organization, many individual bands collected fees from merchants to keep from annoying their customers; they also provided bearers for funeral processions. Each of these bands had leaders who paid protection to the Green Gang and did occasional odd jobs the gangsters requested. But there was no unified "kingdom" and certainly no single "king." [77]

Refugees and Vagabonds in the New Civic Society

Seen through official Chinese eyes, by contrast, Shanghai's beggars were castaways who represented a potential threat to established society, both Confucian and Western. Chinese estimates of the number of beggars in Shanghai varied considerably. In 1931 one Chinese journalist guessed that there were about 5,000 in the city. Government sources estimated the number to be closer to 25,000. Enumeration was difficult because it was hard to distinguish between the persistently poor and the momentarily unemployed. Even the latter varied considerably. In 1929 the Public Security Bureau estimated that there were 250,000 unemployed men and women in the city: 8.7 percent of Shanghai's total population. By 1935 this number was said to exceed 610,000. The PSB tried to control this massive urban underclass by gathering panhandlers off the streets and bringing them to municipal "aid centers" (jiuji suo) and "rest centers" (jiaoyang suo) run by the Bureau of Social Affairs. But their capacity was limited, especially in winter, and "shelters from the cold" (bihan suo) and "soup kitchens" (zhou chang) were organized by private charities as the world depression began to affect Shanghai's economy, and especially its filatures, after 1931. During that period up to twelve thousand people a day ate at the soup kitchens, while many more starved in wretched misery.[78]

The other oft-perceived threat to public order—vagabonds or liumang—were, by the police's own definition, members of brotherhoods (ge and xiongdi) or gangs (bang, dang, and hui) that engaged in extortion and harassment. The police did try to enforce the injunction against illegal shacks and sheds along the waterfront where the "loafer" population was so huge, but the hovels grew there in number from twenty-one thousand in 1928 to thirty thousand in 1935. By 1931 there were over ninety thousand people—many of them refugees from Jiangbei—living in miserable and filthy conditions in these huts made from earth and straw. Here is a report of one of these huts by a Chinese YMCA investigator:

> The house with six inmates—father, mother, and four children—
> occupied a space of about ten feet by fourteen feet. The roof, built
> of bamboo matting and straw, now in a dilapidated state, lined un-
> derneath with soot and cobwebs, lets in water even in a shower.
> The walls, riddled with holes, are caving in and afford no privacy
> and no protection against cold and storms. There is no flooring. Ev-

erything rests on an uneven mud floor. There is no drainage and lavatory. The home is surrounded by garbage heaps and cesspools. One's throat becomes inflamed in this neighborhood in ten minutes. On rainy days water contaminated by refuse and manure enters and floods the house up to a depth of several inches. . . . In this particular working community there are nearly four hundred such "homes." [79]

The municipality did try to provide paupers' housing (*pinmin zhusuo*), but between 1928 and 1931 only 840 units were built.[80] Consequently, even though the authorities frequently burned down these shanty towns, the homeless simply rebuilt them again and again, for lack of any alternative place to live.[81]

The *liumang* who lived along the waterfront were a noisome nuisance to travelers disembarking from the long-distance ferries that carried passengers from the hinterland down the Yangzi. Arriving visitors were usually accosted at the bottom of the gangplank by a horde of shrill *liumang* who would forcibly grab the luggage from their hands and march the hapless strangers off to a non-licensed "hotel" where the bills would be padded until the bumpkins had been systematically fleeced of all their money and could be thrown out onto the pavement to join the rest of the urban poor.[82] Wharf and steamship companies regularly paid *liumang* dividends to ensure against theft, and merchants who opened a new shop had to pay them silver cash to keep them from driving customers away by constant annoyance.[83] They even intruded into high finance: the opening of the stock exchange presented new opportunities to the *liumang*, who invaded its floor in defiance of the police until the stockbrokers called in Du Yuesheng to "provide instruction" (*zhijiao*) and shoo them away.[84] *Liumang* were thought by the police to be behind most of the petty gambling in the city, especially in the vegetable and produce markets.[85]

Indeed, gambling and whoring and drug taking were all part of an existence that Colonel Yuan Liang identified with bad companions and easy money. In a long vernacular handbill, posted on walls along the Bund in 1930, the PSB chief addressed himself directly to the *liumang* by name, telling these "old hands" (*laoshou*) that they had better reform themselves. There were two kinds of civil society in the world at present: Confucian society with its "four people" (*simin*) of scholars, peasants, workers, and merchants; and Western society with its various "professions" (*shiye*) of teachers, lawyers, doctors, and so forth. The *liumang* were outside both of these social formations, and unless they changed their ways they were going to cut themselves off even more from redeemability, falling into robbery and more serious crimes.[86]

"The national government," Chief Yuan warned, "is now paying special attention to Shanghai. It wants to make it a model city, and that's why it's paying even more attention to the Chinese section. That's why it has established a municipal government to completely consolidate peace and order in the Chinese area." With the new PSB and Garrison Command, control was going to become more and more "refined" (*xi*), and the city's population of vagabonds would not be able to get away with their activities anymore. "Change quickly!" he warned the *liumang*. By giving up drugs, prostitutes, and gambling, "you yourselves can actually decide not to be *liumang!*"[87]

Refugees were also linked by the PSB to gambling, whoring, and drug abuse, but by the very marginality of their existence, the *youmin* seemed even more threatening to the police, being identified as well with kidnapping and rape.[88] They were, in effect, humans who had ceased being members of civilized society because of desperate economic conditions, and their numbers were increasing daily as the cost of living went up while employment declined. Their very existence, especially as homeless panhandlers, disturbed "public order" (*zhixu*), and the PSB ordered its officers to see that beggars were arrested and taken to hospices.[89] There were several private vocational schools or reformatories (*xiyisuo* or *xiqinsuo*) designed to return the refugees to civilized society.[90] However, the PSB decided to open an additional *suo* of its own "on a scale of management similar to that of a jail" (*jianyu*).[91]

The reformatory was to be different from a regular jail or prison.[92] (The very establishment of the reformatory in China may have reflected the global utilitarianism that took for granted the efficacy of institutions for social improvement.)[93] The latter were, in the case of the Mixed Court's women and debtors' prisons, places where criminals could continue to smoke opium and gamble as long as they had the means to pay off corrupt wardens and guards.[94] Reformatories—as viewed from an idealistic contemporary social worker's perspective—were meant to be well-regulated hospitals for the infirm.[95] The PSB had taken over the old Songhu Police Prefecture lockup, where people arrested for minor infractions were put in the same holding cells as criminals suspected of capital crimes.[96] One of the new police force's earliest plans was to build new detention centers (*juliusuo*) with proper waiting rooms, interrogation rooms, toilet facilities, and segregated areas for men and women.[97] New jails were constructed, and plans were duly made by October 1930 to build a model prison on sixteen acres, "designed in accordance with the latest Western ideas pertaining to prison construction."[98]

But this Shanghai version of Bentham's Panopticon (that "cruel, ingenious cage," which was "a mechanism of power reduced to its ideal form") was not quite the same as the Public Security Bureau's reformatory or *xiyisuo* (a term which connoted practicing the arts in a repeated and habituating way).[99] This conception of reformation by way of instruction combined the Western penal notion of rehabilitation by teaching inmates a vocational skill and industrial discipline, together with Confucian beliefs about teaching proper moral behavior through instruction.[100] Another word for reformatory was *ganhuayuan,* which suggested an institute of conversion by education; and the term for a house of hope for wayward women, *jiliangsuo,* meant "a place to aid the worthy."[101] Technical vocation and moral education were meant to merge in such reform schools, where policemen were supposed to serve as ethical teachers to redeem the lost rather than as jailers to restrain the lawless or trainers to discipline the shiftless into learning how to work. In other words, in contrast to Western correctional Panopticons, whose "functional inversion of the disciplines" primarily treated their inmates' externalities in an economy of power, the ideal Chinese reformatory addressed the individual's internalities in a community of power; it was supposed to inculcate or introvert values *while* inverting discipline.[102]

> Lately people's minds have been demoralized and virtue has been lost . . . [with] people overstepping the bounds and violating the rules. If you want to restrain them by law, then it will be punishment after punishment without victory. If you wish to use human feelings, then it will be forgiveness after forgiveness without wearing them out. Two complete roads must be chosen as a strategy by immediately establishing each of these institutes and factories [i.e., reformatories] in order to educate and nourish them. Then they will be taught a craft (*yineng*) and they will receive instruction in studies (*xueshi*). The people, having a sense of shame, will correct themselves (*min chi qie ge*).[103]

Since it was impossible to predict how long it would take for a prisoner's "evil nature" (*exing*) to be "transformed" (*ganhua*), the power to reduce or lengthen jail sentences should be vested in the police themselves, whose moral evaluation was more important than the court's more impersonal legal judgment.[104]

Police Paternalism and Social Control

In that same sense, the policeman was ideally supposed to be a teacher (*daoshi*) and nurturer (*baomu*) to the people at large, so that "society's enemies will fear us and the people will love us."[105] In his police manual,

Yu Xiuhao insisted that anyone who entered the service of the police must possess a "true spirit of self-sacrifice" and be ready to "give up the slightest bit of egoism" (*ziwo zhi taidu*).[106] Above all, he must resist the temptation to abuse his "police powers" (*jingquan*) by observing self-discipline and respecting the people's "right to freedom" (*ziyou zhi quanli*).[107] Yu Xiuhao's concern echoed a traditional refrain inspired by the contradiction between Confucian paternalism and Legalist authoritarianism, between instruction and discipline. Guides to the people, Shanghai policemen also had at their disposal an elaborate code of administrative laws (*xingzheng zhi xingfa*) and police regulations that they were authorized to prosecute entirely on their own.[108]

This system of penalties for breaches of administrative law was enforced in Chinese territory by the PSB and not the judicial courts.[109] Principal punishments for violation of administrative law could be detention in the Public Security Bureau for one to fifteen days, a fine of $0.10 to $15.00, or a caution; while accessory punishments could result in confiscation, suspension, or prohibition of a business.[110] The police administrative laws covered many different aspects of daily activity. According to Article 3, it was a police offense, punishable up to fifteen days in jail, to loiter on a highway, beg alms, conduct prostitution, sing indecently, or hold improper theatrical performances.[111] Article 32 prohibited setting off firecrackers in densely populated places, disseminating rumors, and allowing dogs or lunatics to run recklessly along the highway or enter a dwelling.[112] According to Article 34, you could be fined up to $10 and serve ten days in jail if you failed to report your marriage, the birth of a child, or a change of residence to the PSB. The same applied to innkeepers who did not record the names, occupations, addresses, and destinations of their guests. Article 34 also made it a police offense to fail to answer correctly the questions of a PSB officer at a public meeting.[113]

Between July 1927 and June 1928, 4,652 adjudicated trials for breaking administrative laws were judged (*panjue*) entirely by the PSB proper, often within twenty-four hours of the misdemeanor.[114] According to the municipal advocate of the International Settlement:

> In Chinese territory the practice seems to be for the Public [Security] Bureau to order, not arrest, the accused to appear immediately at the nearest station, provided he does not have really important matters to handle and the exact name and address of such accused is known and there is no danger of such accused absconding. The order is mandatory, for if the accused does not comply he is arrested and taken to the nearest station. When the accused arrives at the station he is given an immediate trial.[115]

Simple infringements of police regulations ("breaking police laws" or *wei jinglü*), usually handled on the street by patrolmen, numbered much higher: during the year July 1929–June 1930, police dispensed with some 38,147 cases.[116] And of the grand total of 206,441 crime and misdemeanor cases recorded over the entire period 1927–32, only 18 percent (37,175 cases) were violations of the law, whereas 82 percent (169,266 cases) were infringements of police regulations.[117]

The fines collected by the Public Security Bureau constituted a significant, though not major, source of revenue. During the police year 1930–31 alone, Ch. $138,356 were collected as police fines and used to defray expenses.[118] Needless to say, the PSB's partial dependence upon fines naturally would have led to an increase in the level of enforcement of police-invoked rules (as opposed to that of regular criminal laws), which patrolmen generally tend to underenforce.[119]

This quasi-independent judicial authority gave the Shanghai Chinese police force unusual power to regulate social mores.[120] As agents of the new revolutionary government, the police determined from the outset to "reform" (*gaishan*) Shanghai's unseemly public manners[121] by prohibiting women from walking around with bare arms, by banning dramas that were injurious to public morals, by seizing "inappropriate" or offensive brands of cigarettes from vendors, by forbidding the publication of books considered "wounding to public customs," and by fining pedestrians for spitting on the sidewalk or using obscenities in the streets.[122] The police also targeted entertainers, using business licenses to regulate popular behavior, so that dance-hall girls (*wunü*) were required to register with the police and then wear their license on their blouses or dresses.[123]

But enforcement of these blue laws was not easy and, confounding public propriety with social health, the PSB found that police interference in relatively trivial personal habits infuriated the citizenry beyond normal measure.[124] The police, after all, sought to regulate every aspect of popular culture, from movies and funeral arrangements to astrologers, fortune tellers, and even neighborhood gossips. To control the content in advertisements, the police specifically forbade pornography offensive to public morals, patent medicine swindles, pictures showing "improper liberties" that might deprave young men and women, get-rich-quick schemes, "radical" (*jilie*) appeals dangerous to "order" (*zhixu*) and "peace" (*anning*), as well as "other things forbidden by the authorities."[125] Similarly, they insisted upon putting hotels and theaters under surveillance in order to "reform social customs." They formed a Movie Inspection Committee (Dianying jiancha weiyuanhui) to make sure that Shanghai inhabitants were not corrupted by lewd and licentious films. They even forbade funeral attendants (*yizhang*) from carrying banners or placards that conveyed "any sort of feudal flavor."[126]

Yet as annoying as this police interference was in the lives of many sojourners in this Sino-Western treaty port, few could deny that the abandonment of traditional decorum accompanied modern vices, and the combination undercut the economic foundations of Shanghai citizens' lives. Organized gambling was perhaps the worst of these, especially when it came to personal bankruptcy and familial ruin. This fundamental challenge to the social control of the police, along with other vices that sustained a gigantic network of organized crime, will be examined in the chapters that follow.

3

ORGANIZED "CRIME"

7   Vice

Such unwholesome recreation resorts as roulette houses,
greyhound racing stadiums, cabarets, and dancing saloons,
which are great criminal mills, turning out kidnappers,
robbers, loafers, ruffians, and other undesirable and daring
desperadoes in large number and on a wholesale scale should
be ordered to be sealed without a moment's delay.

China Weekly Review (1930)

All of the law enforcement agencies of Shanghai, including even the Japanese consular police, engaged at one time or another in the regulation of vice, and especially of gambling and prostitution. Each of them, and notably the Chinese Public Security Bureau and the Shanghai Municipal Police, was ultimately frustrated in its effort at control because of the limitations of its own jurisdiction. Suppression in one sector of the city simply meant that the activity moved to another more receptive zone. Or, successful restraint within a jurisdiction was jeopardized by events taking place outside that area, even outside Shanghai proper in the hinterland under Nationalist authority. This story of municipal partition was repeated again and again until it became one of the most salient aspects of Shanghai's qualities as a "capital of vice." Yet it deserves retelling here because genuine police efforts to control the city's entertainment industries illustrate better than practically any other law enforcement activity the limitations imposed upon the Chinese police by extraterritoriality.

Gambling as Entertainment and Crime

During the late 1920s and early 1930s commercialized gambling in Shanghai existed on a scale larger than in any other city in the world.[1] The turnover from professionally conducted gambling exceeded $1 million a week, and some claimed that Shanghai deserved to usurp Monte Carlo's title as the gambling center of the world.[2]

This new entertainment industry was not without its social costs.[3] Not only did gambling encourage both white-collar crime and violent felonies (armed robberies increased appreciably just before the autumn horse races each year);[4] it also fostered the destitution of ordinary urban residents, who all too often lost their money at the dog track, in a casino, or playing popular lotteries[5] like "huahui," and who ended up—in the slang of the time—"taking a jump in the Huangpu River" (*tiao Huangpu*) or leaping off the roof of the Great World amusement center.[6] Westerners liked to believe that they were immune from such feverishness.[7] Contemporary Chinese commentators, by contrast, blamed the foreign authorities, and especially the French, for making these temptations available to fellow countrymen who committed suicide in such large numbers.[8] This was especially so after the effects of the Great Depression began to reach Shanghai in 1930 and 1931, when unemployed white-collar workers—former bank clerks, customs brokers, and so forth—precipitously took their lives.[9]

Casinos frequented by foreigners were often registered in local Latin American consulates so as to take advantage of extraterritoriality.[10] However, a large Chinese clientele patronized these gambling houses as well. There were even "foreign style" casinos managed by Cantonese exclusively for Chinese customers.[11] A private survey of several roulette casinos in the French Concession in 1929 estimated the daily number of patrons as one to five thousand apiece, while approximately $150,000 changed hands in the average gambling house during operating hours, which ran from 3:00 P.M. to 3:00 A.M., seven days a week. More than 50 percent of the patrons were young Chinese women from twenty to thirty years old, and they were mainly identified as being concubines and wives of local officials and merchants.[12]

Like high rollers in Las Vegas, casino habitués received free-of-charge the best cigarettes, wines, liquors, food, and opium available. Du Yuesheng's best-known gambling casino—the three-story Fusheng at 181 Avenue Foch—even provided its big-stake customers with chauffeured pickups and returns in the latest model limousine.[13] Of course, the casino also ran a special "service" shop next door where you could conveniently pawn anything from fur coats to underwear.[14] Especially in the French Concession, but also at first in the International Settlement, such gambling houses were more or less openly tolerated by the police, although they were also rigged with camouflage in the event of sudden raids.[15]

Gambling on horse racing initially served as an amusement of the foreign community.[16] Track meets at the Shanghai Race Club, which with its adjoining recreation grounds covered sixty-six acres of the choicest property in the city, were originally held twice a year, during the first week in May and the first week in November.[17] In the 1910–19 period,

> Every Shanghai gentleman owned ponies (Jardine's had the largest
> stable of course), and a good many of them participated in the
> races. It was a strictly sporting affair: no jockeys were used. . . .
> There were no bookmakers, and one-fourth of the totalizator's in-

come was used for the upkeep of the establishment. The Great
Shanghai Sweepstake was the climax of the season.[18]

Ordinarily the race tracks were segregated. Although other non-whites,
such as Blacks, Koreans, and Indians, could enter the grounds and stroll
through them, Chinese were forcibly kept out by guards—except for race
days. On those occasions, Chinese could line up at the race track window
and buy a one-to-five dollar ticket to get in to bet.[19]

The reason racial barriers were eventually lowered was quite simple:
after World War I the foreign owners realized the important contribution
made by their Chinese clientele to large-scale horse race betting.

> Development of foreign race courses and race club property in
> China is a result of Chinese patronage of their meetings; that is, it
> has been Chinese betting on the races that made the foreign clubs
> prosperous. Probably ninety-five percent of these clubs' revenues
> come from Chinese.[20]

As a result, the Shanghai Race Club was said to be the wealthiest foreign
corporation in China except for one or two banks and shipping companies.
Taking 20 to 25 percent of the money bet on the big "sweeps," the club's
percentage from the four-day autumn meeting alone yielded $250,000.
The net profits from those grosses, invested over the years, had enabled
the club to acquire lands and buildings valued at many millions of dollars.[21]

The prospect of such stupendous profits induced other investors to
form the International Recreation Club and the Far Eastern Recreation
Club in order to open two more race courses at Jiangwan and Yinxiang
outside the International Settlement. Together the two tracks earned revenues of about Ch. $960,000 per year by 1927, but because they had to be
licensed by General Sun Chuanfang, 40 percent of these net profits were
transferred to the Garrison Command. After the Nationalists took power
they continued to levy high taxes on the racetracks and additionally tried
to force the race clubs to absorb central government loans and buy revenue stamps for their admission tickets.[22] This pressure, coupled with
threats of violence and kidnapping, continued until after the Northern
Expedition.[23] Then the Chinese Municipality took over the revenues.
Taxes and "squeeze" thus reduced the profit margin of the extra-settlement Chinese racing clubs, but the returns were still high enough to make
the licensed horse race concessions a good investment.[24]

Greyhound racing proved to be an even more profitable form of track
betting.[25] On September 28, 1927, the Greyhound Association of China

Ltd. was incorporated in Shanghai by, among others, Shanghai Municipal Council member W. R. B. McBain and SMP police officer M. O. Springfield, with a capitalization of $250,000.[26] After the Greyhound Association Ltd. (one of whose board members was SMC chairman H. E. Arnhold) opened a dog track called Luna Park, another group of British investors set up a second called the Stadium. Both of these dog tracks were located in the International Settlement. A third, the Canidrome, was opened about the same time in the French Concession by Le Champs de Courses Français.[27]

The dog tracks featured pari-mutuel betting, which was outlawed in England. The owners, who were mainly foreigners with excellent political connections to the Municipal Council, published daily advertisements in the Chinese and foreign newspapers, with posters on billboards and tramcars. Free admission tickets were distributed to well-to-do Chinese merchants, to Chinese members on the staff of foreign firms, and even to children who took them home and gave them to their parents.[28] The sport quickly became very popular, and on a typical Saturday evening seventy thousand people attended the dog races at Luna Park.[29]

> The average person's programme for his leisure runs something like this: on Monday evening he rests at home after a strenuous weekend. Tuesday evening he attends the greyhound racing at the Stadium and the following evening at Luna. On Thursday evening he may attend the greyhound racing in the French Concession. On Friday, he goes to the Stadium and the following evening to Luna. On Sunday, he goes to the greyhound racing in the French concession.[30]

A meeting at one of the dog courses during good weather had a high turnover, and it was estimated that greyhound racing took about Ch. $250,000 a month out of (mainly) Chinese pockets.[31] In their annual financial report announced on October 31, 1930, the British owners of Luna Park showed a net profit of Ch. $322,000.[32]

Like the horse racing revenues, greyhound receipts could not but attract the new régime's attention. American journalist John Powell remarked, "If General Chiang Kai-shek had a small proportion of the money which will flow into the coffers of the Shanghai race club and the greyhound racing club this spring, he could finance his Northern Military Expedition and probably have sufficient left over to cut a considerable slice off the Chinese national debt." To Powell this would have seemed just deserts since "these institutions annually drain vast sums of money out of China for which little return is made."[33] But Chinese commentators were struck less by the Chinese government's supposed moral claims to foreign gambling revenues than by the connection between the foreign concessions' tolerance of modern commercialized gambling and the urban populace's rack and ruin. "We often read in the Chinese newspapers of suicides, of bankruptcies, of young men, clerks in firms, misappropriating from their employers large sums of money in order to gamble and, after finding that they have lost it all, end their lives by drowning themselves in the Huangpu River."[34]

An even greater cause of suicide, however, was a traditional southern form of gambling called "huahui," which came to Shanghai via Ningbo.[35] Huahui ("flower club") betting appealed to upper and lower classes alike, "ranging from rich people to the poorest rickshaw coolies, for a man may put in a hundred dollars or he may put in one copper."[36] This form of the numbers game especially attracted women who "stubbornly held on to superstition" by burning incense and consulting soothsayers before wagering.[37] According to Chinese police reports, huahui losses were a major cause of female suicide.[38] The huahui lottery (prohibited in the Chinese Municipality) was envisaged as doorways to a house.

> There are altogether 36 doors; to each door there is some special
> name. When lots on these doors are drawn, only one of these
> doors is to be counted. Any gambler may put in any sum of
> money, coppers, dimes, dollars, etc., in any one of these doors. If
> when the lots on these doors are drawn and if it happens that the
> door counted is the very one in which he placed his money, he
> would have back 29 times the sum which he put in before.

The organizers of the lottery, which was drawn every morning and evening, pocketed the remaining 7/36ths wagered or about $48,000 per day.[39]

The headquarters or "big pipe organ" (*datong jiguan*), where the lots were drawn, was located in the foreign concessions. Its many branches were spread throughout Shanghai, providing employment for hundreds of *liumang* who manned these streetside posts to earn commissions on the winnings. Because huahui was also banned in the foreign concessions, the headquarters office was regularly moved from place to place, but everyone knew precisely where it was located. It flourished with such impunity because the SMP and French police were regularly paid off by the lottery's organizers.[40] Efforts by the chief of the Songhu police prefecture, Xu Guoliang, to cooperate with the SMP to close down the "big pipe organ" at Mengjiang Alley in the jurisdiction of the Hongkou police station came to naught because when plans were made for a joint raid, the gamblers were tipped off in advance.[41]

Chinese Efforts to Control Gambling

Although the SMP did try periodically to close down gambling establishments and arrest their operators during the first two years of the new Chinese municipal government's rule, the latter's Public Safety Bureau officers continued to believe that the International Settlement and French Concession police forces were not to be trusted to carry out a thorough-going crusade against gambling.[42] In their view the most effective approach was a characteristically legalistic one. They would only be able to close down the huahui and other gambling rackets by drawing up severe provisions, restrictions, and regulations (see Appendix 1); and then they would compel the Settlement authorities to help them enforce these statutes by securing the support and backing of the Chinese government's highest political authorities.[43]

Partly because of such pressure from the Chinese government, the SMP decided in January 1929 to mount a campaign against the concession's roulette casinos.[44] Although the January 1929 raids did not force all of the International Settlement casinos out of business by any means, they did drive a number of customers across the boundary into the French Concession. There, in response to the SMP crackdown, several Cantonese entrepreneurs opened up their own casinos directed toward a mixed Sino-Western clientele.[45]

The Chinese authorities no doubt appreciated the SMP's campaign against roulette, but they were much more concerned about the new sport of greyhound racing. Advertisements in the Chinese press and distribution of free tickets of admission made the greyhound tracks seem a much greater danger to public morals. In May 1929, consequently, the Chinese government sent a formal protest to the British ambassador, Sir Miles Lampson, noting that greyhound pari-mutuel racing was forbidden in the British Isles and should therefore be outlawed in Shanghai.[46] Sir Miles in turn came to Shanghai to deliver the objection to E. S. Cunningham, American consul general and head of the consular body, and to inform British officials that they would have to stop greyhound racing because of the Chinese official reaction against it.[47] In response to this prompting, British members of the SMC wrote the British directors of the Luna Park and Stadium on May 25 requesting them to restrict their races to one night a week.[48] The greyhound stadium proprietors asked in turn what the council intended to do about other forms of gambling in Shanghai. Less than a day later, in the dawn hours of Sunday, May 26, the Shanghai Municipal Police staged a spectacular siege in front of a casino at 151C

Bubbling Well Road popularly known as "The Wheel," rounding up more than two hundred customers including a dozen consular officials.[49]

The "Wheel Case," which had its first hearing on June 12, 1929, was described in the press as a "gang war" between the British-owned greyhound gambling resorts (whose board members and investors included SMC members and British police officers) and the Latin American and Chinese-owned roulette casinos. The defense attorney for The Wheel's owners, a Mexican citizen named Carlos Garcia and his partner, G. F. del Valle, argued in Shanghai Municipal Court that his clients were being railroaded because certain financially interested members of the SMC were anxious to suppress roulette in order to attract people to greyhound racing.[50] The English-reading public readily accepted this explanation, but that hardly helped poor Mr. Garcia, who learned in Chinese provisional court that the Mexican treaty conferring extraterritorial rights had expired at the end of 1928.[51] Meanwhile, despite the orders to restrict their races to one night a week, the British dog track owners were able to maintain their profits by dint of increasing the number of events they ran on that one night.[52]

The Nationalist government refused to relent.[53] As agitation for the abrogation of the unequal treaties mounted, the Chinese authorities demanded that the Luna Park and Stadium be closed.[54] The SMC tried to stand firm, but the consular body found it difficult not to respond to this pressure. On July 8, 1930, the Nanjing government finally announced that it would stop greyhound racing in Shanghai by issuing arrest warrants for Chinese employees and habitués of the dog tracks. Shares in the two enterprises slumped toward zero, and after the SMC finally ordered the two tracks to shut their gates by March 31, 1931, they went out of business.[55] The French Concession's Canidrome, however, refused to heed the Chinese government's demands.[56] Now, as the only dog track in town, business boomed. The French owners even stopped issuing complimentary tickets and began charging everyone an entrance fee.[57] However, their profits were instantly eaten away by heavy taxes: $574,890 to the Caisse des oeuvres d'intérêt public; $35,900 to the French Municipal Council; and $18,833 to the French police.[58]

Nevertheless, public pressure, especially in *Shenbao* and other major Shanghai newspapers, continued to mount against greyhound racing in particular, and gambling more generally, during 1930. Between October 18 and October 25 the Japanese Self-Preservation Society in Shanghai held a meeting against gambling, and the local newspaper *Nichi-nichi* published a notice that the Japanese consular police were going to attend local dog and horse races and jailai games, and report the names of any Japanese attending for prosecution in Japanese consular court.[59] That same year the International Settlement banned the importation of slot machines. Later, when the import ban proved ineffective, the SMP ordered owners to remove the thousand or so in use around the Settlement.[60]

But the French Concession proper refused to clean up its vice establishments; at the time this was attributed almost invariably to extraterritoriality.[61] French tolerance of vice was also ascribed by at least one contemporary Chinese journalist to a kind of colossal colonial indifference to the sufferings of the native population, and to a gallic willingness to tolerate the most blatant forms of criminality in exchange for bribes and favors.[62]

> First [the French administration] permitted a gang of Chinese opium and dope smugglers to establish themselves in the concession, where under French extraterritorial protection they have consolidated their position to such an extent as to be practically impregnable. Next, the French authorities permitted the opening of gambling houses catering to Chinese, which have become practically as formidable as the drug ring. Now as a final step toward debauchery, the local French officials have permitted the opening of gambling houses catering to foreigners.[63]

This kind of journalistic exposé made the French authorities, and especially Captain Etienne Fiori, chief of police, squirm. A commission of inquiry would soon put the latter's position in jeopardy, and by September 1931 Fiori was promising to close down all of the six to ten big commercialized gambling resorts that flourished in the residential section of Shanghai's French Concession.[64] In fact, as we shall see, except for a few desultory raids, nothing much was done until Fiori was dismissed and a reformist administration appointed by the authorities in Paris managed to get the racketeers out of "Frenchtown."[65]

Of all the Public Security Bureau's campaigns to control the vice industry, the attack on organized casino and dogtrack gambling in the foreign concessions of Shanghai surely counts as the most successful.[66] By 1930–31 the PSB, with the full diplomatic backing of the Nationalist government and working through the British and American consular authorities, managed to get many of the casinos and the greyhound racing tracks in the International Settlement closed, and to bring public pressure to bear upon the French authorities so as to help topple the corrupt Fiori administration. Yet we must also recognize that closing down the casinos in "Frenchtown" meant reopening them in other parts of Greater Shanghai, including South Market and Zhabei, where the Chinese police were soon "blocked" or bribed in much the same way as had been their colleagues on the French and International Settlement police forces. Thus, public gambling continued to be a bane to the Public Security Bureau even after it secured banishment of the vice from areas beyond its direct jurisdiction precisely because of the vulnerability of any Shanghai law enforcement agency to the massive corruption that went with roulette or lotteries.[67]

Chinese Organization of Leisure and Gambling

During the boom years of the First World War—an era typified as "the golden age of the bourgeoisie" in Shanghai—a Chinese medicine millionaire named Huang Chujiu decided to build a modern amusement center for the common folk of the city.[68]

> The result was for those days a tall building, given a Chinese name signifying "the paragon of all such edifices" and embodying a large theatre, open-air cinema, and roof garden where people could sit and gossip over their tea. The venture was a resounding success, and Huang decided to sell out his interest to build a bigger and better center called the New World. This again was so successful that the Peking authorities decided they too would have a modern amusement center, which they built in 1916 under the same name. Meanwhile, in Shanghai the enterprising Huang ceded his New World shares to the widow of his former partner and . . . [built] a new temple of pleasures to outdo all the rest. Completed in record time due to the large bonuses given to construction workers, it was opened on July 4, 1917, as the Great World [Da shijie].[69]

The Great World, a hodgepodge of West and East, expanded gradually, story by story, until it attained its present five floors behind a broad facade with spires on 14,700 square meters of land at the corner of what were then Thibet Road and Avenue Edward VII.[70]

The central attraction of the original amusement center had been a set of several dozen funhouse mirrors imported from Holland.[71] Later, cinemas were added, along with fast-food shops and galleries. The layout of the building resembled one of the modern department stores over on Nanking Road, so that customers moved from floor to floor, shopping from one layer of entertainment to the next: theaters, puppet shows, wrestling, sing-song girls, food shops, and games of chance.[72] Yet there was also an air of the country fair about the building, with a rich offering of regional drama and traditional storytelling.[73]

Shaoxing opera, which had begun as a rural ballad form, was introduced into Shanghai at the time the Great World was being constructed;

and under the influence of both Beijing opera and the naturalistic production style (including stage scenery) of Western theater, it took on a much more dramatic form. A. C. Scott saw his first Shaoxing drama in the Great World.

> The plays were romantic and highly sentimental to the point of being maudlin, concentrating as they did on tragic lovers, betrayed wives, and thwarted passions. . . . Shaoxing drama was a particular favorite with women playgoers; whether they were middle-aged matrons, old grandmothers, simple servant girls, or shop assistants, one and all were assured of a deliciously harrowing hour or two and a colorful stage presentation whenever they went to the theatre.[74]

Storytellers in the Great World, meanwhile, entertained in one of several halls on the second floor. Dressed in long Chinese gowns and carrying a folding fan or handkerchief, they amused their audiences in one of the many storytelling styles of the Yangzi Valley, so that a visitor to the Great World was almost always certain to be entertained in his or her own hometown dialect.[75]

Although an entire entertainment district grew up around the Great World (the Nanjing Movie Theatre and the Casanova Cabaret were on the same crossroads, which was one of the most heavily frequented in the city by Chinese pleasure-seekers), Huang Chujiu went broke in 1931 and had to sell the amusement center to Huang Jinrong, the gangster who had become chief of the French police's Chinese detective squad.[76] Under the racketeer's management the Da shijie became known as "Rong's Great World." The amusement center still featured acrobatics, theatrical performances, and storytelling, but it thrived by becoming more licentious; and the Da shijie quickly acquired a notorious reputation as a midway for gamblers and prostitutes.[77] Like so many other manifestations of popular entertainment in the 1930s, its commercial success became intertwined with Shanghai's vice industries. By 1949, when the Communists turned it into the Municipal Youth Palace, the Great World epitomized Shanghai's wicked petty bourgeois decadence.[78]

The hotels erected in Shanghai became another measure of profound social change. A distinct feature of the twentieth century, the modern hotel afforded an extrafamilial anonymity that subverted the conventional household.[79] The hotel room became, as a short story written in 1940 put it, the central feature of urban life in Shanghai.

> Hotels became not just a place to put up travelling merchants or travelers from far away, but, on the contrary, the center of the cen-

tral place in the life of urban dwellers. Hence, in urban hotels all sorts of tragedies and comedies take place. A young girl is sold after being raped. A college graduate with a bachelor's degree commits suicide by swallowing lysol, following the iron law: "graduation equals unemployment" (*biye jiushi shiye*). After ten years of cohabitation husband and wife accuse each other of abandonment. A certain son of a certain rich person is suddenly abducted. Nearly nine out of ten of all court cases require as witnesses in the court either a hotel owner, a cashier, or a tea boy as witness. The history of the rise of hotels is the history of the disintegration of Chinese families.[80]

Shanghai's hotel rooms were "homes away from home" for secret lusts and chimerical desires, arenas for vice at once both private and impersonal, which was the human condition of modernity.

Dance halls were also notorious centers of vice, even though dancing had quite respectable social roots. The tea dance was one of the first cultural events to bring the Chinese and Western elites of Shanghai together. High society initially met at the Astor Hotel once a week. Soon tea dances were held every day except Saturday and Sunday.[81] As Western dancing became more popular with the introduction of the gramophone record and Victrola, it spread among Shanghai's "petty urbanites" (*xiao shimin*), and dancing schools appeared.[82] As Percy Finch remarked in what is now an anachronistic "old China hand" voice: "Shanghai had started to abandon all the old restraints which kept Chinese girls shy prisoners of their parents or husbands. They swallowed Westernism in large, strangling gulps. It was a period of tea dances, fashion shows that made the clinging Shanghai gown the mode for all China, nightclubs, society affairs on the Hollywood model."[83]

The lavish nightclubs that opened in the 1920s and early 1930s in Shanghai mainly catered to the large and affluent population of Western bachelors.[84]

> Shanghai was the place to give a bachelor all the fun he could possibly ask for.[85] Throughout those turbulent years through revolutions and civil wars, through crises and depressions, Shanghai had gone on with the world's most glamorous, most sparkling nightlife. Beneath a million brilliant lights the cabarets and gambling houses, the theaters, teahouses, dance halls, sing-song places were jammed with customers.[86]

The most famous nightclubs included Farren's and Del Monte's (both casinos), where the dancing partners were White Russian women sheathed in silk and watched over by vigilant Sikh guards.[87]

Del Monte's only really came to life between 3:00 and 4:00 A.M., and Ciro's and Roxy's normally closed at 6:00 A.M.[88] But a typical night out started much earlier with highballs at the St. Anne Ballroom on Love Lane, where the Filipino orchestra played, or a couple of absinthes at the huge semicircular bar at the French Club on Avenue Cardinal Mercier. This would be followed by rounds to the Ambassador, the Casanova, the Venus Café, or the Vienna, "the acme of Chinese cabaret girls' desires," where the untroubled foreign male could nonchalantly choose his companion for the evening from a cosmopolitan assortment of glamorous but ill-fated women.[89]

> You drifted into one of those cabarets an hour or so before midnight. You chose your table not too far from the floor and you looked them over: the pretty Chinese girls with their slit silk dresses and with too much rouge on their soft cheeks; the glorious Russians with their décolleté evening gowns—Chanel and Molineux models, if you did not look too closely; the stupid and touchingly attractive Koreans; the slightly simian half-castes; the quick and clever Japanese. . . . You bought your ticket and danced with them, and if you invited one of them to your table you had to pay something extra and the girl had apple cider that turned into champagne on your chit.[90]

By 1936 there were over three hundred cabarets and casinos in Shanghai's foreign concessions alone.[91]

Those same years, however, saw the rise of the dance halls: "[Shanghai] became also a city of tawdry, sordid dancehalls. The old Carlton closed. It opened again at once as a dancehall with Russian hostesses, a risqué floor show, and became a cabaret of sailors."[92] Public dancing during the 1920s had been more or less monopolized by White Russian women, but around 1930 dance halls on the Western model began to open up in Shanghai and other Chinese port cities with Chinese *wunü* (dancehall girls).[93] "The oldest restaurants are closing down; the number of tea houses and singsong houses is diminishing; and mah-jongg and poker matches now belong to history. These establishments and occupations are gradually being replaced by dancing halls."[94] Eventually, toward the end of the 1930s, Shanghai would have 2,500 to 5,000 taxi dancers, more than 60 percent of whom were believed to be practicing prostitutes.[95]

Similar complaints were voiced about the ten massage parlors licensed by the police in the French Concession and the twenty-six unlicensed massage houses in the International Settlement. The average massage establishment had about six masseuses, and they were open from around noon until midnight. Fees for the massage and bath went directly to the owner. Sexual services were contracted for directly with the masseuses, who made about $25 per month after paying the massage house owners for board, fuel, and servants.[96]

As far as ordinary brothel owners were concerned, this kind of sub rosa prostitution must have represented unfair competition. Massage parlor managers presumably were not liable for such thick "red envelopes" as regular panderers had to pay to the police to stay in business. The same unfair advantage could be attributed later to the "travel agencies" that spread to Shanghai from the United States and Japan after 1935 and that offered women as "guides" to males visiting the city.[97]

Prostitution in Shanghai

More than fifty years ago a young Chinese sociologist pointed out that, in conditions of urban development and commercialization, "a world of men develops and special types of prostitutes appear in order to meet the demands of men in the lower classes who demand sexual satisfaction and yet cannot afford to go through all the procedures of the ceremonial court-ship."[98] As streetwalkers became common in a city where among the reg-istered population there were thirteen to sixteen men for every ten women, the business of prostitution became increasingly impersonal— in Hershatter's words: "What had been essentially a luxury market in courtesans became a market primarily geared to supplying sexual services for the growing numbers of unattached (although not necessarily unmar-ried) commercial and working-class men of the city."[99] (See Figure 3.)

The market in sexual favors was, by all accounts, enormous. Adminis-trative figures of registered prostitutes provide a fractional sense of the numbers involved. In the International Settlement in 1915, for instance, official statistics listed 9,791 prostitutes.[100] Five years later, in 1920, the Shanghai Municipal Council calculated that there were more than 70,000 prostitutes in the foreign concessions: 12,000 high-class *changsan* (see below); 490 second-class *yao'er*; 37,140 unregistered streetwalkers or "pheasants" (*yeji*), of which 24,825 were to be found in the International Settlement and 12,315 in the French Concession; and 21,315 women working in "flower-smoke rooms" (*huayanjian*, where men smoked opium first and visited prostitutes afterwards) and "nail sheds" (*dingpeng* or crib joints that catered to laborers).[101] If these figures are approxi-mately correct, then in the French Concession in 1920, where there were 39,210 female adults on the population registers, one in every three women was a prostitute.[102]

These numbers certainly jibed with Westerners' impressions then and slightly later, when one of the primary motifs of Shanghai for American

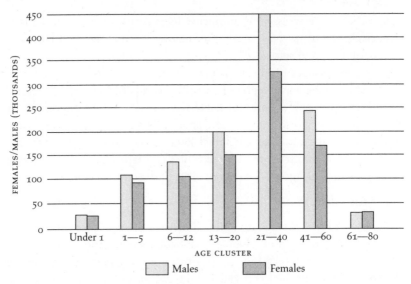

Total population: Males 1,198,908; Females 905,492

FIGURE 3.   Greater Shanghai population, 1936. Source: SAM, Section One.

theater audiences was the miscegenation of the bordello.[103] In 1929, foreigners exclaimed at the degree of public solicitation by prostitutes along
Nanking and Fuzhou Roads from nightfall until midnight:

> The situation is especially bad on the streets around the large Chi-
> nese department stores and hotels and even prevails on the street
> directly in front of the doorway to the Louza Police Station.[104] . . .
> Anyone who would so desire could count at least five hundred Chi-
> nese prostitutes on the public streets of this section of Shanghai
> any evening.[105]

The police—at least in the concessions—appeared to the public to be doing
very little to get these "pheasants" off the streets.

The foreign community was sensitive to its own vulnerability on the
prostitution issue.

> One of the publicly announced reasons for maintaining the present
> foreign régime in Shanghai is that the place would quickly go to
> ruin if the Chinese were running it, but we doubt seriously if there
> is another city anywhere in China under Chinese control where
> such a spectacle of public prostitution is presented on the public
> streets every night in the week and every day in the year![106]

The SMP did periodically round up the prostitutes on Nanking Road, forcing them to spend a night at the station, but the streetwalkers' panderers

paid a trifling fine to gain their release, and they started in again the next evening.[107] Thus, in 1932 of all the women serving time in Shanghai jails, only two were prostitutes.[108] "No one of intelligence expects this international seacoast port of Shanghai to maintain the moral standards of a New England village," *China Weekly Review* complained, "but it does seem that the Shanghai police department, if it really wanted to do so, could at least keep these women off the principal public streets of the city."[109]

While Western commentators found prostitutes on the street offensive, high-class cabarets and brothels along "The Line" (the International Settlement's red-light district) were another matter. Gracie Gale's glamorous bordello at Number 52 Jiangxi Road was properly sedate on the outside, but during the brothel's heyday in the early 1900s the inside was dominated by a richly decorated salon in the best belle époque style. Gracie Gale's Chinese chef provided a dinner that was an authentic social event. When her American girls—Big Annie, Singapore Kate, Lotus from California[110]—rode down Nanking Road summer nights in their open carriages, they set the style for the rest of Shanghai's foreign women.[111] "With energetic finesse, Gracie Gale pushed the American girl to the top of her profession. What Ming was to porcelain and the Rolls Royce to cars, the American girl was to commercial vice in Shanghai."[112]

The era of American madams and prostitutes came to an end with the Russian revolution. As White Russians poured into China, "American houses could not compete, and the American girl vanished from The Line as the buffalo vanished from the great plains of the West. Love became less segregated—and cheaper. A man could keep a Russian mistress for a month on what a night at Gracie's would cost him."[113] Hundreds of White Russian women entered the night life of the city as entertainers, shocking other Western women by "thr[owing] themselves in the arms of white and yellow alike," while at the same time utterly entrancing the city's European gentlemen.[114]

> Many of them were lush, snow-white creatures with hair the color of pale honey and eyes like violets in the spring; and they sent the temperature of Shanghai's night life soaring. . . . Overnight Shanghai became a cabaret town, a city of expensive nightclubs where the most beautiful of the emigrées appeared as entertainers.[115]

The White Russian women themselves often had little choice in the matter, having to support husbands, parents, in-laws, aunts, younger brothers, and sisters. Many opened shops, beauty parlors, and tearooms, but the surplus turned to masculine entertainment.[116] By 1930 there were about eight thousand Russian prostitutes in Shanghai, either working openly in "Russian Houses" (*Luosong tangzi*) in Hongkou and the

French Concession or as taxi dancers selling their sexual services on the side.[117]

American and White Russian prostitutes mainly served Western clients.[118] There was also a special group of Cantonese women in Shanghai, registered by British medical authorities, who exclusively serviced foreign sailors.[119] But the vast majority of Shanghai prostitutes, aligned up and down a social hierarchy that roughly corresponded to the evolution from traditional courtesanship to modern streetwalking, catered to a Chinese clientele.[120]

Chinese Prostitutes

The highest class of Chinese prostitutes during the late nineteenth and early twentieth centuries was composed of singers and storytellers whose private residences were called *shuyu*. This became the term they used for themselves. Westerners called them "sing-song girls," and they were celebrated by contemporary literati (especially during the period 1870–94) on special "flower rolls" (*huabang*) that advertised their beauty and accomplishments.[121]

By the 1920s, the geisha-like *shuyu* had been absorbed into the *changsan* (long threes) class of prostitutes.[122] *Changsan* were specialists in hosting banquets and gambling parties, and they dressed in elaborate costumes. They also continued the tradition of performing classical songs and scenes from opera; and, in this regard, they competed with the singers of *Shen qu* (Shanghai opera), which originated in the 1880s in Pudong as "flower drum plays" (*huaguxi*) performed in brothels.[123] However, like the original *shuyu*, the "long threes" retained the discretion of a courtesan to pick and choose their suitors: patrons desiring their sexual favors had to go through a long courtship process.[124]

Although *changsan* often went from party to party in sedan chairs, they also were to be found in the fancy teahouses clustered along Nanking and Fuzhou Roads. The teahouses, decorated in carved black wood from the South, were entered from the street directly, a wide staircase leading to the second-story restaurant and verandah where customers could chat and sip their wine or tea while looking down on the street below. Foreigners called this the "tenderloin" district of Shanghai.[125]

The next highest class of prostitutes also derived its name from dominoes: *yao'er* or "one-twos," because they were paid one yuan for providing melon seeds and fruit and two yuan for drinking companionship. *Yao'er* houses were most numerous in the French Concession (where they were called "taules" or cathouses) and along Beijing Road.[126]

"Pheasants" (*yeji* or *zhiji*) were streetwalkers who wore gaudy clothes and were thought to go here and there like wild birds. In 1932 their prices ranged from one yuan for a "one-shot deal" (*yipaozhuyi*) to seven yuan for the night. Contemporary Shanghai guidebooks warned visitors to beware of their aggressiveness and to keep a hand on one's wallet.[127]

Below the *changsan* and *yao'er* were the "salt pork shops" (*xianrou zhuang*), where, in the words of a 1932 guidebook: "The price in the shop depends on the taste of the meat. Everyone knows that a slice costs three yuan and an entire night five to eight yuan." Sex, in effect, was flesh for sale, without the benefit of songs or finesse and conducted in cubicles just big enough for a single "pigeon bed" (*gezi peng*). Most of the *xianrou zhuang* were located around the Bridge of the Eight Immortals in the French Concession.[128] The equivalent of "salt pork shops" for foreigners was the "Trenches," in Hongkou down by Suzhou Creek and leading off of Seward Road. The licensed brothels there were patronized chiefly by sailors and naval ratings. Because of the affrays (often between Japanese and American sailors), this red-light district was also called "Blood Alley."[129]

Finally, the lowest class of prostitutes were to be found in the *dingpeng* ("nail sheds"), where sexual intercourse was to be had for Ch. $0.30 as quick as "driving nails"; and in the *huayanjian* ("flower-smoke rooms") where customers combined opium smoking with a visit to a prostitute for quick sex (thirty cents) or the whole night (one yuan).[130]

Many of the girls and young women who worked in Shanghai brothels had originally been sold into prostitution by family members.[131] Others had been seized by kidnappers either in the countryside or just after getting off the boat when they arrived in this strange and confusing metropolis. The kidnappers would spirit their prey off to lockups disguised as small hotels in the French Concession where they would keep the girls until they could be sold to a brothel.[132] Still others were women enticed to Shanghai by offers of lucrative employment, who were then seized and sold off to houses of ill fame in cities such as Hangzhou and Amoy (Xiamen).[133]

The magnitude of the traffic in children and women was extraordinary. During the period 1913–17 the Anti-Kidnapping Society in Shanghai rescued 10,233 women and children: an average of more than 200 cases per month.[134] However, the bordello madams or *laobao* often had connections with the local police to whom they paid "street standing taxes" (*zhanjie juan*) and other informal levies. Consequently, if a prostitute—even a kidnapped one—fled the brothel, she was lucky to make her way to the Door of Hope or some other relief organizations without being picked up by the *laobao*'s gangland friends while the cop on the beat looked the other way.[135]

Brothels, after all, were regulated by the police in the International

Settlement under Bylaw 34, which gave the Shanghai Municipal Council the right to license all commercial establishments. Bylaw 34 was attacked by the Settlement's Moral Welfare League, which opposed the medical examination of prostitutes on the grounds that clients were given a false sense of security which encouraged vice, and that the ratepayers were thereby implicated in a system of approved prostitution.[136] In 1919 the ratepayers voted to establish a Special Vice Committee, which submitted a report in March 1920 advocating the ultimate suppression of brothels by a gradualist method: first, Bylaw 34 would be enforced strictly so that every brothel had a municipal license with an assigned number; second, every year one-fifth of the numbers would be drawn at random and those licenses would then be cancelled. In this way, the Special Vice Committee hoped to eliminate prostitution from the International Settlement altogether within five years.[137] The SMC tried to ignore the report of the Special Vice Committee, favoring regulation over elimination of the brothels on the grounds that if the houses of prostitution had no licenses, they would simply move outside the Settlement. Also, if brothels were not licensed, they would proliferate, and more police would be needed to suppress them. However, in April 1920 the Special Vice Committee brought its report before the ratepayers, who approved the proposal. Protesting, the SMC nonetheless began to take steps in May 1920 to license all brothels per the committee's instructions.[138]

Public reactions to this new policy varied from the support given by the Jiangsu Education Association to the opposition expressed by the Chinese General Chamber of Commerce. The latter conveyed Shanghai shopkeepers' letters arguing that first-class brothels served as meeting places for prominent merchants and gentry.[139] Nevertheless, the SMC ignored these objections and went ahead to sanction the first drawing of brothel licenses in December 1920. Every three months the town hall on Nanking Road filled with Chinese brothel keepers and white madams. The police vice squad used a drum and mixer under the supervision of the Moral Welfare League. Numbers were mixed, then the tap was turned at the bottom, and out rolled a ball with a number on it. The number was yelled out in English and then Chinese, and that license number's house had to shut down. Within a year 210 bordellos had closed their doors.[140]

This had three consequences. First of all, prostitutes took to the streets with—in the words of the police commissioner—"a consequent impossibility of any effective police control."[141] Frank Rawlinson of the Moral Welfare League might well argue that the police were not enforcing a rigorous policy of suppression, but the SMP simply pointed out that, because prostitution itself was not illegal, the police could not take action against unlicensed prostitutes unless they were practicing in an unlicensed brothel. By the end of 1922 even members of the Moral Welfare League were beginning to have doubts about their policies, which seemed to be driving prostitution out of control altogether.[142]

The second consequence was the masking of prostitution behind other urban entertainments and specious service agencies (both in Shanghai and around the world where there was a growing trend away from simple brothels and streetwalking). "The ordinary brothel seeks camouflage by maintaining its operations under the guise of massage houses, dancing schools, travel guide agencies, photograph shops, *chang san* or singsong houses, cafés and bars, traffickers of unemployment agencies, hotels, cabarets, and dancehalls—convenient establishments through which to work."[143]

Third, the brothels soon reopened without any license whatsoever, especially on streets along the Settlement borders; and when the new Nationalist government inaugurated the Chinese Municipality, protests sent to the consular authorities asked them to take steps to close these houses of prostitution.[144] Yet at the same time, the 1928 ban by Chiang Kai-shek's government of prostitution in all the cities of Jiangsu, Zhejiang, and Anhui led to an even greater influx of prostitutes into Shanghai's International Settlement, where by 1937 there would be nearly one thousand unlicensed houses of prostitution.[145]

The result of this uncontrollable influx from Nationalist territory was a schizophrenic social policy on the part of all the police authorities of Shanghai. On the one hand, they ostensibly opposed prostitution, especially after the League of Nations sent a Commission of Inquiry to China in 1930, published a detailed report on prostitution in the Far East in 1933, and then convened a meeting in Bandung in February 1937 attended by thirty delegates from China.[146] On the other hand, they continued routinely to license prostitution. In 1936, the International Settlement Police issued brothel licenses to 697 people, to 558 people in 1937, to 585 in 1938, to 1,155 in 1939, and to 1,325 in 1940. Meanwhile, in a more complicated process that will be examined later in discussing the impact of the Japanese invasion of 1932, the Chinese police tried unsuccessfully to keep prostitution under control in their jurisdiction. By the time the Wang Jingwei puppet régime lifted the ban on solicitation altogether in November 1941, there were probably over 100,000 prostitutes in Greater Shanghai, which truly had become the vice capital of the world.[147]

8   Narcotics

History and moral responsibility apart, opium had a tenacious
hold on China. The International Settlement in Shanghai was
as efficiently policed as any city in the world. Yet no amount
of surveillance could stop smoking after opium became illegal,
just as no amount of policing stopped drinking in the United
States during prohibition. Pipes burned within the shadow of
the central police station.

Percy Finch, *Shanghai and Beyond*

Illustrating Finch's point, the crusading journalist B. L. Simpson reported
that "the Shanghai opium trust has its headquarters in the French concession, where its stocks are safely stored under police immunity. More than
20,000 chests of Persian, Turkish, and Indian opium are stored there annually. In addition, 1,500 chests of Chinese opium are stored there
monthly, bringing a total revenue of 6 1/2 million dollars to those controlling the opium traffic."[1] The sheer volume of this huge contraband
trade surpassed the management capabilities of old-fashioned *wenren*
("celebrities") like Huang Jinrong and other older Green Gang leaders.
Although Huang had been quick to accept the invitation of the Anfu militarists to become a partner in the Joint Prosperity Trading Company, and
although his role as chief of the Chinese detective squad was a crucial
factor in the momentary success of that cartel, he still remained a traditional *banghui* (gangster band) patriarch who did not have the imagina-
tion to conceive of a monopoly over so vast a traffic, which required too
much capital investment for any single wholesale dealer to handle. Nor
could he conceive of the possibilities of producing and marketing new
kinds of refined opiates like the "white drugs" morphine and heroin to
be used with a hypodermic syringe or "red pills" to be smoked in cigarettes.[2]

But Huang Jinrong's closest disciple, the man who sat at his side in the
morning audiences and packed away the "celebrity's" fees in his boss's
suitcase, could easily conceive of such an arrangement.[3] That man—Du
Yuesheng, who had started out as an apprentice in a fruit stand in South
Market—deftly modernized the Shanghai drug trade to create one of the
world's largest illicit cartels.[4] This chapter documents the extent to which
Du's success in reorganizing the expanded opium trade became intimately

connected with political developments in Shanghai that reflected larger shifts in Chinese political power.

Du Yuesheng was born on August 22, 1888, in a shopkeeper's family at Gaoqiao in crime-ridden Pudong, across the river from the Chinese Bund.[5] By the age of nine Du had lost father, mother, and stepmother to various physical and social afflictions; and he was sent to live with a maternal uncle, whose money he began stealing after he had squandered a small inheritance on gambling. Expelled from the household at the age of fifteen, he signed up as an apprentice in a small fruit store on the Shanghai waterfront south of the French Bund near the Little East Gate. After three or four years as a shop clerk and a shorter stint in another fruit store, Du became a "boat" or runner in the numbers racket, going from teahouse to teahouse trying to get people to lay bets on lotteries derived from huahui.[6] In the course of his hustling, Du was "adopted" by the owner of a brothel, and this procuress—his "godmother" (*ganniang*)—brought him together with Chen Shichang of the Green Gang.[7] Once Du swore allegiance to Chen as his *lao touzi* (boss), he joined a band of Green Gang ruffians at the Huangpu steamship docks where they extorted money from the weak and robbed the unwilling.[8] In 1911 Du Yuesheng was admitted into the dope-smuggling Big Eight or Eight-Legged Mob (Bagudang) of Shen Xingshan, superintendent of detectives in the SMP. Du quickly became a police informant or assistant (*huoji*) for the French police.[9] The chief inspector of the Chinese detective squad was, of course, Huang Jinrong; and Du began to curry favor with Huang by paying calls on him at home, carrying his parcels and suitcase, and even participating in meetings of the detective squad.[10] Gradually, he won Huang's admiration and confidence, partly by making himself useful to his boss's wife as her loan collector and enforcer.[11] Eventually, Du was introduced to the Swatow opium merchants as an expert on protecting (and heisting) the drug along the docks of the Huangpu.[12] Although he soon came to dominate the transportation of opium along the waterfront, it was a big step from that to displacing the Big Eight Gang and monopolizing the trade in narcotics altogether.[13]

Du Yuesheng's monopolization of the Shanghai narcotics trade in the 1920s on one level amounted to an agreement between the three *wenren*—himself, Huang Jinrong, and Zhang Xiaolin—to equally divide the spoils, sharing profits among themselves rather than fighting for exclusive control.[14] But before that agreement could be reached, Du Yuesheng had to be able to deal with Huang Jinrong as an equal. In 1923 he was still just a *daheng* (bigshot), a "wise guy" leading his own hijacking raids and banking Huang Jinrong's daily take. What changed his status almost overnight was a totally unexpected incident that led to the momentary downfall of Huang Jinrong and a corresponding elevation of Du Yuesheng as Huang's savior and benefactor.

Playboys, Gangsters, and Warlords

In 1924 among the most dashing playboys of Chinese Shanghai were the young men known as the "four lords" (*si gongzi*)—a term that instantly brought to mind the romantic poets of late Ming Jiangnan.[15] The "four lords" of Republican Shanghai were Yuan Hanyun (son of Yuan Shikai, first president of the republic), Zhang Xueliang (son of Zhang Zuolin, the Manchurian warlord), Zhang Xiaoruo (son of Zhang Qian, the Nantong industrialist), and Lu Xiaojia (son of Lu Yongxiang, the warlord or *dujun* occupying Zhejiang).[16] The most notorious "romantic" of them all was Yuan Hanyun, who compared himself to the son of Cao Cao, having come to the Jiangnan area because he had angered his fathers and brothers. Even after his father's failure to become the Hongxian emperor, Yuan was considered to be a man of great influence in Shanghai, whose position was even higher than that of the three *wenren*, although he sometimes had to sell his calligraphy to support his opium habit. People in difficulty presented themselves like petitioners in front of his house at Houzaili on Baike Road. Many of these were entertainers and artists who were very much at the mercy of their gangster-patrons, and who hoped for a degree of protection that Yuan Hanyun was actually unable to provide when it came to such powerful racketeers as "Pock-Marked Jinrong."[17]

For example, when the Peking opera star Yu Shuyan visited Shanghai he held a performance in one of Huang Jinrong's theaters. It was a great commercial success. Although he thereupon made a verbal agreement to work exclusively for the gangster whenever he came to Shanghai, Yu Shuyan soon after performed in the theater of Huang Jinrong's competitor. When Huang swore to make Yu Shuyan pay for breaking his word, Yu panicked and pleaded for Yuan Hanyun's help. Yuan said that he simply could not afford to have a fight with "Jiu bing" (Nine Cakes, referring to the brand of cakes called Maqiao because Huang Jinrong's face was pitted with smallpox scars or *mazi*). However, he did introduce Yu to his closest disciple, Yang Qingshan, who saw Yu to and from the theater by car. Yu Shuyan also looked to Xu Guoliang, the police prefect (*jingcha tingzhang*), for protection. But not long afterward, Prefect Xu was murdered, and Yu, detecting the fine hand of Huang Jinrong in the assassination,[18] quickly returned to the north and never came south again.[19]

Like Yuan Hanyun, Lu Yongxiang's son Lu Xiaojia was also a patron of actors and actresses, and this too brought him into conflict with "Pock-

Marked Jinrong." At that time, on the eve of the Jiangsu-Zhejiang war and while he was still chief of the French Chinese detective squad, Huang Jinrong fancied a young and unusually beautiful Hankou actress named Lu Lanchun who had come to Shanghai to pursue her career as a Peking Opera singer. Since men and women did not usually act together on the same stage, Huang Jinrong built a special theater for Miss Lu at Jiumudi. The Gongwutai Theater succeeded thanks to Lu Lanchun, whose most famous roles were recorded on one of the gramophone records then all the rage in Shanghai. Huang Jinrong, needless to say, doted on Miss Lu, and many of his evenings were spent in his box attending her performances.[20]

One night Lu Xiaojia (then in his twenties) came, accompanied by two of his bodyguards, to hear Lu Lanchun sing the leading role in *Luoma hu*. Huang Jinrong was also in the audience. The actress performed well enough at first, but halfway through one of the role's most famous arias Miss Lu introduced a variation that struck the young "gentleman" unpleasantly, and he booed aloud. Infuriated by the insulting catcall, Huang called out his own displeasure at the interruption, causing a crowd of red-eyed "heroes" (*haohan*) among his followers to assault Lu Xiaojia on the spot. The attack was so ferocious that Lu's bodyguards were afraid to intervene, and it was not until Lu had been beaten to the ground and kicked several times that they were able to get him out of the theater and on to his carriage.[21]

Two nights later, while Miss Lu was giving another performance, a group of Garrison Command plainclothes detectives forced their way into the Gongwutai Theater and put a gun to Huang Jinrong's head. These military policemen had been sent by the Shanghai defense commissioner He Fenglin, responding to the fury of the young man's father, Lu Yongxiang.[22] The military detectives hustled Huang outside and into a car, which drove to the Longhua garrison, where Huang Jinrong was taken inside, beaten ferociously by the MPs, and thrown into the lockup.[23]

The disappearance of Huang Jinrong threw his followers into a panic. "Like ants on a stove," they rushed about, trying to find out where he had been taken. It was certainly obvious enough to them by now that in a world dominated by warlords, Zhejiang *dujun* Lu Yongxiang was emperor, Shanghai military governor He Fenglin his viceroy, and the *liumang* mere subjects. Green Gang elder Zhang Xiaolin set off for Hangzhou to try to assuage Lu Yongxiang, and Du Yuesheng began making arrangements to appease He Fenglin.[24]

This provided a golden opportunity to Du Yuesheng. Huang Jinrong's humiliation not only revealed how helpless the racketeers were in the face of brute military force (a lesson Du Yuesheng never forgot vis-à-vis Chiang Kai-shek); it also cost Huang some of his reputation among his disciples in the Green Gang.[25] Du Yuesheng arranged for his "teacher's" release, of course, but he did so by undercutting Huang's hegemony over the protection racket in order to establish a much more ambitious marketing set-up of his own. Supposedly assembling the wherewithal to ransom his boss, Du brought together Shanghai's ten major Cantonese opium wholesalers and persuaded them to invest millions of dollars more in a common fund in order to bribe Defense Commissioner He Fenglin into helping them set up an opium monopoly for the entire city.[26]

Meantime, warlord armies continued to swirl around the city, which changed hands repeatedly.[27] The Jiangsu-Zhejiang war that broke out in September 1924 lasted for forty days, ending with the victory of Qi Xie-yuan and Sun Chuanfang while Lu Yongxiang and his officers slipped out by boat to Japan. As word came to Zhang Zuolin in the Northeast that Lu Yongxiang was losing the struggle, the Manchurian warlord realized that the Zhili clique would thereby be free to attack him without fighting a two-front war. Zhang therefore attacked the Zhili forces in north China even before the Jiangsu-Zhejiang war was over. Wu Peifu counterattacked successfully, however, and for a moment it looked as though he was going to defeat Zhang Zuolin and unify China under his Zhili faction's rule. Precisely because of that possibility, he was betrayed by General Feng Yuxiang, who joined forces with Zhang Zuolin and occupied Beijing for the Fengtian faction on October 23, 1924. This not only destroyed the hopes of the Zhili faction of unifying China; it also brought General Lu Yongxiang back from Japan to retake Shanghai under Zhang Zuolin's aegis and to renew the opium agreements that He Fenglin had worked out with Du Yuesheng.[28]

The Reorganization of Crime

The exact date of the founding of the "Big Company" (Da gongsi) is not known, but probably later that year or early in 1925 the Three Prosperities Company (Sanxin gongsi) was formally established, with capital of Ch. $2.7 million, by the ten leading Swatow opium dealers and the three wenren.[29] Thereafter, any other wholesale dealers who tried to muscle in on the Big Company had two opponents to face: the Green Gang itself, and the military police of the Garrison Command. In addition, an alliance forged with the French Concession leadership included the chief of police.[30]

On April 28, 1925, a tense meeting took place at 4 Route Vallon, which was the home of a French pharmacist named Galvin.[31] Two other Europeans were present, Chief Fiori and Dr. Hibert. The Chinese principals, Du Yuesheng and Wang Jiafa, represented the opium syndicate. Monsieur Galvin presented the French offer: in exchange for an initial payment of $35,000 "pour fermer les yeux" (for them to close their eyes), the French police and consular authorities would permit Du and his associates to open five opium shops and a depot. After two weeks' trial, a second $35,000 would be due, and then in two more weeks' time fifteen additional shops could be opened. Du Yuesheng and Wang Jiafa were quick to express their lack of confidence in the protection of the police and insisted upon paying the first $35,000 only after a trial period of ten days. After much further negotiation, and one false start, a second agreement eventually concluded on June 1, 1925, between the two "committees" provided for a three-month contract that paid a lump sum of $140,000 to the Europeans, plus $80,000 per month thereafter as well as $250 for each case of opium unloaded at the depot and $500 per month for each retail shop in operation.[32]

The French Concession arrangement was a particularly lucrative set-up for Du Yuesheng, because in exchange for the police protection he had just bought, he acquired what amounted to a quasi-official system of value-added taxation upon retail consumption.[33] The arrangement functioned, in effect, as a kind of tax farming conducted under his personal aegis. A special "Opium Pipe Company" collected 30 cents per day for each pipe in a den. Every afternoon, after collecting, company officers put a seal on the den's account book.[34] If a den refused to pay, then the company arranged for the French police to stage a raid. Sometimes, police raided regardless, but if they turned up account books with the seal of the Opium Pipe Company on them, the proprietor was not punished. The result was that

> The company's income amounted to about 100,000 [Mexican] dollars per month and all opium smoking dens south of Avenue Edward VII and west of Mohawk Road paid contributions and were permitted to conduct business openly. . . . Du, together with Huang Jinrong and Zhang Xiaolin, amassed considerable strength and numbered among their associates and followers officials, detectives, conductors of gambling dens, shopkeepers, lawyers,[35] armed robbers and kidnappers.[36]

Under such lucrative circumstances Huang Jinrong yielded the first line of leadership willingly, simultaneously resigning from the French detective squad and giving up "social affairs" (*shehui shiye*) for "philanthropy" (*cishan*).[37] This dual retirement did not mean, however, that he simply ceased being a major gang patron. So far as is known, Du Yuesheng did not change the organizational structure of the Green Gang toward greater centralization. Rather, each of the three *wenren* continued to build up their own personal cliques, rewarding their followers with shares of the huge profits from the opium cartel's receipts, which were estimated to range annually from $40 to $78 million.[38] Thrice a year—at Spring Festival, Dragon Boat Festival, and Mid-Autumn Festival—Du Yuesheng would invite the ten major opium merchants to a party. After the formalities were over, Du would tell them that he needed a certain sum of money, an amount that reflected Du's own carefully researched knowledge of the true extent of their profits.[39] Afterward, and always during the festival celebrations, the three racketeers would distribute due amounts of these gains to their individual followers.[40]

In return, Du Yuesheng could guarantee that the shipments of the ten big opium merchants would be transported safely from the port to one of the underground warehouses for storage and sale.[41] In addition to providing Green Gang outriders, the gangsters gave the license numbers of the dealers' trucks to the French Concession Police (FCP), whose Chinese detective squad was still under Huang Jinrong's command.[42] To guarantee their protection, higher French municipal officials, probably including FCP Chief Fiori, received 2 percent or more of the narcotics revenues in payoffs of up to $150,000 a month.[43] Du Yuesheng himself was appointed to serve on the governing board of the French Concession as a full fledged municipal councilman in his own right.[44]

Crime and Politics

Du Yuesheng's crucial role on Shanghai's political stage became recognized formally during the purge of the left wing after the Northern Expedition. The story of Chiang Kai-shek's utterly unexpected "White Terror" in Shanghai, when he purged the GMD of its Communist members, has been told many times, and it will only be briefly discussed here.[45]

As the Northern Expedition neared Shanghai, the leaders of the Green Gang debated among themselves how best to respond. They had cooperated with Sun Chuanfang, the warlord who had driven out the Fengtian forces and occupied Shanghai in October 1925.[46] They had also agreed to help the French in exchange for armaments.[47] Detectives, who were members of the gang, had infiltrated radical circles in Pudong and Zhabei and provided intelligence on the workers' movement.[48] But at the same time, during the winter of 1926–27, they also provided intelligence to Guomindang espionage.[49] They were even contemplating an alliance with the Communists until the March 1927 uprising, when the syndicalists took over the police stations in Chinese Shanghai.[50] That the Green Gang and the police were such close allies helped turn the racketeers against the Communist-led unions and toward Chiang Kai-shek, who had appointed the *wenren* his "resident special agents" in Shanghai and who may have promised to recognize their opium monopoly as well.[51]

Chiang entered the French Concession on March 26, 1927, coming downriver from Hankou on the gunboat *Zhongshan*.[52] After conferring with T. V. Soong in his residence on Rue Molière, Chiang met with Yu Xiaqing and other prominent businessmen, who promised him financial support if he would break with the Communists.[53] He also reportedly conferred with Huang Jinrong and perhaps saw Du Yuesheng (who was by now an honorary member of the French police force).[54] Meanwhile, Captain Fiori arranged a meeting between SMC Chairman Stirling Fessenden and Du Yuesheng, who agreed to provide members of the Green Gang, supported by detectives from the French police, as cadres in the purge of the strikers that followed.[55]

In the early morning hours of April 12, 1927, armed Green Gang activists, enrolled as members of what had been Chen Qimei's revolutionary political club, the China Mutual Progress Association (Zhonghua gongjinhui), were allowed to pass out of the French Concession and through the International Settlement into Zhabei, where the syndicalists had established their headquarters.[56] The gangsters and detectives were backed up by regular military units under General Yang Hu, who was one of Chiang's most trusted lieutenants.[57] Yang Hu was also chairman of the special seamen's party branch—a position he owed in part to his high rank in the Green Gang.[58] During that morning and through the days that followed, Yang Hu's shock troops and the Green Gang's paramilitary forces raided left-wing centers, taking the prisoners that they seized out to be shot.[59]

Within Shanghai proper, the purge was put under the formal direction of a Committee to Purify the Party (Qingdang weiyuanhui), founded on April 14, 1927, under the direction of Chen Qun.[60] Chen was Zhang Xiaolin's secretary, Du Yuesheng's sworn brother, and a friend of Yang Hu.[61] Du, in fact, lent Chen Qun his chief Green Gang lieutenant, Rui Qingrong, who commanded the committee's "action squad."[62] Throughout April as many as four thousand leftists were killed in Shanghai and hundreds elsewhere as the White Terror spread to other coastal cities.[63] By May, Chiang Kai-shek had firmly established control over the littoral of Jiangsu.[64] In late June, Yang Hu's squad of fifty executioners brought Ningbo into line and Communists were being killed all over Zhejiang province.[65]

At the same time, Chiang Kai-shek also used the White Terror to force some of the major capitalists of Shanghai to contribute more than Ch. $50 million (or about £2.7 million) to his war chest and political coffers.[66] Bankers and industrialists who sought asylum in the foreign concessions could evade arrest as counterrevolutionaries, of course, but extraterritoriality was no hindrance to Chiang's allies in the underworld, who could threaten kidnapping across concession boundaries if a financier refused to buy one of Chiang's relatively worthless bond issues.[67]

The April 12 purge had been an important test for Du Yuesheng. When he passed it successfully, he felt as though he had "climbed the dragon gate" (shang longmen) and had become a truly durable figure.[68] According to hearsay, he was now advised by certain important "people" to gain respectability by engaging in more conventional commercial activities such as banking. The "people" included Qian Xinzhi (Qian Yongming), manager of the Sihang Savings Association and a fellow townsman of Chen Lifu and Chen Guofu. Qian Xinzhi probably helped Du Yuesheng open the Zhonghui Bank in February 1929, using narcotics and gambling casino profits and selling bank directorships at Ch. $500,000 each to Shanghai businessmen who wanted Du's protection. For, hereafter, Du Yuesheng was regarded by many respectable financiers as being a kind of "gate spirit" (menshen) who inspired fear and respect and could ward off unwelcome presences. By the eve of the Sino-Japanese War, Du held directorships himself in more than twenty banks, coin shops, and trust companies.[69] He also served prominently in the Shanghai Bankers Association and the Shanghai Chamber of Commerce.[70]

Within the French Concession, Du's personal standing also acquired new political respectability thanks to the activities of the Chinese Ratepayers Association (CRA). The CRA had been established in January 1927 to represent the Chinese ratepayers' interests in the French settlement, which now had over 300,000 Chinese residents. The three Green Gang leaders jointly chaired the CRA Preparatory Committee, which operated out of Du's residence on Rue Wagner.[71] From April through July, just after the purge, Du Yuesheng negotiated with the French authorities on behalf of the CRA over a tax increase. In exchange for accepting a temporary 2 percent increase in rates in July 1927, the CRA was given the right to elect nine Chinese advisers to the Concession's Provisional Commission. Four of the nine—including Du Yuesheng—were Green Gang members.[72]

The CRA continued to press for actual Chinese membership on the Provisional Commission in the name of self-government. When the French sought to continue to collect increased rates in January 1928, a second deal was negotiated. This time Green Gang boss Zhang Xiaolin was appointed by Consul General Naggiar to the commission as a regular member. Both this appointment and Du Yuesheng's own nomination to the Provisional Commission in July 1929 were widely regarded as the French authorities' quid pro quo for the services rendered by the Green Gang during the April 1927 crisis. Du Yuesheng, meanwhile, deemed this a major personal victory over the Gentry-Councillor Clique, whose leading member, Wei Tingrong, was abducted to Pudong a week after Du took his seat on the commission.[73] Wei was eventually released, after the French threatened to close down the opium trade, but Du Yuesheng rightly concluded that his own influence on the Provisional Commission was greater than his rival's.[74]

Just as important to Du Yuesheng's increasing prominence and durability was the Green Gang's importance in the labor unions, where it undermined the Communists.[75] On April 14, 1927, after the Communist-dominated Shanghai General Labor Union was outlawed, the Political Department of the Nationalist army in Shanghai set up a "Shanghai Labor Organizations Unification Committee" to purge the unions of leftists. The local Guomindang party branch, which was dominated by the "CC" clique of Chen Lifu and Chen Guofu, saw this as a military incursion upon its turf and therefore established a rival "Shanghai Federation of Workers." While the two of these struggled against each other for supremacy, it became clear that the only effective force to supplant the underground Communists in Greater Shanghai was the Green Gang.[76] As Emily Honig has observed:

> There was virtually no one else who could do the job of undermining the power held by the Communists in Shanghai at that time. Shanghai's treaty port status partially accounted for this predicament. . . . One of the peculiarities of foreign domination was to render official institutions impotent. It was in this context that an organization such as the Green Gang could assume such wide ranging powers.[77]

The Green Gang leaders themselves competed to control Shanghai unions.[78] By the end of 1927 Du Yuesheng and Zhang Xiaolin had allied against Huang Jinrong, displacing his authority over such important labor organizations as the British-American Tobacco union in Pudong.[79] Huang Jinrong later complained bitterly that

> Originally Du Yuesheng called me "Uncle Huang." Later, my follower Chen Peide and Du's followers Lu Jingshi and Zhou Xuexiang became bosses in the Shanghai labor unions, but Chen's ability fell short of Lu's . . . and Du's prestige outstripped my own.

From this point on when Du spoke with me on the phone he no longer called me "Uncle Huang," but changed the term of address to "Elder Brother Jinrong." This left a bad taste in my mouth.[80]

Although these close ties between politics and crime may suggest parallels with the Italian Mafia—especially with regard to the Mafia system of *fari vagnari a pizzu* (wetting the beak) by dipping into every business venture—the Green Gang was in certain respects quite different. First, and most important of all, there was no single *capo di tutti*. Du Yuesheng was not an absolutely paramount chief of chiefs like Don Vito Cascio Ferro in Sicily at this same time. Second, Du's personal power did not pose a direct challenge to Chiang Kai-shek's political authority. Legend had it that Mussolini could only visit Mafia strongholds in Sicily with Don Vito's permission; Chiang Kai-shek came to Shanghai, so to speak, anytime he pleased.[81] Du Yuesheng savored his connection with Chiang because it gave him respectability, but he hardly took it for granted. Indeed, he valued intermediaries like Qian Xinzhi precisely because they helped "sew the stitches" between him and Chiang Kai-shek more closely.[82]

As a result of the April 12 coup de main, much has been made of the great debt that Chiang subsequently owed the Green Gang bosses as a whole.[83] Certainly, the linkages between the Green Gang and the Guomindang were considerably strengthened by the purge.[84] The Green Gang bosses received military titles with the rank of major general (*shaojiang canmou*) in May 1927, and reliable rumors had it that Chiang Kai-shek and Du Yuesheng cut a special deal in May 1931 when Chiang appointed Du chief Communist suppression agent for Shanghai.[85] According to the newspaper *Dagong bao*, at a conference held in Nanjing shortly before this, Chiang agreed to pay Du $1 million to organize anti-Communist terrorist activities while recognizing the racketeer's opium monopoly in the Yangzi Valley.[86]

But this arrangement to trade opium monopoly rights for criminal assistance against the Communists was not so much a payoff for tasks performed as an alliance between the government and the underworld for services to come. In other words, Chiang Kai-shek's determination to suppress the CCP was forcing his security authorities to ally themselves with China's major drug dealers, thereby sacrificing the Shanghai PSB's campaign against narcotics to political warfare against the left.[87]

This alliance between the military and the drug kings put political leaders in an awkward position. Not long after the April 1927 purge, Chiang Kai-shek and his military supporters found that the special purification committees set up under the Green Gang to "cleanse the party" (*qing dang*) executed so many left-wing "reactionaries" that other Guomindang leaders could not tolerate the level of killing.[88] Moreover, the Mutual Progress Association had posed the threat of forming a national network of Green Gang branches capable of taking the law in their own hands.[89] These developments prompted the establishment of the new police force in the Chinese Special Municipality of Shanghai in the summer of 1927 to bring unrestrained White Terror under control.[90] By the following September 27, a special order of the GMD Central Committee dissolved the Committee to Purify the Party, and its operations were assumed by the local party organization.[91]

Policing the Opium Trade

However, the means of exercising that control required a high degree of criminal co-optation. We have examined, in earlier chapters, the efforts made to create new policing operations in Shanghai. Despite the influx of northern policemen and the emphasis on patrol constables rather than detectives, however, "foul elements" persisted among the Shanghai police. A number of prominent Du followers worked in the Public Security Bureau, including the head of the Jiangwan police station, An Taidong; and many policemen joined or tried to join the Green Gang both for professional connections and personal enrichment.[92]

The opportunity for personal gain came with the beat, as it were; the confluence of policing and the drug trade provided a chance for the marginal to get rich in a city otherwise dominated by middle-class commerce and finance. Trade in narcotics was the lifeblood of the Shanghai underworld, and as racketeers like Du Yuesheng organized factories to refine the raw drug into ever more potent commodities for consumption, the business of marketing morphine and heroin could even be seen as a metaphor for the freebooting entrepreneurship of Shanghai itself, conducted by extracting and processing the resources of a hinterland red with poppies.[93] The profits from its traffic not only impoverished peripheral regions;[94] they corrupted all of the police forces of Shanghai.[95] As the journalist G. W. Woodhead pointed out at the conclusion of a series of articles on the Shanghai drug problem in 1931 in the *Shanghai Evening Post and Mercury*:

> The profits accruing from the illicit drug traffic in Shanghai are so enormous and its ramifications so extensive that it can hardly be supposed that all the police of all the areas concerned have remained immune from corruption.[96] . . . It is, I believe, the considered opinion of some of Shanghai's most experienced foreign police officials that if it were not for the illicit traffic in drugs, serious

crime, such as kidnapping and armed robbery, would be reduced by half, if not almost completely eliminated. The drug traffic attracts thousands of the worst criminal elements to Shanghai and fosters the formation of criminal organizations which are a constant menace to the peace and security of the law-abiding public.[97]

When the Nationalists took over in 1927, the northern military officers who manned the new PSB were determined to help stamp out the traffic in drugs, and its leaders vowed to give full support to the national opium suppression effort that was launched that same year. The effort was controversial, however, because it meant establishing a government monopoly and selling the drug through a system of permits, while at the same time preventing new smokers from getting hooked and helping old addicts to kick the habit.[98]

The Shanghai Opium Suppression Bureau was opened on August 21, 1927, in the old coal merchants guildhall in South Market. The chief of the Public Security Bureau, Shen Yulin, was named director of the Opium Suppression Bureau, which proceeded on August 27 to order all of the opium shops in Greater Shanghai to deposit securities from $500 to $3,000 with the bureau. Addicts were also told that they would have to register and get permits in order to buy opium legally.[99] There were revolutionary precedents for such licensing, especially if it was deemed part of a program of eventual suppression that ended by curing the addicted. Most important, as Garfield Huang of the National Anti-Opium Association frequently reminded leaders of the Guomindang, Sun Yat-sen had made the absolute suppression of opium a cardinal principle of the party's platform.[100]

Chiang Kai-shek himself seems to have been ambivalent about the ultimate goal of licensing.[101] On the one hand, it was a very effective way for the Nanjing government to raise revenue: during the period of legalization, from August 1927 to July 1928, the government is said to have made over $40 million.[102] On the other hand, unless the government carried the program through to detoxification and rehabilitation, with a lot of administrative self-policing along the way, legalization was tantamount to condoning the opium habit. Opponents of legalization, including the leadership of the National Anti-Opium Association (which was inspired by missionaries and subsidized by the American Boxer Fund) insisted that the failure of China to wipe out opium addiction was due to the failure of officials to enforce existing laws. Garfield Huang, the association's secretary, also frequently voiced the fear that the government would become fiscally addicted to the drug monopoly system because it could not afford to give up the extra revenue.[103]

Under the terms of the monopoly, at least, the new municipal government was serious about suppressing the drug traffic; and the PSB cooperated with the Customs Service in seizing and destroying illegal shipments
of opium, heroin, and other narcotics smuggled through Shanghai.[104]
However, public opinion was turning against legalization. In July 1928
the national government succumbed to public pressure and discarded the
policy of monopoly and taxation of the drug, and the following month a
National Opium Suppression Committee was formed under the honorary
chairmanship of Chiang Kai-shek himself. At the Opium Suppression
Conference that opened in Nanjing in October, the Generalissimo said:
"The National Government will not attempt to get one cent from the
opium tax. It would not be worthy of your confidence if it should be found
to make an opium tax one of its chief sources of income."[105]

A few weeks later, the working chairman of the Opium Suppression
Committee, Zhang Zhijiang, received a tip from his sponsor, the "Christian warlord" Feng Yuxiang, that a shipment of twenty thousand ounces
of opium from Hankou was going to be unloaded on the night of November 21–22 at the wharves along the Chinese Bund of Shanghai.[106] The tip
was passed on to the Shanghai PSB authorities, and on the night in question, Chief Dai Shifu carefully hid his men in the shadows between the
wharves and the warehouses beyond. Soon a China Merchants Steam
Navigation vessel, the *Kiangan*, pulled up alongside the docks, and crews
of coolies, flanked by armed guards, began to carry chests of the drug
ashore. At a signal, the PSB agents rushed out to arrest the convoy, blow-
ing their whistles and shouting that they were policemen. To their surprise, the thirty fully armed guards around the convoy instantly flourished badges of their own that proclaimed them detectives of the Garrison
Command. The MPs insisted that the millions of dollars worth of opium
was an official shipment consigned to the Shanghai garrison commander,
Xiong Shihui. When the civilian policemen objected, they were put under
arrest by the larger and better armed group of military detectives and
taken off in custody to the Military Police Bureau at the West Gate, where
they were detained. The chests of opium were spirited off quickly into the
French Concession for storage.[107]

News of this fracas hit the Shanghai press, making it obvious that the
military and police were completely at odds with each other. "The military now accused the police of intercepting opium which they claim was
being officially seized, while they, on the other hand, are denounced by
the police as having protected the smuggling of the drug."[108] It was also
obvious that the Chinese PSB chief Dai Shifu and Mayor Zhang Dingfan
(a member of Bai Chongxi's Guangxi clique) were in a serious quan-

dary.[109] The military Garrison Commander, Xiong Shihui, was also identified as a Guangxi man, but he was even more visibly known to be a
member of Chiang Kai-shek's personal clique. Whether or not the Generalissimo knew of the drug shipment (many thought that he did, and that
"Chiang's opium" was going to be used to finance ordnance purchases),
he would surely want to protect his own army lieutenants.[110]

Such proved to be the outcome, even though the Nanjing government
had just passed, on November 24, a new opium suppression act. The State
Council did appoint a special investigation team headed by Zhang Zhijiang, who announced:

> I intend to make this a test case for the National Opium Suppres-
> sion Committee, the usefulness and the necessity for the existence
> of which will be determined by the result of our present investiga-
> tion and the subsequent action taken by the central authorities
> with regard to our findings and the judgment of the proper authori-
> ties for adequate punishment of the offenders.[111]

Also, the head of the Shanghai Social Affairs Bureau and representative
of the local *dangbu* (GMD party apparatus), Pan Gongzhan, publicly encouraged the press to print stories about the case.[112]

The same sort of public encouragement of the investigation was, oddly
enough, expressed by Green Gang sources for a very simple reason. What
was rapidly coming to be known as the *"Kiangan* Incident" was a huge
embarrassment for the Green Gang bosses, who were turned into objects
of humiliation and who feared that their quiet arrangements with key
figures in the Nanjing government would be jeopardized. They consequently tried to turn attention away from themselves by calling for the
punishment of those involved among the military and police.[113]

Despite the public outcry, the result was indeed half-hearted. Zhang
Zhijiang's committee of investigators came out with a mixed and desultory report. They found that the chief of the Intelligence Corps of the
Shanghai Military Police, Fu Shuxian, was at fault for having arrested one
of the PSB officers.[114] But they also criticized Public Security Chief Dai
Shifu for too readily alleging that the military police had protected the
opium without evidence. Chief Dai Shifu was very close to Zhou Yong-
neng, the chief of Mayor Zhang Dingfan's secretariat; and Zhou in turn
had served in Canton under Chiang Kai-shek. This connection did not
save Colonel Dai from being suspended as director of public security along
with Colonel Fu; Mayor Zhang Dingfan resigned in short order thereafter.[115]

The central government—and certainly Chiang Kai-shek—thus refused to support the Shanghai municipal authorities vis-à-vis the Garrison Command.[116] The consensus of public opinion at the time was that Zhang and Dai's successors would neither dare to challenge the opium syndicate because of its close connection with central government leaders, nor would they feel obliged anymore to turn down the usual bribes and blandishments that had suborned members of the foreign police forces in the city.[117]

Zhang Zhijiang also resigned as head of the Opium Suppression Committee because he discovered along the way that Feng Yuxiang had told him about the drug shipment only because he, Feng, had secretly been hoarding stocks of Gansu and Shaanxi opium and wanted to drive the price of the drug up in Shanghai by forcing his rival's supply off the market.[118] Meantime, succeeding PSB directors scored the bureau for continuing to be corrupt, knowing full well that the leaders of the national government were not behind their efforts to "thoroughly rectify" (*zhengdun*) the Shanghai police.[119]

The Chiang government's evident hypocrisy about the "*Kiangan* Incident" did not shock very many at the time.[120] The narcotics problem was simply there to stay in most observers' eyes.

> The Chinese city was wide open. Under military control opium was purely and simply a business arrangement. The warlords collected direct from the combine, millions going to lesser officials in the long chain of authority from mayor to the underpaid cop on the beat. . . . With the Nationalist government, conditions did not change much. Under the guise of regulating the opium traffic, the monopoly was still the perquisite of the French concession gang, which supported Chiang Kai-shek and removed serious underworld competitors who might discredit Nanjing's make-believe efforts.[121]

Occasionally raids were conducted, and the PSB did make 1,678 opium arrests from July 1, 1929, to June 30, 1930.[122] But this barely was noticed against the more distressing backdrop of pervasive drug addiction.

By then opium was the official standard of value set by the Chamber of Commerce of Guizhou. In Yunnan, 90 percent of adult males smoked and many babies were born addicted. In Hankou, the special opium tax bureau collected $3 million in opium revenue, half of which went to Nanjing, 30 percent to the government of Hubei, and 20 percent to the Sichuanese warlord who supplied the drug in the first place.[123] Narcotics not only dominated the political economy of Shanghai; illicit drugs sapped the energies of the entire nation.[124]

9   Reds

Chiang Kai-shek's henchmen, supported by the international
police, were combing the textile factories by day and the
Chinese Quarter by night in search of Communists. Those
who were caught faced a horrible choice: to become traitors or
be killed. Thousands of the best Party cadres in China had
already suffered the same fate. Gangster bands, with whom
the Kuomintang had been working for a long time, and Chiang
Kai-shek's fascistic "Blueshirts" assisted the police. This
systematic extermination campaign, which had continued
unchecked since 1927, forced the Communists into deepest
secrecy.

Otto Braun, *A Comintern Agent in China, 1932–1939*

During these years the Nationalist government was expending a large
proportion of its resources on the extirpation of Communists and other
progressives, who were either jailed or killed, or offered the choice of
defection and betrayal with its material rewards. A sophisticated, cynical
observer at the time might have supposed that official toleration of Shanghai's various opiates was surreptitiously intended to weaken the militant
asceticism of Communist agents and divert the urban populace from radical social concerns.

The thought at least occurred to Mao Dun, whose short story "Comedy" portrayed down-and-out Mr. Hua just out of jail and trying to get
his friend Chin to help him find a job. Mr. Chin could not be of much
direct help himself, but he suddenly had a great suggestion for his progressively minded friend. "Didn't you tell me that someone accused you
yesterday of being a Communist?" When Hua answered affirmatively,
Chin went on to say: "That's fine. Now you say that you are a Communist who wants to go over to the government. Then there'll be no difficulty about a job." With that the two friends decided to go to a cabaret and
celebrate, Mr. Chin humming "Rio Rita" along the way. Hua is utterly
entranced by the cabaret and its fleshly delights, and all thoughts of social
reform are swept away. "When he emerged on the street again, Hua had
experienced another transformation in the few hours that had passed. His
pockets were still empty, and his brain was also emptied of all his old

questions. Instead it was crammed with notions of gold and beautiful women."[1]

But as the New Life Movement was later to show, in the eyes of the Nationalist right wing, political radicalism and cultural permissiveness were cut from the same cloth. The Chinese Communist movement was deliberately smeared by its association with foreign Bolshevism, and both were in turn linked in Nationalist propaganda with attacks upon the Confucian family and with the advocacy and practice of free love. In short, Chiang Kai-shek's most devoted followers were far too righteously conservative to consciously promote sexual license as a diversion for the masses.

Policing as Political Control

Instead, attention concentrated increasingly on censorial control of political opinions. Reforming public mores was held to be the positive side of a continuing attack on the enemies of social order, which had commenced with Chiang Kai-shek's anti-Communist purge of April 12, 1927.[2] One of the Public Security Bureau's eight stated reasons for the difficulty of keeping the peace in Shanghai was the presence of the Communists; and although we shall argue that concern about left-wing activities eventually turned into an obsession that hampered regular police work, it is obvious that worry over ideological dissension and radical political protest was present among PSB leaders from the very first summer of the bureau's existence. The March 7, 1928, Emergency Law clearly defined the spreading of doctrines incompatible with the Three Principles of the People as a political crime, commission of which caused one to be sent directly to the headquarters of the Garrison Command for "severe punishment" (*chengban*) under military justice.[3]

From the very beginning, too, the Garrison Command had insisted upon the establishment of a special postal inspection committee (*youzheng jiancha weiyuanhui*) with the help of the PSB in order to prevent both the transmission of espionage reports and the dissemination of Communist or "reactionary" propaganda.[4] Soon, even closer ties were being forged between the Nationalist military authorities and the Public Security Bureau after plans were drawn up on July 7, 1930, to use the graduates of the police affairs group (*jingwu zu*) of the Central Army Officers School as police personnel.[5] On August 9, 1930, the first graduates of the *jingwu zu* were tested and assigned by the central government to posts in the Shanghai Chinese police force officers' corps, and a Special Services Group was created to gather "intelligence" (*qingbao*).[6] At the same time, the Guomindang Special Services Department—which was the forerunner of the Central Statistics and Investigation Bureau (Zhongtong)—set up a counterespionage unit in Shanghai. Xu Enzeng, a graduate of Jiaotong's Engineering Department who had studied factory management at the Carnegie Institute of Technology and had worked for Westinghouse in the United States, was selected by his cousin Chen Lifu to head this unit in order to conduct "investigative work" (diaocha gongzuo) against the Chinese Communist Party underground.[7]

The advent of these new military and civilian security personnel alone may have been enough to account for the heightened concern about "reds" (chizi) or "red elements" (chihuafenzi) that springs out from the pages of the PSB police reports during 1930–31, but that seems doubtful. Rather, their arrival coincided with a growing obsession with Communist subversive activity, in contrast to the previous three years when ordinary criminals and social order were the Chinese police force's primary worry.

The basic cause for this new concern ("Communist agents are hiding in ambush on all sides, taking every opportunity to wriggle like worms") was the growth of Communist soviets in the interior. On the one hand, the Chinese police believed that many Communists were taking flight from counterinsurgency campaigns in the countryside by seeking refuge in Shanghai's urban labyrinths.[8] On the other hand, the Nationalist authorities responded to secret orders from Nanjing. On August 1, 1930, a "Secret Order from the Nationalist Government, Character MI, Number 11," addressed to the defense commissioner of Wusong and Shanghai, was signed by the presidents of the Executive, Legislative, Judicial, Examination, and Censorial Yuan. The directive noted that military operations had not been eased and that the Communists were creating disturbances everywhere. Therefore, drastic steps were needed to preserve public order.

> Concerning Communists arrested in various places, if the circumstances warrant it, they should be immediately dealt with, according to military law. In case the principal culprit has already been sent to a court, then he should be dealt with immediately in order to put an end to disturbances. Besides secretly ordering the various organizations, you are hereby ordered to act accordingly, and we expect you to order your subordinates to do the same.[9]

Public measures followed in turn. By January 9, 1931, it had already been decreed a crime to criticize the Nationalist Party in the press, while sedition included publishing and disseminating "reactionary printed materials."[10]

Three weeks later, the central Government Council (Guomin zhengfu huiyi) decided to promulgate a new Emergency Law for the Punishment of Crimes against the State, which would take precedence over the criminal code. Persons found guilty of disturbing public law and order "with a view to subverting the Republic," of conspiracy with foreign countries, and of inciting troops to desert or rebel would be liable to the death sentence. And persons guilty of inciting others to disturb the peace "by means of pictures, books, or speeches of subversive propaganda against the state" were to be punished with death or life imprisonment. Partly this created a legal weapon to be applied to the "bandit suppression zones," where the highest military organ in the district was to be responsible for the trial of suspected traitors. Partly also it helped set the security forces of the government above regular criminal procedures.[11]

Whether in the bandit zones of Jiangxi or the working-class districts of Shanghai, "reds" were to be found everywhere, constantly threatening public order and tranquility.[12] The Chinese Nationalist authorities in Shanghai carried the conviction that radical leaders would use any opportunity to stir the masses to action.[13] These fears focused on important revolutionary anniversaries commemorating the 1911 Revolution, the October Revolution, the death of Sun Yat-sen, and so on, with the month of May (the May Fourth Movement, the May Thirtieth Movement) provoking the greatest edginess.[14] Orders would go out to precinct stations and reserve units to maintain special vigilance on those days, when public processions offered an occasion for Communist "reactionaries" to incite the Shanghai mob against the authorities.[15] And on ordinary days, when the police were not trying to anticipate radical demonstrations, more and more of their efforts were directed toward keeping track of suspected Communists, making raids on left-wing bookstores, strengthening "red squad" units in the detective squads, and sending out undercover cadres to find out what the "red elements" were planning.[16]

New Collaborations—The PSB and the SMP

This anti-Communist hysteria had two extremely important consequences. First of all, it blunted the nationalistic zeal of the PSB, which until then had been acting as a force for recovering sovereign rights from the International Settlement and Concession authorities.[17] As the once-revolutionary Guomindang purged its own left wing and began to take on some of the same anti-Communist fears that the British and French had experienced all along, the Chinese municipal authorities found that they shared far more with the foreign police than they had imagined.[18] Sensing

these common fears, the PSB began to make special requests for cooperation in controlling access to and from the Chinese-governed parts of the
city on revolutionary anniversaries.[19]

Gradually, too, more and more information about "radicals" passed
from one police force to the other.[20] Although all of the police forces of
Shanghai used "third-degree" methods of interrogation, the Chinese police probably had more latitude to question with torture, especially once
"special service" elements began infiltrating the detective squad after
1930.[21] Information extracted by less squeamish military secret service
interrogators was thus passed on to inspectors in the Chinese detective
squad in the SMP, and the latter in turn disclosed their intelligence to
Chinese colleagues in the detective division of the PSB.[22]

Within the SMP the critical officer in this liaison was Deputy Superintendent Tan Shaoliang, a Cantonese who held the highest Chinese rank
in the Special Branch and who supervised a staff of his own detectives
(*tanyuan* or *tanmu*) mostly recruited through secret examinations.[23] Better educated than the "hired snoops" (*bao dating*) on the detective squad
of the regular CID, who usually rose from the ranks of regular patrolmen,
the Special Branch detectives were picked for their literacy and political
sophistication. After taking an entrance examination, they usually spent
a year or more waiting for their identification "cards" (*ka*) as regular
detectives. Tan himself earned a graduate degree and worked as a civilian
interpreter before becoming a political police official. A public figure with
flair and a certain bearing, Tan Shaoliang was thus very different from an
earlier generation of chief detectives, active in the early 1920s: officers
such as Liu Xingfu and Chen Yunzhong who were used to dealing with
straightforward criminal activities and who were more down-to-earth and
unpretentious.[24]

Tan Shaoliang was also very different from his counterpart in the CID,
"fat, jovial, beer-drinking" Lu Liankui.[25] Deputy Superintendent Lu had
been a beat cop, "rolling the flowery club" (*nie hua bangchui*) as a uniformed policeman on the street.[26] Hailing from Huzhou, southwest of
Shanghai across the border in Zhejiang, Lu Liankui was big for a south-
erner and could easily hold his own alongside patrolmen from Shandong
or Subei. In fact, he didn't care who crossed his path. With criminal suspects he was quick to use his fists or gun, and contemporaries chronicled
his rise from patrolman to detective, senior detective, chief of detectives,
and eventually deputy superintendent by counting the broken bodies of
interrogated prisoners and victims of the third degree, and the corpses of
kidnappers, robbers, and petty gangsters.[27] Yet as we shall see, both Lu

Liankui and Tan Shaoliang were to end up in exactly the same predicament after 1932.[28]

Tan Shaoliang worked well with his political intelligence counterparts in the Public Security Bureau. Through their combined efforts, case by case, the mutual hostility that had initially characterized relations between the police agents of the new Chinese municipal régime and the Settlement authorities, and had found expression in the disputes over licenses and boundary rights, gave way to a sense of common purpose in the shared endeavor against international Bolshevism and Chinese Communism.[29]

A second, unanticipated consequence of this shift in 1931 to controlling urban radicals was the increasing emphasis placed upon plainclothes ideological surveillance by the very detectives suspected of corrupt connections with racketeers and gangsters. This in turn led to an attenuation of efforts by PSB officers with outside military training to ease out of the detective squads old Shanghai hands with strong local connections. The bureau tried hard to keep the Japanese police-box system in operation, relying upon northern patrolmen on the beat to prevent ordinary felonies from being perpetrated, but Hebei or Shandong patrolmen, unable to understand Shanghai dialect, were unfit for assignments at rallies, during demonstrations, or around railroad stations where travelers' stray conversations could provide clues about the enemy's political conspiracies.[30]

On days of special concern, like the anniversary of May Thirtieth, the PSB actually had to muster detective patrols, sending squads of two or three plainclothesmen out into the city as undercover agents or *mitanyuan* (secret detectives) to stave off riot and rebellion by keeping a watch on telephone booths and monitoring travelers' movements.[31] The detective squad's growing workload meant assigning more and more police cadets to plainclothes duty. That required recruiting greater numbers of Shanghainese vulnerable to underworld blandishments, as well as paying higher salaries from an already overstretched police budget—thereby diverting resources from ordinary crime prevention and from municipal modernization.[32]

The accentuation of the Public Security Bureau's concern with "reactionary" left-wing conspiracies occurred just as the International Settlement's police force was also becoming more than usually worried by what it took to be signs of increased Communist activity in China's foreign concessions.[33] Police statistics from various concessions indicated that more than forty victims had been attacked by Communist death squads since 1928, and at least thirty of these had been killed. Several of these assassinations, which were attributed to a group within the CCP identified by France's Services de Renseignments Politiques as the "Chinese GPU" (better known as the GRU, the Glavsnoie Radzdivateinoie Oupravienie, or Red Army's secret service founded by Trotsky), were singled out for special attention. The first had been the murder of Yang Kiamoh, Inspector No. 1 of the French Tramway Company, in May 1928. Inspector Yang had given the French authorities the names of the Communist leaders of the French Tramway Union. The second was the shooting of two dissenting members of the Zhili Committee of the CCP on March 1, 1929, in the French Concession in Tianjin.[34] In that case the assassination led to the discovery and arrest of several members of the Provincial Bureau of the Communist Party, which paralyzed CCP activities for a short period of time in Tianjin and several Zhili counties. The third was the particularly bloody homicide on November 11, 1929, of Bai Xin, the defector who had brought about the arrest of Peng Pai on August 24. Bai Xin was murdered along with a servant, his bodyguards, and a detective from the Shanghai Public Security Bureau.[35] The Communist leader believed to be responsible for these murders was the founder and leader of the "Chinese GPU," Gu Shunzhang.[36]

Gu Shunzhang, an alternate member of the CCP Politburo, leader of the Communists' secret service, and special assistant to Zhou Enlai, was a machinist from Songjiang who ostensibly worked for the Nanyang Brothers Tobacco Company.[37] He had joined the Communist Party cell at Nanyang shortly after it was organized in 1924, and was subsequently sent to Canton, where he became an "action cadre" (*xingdong ganbu*) and served as a bodyguard for Michael Borodin. Borodin arranged for Gu Shunzhang to go to Vladivostok in October 1926 to take a complete GPU training course on espionage and methods of armed insurrection. In 1927 Gu served as commander of the Workers' Picket Line Brigade (Gongren jiuchadui) during the three uprisings of Shanghai workers.[38] A Green Gang member with the winning air of a Shanghai playboy, Gu was a master of disguise and deception. Just under thirty years old and well built, he often posed as a famous magician named Hua Guangqi—an illusionist who performed regularly in the Roof Garden Theater of the Sincere Department Store, appearing on stage dressed like a Western gentleman in formal clothing. Gu was eloquent, articulate, well spoken: a dazzling performer whose affability and charm were appreciated.[39] His ability to move secretly and unnoticed past the police of a dozen different foreign concessions was legendary.[40] His skill as an assassin was notorious: he was said to be able to fire a weapon in silence, and he could strangle a victim without leaving any marks at all.[41] He relished killing people: if

"Xiao Gu" was mentioned in those years of frequent "wet work," people paled.[42]

In 1928, after the Communist Party went underground, Gu Shunzhang served directly under Zhou Enlai's direction. His task, in the first few months after the CCP's definitive rupture with the Guomindang, was to create a "red special services" (*hongse tewu*) organ to conduct "political protection work" (*zhengzhi baowei gongzuo*) for the party's leadership.[43] In addition to this primary task, the tasks of Gu's Special Services unit (or Red Brigade [Hongdui] of the Central Committee, which answered directly to the Politburo) were both to support underground work by providing safe houses, documents, weapons, and even food and clothing, and to survey the loyalty of party members.[44] The last of these duties was declared to be especially important after a Central Committee directive was issued on October 17, 1928, which declared that "surrendering to the enemy and defecting" (*zishou panbian*) had become a "serious problem" in the CCP ranks and was punishable by death.[45]

According to French intelligence sources, the Communist Special Services Committee (Tewei) or Red Brigade—the "Chinese GPU"—was organized into four departments. The Organization Department was concerned with overall supervision of each of the offices (*ke*) of the Red Brigade. The Intelligence Department gathered information from various enemy camps and maintained surveillance over traitors to the party. The Operations Department protected Communist Party leaders and bureaus, maintained surveillance, found and secured locations for clandestine meetings, and executed sentences against traitors to the party. The Liaison Department maintained communications with the superior organs of the CCP, and especially contacts between white and red zones.[46]

The Red Brigade mainly operated in big cities where its agents could set up furniture stores, real estate agencies, rice stores, department stores, and clinics to provide the necessities for the CCP's underground cadres, who had no outside jobs themselves. Often the manager of the store or agency was not even aware that the enterprise had secretly been established by the Communists.[47] These shops were both a fairly secure cover (especially since CCP Red Brigade agents did not engage in activities such as labor organizing that would have drawn the authorities' attention) and a good source of supplementary income. The income was important. No one on the Communist or the Nationalist side knew the full amount of funds that were coming into the CCP's coffers. Under Guomindang Special Services interrogation, the secretary-general of the CCP confessed that in 1930 the Comintern subsidy was US $45,000 per month, to which were added funds seized in the field by the Red Army or remitted by the

Jiangxi and Fujian soviets to Shanghai.[48] Red Brigade agents also supplemented their business income and subsidies with booty from robberies, which were intended as well to disturb "public order" (zhixu) and thereby undermine the authority of the Nationalist régime.[49]

The Red Brigade also established safe houses and "secret command posts" (bimi zhihuisuo) under conditions of extremely tight security. Party leaders would order a Red Brigade cadre to send agent A (jia) to set up the safe house. A would in turn send agent B (yi), who worked undercover in a CCP real estate agency, to lease the dwelling. Another agent, C (bing), would be sent by A to rent furniture. Neither B nor C would know each other, and if their paths accidentally crossed they usually assumed the other to be a bona fide businessman. Meanwhile, another Red Brigade group, rigidly limited to vertical contacts with one agent above (B and C only needed to know one CCP member, agent A) and strictly prohibited from horizontal connections, would pull together servants, cook, relatives (including children and grandparents) for a household of eight. Some of these were party members; some might also be dependents of party martyrs. Once mobilized, this perfectly ordinary-looking family would move into the residence and set up house. Ever alert and vigilant, the personnel running such a CCP safe house could have it completely vacated, along with all documents, within two hours of receiving notification from a party informant in the police or investigative services of an impending raid. Within four hours the house could be entirely stripped of furniture and personal belongings. By the time the police arrived they found only an empty house.[50]

The Red Brigade was specifically assigned penetration targets ranked in order of importance. Of the highest priority were command staff (canmou) and logistical (houqin) departments of military units. Second came police intelligence units. The third priority consisted of finance, economics, tax collecting, and currency units in regular administrative offices.[51] By 1930, the "Chinese GPU" had already achieved several successful penetrations. The most spectacular was the placing of a mole high in Xu Enzeng's Guomindang Special Services Bureau (Tegong bufen—SSB).[52]

The mole was an extraordinary young man named Qian Zhuangfei, from Huzhou, which was Guomindang Special Services Chief Xu Enzeng's native place as well. Qian entered National Beijing Medical College in 1914, and after graduating in October 1919 he had both a private medical practice and a position working in a small hospital off Suitie Road. He also taught anatomy in a Beijing art academy, which engaged his continuing interest in calligraphy and painting. At the same time Qian dabbled in wireless radio transmission and filmmaking. In fact, he and his wife,

Zhang Zhenhua (who was also a doctor), helped to support a small Beijing film company and actually acted in several of its movies.[53]

In 1925 Qian Zhuangfei and Zhang Zhenhua secretly joined the Chinese Communist Party. They found both the acting and their medical practices very useful covers for their underground party work. One of their best friends, Hu Di, also joined the party at this time, and worked closely together with them.[54] After the White Terror spread to Beijing in the wake of the April 12 purge in Shanghai, Qian and Zhang had gone to Kaifeng to work on Feng Yuxiang's medical staff, but salaries were too low to get by. At the end of 1927, therefore, the couple moved to Shanghai, where they were joined by Hu Di. Shortly after reaching Shanghai, Qian Zhuangfei tested into Xu Enzeng's Wireless Radio Training Unit (Wuxian xunlian ban), where he excelled. In fact, he did so well that when his fellow townsman, Xu Enzeng, was named chief of the Shanghai Wireless Bureau, Qian was made his secretary.[55]

Meanwhile, through Hu Di, Qian Zhuangfei had come into contact with another experienced CCP underground worker, Li Kenong, who in November 1929 was attached to the Propaganda Committee of the Huazhong Regional Committee of the Communist Party.[56] Li, who was to work closely with Zhou Enlai on security and intelligence matters during the 1930s, seemed to Qian to be a perfect candidate for entry into the Wireless Radio Training Unit. By December 1929, Li Kenong had passed the entrance exams and was working as an editor for Broadcast News (Guangbo xinwen), which was another one of Chen Lifu's intelligence organs operating in the Shanghai area.[57]

The winter of 1929–30 saw Xu Enzeng expanding his intelligence operations on all sides, and especially throughout the Yangzi Valley. Operations were coordinated from Guomindang Special Services headquarters in Nanjing via a clandestine radio transmitter operated there by Xu's recently trained technicians. It was at this point that Qian Zhuangfei was given the title of "confidential secretary" (*jiyao mishu*) and assigned the task of gathering intelligence on the Communists and other opposition parties by setting up local secret service units disguised as "news agencies" (*tongxun she*). As a result, the central intelligence headquarters (where Qian Zhuangfei was chief coordinator), the Shanghai intelligence organs (where Li Kenong ran the Broadcast News service), and the Tianjin listening post (which was run by Hu Di as the Great Wall News Agency) of the Guomindang were all manned by Communist moles.[58]

In addition to this still-secret triumph at deep political penetration of the enemy's most strategic intelligence bureaus, the Red Brigade also targeted the imperialists' police and intelligence organs. By that same time, the Communists had organized a party cell within the Shanghai Municipal Police.[59] And the CCP's auxiliary organization, the League against Imperialism and for Colonial Independence, was circulating anti-imperialist propaganda among Annamite troops and policemen garrisoned in the French Concession.[60]

Imperialism and Anti-Communist Policing

There was nothing novel about the French Concession Police's worry or the SMP's concern over subversion by revolutionary nationalist groups— whether Indochinese revolutionaries defying French colonialism or Indian nationalists opposing the British Raj. But in November 1930 the prospect of Communist secret agents inciting Indochinese mutineers helped persuade the French Political Intelligence Services to cooperate with the Nationalists in putting together an authoritative study of the structure and situation of the Communist Party and its affiliated organizations in the Yangzi Valley.[61] And at the same time, the SMP's Special Branch (the so-called political police) began to seek common cause with the Nationalist Public Security Bureau against the Communists who appeared to be fomenting unrest among the thousand or so Indians living in Shanghai.[62]

This was not a surprising convergence since the Shanghai Municipal Police and the French Concession Police were both part of global colonial networks of imperial control systems.[63] The head of the SMP frequently had seen service in other parts of the British Empire such as India or Singapore, and many of the officers had originally been recruited in England or Scotland to work for the East African or Hong Kong police before they moved on to Shanghai.[64] Typically, these were men of relatively modest backgrounds: former factory apprentices or soldiers who were eventually drawn to Shanghai because it was "viewed as an arena more accommodating than Hong Kong to the adventurous and ambitious."[65] They were also of a recognizable type, especially during the waning years of the British Empire, strongly attracted to security work. Little wonder, then, that Section One (S.1) and Section Two (S.2) of the Special Branch were in close communication with the Criminal Investigation Department in Delhi and with the central police bureau in Singapore.[66] The former frequently directed the harassment and arrest of Indian nationalists in Shanghai by the SMP.[67] And the latter functioned as a kind of distant early warning system for detecting revolutionary nationalists and other "radicals" coming out to China by steamer through the Malaccan Straits.[68]

During the winter of 1926–27, in fact, a special "Indian section" was set up within the SMP's Special Branch for "collecting information on

Indian seditionist movements, etc., which became intensified coincident with the success of the Chinese nationalist movement."[69] The intelligence group, which was top secret and only identified as Section Four (S.4), worked closely with the British Consulate.[70] It originally consisted of four Sikh staff members under D. I. Sullivan, and their primary task was to infiltrate "clandestine meetings of seditious character" held by "such notorious individuals as Gajjan Singh, Ishar Singh, Hari Singh, and others" in Jessfield or Hongkou parks.[71]

One of S.4's first triumphs was the conviction for sedition in July 1927, and ensuing deportation to India in April 1928, of "three rabid individuals": the Gajjan Singh mentioned above, as well as two other Sikh leaders, Gainda Singh and Dasaundha Singh. This was said to have had a "strong moral effect" on the local Indian community, but the actual result was quite the opposite. Despite an order to the contrary from the British consul general and an armed cordon of police and soldiers, the Sikh community managed to reopen the Paohsing Road Gurdwara (temple) on April 27, 1928. Thereafter two S.4 Sikh undercover agents attended and reported on all the meetings held in the Gurdwara by the Indian nationalists, five of whom were sentenced to imprisonment and deportation in May 1929. At the same time, at the behest of Vice Consul Blackburn of the British Consulate, S.4 collected two thousand photographs and prepared one thousand biographies of members of the Shanghai Indian community, while managing simultaneously to "visit" all incoming ships whose passenger lists contained Indian names. Success led to expansion: by the end of 1929 the "Indian section" consisted of one detective subinspector, two detective sergeants, five Indian detectives, two Chinese detectives, and one Chinese secret agent.[72]

A certain overlapping of personnel occurred in these imperial control systems. The deputy commissioner in charge of the Shanghai CID in 1928, for example, was Captain W. G. Clarke, who had served in the Indian police before becoming head of the Sikh branch of the SMP.[73] French Concession police chiefs—who were often Corsicans—usually had a colonial military background with service in North Africa or Indochina.[74] Tall, elegant, mocking Etienne Fiori, commissioner of police from 1919 to 1932 and an artillery captain in the army reserve who had served in Morocco, was an "honorable member" of the French Intelligence Service.[75] Fiori devoted a respectable part of his resources at Rue Stanislas Chevalier to collecting political intelligence on the international Communist movement, and his office maintained close contact with the headquarters of the Sûreté in Hanoi.[76]

Both the SMP and FCP routinely exchanged daily and weekly intelligence reports, which were sometimes also shared with the British, French and American consuls, and with the offices of the military attachés in Nanjing.[77] These reports were based upon information provided by a network of paid secret agents to intelligence officers serving in Section One of the CID as special Chinese inspectors.[78] As Superintendent T. Robertson spelled out in a 1931 memo concerning Detective Sub-Inspectors Sih Tse-liang and Kuh Pao-hua who had been promoted to inspectors in S.1:

> The duties of these two officers are of an exacting nature and include the drafting of political and other miscellaneous reports submitted by agents and compilation of statistics on matters appertaining to military, naval, labor, political, and quasi-political, and the Settlement food supply. Other duties are assisting in raids on communistic bases and interrogation of persons apprehended and translation of documents seized, in addition to which they are called upon to carry out occasional special investigations.[79]

These Chinese inspectors, who themselves were the single most important source of political information for the higher leadership of the SMP, directed a large staff of clerks who processed field reports and translated documents in a secret unit of the SMP called the "Intelligence Office."[80]

The field agents "run" by these Chinese inspectors were typically younger men in their twenties hired to maintain surveillance over assigned portions of the city (including the Chinese-run districts), to keep watch over the docks and railroad stations, and to report on political rallies and popular assemblies. Often posing as reporters, they built up their own networks of acquaintances across jurisdictional boundaries: that is, Chinese field agents working on commission for the International Settlement, French, and Chinese police forces (including the Garrison Command Military Police) helped each other out, trading favors and information in what was an extremely hazardous calling. Although these field agents were ultimately dispensable, their superiors among the Chinese inspectors tried hard to protect them through their own informal contacts in other police and intelligence services in the event of their being compromised.[81]

Intelligence Gathering as Part of Shanghai Life

There was little ignorance of the intelligence-gathering function of the SMP among readers of the English-language press in Shanghai at the time. The *China Weekly Review* informed its readers that

> For those who do not know what the initials "CID" stand for, we will explain that they mean *Criminal Investigation Department* of

the Shanghai Municipal Council. Although this department receives its pay from local tax revenues collected from local taxpayers of all nationalities including the Chinese, it actually serves as an unofficial branch of the British political intelligence and propaganda service.[82]

Deputy Commissioner W. G. Clarke, the head of the CID, was assumed by many knowledgeable Shanghai residents to be a leading SIS (Secret Intelligence Service) agent in China.[83]

For their part, the political branch officers in the SMP were convinced at the same time that the Nationalists' Northern Expedition Army contained "subversive foreign agents, who for almost a decade have been propagating Communism among Chinese, [and who] have for the past year extended their activities to the creation of discontent among the Indian community in China."[84] In April 1927 an Indian named Harbant Singh, "who undoubtedly was acting at the instigation of the seditious elements," shot dead Senior Indian Inspector Sirdar Sahib Buddha Singh at the entrance to the central police station. This was considered by the SMP to be the prelude to a strike movement among Sikh policemen led by Indian agitators sent from Hankou and accompanied by a Russian GRU agent.[85]

Hankou then was the seat of the United Front government, soon to be purged by Chiang Kai-shek, and it was viewed as both an outpost of the Comintern and a source of anti-imperialist Asian revolutionary nationalism. Even after the Nationalist government was established, the British authorities in charge of the SMP remained alert to the danger of Guomindang support for the Indian nationalists through organizations such as the Eastern Oppressed People's Association in Nanjing.[86]

The Chinese police were understandably reluctant to cooperate with the SMP in its campaign against Indian nationalists, who were subject to deportation back to India and a colonial prison sentence if convicted of "acting in a manner prejudicial to public safety."[87] In a meeting held on December 16, 1930, the Public Security Bureau decided to release captured Indian nationalists as long as they were not suspected of Communist activities.[88] At the same time, however, the PSB was becoming ever more eager for help from the International Settlement and French Concession police against "reactionary elements" and Communist agents in the foreign-run sectors of Shanghai. This eagerness stemmed in part from security concerns within the Garrison Command and the police proper.[89] It also resulted from requests, coinciding with the 1929 suppression of the left wing of the Guomindang in Jiangsu province, that emanated from the Shanghai Nationalist Party branch and came to the SMP via the Shanghai

Provisional Court. These requests marked a pivotal turning point in relations between the Public Security Bureau and other Shanghai police forces, and the beginning of a policy of official collaboration that would virtually exterminate the Shanghai branch of the Chinese Communist Party.[90] Indeed, GMD Special Services Chief Xu Enzeng would later observe that "it was only because we had the full and vigorous cooperation of the concessions' authorities that we were able to destroy even more [of the Communist Party underground groups in Shanghai]."[91]

The early years of Nationalist rule in Shanghai coincided with the heyday of the so-called "great illegals": Russian secret agents like Theodore Maly, Richard Sorge, Deutsch, "Otto," Alexandor Rado, Leopold Trepper, Ignace and Elisabeth Poretsky, "Sonia" (Ruth Werner), the Piecks, and Walter Krivitsky—many of whom worked in or passed through Shanghai as agents of Red Army Intelligence of the GRU's Foreign Section (INO), or of the Communist International's Liaison Section (Otdyel Mezhdunarodnoi Svyazi—OMS).[92] After the All-Russian Cooperative Society raid in London in 1928, when MI5 (Counter-Intelligence) smashed most of the Russian embassy-run espionage apparatus in England, Moscow decided that its diplomatic quarters abroad were no longer safe centers from which to control agents.[93] From then on, its agents were run by a variety of case officers posing as journalists, brokers, educators, and so forth.[94] The best of these secret agents were known as the "great illegals," who often held Russian citizenship but regarded themselves as acting on behalf of international Communism and the Comintern.[95]

Working under cover, sometimes considering themselves Trotskyists, they organized a series of high-grade spy rings around the world: the Rote Drei in Switzerland, the Ring of Five in Britain, the Rote Kapelle in Germany, and Richard Sorge's networks in Shanghai and Tokyo. Although many of them were eventually, in 1938, recalled one by one to Moscow and executed by Stalin, they were the finest recruiters and controllers the Russians ever had, and from 1928 to 1933 Shanghai was one of their key communications hubs.[96] The Comintern's Far Eastern Bureau in Shanghai was charged by the Executive Committee of the Third International with guiding the work of the Chinese, Japanese, Formosan, Indochinese, Philippine, and Malayan Communist Parties. Part of the bureau's task was disbursing the 1,375,000 francs (Gold $55,000) it received per year in reichsmarks, gold dollars, Mexican dollars, and yen.[97] Liaison with the Comintern was maintained by couriers who frequently traveled between Moscow, Berlin, and Shanghai, and by coded letters sent to and from Berlin through postal boxes which the Far Eastern Bureau rented under different names in the Central Chinese Post Office in Shanghai.[98]

The Noulens Affair

In 1931 the central operator of this communications system—the Organization Department of the Comintern's Far Eastern Bureau—was a man known as Hilaire (Hillyer) Noulens, operating in Shanghai under the cover of secretary-general of the Pan-Pacific Trade Union.[99] The Shanghai Organization Department functioned like a massive switching operation, channeling funds and agents through the city and throughout Asia, and using safe houses and cutouts to maintain security. Noulens, also known to Shanghai Comintern agents as Paul Ruegg, was an extremely tense man in his late thirties, "forever moving about and switching from one to another of his three languages apparently without noticing."[100] He had arrived in the city with a stolen Belgian passport featuring his photograph under the name of Ferdinand Vandercruyssen, and he had many aliases, including four different passports under the names Charles Alison, Donat Boulanger, Samuel Herssens, and Dr. W. O'Neill.[101] In Shanghai he had rented seven separate homes for which he paid Gold $1,300 in rents every month under different names, eight different post office boxes, four telegraphic addresses, and ten separate bankbooks, with deposits totaling $50,000.[102]

The French police's first inkling of the existence in Shanghai of the Far Eastern Bureau of the Comintern was acquired in April 1931 when a group of Annamite Communists arrested in the French colony divulged under interrogation that liaison between the Indochinese Communist Party and the Third International was carried out through an "Oriental Bureau" located in Shanghai. The French Concession Police were immediately ordered to try to locate this bureau, but they failed to find it. On June 6, 1931, however, they did discover in the papers of Le Quang Dat, an Annamese Communist agent arrested by the Political Service of the French police, a sealed envelope containing instructions from Moscow. These confirmed the existence of an "Oriental Bureau" in Shanghai.[103]

Five days earlier, moreover, the British Special Branch in Singapore had arrested a French Comintern agent and courier named Joseph Ducroux, alias Serge LeFranc (Lefranca).[104] When the police searched LeFranc they found two scraps of paper: one contained a Shanghai telegraphic code address—"Hilonoul, Shanghai"; and the other read "P.O. Box 208, Shanghai."[105] Armed with this information, the SMP's Special Branch began a joint operation with the French Concession Police to track down the person who had rented the box. Surveillance identified the box-holder as a "professor of French and German" named Hilaire Noulens whose home in the International Settlement was located at 235 Szechuan

Road. Further surveillance led to another address: 30 C, Central Arcade (49 Nanking Road). On June 15, 1931, the SMP arrested Professor Noulens in his rooms at 235 Szechuan Road, and seized the contents of the office in the Central Arcade. The three steel boxes that they found there turned out to be the archives of the Far Eastern Bureau and the Pan-Pacific Trade Union.[106]

Noulens's files yielded the addresses of the other safe houses he had rented, and these were swiftly raided. Not only was Madame Noulens discovered and seized; quantities of important Communist documents in various foreign languages concerning the Communist movement throughout the Far East were also found. The French and British had intercepted Comintern communications earlier, of course, but they had been unable to decode them. This was because the ciphers consisted of two different cryptographic systems involving one code to correspond with Comintern workers in Asia, and a second set to correspond with Comintern leaders in Moscow and Europe.[107] Now, having discovered the keys to these ciphers, French Intelligence broke down the codes and secured the names of couriers and agents throughout the region. They and the British discovered that each agent had several noms de guerre, and often carried two or three passports. The pseudonyms differed according to accounts and correspondence, and even the branches of the Comintern to which they reported in Berlin and thence to Moscow were given personal names like "Alexander" rather than functional administrative designations. They also discovered Noulens's payroll records, which revealed the names of his agents in various Chinese government organizations including the secret services, as well as in bureaus of the Shanghai Municipal Police.[108]

The French police believed that Hillyer Noulens's "true" name was Paul Ruegg or Rugg, and that he was born in Zürich on March 30, 1898. According to their Intelligence Service records, he had surfaced for the first time in 1922 in Basel as a member of the Central Committee of the Swiss Communist Party. Two years later he had left Switzerland for the USSR where he disappeared from sight for five years. In December 1929 "Ruegg" had reappeared in Brussels where he had managed to acquire a Belgian passport that in turn had gotten him to China via Berlin, Moscow, and Manchuria. He had arrived in Shanghai on March 19, 1930. French Intelligence did not claim to know the "true" identity of Madame Noulens, who had two Belgian passports in her possession at the time of her arrest: one bearing the name of Sophie Louise Herbet (née Lorent), and the other made out to Marie Vandercruyssen (née Dusand).[109]

Their identities, in fact, remained a mystery to most Comintern agents, who only were told that the secretary-general of the Pan-Pacific Trade

Union and his wife, both Swiss citizens, had been arrested in Shanghai. Willy Münzenberg (member of the Communist faction of the Reichstag and secretary-general of the League against Imperialism and for Colonial Independence), who eventually directed the International Red Help Society's campaign to get the two released, did not even know that Noulens or "Ruegg" was actually a Ukrainian NKVD agent named Luft who had served as a Balkan trade unions specialist in the Soviet Embassy in Vienna between 1925 and 1929. Luft had met his wife "Madame Noulens," a graduate of a St. Petersburg finishing school for the daughters of the aristocracy, in Rome, where she was the secretary of the Soviet[110] Embassy.

After they were arrested the Noulens declared that they were called Vandercruyssen and demanded to be brought before the Belgian Consular Court. The Belgian consul, however, said that this was a false declaration. Consequently, when the Noulens were arraigned before the Chinese Court in the International Settlement on June 19, 1931, their lawyer, Dr. Karl Wilhelm, claimed that Mr. Noulens's real name was Xavier Alois Beret and that the two were Swiss citizens. The Swiss chargé d'affaires rejected that claim as well. On August 12 the Noulens were brought before the Chinese authorities who decreed that they be tried before a military court. Two days later they were transferred to Nanjing and incarcerated in the capital's model prison while awaiting a court martial to be held in October.[111]

The Noulens's attorney, Wilhelm, belonged to a firm of lawyers (Musso, Fischer, and Wilhelm) that was identified by French Intelligence as frequent defenders of Soviet interests in Shanghai courts. On July 3, 1931, Fischer left Shanghai for Moscow accompanied by a Polish Comintern agent named "Stewart" who carried an American passport. Fischer's mission was to ask the Third International what line of conduct he and his colleagues should adopt as the Noulens's lawyers, to arrange for payment of legal costs, to establish if possible proof of the Swiss nationality of the Noulens, and to help organize a campaign in Europe in favor of their release.[112]

Fischer's mission succeeded. On August 20 a Noulens Defense Committee was announced in Europe, directed by Henri Barbusse, Victor Margueritte, and Jacques Sadoul; and the following day an international campaign was launched.[113] Elisabeth Poretsky, one of the few survivors of Stalin's purges who knew the Lufts, described the campaign nearly forty years later:

On 21 August Willy Münzenberg produced an article in *Imprecor*, the Comintern journal, that set off the campaign. He had no idea who Paul Ruegg was, nor did it make matters any easier when the Shanghai police announced that Ruegg also used the name Noulens and claimed Belgian nationality, but his publicity was superbly effective. The world at large soon believed that the Rueggs, although they might have been Communists, had been engaged in straightforward labour union work and were being unjustly accused for no other reason than their allegiance to trade unionism. In order to get rid of trade unionists, so the argument went, the Chinese had framed the two Swiss as Soviet spies.[114]

By September 1931 radical circles among foreigners in Shanghai had formed a committee of help for the "secretary of the Pan-Pacific Trade Union." Among its members were Agnes Smedley, J. B. Powell, Edgar Snow, and Harold Isaacs. Soong Ching-ling, Sun Yat-sen's widow, who had received numerous telegrams from organizations and notables in Europe asking for her intervention, organized a Committee for the Defense of Paul and Gertrude Ruegg (Noulens), which was composed—among others—of George Finch (Secretary of the YMCA) and Theo Thackery (editor of the *Shanghai Evening Post and Mercury*) and which attracted the support of Sun Fo, Cai Yuanpei, and Ju Zheng (president of the Judicial Yuan).[115]

Meanwhile, the Noulens were brought to trial before a military court in Nanjing, which in late October condemned Hilaire Noulens to capital punishment and Madame Noulens to life imprisonment. Willy Münzenberg promptly sent a telegram in the name of the Committee for the Defense of the Noulens to Chiang Kai-shek, protesting the death sentence and asking for his liberation as an innocent person. As the international clamor for the Noulens's release increased, the Generalissimo decided in December 1931 that the case should not have been tried before a military tribunal. On July 5, 1932, the Noulens were tried before the Jiangsu High Court in Nanjing. On July 17 they were both sentenced to capital punishment, but by application of a general amnesty promulgated the month before, the sentence was commuted to life imprisonment.[116] Ultimately, the Noulens ended up serving only five years of that sentence. When the Japanese took Nanjing, the Noulens were somehow released from jail and reappeared briefly in Shanghai before disappearing again, probably headed for the Soviet Union and eventual death in Stalin's Gulag.[117]

Altogether, according to the French Concession Police report of the case, "the arrest of Noulens has led to the discovery of a quantity of precious information on the situation of the Communist movement in China and has destroyed for a certain amount of time the technical apparatus of liaisons of the Comintern in the Far East."[118] A number of Communist couriers and liaison agents were discovered or arrested during the summer of 1931. One of Noulens's Hong Kong correspondents, Nguyen Ai Quoc (Ho Chi Minh), turned out to be the head of the Indochinese Communist Party when he was arrested in the Crown Colony by English police on July 6, 1931, and sentenced by the Hong Kong Military Tribunal to two years of prison.[119]

The arrests of liaison agents momentarily severed connections between the Comintern and local Asian Communist parties and for awhile, at least, closed down the Far Eastern Bureau. Indochinese Communist Party representatives sent to Shanghai in August 1932 to try to reestablish contact with the Far Eastern Bureau were directed to the Central Committee of the Chinese Communist Party, which gave them their instructions. It appeared, therefore, that for a significant hiatus after the arrest of Noulens, the CCP's Shanghai headquarters acted as the Comintern's Far Eastern directorate.[120]

The Gu Shunzhang Affair and the White Terror

It was a measure of the disastrous state of the Comintern's Far Eastern Bureau that control of its agents had to be temporarily turned over to the Chinese Communist Party branch, which was in nearly as dire a condition. For, just as the Noulens affair was being exposed by the Special Branch and Sûreté, another equally damaging domestic Communist case was being broken by the Nationalist intelligence services with the help of the Shanghai Public Security Bureau. In April 1931, just two months before Noulens's arrest, Gu Shunzhang, the man in charge of the CCP's Red Brigade, fell into the hands of the Guomindang's Special Services Bureau (SSB).[121] The Gu Shunzhang Affair began with an attempt to assassinate Chiang Kai-shek. When the "bandit suppression" campaign against the Communist soviets in Jiangxi commenced in 1930, Chiang Kai-shek went to Wuhan. In December Gu Shunzhang received orders from Communist Party Center—that is, Li Lisan—to lead a team of Red Brigade agents to Wuhan to assassinate Chiang.[122]

Shortly afterward, in January or February 1931, a traveling troupe of performers arrived in Hankou. The star of the show was a magician called Li Ming who appeared on stage dressed as a foreigner with a big nose and a small mustache. The show was a success but, though it ran for several months, Li Ming seldom left his room in the Pacific Hotel (Taiping yang fandian) other than to go to the theater. Instead, he received a steady stream of daily visitors, including several suspected Communists and some high-ranking Guomindang members. These callers attracted the attention of the head of the Guomindang SSB in Wuhan, Cai Mengjian, who put Li Ming under surveillance as an "element in touch with the Communist Party." He also managed to have a photograph taken of the magician when the performer left the hotel for a walk. Cai sent the likeness to SSB headquarters in Nanjing to see if anyone there could identify Li Ming, and word came back that he was actually Gu Shunzhang, dreaded chief of the CCP's Red Brigade. Cai Mengjian was ordered by SSB Director Xu Enzeng to seize Gu and bring him immediately downriver to Nanjing on the next China Steam Merchants Navigation Company ferry.[123]

Gu Shunzhang was arrested on Friday, April 24. He immediately warned SSB officer He Chengjun not to cable the news of his arrest to Nanjing lest it be intercepted. Hoping to gain favor with Chiang Kai-shek, He Chengjun went ahead anyway and sent a telegram announcing the arrest to Nanjing. When Gu heard about this he stamped his foot and angrily exclaimed: "That does it! You'll never lay a hand on Zhou Enlai now." Gu explained that one of Chiang Kai-shek's "confidential secretaries" (*jiyao mishu*) was a Communist agent, although Gu did not know his name, and that if the agent intercepted the telegram he would warn the CCP leaders in advance that Gu had been captured.

The telegram reached the SSB office in Nanjing at 6:00 that evening. Xu Enzeng had already left the office to go to a dancing party, so the cable was delivered to confidential secretary Qian Zhuangfei instead. Qian instantly realized the implications of Gu Shunzhang's detention. That same Friday evening Qian sent his son-in-law, Liu Qifu, to Shanghai by express train to alert Li Kenong, who in turn told Chen Geng and Zhou Enlai about Gu Zhunzhang's arrest. The Communists immediately began closing down their safe houses in Shanghai and going into hiding.[124]

The next morning, Saturday, Xu Enzeng went in person to the Nanjing docks to pick up the prisoner, who was brought ashore by two SSB agents in a tender. According to Director Xu's own account, which was far from disinterested, he had succeeded numerous times in persuading captive Communists to defect.[125] But this time he felt unsure of himself because of Gu's reputation as a ruthless and fanatical CCP leader. Xu Enzeng had insisted that his staff make the secret office used for the interview look like a regular reception room, keeping the usual interrogation equipment out of sight. He also insisted on meeting with Gu alone, one on one. For his part, Gu Shunzhang, as cool and experienced as he was, came to the interview filled with terror imprinted in him by the CCP, sure that he was about to be tortured to death. The very fact that Xu Enzeng was so unintimidating and the room so ordinary began to shake Gu's faith in the Communist Party.[126]

Xu Enzeng felt that he needed both a psychological assessment of the thirty-six-year-old prisoner and some comprehension of his political views.[127] In the course of a polite discussion that began to move across a spectrum of topics, the American-trained engineer, who had turned himself into a counterspy and expert in expounding the Three Principles of the People while exposing the "errors" of Communism, thought he discovered that Gu Shunzhang did not have a very deep understanding of Marxist-Leninist concepts. Although a genius at secret service work, Gu was relatively simpleminded about ideology. All he could speak of was the "class hatred" taught him by CCP organizers when he joined the party. According to Xu Enzeng, Gu thus had few conceptual defenses when the SSB interrogator contrasted the unitary nationalism of the Guomindang with the divisive way in which the Communists had "sold out China" (*mai guo*) to the Russians in the name of class struggle. Xu drew an end to the conversation by quietly telling Gu that he had two hours to choose his future course. If he continued to be a "tool" of international Communism, he would be traveling down a road marked for death. If Gu left the Communist Party and returned to the side of his nation, he would be warmly embraced.[128]

Two hours later, when Xu Enzeng returned to the secret office, Gu Shunzhang told him that he wanted to "change sides" (*zhuanbian*). Elated, Xu took Gu, accompanied by two Nationalist agents, to Nanjing's largest hotel, the Zhongyang fandian (Central Hotel), where Xu's boss, Chen Lifu, was staying. By now it was close to noon, and Gu Shunzhang spent the next two hours in the hotel room with Chen and Xu Enzeng, while the two agents stood guard outside. During those two hours Gu swore an oath of loyalty to the "nationalist revolution" (*guomin geming*). He also gave proof of his sincerity by revealing the identity of the Red Brigade's most highly placed mole in the Guomindang's Special Services Bureau. Gu disclosed that Director Xu's confidential secretary was a CCP agent sent to infiltrate Chen Lifu's counterespionage organization. Xu Enzeng could hardly believe his ears. He had always taken Qian Zhuangfei to be a sedulous, dedicated person, who stuck to his business and was absolutely trustworthy.[129]

Xu Enzeng instantly sent for Qian Zhuangfei, only to learn that his closest aide had sneaked away that very morning.[130] Gu Shunzhang was intensely alarmed by this news. Knowing himself how the Communist Party Center was likely to react, he said he now feared for the lives of his wife, son, parents-in-law, and brother-in-law back in Shanghai. Xu Enzeng immediately sent SSB agents to Shanghai to pick up the family.[131] Seven hours later, when the Nationalist agents reached the addresses in Shanghai that Gu had given them, each dwelling was deserted.[132] Gu

Shunzhang vowed to take revenge upon the Communist Party, and the hunt was on.[133]

Gu Shunzhang's defection meant that the Nationalist secret service was no longer blindly fighting the Communist Party in the dark.[134] As their guide, Gu had a formidable knowledge of the middle and upper levels of the CCP organization.[135] He himself had served in, been involved with, or knew about many of the most active bureaus: he was a "living dictionary" when it came to party rosters.[136] He provided the Nationalists information that enabled them to break up ring after ring in Hankou, Nanjing, Tianjin, Beijing, and Shanghai.[137] One success led in turn to the next "so that the underground organizations of the CCP in every locale throughout the entire country experienced the heaviest attacks that they had ever endured."[138]

The Communist Party tried to fight back, but much of its energy was directed against "deviant" (*yiji*) elements in its own midst.[139] As soon as Party Center learned of Gu Shunzhang's defection, it assigned to Zhou Enlai the responsibility of reorganizing the Communist Special Services Committee (Tewu weiyuanhui), which had originally consisted of Zhou, Secretary-General Xiang Zhongfa, and Gu Shunzhang, and which had supervised the Red Brigade unit.[140] The new Special Services Committee was chaired by Liao Chengyun. Yang Sen was named head of the Social Tradecraft Department (Shehui gezhong jishu). The Espionage Department (Zhentan) was run by Pan Hannian.[141] The head of the Red Brigade was Zhao Yun, and Communications, department number four, was under Chen Shouchang.[142] Because of its mission as an assassination squad to execute party traitors and potential defectors, the Red Brigade was also known as the "dog-killers squad" (*dagou tuan*).[143] A French Intelligence digest remarked:

> It is interesting to note that the [Chinese] GPU recruited its agent-executors among people of the lower classes. These agents were fed and nourished by the GPU and received fifteen dollars a month as salaries. They did not know the names or the circumstances of the persons that they were going to assassinate, and it was not until the day afterwards that they learned via the newspapers the names of their victims.[144]

The membership of the Red Brigade was entirely secret.[145]

The Red Brigade's assassination schemes notwithstanding, the Communist Party was almost defenseless once its former security chief went over to the Nationalists. Often a major Nationalist victory would result from a small raid thought at the time to be inconsequential. Photographs taken of the people seized during the raid were routinely sent to Gu, who frequently recognized them as major Communists who had changed their names.[146] This intervention thus changed the entire complexion of any number of cases and caused widespread damage to the Communist Party.[147]

Harold Isaacs once described the White Terror of these years as "having no parallel in history except perhaps the invasions and slaughters staged by the Huns in the fourth and fifth centuries."[148] Those words were written before the Nazi Holocaust, of course, but they seem slightly less hyperbolic when we read the authoritative French intelligence summary of the 1931 campaign against the Chinese Communists: "[It's worth] remarking that all Communist affairs were judged during this period by courts martial, often specially organized towards this end and that the judgments that were handed down by these courts were extremely severe. Although the numbers of persons accused of Communism and executed during the months of June, July, and August has never been divulged, it can be estimated at several thousands."[149]

Thus on June 22, 1931, one week after the seizure of Noulens, the French Concession Police arrested Xiang Zhongfa, secretary-general of the Chinese Communist Party.[150] Xiang was promptly extradited, and just one day later, after interrogation by the Nationalists, the "Chinese Stalin" was executed in the military garrison at Longhua.[151] French Intelligence authorities regarded Xiang's arrest, confession, and execution as "a blow no less serious" than Gu Shunzhang's defection.[152] It was quickly followed by more arrests, especially in Tianjin where more than twenty leading Communists were arrested, including the Hebei party secretary and members of the Hebei CCP Military Affairs Commission.[153] In Shanghai, where the so-called red days (*journées rouges*) of July 1931 passed mainly in silence, the most important organs of the CCP seemed "hors de combat."[154]

Aftermath of the Gu Shunzhang Affair

Most members of the Central Committee of the Chinese Communist Party precipitously left Shanghai after the arrest of Xiang Zhongfa. Some of them sought refuge in the interior of Jiangsu; others went to Hong Kong. The Politburo had the party archives taken south, and provisionally confided the duties and responsibilities of the Central Committee to a special commission composed of young members of the party who were hardly known to the authorities, but who were sufficiently energetic and engaged to assure the functioning of the Central Committee under extremely hazardous conditions. At the same time the Politburo ordered provincial committees in Jiangsu, Anhui, Hubei, Guangdong, and Hebei to intensify their activities as much as possible in order, first, to draw the attention of the Nationalists away from the Soviets in Jiangxi; second, to show the masses that despite the measures taken by the régime, the activities of the party were not totally curtailed; and third, to maintain the combative spirit of party members and their sympathizers.[155]

In truth, however, the Communist Party was mortally wounded in China's cities; the Nationalists' "resolute, timely, and decisive application of repressive measures" had worked against a determined revolutionary urban movement.[156] Altogether, more than forty high-ranking party members had been arrested at the central level, and another eight hundred important CCP members were being rounded up at local levels.[157] Communists who had used the foreign settlements as a refuge found themselves the targets of the combined Shanghai police forces whose officers acted on the tips provided by the intelligence services to raid one safe house after another.[158] In October, Zhou Enlai left his Shanghai hiding place disguised as a priest and headed, like so many other urban party leaders, for the mountains of Jiangxi.[159] By early 1932 there were only two Central Committee members remaining in Shanghai: Kang Sheng and Li Zusheng; and there was a nearly complete rupture between the central organs of the CCP and the party's provincial members.[160]

Profound consequences emerged from this urban defeat at the hands of the régime's police, working together with newly found allies among the French and British "imperialists." A different branch of the Chinese Communist Party, with a totally distinct political strategy and under new leadership, would eventually emerge from China's vast countryside and reclaim the cities with military force. However, this rural threat to the Nationalist government, and to the foreign powers that continued to dominate modern Shanghai, was barely discernible in 1931, when the urban elements of the Chinese Communists were in such disarray. With the enemy so thoroughly routed, one would have thought that the Sino-Western alliance against Bolshevism, especially among the police and intelligence services of Shanghai, might have attenuated. Yet the anti-Communist collusion between the Guomindang régime and Shanghai's foreign authorities was tightened all the more by the Gu Shunzhang Affair and the ensuing White Terror. Why did this paradox occur?

First, by late 1931, outlines of a new urban Communist strategy were already being adumbrated. After the Manchurian Incident (see Chapter 10) that September, there existed the prospect of future united front alliances against Japanese aggression that would provide a renewed Communist movement in Shanghai with opportunities to infiltrate and lead patriotic movements of the "national bourgeoisie."[161]

Second, the White Terror continued well into the mid-1930s. The year 1931 was a turning point, but it did not mark the total eradication of the militant urban Left. Indeed, the Communists continued to fight back even within Shanghai, where the Red Brigade imported specially trained assassins from the Jiangxi Soviet area and used them to hunt down Guomindang secret policemen.[162] On November 25, 1932, for example, a team of five killers from the Red Brigade raided the headquarters of the Guomindang Special Services in Shanghai, shooting station chief Zeng Boqian to death through the left eye, while gunning down three other special agents as well as Zeng's wife.[163]

A third reason for the growing anti-Communist alliance between the Shanghai Public Security Bureau and the French and International Settlement police forces was the public's perception of an increased threat to law and order posed by the revolutionaries. This, too, was an offshoot of the Gu Shunzhang Affair, as a result of the vengeance taken by the Communist Party against Gu's family after he defected to the Nationalists.[164]

On September 28, 1931, the Shanghai Municipal Police arrested a suspected Communist named Wang Zhuyou. When his photograph was sent to SSB headquarters in Nanjing to be studied, Gu Shunzhang exclaimed, "If there is any news about my family, this man is the one to know about it!"[165] Gu explained that Wang Zhuyou was actually Wang Shide, a fellow townsman from Songjiang who had worked under him in the Red Brigade and who had been one of the few people permitted to visit Gu at home. Wang, who was just over forty years old, had been trained at Sun Yat-sen University in Moscow. He was one of the Communists' top assassins.[166] A cable was quickly sent to the SSB station in Shanghai to bring Wang Shide to Nanjing. When he arrived in closely guarded custody, Wang was taken to see Xu Enzeng. Director Xu was nonplussed by the sincere and quiet manner of the arch-assassin, who in person seemed like a meek if somewhat pedantic *sishu* (old-style private school) teacher.[167] Wang Shide was then brought to Gu Shunzhang. Gu asked him about the disappearance of his family. Wang told his former chief that he only knew Gu's family was in the custody of the party. He was not privy to any other information because, as one of Gu's lieutenants, he had been taken out of action by the party after Gu's arrest.[168]

The Nanjing agents thought the story was fishy, but when one of them suggested torturing the truth out of Wang Shide, Gu Shunzhang objected.

Gu said that Wang was an "experienced and cool-headed" operative who would not readily yield to "hard" methods. Consequently, the assassin was confined but not physically mistreated. Instead, another fellow townsman from Songjiang, SSB department chief Guo Deji, decided to try the opposite approach. When Wang Shide was delivered to the Nanjing SSB in the first place, Guo Deji had recognized him from schoolboy days. Wang Shide had been the second-year teacher at Songjiang's Mingde School, from which Guo Deji had graduated. Now, Guo greeted Wang Shide deferentially as a former teacher, and identified himself by his school-name ("Guo Jianhua"), while he reminded Wang that he had gotten very good grades at Mingde. The Communist assassin was startled, and then touched when Guo asked after Wang's younger brother, who had also gone off to Moscow for training and was now dead. From there, Guo Deji went on to mention other families of mutual acquaintances in Songjiang as Wang gradually let his guard down. Eventually Guo argued that if Wang was willing to "turn around" (huitou), then Guo would guarantee his life and personal safety. This would mean working with the Nationalists as an agent, of course, because if the SSB released him, the other side would kill him for having turned coat. After he was moved to more comfortable surroundings and given time to ponder his options, he declared that he was going to change sides.[169]

Once he had decided to defect, Wang Shide had to tell the truth to Gu Shunzhang about his family. According to Wang Shide, all but the son were taken to a house in the French Concession and murdered. "Your family members were completely executed a long time ago."[170] Gu Shunzhang was deeply grieved and enraged, but he did not direct his anger against Wang Shide. He knew what it meant to be under Red Brigade orders. The next day he, Wang, Guo Deji, and several Nationalist agents took the train to Shanghai to exhume the Gu family's corpses.[171] Wang Shide directed them to a quiet residence district off Gaston Road. The house at 11 Haitang Lane (Aitangcun) was deserted. Inside the gate was a small patch of green grass enclosed by a cement walk: what Shanghainese called a "field-well" (tianjing) in a play on words with the "well-field" (jingtian) system of feudal times.[172] When the agents asked Wang Shide where the bodies were buried, he pointed to the grassy spot. Because it was by then quite dark, they decided to return to their hotel and start their investigation the next morning.[173]

The excavation began at ten in the morning. A large crowd quickly gathered, some climbing nearby trees to get a better view.[174] After half an hour, when the workmen had dug three to four feet (chi) deep, they unearthed a tooth. The journalists crowded around excitedly, but the incisor turned out to be a dog's tooth. Some of the workers wanted to give up digging at this point, but Wang Shide quietly said that they would have to go down at least seven or eight feet more.[175] After another half-hour of digging, the soil abruptly changed texture and took on an ocher color. The workmen's shovels struck concrete. When they broke through the cement cover a terrible stench made some of the bystanders vomit. One of the workers groped into the cavity beneath the cement and felt a human leg. Four decapitated corpses were brought out of the ground naked. They were bound together two-by-two, the one folded into the other with neck tied to leg and vice-versa. As they matched the heads with the necks and arms, Gu Shunzhang stood by, tears running down his face, saying, "That's my wife. That's my mother-in-law. That's my father-in-law. That's my brother-in-law."[176] Only his son, Asheng, had been spared. Wang Shide explained later that he could not bring himself to execute the boy, who had secretly been sent back to Gu Shunzhang's natal home in Songjiang.[177]

This was not the end of the day's wrenching exhumations. Wang Shide led the secret service team into the International Settlement to 32 Wuding fang, the first of five other burial sites. At each site, helped by the Shanghai Municipal Police, the team dug up more bodies: five here, half-a-dozen there, and so forth. The corpses were mostly too decomposed to recognize, and Wang Shide only knew of them as anonymous "rebellious elements" (*panni fenzi*) from within the Chinese Communist Party. According to Wang the victims were people who had opposed Party Center. Often they were cadres directly under the command of Zhou Enlai, who had ordered their deaths because the CCP leadership believed that such drastic punishment was necessary in order to keep the underground party a disciplined force.[178]

The International Settlement police accompanying the secret service team grew increasingly disturbed as corpse after corpse was pulled out of Shanghai's watery soil. Crowds gathered wherever they dug. Reporters surrounded them. The SMP authorities believed that people would say that the International Settlement police could not maintain order in their own domain. They would "lose face" (*shi mianzi*) before the populace. At the fifth burial site, the SMP ordered the Nationalist secret service team to stop digging. By then more than three dozen bodies had been unearthed.[179]

The Gu Shunzhang Affair and its grisly aftermath had two immediate consequences. The first was popular horror and dismay. The newspaper coverage was sensational, including many graphic photos of the CCP's victims. According to Xu Enzeng, the discoveries had a tremendous impact on public opinion. Many Shanghainese revised their views of the Communists and judged them thereafter to be implacable and cruel. There was also a swelling support for the authorities' anti-Communist crusade—or at least so claimed the Nationalists among themselves.[180]

Law Enforcement Alliances

The second immediate consequence was the transformation of the two police forces' growing anti-Communist consensus into a law enforcement alliance directed against the Communist Party. According to SSB section commander Guo Deji, the Nationalist secret service agents only agreed to stop the search for more corpses after they were assured by the SMP that the Settlement authorities would cooperate with them in the future. "They consented that thereafter they would be willing at any time to accept our requests (*yaoqiu*) and cooperate in restraining (*fangzhi*) Communist Party activities."[181]

SSB Chief Xu Enzeng was even more explicit. He said that the secret service team only agreed to stop digging after the International Settlement authorities entered into a "gentleman's agreement" (*junzi xieding*) to provide their "entire help and collaboration" in the campaign against the Chinese Communist Party.[182]

The new collaborative policy was personified on the International Settlement side by Patrick T. Givens, the charming Irishman from Tipperary who was then in charge of the Special Branch.[183] Givens had joined the SMP on March 31, 1907. After three years in ordinary police service, he was promoted to the CID where his foremost duties in the Special Branch were to investigate Communist activities. Chief Inspector Givens was appointed assistant commissioner in August 1927, and as head of the Special Branch he was given credit for handling the Noulens case.[184] Patrick Givens, who was caricatured later by Hergé in *Tintin et le lotus bleu* as a venal cop completely in the pockets of the Japanese, was also a member of the British Secret Intelligence Service.[185]

When Assistant Commissioner Givens eventually retired in 1936, he was presented with a Chinese medal of honor along with a letter of appreciation from the mayor of Shanghai recognizing that "in the course of his duties in securing evidence against Communists, he frequently worked in close cooperation with the Bureau of Public Safety [PSB]."[186] Harold Isaacs, radical editor of the *China Forum*, was outraged by the commendation: "Nothing, perhaps, has more clearly revealed the close alliance of the Nanjing government with foreign imperialism than the award last December 13 of the First Class "A" medal of the Chinese military naval and air forces to . . . Patrick T. Givens, assistant commissioner of the imperialist Shanghai Municipal Police, for [his] 'excellent' work in hounding down Communists and suspected 'reds' and bringing them to 'justice'—which in the vast majority of cases has meant death."[187]

There was no single counterpart to Patrick Givens on the Chinese side, but just as the CID was criticized for putting political intelligence work above crime investigation so was the PSB's *zhenjidui* (detective squad) faulted for devoting too little attention to solving criminal cases.[188] Matters from that perspective only worsened as the police department's national concerns with political espionage and counterintelligence work overshadowed routine commitments to local law and order.[189]

4

IMPLICATIONS OF POLITICAL CHOICES FOR POLICING

10   Making Choices

Fully aware of the probable seriousness of the coming
situation on May 1, high officials of the International
Settlement, the French Concession, and Chinese territory
yesterday held a joint conference in the office of the director-
general of the Shanghai Municipal Council, at which plans to
circumvent the Labour Day schemes of Communists and
agitators were discussed and the closest cooperation pledged by
all in order to minimize or completely check disturbances and
demonstrations on that day.

Shanghai Times, April 1930

As strategic political concerns occupied more and more of the government's attention, the nature of policing in Shanghai shifted significantly.
A range of choices faced Chinese leaders and, as each choice was made,
together they moved the policing of Shanghai in a direction quite different
from its early intentions. The first choice, as we have seen, was between
the maintenance of social order and law enforcement. Just as there was a
distinction between law enforcement and order maintenance, so the second choice was prompted by discord between the Public Security Bureau's
social duty to control crime and its political mission to suppress the
Chiang Kai-shek régime's enemies. And in defining enemies, the third
choice became a question of whether to focus on the Communists or on
the Japanese.

Such choices had to be made, because the police could not take on all
of these distinctive tasks at once. Simply put, with a roster of about four
thousand patrolmen, the PSB was not large enough to do everything in a
city the size of Shanghai.[1] Colonel Yuan Liang, who was personally familiar with the police system in north China, pointed out that although Beiping[2] had roughly the same population as Shanghai municipality (and
only a third the area without any of the divisional problems posed by the
concessions), the former capital had two to three times as many policemen
to maintain law and order.[3] In Yuan's opinion, the Shanghai Chinese police force was simply insufficient.[4] Yet with only one uniformed officer
for every 425 inhabitants in the Chinese-administered portions of Shanghai, the PSB still continued to put an enormous strain on the municipal

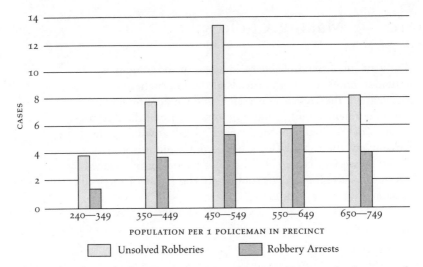

FIGURE 4. Police density and robbery, Shanghai, 1929. PSB unsolved crime and arrest records. Source: *SSG*, vol. 3, 102–8.

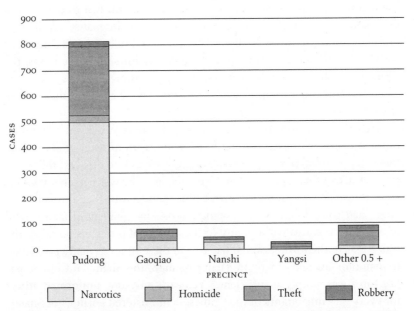

FIGURE 5. Shanghai PSB precinct crime rates, 1929. Source: Third Section, PSB, in SAM, Section Three.

budget, being the major cause of its perennial deficits.[5] (See Figure 4 and Figure 5.)

Contradictory Pressures

Shanghai's municipal deficits were far from exceptional. Nanjing was in the same position, although certain benefits accrued to it as a result of being the national capital. Also, its police force was directly under the Ministry of the Interior. Nevertheless, Nanjing was in deficit six years out of ten, especially from 1927 to 1931. In Hankou, the provincial government ordered the municipal government to reduce the services of six bureaus to three sections in order to cut down the expenses of the city's administration; and in Beiping the municipality had a deficit of Ch. $1.6 million for the fiscal year 1931–32.[6] All of these municipalities were under continuing pressure to devise rational accounting systems.[7]

In the case of Shanghai, the new Bureau of Finance (Caizhengju) had tried in 1927 to establish a centralized accounting system for each of the bureaus, requiring fortnightly and monthly reports as well as annual budgets in advance.[8] The individual municipal taxes (light tax, street cleaning tax, refuse removal tax, and so forth) that existed before the Nationalists took over had been replaced by a general tax of 6 percent on the rental of houses and 10 percent on the rental of shops.[9] Later, the rates were increased to 10 percent on houses and 14 percent on shops, with the promise that most of the increased income would be used to defray public safety costs.[10]

Although there now existed a general municipal tax fund, it was persistently short of cash and had little recourse to provincial sources of revenue.[11] Within Shanghai, therefore, individual bureaucratic units levied taxes on an ad hoc basis: that is, from 1928 to 1939 (when a Municipal Treasury or Shijinku was formed) each of the bureaus collected taxes on its own to pay for services performed.[12] The PSB, as we have seen, relied upon fines collected for breaking police regulations.[13] During the fiscal year 1930–31, for instance, the police collected Ch. $138,356 in fines. However, that income only defrayed 7 percent of total annual PSB expenses of Ch. $1,974,918, and expenses continued to climb year by year (see Table 2).[14]

The largest item in the PSB budget was the cost of personnel, which constituted 87 percent of the bureau's costs in 1927–28.[15] In March 1928, for example, the Nationalists had to allocate Ch. $75,000 in credits to the PSB to cover monthly expenses.[16] Of this amount, Ch. $12,000 was for administrative costs and 63,000 for personnel expenses, including salaries.[17] The overall costs of professionalization, which elevated the quality of police performance, increased this burden. In 1930, Yuan Liang's fancy new police uniforms alone cost Ch. $172,983, while the expense of taking on the Public Health Bureau's street-cleaning duties added another Ch. $59,664 to the PSB's budget.[18] New policemen and policewomen were added to the PSB roster that year, but the bureau continued to be short-handed and overworked.[19]

The Public Security Bureau was also overstressed, reflecting the hazards of police work in Shanghai, where running gunfights between criminals and law enforcement officers of the French, International Settlement, and Chinese police were so common as to appear almost casual to bystanders frequently wounded in the affrays.[20] According to critics of the International Settlement police, such a readiness to open fire reflected the devaluation of Chinese lives by European police.

> The actions of the Shanghai police in firing into crowded streets indicated a callous disregard of human life unequaled anywhere else in the world. . . . To make the matter more specific, no member of the Shanghai police force would think of firing into a crowd of foreigners in Shanghai, but he doesn't hesitate to do so when the crowd is Chinese.[21]

Every SMP officer in Shanghai carried a pistol, often a Colt .380 semi-automatic, sometimes accompanied by orders to take the safety catch off whenever he went on duty.[22]

But the Chinese police were heavily armed as well, and they too patrolled under the constant menace of encountering armed robbers.[23] Part of the problem was the difficulty of spotting likely suspects. "The most dangerous and successful robbers often [wore] well-cut silk gowns," and looked like "good-class Chinese gentlemen." Moreover, their long sleeves enabled them to carry their pistols in their hands concealed and cocked. "When whistles are blown at night, every man runs toward the sound with his pistol in his hand. Should he meet the robbers in flight, he can be certain they will open fire on sight and he knows he has to stand up and return the fire."[24] Under such circumstances, the rate of indiscriminate casualties was unusually high.[25]

Such hazardous working conditions must have contributed to the high turnover rate of personnel. Although the bureau encouraged policemen to stay on for at least five years of service by offering public primary school tuition waivers to their children after that term, patrolmen and office workers alike frequently resigned or were dismissed.[26] In 1930, the PSB chief estimated that an average of one hundred policemen were dismissed or retired each month.[27]

The Political Threat of Dissent

Under these circumstances, the ability of the Chinese police to enforce regular criminal laws was sorely taxed. Yet the Public Security Bureau was not only under public pressure to cut down the crime rate; it was also the recipient of continuing and growing demands by the Nanjing government to extend its activities into the political realm by suppressing dissident publications and arresting such "reactionary" opponents of the Chiang régime as the Communists and the Reorganizationists headed by Wang Jingwei and members of the Guangxi clique. These demands, which were transmitted to the PSB on the part of Chiang Kai-shek, were also sent to the International Settlement police in the form of requests forwarded by the Shanghai Provisional Court.[28]

The first formal request to the SMP for cooperation on a political matter came on February 20, 1929. That day the Provisional Court forwarded two sets of documents to the Criminal Investigation Department of the Shanghai Municipal Police. The first, dated February 4, from the Shanghai Special Municipality, cited an order from the national government, signed by Chiang Kai-shek, calling for the suppression of the "reactionary" Communist periodical *Xuechao* (*Tide of Blood*), published by the Liqun Bookstore at 142 Kuling Road. The second communication, also an order from the national government, referred to a dispatch signed by Chiang Kai-shek on February 9 about editorials calling for the "reconstruction of the Guomindang." These were published in the periodical *Juedou,* said to be a journal of the Decisive Struggle Club (Juedoushe), a creation in turn of the Wang Jingwei-led Association for the Reorganization of the Guomindang (Zhongguo Guomindang gaizu tongzhihui), established in Shanghai the previous spring. Saying that the editorials in *Juedou* were "absurd and detrimental, [and] therefore its issuance should be prohibited," the Chinese government requested that the Shanghai Provisional Court seal the premises of the Juedoushe, which was supposedly located on Canton Road.[29] The SMP agreed to comply with both these requests. That is, their CID not only tried to find the Communist bookstore; it also launched an investigation of the Reorganizationists—a group supported by the Guangxi clique and opposed to Chiang Kai-shek, but hardly more inimical to British interests, as such, than the orthodox Guomindang local branch, which was dominated by militant young intellectuals affiliated with Chen Guofu and Chen Lifu.[30] Neither investigation yielded major results.[31]

Although these investigations did not create a direct connection between the SMP and the PSB, this was achieved nine months later. The two police departments were brought together in investigative cooperation for the first time on November 2, 1929. Once again, however, the two causes—anti-Communist, anti-Reorganizationist—were linked, with the Chinese authorities providing enticing intelligence on putative Communist activities in exchange for help against Chiang's enemies within the Guomindang and among the Guangxi clique. In a two-part intelligence report Chief Yuan Liang provided the address of Huang Huiping and explained that the former secretary of the Shanghai Guomindang headquarters had been bribed by the Guangxi clique's Reorganizationists to induce members of the GMD to engage in reactionary activities. Shortly after that Showin Wetzen Hsu, president of the Provisional Court, requested the International Settlement commissioner of police "to give orders for strict and secret investigations and apprehensions to be made" of the Reorganizationists.[32] The second part of Chief Yuan Liang's intelligence report described Communist plans for a demonstration on November 7 to commemorate the twelfth anniversary of the Bolshevik Revolution. Over three hundred unemployed workers had supposedly been sent by the Communist Party's district committees to Ferry Road, Robison Road, Jessfield Village, Pudong, and Zhabei to instigate a general strike. At the same time, CP cell members at various educational institutions were preparing to mobilize student support. The PSB therefore requested the cooperation of the SMP in banning these demonstrations.[33]

The response of the SMP to this information was quick and direct. R. C. Aiers, assistant director of Criminal Investigation, told his men to be on the lookout for Communist activities.[34] Shortly after this, when Judge Hsu's request for compliance with the central government's order to suppress the "Reactionary Party" came in, the director of Criminal Investigation of the SMP wrote back: "I have to acknowledge receipt of your letter of November 26 requesting assistance from the municipal police in suppressing the activities of certain reactionaries who are in the habit of fabricating rumors defamatory to the national government and to prevent the circulation of propaganda in the form of literature prepared by these parties, and to inform you in reply that the matter is now receiving attention."[35]

It was clear, then, that as far as the CID was concerned, information from the Chinese police about Communist activities within the International Settlement provided both ammunition against a mutual adversary, and an inducement to cooperate in suppressing the Reorganizationists. The International Settlement police's Special Branch, after all, was ultrasensitive to all matters concerning the Communists' influence upon college students.[36] The slightest suspicion of Communist activity on Shanghai university campuses was enough to call down a full-scale investigation by the CID.[37]

The SMP also continued to concern itself with stemming the dissemination of Communist propaganda, and as of 1930, assigned censors to the post office to make sure that the mails were not used to spread subversive ideas.[38] This was, after all, a year that saw the formation in Shanghai of the League of Left Artists, which published its own magazine and founded reading clubs; a union of bookshops engaged in publishing and circulating left-wing literature and magazines; the Left Dramatic League, led by Tian Han; the All-China Social Scientists League's school for workers and students; and the Left Cultural Federation of China.[39] The International Settlement police force's main fear was that all these anti-imperialist influences would engender demonstrations and inflame eruptions, especially during the early days of May when so many radical anniversaries could be commemorated.

New Police Collaboration to Control Dissent

On April 27, 1930, the CID received a warning from the Chinese Public Security Bureau that the Communists were planning to stage demonstrations during the next three days. These demonstrations to usher in May Day would supposedly involve students from Great China University and the Anti-Imperialist League in the Western District, members of the School of Arts and Youth League in the French Concession, representatives from the Freedom League and the General Labor Union in the International Settlement, cotton mill workers in Yangshupu, the Boy Scouts in Zhabei, and delegates of peasant groups in Pudong. Consequently, a special meeting was held at the SMC offices with Colonel Yuan Liang, Major Gerrard, and Captain Fiori to coordinate the police forces of the Chinese, international, and French sectors of the city to stave off radical demonstrations on May 1.[40]

On the morning of April 29 the SMP took preemptive action by raiding ten "suspected communistic bases" in the International Settlement. Five of the "bases," including one middle school, yielded nothing suspicious. At a sixth, on 386 Burkill Road, nine persons were arrested in the act of holding a meeting. The seventh, eighth, and ninth addresses contained "communistic literature."[41] The tenth raid was on 866 East Yalu Road, which turned out to be occupied by members of the Shanghai Power Company Employees Union. There the police seized seven hundred copies of "communistic papers" (*Shanghai bao* and *Hongqi bao*) and a printing press, and arrested sixteen people.[42] Four of the sixteen were identified as simple residents and released. The remaining twelve were detained: an unemployed butcher named Xu Asan, ten employees of the utility company, and a thirty-two-year-old unemployed pawnshop assistant named Wang Lisheng who was found sleeping on top of a table that covered the "communistic papers." One of the power company workers gave the police the names of the union president and vice president, and the SMP managed to arrest the second of these and obtain the names of ninety present and former members of the group—names that were forwarded to the English manager of the company "for his information."[43]

The twelve men arrested at the East Yalu Road address meanwhile were arraigned the following day at a preliminary hearing before the branch high court of the Harbin Road station. "Representatives of the Military Authorities from Longhua" were present at the hearing together with an informer who identified Wang Lisheng under another name as a person wanted by the Chinese police. The three Chinese judges sentenced Mr. Wang to two years' imprisonment for possession of the "communistic literature" he had been sleeping on, and after an additional hearing, he was handed over to the Garrison Command representatives for extradition.[44]

When the Guomindang revolutionaries first came to power, the Settlement authorities had not honored extradition requests.[45] In September and October 1927 the Shanghai Garrison Command had asked for the extradition of two thousand to three thousand Chinese prisoners in Settlement jails, ostensibly in a joint effort to make room for more miscreants so as to clean up Shanghai's criminal elements. The request was peremptorily rejected.[46] Policy began to change as of New Year's Day, 1928, when the Municipal Council announced that from then on, it would be willing to maintain closer relations with the Guomindang government.[47]

Now, the Yalu Road case seemed to establish a precedent for extradition by the Shanghai Garrison Command if a person were charged with possession of Communist propaganda.[48] The principle was challenged less than two months later, however, when the Jiangxi authorities sent a dispatch warrant to the Shanghai Military Police for the arrest of four suspected Communists whose names had been gotten through the interrogation of other Communists seized in that province. The Shanghai Garrison Command handed the warrant over to the Public Security Bureau, which requested the help of the SMP in arresting the suspects, who turned out to be in possession of incriminating documents. The PSB thereupon asked for extradition, but when the case came before Judge Yih of the Shanghai Municipal District Court, deputy municipal advocate Paul Y. Ru argued that "the Bureau of Public Safety was not a law court, nor was the Shanghai and Woosung gendarmerie's commissioner's yamen, and they had absolutely no jurisdiction in the matter." The accused should not be handed over—Ru insisted—unless two courts had concurrent jurisdiction, in which case the Jiangxi High Court, and not the PSB or Garrison Command, would have to make application. Judge Yih promised to consider the matter.[49]

The last months of 1930 saw a renewal of right-wing terror throughout China.[50] At Beiping National University sixty students were imprisoned for trying to form a branch of the Social Science League. A dozen more were arrested in Tianjin for the same reason. Slaughter continued in Hankou. Canton forbade all newspapers to publish news of the arrests and executions of youth. In October Sichuanese military authorities offered $50 per head for Communists and gave soldiers and policemen the authority to kill them on the spot. As a result, during the next two months, two thousand men and women, chiefly students, were butchered in the major cities of that province.[51]

Meanwhile, the Public Security Bureau continued to concern itself as obsessively as ever with the suppression of "reactionary" publications.[52] A new municipal Information Investigation Office (Xinwen jiancha ju) was charged with the responsibility of censoring thousands of suspect periodical articles.[53] Requests continued to be sent to the International Settlement police for cooperation in this effort to silence the "deviant talk (*xieshuo*) [that] has for a long time been penetrating deep into people's minds."[54] On October 2, 1930, Chief Yuan Liang wrote to Commissioner Gerrard listing the names of eight "reactionary" and "communistic" newspapers, including *China Soviet Weekly*, singled out by the postal censors attached to the Garrison Command, and asked that Gerrard give instructions for them "to be strictly suppressed."[55] Gerrard evidently complied, and other titles were added in the following weeks.[56]

Cooperation continued to increase through the winter of 1930–31. On December 7, 1930, for example, the Zhabei Public Security Bureau carried out a major raid against the Renji Printing Company at 9 Linping Road, where *Red Flag Daily* (*Hongqi ribao*) was being run off. Plates were seized and a total of thirteen persons were arrested and interrogated by the security authorities.[57] Using the information gathered during this raid, the Chinese police secured the support of the SMP in raiding and closing down some twenty bookshops publishing or circulating books bearing such "ominous" titles as: *Materialistic Philosophy, Materialism and Religion, Oulinoff the Materialist, Soviet Farmers,* and *Women.*[58] By January 1931, in other words, the International Settlement's CID was beginning to comply on a routine basis with requests from the Songhu Garrison

Command and the PSB, cast in the form of nameless warrants, to search bookstores suspected of selling "reactionary" works, and to arrest booksellers whenever incriminating materials were found.[59]

The International Settlement police were not only complying with the PSB and Garrison Command's requests for bookstore raids and random arrests; they were also arresting suspected Communists on their own and, moreover, keeping the PSB fully informed in turn.[60] On February 10, 1931, for instance, President Yang Shaoshun of the Shanghai Special District Court informed the SMP that the Guomindang's Central Propaganda Bureau had good reason to believe that the Wo Sing (Huaxing) Bookstore, at the east end of Connaught Road, was a major propaganda organ of the Communists that had published many of "Linin's" (*sic*) works.[61] Forwarding a list of thirty-seven titles to be found in the store, which included three books by Lenin and a number of studies of the Communist movements in Russia, India, and Korea, President Yang asked that "necessary steps" be taken by the International Settlement police.[62] The SMP thereupon proceeded to seal seven bookstores on Fuzhou Road and authorized the arrest and extradition of one or two more bookstore clerks and acting managers.[63]

These raids coincided with the SMP Special Branch's apprehension that, as of January 15, 1931, there had been a change of policy in Moscow.[64] British Intelligence was convinced, thanks to "a very reliable source," that henceforth the Soviet government was going to devote most of its funds for subversion to foster sentiments and movements hostile to the "so-called" imperialist nations. It was expected by the police that this change of policy would lead the Soviets to concentrate their energy on demands for the restoration of the concessions and the abolition of extraterritoriality. The instruments of this agitation would be various antiimperialist leagues, oppressed people's associations, and other societies masquerading as "patriotic organizations."[65] Two nights later, on January 17, thirty-six Communists, of whom seven were women, held a secret meeting in the Eastern Hotel. The SMP's Special Branch raided the hotel before the revolutionaries could scatter.[66] All thirty-six were arrested and handed over to the Nationalists, who incarcerated them in the garrison headquarters at Longhua. Three weeks later, during the night of February 7, twenty-three of the suspected Communists (including three women) were taken out and shot. At the time there was not a single word about this execution in Shanghai newspapers, and it was not until April 25 that the death of the revolutionary martyrs was publicly revealed in a special magazine founded for this purpose by the League of Left-Wing Writers and called *Outpost (Qianshao)*.[67]

Questions of Legality in Policing Dissent

Meanwhile, disturbed by the questionable legality of these raids and arrests, Deputy Municipal Advocate Paul Y. Ru continued to raise protests before the Shanghai Municipal District Court, arguing that it was contrary to Chinese criminal procedure to have the municipal police arrest an innocent person on a nameless warrant in order to get information on the whereabouts of suspected Communists. Furthermore, these warrants represented charges being brought not by the Settlement police but by extra-settlement authorities such as the Public Security Bureau. The warrants were not issued in the accused person's name, but for any person in charge of the store, who was then seized and taken off by PSB detectives regardless of complicity.[68] The SMP continued to turn a deaf ear to Advocate Ru's legalistic objections, although officers did express uneasiness about the arbitrariness of the arrests.

> Great difficulty is experienced in the execution of this class of warrant, for apart from the name or names contained thereon, we have no means of identifying the wanted persons. . . . Invariably the Public Safety Bureau detectives know nothing of the person wanted and less of his habitual address.[69]

This ambiguity took on added importance, given that any suspect, and especially students, faced torture and possibly death if turned over to the Nationalists' civilian and military police.[70]

This is not to say that the SMP jailers were above mistreating their own captives.[71] A woman arrested by the SMP on suspicion of kidnapping described how she was initially shoved into a holding cell with twelve men and one other woman. The men had been beaten. The police forced urine and feces into her nose, and after being transferred to the regular SMP prison she found people in terrible physical condition, the bedding filled with bugs and lice, food containers used as bedpans, and so forth.[72] But it was much worse when, after three days, she was turned over to the Public Security Bureau. The minute she arrived she was taken to a room and without a word, the new prison guards beat her. Then she was given the tiger's bench: "they pull the ligaments under the knee in opposite directions." When she recovered consciousness she found herself among a group of prisoners sobbing from pain. "During the whole day I heard only the sound of iron shackles, moaning voices, the beating and threats of the guards. This place is the high command for massacring the people, and they have the power to kill anybody they wish, so oftentimes we can hear the shooting as prisoners are executed not far away."[73]

Despite nearly certain knowledge of these brutalities, the British police officers in charge of the SMP hastened to increase cooperative activities with the PSB. They had compelling reasons of their own for wanting to collaborate with the Chinese police in suppressing "Communist activities" at this particular time, prompted by the leafletting of British and American military men. The leaflets urged these sailors and soldiers to support the Chinese Red Army because it was "the armed force of the Chinese workers, peasants, and revolutionary masses."

> What are your ideas? Are you willing to help the ruling classes, capitalists, and imperialists to slaughter your class brothers, the Chinese Red[s], or to support the Red[s]? Think it over, please. You are oppressed by your ruling classes as bitterly as the Chinese workers and peasants. . . . Don't be the tools or running dogs of the capitalists and imperialists any more. You are men. Try to learn how to be a man.[74]

The Settlement police were unable to trace the source of the handbills, even though they continued the search for some time as part of a general preparation for Communist demonstrations expected to take place in May.[75]

Meanwhile, on April 28, 1931, PSB Chief Chen Xizeng addressed Commissioner Martin of the Shanghai Municipal Police asking that "precautionary steps be taken to prevent the Communists from carrying out their plans for strikes, etc. on the various commemoration days in the month of May."[76] Chief Chen's letter was acknowledged "with thanks" by Assistant Commissioner Patrick T. Givens, the current head of the Special Branch, who said that the problem was "receiving attention" on April 30, 1931.[77] During the following month, the SMP routinely pulled policemen off traffic duty and held them on reserve in the stations and barracks; had senior officers constantly patrol their districts by car or motorcycle; drew the attention of all ranks to the use of firearms; cancelled monthly leaves; and announced its intention to disperse all gatherings (with baton charges if necessary) and arrest any who resisted.[78] And together with the French Concession police and the Public Security Bureau, the SMP cooperated in the seizure of over one million handbills and pamphlets, which was "believed to have been one of the most important factors in prevention of the usual disturbances in Shanghai on the anniversary of the student incident of 1925."[79]

The annual police alert over "May days" subsided in 1931 just as it had the year before, but in the course of that single year the working relationship between the International Settlement police and the Chinese

Public Security Bureau had undergone a major change.[80] Not only were bookstore raids routinely and zealously carried out in full cooperation; suspected Communists were arrested on the flimsiest of evidence by the SMP, which regularly accepted nameless and open-ended warrants presented by the PSB or dispatched by the Garrison Command via the Shanghai District Court.[81] By June 5, 1931, the court was even sending in lists of suspected Communists from the provincial government, requesting that the Special Branch "be good enough to give instructions to the various police stations to effect the arrest of these [twenty-five] names," who were "to be brought before this court when they are arrested."[82]

Although cooperation between the SMP and PSB became increasingly routinized, the International Settlement police were more concerned about clandestine subversion than public agitation and propaganda. The Public Security Bureau, on the other hand, continued to fret over "reactionary" publications and continued to call for the keenest month-by-month vigilance against the celebration of "international red" (*guoji chise*) days, even though protests and demonstrations lessened dramatically after June 1931.[83] The Shanghai Municipal Police certainly had no plans to alter its policy of cooperation with the PSB, but at the very least its officers were growing slightly skeptical about the truly "communistic nature" of the literature they were confiscating during their various raids, and becoming concerned about the resources diverted from ordinary criminal investigation to political policing.[84] When they actually read some of the materials collected in one of their bookstore raids, including a copy of Lenin's *Materialism and Empirio-Criticism*, police inspectors concluded that such works did not constitute an offense against "the Internal Security of the State."[85] Thereafter, the SMP was far less likely to accept the word of the PSB alone that such and such materials were "communistic," though it did not overtly challenge the reliability of lists of "communist organizations" that were forwarded by the Chinese Municipality of Greater Shanghai with the usual requests for suppression.[86]

The PSB's Shifting Priorities

The Public Security Bureau's obsession with "reactionary" propaganda diverted its officers from other police work. According to its own records for the police year 1930–31, the PSB sent out detectives to make preemptive arrests on 123 different occasions, seizing 1,471 sets of printed materials such as handbills meant to be distributed at public demonstrations. Ordinary police work continued to try to cope with Shanghai's rising crime rate, but more and more resources were being devoted to "red squad" activities.[87]

As a result of this increasingly obsessive attention to political duties, the priorities of the Shanghai Public Security Bureau shifted perceptibly. Ordinary crimes continued to occur and even to increase, but more and more time was spent ferreting out Communist "reactionaries" and combating conspiracies. Between 1927 and 1932 there was a total of 686 cases dealing with Communists, and 988 cases of "uncovering conspiracies" or *pohuo*.[88] But the distribution of these political cases was uneven over the span of time, reflecting the PSB's altered sense of mission. The official annals of police affairs for the years 1927–30 reflected the social activism of that period, being filled with accounts of traffic modernization, moral regeneration, and urban improvement. The annals for the police year 1930–31 were quite different in emphasis. Not only were fewer criminal arrests listed; almost all of the entries either concerned political repression or routine personnel transfers and administrative changes. The police's conscious view of themselves as revolutionary social activists visibly declined.[89]

It certainly was not true that fewer crimes were systematically recorded. The reporting of crimes was standardized and statistics were carefully—even compulsively—kept up to date.[90] The provenance of criminals was noted; most came from Jiangsu and Zhejiang, of course.[91] Their age groupings were analyzed; roughly four out of ten miscreants were between twenty-one and thirty.[92] And they were sorted and divided by occupations: workers, 43 percent; unemployed, 42 percent; merchants and vendors, 9 percent; peasants, 4 percent; and miscellaneous, 2 percent.[93]

Thus, even as more attention was being paid to alleged political conspiracies, a steady increase in crime was being recorded. Between 1929–30 and 1931–32 the number of cases prepared for preliminary court hearings by the PSB increased 81 percent, from 4,713 to 8,528 (see Table 3). Nine out of ten of these crimes were committed by men, with women mainly being arrested for crimes related to public morality, drugs, and prostitution (see Tables 4 and 5). And although there was a below-average rise or even decline in cases of illegal flight, concealment of felons, counterfeiting, forgery, narcotics, and homicide, there was an above-average increase in cases of gambling, battery, theft, squatting, and extortion—all relatively petty offenses that required very little time to detect and solve.[94] In other words, crime rates, as represented in cases brought to arraignment, nearly doubled during those two years, the main increase being in cases of relatively conspicuous criminal behavior that came to the attention of the uniformed police rather than to the politically distracted detective squad (*zhenjidui*).

The contradiction between criminal investigation and political policing did not escape contemporaries' attention. It was most visible in the case of the International Settlement police's Criminal Investigation Department, and as usual it was the *China Weekly Review* that brought the matter to the public's attention as early as December 1928, shortly before the SMP and PSB began taking their first hesitant steps toward political cooperation.

> The "CID," as its name implies, should be a purely police investigation service confined to matters pertaining to crime exclusively. If the British government wishes to maintain a political intelligence and propaganda service in this part of the world, that's the business of the British government. But it should be financed by the British government and not by the Shanghai Municipal Council.[95]

By the end of 1931, nonetheless, cooperation was quickly turning into collaboration. Public misgivings regarding the political mission of Shanghai's police departments had by this time abated somewhat, given the impact of the sensationalist Noulens and Gu Shunzhang Affairs. The choice to combat international and domestic Communism over local crime was vindicated by these two cases of counterespionage.

More problematic, however, was the Chiang Kai-shek régime's decision to define as the greater enemy to the state the Chinese Communist Party, rather than potential Japanese aggression. Several important changes in the structures for policing Shanghai emerged from this focus on anti-Communist strategies. Not the least among these was the Public Security Bureau's decision to subsume control of what remained of the urban militia within the municipal administration, which amounted to a further militarization of the police and yet another blow to the autonomy of merchant street associations and their allies within the local Nationalist Party branch.

In September 1929 the central government decreed that local militia throughout China should be put under official county or municipal authorities.[96] On September 12 the decree was promulgated in Shanghai along with an announcement by the Shanghai-Wusong Garrison Commander Xiong Shihui that control of the militia would be transferred to the Public Security Bureau.[97] The Shanghai militia chief, Yao Wennan, who was on very poor terms with PSB Chief Yuan Liang, instantly opposed this move. The local branch of the Guomindang joined with guilds, street unions, and the merchant association (*shangmin xiehui*) to form a Shanghai general assembly.[98] The assembly in turn elected party member Jiang Huaisu president and unanimously rejected the decision to transfer the militia on the grounds that it was a voluntary army and not a police force. The assembly, arguing that a local notable should head the militia, simultaneously accused Yuan Liang of moral and political corruption.[99]

This accusation of personal corruption by the Guomindang-merchant coalition probably referred to Yuan Liang's involvement in the Wang Yansong case, which came to a head the very day that the militia-transfer decree was announced. Wang, a prominent member of the sixth district Guomindang, was arrested on the morning of September 12, 1929, when he presented himself at the PSB together with Zhang Baoshi, the widow of a Chinese general who had been killed in a brawl by British soldiers. The case was a complicated tangle of interests involving a group of self-serving Guomindang political representatives (Wang Yansong, Zhang Hongkui, Shen Tingkui, Jiang Ruzhi, and Zhang Lian'en—all members of the sixth district GMD) and two fellow townsmen of Madame Zhang from Tongzhou (Yan Guitang and Cui Wenjun). Both groups of men were helping Madame Zhang press a claim against the International Settlement. On September 6 the SMC's Foreign Affairs Bureau had paid Zhang Baoshi a solatium of $5,000, which led the two groups of men to quarrel over the spoils. Wang Yansong eventually forced Madame Zhang to give him a large portion of the cash, which he pocketed. When the two Tongzhou men objected to this, Wang went to the Chinese police and accused the two "rowdies" of being swindlers. The PSB had no reason to doubt the word of a leading GMD member, and promptly arrested the Tongzhou men. However, when Madame Zhang was asked to verify the story, she exonerated the prisoners and accused Wang and his accomplices of extortion instead. Colonel Yuan Liang thereupon issued warrants for Wang Yansong's arrest, and when Wang presented himself in person at PSB headquarters to try to bluff the matter through, Yuan Liang had the Guomindang leader seized.[100] The local party branch immediately issued a protest, but Colonel Yuan ignored their complaints and as of September 20 Wang Yansong was still being detained.

By then the case had caused a major rift between Colonel Yuan Liang and the Nationalist Party headquarters in Shanghai, and there was good reason to believe that Yuan Liang would lose his job—especially since the fate of the urban militia was also at stake.[101] In the next two days, however, a settlement was mediated by the director of the Shanghai Telegraph Bureau (Dianbaoju), Chen Xizeng, who was a "disciple" (*tangfang xiong-di*) and fellow townsman of Chen Guofu and Chen Lifu, and who was eventually to succeed Colonel Yuan Liang as director of public security.[102] On September 22 Wang Yansong was released, and the British Intelligence Service subsequently commented: "As a result of the reestablishment of friendly relations between the municipality of Greater Shanghai and the Kuomintang, the danger of Yuan Liang, chief of the Public Safety Bureau, losing his position has been removed for the time being."[103] Although the resolution of the Wang Yansong case eased some of the tension between Yuan Liang and the Guomindang, their conflict over control of the militia continued.[104] The militia ignored repeated orders to be transferred to the police. Mayor Zhang Qun (Zhang Yuejun), arguing that the militia were being reorganized in order to be more efficacious, said that he was ready to entertain negotiations.[105]

As a result, the influential merchants who had run the militia since 1911—Yu Xiaqing, Wang Binyan, and Gu Xinyi—sent the executive directors of the South Market and Zhabei self-defense corps, Ye Huijun and Wang Xiaolai, to represent them in discussions with the mayor's office.[106] After a month of negotiations by these two, a Peace Preservation Corps Reorganization Committee (Baoweituan zhengli weiyuanhui) was formed consisting of five local notables, a Guomindang representative, and three members of the municipal government, including Yuan Liang.[107] Missing from the committee were the government's most vociferous opponents, including militia director Yao Wennan himself.[108]

The municipal government's strategy of dealing only with "responsible" elements among the city's merchant elites worked. In January 1930 the Reorganization Committee announced its decision to hand over control of the militia to a Peace Preservation Corps Management Committee (Baoweituan guanli weiyuanhui).[109] It required another year of negotiation before this last step was taken, but the Management Committee eventually took over; it was composed of the director of public security (by then Chen Xizeng), Sun Baorong, Luo Jingyou (representing the mayor's cabinet), Yu Xiaqing, Wang Xiaolai, Ye Huijun, Yao Mulian, and Wang Binyan.[110] Within two years, by 1933, Mayor Wu Tiecheng transformed the urban merchant militia into an auxiliary armed force fully integrated into the PSB local police apparatus.[111]

Advent of the Japanese

On February 3, 1931, Chen Xizeng succeeded Colonel Yuan Liang as chief of the PSB.[112] The fact that he was a disciple of the Chen brothers, a member of the "CC" clique, and probably therefore connected with the party counterintelligence organization that the brothers had set up, may have had something to do with the growing obsession of the PSB with "reds."[113] But through the late summer and fall of 1931 the Chinese police chief's concern with internal subversion was gradually overwhelmed by the difficulty of coping with the Japanese.

The 1920s had seen a changing relationship in Shanghai between the

British and the Japanese as the latter gained in numbers and influence at the expense of the former. In 1890 there had been eight hundred Japanese in Shanghai; thirty years later, in 1920, there were ten thousand.[114] By 1931 Japan was annually shipping 124,000 bales of cotton yarn to Shanghai, where they had invested more than one billion yen in thirty-two cotton mills, superior in efficiency and equipment to the twenty-two Chinese-owned and five British-owned mills in the city.[115] In the Yangzi Valley—once taken by the British to be their own economic preserve— Japanese businessmen controlled ironworks, railways, a land investment company, a paper mill, a machine plant, and power plants for twenty-four cities.[116] Twenty-seven different Japanese steamships linked the river ports with Shanghai, where all the major shipping firms had their head offices. During those years Japanese companies also bought three wharf frontages (one at Yangshupu and two at Pudong), and the number of banks owned by Japanese increased steadily.[117] By 1930 the Japanese community in Hongkou totaled thirty thousand people, nearly three times the number of British living in Shanghai.[118]

As relations between China and Japan worsened, the Shanghai Public Security Bureau found this large Japanese community to be a frequent cause of distress. "Police sovereignty" (*jingquan*) was sometimes at stake in disputes concerning the Imperial Japanese Navy, Marines, and Military and Consular Police.[119] More often, however, the source of difficulty was the population of Japanese adventurers (*rōnin* or samurai without masters) inhabiting "Little Tokyo."[120] For, along with the businessmen and bankers came the gangsters and *yakuza*, the arms dealers and drug runners.[121] The Japanese consular police, under Chief O. Muraji, had claimed earlier, in 1926, to have cleaned out these denizens of Little Tokyo's underworld.[122] But in reality, the Japanese police worked closely in Shanghai, as they did in Japan proper, with gangsters who shared their ultra-patriotism and right-wing ideals.[123] *Yakuza*—gangs of "tough-looking loafers [*liumang*]," which included Taiwanese and Koreans alongside low-caste Japanese—worked as bouncers and Chinese-language interpreters in the brothels for Japanese sailors and marines along Darroch Road.[124] Other "ruffians" were employed as croupiers and dealers in the gambling casinos behind the Isis Theater on Haskell Road, while yet another group of *yakuza* allegedly served as strong-arm thugs for the Japanese Gendarmerie.[125] After the Manchurian Railway Incident on September 18, 1931, these and other ultra-nationalist elements among the Japanese civilians in Hongkou engaged in a steady spate of altercations with the Chinese police in Zhabei, seemingly seeking out quarrels with PSB men intentionally.[126]

At the same time, the police were having even greater difficulty holding Shanghai's outraged citizenry in check. Anti-Japanese associations dating from the May Thirtieth Movement had resumed their activities in July 1931 at the time of the Yangzi floods and of the scission between Nanjing and Canton and after ethnic conflict broke out between Korean and Chinese farmers at Wanbaoshan along the border near Kirin.

> As soon as the news of the conflict between the Chinese peasants and the Koreans over the question of farming rights in certain parts of the [Wanbaoshan] district, Kirin, on July 2, 1931, reached Shanghai, the anti-Japanese feeling, which appeared to have subsided since the anti-Japanese agitation in 1928–1929, resulting from the dispatch of troops by the Japanese government to Shantung in April 1928, and the subsequent collision with the Nationalist troops at Tsinan on May 3, 1928, revived among the local Chinese community.[127]

News from the northeastern provinces spoke of Chinese being killed by Koreans, who allegedly disguised themselves as Japanese policemen.[128] An anti-Japanese boycott organized by various local groups including the Shanghai Chamber of Commerce, and headed by Yu Xiaqing, was launched on July 13, supported by the local branch of the Korean Independent Party, which blamed the attacks on the Chinese to Japanese instigators.[129] During the next three weeks anti-Japanese boycott pickets boarded tenders along the Huangpu River and seized Japanese textile goods, including cotton yarn.[130] In early August, the Guomindang began broadcasting anti-Japanese speeches over local radio stations; and on August 10 a group of Chinese workers assaulted two uniformed Japanese marine officers after they began tearing anti-Japanese posters from the wall of a factory off of Ward Road.[131]

In other words, Chinese nationalistic passions against the Japanese were already inflamed weeks before news of the Manchurian Railway Incident reached Shanghai on September 19, 1931. Thirty local university representatives immediately gathered at the Shanghai Baptist College to form the Committee to Resist Japan and Save the Nation (Fan Ri jiuguo lianhehui), which organized propaganda teams to mobilize support for the patriotic movement.[132] Two days later thirty-seven secondary school representatives founded an equivalent umbrella group, which urged its members to "stop classes to propagandize."[133] The committee put up posters, distributed handbills, made speeches in the streets, staged anti-Japanese dramas, and held a series of rallies that culminated in a General Assembly of the Citizens of Shanghai (Shanghai shimin dahui), consisting of 200,000 persons who demanded the retreat of Japanese troops or a declaration of war, the rupture of economic relations with Japan, and the political reunification of China.[134]

The impact of the boycott of Japanese goods on the Japanese community of Shanghai was unprecedented. In 1930 29 percent of Shanghai's total imports came from Japan. By December 1931 this had decreased to 3 percent. More than 125 Japanese-operated factories in Shanghai suspended production, and 90 percent were completely closed down; another nine Japanese cotton factories shut their doors a month later. Japanese residents of Shanghai organized their own "Committee on the Current Situation," which demanded that the Japanese government "take resolute steps to punish China's intransigence." On October 10, 1931, the Japanese minister to China, Shigemitsu Mamoru, warned the Nanjing government that it would be held responsible for controlling the boycott and for protecting the property and lives of Japanese residents. The Chinese response was tart and unyielding.[135]

As word spread of an imminent Japanese invasion of Shanghai, Mayor Zhang Qun twice decreed martial law and assigned Public Security Bureau agents to trace the source of the rumors.[136] On October 16, Chen Xizeng told his precinct chiefs that public order now had become a diplomatic issue at the national level, and he ordered them to take special measures to prevent incidents that could give the Japanese a pretext for further aggression.[137] At the same time, the mayor tried to keep Shanghai's students from going on strike, but was unsuccessful.[138] More than ten thousand students demonstrated, occasionally coming into violent conflict with Japanese military patrols. The authorities grew ever more concerned that there would be a provocation similar to events in Tianjin, where the Chinese police and Japanese marines had engaged in an armed confrontation. A special liaison bureau was established in Zhabei where the risks of conflict were the greatest.[139]

The fall and early winter of 1931 was a time of great strain for Shanghai, precisely because of this confluence of national and local concerns. Communists again took to the streets, smashing trams, shouting slogans, and fighting the police.[140] Student demonstrations in favor of a strong response to Japanese aggression and against the Chiang government's cautious foreign policy continued to mount. Tens of thousands of students poured into Nanjing from Shanghai and other cities besieging government offices and threatening to riot.[141] On December 9, 1931, the day after policemen and Guomindang toughs descended on a rally at West Gate and seized one student and badly beat another, Shanghai students surrounded the Chinese municipal town hall overnight and sacked and wrecked the Guomindang headquarters.[142] The next day they held a kangaroo court that interrogated and beat a PSB detective. They also issued a warrant for the arrest of the commissioner of police.[143] That afternoon, December 10, General Zhang Qun stepped down as mayor of Shanghai, and a continuing spate of other demonstrations and public processions helped precipitate Chiang Kai-shek's resignation as head of the national government and his retirement to his hometown twelve days later.[144]

Governmental Chaos

The Canton faction of the Guomindang promptly stepped in, and Sun Ke (Sun Fo, Sun Yat-sen's son) took over the leadership of the national government.[145] Immediate repercussions emerged in the Shanghai police and army commands. PSB Chief Chen Xizeng, whom many blamed for the December 9 affair, left office, while Xiong Shihui, the head of the Wusong Garrison Command and a Chiang loyalist, also resigned. Sun Ke's government replaced Xiong and his men with 33,500 southern troops of the Nineteenth Route Army under the command of Generals Jiang Guangnai and Cai Tingkai.[146] General Cai, who had an impressive combat record, had been in and out of every faction of the Guomindang before he finally joined the Canton group.[147]

Chiang Kai-shek began to return from retirement early in January 1932. The key to the situation then, from the vantage point of Nanjing, was financial.

> The southern faction, which was so sure of itself and so insistent that the old régime should vacate, so as to give "new blood" and higher ideals a chance, has been in office now only a few weeks, and it has found itself up against, not a theory, but the plain, hard fact that its government is on the brink of bankruptcy, with its outgoings three times its income, and without the help of the people whom its supporters so furiously opposed, to improve its financial situation.[148]

Sun Ke, who spent most of the week of January 9–16 in Shanghai, admitted on January 12 that the monthly revenues of the Nanjing government came to only $6 million, whereas expenses amounted to $22 million. He and others, therefore, began to pin their hopes on returning to power Chiang Kai-shek, along with Wang Jingwei (who claimed to be suffering from diabetes in Shanghai but who had called a meeting of his Reorganizationists early in December) and Hu Hanmin (who continued to remain in Hong Kong supposedly recovering from high blood pressure); these three could persuade Shanghai's financiers to help them out.[149] That same day Sun Ke sent General He Yingqin, minister of war, and Zhang Ji, president of the Legislative Yuan, to Fenghua to plead with Chiang to return to Nanjing. The Generalissimo simply sat stone-faced when they delivered their entreaties.[150]

One reason for Chiang Kai-shek's reluctance to return immediately was a dispute over the military control of Shanghai, which was so obviously one of the flashpoints in the smoldering conflict between the Chinese and Japanese. Chiang wanted to have his own men in control of the area. The Nineteenth Route Army, however, refused to leave Shanghai until they were given the back pay owed them.[151] One compromise emerged over the office of mayor: Mayor Zhang Yuejun was willing enough to surrender his office when he was told by the central government that he would be replaced by Wu Tiecheng, the military officer and police expert who was one of Chiang's most loyal supporters.[152] As a Cantonese, General Wu was also acceptable to Sun Ke.[153] On January 7, 1932, the new mayor took his oath of office at the city government's headquarters at Fenglin Bridge, and turned the Public Security Bureau over to Wen Yingxing, who would remain director until September 3, 1932.[154]

Wen Yingxing, forty-eight years old, was born in 1887 in Xining (Guangdong). After studying engineering at Nanyang College in Shanghai, he enrolled at the Virginia Military Institute, and then upon graduation in 1904 entered West Point where he also received an engineering degree. Wen served as an instructor in the military academy in Canton in 1910, and, after participating in the 1911 Revolution, moved up the ranks to become chief of staff of the military government of Shanghai and secretary to Sun Yat-sen. By 1923 he was a brigadier general under the Beiyang government and chief of police of the special zone in Manchuria. Eventually, after serving as president of Qinghua College and as a senior official in the Nationalist Ministry of Finance, he was appointed superintendent of the military police school. At the time of the Manchurian Railway Incident, Wen Yingxing was in charge of the military police and police sections of the Central Military Academy.[155] A short, vigorous man, with a bald head and a penchant for bow ties, Chief Wen may have had excellent qualifications for his new post as chief of the Shanghai police, but in the public's eye he was too loyal to his Cantonese cronies.[156] As soon as Wen Yingxing became director of public security, the number of Cantonese on the central staff rose from four to forty. Many of these men had Wen's surname, and six of them even shared his generational name.[157] Such blatant nepotism brought the new chief of police instant notoriety.[158]

The public's attention was quickly distracted, however, by the growing crisis in Sino-Japanese relations. As far as many Chinese were concerned, Japan seemed bound and determined to "colonize" (*zhimindihua*) China.[159] The Japanese living in China, on the other hand, were offended by the interminable slights and insults cast upon them by their erstwhile hosts. On January 9, Japanese residents in Shanghai were infuriated by an article in *Minguo ribao* about a Korean assassin's effort to take the emperor's life the previous day. The writer commented: "Unfortunately the bullet hit only an accompanying carriage." In order to satisfy the enraged Japanese, Mayor Wu had to apologize repeatedly and punish the journalist who wrote the article.[160]

The following day, January 10, 1932, a patriotic rally at the West Gate public recreation ground in South Market to mourn the death of Yang Tongheng, the student killed during anti-Japanese demonstrations in Nanjing on December 17, turned into a confrontation with the International Settlement police.[161] Thousands of high school and college students assembled in front of the coffin and portrait of their dead comrade.[162] Then, flanked by French and International Settlement police and detectives, they marched through the foreign concessions, shouting "communistic slogans" that attacked Japanese imperialism in Manchuria, and called for the release of compatriots jailed by Sun Ke's government.[163]

The police were forced by the crowd to release one man they had arrested, and "in view of the fanatical utterances of the mob and its general hostile attitude," they dared not intervene when the demonstrators proceeded boldly down Nanking Road before turning toward Hongkou. When the procession reached the Hongkou Bridge, the SMP Reserve Unit suddenly charged the parade with batons. The demonstrators scattered, leaving their wounded behind.[164]

Tensions continued to mount, and consular authorities advised Japanese residents to leave China for their own safety.[165] On January 18 more violence erupted.[166] Five Japanese Nichiren priests chanting Buddhist sutras on Mayushan Road were attacked by a Chinese mob. One monk was killed and two were seriously wounded. The attack was secretly instigated by Japanese special services Major Tanaka Ryūkichi to divert foreign attention from Manchuria, where the new puppet state was being set up. The site of the attack was chosen because it was near the Sanyou Towel Company, which was famous for its anti-Japanese workers' militia. The following night, in a heavy rainstorm, a Japanese youth group controlled by Major Tanaka invaded the Sanyou Company and set fire to the storage rooms. The youths clashed with SMP police after the raid in the early morning hours of January 20, and that same afternoon the International

Settlement police fought yet another mob of a thousand or more Japanese residents who were on their way to present demands for military intervention to the Japanese consular, army, and navy authorities.[167]

Three days later, on January 23, just as the Public Security Bureau was trying to prevent a commemoration for Lenin from turning into an anti-Japanese riot, the Japanese consul general served an ultimatum to Mayor Wu Tiecheng, demanding that he silence anti-Japanese propaganda, suppress the boycotts, dissolve the Committee to Resist Japan and Save the Nation, pay reparations, and punish the culprits in the January 18 incident.[168] Even as the mayor heard the ultimatum, increments to the original Japanese standing fleet of two warships arrived in the Huangpu River in the form of eleven other vessels; thirteen additional warships were steaming on their way from Japan to join Rear Admiral Shiozawa Kōichi's Shanghai command.[169] The fleet moored off the Hongkou wharves, where the waterfront was connected by a secret underground tunnel to the huge cement-and-steel Japanese military headquarters and arsenal on Jiangwan Road.[170]

Choosing a Position Regarding the Japanese

Wu Tiecheng thus found himself between the Scylla of Japanese imperialism and the Charybdis of Chinese nationalism. He consequently consulted Nanjing for advice, throwing the national government into a similar dilemma. The minister of foreign affairs, Chen Youren, wanted to declare war; when Sun Ke demurred, Chen resigned. Sun Ke followed Chen to Shanghai, attempting to draw him back into the government, and when that failed, he too submitted his resignation on January 25, leaving the government without a head.[171]

On January 27, 1932, the Japanese consul general reiterated his ultimatum, including the demand that the Committee to Resist Japan and Save the Nation be dissolved, and insisted upon having an answer by 6:00 the following afternoon. Wu Tiecheng was clearly running out of time, and, after consulting his supporters among the Shanghai bourgeoisie, he decided to risk uprisings and strikes rather than to go to war with Japan over Shanghai. At midnight on January 27, under his orders, the Public Security Bureau took over the various seats of the Committee to Resist Japan and Save the Nation, expelled its members, and sealed the doors.[172] Cowed or replaced, Mayor Wu's opponents within the local Guomindang branch remained silent, and thereafter nearly all political initiative in the city remained firmly in the hands of the municipal government and its leaders.[173] The next day, at 3:00 P.M. on January 28, Wu Tiecheng officially told the consul general that the municipal government had accepted all of his demands.[174]

By now, however, the Japanese were already on the move.[175] That same day Admiral Shiozawa told his British counterpart on the Shanghai Defense Committee that Japanese marines would go into action on January 29. The chairman of the Shanghai Municipal Council proceeded to place the International Settlement under martial law as of 4:00 P.M. on January 28.[176] At 8:30 P.M. Admiral Shiozawa issued two declarations: one ordering the Chinese army to evacuate Zhabei, and the other prohibiting public meetings. At 9:00 P.M. 468 Japanese marines were ferried in from the fleet to join the 1,365 marines already ashore.[177] At 11:25 P.M. Admiral Shiozawa delivered a note to the Public Security Bureau demanding the withdrawal of all Chinese troops from Zhabei and the removal of all "hostile defenses" in the form of sandbags and barricades. Five minutes later, the Japanese marines began preparations to move into their assigned positions.[178]

Some elements of the Chinese Nineteenth Route Army had already moved out of Zhabei, but the majority of the thirty-three thousand soldiers were still waiting for arrangements to be made with local merchants to provide them with back pay. The moment it became clear that the Japanese were going to invade the Chinese sectors of Shanghai, the international forces in the International Settlement set up a defense perimeter and the Chinese forces under Cai Tingkai began smuggling their own men in civilian clothing into Hongkou.[179] Other Nineteenth Route Army soldiers erected sandbagged barricades around the North Station just across the border between Hongkou and Zhabei.[180]

Twenty minutes after Admiral Shiozawa's request, at quarter to midnight, four hundred Japanese marines boarded eighteen military trucks in front of the Jiangwan arsenal. Huzzahed with repeated "banzai" from the civilians watching in front, the convoy set off accompanied by armored cars.[181] Shooting broke out before the marines reached the station, with the Chinese claiming the Japanese had fired first and vice-versa.[182] It seemed initially as though the Japanese bluejackets would have no trouble moving ahead. Indeed, the Japanese commander had proclaimed that the Chinese city would be his in four hours.[183] But as sea planes overhead reported their advance to the admiral's flagship, the bluejackets bogged down five hundred yards from their objective.[184]

By the morning of January 29, planes from the aircraft carrier *Notoro* were thundering over North Station at rooftop height, dropping their bombs from three hundred feet.[185]

> The whole of Shanghai is fully illuminated by the flares in Chapei, which are rising twenty to thirty yards into the sky. The roar of the flames can be heard at a great distance. The Chinese refugees who are streaming from Chapei into the Settlement report that vast numbers of the 200,000 population of Chapei have been slain, and that the dead and dying number thousands. Eye-witnesses tell of scenes in the nearest medical stations where the bodies of women, children, and infants, riddled with bullets, have been deposited.[186]

Many sections of Zhabei were laid waste, including most of the major industrial factories and the modern printing plant of the Commercial Press.[187] Those who escaped from the bombs and artillery fire had to submit to the cruel exactions of Japanese marines and their aides, the reservists who served as militiamen.[188] Brutalized and terrified, more than 230,000 refugees streamed across Suzhou Creek seeking the safety of the Settlement while the fighting north of the creek continued.[189]

The Chinese military lines, however, held.[190] During the first ten days of the war the Japanese had less than three thousand men in Shanghai, and not until February 15 did reinforcements arrive in the form of the Ninth Division of the Imperial Japanese Army under the command of Lieutenant-General Ueda Kenkichi.[191] Nevertheless, the stalemate continued, and five weeks after the attack Zhabei's North Station was still in the hand of its defenders while the Japanese rushed two more divisions in by sea to break the impasse.[192]

Of course, the Shanghai municipal government had to abandon Zhabei, which was put to the torch, but Mayor Wu Tiecheng—who had not been in office for a full month by the time war broke out—managed to organize a temporary headquarters under the cover of a social club or *lianshe*. The club's employees were all former members of the secretariat or of other municipal bureaus, and in their own eyes they constituted an elite group working throughout the emergency.[193] Thanks to the office's efficiency, the mayor devoted all of his attention to propaganda work. With the help of Secretary-General Yu Hongjun and an experienced newspaperman, Zhang Tingrong, the mayor held daily press conferences that played no small part in mobilizing international opinion against the Japanese.[194] Needless to say, internal opinion was already highly aroused. For many, especially students and "petty urbanites" (*xiao shimin*), the salvation of the nation appeared to be at stake. After the Japanese bombing of Zhabei on January 28, 1932, "the dancing girls disappeared from our cinema"— claimed Communist filmmaker Xia Yan—"and we started on the new road of courage."[195]

In addition to mobilizing public opinion, the Chinese municipal government helped organize refugee camps through a general mobilization, which was quite spontaneous, of the Chamber of Commerce, guilds, charitable organizations, regional associations, the Red Cross, the Red Buddhist Swastika, and so forth.[196] Some of these organizations had already accumulated considerable experience at fund-raising during the catastrophic North China famine of 1928–30, when as many as 6.5 million people perished in Henan, Shaanxi, and Gansu alone. During that crisis Shanghai philanthropies had organized car parades down Nanking Road, established "merit boxes" (*gongde xiang*) in department stores featuring window displays of photographs of famine victims, collected "pagoda donations" (*baota juan*) in Buddhist temples, and amassed charitable donations from a public-spirited populace that was rapidly acquiring a new sense of national responsibility.[197] Relief organizations also became accustomed to running refugee shelters during the cataclysmic floods of the summer of 1931, when the Yangzi ran twenty feet over the dikes at Nanjing and a quarter-million people were drowned or physically injured.[198] But the scale and pace of the human need in January and February 1932 were quite different. While the municipal government put all of its schools and commissariats at the disposition of the aid associations, the Public Security Bureau policed the seventy camps that were in place by early March to house more than thirty thousand refugees from Zhabei. The Bureau of Social Affairs organized the collection and distribution of clothing, blankets, and utensils; and the health services inoculated against smallpox, meningitis, and cholera the more than 200,000 people who were transited through these centers.[199] Even the Bureau of Education played an important role, reaching a population normally outside its sway by organizing classes for both children and adults among the war refugees.[200]

The fighting, meantime, was ferocious. Ernest Hauser described the street and alley combat in devastating terms:

> Dogs and rats were celebrating a holiday of their own; there were places where one could no longer distinguish the corpses beneath the ravenous packs. Fires were raging throughout the section which was, since the beginning of the war, completely under Japanese "control." The municipal police had withdrawn south of Soochow Creek, although Hongkew, officially, was part of the Settlement. For the time being it seemed to be administered from the Japanese club on Boone road, where the Japanese shopkeepers, bank employees, and clerks met to get their rifles and become Ronins. Terror ruled north of the creek.[201]

Chinese vigilantes were organized in turn, and certainly with as much zeal as the Japanese mustered.[202] Green Gang leader Du Yuesheng dispatched squads of snipers to ambush Japanese patrols, and the Chinese militiamen were even able to inflict some damage on Japanese river vessels.[203] Still, the Japanese "Ronins," in Hauser's lurid and directly addressed description, "perpetrated their cruelty" upon the Chinese.[204]

> No—you would not have recognized Sato-san and Kato-san as they tramped through the narrow streets, big black Mauser pistols in their hands. You would not have recognized them as they forced their way into the Chinese shops and houses, pulled out a couple of trembling coolies, shot them in cold blood. You would not have recognized the thousands of Sato-sans and Kato-sans who had armed themselves with rifles, old-fashioned swords, baseball bats, or just plain walking canes. They were the Japanese volunteers, the "Ronins."[205]

At the same time the Chinese police had their hands full dealing with looters who were often identified as "traitors" (*hanjian*)—collaborators who had deliberately gone into the combat zones "to make trouble" and to work for the Japanese.[206] After General He Yingqin cabled the municipal government that the Japanese were sending two hundred of their Chinese secret agents from northern Jiangsu and Anhui, the PSB and Military Police Bureau arrested numerous spies who were publicly executed in order to let the "masses" (*minzhong*) know the penalty of treason.[207] And the police continued to make every effort to keep "reactionary elements" from "taking advantage of the opportunity to riot."[208] There were even conspiracies within the Public Security Bureau to link up with restive army officers and make use of the public disorder to occupy parts of South Market and Pudong in a military coup planned for the early hours of March 13, 1932.[209]

Intelligence Efforts against the Japanese

Mostly, though, the Chinese struggled to gain information about the enemy's military plans. There was a proliferation of listening posts and intelligence gathering units within Shanghai, quartered in teahouses and hotel rooms. The detective squad (*zhenjidui*) of the Songhu Garrison Command, for instance, set up such a post in the First-Class Fragrance Hotel (Yipinxiang lüshe) on Thibet Road.[210] The rooms they rented were supposedly meant to be an off-duty club to provide women and gambling for military personnel "as a respite from official activities." The real purpose of the suite, through which there was a constant coming and going of people from all walks of life, was to collect intelligence reports from field agents. The existence of the Garrison Command intelligence post was known to SMP Detective Superintendent Tan Shaoliang, from whom very few secrets were kept in the International Settlement.[211]

One evening, as was his wont, Detective Tan dropped by the suite to chat with the duty officer, who that night happened to be an officer named Lu Yuanhua. When Tan asked him if there was any news to report, Lu— wanting to appear to be in the know—made up a story that Nanjing had transferred a fresh regiment (*tuan*) of soldiers to the front lines and that they were being billeted in the Huzhou provincial guildhall in Zhabei. The very next morning, Japanese bombers swooped down out of the dawn's light and completely demolished the guildhall and its surrounding neighborhood.[212]

Nationalist Intelligence officials were piqued by the bombing raid. Why would the Japanese go to such trouble to bomb the guildhall, which was deserted save for the corpses (including the remains of the murdered relatives of Red Brigade leader Gu Shunzhang) in the attached mortuary? The security officers' curiosity was satisfied when Lu Yuanhua reported his conversation with Tan Shaoliang, for surveillance soon disclosed that the famed detective superintendent had been suborned by the enemy. Tan Shaoliang, the most important single officer in the Special Branch of the Shanghai Municipal Police, had been recruited as a spy by the Japanese.[213]

Chinese Military Intelligence officials mulled over their dilemma. Tan Shaoliang would continue to supply the Japanese with valuable military information unless he was silenced, but at the same time he represented the prime link between the Nationalist Special Services Bureau and the SMP in the fight against domestic Communists. Should the secret servicemen, for the sake of Chiang Kai-shek's policy of *annei rangwai* (first subjugate the internal enemy, then expel the external enemy) keep Tan's treachery a secret to themselves? Nationalist Military Intelligence officials checked with their superiors in Luoyang, where Chiang Kai-shek had temporarily moved his capital while Nanjing fell under the barrels of Japanese gunboats, and the answer clearly was: do not expose Superintendent Tan as long as our highest priority is the suppression of the Communists.[214]

Meanwhile the fighting raged on in Zhabei, where the Nineteenth Route Army's valiant defense of the railway station drew the country's patriotic support.[215] On February 18 British Minister Sir Miles Lampson arranged for a meeting between representatives of the Nineteenth Route Army and the Japanese Ninth Division. When the Japanese ordered the Chinese to withdraw twenty kilometers beyond the International Settlement's borders, the Chinese refused to accept the ultimatum. On February 20 General Ueda confidently attacked Cai Tingkai's positions in the Jiang-wan area. The Chinese fought back tenaciously and heroically, holding their lines for two days until the Japanese shifted their attack north of the area on February 22. General Ueda was unsuccessful there, too, and the northern wing of his forces barely repelled a Chinese counterattack on February 23.[216]

Admiral Nomura Kichisaburō, who had replaced Admiral Shiozawa as commander of the Third Fleet, urgently radioed Japan:

> Unless we give them a decisive blow, Chiang Kai-shek will increase his assistance and his popularity will grow with talk of victory, leading eventually to war between the two countries. Under the cir-cumstances it is imperative that hostilities be brought to a quick conclusion by employing an army force of sufficient size and strength.[217]

On February 23, the Japanese cabinet received the emperor's approval to send the Eleventh and Fourteenth Divisions to Shanghai.[218] By March 1 the Japanese forces there, now under the reorganized command of General Shirakawa Yoshinori, numbered nearly ninety thousand men.[219] On March 2, before they could be encircled by the Ninth and Eleventh Divisions, the Chinese Nineteenth Route Army began a general retreat. At 2:00 P.M. on March 3, 1932, the Japanese declared a unilateral truce.[220] The Empire of the Sun had finally, with a huge diversion of men and weapons, won the Battle of Shanghai, but only after the Chinese Nine-teenth Route Army, with help from the Eighty-seventh and Eighty-eighth Divisions, had brought Hirohito's army and navy to a standstill for thirty-five days. The lesson of the 1932 Shanghai campaign was clear enough: Chinese soldiers could fight bravely and well if given proper weapons and able leadership.[221] The price of their resistance in casualties both civilian and military, however, was extremely high, including the cost of bringing law and order back to the battered city once the Japanese troops withdrew.

The Shanghai Bund. Green, *Shanghai of Today*, plate 15.

Foochow (Fuzhou) Road ca. 1927. The three large banners left to right advertise musical instruments and phonograph records, medicinal tonics, and a locksmith's shop. Green, *Shanghai of Today*, plate 22.

The purge of April 12 through 15, 1927. Troops loyal to Chiang Kai-shek, along with Green Gang elements, arrest activists among the "revolutionary masses." *Shanghai renmin geming shi huace,* 135.

The Longhua Garrison Command. *Shanghai renmin geming shi huace,* 174.

Autumn Fashions in Shanghai, 1930. *Liang you* 50:23.

Huang Jinrong. *Haishang mingren zhuan,* 61.

The Great World. *Shanghai xin mao,* 33.

Du Yuesheng. *Haishang mingren zhuan,* 13.

"An Alluring Pose": Movie star Ye Xieyan in her dressing room.
Zhonghua tuhua zazhi, July 1930, 25.

Zhang Xiaolin. *Haishang mingren zhuan*, 47.

"An Enticer." *Zhonghua tuhua zazhi,* November 1930, 25.

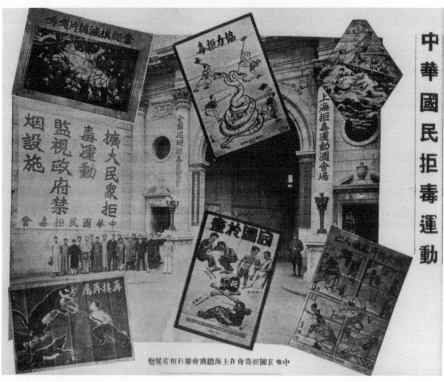

中華國民拒毒運動

Shi Liangcai before his assassination by the
Nationalist secret service. *Shanghai renmin
geming shi huace*, 201.

Opposite, top: Qian Zhuangfei, the Communist
"mole." *Shanghai renmin geming shi huace*, 146.

Opposite, bottom: War on Drugs, April 1930.
Liang you 41:9.

A Japanese garden in "Little Tokyo." Green, *Shanghai of Today*, plate 36.

Opposite, top: Mayor Wu Tiecheng. *Songhu yu Ri xuezhan da huabao*, 39.

Opposite, bottom: "Military police arrest a traitor instigated by the Japanese to incite disturbances in the rear areas." *Shanghai zhanshi huakan*, 29.

General and Madame Chiang Kai-shek implementing the New Life
Movement in Nanchang. *Zhonghua minguo shi hua*, 555.

Shanghai students demonstrating on December 19, 1935, in favor of resistance to Japanese aggression. *Shanghai renmin geming shi huace,* 204.

The Generalissimo and the Madame after the Xi'an Incident.
Kangzhan huace, 2.

Chiang Kai-shek at Lushan on July 19, 1937, announcing over national radio the declaration of the War of Resistance against Japan. *Jiang zongtong xunye huaji,* 28.

August 1937: "Our army's bloody war of resistance before the retreat from Zhabei." *Zhanshi huabao,* 10.

Opposite: October 2, 1949: "Amidst a chorus of firecrackers and martial music, the red flag is hoisted over the Shanghai People's Government's city hall." The calligraphy reads: "Return the fruits of the people's labor to the people." Smaller banners, barely legible in the photograph, read: "Defend world peace," and "Congratulations on the foundation of the central people's government of the People's Republic of China." *Yi nuli fazhan shengchan lai qingzhu Shanghai jiefang zhounian.*

把人民勞動的成果
歸還給人民

在爆竹與軍樂齊鳴聲中，紅旗在上海市人民政府的大廈上升了起來。

The Impact of the Japanese on
     Municipal Policing

I watched the Japanese deliver the final air assault. . . . I saw a
plane swoop down on the three-storey building, its wide
balconies crammed with troops. A direct hit tore a gaping hole
in the roof; two more hits on the south end and the wall
collapsed on the platform. The sky was full of climbing and
diving planes and the air thick with dust and smoke. At long
last, moving from their five-week-old positions, Japanese
bluejackets crowded into the station compound and the
remnants of Cai's army retreated down the railroad track and
through the city, fighting from house to house and slowly
abandoning the area. Fires started earlier gradually gathered
strength until most of Zhabei was ablaze. It was a sad, costly
funeral pyre of Shanghai's initial hope of resisting Japan.

Percy Finch, *Shanghai and Beyond*

Despite the valor of the Chinese defenders, who inflicted four thousand
casualties on the aggressor while incurring fourteen thousand of their
own, the Japanese eventually took North Station.[1] There was not that
much left to hold. By March 5, 1932, when the Japanese and Chinese
accepted a League of Nations resolution calling for the opening of truce
negotiations, Zhabei was "a smoking shambles, reeking with the foul odor
of death and destruction."[2]

Under the supervision of an international committee, the Japanese and
Chinese formally met in Shanghai on March 24.[3] China's strategy was
to try to shift the armistice talks from Shanghai to Geneva where the
international committee (the so-called Committee of Nineteen) of the
League of Nations could intervene. The Chinese believed that they could
earn the committee's sympathy and support by emphasizing how much
they had already conceded in Shanghai to the Japanese. They also believed
that they could play upon the embarrassment of the foreign authorities
of the International Settlement, whose Defense Committee had invited
the Japanese navy to defend a sector which included a piece of the Chinese
municipality. Once hostilities began, the foreign authorities were obviously unable to keep the Japanese forces from usurping the authority of
the SMC in their defense area as well as from conducting military opera-

tions into Chinese territory. But now that hostilities had ended, the Chinese counted on foreign support, and especially British backing, to prevent the Japanese from transforming their de facto encirclement of the city into a de jure zone "neutralized" under international control and closed to Chinese civil and military officials.[4]

The Chinese strategy succeeded. On April 11, the Nationalist representatives requested that the Committee of Nineteen be convened. This shifted the talks to Geneva, where the committee adopted a resolution proposing an armistice settlement on April 19. The Japanese army considered this a violation of its right of supreme command, and threatened that Japan would withdraw from the League of Nations. A compromise provided for the league's committee to call violations of the troop evacuation process to the attention of China and Japan. This shifted the talks back to Shanghai, where the arrangement was almost scuttled when a Korean terrorist's bomb exploded at the emperor's birthday party celebration in the Japanese Consulate on April 29, killing General Shirakawa and wounding several other officials.[5] But by now the evacuation process was already in motion. The Twenty-Fourth Mixed Brigade and the Eleventh Division had already returned to Japan, and the Fourteenth Division had been sent to Manchuria. Consequently, when China refused to accept the Imperial Japanese Navy's demand that Chinese troops be kept out of the Pudong area, and when Great Britain backed China up, the Japanese naval officials in Shanghai had no choice but to give in. The armistice agreement was signed on May 5, 1932.[6] According to one war correspondent: "The Chinese government had at least saved its face by winning the point that Chinese sovereignty and Chinese police rights were to be restored in the demilitarized zone."[7]

Japanese Control of Shanghai

Nevertheless, Japan managed to impose a kind of neutralization upon the Nanjing authorities, who eventually had to agree, in March 1934, to refrain from stationing troops in certain parts of Shanghai and to notify Japan each time its troops passed through those sections.[8] In exchange for this, Greater Shanghai was to be restored to the Chinese, who were to form a Peace Preservation Corps (Baoandui) to maintain law and order while the Japanese withdrew all of their army and navy units except for the regular Shanghai garrison.[9] Although the closure of Shanghai to Chinese troops affronted Chinese sovereignty, the national government did feel that this would keep Japan from launching further attacks in the Jiangnan area, while freeing Chiang Kai-shek's forces to commence—once the May 5, 1932, "Peace Agreement" was signed—a Fourth Extermination Campaign against the Communists.[10] At the same time, the peace agreement made provision for the Japanese to evacuate their forces from the area across Suzhou Creek west of the Settlement boundary by May 16, 1932.[11]

Over the course of the preceding three months, however, the Japanese had entrenched themselves throughout the Chinese sector—their sixty to seventy thousand soldiers occupied forty-seven public and private buildings, all of the municipal and administrative buildings still standing, and 110 elementary and secondary schools.[12] And although they disclaimed having created a puppet city government, they had actually set up a collaborationist police force to patrol the Zhabei area. By their own account:

> The Japanese Authorities have never sought to set up, nor give assistance to set up, a political or administrative form of government whatever, at Chapei. The Japanese occupation has confined itself to military necessities, at the same time considering it desirable that the Police be reorganized, in order to ensure that order and the circulation of the traffic be maintained.[13]

The puppet police force was initially supposed to have been organized as a Chinese Gendarmerie Brigade (Huajingdui) under Wang Binyan, former commander of the Zhabei Merchant Volunteer Corps and a member of the Zhabei Chamber of Commerce.[14] Wang refused to lend his name and reputation as a merchant militia leader to the Japanese, who sponsored instead the Zhabei Citizens' Maintenance Association (Zhabei shimin weichi hui)—an unsavory collection of "notorious bad characters of the former Chapei district," including opium runners, gun smugglers, and former members of the PSB detective squad who were mainly engaged in turning occupied Zhabei into a haven for opium den owners and gambling casino operators.[15]

The Zhabei Citizens' Maintenance Association, also known as the Shanghai Northern District Citizens' Maintenance Association, began— ironically enough—as a street-cleaning operation. On March 24, the Japanese army engaged 150 Chinese coolies to sweep the streets from Suzhou Creek all the way up to North Station. They were supervised by Chinese foremen, probably Subei gangsters, and paid fifty cents an hour from funds generated by a monthly tax of two dollars levied on all of the street traders in Zhabei. The operation was being run out of the former office of the Zhabei branch of the municipal finance bureau at 66 Minli Road by an organization called the "Great Japan New Political Affairs Bureau," which was a puppet "municipal organ" guarded by Japanese soldiers but manned, after April 1, by Chinese collaborators.[16] Among the leading puppet administrators were the following:

> Hu Lifu, chief administrator. Mr. Hu, who was either forty-five or fifty-two years old, formerly owned a leather factory on Ferry Road along with the Wulong Bath House at 522 Nanking Road. Since most bath house owners in Shanghai were from north of the Yangzi ("Jiangbei," "Subei"), or what was contemptuously called "Kompo" in Shanghainese, Hu Lifu was thought to be a native of northern Jiangsu. Hu was actually from Anhui. A close friend of opium smuggler Cheng Agen (see below), "he is also said to be an associate of Japanese undesirables in Hongkew who earn a living in smuggling morphia."[17]

> Wang Du, chief of general affairs. Wang, from Funing, had worked for the Yokohama Specie Bank and spoke Japanese.[18]

> Chang Yuqing, chief of police. Chang, also called Chang Guoqing, was described in an SMP police report as "a notorious Kompo loafer" about forty years old. He also owned a bath house, the Da-guanyuan Baths at 260 Thibet Road. Formerly a wharf coolie, he had a number of "local bandit" followers. At one time he had owned a theater on Foochow Road, and he had once been arrested in connection with a threatening letter case. He was chairman of the North Jiangsu Residents Guild, and a close friend of Gu Si, "a theater proprietor and one of the most prominent loafer leaders in Shanghai."[19] Gu Si ("Gu Number Four") was the alias of Gu Zhu-xuan, the Subei gang leader.[20]

> Cheng Achang, superintendent of traffic. Cheng—also known as Cheng Xizhi, Cheng Agen and Feilong Agen (Flying Dragon Agen), was the former proprietor of the Feilong Garage on Avenue Edward VII or Zhejiang Road. A native of Ningbo, about forty-five years old, he started out as a chauffeur. "Between 1920 and 1924 he acquired considerable wealth through opium smuggling from Liu Ho to [the] French Concession and subsequently became proprietor of public hire garages on Hupeh Road, Moulmein Road, and Avenue Edouard VII, and built houses and [a] workshop in Yu Yuen Road."[21] In 1924 General He Fenglin issued a warrant for his arrest on charges of committing armed robbery of an opium shipment. Cheng went into hiding and his garages were sealed by court order. Eventually Cheng bribed General He and was able to come back into the open. However, at the time of the Japanese attack two of his garages were again closed. "[He is] an associate of loafers of

both the International Settlement and the French Concession."[22] Cheng was thought to have bought Portuguese citizenship.[23]

Yao Zhitu, chief of detectives. Yao, also called Yao Asheng, Yao Zidu and Yao Wu, was a native of Jiangbei. About forty years old, he had joined the Shanghai Municipal Police as a constable in 1907. Later he became a Chinese Detective Inspector in the CID. "His services were terminated on February 9, 1928, owing to suspicion of his having become an associate of criminal elements. In April 1929 a warrant was issued for his arrest on a charge of being an associate of armed robbers and is still on file at the Shanghai Special District Court."[24]

Li Fei, chief inspector of police. Mr. Li, whose aliases included Li Pengfei and Tianjin Erbao ("Tianjin's Number Two Treasure"), was of course from Tianjin. Formerly a musician in sing-song houses, he was a follower of the notorious gang leader Ji Yunqing. In 1927 he had become chief of the bodyguard of General Yang Xiaotian; and then, when Yang retired, he had become one of the croupiers ("conductors") in a roulette casino at 209 Rue du Consulat. Li Fei was a well-known arms and drug smuggler.[25]

The ostensible purpose for this rogue's gallery of puppet administrators to form a Zhabei Maintenance Association was announced in notices posted on shop shutters: "Owing to the lawlessness obtaining in [Zhabei] as a result of the Sino-Japanese hostilities, a committee of citizens has been formed with Hu Lifu as chief and Wang Du as his assistant to combat the lawless element and make the district fit for residence."[26] In order to pay for the small police force of twenty to twenty-five khaki-uniformed constables and forty male and female detectives who had already been recruited, the Maintenance Association proposed to charge fees for permits to remove goods from the area, for vehicle licenses, and for the sale of goods.[27]

But the fees, which were 1 percent of the value of the goods to be removed and an average of $2 for each permit, were small change as far as these gangsters and former policemen were concerned. The backers of the association were much more interested in promoting the licensing of opium and gambling dens. Three prominent racketeers were involved: Gu Zhuxuan, his brother Gu Songmao, and Wei Zhongxiu. Gu Zhuxuan, the "emperor of Subei," was the most infamous "Kompo" gangster in Shanghai. Gu Songmao, alias Gu San (Gu Number Three), was his brother. Formerly a rickshaw coolie, he worked as a foreman in the Star Rickshaw Company and was "proprietor of a Kompo theater in Chapei and a notorious loafer."[28] Wei Zhongxiu, also a native of Jiangbei, "formerly Chief Detective of the Public Safety Bureau, is a follower of Doo Yuet-sung [Du Yuesheng] and the French Concession Opium Gang."[29]

Little wonder, then, that the general public tended to believe that the collaborators with the Japanese occupation forces of Zhabei were mainly "Kompo traitors": natives of Subei, the area north of the Yangzi River.[30] Even foreigners made that identification, as one SMP English detective's confidential report on the puppet police would suggest: "Seeing that the majority, if not all, of the persons in office [in the puppet organ] are of Kompo loafer class, it is inconceivable that their administration can produce any relief for the ex-population of the Chapei areas."[31]

Actually, the Maintenance Association did make a gesture of providing social welfare. On April 7, when nearly a quarter of the small shops in western Zhabei had opened their doors for business and over five hundred rickshaws were again available for hire, the Shanghai Northern District Citizens' Maintenance Association reopened the congee kitchen at Jiaotong Road, providing meals for about three hundred indigents.[32] That same day, however, Mayor Wu's municipal government instructed the Public Security Bureau to arrest the "undesirables" who were running the association "in conspiracy with certain foreigners."[33]

The price the backers of the Maintenance Association had to pay the Japanese for the opportunity to open up opium dens and casinos was highly visible support to the occupation troops. A group of the women detectives working for the puppet police was posted at the north end of Markham Road Bridge to help Japanese marines search Chinese female pedestrians. Thirty of the male detectives were assigned to the entrances of various streets in Zhabei to vet and search people entering the area or to remove belongings or goods that did not have the special permit issued by the occupation authorities.[34] By April 10, when the total number of puppet police officers had been increased to 110, the collaborators had opened up a precinct office in the former first substation of the fifth district Public Security Bureau on Jukong Road. The precinct chief, SMP investigators reported, was another "Kompo loafer."[35]

But even though Gu Zhuxuan himself may have found it an embarrassment to be identified as a collaborator, the rewards were lucrative.[36] According to a confidential SMP detective report, the gangsters had opened up more than twenty "good-class smoking dens" at the end of Chaofeng Road, opposite a big gambling casino at 118 Derun Road. Two other big opium shops had opened at Wuhua Road: one of these had just been moved from the French Concession, and the other was being operated by a man named Zhang whose brother-in-law, a Portuguese subject,[37] also sold opium through the Tongtai hang (hong) at 125 Yuen Fong Road, which was under the protection of the Chinese head of the puppet detective squad—the former SMP Chinese detective inspector known to the British as Yau Ts-doo (Yao Zhitu). Yao, who was also president of the Regional Association of Jiangbei (Jiangbei tongxiang hui), visited the opium and gambling dens every afternoon "accompanied by four Japanese soldiers for protection."[38]

One reason for the sudden expansion of opium smoking dens was the low daily license fee of only fifty cents per pipe charged by the puppet police. Many opium smokers from the French Concession and International Settlement went to Zhabei because it was cheaper to support their habit, and as a result rents of houses increased dramatically. In fact, these illicit ventures did so well altogether that Du Yuesheng, who was holding a series of conferences with the French authorities over gambling and opium, considered the possibility of moving "gambling, opium hongs, and smoking dens" into Zhabei in the event of a deadlock with the French.[39]

Du Yuesheng had come to dominate the gambling and narcotics rackets in the French Concession under the protection of Chief Etienne Fiori and Consul General Koechlin.[40] About a year after the April 1927 purge the Green Gang boss had gotten the help of certain Cantonese investors and opened four gambling houses in the French Concession. They were operated in a neat and orderly fashion under the watchful eyes of armed "protectors" in each casino who prevented *liumang* from causing a ruckus or offending the customers, who were treated to free food, drinks, and even women and drugs. Each gambling house quietly paid a daily protection bribe of $2,500, which was discreetly passed on to the highest authorities by Du Yuesheng himself.[41]

During the following two years things only got better for Du, who reputedly cured himself of his own addiction to opium in 1931.[42] According to a secret memorandum in the Shanghai police files,

> 1930 and 1931 were the most flourishing years of Mr. Tu Yueh-sung's [Du Yuesheng's] reign in the French Concession; he was frequently requested by rich people in the Concession to settle disputes arising over the division of inherited property, divorce, etc. In cases such as these he considerably enriched himself.[43]

Much more important than his arbitration of divorce and property disputes, however, was Du Yuesheng's role as a labor negotiator. Du's mediation of the strikes in December 1928 and June–August 1930 at the French Tramways and Electric Light Company led to his control of the French Tramways Union, as well as Consul General Koechlin's agreement to permit the Chinese Ratepayers Association—which was controlled by the Green Gang—to elect Chinese members to the Provisional Commission. The CRA convened on November 18, 1930, formally endorsed the five sitting Chinese members (including, of course, Du himself), and elected nine special advisers to the commission's various committees. Du Yuesheng now controlled the Provisional Commission, completely overshadowing the Gentry-Councillor Clique and dominating the French administration of the Concession.[44]

Du Yuesheng celebrated that dominance and his growing respectability on June 9, 1931, with a huge and elaborate parade to commemorate the completion of his family shrine in Pudong. Chiang Kai-shek instructed military and civil governors, along with Guomindang branches throughout the area, to send congratulatory telegrams to the gangster-philanthropist. The parade itself involved thousands of Green Gang members, businessmen, government officials, British constables, Annamese policemen, and Chinese infantrymen. The orderly retinue passed from Du Yuesheng's house on Rue Wagner through heavily guarded streets. Marchers in the van of the procession, led by Mayor Zhang Qun, carried congratulatory scrolls from Zhang Xueliang, Dr. C. T. Wong, and Chiang Kai-shek.[45]

Removing Du from the French Concession

Du Yuesheng's influence in China was unmistakable, but his reach did not extend far abroad. The authorities in Paris were aware that matters were amiss in Shanghai, where the entire French Concession seemed to have been turned over to Chinese gangsters.[46] Someone in the colonial government in Hanoi, perhaps a disgruntled legislator, had already complained about the corruption.[47] Strong metropolitan pressure, then, pushed Koechlin to join with the British in the crusade against gambling during the winter of 1930–31. The pressure continued to grow during the summer and early fall of 1931, when an ephemeral Shanghai journal called *La Vérité* delivered weekly tirades against the French chief of police for dilatoriness in suppressing gambling.[48] Apparently succumbing to this pressure, Captain Fiori finally announced on September 16, 1931, that he would lead a crusade against the Green Gang's casinos: "Not a single Chinese or foreign gambling house in the Concession will be open by the end of this week."[49] Purely as a publicity stunt, Captain Fiori proceeded to close down ten small dives and left Du's casinos utterly alone.[50]

Once hostilities began with Japan on January 28, however, Vice Admiral Herr, commander of the French Far East fleet, declared martial law in

Shanghai and proscribed gambling and drugs. When more than a thousand of Du Yuesheng's gangsters, armed with weapons and tricolored armbands supplied by the French police, rallied in support of Consul General Koechlin, Vice Admiral Herr simply had his forces clear the streets. Koechlin promptly called for Du Yuesheng's resignation from the Provisional Commission, which he received on February 15, 1932; but before the resignation was announced, Koechlin himself was relieved of his post and replaced by Henri Meyrier, the French consul general in Tianjin. Captain Fiori also had to resign, giving way to Louis Fabre, the chief of the Tianjin French Concession Police.[51]

Consul General Meyrier and Chief Fabre, aided by Commissioner Robert Jobes, were said to be incorruptible.[52] Although Du Yuesheng was supposedly trying to grease the wheels in France with bribes to certain metropolitan officials, Paris was too far away from his sphere of influence.[53] His French Concession rackets clearly depended upon the personal protection of Koechlin and Fiori, and now they had failed him altogether. In mid-February 1932, Du gave a luncheon at his mansion on Rue Wagner for Georges-Marie Haardt, leader of the Citroen Motor Company automobile expedition that had retraced the Silk Route to China, reaching Beiping on February 12. Among the guests were former Consul General Koechlin and Commissioner Fiori. One of the dishes served that afternoon was made with Ningbo mushrooms, and of those who ate the delicacy four died shortly afterwards: Consul General Koechlin, Colonel A. Marcaire (commander of French land forces in Shanghai), M. du Pac de Marsoulies, and Haardt, who managed to make his way to Hong Kong before succumbing to pneumonia on March 16, 1932, at the Repulse Bay Hotel. Etienne Fiori was extremely ill, but he survived the banquet and returned to France to enjoy the fruits of his Shanghai years in a villa at Cagnes-sur-Mer, far from Du Yuesheng's murderous domain.[54]

Although these deaths and illnesses could be attributed to unintentional food-poisoning, Shanghai buzzed with the gossip of Du Yuesheng's revenge; and the case of the poisonous mushrooms soon became part of the lore surrounding the mysterious racketeer.[55] There was no evidence to substantiate such rumors of homicide, but Consul General Meyrier did pay tribute to Marcaire and Koechlin for having "died for France in the service of our Concession."[56]

In his inaugural speech on March 14, 1932, before the Provisional Commission, Meyrier pledged to restore good government to the French Concession, starting with a reform of the police force. Large numbers of corrupt policemen were dismissed by Chief Fabre, and new officers were

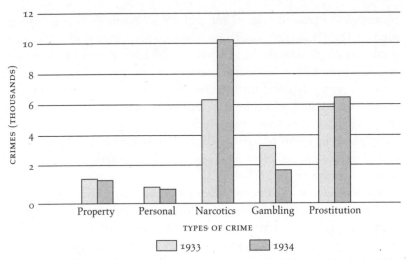

FIGURE 6.   French Concession crimes, 1933–1934. Source: Shanghai shi nianjian weiyuanhui, 1935, L30–33.

selected with care. The chain of command within the police force was strengthened and new sanctions were instituted, effectuating the best discipline and control the police force had enjoyed since World War I.[57]

At the same time, while intensifying their crackdown on vice (narcotics, gambling, prostitution), the French police opened negotiations with Du Yuesheng to remove the Three Prosperities Company from the French Concession. (See Figure 6.) Du tried to come to an accommodation with Meyrier and Fabre, who were alternately offered bribes and threatened with death. Eventually, Du Yuesheng came to realize that the order to cease gambling operations, which had been issued in compliance with the decision of the metropolitan French government, could not be circumvented. One way out, of course, would be to transfer his operations to Zhabei where the Japanese appeared to be tolerating a wide-open city under unsavory puppet police rule. That choice, however, lacked a certain respectability, which was important to Du at a time when he was getting such bad press in Shanghai. His own syndicate of Cantonese casino owners had deposited their capital of $4 million with him, requesting him to negotiate a cancellation of the order to cease gambling in the French Concession. But as that prospect grew dimmer, Du Yuesheng decided to divert the capital into one of his more legitimate enterprises by using the money to construct the Zhonghui Building, which housed the bank he had founded four years earlier. The casino owners dared not raise objections to this, and they were subsequently paid back fully in five yearly install-ments.[58]

Another possibility was to put pressure on the French to help Du make new narcotics arrangements with the Chinese municipal authorities. There were a number of small factories—often only a single room just large enough to contain a laboratory—scattered around the French Con-cession where crude morphine manufactured in eastern Sichuan was re-fined into morphia and heroin by Chinese, Japanese, German, and Russian chemists.[59] If the Nationalist authorities, who had been trying once again in 1931 to establish a legal opium monopoly, could be persuaded to come to an agreement with Du Yuesheng, then these refineries might be relo-cated outside the French Concession in Greater Shanghai.[60]

This became the final outcome, arrived at after the hostilities with Ja-pan ended. By using the ploy of calling the French Tramway Union out on strike that following summer, Du managed to force Consul General Meyrier to meet with Mayor Wu Tiecheng. The two of them ultimately agreed that Du could move his narcotics operations to South Market. The French agreed to transport the opium out of the Concession. By the end of 1932, the Three Prosperities Company was to be dissolved, and the narcotics operation would be run by a Special Services Department under the Shanghai Peace Preservation Corps commanded by Yang Hu.[61] Ac-cording to a Shanghai Municipal Police report:

> Realizing that armed protection was necessary for the transporta-tion of opium, [Du Yuesheng] succeeded in nominating General Yang Hu as commander of the Shanghai Peace Preservation Corps. A "special service department" was then formed by the corps; this department took over the work of the San Shing Company, which was "wound up." The special service department was, however, an-nexed and incorporated into the Bureau of Public Safety in the mid-dle of December 1932 by the order of mayor Wu Te-chen [Tie-cheng].[62]

This reputedly went hand in hand with the "deal" (see Chapter 8) between Chiang Kai-shek and Du Yuesheng according to which Du agreed to orga-nize anti-Communist terrorist activities in exchange for Chiang's recogni-tion of his drug monopoly in the Yangzi Valley.[63]

The End of the Puppet Police

Meantime, the Zhabei collaborators were growing more and more embar-rassed by their own disreputability: "The original promoters of the Shanghai Northern District Citizens' Maintenance Association, realizing that their reputation was against their successfully running the Chapei Administration, are considering the necessity of reorganizing the association."[64] Hu Lifu, the leading member of the Maintenance Association, was said to be extending invitations to a more distinguished group of Shanghainese to join them, including Wang Binyan; Fan Huichun, the largest shareholder of the Far Eastern Recreation Ground and an intimate friend of gangster Huang Jinrong; Shi Liangcai, publisher of *Shenbao*; and Li Shuyi, the comprador of the Mitsui Bussan Kaisha of Tianjin.[65]

The public had by then become so "dissatisfied with the foul tactics of these traitors" that the Japanese decided on April 10 to dissolve the Maintenance Association at the behest of the American and British consuls, whose nationals denounced the financial exactions of the carpetbaggers.[66] Hu Lifu and his friends, however, continued to receive secret Japanese support, and five days later reorganized themselves as the Zhabei Refugee Provisional Relief Association, which was also known as the Association for the Promotion of the Local Self-Government of Zhabei (Zhabei zizhi xiejin hui), and which had offices guarded by Japanese marines at the premises of the former Fifth District Public Security Bureau near Minli Road.[67] Under the association's aegis the rackets continued to flourish: three more big gambling dens were opened, and the biggest of these, the Dali Company Club, was allowed to offer opium, gambling, and prostitutes to its customers—a privilege for which the club paid $300 daily in tribute to the authorities. The Association for the Promotion of the Local Self-Government of Zhabei also planned to collect taxes, establish a huahui lottery, license prostitution, and authorize the open sale of opium. The Japanese, meanwhile, insisted that there was no authority in Zhabei other than that wielded by the Japanese military themselves.[68]

Nevertheless, in their guise as members of the Refugee Relief Association, Hu Lifu and his cronies continued to hold secret meetings at 211 Yuezai Road, planning to extend their puppet administration even as the Chinese and Japanese began to prepare for ceasefire negotiations.[69] On April 28, Hu Lifu presided over a meeting that passed seven resolutions sketching out a complete program, from a volunteer corps to investigation and intelligence sections.[70] Two days later the Refugee Relief Association (its membership list still concealed from SMP secret agents) met again and passed four more resolutions regulating the conduct of brothels and opium smoking houses under the protection of the Japanese Military Police.[71]

Within two more days, however, the peace agreement had been signed and the puppet police's days were numbered.[72] The gambling—especially at the big Dali casino at 118 Derun Road—had become so blatant that the

SMP felt obliged to discuss the racketeering with the Japanese. On May 19, SMP Chief Detective Inspector Nakagawa paid a call at the Japanese Consulate and interviewed Inspector Okumura, chief of the Judicial Department of the Consular Police. Given "the imminence of their withdrawal from Shanghai and consequent pressure of work in having to make arrangements for departure," however, the Japanese refused to take action.[73] Thus the effort to curb this new wave of racketeering in Zhabei had to await the restoration of Chinese police control now that the 1932 hostilities were over.

Resumption of Chinese Authority

The Chinese had already begun to prepare for the resumption of their authority over Zhabei, which meant reconstituting a police force to restore law and order, and to deal with what were bound to be numerous potentially hostile encounters with Japanese military and civilians.[74] During the negotiations the Japanese themselves resisted Chinese efforts to bring back the old PSB forces with whom they had had such bitter encounters. One solution, proposed by Dr. Rudolph Muck, Nazi police adviser to the national government, had been "that a special office be formed with foreigners (Europeans) employed as members so as to deal with cases wherein foreigners are involved."[75]

Although Chief Wen rejected that suggestion, he readily agreed with Dr. Muck's second proposal, namely, that the Shanghai PSB recruit 500 policemen from Beiping.[76] Officers were sent north to the former capital to recruit constables, while professional Beiping police officers were brought to Shanghai to staff important Zhabei PSB posts.[77] By mid-May 448 Beiping policemen would be brought in to reoccupy the Zhabei area under the command of General Lu Lu, and the police station opened at 118 Linping Road would be placed under the command of Inspector Wu Tingxun of the Beiping police.[78]

On May 2, "with the object of restoring the police administration in Chapei and Woosung in case of Japanese evacuating these areas," the Chinese Public Security Bureau constituted a ten-member committee including Wang Zhijing (chief of the Second Section), Lu Ying (chief of detectives), and Dr. Hong Qi (secretary for foreign affairs). The Japanese Consulate denied formal permission to Wang Zhijing for the committee to visit Zhabei for inspection purposes, but PSB officers did informally tour the area and were able to provide the committee with an estimate of the number of people required to reorganize the police force and reestablish new stations in the combat zone.[79] This information was all the more necessary because the Japanese inserted into the May 5 accord the provision that the Chinese would create the Peace Preservation Corps to take responsibility for the security of the inhabitants of Zhabei.[80]

Chief Wen Yingxing served as a member of the joint commission to oversee the Japanese evacuation, but it was in his capacity as director of public security that he accepted notification that the Japanese forces would move out on May 16.[81] The PSB proposed using 750 men to police the evacuated area—that portion of Zhabei bounded by the railway line on the north, Suzhou Creek on the west and south, and on the east by a line formed by the Zhabei settlement boundary from Suzhou Creek to Haining Road extension and continuing directly north to the railway line.[82]

On May 14, 1932, Wen Yingxing wrote of these plans to SMP Commissioner Gerrard, indicating that the police force, armed for duty, needed to move from South Market through the French Concession and International Settlement via Thibet Road.[83] The next morning, May 15, the contingent of 750 policemen, including 448 Beiping policemen armed with rifles and Mauser pistols, arrived at the South Market Bund by boat from Kunshan. They were billeted in the coinshop guild at 676 Longhua Road, and that afternoon they were inspected by Mayor Wu Tiecheng, Secretary Yu Hongjun, and Chief Wen Yingxing.[84]

At 7:30 on the morning of May 16 the first convoy crossed the foreign concessions. The ten furniture vans filled with equipment and armed Chinese police in full uniform were not escorted by the SMP, who had taken a different route. After the Chinese transports crossed Markham Bridge and entered Zhabei, the Japanese withdrew their marines at 8:00 A.M. from their posts on the bridges in the district. Two more trips were made by the Chinese vans that morning under police escort from Sinza station.[85]

Meanwhile, Huang Ming, the officer in charge of the reserve unit of the PSB, called at the headquarters of the fifth company of Japanese marines in the former police training depot on Kungwu Road. The Japanese exchanged documents with Huang Ming, and then the 200 marines proceeded eastward, leaving the Chinese free to take back their police posts, stationing one local constable and one Beiping policemen, each armed with a rifle, at crucial traffic points. By 10:00 that same morning, as motorcycle patrols armed with machine pistols circulated through the streets, the PSB had already begun to distribute census forms from its seven newly reopened offices (see Table 6).[86] During the afternoon a crew of 150 street cleaners set to work clearing away debris, removing corpses, and scattering disinfectant. And by nightfall Chinese martial law was in effect over most of Zhabei.[87] Within a month, after 1,700 workers had spread more than eleven tons of lime to prevent a major epidemic, the Fifth District had been recovered with another three police companies of 360 officers and men armed for duty, and the district west of Suzhou Creek and east of the Shanghai-Wusong railway line was occupied with 100 armed policemen under the command of senior officers.[88]

The Chinese police's recovery of Zhabei after the Japanese evacuation was an impressive accomplishment, aided in no small part by the contingent of Beiping policemen brought in—like the Baoding officers in 1927—to keep local forces in check. The Chinese city they entered, however, was now devastated. The empty and deserted streets were overrun with fat, sleek rats in the dim light of late afternoon. More than 12,000 residences, 4,000 stores, 240 schools, and 600 factories had been destroyed; and most schools, municipal bureaus, and police stations were buried beneath the rubble.[89] In Zhabei alone, 85 percent of the inhabitants had fled; and of the total of 801,839 persons registered as living in the affected zones, 540,000 had left.[90]

The January-February war dealt a severe financial blow to Western and Japanese businessmen in Shanghai. Shanghai's trade had temporarily been ruined, as godowns with their contents were destroyed. European and American steamship lines had simply taken Shanghai off their schedules, dumping cargo in other ports. Industrial production stood still and two hundred thousand workers had lost their jobs.[91] The Japanese had incurred a loss of £18 million, and half of the thirty thousand Japanese residents had gone home.[92]

As far as the Chinese municipal government was concerned, the 1932 war over Zhabei was an economic catastrophe that momentarily paralyzed the Nationalists' plans for urban modernization.[93] The moment the ceasefire was signed, former residents began returning to ruined homesites where "dashing thunder and flying flame had left mortal men slain."[94] Thousands of straw huts sprang up in Zhabei practically overnight.[95] Yet a comparison of the total registered population (including hut dwellers) living in the Chinese-administered portions of Shanghai during the six months before the January incident and the six months afterward still shows a drop of 43 percent (see Table 7).[96] The Chinese sectors were especially hurt commercially.[97] Over one-third of the Chinese-registered jewelry stores and food shops were closed down, and half of the pawnshops and hotels ceased to exist. Other amenities of popular life were also harmed: of the Chinese city's recreational facilities, including theaters and movie houses, 60 out of 110 were dropped from the police registries, presumably because they went out of business or were destroyed during that six-month period (see Table 8).

The city did recover. As the refugees returned to Zhabei and Hongkou, the shell holes were filled in and the houses rebuilt; and ocean liners once again steamed up the Huangpu.[98] But the financial situation of the municipal government was disastrous.[99] Monthly receipts were only coming to about Ch. $100,000, or just one-sixth of the city's income before the war.[100]

Yet a steady stream of Zhabei merchant delegations asked the city government for total noncollection of taxes. On June 21, 1932, the municipal government announced that the tax on habitations was totally forgiven for the first six months of the year, the tax on vehicles would be levied as of June, and the other taxes on boats, markets, and so forth, were to be collected only when those activities resumed. As for the Chamber of Commerce's request for total noncollection, secretary-general Yu Hongjun responded that the municipal government had already lost an enormous amount of income, and that some tax collection was necessary. Mr. Yu was, in effect, insisting upon the collection of the residential tax, and in the end he prevailed. The municipal government did pay Ch. $150,000 in rebuilding subsidies, which was added to the Ch. $300,000 contribution by the local preservation society. It also ordained a three-month rent furlough in the actual combat zones. But it quickly resumed real estate tax collection that July in an effort to gain some headway on the municipal deficit of Ch. $3 million.[101]

Help emerged from other sources: Ch. $500,000 from the national government; Ch. $150,000 from the provincial government; and Ch. $300,000 from the *difang weichi hui* (local preservation society).[102] Yet new expenses ate into those sums immediately, including the costs of paying for the Peace Preservation Corps that the May 5 agreement had called for in place of a Chinese Garrison Command. For, despite Mayor Wu Tiecheng's pleas to the national government for help, Nanjing refused to give the slightest financial contribution to this new force composed of policemen whose salaries, arms, and clothing had to be paid by the city.[103]

In June 1932 it was announced that the corps would consist of two units of 1,500 well-armed men who would be stationed throughout Greater Shanghai, including the outlying districts.[104] They would be "so equipped and placed that they will be able to concentrate at a moment's notice, ready for action against bandits or similar lawless elements which have been considerably increased in number as the result of the recent war in and around Shanghai."[105] The core of the Shanghai Baoandui was to be the special police from Beiping, who eventually formed the second battalion of the first infantry regiment. They were to be supplemented by recruits who already had military and police training and could form a special constabulary of riflemen and machine gunners, backed up by mounted units, motorcycle squads, and armored car sections.[106] A major source of these recruits, in fact, turned out to be members of the regular military police who formed the bulk of the second infantry regiment.[107]

The Shanghai Municipality Peace Preservation Corps that was finally formed on July 5, 1932, thus turned out to be a formidable military group. Its first infantry regiment, formally organized under Colonel Huang Ming, consisted of three battalions divided into four companies each with 124 policemen.[108] A second regiment, also enrolling three thousand men, was to be organized out of the sixth regiment of military police that had returned to Songjiang from its bandit suppression campaigns in Jiangbei.[109] The entire military force on July 5 was put directly under the Chinese mayor of Shanghai and his deputy, Chief Wen Yingxing, strengthening their power in the city beyond all expectations.[110] Within six months, by December 1932, Mayor Wu Tiecheng and the police chief controlled nearly four thousand soldiers equipped with automatic weapons and heavy machine guns, and barracked in temples and guilds all around the city (see Appendix 2).[111]

This recovery seemed miraculous, given the widespread devastation in Shanghai. The Japanese attack on Shanghai in 1932 showed that—as one historian put it—"the municipal administration could successfully cope with a multitude of problems under the most difficult conditions."[112] From the perspective of the Public Security Bureau, the January-May crisis tested their abilities sorely. In their own chronicles, the Chinese police congratulated themselves on their ability to combat the conspiracies on all sides by "reds" who wished to take advantage of the chaos to "destroy public order."[113] This illustrates the continued preoccupation with the Communists, for when it came to basic crime suppression, July 1931–June 1932 turned out to have been a dismal year. Crime rates were up more than 80 percent in two years (see Table 3). During a good part of the time, while puppet police encouraged gambling and narcotics at a cheaper-than-ever payoff rate, the Public Security Bureau's men became, as Chief Wen Yingxing candidly reported, rear-line auxiliaries to the soldiers of the Nineteenth Route Army, policing wherever and whenever they could.[114] And when the fighting was over, and the Nineteenth Route Army and Garrison Command moved out, the PSB found itself more than ever militarized, playing now more of a back-seat role to the military police (which were expanded considerably by Chiang Kai-shek in 1931) and to the Beiping professionals brought in to restore order to Zhabei and to form the new paramilitary Peace Preservation Corps.[115]

Although there were similarities, however, this new re-militarization of the police was not a throwback to the days just after the Northern Expedition, when Shanghai's civilian police had been forced to accept northern constables. In the first place, the mayor and police chief's office were both considerably strengthened vis-à-vis local interests. One of the unexpected results of the crisis of the winter of 1931–32 was the overturning of the relationship between the municipal government and the local section of the Guomindang, which had already been tarnished by the kidnapping of students during the December 1931 riots in front of city hall. The Shanghai section of the party was reorganized under the new director of social affairs, Wu Xingya, who was affiliated with the Chen brothers and who had been specially delegated by Nanjing to bring the local *dangbu* (party branch) under control.[116] The new executive committee was composed both of former members who controlled the internal affairs of the party apparatus, and of new and more moderate members like Yu Hongjun who came out of the municipal government. Henceforth the GMD no longer interfered in the administrative affairs of the municipality.[117]

The municipal government was also strengthened vis-à-vis the city's local notability. The Shanghai businessmen and civic leaders who had helped mediate a compromise over the militia issue were appointed by the mayor to a provisional municipal council.[118] Even though this did not fundamentally change the distribution of municipal power, it gave the Jiang-Zhe financial elite a new, albeit relatively informal, role in municipal government. But the compromise was definitely weighted on the side of Mayor Wu Tiecheng and Chief Wen Yingxing, and it came about precisely because local elites had learned to recognize their limitations against municipally centralized police authority under the command of a centrally appointed mayor connected to the national political system via patronage networks.[119]

Taken together, these various shifts underscored a single, most important change in the role of the Shanghai Public Security Bureau over the first five years of its existence: the strengthening of administrative authority at the expense of civil society. Municipal autocracy, not municipal democracy, stood the winner.[120]

12   A Second Chance

The Administration of Mayor Wu Tiecheng

In spite of all these handicaps, most observers in Shanghai are agreed that in the short space of about eight years the Chinese have made notable advances in the conduct of a modern municipal government. Residents of the Chinese municipal area have profited by better police protection, better health protection, and improved public services and transportation facilities. It has been demonstrated that properly trained Chinese officials when free from political pressure can do their work efficiently. There has been definite improvement in the relations between the Chinese city officials and the foreign authorities. The development of the Chinese municipality of Greater Shanghai has progressed beyond what many foreigners believed possible.

William Johnstone, Jr., *The Shanghai Problem*

The need to rebuild Zhabei after the 1932 conflict appeared to offer enlightened municipal governance a second chance in Shanghai. Many dared to believe that under military pressure urban leaders had pulled together an administrative structure capable of accomplishing new policy goals, as evinced by the speedy recovery from the Japanese devastation of Zhabei. The tenure of General Wu Tiecheng, the fourth and last mayor of Shanghai before the Sino-Japanese War of 1937, was thus a time of renewed hope for political recovery and municipal modernization. Once General Wu arrived in office, and especially after the crisis with Japan was resolved in May 1932, the municipal government saw a fresh burst of authority and activity. The secretariat was replaced, except for Secretary-General Yu Hongjun, and all of the bureaus, save Health and Public Works, received new directors.[1] Like Wu himself, seven of the directors were born in Guangdong, and two were from Anhui, where Wu had been raised. They were relatively young and fairly close in years, the median age being forty. Most came from the coastal zones, almost all had a university education, and five of the leaders of the newly reorganized local Guomindang branch had graduated from the same law school in Shanghai, probably during the same year.[2]

By all accounts, this group of lawyers, officers, engineers, and politicians worked well together and shared each other's technocratic enthusiasms for building a new Shanghai out of the ruins of the old.[3] Mayor Wu even spoke of this period of reconstruction as being a turning point for Shanghai, a time when a new "Chinese Renaissance" would take place.[4] "If you will permit me to guide your thoughts into a state of idealism," he told his fellow citizens, "you will form a picture in your mind of a city, a sort of Utopia, which embodies the world's latest and most approved form of municipal government. . . . Such is the Greater Shanghai that we would like to see."[5]

Visions of Shanghai's Future

But in the temper of the times, Shanghai still really appeared to be two cities: "a heaven on top of a hell."[6] Writing after the destruction of 1932 and in view of Wu Tiecheng's commitment to build a new and even better civic order, the editors of *Xin Zhonghua* saw on the one hand that the world's sixth largest city served as "international imperialism's basic garrison directed against Chinese trade," constantly "flourishing and Europeanizing" (*Ouhua*). But they also saw the nether side: a growing urban populace of starving and homeless, living side by side with the affluent and idle rich.[7] Just as the city enjoyed a tremendous import-export trade while whole sections of business were insolvent, so did the "masters," the upper-class Chinese, daily pass by "the slaves," Chinese shriveled up in the streets on the verge of death.[8]

In the early 1930s the sanguine rested their hopes for the future on a kind of natural political and technical evolution. Eventually, the essayist Lu Xun hoped, foreigners would gradually return home, the concessions would revert to the Chinese, while the world of vice and "evil demons" (*emo*) quickly disappeared. Replacing the strips and concessions, the Shanghai of the future would be shaped in a concentric ring with wide boulevards marking the boundaries between an administrative district in the center and outer layers containing hospitals, schools, gymnasiums, amusement centers and, beyond those, the commercial sector, and an outlying industrial section. The Shanghai of the future would be a city of cars with the outer layers connected to the administrative hub by a few broad boulevards radiating from the center to the periphery, conveying automobiles to and fro. The individual family—a nuclear husband-and-wife unit—would each possess a *jiating qiche* (household automobile) that would solve the transportation and housing problem simultaneously: when night fell the family unit would simply park its car in some quiet place and sleep, secure in the public law and order observed by the entire populace.[9]

It was not difficult to parody such utopian fantasies. Ming San wrote that the Shanghai of the future would be "modernized" (*jinhua*), "the streets would be filled only with the most illustrious, with celebrities, with the most successful, with the gentry; with philanthropists, and with the geniuses of the International Settlement including great foreign men and their wives." Youth would be "modernized" (*modenghua*) into the "modern boy" (*mopu*) with a foreign suit and mustache, and the "modern girl" (*moge*) with a permanent wave and high-heeled shoes; and when these members of the opposite sex met each other, they would speak together in a foreign language.[10] Meanwhile, the shanties and huts of Zhabei and Xujiahui would all have been torn down and replaced by entertainment centers. All of the buildings would be constructed ten stories high according to prescribed rules, and in a mixture of Eastern and Western styles.[11] The rickshaws would all have been replaced by automobiles or public air buses. At every crossroad there would be enormous billboards advertising English, American, Japanese, and French products at bargain prices. Even the coffin companies would advertise two for the price of one. And each of the schools and universities would have large neon signs at their gateways advertising special reductions in tuition.[12]

Ming San's satirical jauntiness was exceptional. Much more typical of those who wrote about Shanghai and its future was the saturnine journalist Yang Yuansheng who darkly depicted the tall buildings and broad streets as built with the blood and sweat of the workers. The peace and orderliness of its streets were the result of the guns and sticks of its policemen and the gunboats and artillery of the imperialists. "Can we not see the masses' wounds still glistening with blood?"[13] Were not the bordellos, the massage parlors, and the dance halls all signs of this capitalist exploitation? Could the Chinese masses rise and destroy this capitalist fortress and its desperate defenders? Yes, but only at the cost of many innocent lives.[14]

Yang Yibo, another pessimistic essayist, found it hard to imagine how the forces of revolution would be able to defeat the forces of counterrevolution, and yet the necessity for that struggle—which would certainly surpass January 28, 1932, in ferocity and destructiveness—seemed unavoidable.

> Shanghai is a seething cauldron. Did you not see the phenomenon several months ago when the Huangpu River in raging tide over-

flowed its banks and completely washed away the major roads? This appears to be exactly like the first act of the great masses of China taking back Shanghai by force. . . . I hope to utterly destroy this old Shanghai, to smash asunder this oriental bastion of imperialist domination, to inter forever those golden dreams of bloodsucking vampires![15]

And Yang Yibo concluded: "Shanghai will finally have, in the future soon to come, a day of rage!"[16]

Less apocalyptic, though strikingly Kafkaesque, was Liu Mengfei's prognostication of Shanghai's future, when there would no longer be a distinction between "masters" and "slaves," between "high-level Chinamen" and the shriveled beggars of the sidewalk—or what Liu called the "black insects."[17] The poor people would move from their ratholes to the "high-rise mansions" (*gaolou dasha*) of the "playboys" (*anlegong*), who would flee by airplane to some distant place where they could continue to be pampered. The imperialists' barracks would be blown up and the foreign banks would be taken over by the masses, the "black insects," who would also run the textile firms and newspapers. The gerontocrats would lament the loss of morality and the advent of social chaos. The scholars with Ph.D.'s in "pragmatism" (*shiyongzhuyi*) would express their hatred for "people's rights" (*renquan*), and the psychologists with doctorates in "behavioralism" (*xingweizhuyi*) would regret not being able to carry out any more experiments on the "black insects." But never mind: victory in the end would go to the masses.[18]

Elite Alliances for Governance

Mayor Wu Tiecheng and his cohort of reformist technocrats had another scenario in mind. Their plan for Greater Shanghai was neither to turn the keys of the city over to the masses, nor even to consult the middle classes through popular elections. Rather, Mayor Wu preferred to work with elements of the city's financial elite—the Ningbo banking patriciate—through permanently appointed committees and councils. After the hostilities with Japan concluded, and after consultation with his predecessor Zhang Qun, Wu Tiecheng sought the advice, support, and monetary backing of the higher bourgeoisie of Zhejiang and Jiangsu who mainly lived in the International Settlement and French Concession. He demanded and received authorization to name a provisional Municipal Council provided with a perpetual mandate; that is, it could not be dissolved until a regular Municipal Council was elected.[19]

The announcement of this new mayor-appointed council met with consternation and opposition on the part of some municipal officials and many of the Chinese citizens of Greater Shanghai. They protested the domination by persons living in the concessions and demanded that the council be enlarged to include at least representatives from Zhabei and South Market, not to mention other urban zones administered by the municipality. They received no response.[20] Instead, the mayor's office revived that old and tired cliché of gentry home rule, "local self-government." Only this time, no pretense of involving local elites, as had been the case three decades earlier, was made at all. In fact, "natural" local communities were administratively amalgamated by redividing existing districts such as Wusong, Qingpu, and Baoshan, and by combining South Market and Zhabei into a singly administered "Chinese" Greater Shanghai with a total area of 494 square kilometers and a population of 1,655,070.[21]

At the same time, Mayor Wu set up a new group called the Committee of Preparation for Local Self-Government (Choubei zizhi weiyuanhui), composed entirely of members of the municipal administration and headed by Secretary-General Yu Hongjun. These bureaucrats together drew up plans for the creation of forty municipal zone offices (*qu gongsuo*), each to be staffed by a zone chief (*quzhang*), an assistant, and a group of policemen to make a census of the local population. The census taking was supposed to be completed within four months, and local elections were supposed to be held after the new year. This window dressing did not impede Mayor Wu's autocratic proclivities. Lack of funds, however, prevented any of these top-down "local self-government" plans from being implemented, and elections never took place. Moreover, the mayor's provisionally appointed Municipal Council became permanent—at least until the Japanese attacked five years later.

Supported by key members of the Shanghai commercial elite, Wu's centralizing reforms reined in those who would resist cooperation with the concessions' authorities and appealed to "old China hands" who were impressed by his fluent English and sociability with Westerners, and charmed by his wife at the elegant soirées he hosted in their mansion on Avenue Haig. Thanks to him, they thought, the Chinese police would be "enjoined to refrain from acts calculated to affront or inconvenience foreigners."[22]

In fact, this warming of relations between the Chinese and foreign authorities in Shanghai even made it possible to move a good way toward solving the vexing extra-settlement roads issue. The first step had been taken the previous summer, coinciding with the SMP and PSB's collaborative campaign against the Communists after Gu Shunzhang's defection. On July 24, 1931, Director-General Fessenden sent a confirmation to the

Jiangsu Foreign Affairs Bureau that the SMC had instructed Public Works Commissioner Harpur "to formulate definite proposals regarding the extra-settlement roads and to invite discussion of such proposals with representatives of the Municipality of Greater Shanghai."[23] The SMC-Special Municipality discussions eventually resulted in an acceptable agreement, a year later, after the Sino-Japanese hostilities concluded. The agreement stipulated that the city government of Greater Shanghai would establish a police administration with substations in different parts of the extra-settlement roads area. The police administration would be under the control of the Public Security Bureau, although the SMC would have the right to dispatch constables of its own in case of an emergency. The SMC was also given exclusive authority to collect taxes on behalf of the Chinese municipality at rates set by the latter, and to administer road maintenance services such as sewage disposal. Public utilities would be franchised by the Greater Shanghai Municipality.[24]

The July 1932 "modus vivendi" agreement was taken as a great victory for national sovereignty by the Guomindang. To members of the Executive Committee of the Shanghai party branch, the establishment of jurisdiction over the extra-settlement roads was an instance of recovery of ownership rights over Chinese territory; and in the absence of de facto abolition of extraterritoriality, which was not to come until the Japanese rewarded Wang Jingwei's puppet régime during World War II, this evidence of Nationalist independence was much cherished.[25] Others outside Shanghai, and especially in cities where there were large foreign concessions, agreed. Professors at National Wuhan University requested, through their own city government, copies of the diplomatic correspondence to learn how Shanghai had "recovered management rights (*guanli quan*) and administration rights (*xingzheng quan*) over the extra-settlement roads."[26] The municipal administration of Tianjin also asked for documents from Shanghai explaining how to recover "police and administrative sovereignty."[27]

The mayor's office was only too happy to comply, even though the "modus vivendi" agreement was never implemented owing to Japanese opposition. The Japanese, too, were establishing themselves in extra-settlement road areas north of Hongkou. By 1930 a number of Japanese factories and 5,690 Japanese residents existed there, and, by 1933, a Japanese military barracks sat on Jiangwan Road while naval and consular police conducted regular patrols.[28] The Japanese authorities consequently found the "modus vivendi" agreement, especially its provisions for a special joint police administration under the PSB commissioner, to be quite unacceptable; and they demanded that the deputy commissioner and the senior

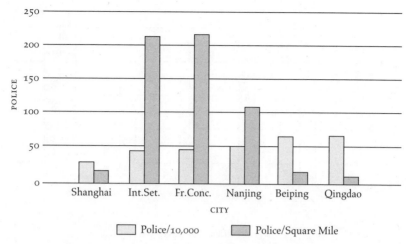

FIGURE 7. Police ratios, 1935, area/population. Shanghai, Nanjing, Beiping, Qingdao. Source: SAM, No. Diwei 1 2660 DEPT 895.24, File 15.

officers of the joint administration be Japanese nationals. Complicated triangular negotiations during 1933–34 failed to break the deadlock. The British and Chinese agreed that the majority of senior foreign officers, except for the deputy commissioner, would be Japanese nationals.[29] In October 1934 the Japanese consul general made a counterproposal that the SMC (in which his countrymen were acquiring an increasingly powerful voice) have the right to nominate the deputy commissioner and one of the two assistant commissioners, and that foreign nationals with extraterritoriality be placed under the jurisdiction of the deputy commissioner.[30] The Chinese and international negotiators in turn proposed a special tax arrangement. When the Japanese insisted that Mayor Wu approve both agreements simultaneously, he naturally rejected both.[31]

Japanese obstruction of the "modus vivendi" agreement meant constant petty jurisdictional conflict in western Shanghai between the concession authorities and the Chinese during the five years after July 1932. The SMC and Special Municipality bickered over tax collecting rights, while the Shanghai Municipal Police and the Public Security Bureau quarreled about the licensing of vendors, the serving of warrants, access to certain roads, and so forth.[32]

Partly these were issues of police sovereignty and partly questions of access to scarce resources, especially during the difficult winter of 1936–37 when the world was sunk in economic depression. The Shanghai Municipal Police had been living for years off the Ch. $81 million reserve fund generated by the sale of the electric power plant in 1929. In order to

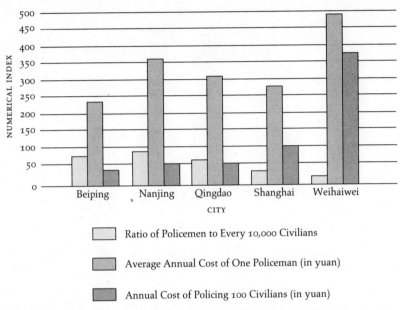

FIGURE 8.   Comparative policing costs. Source: NTN, 12(6)-21952-1935.

avoid another annual deficit, the SMC had tried to raise land taxes in 1936 from 14 to 16 percent, but the Japanese ratepayers had strenuously objected.[33] Since the International Settlement's net indebtedness—which was secured by the Ch. $67 million worth of land and buildings owned by the SMC—was already $39,692,284 in June 1936, the council had no choice but to dip into its electricity plant reserves for another $2 million to balance the budget. The same was true for the 1937 budget which would eat up another $3,250,000 of the rapidly diminishing reserve fund. In late November 1936, therefore, the SMC adopted special measures to economize, including a police pay cut of 8 percent and the reduction of various police allowances.[34]

The Public Security Bureau was less strapped, even though its 1936–37 budget was cut by 5 percent to Ch. $3,463,670.[35] At the same time, however, its resource needs were much higher than the SMP's, both in terms of territory covered and population governed. (See Figure 7.) Per capita, less was currently budgeted for police costs in the Chinese municipality of Shanghai than practically any other major city in China—a factor which helped account for Shanghai's soaring crime rates. (See Figure 8.) The ability of the PSB to extend police sovereignty into western Shanghai thus carried both the promise of fresh sources of short-term revenue in the form of fines and license fees, and the guarantee of added long-term expenses for extra patrols and more equipment.

Anti-Communist Collaboration

For both police forces, then, competition was costly; suburban skirmishes were an unaffordable diversion. Consequently, during the five years after July 1932, there was a much more basic impulse shared by Wu Tiecheng and the concessions' authorities to cooperate across a broad spectrum of common concerns about public order in the central city and political stability at the core. To begin with, the leaders of the Shanghai Municipal Police agreed strongly that one of their primary duties, as guardians of law and order, was to combat international Communism. British Intelligence agent H. Steptoe wrote in 1935 to Commissioner Givens:

> Broadly speaking, the function of the Comintern is to act as the mainspring of an illegal conspiracy against international law and order. The function of the Police is to preserve that law and order, locally, and as far as possible internationally, and it will, in my opinion, be a profound pity, if and when information concerning the presence of Comintern agents here is made available to the local Police from any source whatever, the utmost endeavour is not made to discover everything possible concerning these people.[36]

It followed logically, then, that this duty to combat international Communism, shared with their colleagues on the French and Chinese police forces, naturally extended to an obligation to help the Nationalist authorities crush domestic Communists.[37]

This collaboration became necessary because, despite the blows suffered by its urban cells just after Gu Shunzhang's defection, the Chinese Communist Party experienced a temporary recrudescence during the crisis with Japan between September 1931 and May 1932. The first sign of this revival was the nomination of Zhou Enlai to the post of secretary-general, which had been vacant since the execution of Xiang Zhongfa.[38] The task the CCP set itself after September 1931 was to work in adverse circumstances among the masses in order to fight for the daily needs of the workers, to reinforce and consolidate the red unions, to create Communist cells in the "yellow unions," and to intensify propaganda among the workers. The volume of its propaganda provided the most visible evidence of CCP activity. In August 1931, still reeling from the attack upon its Agitprop Department, the party had not issued any publications in Shanghai at all. By September, however, during the public protests against the Japanese invasion of Manchuria, Shanghai police confiscated sixty-six different types of Communist publications.[39] Some of this propaganda work was directed at foreign troops in Shanghai, including Japanese troops.[40] Police found Annamite troops, for example, carrying anti-imperialist tracts published in French and English in April 1932.[41] When the SMP and French police raided the headquarters of the Communist committee in charge of conducting propaganda among foreign troops garrisoned in Shanghai, they also found copies of extremely detailed minutes of the Nationalist military conference held at Lushan on June 16–17, 1932. This top-secret meeting of Chiang's troop commanders charged with the suppression of the Red Army had obviously been infiltrated by CCP agents, who sent back intelligence of the most sensitive character about the Nationalists' most confidential military and political plans.[42]

Discoveries of this nature strengthened the connection in the eyes of police officials between international Communist attacks on Western imperialism and the domestic CCP insurrection against the Nationalists, and that of course made cooperation all the more sensible. As a result, from May 1932 to October 1933, sixteen operations were secretly hailed by French Intelligence as a sensational joint victory over the Communists.[43] They comprised the detection in the International Settlement of the offices of the Committee of Revolutionary Foreign Soldiers in Shanghai, which had been reestablished after its destruction in June 1931; of the central office of the League of Chinese Communist Youth; and of the Agitprop committee charged with propaganda work among foreign troops.[44] And they also included thirteen very important sets of arrests, ranging from Chen Duxiu, the first Secretary-General of the CCP, along with eight members of his group (arrested on October 15, 1932, in the International Settlement), to Miss Zhang Jinglan, member of the CCP Central Committee (arrested on November 20, 1932, in the International Settlement), and Chen Gang, chief of the Second Department of the Chinese GPU (arrested on March 2, 1933, in the International Settlement).[45]

The Communist Party reacted by tightening its own disciplinary rules and sanctions. In 1932 and 1933 the CCP's Red Brigade ("dog-killers squad") accelerated its attacks against former party members working for Nanjing. This campaign was designed both to destroy the Communist Party's enemies and to terrorize "indecisive" party members, but it actually became entangled with factional struggles within the CCP after Chen Shaoyu (Wang Ming) took over and drove many to go over to the Guomindang in self-defense.[46] The government, meanwhile, had changed its accustomed policy from executing arrested Communists to proposing that they submit and collaborate for the "health of the nation."[47] Many did, including a long list of prominent CCP members—Wang Ping, Hu Chongyao, Song Zeming, Wang Yongcheng, Xu Binggeng (member of the Central Committee), Li Ping (editor of *Red Flag*), Lu Fowang (alias Li

Yufong, member of the Politburo), Wang Yeucheh (alias Shao Kikwei and Chen Kwang, secretary of the General Red Syndicate of Chinese Workers in Shanghai), and seventeen others—who in March 1933 issued a public avowal of their decision to join the Guomindang and oppose the methods of the Central Committee of the Communist Party.[48] The most notorious turncoat of all, of course, was Gu Shunzhang, whose whereabouts were top secret. A protected witness in effect, he was kept undercover in the capital, where he married the pretty daughter of a Nanjing tailor and was reunited with his son, Asheng.[49]

One of Gu Shunzhang's disciples who also defected was Ma Shaowu, formerly a special delegate of the CCP Central Committee. Like Gu, Ma Shaowu was able to help the Guomindang Special Services Bureau seize or "turn" numerous party members after he became a member of the Nationalist secret service. He and another defector specializing in security work, Wang Yonghuan, were specially detailed to Shanghai by the Guomindang "to hunt down Communists"—a task which they performed zealously and with scant regard for legal niceties, despite their positions as inspectors in the Special Services Department of the Public Security Bureau.[50]

On May 14, 1933, police agents raided an apartment on Kunshan Road and seized the left-wing writer Ding Ling, her husband Feng Da, and an anonymous Communist friend—all of whom completely slipped from public view. The kidnapping was protested by the Secretary-General of the League for the Protection of Human Rights, Yang Xingfo, but the protest was met with official silence and Yang himself was assassinated soon afterward by one of Dai Li's hit teams.[51] One of the witnesses of the Ding Ling kidnapping, however, noted the license number of the automobile. That number, 4223, turned out to be the license of a car belonging to the Special Municipality of Greater Shanghai, and on the night Ding Ling disappeared the car had been checked out to Inspector Ma Shaowu.[52] One month to the day after the Ding Ling abduction, Ma Shaowu pulled up before the "Sweetheart," a sing-song house just off of Foochow Road. As he was getting out of his car, men stepped out of the shadows of an alley and opened fire. Inspector Ma was shot down before he could draw his own service pistol—a victim, the public surmised, of the Communists' revenge. At his funeral, attended by many officials, Chief Wen Hongen paid tribute to Ma's zeal and efficiency.[53] Ma Shaowu was succeeded as head of the secret service department of the Public Security Bureau by fellow-defector Wang Yonghuan, who continued the crackdown on Communists. At 11:15 on the night of August 23, 1933, however, as Inspector

Wang rode in an elevator after visiting a friend at the Sun Sun Hotel, he and his bodyguard were fatally shot four times by two assailants, who escaped unscathed.[54]

The Ma and Wang assassinations shocked the public and alarmed the police on both sides of Suzhou Creek, targeting so directly as they did the security authorities. Perhaps even closer cooperation, especially between the concessions' police forces and the Nationalist secret service, was necessary. After yet another assassination of a PSB secret agent on September 11, and the discovery of bombs planted in Settlement police stations, Chen Lifu's lieutenant, Xu Enzeng, and the Western police entered negotiations. On the Chinese side, Xu got authorization to have his secret service agents penetrate the two concessions. The French and Anglo-Americans, at the same time, agreed to join in launching a major operation against the Red Brigade. On November 7, 1933, the Chinese police, with the help of the SMP, arrested in the International Settlement five heavily armed Red Brigade terrorists. Their interrogation established that these individuals had taken part in six assassinations, including the murder of Ma Shaowu and Wang Yonghuan. Further information, culled from these prisoners and other Red Brigade agents taken into custody in the concessions, gave the SMP and PSB special services a chance in May–June 1934 to seize and "turn" two of Kang Sheng's lieutenants—Li Shiqun (alias Slavine) and Ding Mocun—and to close down the central communication headquarters (confiscating seven radio transmitters) that linked Moscow and the Shanghai Communists.[55] And the following year, after one of Dai Li's double agents was murdered in his hospital bed, Juntong (Military Statistics) secret servicemen and French Concession Police detectives seized four remnant members of the "dog-killers squad" in a jewelry store on Avenue Foch and eventually had them executed.[56]

At the Special Municipality's regular weekly Sun Yat-sen memorial service on August 28, 1933, Mayor Wu Tiecheng had paid special tribute to Ma Shaowu and Wang Yonghuan, among other PSB officers killed in the line of duty. Their sacrifices had, nonetheless, brought relative peace and order to Shanghai during the past year or so. Mayor Wu claimed that this could be attributed to two factors. First was the realization on the part of Shanghainese that peace in Shanghai was the key to peace in China. Second was the fact that "there had been close and harmonious cooperation from and with the authorities and the police of the International Settlement and the French Concession in ridding the city of undesirable elements and lawless characters." Mayor Wu concluded by praising the "faithfulness and devotion" of PSB members that "had led them to face danger and risk their lives in the performance of their duty in order to keep robbers and Communists in check."[57]

Suppressing Anti-Japanese Protest

The policy of cooperation and the conflating of felony with political radicalism continued to characterize the programs of the Public Security Bureau under Wu Tiecheng's second police chief, Colonel Wen Hongen. Like his predecessor (who had resigned because of the malfeasances of an associate), Colonel Wen was from Guangdong. After graduating from the Yunnan Military Academy (Yunnan lujun jiangwu xuexiao), Wen Hongen served as a general staff officer in the police and then commanded a regiment in the National Revolutionary Army. In 1929, after a stint as commander of an army division, Wen was sent to Europe for three years of study and training, mainly in France. He was forty years old when he became director of the Shanghai Public Security Bureau on September 4, 1932.[58] Colonel Wen took over PSB in the midst of an anti-Japanese boycott and "national salvation" demonstrations that had been growing steadily since spring and that were constantly being raided by the police.[59] The largest raid was carried out on July 17, after Zhabei was recovered. Chinese authorities broke into a meeting of representatives of anti-imperialist organizations, convened by the Communist-infiltrated Federation of Shanghai People to Oppose the Agreement to Cease Hostilities in Shanghai and to Support the Volunteer Armies in the Northeast, held at Huang Jinrong's Gongwutai Theater on Robison Road. The Public Security Bureau took ninety-three members of the group into custody, and four days later requested the help of the International Settlement police department to arrest members of eleven different Shanghai organizations suspected of harboring communists.[60]

Authorities throughout Shanghai feared "possible communistic uprisings" on September 18, 1932, the first anniversary of the Manchurian Railway Incident at Mukden, especially since there were diplomatic rumors that Japan intended to sign a treaty of recognition with the puppet government of Manchuria a day or two before then. On September 15, Colonel Wen wrote to SMP Commissioner Gerrard: "Fearing our patriotic people might become enraged at Japan's recognition and that they might be utilized by reactionary cliques, I have altered the date for the enforcement of special martial law in the districts under the jurisdiction of this Bureau from September 17 to September 19."[61] That same day, September 15, at 7:30 in the evening, a crowd assembled outside the Guanghua Movie Theater was dispersed by the SMP; several groups of demonstrators moved down Manila Road and Avenue Edward VII into the French Concession, where detectives from the political section arrested five activists carrying "communistic tracts" and a banner inscribed "Eastern District Committee of the Shanghai Anti-Imperialist League."[62] Other incidents followed. For instance, less than two hours later, more demonstrators assembled outside the Great World, shouting, "Down with imperialism, support the Chinese Communist Party," and four activists were arrested.[63]

By September 18, all of Shanghai's police authorities, including the Japanese consular police, were on emergency standby. Their presence was so overwhelming that only one incident occurred: an effort by twenty persons "of the worker and student classes" to demonstrate at the corner of Nanking and Shansi Roads. A few "communistic slogans" were shouted, but further activities were cut short by the approach of the SMP. The Japanese were much relieved. Captain Sugisake, commander of the Naval Landing Party, sent one of his lieutenants who acted as liaison between Japanese Naval Intelligence and the Special Branch of the SMP to express to Superintendent Givens "appreciation of the assistance rendered during the past few days by the Municipal Police to the Japanese forces." And another Japanese spokesman told the press that "at no time in the recent local history has there ever been seen such effective cooperation taken by the authorities of different nations for the preservation of peace and order in the city."[64]

That policy of cooperation, for reasons of legitimate self-interest, extended as well to the Shanghai Public Security Bureau. As we shall see, throughout 1933 and 1934 the PSB continually endeavored to keep Shanghai's students, petty urbanites, and workers from conducting boycotts, demonstrations, and strikes in order to avoid providing the Japanese with a pretext for another devastating military intervention that would surely undo the accomplishments of Mayor Wu Tiecheng's municipal administration.[65]

5

THE LIMITATIONS OF THE NEW CIVIC ORDER

13 The New Life and National Salvation Movements

The Shanghai police must be assembled for training because in the past there has not been that great a difference between the police and ordinary people. Listless, apathetic, heartless, humpbacked, stooped, and lame, they walk along tottering from side to side. They are not suited to serve as modern policemen. Secondly, their hearts are not content with their salaries but rather are bent upon forming connections with bad people to carry out corrupt activities. . . . We must devise ways of abolishing this kind of unconscionable behavior. . . . They must all have the physique, the ability, and the revolutionary integrity of a military man. Only in this way will we be able to enforce the law and transform social customs.

General Cai Jingjun, 1936

The leaders of the Shanghai Public Security Bureau were convinced, and not without cause, that the Communists were donning the cloak of patriotism to turn the National Salvation Movement of resistance against Japanese aggression to their own purposes.[1] By 1933 the Shanghai Party Center had to move to the Soviet area, and during the following year the Jiangsu and Shanghai underground party committees were almost completely wiped out. Individual Communist Party members and leftist intellectuals shifted their attention to national salvation movements headed by nonpartisan "social notables," and substituted "struggle through unity" for the failed policy of confrontation.[2] As Cai Jingjun, who became chief of police after Colonel Wen passed away in the fall of 1934, told his officers and men: "We have no doubt that students are patriotic, but upon investigation it is clear that complicated forces are behind the student movement: namely, after the red bandits had to flee the Soviet zones under Nationalist military attack, other [Communists] came into Shanghai under cover of the slogans of National Salvation."[3]

The third of Wu Tiecheng's police chiefs, Lieutenant General Cai Jingjun was also from Guangdong (Hainan). Because he began his military career as a cadet at the Guards Army Military Academy founded by Wu Tiecheng in Guangzhou, Cai regarded himself as Mayor Wu's lifelong student. When the Guards Academy was merged with the Huangpu Mili-

tary Academy, Cai continued as a Guomindang cadet and graduated with
the first Huangpu class. After a stint abroad studying military science in
Germany, Italy, and the Soviet Union, Cai was named head of the First
Section of the Staff Office of the Northern Expedition, and then director
of the Bureau of General Affairs in the Nanchang provisional headquarters. A tall, thin, severe man in his early forties, General Cai arrived in
Shanghai on February 24, 1935, and formally assumed his duties on
March 1. He served as director of the Public Security Bureau until No-
vember 1937.[4]

Renewed Police Reform

General Cai came into office at a moment when the high tide of the New
Life Movement coincided with a second wave of police reform. This second wave had begun to surge during the last months of Colonel Wen
Hongen's tenure in 1934, and it clearly reflected Mayor Wu Tiecheng's
belief that a strong police system was crucial to national "wealth and
power." One had only to look at the example of two such great "police
countries" (*jingcha guojia*) as Germany and Japan.

> These two countries have relied on the strength of their police to
> create stable societies and rich and powerful nations. Our country
> is unusually weak as a nation. Our society is not yet stable. Com-
> pared to Germany and Japan our need for police is even keener.[5]

The Chinese people's greatest weakness was their lack of "strength to
govern themselves" (*zizhi li*) and of "strength to organize themselves"
(*zuzhi li*). If China wanted to "revive" (*fuxing*) and become "rich and
powerful" (*fuqiang*), then this weakness would have to be extirpated.[6]
Since the police, after all, are the "officials closest to the people" (*qinmin
zhi guan*), then it is their sacred duty to "guide" (*zhidao*) the people to
acquire those two strengths.[7]

Invoking the difficulty of maintaining public order in such a culturally
diverse city, the mayor ordered the PSB to improve the quality of its
personnel both by stiffening the local entrance examination requirements
for the police academy (*jingshi jiaoliansuo*) and by recruiting students in
Beiping. On October 8, 1934, Wu Tiecheng convened a group of police
instructors in the Songhu Garrison Command and authorized them to
send a four-man mission to Beiping on October 31 to recruit 250 students.[8] (See Figure 9.) With the permission of Beiping's mayor, 732 appli-
cants were registered and tested on January 5, 1935. On February 3, the
top 250 were brought down via Nanjing, put in training classes in the

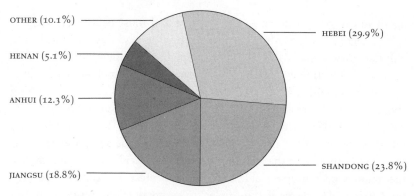

OTHER (10.1%)

HENAN (5.1%)

ANHUI (12.3%)

JIANGSU (18.8%)

HEBEI (29.9%)

SHANDONG (23.8%)

FIGURE 9.   Provenance, Shanghai PSB, 1934. Source: SMA.

Shanghai PSB Police Academy, and eventually given regular police assignments.[9]

Meanwhile, the PSB trained its own ballistics specialists so as not to have to use the SMP's Ballistics Office;[10] it instituted new clothing regulations that required the wearing of "national clothing" and of the Zhongshan jacket;[11] it acquired two new fire trucks at a cost of Ch. $10,000 each;[12] at Mayor Wu's order, it set up new-style *baojingting* ("like the Concession's 'police box' ") in the city's central districts and near dormitories for bank clerks;[13] it established regular police boxes (*paichusuo*) near high schools to guarantee the safety of students and in neighborhoods where the ratio of population to police was too high;[14] and it decentralized the main detective brigade (*zhenjidui*) by forming a headquarters squad (*zongdui*) with separate detective units (*fendui*) attached to each precinct (*fenju*) and police station (*jingcha suo*).[15]

Cai Jingjun was resolved to continue and deepen these reforms, first of all, by an expanded program of police training along scientific Western lines that would prepare the police in the event of a crisis such as the 1932 invasion.[16] Despite earlier rhetoric, less than one-quarter of the current members of the police force had actually received proper training, mainly because they had been hired on a temporary basis. After Chief Cai received Mayor Wu's approval to increase salaries to attract better personnel, he also organized four special training classes for those who had not graduated from the regular police academy.[17] Aware that after thirty years of modern training programs the Chinese police were still regarded with "dread and abhorrence" by the public, Cai candidly divided the members of his force into three categories, ranging from the most fit and intel-

ligent in category A down to the weakest and most elderly in category
C.[18] Category C elements were to be retired at once, and in the future
only category A candidates would be acceptable for admission to the police
academy.[19] Meeting with each of his precinct captains to discuss individual
training programs, Cai stressed that the Shanghai police force's training
should not only stress police theory and techniques, but should also emphasize general knowledge about telecommunications, fire prevention, air
raid defense, and riot control.[20] Meeting with the cadets themselves, General Cai promised that the training they were receiving would help change
them into good policemen, able to serve and protect the "common people"
(laobaixing). However, if they failed to respond to the training by not
reforming themselves and if they behaved corruptly toward the "common
people," he would personally see that they were remanded to the police
headquarters of the Garrison Command for military punishment.[21]

Coming in fresh from the anti-Communist "front" at Nanchang, General Cai approached the problem of "maintaining social order" (weichi
shehui zhixu) in Shanghai with a soldier's distaste for the city's commer-
cialism, Sino-foreign social intermingling, and debased popular customs.
In his inaugural speech at the Public Security Bureau on March 1, 1935,
the new chief declared that "our most important task is to guard against
disaster in advance" by "transforming social customs" (zhuanyi fengqi)
through the New Life Movement.[22] And he told his men in January 1936
that the police had four tasks to perform, the first of which was to implement this movement as thoroughly as possible.[23]

The New Life Movement

Much the same impulse to "police" social behavior on the one hand, and
to "train" people's habits on the other, characterized both the PSB and
New Life Movement.[24] The Public Security Bureau, as we have seen, had
been concerned with the control of popular mores long before the New
Life Movement was formally launched in Nanchang by Governor Xiong
Shihui and General Chiang Kai-shek in February 1934.[25] The Shanghai
PSB continued after the 1932 Japanese invasion to concern itself with the
public's physical and moral health and with changing and controlling
fengsu (customs).[26] It responded with alacrity and a kind of shock of recognition, consequently, when the national New Life Movement was
brought to Shanghai by the local party branch of the Guomindang on
April 8, 1934. A series of meetings of different sectors of the urban population were to be convened: merchants at the Chamber of Commerce on
April 11; farmers in the Su-Song Middle School on April 12; politicians
and GMD cadres on April 13; and so forth.[27] By April 11, more than five

thousand people had registered with the Shanghai New Life Movement Acceleration Association; and a meeting that afternoon passed a series of resolutions including a request that the Bureau of Education order local schools to teach the New Life song composed by Chiang Kai-shek.[28] On April 12, 13, and 14, the Acceleration Association organized public propaganda meetings on the recreation ground in Wusong, followed by lantern processions through the streets.[29]

Culminating this initial activity, at the end of the first week of the New Life Movement a morning meeting was held in the Chinese Chamber of Commerce on North Henan Road. While Chinese police constables maintained proper order and while the Public Security Bureau band played medleys, an audience of more than three hundred persons listened to speeches from GMD members asserting that the New Life Movement was the only way to reform the Chinese nation. The audience responded in unison to shouted slogans, and many members later participated in another lantern procession involving more than six thousand people, including five hundred members of the Peace Preservation Corps, three hundred PSB policemen, and one hundred military policemen. The parade began at 6:00 P.M. and wound its way through South Market, breaking up at 10:10 P.M. at West Gate.[30]

The government and party-sponsored movement continued to try to work through professional, labor, and commercial organizations while centering the Shanghai focus of New Life activities on the new town hall out at Jiangwan.[31] On April 17, eleven members of the Acceleration Association met in their offices off of Route Ghisi and resolved that local military, political, GMD, and other public organizations be notified to form branches and that Jiangwan or Wusong be made an experimental district where the New Life Movement could be uniformly implemented.[32] Two days later the local press reported that more and more citizens were joining these branches.[33]

The symbolic setting of this movement became the new civic center at Jiangwan. The town hall had been finished and inaugurated in October 1933, and shortly after that all of the municipal services, with the exception of the Bureaus of Finance, Public Utilities, and Public Security, moved from the old city to the new center. More construction was to come. On December 1, 1934, the first stones were simultaneously laid for the library and museum, and the ground was broken for the municipal stadium, gymnasium, and pool—all of which were barely finished in time for the sixth national All-China athletic meet in August 1935.[34] By July 10, 1937, the tenth anniversary of the foundation of the Greater Municipality of Shanghai, the new city center served as a perfect site for the commemoration of such a civic occasion. Thousands of persons made the trip out to Jiangwan to join in these celebrations, which were held just three days after the Marco Polo Bridge Incident led to war between China and Japan, and which thus inadvertently but ironically marked the end, rather than the beginning, of an era of urban development.[35] Neverthe-less, the Jiangwan civic center was not really ready in 1934 to accommo-date the New Life Movement in a grand and ceremonial way. The move-ment itself, most would agree, lacked spontaneity. A top-down affair, organized with the help of municipal bodies such as the police and the local party organization, it worked mainly through professional groups, educational institutions, and other organs open to GMD manipulation.[36]

Propaganda issued by the party branch of the Peace Preservation De-partment of the Special Municipality outlined the rationale for the New Life Movement. At present, it said, other countries regarded the Chinese people as "barbarians" (*yeman*), a "backward race" (*luohou minzu*) that lacked a scientific and civilized spirit. The failure to "nurture scientific personnel" (*peiyang kexue rencai*) occurred because the Chinese had paid insufficient attention to the basic spirit of their civilization. By contrast, the Japanese had been able to modernize their country during the Meiji Restoration by copying the West while simultaneously preserving their "Japanese soul" (*He hun*).

> Speaking bluntly, ever since the time of Zeng Guofan at the end of the Qing, we have been making an effort to nurture scientific tal-ent. For several decades now it has been like this. How is it that we are still unable to save the country? It is for no other reason than this: we have forgotten how to nurture talent, and we have lost our own [national] spirit (*jingshen*).[37]

As Chairman Chiang Kai-shek had demonstrated in "exterminating the Reds," only comprehensive solutions sufficed. Minds and material condi-tions had to be addressed simultaneously; the patient had to be treated as a whole. And that was why Chairman Chiang was promoting the New Life Movement.[38] The movement continued through May 1934, though it began to falter and become routinized toward the end of that month.[39] There were numerous New Life gatherings, but the impression one gleans from accounts of these meetings is that they were increasingly perfunc-tory and desultory.[40]

This is not to say that the New Life Movement ceased to be an im-portant phenomenon, as a party-led and police-run set of exercises, in the everyday life of Shanghai's urbanites. One has only to look through the

Ministry of Interior archives in Nanjing to discover how thoroughly and precisely the New Life Movement directives governed everything from the management of bean-curd shops to the size of public hat racks.[41] But while New Life rules thoroughly regulated public activities, they probably failed to penetrate very deeply into the individual's private political consciousness. On February 21–23, 1935, for example, when the Shanghai Peace Preservation Office (Baoan chu) wished to commemorate the first anniversary of Chiang Kai-shek's Nanchang announcement, the best that they could come up with was a "cleaning up" (*qingjie*) effort to sweep the streets and collect garbage.[42]

The more the general public remained ideologically indifferent to the New Life Movement, the more zealously it was promoted by such right-wing groups as the Blueshirts (Lanyishe). The core organization of these fanatically devoted followers of Chiang Kai-shek was the ultra-secret Society for Vigorous Practice (Lixingshe), founded in March 1932.[43] The two most important front groups created by the Lixingshe's core members (all former Huangpu Academy cadets) were the Renaissance Society (Fuxingshe) and the Chinese Culture Study Society (Zhongguo wenhua xueshe), formed in July 1932 and December 1933 respectively. Coordinating the activities of these groups around the New Life Movement was regarded as one of the Blueshirts' major responsibilities.[44]

If the Renaissance Society were successful, the New Life program would create "a new atmosphere" which would eradicate such "evil customs" as extravagance, greed, laziness, deception, treachery, gambling, lust, and all that "longing for leisure and abhorrence of labor" characteristic of the "feudal gentry." Under this new moral order, which would do away with waste and patronage, men and women "would revive our ever self-generating and self-renewing national spirit . . . to recover a confidence, lost since the Opium War, in the nation's ability to survive."[45]

National Revival and Fascism

The primary goal of the Chinese Culture Study Society (CCSS) was, correspondingly, to "renew life" by moving people's hearts and minds to common public purpose. The essence of this effort was a program of "militarization" (*junshihua*) that would be extended to the public at large through the mechanism of the New Life Movement Promotion Association. This association implemented many of the most controversial and intrusive measures of the New Life Movement, including restrictions on smoking, dancing, and the wearing of certain kinds of Western clothing.[46] The Blueshirts were consequently blamed by foreigners, and especially the American missionary community, for having subverted the original intent of the New Life experiment by turning it into a fascist-dominated movement.[47]

The Blueshirts were well established in Shanghai.[48] In January 1932, the "preparations department" (*choubeichu*) of the Lixingshe had begun to build up an organization there to control the student movement.[49] Two years later, according to Japanese reports, the Blueshirts held an executive committee meeting in Shanghai.[50] The meeting adopted a set of group principles, drew up a table of organization, and established membership rules and categories. The Japanese claimed that the Blueshirts' principles included the declaration that "fascism shall be adopted as a step toward the materialization of the dictatorship." In order "to materialize the new social order as well as a state based on fascism as soon as possible," the Blueshirts were to engage in intelligence, propaganda, and execution activities as the need arose.[51]

Meanwhile, Xiao Zuolin, the Secretary-General of the CCSS (nominally chaired by Chiang Kai-shek), was transferred from Nanchang to Shanghai in order to open a branch of the new society there with the help of Liu Bingli (the editor of *Future* [*Qiantu*]), Ni Wenya, and other local Blueshirts.[52] According to Xiao Zuolin himself, the organization of the CCSS coincided with the "high tide" of the Renaissance Society's "fascist propaganda movement," when the Blueshirts attracted the most followers and exerted the greatest influence on public opinion in Shanghai.[53] After opening up a bookstore and publishing house at 50 Huanlong Road, the CCSS began issuing a regular bulletin, along with collections of titles on youth (*Qingnian congshu*), military affairs (*Junshi congshu*), democracy (*Minzhu congshu*), and so forth. The society also published a number of works in translation through the central headquarters of the society under Wu Shoupeng in Nanchang.[54]

Xiao Zuolin, meanwhile, moved the editorial offices of *Youth and War* (*Qingnian yu zhanzheng*) to Shanghai, along with the "official" newspaper of the Fuxingshe: *The Chinese Revolution*. The Chinese Culture Study Society supported as well an arts monthly, *Chinese Literature* (*Zhongguo wenxue*), and a literary magazine called *Cultural Intelligence* (*Wenhua qingbao*).[55]

The Renaissance Society hoped to use the Chinese Culture Study Society to launch a "cultural movement" (*wenhua yundong*) that would give Blueshirt intellectuals an opportunity to lead a national revival movement by exercising control over the reading public's thought and behavior. The program was vaguely put forth in the form of a special issue of the Fuxingshe's monthly, *Future*, to which Wu Tiechang, Liu Bingli, He Zhong-han, and so forth, contributed essays with titles like "Cultural Control (*wenhua tongzhi*) in Chinese History" and "Controlling Culture in Order to Lead to a Plan for Salvation from Extermination."[56] Common to all of these essays was the simple notion of *tongzhi*, a vague sense that the Fuxingshe ought to somehow gain control over the intellectual life of the country, as well as the much more particular notion that the Blueshirts should take charge of a new thought movement in the major cultural center of China at the time, Shanghai proper.[57]

That some of these ideas were shared with the leaders of the Public Security Bureau came as no surprise: the use of common terms and a shared rhetoric strongly suggest that high police officials were either Blueshirts themselves or steeped in this literature of cultural control and moral revival.[58]

Chen Guofu, Chen Lifu, and members of their "CC" clique were well aware of this challenge to their own political prerogatives and prepared to respond to it. Just as soon as the Chinese Culture Study Society was founded by the Renaissance Society, members of the "CC" clique formed a Chinese Cultural Construction Association (Zhongguo wenhua jianshe xiehui). When Xiao Zuolin came to Shanghai in 1934 to establish a Chinese Culture Study Society branch there, he was followed almost immediately by Chen Lifu, who set up headquarters at 45 Rue Victor Immanuel III for a Shanghai section of the Chinese Cultural Construction Association, with the intention of competing with Xiao Zuolin's group to win over "distinguished scholars" (*mingliu xuezhe*) in literary and cultural circles.[59] The "CC" clique also established a "special body" whose duty it was "to investigate the political inclinations of Chinese literati."[60] The "special body" later came to include among its members Wang Xingming, the editor of *Chenbao* (*Shanghai Morning Post*); He Bingsong, chairman of the editorial committee of the Commercial Press; Wu Yugan, Professor of Political Science at the Central University in Nanjing; Sun Hanbing, Dean of Law at Fudan University; Huang Wenshan, Dean of Social Sciences at the Central University; Tao Xisheng, Professor of Journalism at Beiping University; Zhang Yi, Dean of Education at Fudan; Chen Gaoyang, Professor of Law at Ji'nan University; Fan Zhongyun, editor of *Wenhua jianshe yuekan* (*Cultural Construction Monthly*); and Sa Mengwu, Professor of Political Science at the Central University.[61]

The formation of a rival cultural society by the "CC" clique posed a particularly awkward problem for Mayor Wu Tiecheng and the university presidents who had already joined the preparatory committee for the Renaissance Society. They and a number of more prominent professors promptly took the safest course and joined both societies. However, the

Blueshirts' Chinese Culture Study Society turned out to be much more adept at arousing support in Shanghai among university students, especially those at the large specialized schools.[62] At Ji'nan University, for example, the Blueshirts were able to capture the allegiance of a majority of student activists, and because the CCSS cadres were mainly former military students themselves, they were able to organize and discipline their supporters more effectively.[63] When the "CC" clique supporters attempted to fight back, open warfare erupted: the CCSS cadres simply arrested and locked up the Chinese Cultural Construction Association members on the campus, to the dismay of Wu Xingya and Pan Gongzhan, the chiefs of the party's Social Affairs Bureau and Education Bureau.[64] It was only after Mayor Wu Tiecheng interceded and brought the Fuxingshe members to the negotiating table that the imprisoned students were set free.[65]

The Shanghai Blueshirts were also better at organizing support among police and military elements there and in nearby cities, including Hangzhou, where they established a branch of the Chinese Culture Study Society shortly after the Shanghai group was formed, and where the Cultural Vanguard Brigade (Wenhua qianwei dui) was also set up with students from Zhejiang University and other local schools.[66]

Even though the "CC" clique could not compete successfully against the Blueshirts when it came to organizing student support through these cultural front organizations and through the rank-and-file of the Nationalists' expanding police system, the Chen brothers could resort to Chiang Kai-shek's own plan for assigning intellectual work to themselves while restricting the Blueshirts and their various affiliates to military indoctrination and surveillance. Stymied at the level of mass organization, Chen Lifu therefore went to the very top and persuaded Chiang to issue orders dissolving the Chinese Culture Study Society around June 1934, just at the very time that the New Life Movement was burgeoning in Shanghai under the official auspices of the Shanghai Public Security Bureau.[67]

Nonetheless, the Blueshirts continued in various covert and overt ways to impose New Life standards upon public culture in Shanghai. The Blueshirts had been actively engaged in attacking left-wing movie productions since the previous year. The founder of Lianhua—one of the two major film companies of the 1930s—had close ties with the Blueshirts and managed to keep the League of Left-Wing Writers' Film Group from dominating the studio until 1936.[68] The Yihua Film Company, which was dominated by underground CCP members, was raided in 1933 by a group that called itself the Society for the Eradication of Communists in the

Film Industry (Yingjie chanchu gong tongzhi hui), which was really a creation of the Blueshirts. In addition to attacking that particular studio and establishing a film company of their own (Xinhua), the Blueshirts also issued a warning that the Society for the Eradication of Communists in the Film Industry would "cleanse the cultural world" of makers of leftist films.[69] These bully-boy tactics went hand-in-hand with the work of the Guomindang censors, who rejected eighty-three film scripts and closed fourteen film studios between 1934 and 1935.[70]

The Left fought back as best it could. Censors were bribed, pseudonyms were used, and "pigeon films" were made to draw the censors' fire on purpose so that one's key line of protest in a serious film would get through. Xia Yan conducted the greatest leftist coup in the cinema world when he got the support of Chiang Kai-shek and Madame Chiang for a film released at the beginning of the New Life Movement. Chiang was so pleased by the "Morals of Women" that he had special funds directed to Xia Yan's studio, thereby unintentionally sponsoring that entire circle of left-wing directors.[71] Meantime, filmmakers also had to cope with the censors of the International Settlement and French Concession who had sway over seventeen and eight cinemas respectively. In 1937—a year for which we have reliable figures—the SMP and French police censored 451 feature films, 932 shorts, and 269 newsreels. One hundred thirty-two films were approved after objectionable parts were deleted.[72] Nevertheless, thanks to directorial ingenuity and the intricacies of censorial politics, many trenchantly critical films did appear. Xia Yan's *Street Angel* played in Shanghai in July 1937, just a month before the Japanese invasion.[73]

Attacks on movies formed, of course, part of a larger effort at censorship that deeply affected the cultural life of Shanghai's Chinese residents, who constituted a newspaper-reading population of about 300,000 people.[74] In February 1934 the Guomindang banned 149 books in Shanghai and forbade the circulation of seventy-six magazines including *The Dipper* and *Literature Monthly*.[75] During that year there were 2,709 Public Security Bureau cases forbidding "reactionary works," and more than twenty-five bookstores were threatened with closure because they sold the works of Lu Xun, Guo Moruo, Mao Dun, and Ba Jin.[76] In June 1934, just after the New Life Movement began to wind down, a law made it compulsory for publishers to submit all manuscripts for books and magazines to a special committee for inspection before they could be printed.[77] The main targets of Chinese Nationalist censorship were Communist and a much vaguer category of "National Salvation" publications.[78] The Public Security Bureau frequently requested the International Settlement police's aid in seizing such materials, but the SMP itself needed no special urging to ferret out Communist propagandists.[79]

Acting on warrants issued by the Chinese Special District Court on July 22, 1935, the SMP participated enthusiastically in a number of raids carried out against various offices of the Communist Party. Although most of the twenty-four persons arrested denied being members of the CCP, saying that they had only recently arrived in Shanghai, the seizure of "communistic literature and documents" led the International Settlement police to request of their own volition that the Second Branch of the Jiangsu High Court detain and try the prisoners on suspicion of being Communist Party members.[80]

There was thus no hesitation on the part of the International Settlement police when it came to joint SMP-PSB operations against suspected Communists.[81] Raids to seize "reactionary literature" in general, and "National Salvation" materials in particular, were pursued less enthusiastically. On April 2, 1937, Special Branch officers, accompanied by representatives from the PSB and the Chinese Bureau of Social Affairs and carrying search warrants issued by the Special District Court, raided three bookstores in the International Settlement. The only materials to be found were publications of the National Salvation Federation, such as *Guonan xinwen* (*National Crisis News*) which was directed toward the incipient conflict with Japan. The British eventually decided to send the National Salvation materials to Guomindang headquarters for examination, but no arrests were made and at least one of the warrants was returned to the Chinese unused.[82]

Annei Rangwai

The International Settlement authorities were reluctant to persecute "National Salvation" patriots because the line between patriotism and radicalism became increasingly blurred as the Imperial Japanese armies expanded into North China and as the Nanjing régime stolidly stuck to its determination to first *annei* (subjugate the internal enemy, the Communists) before *rangwai* (expelling the external enemy, the Japanese).[83] Gradually the New Life Movement paled beside this much more striking national issue, especially after the December Ninth Movement erupted in 1935. The devastating public outrage in November of the following year, when Chinese police arrested seven "National Salvationist" leaders, including journalist Zou Taofen, demonstrated how fervently most Shanghainese were opposed to the régime's *annei rangwai* policy.[84] The Nationalist authorities in Shanghai were hard put to find alternatives to the patriotic demonstrations and publications that increasingly called upon the Chiang régime to put aside its fight against the Communists and concentrate upon the struggle with Japan.[85]

One set of alternatives consisted of government- or party-organized counter-holidays to reinforce the régime's own vision of the new municipal civic order. For example, the Shanghai branch of the Guomindang notified various public bodies on May 3, 1936, that

> May 5 being the anniversary of the inauguration of our revolutionary government, the local party branch will convene a meeting of representatives of various circles at its auditorium at 10:00 A.M. to celebrate the occasion. All government organs, public bodies, schools, and the various grades of the party branch are hereby requested to detail three representatives each to participate in the function. The national flag should be hoisted, and separate meetings should also take place to celebrate the anniversary.[86]

The orchestration of this and other ceremonial gatherings was conducted by the Wusong-Shanghai Garrison Command, which had convened a meeting in late April 1936 of officials from the Public Security Bureau, the Peace Preservation Corps, and the Merchants Volunteer Corps "with a view to maintaining peace and order in the districts in the month of May which is fast approaching."[87] Their extra precaution proved effective: no major disturbances of the peace marred that revolutionary month. Yet the officially managed ceremonies that did take place, such as the gathering of pupils and teachers from the May 30th School at the martyrs' tomb where Guomindang leader Wang Xiaolai offered sacrifices, seemed lackluster and formulaic. The régime could muster participants, but it seemed unable to stir their hearts.[88]

The Xi'an Incident, when Chiang Kai-shek was kidnapped by supporters of a united front with the Communists against the Japanese, changed this apathy virtually overnight.[89] After Chiang Kai-shek was released on Christmas Day, 1936, there was an enormous and unmistakably spontaneous surge of public support for the Generalissimo. In Shanghai a number of local business and professional organizations asked for permission to hold a meeting in the Chamber of Commerce on December 26. This would have been on the same scale and along the same lines as the New Life efforts two years earlier. The Guomindang branch office realized how different this occasion was, however, and party leader Wu Kaixian refused them permission, deciding instead to hold a mass meeting on December 28 at the public recreation grounds.[90] The following morning a caucus of twenty representatives of local public bodies was held in the GMD headquarters in South Market to discuss preparations for the mass meeting. All local schools were told by the Bureau of Social Affairs to give their students a holiday on the afternoon of December 28. Members of local organizations and university students were instructed to be prepared to attend the mass meeting each carrying a small national flag. And while other mass meetings were called for Jiangwan, Wusong, and Pudong, the PSB and the Merchants Volunteer Corps were charged with maintaining peace and order at all these civic gatherings.[91]

The mammoth meeting held at the public recreation grounds near St. Catherine's Bridge at 2:15 P.M. on December 28, 1936, was attended by up to 150,000 people.[92] The crowd opened by singing the Guomindang anthem to music played by military bands, followed by bows of respect to the national and party flags and to the portrait of Sun Yat-sen. After three minutes' silence in honor of the comrades killed in the Xi'an Incident, Dr. Sun's will was read aloud and members of the presidium made a report to the audience, Wu Kaixian gave an oration, and short speeches were delivered by representatives of local public bodies. The crowd passed a resolution to send a telegram to General Chiang, welcoming him back to Nanjing and hailing him "as the sole national leader of China in view of his great personality and the meritorious service he had rendered to the country." The meeting was adjourned at 2:45 P.M., and "the enormous crowd afterwards formed a long procession, shouting slogans and marching to the accompaniment of drums and band music and holding up traffic on all thoroughfares for several hours." The *Shanghai Times* called it "one of the biggest and most colorful parades ever staged in recent years in Shanghai," and described how the procession, led by the bands of the PSB and Shanghai-Wusong Garrison force, wound its way for nearly four hours to the West Gate of South Market while two airplanes chartered by the China Aviation Club scattered colored paper slips with pro-Chiang slogans along the way.[93]

The December 1936 rally celebrating Chiang's release from captivity in Xi'an was one of the most successful examples of a party-led and municipally planned counterprocession ever held in Shanghai. Like the radical political assemblies it was intended to displace or rival, the Xi'an rally and parade showed how political mobilization could create a certain sense of civic culture.[94] When we compare the rally in particular to urban activities of any sort in Chinese cities before the fall of the imperial system, we realize how different this new civic culture was from the liturgical ceremonies and religious festivals of nineteenth-century market towns and cities.[95] The robustness of Republican China's urban public culture was, however, questionable—at least when it came to Shanghai. There, civic culture fundamentally rested on two self-opposed axes. First, the city authorities' wish to nurture the people's *lizhi* (strength to govern themselves) contested with the municipal administration's impulse to mold subjects rather than citizens. Second, the city government's need for spontaneous participation and support in patriotic rallies conflicted with its appetite for order (*zhixu*) and control (*zhi'an*).[96]

14   Nationalizing the Police and Making Criminality Respectable

The police must understand that their position in the country
is more important than that of the army. The army is only
used against the outside to protect the country internationally.
The police are used within the country to maintain social order
and to protect the people's lives and property. Otherwise,
social order would not be maintained, the people's lives and
properties would not be protected, and the country would then
become chaotic.

Chiang Kai-shek, 1936

Two distinct developments intersected in Shanghai during the 1930s. The first resulted from Chiang Kai-shek's efforts to nationalize the police, which led to a series of complex innovations shaped by national desires and local realities. The second, more strictly localized, emerged from the efforts by Shanghai racketeers to become respectable, and to be integrated into bourgeois society. The convergence of these two created a new set of circumstances in Shanghai which made it difficult to distinguish between policing and criminality, between patriotism and terrorism.

In 1928 the Nationalist régime had taken the first step in what was to be a nine-year effort to create a unified national police system. A national commission of police experts had been established, consisting of four capital officials and eight provincial officials under the chairmanship of the director of the Department of Police Administration in the Ministry of the Interior.[1] The following year regulations were promulgated calling for the uniform education of all police officials and recruits; and police academies were established in Zhejiang, Jiangsu, Shanxi, Guangdong, Jiangxi, Hubei, Shaanxi, Shandong, Yunnan, Hebei, Gansu, Zhahar, Qinghai, Fujian, and Guangxi. At the same time the central government decreed that local militia throughout China should be put under official county or municipal authorities who reported directly to the Ministry of Interior, and the central leadership of the Guomindang ordered the Ministry of the Interior to take over direct administration of the Capital Police Department in Nanjing.[2] In January 1931 the Ministry of Interior convened in Nanjing the First National Conference on Internal Affairs (Diyici quanguo neizheng huiyi) to discuss police administration. This was followed in December 1932 by a second conference, consisting of more than one hundred delegates from various cities and provinces who made proposals for the countrywide introduction of pension systems for police, the use of new weapons, the hiring of policewomen, and the unification of the fingerprint system.[3]

Of all the provincial police academies established by the Nationalist régime, the Zhejiang Police Academy was considered the best. It had been founded by Zhu Jiahua, administrative director of Zhongshan University in Guangzhou who in 1927 was named chief of internal affairs for the newly liberated province of Zhejiang.[4] By 1934 the academy was a model of its kind in Chiang Kai-shek's eyes.[5] Run along military lines, it had several foreign-trained police experts (including August Vollmer's students from Berkeley, Feng Yukun and Frank Yee), who added forensic science courses to the school curriculum along with the latest police training methods from abroad.[6] In September 1934 the Nanjing National Police College and the Central Military Academy were amalgamated into a single institution, leaving the Zhejiang Academy as the primary "national police institute in the field" to draw students from all over the country, including sergeants from a number of local police forces chosen after a battery of physical and mental examinations such as the U.S. Army Alpha test.[7]

Local Control and a National Police System

The following year Chiang Kai-shek decided to merge the Zhejiang Police Academy with the Jiangsu Police Academy to form a new Central Police Academy (Zhongyang jingguan xuexiao) in Nanjing. Chiang's decision to create a central police training institute apart from the military stemmed from his wider vision as a state builder of a countrywide police system that would integrate other systems of local control and stand alongside the army as one of the two critical buttresses of his régime.[8]

In May 1936 Chiang summoned a special Conference of Higher Local Administrative Officials (Difang gaoji xingzheng renyuan huiyi) to discuss local police and security problems.[9] The meeting took place within the context of a long-standing debate between officials from the central government and provincial leaders over the retention of the Peace Preservation Corps (Baoandui or Baoantuan).[10] Provincial officials naturally favored preserving local militia that they themselves funded and controlled. Huang Shaohuang, the governor of Zhejiang, went so far as to propose that the police forces be abolished altogether and their funds transferred to the *baojia* and militia system.[11] Representatives of the central government opposed the Baoandui and argued for the creation of regular police departments that would be directed and trained by the new Nationalist government, albeit financed with local resources. After hearing both sides of the argument, Chiang Kai-shek came down on the side of police nationalization.[12]

The Executive Yuan duly approved a proposal that required the provinces to submit plans for police reform according to principles worked out by the Department of Police Administration, which was placed under the direction of Vollmer's student, Feng Yukun.[13] The latter proclaimed that as of the end of 1936 the peace preservation corps would be abolished and over three years their duties would gradually be taken over by the regular police. As each *baoandui* was dissolved, its budget and arsenal were to be transferred to the county police departments, which would be made as consistent as possible in salary, ranks, and training. In order to improve the quality of these local police forces, the Department of Police Administration planned to put all recruits through training courses in the provincial capitals and cities, while all higher-ranking police officials would receive educations in the new Central Police Academy. This would also, needless to say, be a further step toward the national integration of public security forces.[14]

The most important item in the new local police regulations of July 25, 1936, was Article 8, which ordered each *xian* (district) to set up a police *ju* (bureau) apart from the regular local government and the former *baoantuan*. This bureau required permission from the provincial government regarding all important police matters, yet at the same time it was supposed to answer to the local magistrate, who had his own separate "police assistant" (*jingzuo*).[15] Although that created a problem of divided authority within the regular administrative system, the new police bureau structure was an important preliminary step toward effectively integrating local police forces into the central government's regular chain of command.[16]

But it was still only a preliminary master plan, and the gap between Chiang Kai-shek's vision of a vertically integrated, nationally centralized police system and the weakly linked or informally arranged district police forces was simply too wide. In reality, rural police stations (*suo*) were often indistinguishable from the guards office (*jingweigu*) of a local *bao* (mutual responsibility unit) leader, and the magistrate's police assistant more often than not turned out to be an informal and personal aide (*muliao*) like the "tent-friends" (*muyou*) of Zeng Guofan's time.[17]

The urban police forces in areas under direct Nationalist control were much closer to Chiang Kai-shek's ideal, but they were still not part of a centralized national system. There were no unified police administrative regulations, no common set of patrol systems, no mutual communication protocols. Top police officials, meeting in Nanjing after Chiang's decision to support the national police over the provincial militia, agreed that with the exception of the capital police force, all other police forces had fallen under the control of local administrative organs. Consequently, the assembled police luminaries decided that the best they could do for the moment to help bring about national "unity" (*tongyi*) would be to organize a Chinese Police Joint Advancement Association (Zhongguo jingcha xiejinhui).[18] This association, renamed the Chinese Police Study Society (Zhongguo jingcha xuehui) in June 1937, would at least serve to keep police officers in closer touch, help standardize procedures, and maintain uniform professional standards.[19]

The Impact on Shanghai

Nanjing's formal efforts to centralize national police administration during 1935–37 had a modest but discernible effect on the operations of the Shanghai Public Security Bureau. When the Ministry of Interior ordered that local district police offices (*qusuo*) be changed into direct branches (*fenju*) of central headquarters, the PSB duly changed nomenclature and added individual street "police units" (*jingcha suo*) that left the recently renovated police-box system intact.[20] At the same time, and directly under General Cai Jingjun's instruction, the new *fenju* were brought into a more centralized chain of command. Before 1935, all police matters in the northern precincts at Xinzha station, North Station, and the city centers at Jiangwan, Wusong, and Zhenru were sent to a special *fenke* (branch post) set up in Zhabei at North Chang'an Road. That *fenke*, which had its own arsenal and holding cells, functioned as a kind of secondary headquarters for the northern sector of the Special Municipality. As of May 9, 1935, at Chief Cai's order, all cases involving violations more serious than the infringement of police regulations were routed to the new central police headquarters in what had formerly been the Shanghai district (*xian*) yamen, and the *fenke* was stripped of equipment and closed.[21]

Centralization of the chain of command within Shanghai not only suited General Cai's military habits; it also coincided with an increasing militarization of police activities, starting early in 1936. This partly increased the force's quasi-military capacity to deal with critical events such as civil commotions (a task which the PSB perhaps performed better than it did ordinary law enforcement), and partly prepared for wartime conditions.[22] In January the PSB began training anti-aircraft cadres in aircraft intelligence, communications, fire control, camouflage, and the firing of anti-aircraft weapons.[23] The following month further measures were taken to prepare for national defense readiness on the part of the police, including telecommunications training.[24] At the same time, the Nanjing government secretly ordered Mayor Wu to continue to construct a clandestine perimeter of pillboxes disguised as houses and temples around the city from Wusong in the North all the way to Longhua in the South.[25] The central government also agreed to provide the Public Security Bureau with Ch. $113,732 to acquire an armored river patrol boat and twelve armored six-wheel trucks.[26]

Meanwhile, the police and military forces of Shanghai came to occupy an ever more central role in the city's urban ceremonies. For example, in the centerfold pages of the special press supplement celebrating the tenth anniversary of the Special Municipality, only one of the fourteen photographs failed to feature a review of police, paramilitary, or military units. As Mayor Wu Tiecheng is sent off on April 10, 1937 to become chairman of the Guangdong provisional government, two pictures illustrate him being greeted by foreign and Chinese SMP units and by the Shanghai Volunteer Corps. Mayor Wu is photographed reviewing the French troops and military band, as well as the Chinese South Market PSB and Peace Preservation Corps. Seven shots show the Shanghai Volunteer Corps' annual parade, with kilted Scotsmen, light horse troops, and mobile machine gun units. There is even a picture of the arrival on April 12 of Giuliano Cora, the new Italian ambassador, greeted by a Fascist guard of honor.[27]

General Cai's penchant for "militarization" (*junshihua*) extended to his own detective squad, which was more or less unwittingly brought into the central government's military intelligence system by spymaster Dai Li. Cai's predecessor as chief of police, Wen Hongen, and his chief of detectives, Lu Ying, had been reluctant to cooperate with Dai Li and the Shanghai Station of the Military Statistics Bureau (Juntong) in 1933.[28] Dai Li was therefore forced to ask his Shanghai Station Group One leader, Chen Zhiqiang, to use his Green Gang connections to link up the military secret service with individual detectives on the PSB detective squad.[29]

Group One, which was also known as the South Market Group (Nanshizu), was located directly in South Market on Penglai Street, and its main responsibility consisted in looking after affairs in the old Chinese city proper. Chen Zhiqiang used his racketeering connections to carry out special service activities and employed his police and government *guanxi* to protect fellow gang members who had gotten into trouble because of their involvement in the narcotics traffic. Through the gang linkage, Chen Zhiqiang was especially well connected with the French Concession Police. His highest-level contact was Fan Guangzhen, chief of the Chinese detective squad, who had been introduced to Dai Li by Du Yuesheng. Fan professed to cooperate with Juntong and was a source of valuable intelligence; but as Dai Li saw it, Fan was more devoted to the French colonial authorities than he was to the Chinese secret police. If Fan were put under too much pressure, then he might feel forced to sacrifice his Chinese relationships in order to maintain his bread-and-butter ties to his foreign employers. Therefore, Dai Li's men only had recourse to Fan when it was absolutely necessary: asking him for an occasional lead into the underworld, and requesting cover and help whenever the Shanghai Station carried out a kidnapping in the French Concession.[30]

Because of Fan Guangzhen's unreliability, Dai Li believed that it was necessary to introduce someone he could really trust into the ranks of the Chinese detectives division of the French police. Dai turned to a Whampoa classmate, Ruan Zhaohui, whose first assignment had been as a communications officer in the Nanjing headquarters of the military secret service. Offering Fan Guangzhen $500 as a bribe, Dai Li managed to get Ruan an appointment as a regular detective. As a result, Chen Zhiqiang and other leaders of Juntong's Shanghai Station secured routine access to intelligence about suspected Communists who had sought safety in the shelter of the French Concession, and they used Ruan to protect Juntong agents who were vulnerable to arrest on charges of abduction or assassination.[31]

Chen Zhiquiang also had close personal connections with members of the Chinese police, including several precinct chiefs (*fenjuzhang*) and the head of the chief detective brigade (*zhenji zongdui*) at PSB headquarters.[32] As long as Wen Hongen was director of public security, however, there had been no opportunity for the Nationalists' military secret service to acquire formal connections with the PSB. General Cai Jingjun, however, proved more willing to cooperate with Dai Li and the Military Statistics Bureau. Gradually, he allowed Juntong agents to assume positions in the police training unit (*jingshi jiaoxun suo*); and eventually Dai Li had his agent Chen Zhiquiang named chief of indoctrination in the PSB while two other secret service officers were made the leading political instructors (*zhidaoyuan*) in the Shanghai Police Academy.[33]

Until 1935, nonetheless, Juntong lacked direct police authority anywhere in the Shanghai area, and if the secret service wished to arrest and interrogate a suspect, that person had to be illegally kidnapped and secretly transported to Nanjing. This fundamental weakness in the Nationalists' secret service operation in Shanghai was not remedied until Chiang Kai-shek authorized Juntong to take discreet control of two major law enforcement groups: the Shanghai Military Police detectives division and the Shanghai transport police.[34]

Creating a Secret Police

Early in 1935, General Chiang granted Dai Li personal authority over the main detective brigade of the Songhu Garrison Command (Songhu jingbei silingbu zhencha dadui). Wu Naixian—chief of Juntong's Shanghai Station—was named commander (*daduizhang*) of the entire division, which was housed in the Baiyunguan on Fangxie Road in South Market.[35] In principle, all of the military detectives in the Shanghai area were now subject to Juntong's commands. In practice, however, Station Chief Wu simply took charge of the detective brigade at the very top. In order to attain operational authority, the secret service commander needed to control the intermediate sections of the brigade by placing his own secret agents in the posts of detective superintendents (*ducha*). This occurred when Wu Naixian was succeeded as detective brigade commander by Weng Guanghui.[36] Weng had been Juntong's first Shanghai Station chief in 1932 until being disgraced for having tried to transmit a piece of valuable intelligence to Chiang Kai-shek without first going through Dai Li himself.[37] Now back in favor, Weng Guanghui brought with him four top Juntong agents to be appointed *ducha:* Shen Zui, Cheng Muyi, Lin Zhijiang, and Ni Yuanchao. But that was still insufficient. The new inspectors quickly encountered two impediments to their plans to turn the Garrison Command's detective squad into a political and paramilitary secret police unit: the recalcitrance of the deputy brigade commander, and the reluctance of the regular detectives already on the roster.[38]

Solving the first problem entailed squeezing out the deputy commander and replacing him.[39] The regular inspectors (*jichayuan*)—the old-timers in the military police—posed another sort of problem. In their outlook and training they were mainly devoted to maintaining local law and order (*zhixu*). It was offensive to them to think of turning the detective brigade into an instrument of terror and coercion that used its powers of arrest as a substitute for illicit kidnapping, and transformed acceptable interrogation procedures into techniques of torture. Their own crime detection suffered as a result, but when Shen Zui reported that they needed to pay more attention to solving felonies, Dai Li said offhandedly: "Do you think we took control over this organization just to nab petty crooks and pickpockets on behalf of others?"[40]

Yet the regular inspectors could not be readily dismissed nor replaced. Many of them had developed close working relationships with detectives in the French Concession Police and the Shanghai Municipal Police. This made arresting suspects in the International Settlement a lot easier for Juntong, while it also made the Shanghai Station agents leery of arousing the suspicions and hostilities of the foreign concessions' police by suddenly getting rid of old friends and acquaintances in the military police.

The decision was taken therefore to proceed very slowly in culling the detective brigade ranks and to try whenever possible to get former military detectives to allow themselves to be co-opted into the Shanghai Station. Gradually, then, after Wang Zhaohuai took over the brigade, a dozen or so new inspectors were brought in from regular secret service ranks, and a number of important *jichayuan* of the former brigade, such as Zhu Youxin and Wang Kaiming, were enrolled as full-fledged members of Juntong. As its ranks were infiltrated and misgivings allayed, the military detectives division was transmogrified into a true secret police, functioning as an outer service organ for the Shanghai district headquarters of Juntong. Whenever the Shanghai Station wanted to transform a kidnapping into an arrest, the military police's detective brigade simply requested the Garrison Command to sign an arrest order. The latter invariably complied. Now, the umbrella of authority protected licit and illicit alike.

Occasionally, when there were cases of gross injustice, the secret police turned to the Martial Law Department (Junfa chu) or military court of the Garrison Command for public support. The chief of that department was Lu Jingshi, a disciple of Du Yuesheng who was very close to Wang Zhaohuai, the head of the detective division. If the secret police felt that they had to release a prisoner, beaten nearly to death while under arrest, they would ask the Martial Law Department to take over. Lu Jingshi complied happily, although his lieutenants grumbled constantly, complaining that they were forced to act as a front for the Shanghai Station's secret police. Nevertheless, Dai Li's men thereby came to possess full and unimpeachable powers of arrest, which actually superseded the authority of the Shanghai Municipal Public Safety Bureau, and which gave them carte blanche to turn the Shanghai Station into the fearsome Leviathan that Juntong was rapidly becoming in areas directly under Nanjing's control. Political criminals could now be incarcerated and tortured with complete impunity on the spot.[41]

Expansion of the Shanghai Station

Dai Li took over the transport police in Shanghai the same way that he had taken over the Garrison Command's detectives: in the autumn of 1935 he had Wu Naixian appointed head of the Nanjing-Shanghai-Hangzhou Railroad Police (Jing-Hu-Hang tielu jingcha). This was a major administrative job, and it meant turning over Wu's responsibilities as the military police detective brigade commander to Weng Guanghui and as

Shanghai Station chief to Wang Xinheng.[42] Shortly after that, the police inspectors' office of the China Steam Merchants Navigation Company was also turned over to Dai Li's men, who staffed leading posts directly from Nanjing. Henceforth, Juntong agents traveled free of charge on the railway and on steamboats, and whenever prisoners of the secret service had to be transported from Shanghai to the capital, the Shanghai Station agents had the complete support and aid of the railway police, with special compartments in the sleeping cars turned over to them for clandestine use.[43]

The acquisition of the detective brigade and the staffing of the transport police vastly increased the responsibilities and duties of Juntong's Shanghai Station, which flourished under the direction of its energetic new chief, Wang Xinheng. A former Communist who had studied at Sun Yat-sen University in Moscow, Wang was a native of Ningbo who had many contacts among merchants from that city in Shanghai.[44] Also well connected with the Shanghai underworld, he formed a close friendship with Du Yuesheng and was a warmly welcomed guest of the Hengshe (Constancy Club), organized by the Green Gang. Thanks to these links, Wang attracted a much broader membership to the secret service, enlisting agents among students who had been in the USSR, merchants, working-class leaders, gangsters, members of the Shanghai Postal General Union, writers and entertainers, and so forth. New clandestine district offices were opened in Hongkou, Zhabei, and southern Shanghai (Hunan). A dozen or so individual stations (*zhan*) were attached to military investigation groups (*diaocha zu*). A large wireless broadcasting station was established to form a central communications network. Altogether, the personnel of the Shanghai Station increased five-fold, from one hundred to five hundred members working full time at headquarters or in the field.[45]

Dai Li's appointment of a Communist "renegade" or *pantu* like Wang Xinheng to direct the Shanghai regional office of the Military Statistics Bureau reflected the secret service chief's belief that no one was better equipped to deal with the underground than a former CCP member. In that respect, Wang was just one among many Communist Party defectors such as Liang Ganqiao, Xie Ligong, Ye Daoxin, Lu Haifang, and Cheng Yiming, who became senior Juntong agents in the 1930s.[46] This contrasted sharply with the practice at the party's Special Services Department (Zhongtong or Central Statistics Bureau)—where Chen Lifu's emphasis on ideological adherence to the Three Principles of the People prevailed—of using Communists only as advisers and not giving them field commands. Thus, former Red Brigade leader Gu Shunzhang had no real political position within Zhongtong; he had no men at his command.[47] Over time this proved intensely frustrating to Gu, who became restless and disappointed.[48]

Perhaps because Juntong was more likely than Zhongtong to give him a field assignment, Gu Shunzhang secretly offered Dai Li his services. Among other assets, he offered to divulge to the military secret service chief all that he had learned from the Russians about special operations.[49] Former Juntong officers believe that his information was so valuable to Dai Li that it may have cost Gu his life. Not long after joining Juntong as the top Communist "renegade," Gu Shunzhang was killed. Juntong lore has it that Gu Shunzhang was dispatched by Chen Lifu, who had never forgiven the defector for offering his talents to Dai Li and who wanted to keep the other spymaster from milking the Communist's secrets.[50]

This has been denied by Chen Lifu, who suggested to the author that Gu Shunzhang had to be dispatched because he was a pathological killer.[51] The true story, which was uncovered in the Bureau of Investigation Archives at Xindian (Hsin-tien) recently, is that Chen Lifu found out about the defector's plans to work for "another special services organization" and "exposed Gu Shunzhang's tricky plot." Doubly frustrated, Gu decided, in the spring of 1936, to get secretly in touch with the Communist Party.[52]

Soon afterward, Zhongtong agents raided a Communist safe house in Shanghai. The documents they routinely seized contained evidence that a high-level agent, probably a defector, within Zhongtong was passing secrets to the Communists. Gu Shunzhang was suspected of being the traitor, but Zhongtong chief Xu Enzeng insisted that Gu be left alone because the evidence was scanty, and because the other fifty to sixty ex-Communist defectors in Zhongtong looked to Gu as a bellwether. More incriminating evidence was supplied by a newly captured Communist, and Xu Enzeng privately warned Gu Shunzhang to change his ways, but the former Red Brigade leader was not arrested.[53]

Finally, however, a defector in his twenties named Lin Jinsheng—a former Communist agent who had been trained by Gu Shunzhang himself—reported to Xu Enzeng that Gu was planning to assassinate the "person responsible for special services work" and then flee to what remained of the Soviets in the mountains of Jiangxi. The "responsible person" (*fu-zeren de*) was, of course, Chen Lifu, who promptly called a meeting of his senior agents and advisers, including Gu Shunzhang. The meeting was ostensibly designed to present work reports. When it was the turn of Guo Deji, who had supervised the exhumation of the corpses of Gu Shunzhang's family, the secret service officer suddenly stood up and demanded that Gu express his frank attitude toward his comrades in Zhongtong. Gu Shunzhang colored and made a violent gesture toward Guo Deji, who drew his service pistol and tossed it on the table between them. "Do you dare to touch it?" he challenged. Guo Deji then ordered Lin Jinsheng to the front of the room and there, in front of Gu Shunzhang, the young ex-Communist told of the assassination plot. Gu's defiance utterly slumped, and in a shrunken, defeated tone of voice he confessed his guilt. It only remained for the "responsible person," Chen Lifu, to report the treachery to "the highest authority" (*zui gao dangju*), Chiang Kai-shek, and then to hand Gu Shunzhang over to the Jiangsu Peace Preservation Garrison Command (Baoan silingbu) for secret execution by firing squad.[54]

Criminal Respectability

Throughout the complex fabric of these events, linking the public security authorities with the secret police of Dai Li and Chen Lifu, ran a single reappearing strand. A thread here, a string there, a cord at the points of strongest attachment, this strand was the criminal connection woven principally by Du Yuesheng.

In this respect, two different processes distinguished 1932–37 from the previous five years of Nationalist rule in Shanghai. The first was the melding of the "respectable" gentry with the racketeering element which developed amidst the bureaucratization of the city's financial elite as politics and banking were taken over by the government (see Appendix 3).[55] This melding was facilitated by the deference with which Chiang Kai-shek treated the racketeers.[56] In 1931, for instance, Chiang Kai-shek presented a stele of his own calligraphy to Huang Jinrong to be placed in front of Huang's recently completed palatial mansion in Caohejing in the south-western suburbs of Shanghai.[57]

A second process further enabled the integration of respectable society with the racketeers: the creation and elaboration of an official narcotics monopoly that bureaucratized criminality while it criminalized the government.

Du Yuesheng's role in these developments had been signaled in 1932 by two events. One was the entry of Du for the first time into the Chinese Municipal Council.[58] The former *liumang*'s commingling with the bankers, entrepreneurs, and tycoons appointed by Wu Tiecheng provides good evidence of the melding process. The second was the foundation in November of the Hengshe or Constancy Club, ostensibly to promote philanthropy and social welfare as well as loyalty to the country.[59] The Hengshe was one of several fraternities organized in Shanghai after 1929 that represented a new stage in the evolution of the Green Gang and its leaders, who were becoming ever more respectable members of what might be called the Guomindang's Shanghai Establishment. The old Green Gang remained intact (though its rituals were modified), but a new set of satellite organizations, a bit like the "front groups" for the Blueshirts' Lixingshe, became attached. Shanghai's gangsters founded fraternities, however, less to provide a cover for clandestine activities than to attain social respectability; to bring "fresh blood" (*xin xue*) into their retinues; to provide an organizational format for extending master-disciple ties into the many new and different social strata of the city; and to combine social, economic, and political relationships into a single institution.[60]

At the simplest level, the foundation of the Hengshe served as merely Du Yuesheng's response to the growing numbers of compradors, officials, politicians, military officers, intellectuals, businessmen, economists, and trade unionists who flocked to his house on Rue Wagner seeking to become his disciples.

The same was true for the other clubs, which were legally registered with the government. The Rongshe (Glory Club), primarily founded by Huang Jinrong, accommodated a membership of middle-level merchants, brokers, people in the entertainment industry (employees of theaters, amusement parlors, dance halls, and hotels), and detectives—in other words, his regular clientele.[61] However, a key difference distinguished this membership from the ordinary Green Gang: the fraternities were deliberately intended to exclude hard-core gangsters and "vagabond" types while attracting higher-status followers. Gangland boss Zheng Jinghu had about three thousand followers within his faction of the Green Gang. Of these, only about two hundred were allowed to join Zheng's Humane Club (Renshe), the eligibility requirements for which stipulated that a military person hold major's rank or higher, that a bureaucrat be of a definite official rank, that a businessman have a certain social standing, and so forth.[62]

At a slightly more complex level, the racketeers' fraternities formed a "respectable" counterpart to the jewelry stores and teahouses they had used earlier in their careers as meeting places with the clients, criminals, and cops who formed part of their underworld network. For the Renshe or Hengshe functioned strictly aboveground. In the Renshe's clubhouse at 1535 Bubbling Well Road, the chief of detectives and the head of the first bureau of the PSB were to be seen together with the former defense commissioner of Tongzhou or the former chief of the Songhu Garrison Command. In the Hengshe's quarters at 39 Rue Brenier de Montmorand, Mayor Wu's personal secretary rubbed shoulders with Lu Jingshi, the head of the Shanghai garrison's military court, while the chairman of the

General Labor Union, Zhu Xuefan, consorted readily with Wang Zhao-huai, chief of the military police's detective squad.[63]

The fraternities eventually took on distinct professional characteristics, and the institutional model extended downward into particular vocations.[64] For example, General Yang Hu, with the help of the chief Chinese inspector of the political section of the French police, tried to form a Xing-zhongshe (Revive China Club) to recruit followers among seamen and shopkeepers, but he failed to get a license from the French authorities. Du Yuesheng and Zhang Xiaolin, on the other hand, founded a Livelihood Mutual Aid Club (Shenghuo huzhu she) in August 1936, run primarily by members of the Shanghai branch of the Guomindang out of quarters at 434 Rue Boppe. The club in turn in March 1937 formed a Shanghai Eastern District Chauffeurs' Committee (Hudong siji weiyuanhui) to organize drivers working for taxi services and for public transportation firms. The SMP was particularly concerned about this committee, which was "completely subject to the influence of Mr. Tu Yueh-sung [Du Yuesheng], one of the local influential leaders of the Green Pang [bang], as the majority of the promoters are his followers . . . [who] hold official posts in the local Tangpu [dangbu] or other government organs."[65]

This kind of organization attracted the attention of the International Settlement authorities not only because it was the racketeers' personal instrument in the critical transport sector of the urban economy; but also because it represented an emerging alliance of Shanghai's petty urbanites and workers with the city's heterogeneously melded elites and even the Nationalist government, against the increasingly menacing presence of Japan. Although the Japanese themselves were quick to see a Blueshirt behind every Green Gang member, their journalists were not amiss when they reported on March 30, 1937, that Du Yuesheng had set up the Livelihood Mutual Aid Club "to organize motorcar, bus, and tramcar drivers in order to prevent them from working for the enemy in time of war."[66]

Intermingling Criminality and Patriotism

The mantle of patriotism amply enveloped the rapid expansion of Du Yuesheng's activities beyond the underworld and the public verification of his mixed-elite status after 1932, when abundant opportunities arose to demonstrate his public loyalty to the nation and his personal allegiance to Chiang Kai-shek. In 1933, for example, when Chiang Kai-shek announced a national lottery to raise money to buy military airplanes, Du Yuesheng joined with Dai Li to form the Dayun gongsi (Big Transport/Luck Company), ostensibly to sell lottery tickets on commission for the government, but also to serve as a drug distribution operation. Du Yue-sheng contributed his share of the commissions to Dai Li (with whom he and Yang Hu swore blood brotherhood in 1927), who used them to subsidize covert operations such as the assassination of Yang Xingfo, chairman of the Chinese League for the Protection of Human Rights, on June 18, 1933.[67]

On August 12, 1933, the newspaper *Xiao gongbao* claimed to have gotten hold of the assassination plans of the Blueshirt Society, which had been training agents to attack Chiang Kai-shek's enemies.

> Since their return to Shanghai from Lushan to await instructions from General Chiang Kai-shek, local assassination members of the society have been becoming increasingly active. Drastic training of secret service members is underway in the headquarters of the society, and the selection of assassination members to carry out the work in all districts is being made.[68]

This elaborate scheme listed fifty-seven agents, divided into fourteen different corps under the leadership of Dai Li and Zhao Yongxing: six corps in the French Concession, five in the International Settlement, and three throughout the Chinese parts of the city.[69] These terrorists, said to be armed with pistols, supposedly disguised themselves as rickshaw coolies, fortunetellers, hawkers, and other members of the city's lowlife. Their assignment was to locate the whereabouts of persons on the Generalissimo's hit list, and then kill them on sight.[70]

Whatever the truth of sensational accounts such as these, which fed upon public rumor and concern, there was substance to the fears that another major opponent of the régime would be struck down by Dai Li's men. Despite the negative public opinion, Chiang Kai-shek had by the time of these reports already ordered that preparations be made to murder a second leading member of the League for the Protection of Human Rights: the editor of Shanghai's leading daily, *Shenbao*, Shi Liangcai.[71]

Shi Liangcai incurred Chiang's wrath for his newspaper's vociferous condemnation of the government's assassination of Yang Xingfo, for his vigorous public support for strong resistance against Japanese aggression, and for his spirited opposition to the crackdown on students and universities orchestrated by Minister of Education Zhu Jiahua.[72] The conjunction of all three causes, and especially *Shenbao*'s dramatic analytical linkage of internal persecution of liberal human rights proponents to external appeasement of the Japanese, constituted a direct provocation to Chiang Kai-shek.[73] Sometime in the fall or early winter of 1933, consequently, Chiang commanded Dai Li to prepare to assassinate Shi Liangcai, who was then serving in one of the most prominent public positions in Shanghai as head of the Chinese Municipal Council.[74]

Dai Li originally planned to carry out the operation against Shi in Shanghai, but the courageous editor lived in the International Settlement where police protection was difficult to circumvent. The secret police chief had to wait until October 1934, when Shi left the sanctuary of the International Settlement to take his family for a holiday to Hangzhou's West Lake. Dai Li moved quickly. An operations squad of six men headed by Zhao Lijun and his deputy Wang Kequan was sent to Hangzhou. A request for assistance was cabled to Zhao Longwen, the chief of the provincial police force and a protégé of Minister Zhu Jiahua. And a Special Services Department chauffeur drove a black Buick limousine from Juntong headquarters in Nanjing down to the Hangzhou Police Academy where the car was fitted with license plates from the Salt Gabelle Bank (Yanye yinhang).[75]

On November 14, 1934, Shi Liangcai and his family wound up their holidays and prepared to return to their Shanghai residence by automobile. Shi's party—his wife Shen Qiushui, his son Shi Yonggeng, his niece Shen Lijuan, and the son's schoolmate Deng Zuxun—took the Hu-Hang highway. When the car drew near Boai zhen, not far from the harbor of Wenjia in Haining county, they came across another automobile drawn across the highway. As Shi's chauffeur slowed down, the doors of the other car opened and the assassins jumped out with drawn guns. In the first hail of bullets the chauffeur and school-chum were shot down dead. The others tried to flee across a nearby field. Mrs. Shi was hit and fell wounded, as did her niece Shen Lijuan. Shi Yonggeng, the son, managed to run to safety. But Shi Liangcai was killed on the spot, and his body was dropped into a dry cistern. Although alarms were quickly sounded, Police Chief Zhao Longwen had managed to tie up all of his mobile brigades by calling a prior meeting of the Hushu and Xiaohe police precinct stations as well as of the motorcar inspection personnel (*qiche jiancha zhan renyuan*), so that the assassination squad drove back into Jiangsu without being stopped. By then Dai Li already knew that the mission was successful, for Chief Zhao had sent a coded message to Juntong via Dai's brother-in-law, Mao Zongliang, reporting that "one set of the twenty-four [dynastic] histories has already been bought at Hangzhou."[76]

Somehow, for all of their planning, Chiang Kai-shek and Dai Li had failed to foresee the tremendous hubbub prompted by the brutal killings and woundings of Shi Liangcai and his family.[77] As one public figure after another expressed outrage over the terrorist act, the entire body of members of the Shanghai Chinese Municipal Council resigned in protest.[78] Their resignations were rejected by the municipal government, but Nanjing was forced to make other gestures to placate such overwhelmingly hostile public opinion. Chiang Kai-shek cabled mournful condolences to Shi Liangcai's family while charging the chairman of the provincial government of Zhejiang, Lu Diping, with special responsibility for solving the heinous crime. Zhao Longwen made a great show of trying to run down the murderers, offering Ch. $10,000 in reward for information leading to the arrest of the assailants. But he himself had to flee the glare of public opprobrium by leaving for England to join H. H. Kong in attending the coronation ceremonies of George VI in May 1937.[79] Because the case never was broken, Lu Diping felt duty-bound to resign as governor. Lu went on to become head of the Military Affairs Commission Staff College (Junshi canyiyuan), but he was still in disgrace when he died of illness shortly afterward.[80]

One immediate beneficiary of Shi Liangcai's murder was Du Yuesheng, who took over the chairmanship of the Municipal Council upon Shi's death. Du also became deputy director of the Chinese Red Cross (Zhongguo hongshizi hui) at this time, as well as head of the board of directors of the China Trading Bank (Zhongguo tongshang yinhang) and director of the Shanghai Opium Suppression Bureau.[81] As implausible as it seems at first glance, Shanghai's biggest narcotics dealer was at the same time the city's major civilian drug enforcement agent. This paradox can only be explained by showing how Chiang Kai-shek himself decided to use a national opium suppression campaign to create his own opium monopoly, an act of stupendous government criminalization that, in the long run, may have delegitimated the Chiang régime as much as the brazen assassinations of Yang Xingfo and Shi Liangcai.[82] The decision to legalize opium led directly to the "degeneration of the virtue of the Party-state" (*Dangguo daode zhi duoluo*)—at least in some contemporaries' eyes.[83]

15   Criminalizing the Government

By means of secure domination of the opium traffic [Chiang
hopes] to increase the political power of the national
government over provinces whose allegiance is doubtful. . . .
No local government can exist without a share of the opium
revenues. If the central government can control the opium
supply of a province, that province can never hope to revolt
successfully.

U.S. Military Attaché Joseph Stilwell

Three critical junctures marked the development of the international
drug traffic in the early twentieth century. As we have seen in Chapter 3,
the first was the Anglo-Chinese agreement of 1907 to phase out Indian
imports and curb domestic opium production in China. The dearth of legal
opium created a demand for smuggled opium, morphine, and heroin,
which was met by Japanese and European traffickers who bought opiates
from legitimate pharmaceutical manufacturers and smuggled them into
China.[1]

The second was a supply crisis in Europe beginning in 1927 as measures sponsored by the League of Nations curtailed legitimate European
factory production by 1932 to about half of what it had been in 1928.
European traffickers consequently began to look for new sources of drugs
in Turkey and Bulgaria, where the heroin factories around Sofia imported
enough acetic anhydride to meet more than twice the legitimate requirements of the entire world.[2]

The third critical juncture came after international publicity forced the
Bulgarian government to close down its heroin factories. Although Persian opium made up for some of the difference, the decision of the governments of China and Japan in the 1930s to allow drug manufacture and
trafficking to expand in their territories led to a replacement of European
and Middle Eastern narcotics by East Asian opiates.[3] This dramatic change
was tersely noted by Eli Liopoulos, the most successful European drug
dealer of the 1920s, who attributed the shift to the effects of the world
depression and the relative decline of silver (see Appendix 3).[4]

> European or Turkish [drugs] cannot be imported owing to the gen-
> eral depression and particularly to the decline of silver, so that Chi-
> nese interests are unable to pay prices which would be attractive to

European producers. As a result, the Far Eastern traffickers have turned to Chinese opium for their raw material and many factories have been established in China for the manufacture of narcotic drugs. It will not be strange if the Chinese, in a short time, will start exporting narcotic drugs to Europe and America similar in quality to those made in Europe.[5]

Liopoulos was quite prescient: arrests in 1933 in San Francisco exposed the China connection, which later implicated the Chinese consul general in San Francisco and nearly resulted in his conviction on narcotics charges.[6]

Chiang's Drug Policy

On the surface, at least, the Chinese government continued to pursue an aggressive campaign against the opium traffic. On June 18, 1932, the régime threatened officials with severe punishment if they neglected to enforce the opium laws. "It is therefore hereby ordered that all the responsible local officials must hereafter obey and carry out faithfully the various laws and ordinances relating to opium suppression and that they must not regard such as dead laws to be treated only as pro forma but ignored de facto."[7] During that year, the authorities reported that they had seized 30,719,925 ounces of opium, 157,472 ounces of morphine, 360,425 ounces of heroin, and 12,578,995 ounces of other "powerful drugs."[8]

Yet at the same time, SMP Superintendent Aiers could routinely report that

> Opium successfully transported from various ships is delivered to various combines in the French concession. These combines usually notify Mau Zang Sung who inspects or checks the opium and charges from 8/10¢ per ounce commission. He then pays gangs accordingly less his own share. Mao Zang Sung is a follower and deputy of Doo Yeu Sung [Du Yuesheng].[9]

The opium runners working along the docks of the Bund paid protection fees initially to the "Old Company" (Lau koongts—Lao gongsi), which ran smoothly until the protection that it in turn had to buy from SMP Chinese detectives grew excessive. The "Old Company" decided then to try to use the river instead, bribing the Jiangsu River Police to let them land drug shipments away from the Bund. This left a vacuum quickly filled by a "New Company" (Sing koongts—Xin gongsi) managed by two SMP Chinese detectives who allegedly bribed other members of the force with monthly presents while passing on payments to the "loafers" who reported to Du Yuesheng.[10]

In 1932, then, no contradiction existed between a government somewhat helplessly calling for enforcement of the laws against opium smuggling, and the flouting of those laws by Chinese policemen working for the foreign settlement authorities. What changed in 1933 and 1934 was the intensification of governmental efforts, led by Finance Minister T. V. Soong, to suppress drug addiction on the one hand, and the establishing of a government monopoly to control the distribution of narcotics on the other.[11]

In January 1933, Minister Soong brought Hankou's special tax bureau under Chiang's general headquarters; the following month complete control of all opium suppression was given over to Chiang Kai-shek as chairman of the Military Affairs Commission.[12] In May 1933 Chiang Kai-shek ordered that a general warehouse be established at Hankou to store incoming opium. The warehouse was managed by a major drug dealer and supervised by former Shanghai police chief Chen Xizeng, director of the Hubei Public Security Bureau and head of the local Blueshirts. Chiang Kai-shek planned to monopolize opium collection and license the existing middlemen—the "forty-eight houses" in Hubei—and sellers. The trade would be the same as before, but the government would now take a large share of the profits.[13]

The two efforts at controlling the drug trade supposedly supplemented each other. That is, addicts were supposed to be registered and their dosages controlled and gradually reduced by the government, which would be the country's sole supplier of opiates. On November 1, 1933, *Shenbao* published an order from Chiang's general headquarters calling for suppression of the unauthorized trade in opium. The proclamation admitted that the government's campaign against the Communists in Jiangxi was largely financed by the opium tax. The Opium Suppression Bureaus in the ten provinces under Nanjing's control were henceforth to deliver their opium revenues to the Agricultural Bank to be used by the Nanchang provisional headquarters in the Bandit Suppression Campaign. In other words, the Nanjing government was bent upon creating an opium monopoly in order to generate additional revenue by selling the drug to licensed addicts, while the Suppression Bureaus, backed by the military police, cut off illicit sources of the drug.[14]

> Since the government had been able to divert the opium from the producing provinces to Yangtze control ports, which were under government supervision, it could monopolize the distribution of a great deal of China's production and by 1937 it had at least four million customers. No figures were given out by the Chinese government regarding opium revenues during this period, but from

1934 to 1937 net profits must have been well over 500 million [U.S.] dollars.[15]

Once the opium revenue—as much as Ch. $30 million per month in 1933—became an adjunct portion of the government's regular income, the pressure to continue the monopoly would be virtually irresistible.[16] Or, as one critic of the policy, Ma Yinchu, put it: "Do not hope for the revenue from the public sale of opium—the evil consequences of that would be endless."[17]

In Shanghai, as we have seen, Du Yuesheng's Three Prosperities Company (Sanxin gongsi) had been dissolved after he moved his operations outside the French Concession, although Chiang Kai-shek had already recognized Du's drug monopoly throughout the lower Yangzi delta.[18] In July 1932 the Ministry of Finance introduced a scheme to sell opium publicly in Jiangsu, where the provincial government was authorized to conduct an auction of confiscated supplies of the drug on September 1. Du Yuesheng negotiated with representatives of the provincial government and managed to secure the opium monopoly for Shanghai—a deal that he confirmed at the national level after a meeting in Hankou at which he promised to pay $3 million directly to the Ministry of Finance in exchange for government protection of opium shipments downriver from Sichuan.[19]

With the blessing of the Nanjing Ministry of Finance, Du Yuesheng then reopened the Three Prosperities Company's office in South Market and resumed business as the "chief distribution office and supply agent for opium in Shanghai." In exchange for a now-licit license to distribute company opium stamps to protected runners and dealers, Sanxin (Three Prosperities) allegedly disbursed about $200,000 per month to Chinese government authorities at the local and national level. The old French connection was completely severed by now and the center of the Green Gang's opium distribution business was squarely in South Market.[20]

Double-Dealing with Chiang's Government

The other facet of the narcotics business was the acetylation of opium and crude morphia into morphine, "red pills" (morphine and strychnine), and heroin. As Chinese- and Japanese-grown crude opium replaced Middle Eastern sources in the 1930s, so did East Asian refineries manufacture substitutes for earlier European narcotics imports. The Nanjing régime's Opium Suppression Bureaus, now under Chiang's direct military control, had already commenced the practice of turning over large amounts of confiscated opium to Du Yuesheng for refinement into heroin.[21] Now, according to SMP intelligence reports, Chiang Kai-shek authorized Du Yuesheng to refine opium shipments seized by Guomindang Opium Suppression Bureau officials into morphine and heroin which were ostensibly to be sold for medical uses, but the profits of which were "intended for the use of the Blue Shirt Society."[22]

> The morphia factory on the Chinese Bund has been in existence for the past six months, permission to run this establishment having been obtained from General Chiang Kai-shek through Col. Huang Tseng-shing [Huang Zhenxing, former Commissioner of Public Safety,] at the request of Tu Yueh-sung [Du Yuesheng]. . . . According to rumor, Mayor Wu Tien-chen [Wu Tiecheng] had promised to close his eyes to the continued operation of the drug establishment.[23]

A special subsidiary firm, the Xiaji ("Yah Kee") Company, was set up to run this and other drug factories in South Market. Naturally, the Xiaji Company enjoyed the highest local support. SMP informants reported that the company was owned by Du Yuesheng, Zhang Xiaolin, SMP Assistant Superintendent Lu Liankui, Mayor Wu Tiecheng, and T. V. Soong. In order to safeguard the running of the factory, Du Yuesheng and T. V. Soong "worked energetically to secure the position of the Garrison Commander of [the] Woosung-Shanghai Areas for Mayor Wu Tieh-chen [Wu Tiecheng]."[24]

Du Yuesheng had been given six months, until the morning of November 17, 1933, to refine the opium or crude morphia into morphine, heroin, and red pills. During that time, his drug factory at 104 Taiping Long in South Market received the complete protection of the Chinese authorities while garnering a daily profit of $50,000, a good portion of which was supposed to cover Chiang's military expenses.[25]

Du Yuesheng saw the possibilities of even greater profits in this scheme—profits that would help him make up the huge payments that he had agreed to hand over to Chiang's forces in order to preserve his monopoly. He had already fallen nearly a million dollars in debt to Chiang's government. Thinking now that he could pull the wool over Chiang's eyes and postpone the processing of the Nanjing-seized opium by pretending local prices had fallen, Du Yuesheng arranged a secret deal with the brother of General Zhang Xueliang, Zhang Xueming, who was the chief of the Tianjin police force. The arrangements were to transport a large quantity of morphia from Zhang Xueming's stocks in Tianjin and use the Nanshi (South Market) factory to refine it in place of the supply seized by Chiang Kai-shek's men, which had a much lower margin of profit.

According to the SMP, Mayor Wu Tiecheng received $10,000 a month "to connive at this deception."[26]

Before the six months had elapsed, therefore, Mayor Wu applied to Chiang Kai-shek for an extension of the November 17 deadline on the grounds that the market for the drug was at an ebb and refining therefore had to be postponed in order to increase their profits. Chiang approved the application, but in mid-autumn he received information—perhaps from Dai Li and Huang Jinrong—about the swindle.[27]

Chiang Kai-shek, already angered by the open talk in criminal circles about his government's complicity through T. V. Soong and Wu Tiecheng with the underworld in the narcotics racket, became enraged by this kind of double-dealing, especially since it represented an integument of Shanghai interests that included his own brother-in-law and one of his closest followers. The Generalissimo decided, therefore, to intervene militarily from the outside. As the original deadline drew near, Chiang sent a battalion of 504 men from the first regiment of the Central Military Police at Nanjing to raid the Xiaji factory. At midnight on November 17, less than twenty-four hours after the deadline had passed, the military police disarmed, photographed, and confiscated the badges of the four PSB constables guarding the entrance to the factory. They also arrested nineteen "inmates" inside the drug refinery and seized morphine and red pills estimated to be worth $5 million.[28] The four constables were handed over to the first district PSB station; the military police detained the other prisoners at the Longhua garrison.[29]

As soon as word reached Du Yuesheng of the surprise raid (which he probably attributed to greedy local commanders), Du pressured the chief adjutant of the Wusong-Shanghai Garrison Command, Colonel Wen Jian'gang, to issue instructions to release three of the prisoners, one of whom was Du's own nephew. The instructions were chopped with the seal of the Shanghai mayor, General Wu Tiecheng. On November 19, Colonel Wen called upon the military police headquarters at Longhua and requested an interview with the prisoners. When this request was refused, the chief adjutant left and came back with eight armed military police attached to the Songhu military headquarters, demanding to see the prisoners, who by then had been moved elsewhere. Colonel Wen left the Longhua garrison empty-handed, and the altercation was at once reported by the Nanjing MP commander to General Chiang Kai-shek at Nanchang. Upon instructions of Chiang's delegate, the military police detained Chief Adjutant Wen; arrested the chief of staff of the Wusong-Shanghai military headquarters, General Jiang Qun; and put Mayor Wu Tiecheng under surveillance.[30]

Chiang Kai-shek furiously demanded an explanation in person, and on November 23, 1933, Wu Tiecheng, Du Yuesheng, and Zhang Xiaolin boarded an airplane at Hungjao (Hongqiao) Aerodrome to fly to Chiang's provisional headquarters at Nanchang.[31] The interview must have been tense and difficult. How could Wu Tiecheng have authorized his own military aide, the chief adjutant, to try to pry loose gangsters and miscreants from the hands of Chiang Kai-shek's military police? Wu Tiecheng had no choice but to sacrifice his military aides to Chiang's anger. "The mayor," explained an SMP report, "excused himself by stating that he had no knowledge of the morphia factory and that one of his chops, which was usually kept by the Chief Adjutant for office use, had been used without his knowledge."[32]

Chiang Kai-shek accepted Wu's scapegoat ploy. After Wu Tiecheng, Du Yuesheng, and Zhang Xiaolin flew back to Shanghai on November 26, forty-two members of the Central Military Police escorted the twenty-one prisoners at Longhua (the nineteen seized in the raid plus Colonel Wen Jian'gang and General Jiang Qun) to Nanchang by rail. When the prisoners reached Chiang's provisional headquarters, the two military aides were questioned and then shot at the orders of the Generalissimo.[33] The next day, Mayor Wu sent a telegram to Nanjing, tendering his resignation from the posts of mayor of Greater Shanghai and commander of the Wusong-Shanghai garrison.[34] There were plenty of Nationalist officials who would have welcomed Wu Tiecheng's resignation because they wanted to be mayor themselves.[35] But T. V. Soong thought otherwise, if only because of Wu Tiecheng's closeness to the Cantonese faction whose support had to be sought at this time due to the secession from the republic of Fujian province.[36]

The Fujian Rebellion and Mayor Wu's Survival

Earlier in November, Li Jishen and Chen Mingshu had led the Nineteenth Route Army—which was, of course, a predominantly Cantonese force— in a movement to create an independent government in Fujian province, dedicated to the overthrow of Chiang Kai-shek. Many observers believed that the political leaders in Guangdong would remain neutral as long as the Fujianese troops did not advance to Chaozhou. Also, the Fujianese vanguard, the Fifty-sixth Division under Liu Wuding, had massed at Pucheng, below the Xianxia Pass on the Fujian-Zhejiang border. This rebellion constituted the most severe threat yet to Chiang's power, and Shanghai political mavens speculated that Chiang would be reluctant to humiliate Wu Tiecheng and his Cantonese followers at such a juncture, even though Nanjing insiders claimed that they had already bought over key secessionist leaders so that the rebellion was doomed to fail.[37]

This was in fact so, thanks to Juntong chief Dai Li who had taken a team of agents headed by his deputy Zheng Jiemin to Jian'ou, about eighty kilometers south of Pucheng. The team, which was called a *cefan zu* (group to incite defection) and was divided into four action units under Ma Xiong and others, went into the area controlled by the Fujian People's Government (Fujian renmin zhengfu) to try to enlist turncoats and subvert the rebel enterprise. Dai Li himself, accompanied by Shen Zui, set up his own headquarters on Gulangyu, the island resort just off Amoy (Xiamen) dotted with the residences of foreign diplomats, businessmen, and missionaries who sought relief from the summer heat of Fujian along the seashore. The defection team followed Dai Li's dictum by trying to win over the *shi* (masters) of the rebel forces, and succeeded in bribing two key officers in the Nineteenth Route Army: Huang Qiang, one of the commanders; and Chief of Staff Fan Hanjie.[38] Within days of the inception of the revolt Dai Li's men had in their hands the codebooks of the enemy and were able from their perch on Gulangyu to intercept all of the battle plans for the deployment of the Nineteenth Route Army. In addition, Dai Li also subverted the military commander at Mawei, opening the gateway to Fuzhou, which was handily occupied by Chiang Kai-shek's army in January 1934, bringing the rebellion to a rapid end.[39]

But none of this had actually been realized by November 27, and Wu Tiecheng's position vis-à-vis the Fujian Rebellion may have been one of the considerations that prompted Chiang Kai-shek to reject his resignation on November 28.[40] After an indignant flurry when he discovered that several of his Central Military Police officers assigned to guard the Xiaji Company morphine cache had actually stolen $200,000 worth of the drugs themselves (four escaped, four were caught and executed), Chiang Kai-shek allowed business to return to normal.[41] Du Yuesheng negotiated a deal with the Generalissimo for the return of the seized morphine and red pills, and the Sanxin Company opium monopoly stamps (which had disappeared from the Shanghai market after November 18) reappeared as of December 2, 1933, on local shipments of drugs, which were guarded by twenty members of the Opium Suppression Bureau/Special Service Corps under the direct control of PSB Chief Wen Hongen.[42]

The vicissitudes of the Xiaji drug case reflected Chiang Kai-shek's ambivalence about his government's official drug monopoly. On the one hand, he sincerely abominated the use of morphine and red pills.[43] But on the other hand, as his brother-in-law kept reminding him, the drug monopoly represented a stupendous source of revenue for the government—income that could cover the increasing costs of the campaigns against the Communists in Central China. Chiang's war against his internal enemy dictated a certain degree of expediency, which in turn demanded that he set aside personal qualms in order to succeed. It was a classic instance of ends over means, which Chiang's enemies privately appreciated but publicly condemned. By selling opium—the "foreign mud" that Western imperialism had imposed upon China—in order to pay his troops, Chiang handed the Communists a huge symbolic victory. The Communists may themselves have trafficked in opium in Yan'an to raise funds, but they operated so secretly (e.g., opium was always referred to on manifests by some other term such as "soap") that they were able to accuse Chiang with strident impunity.[44]

Chiang's own twinges of conscience never entirely disappeared, which may account for his periodic rages over stories of corruption emanating from the Wu Tiecheng administration in Shanghai. In December 1934, for example, the Generalissimo again expressed profound dissatisfaction at the accounts "of corruption prevailing in the administration of the Public Safety Bureau," which he blamed upon Mayor Wu. In this particular case, the assistant police commissioner in charge of the "A" division of the PSB, Guan Gong, was believed to have forced his way into the Xiaji Company morphine warehouse and stolen some of the drugs that had been sealed up after the raid the year before.[45] At the launching of an official inquiry, Guan Gong disappeared. Since Guan Gong was Mayor Wu's brother-in-law, most people believed the story that the mayor tipped off Guan in advance, advising him to go into hiding or to leave Shanghai.[46] Once again Wu Tiecheng had to present himself to the Generalissimo and tell his side of the story, and once again his continued tenure was called into question. But expediency prevailed and Mayor Wu remained in office.[47]

Drug Use and the New Life Movement: The "Six Year Plan"

The announcement of the New Life Movement in February 1934 coincided with the promulgation of a new "Six Year Plan" to reduce opium addiction by means of registration and licensing. As part of the New Life Movement, the opium suppression campaign gained some headway among nationalistic youth by identifying the smoking of opium as an unpatriotic act and by accusing the Japanese of peddling heroin and morphine to demoralize and stupefy the Chinese people.[48] But the Nationalists' Six Year Plan to extirpate opium addiction in China by 1940 was not primarily a response to the new traffic in Japanese-manufactured drugs. It ostensibly resulted from the successful suppression of opium in the three provinces where the Military Affairs Commission had taken control of "bandit extermination" in the four-year campaign against the Communists. In January 1934 the National Opium Suppression Commission petitioned the Executive Yuan, requesting that the task of suppressing opium be transferred to the president of the Military Council, who in turn would establish a new Central Commission for Opium Suppression under the aegis of the central government.[49]

The crux of the Six Year Plan was temporary legalization of opium addiction through a state monopoly of the drug, which would be sold to registered users in exchange for their submitting to detoxification over a mandated period of time. Only those officially registered as addicts would be allowed to purchase the drug through local offices of the Opiums Suppression Bureau headquartered in Hankou.[50] Registered smokers under the age of forty-five were supposed to forsake their habits by the end of 1938, under fifty by the end of June 1939, under fifty-five by the end of 1939, under sixty by the end of June 1940, and sixty and over by the end of 1940.[51]

Opponents of legalization decried this program for turning the opium trade into a regular national budget item, amounting in 1934 to annual revenues of over $100 million.[52] But Chiang Kai-shek, who named himself national opium suppression commissioner, insisted that this new monopoly control system, to be accompanied by a program of hospices to cure addicts, would eventually wipe out the opium menace. Even the so-called frontier provinces (Shaanxi, Yunnan, Sichuan, and so forth) were supposed to be free from opium production by 1940 under a system of inspection by secret agents and of sanctions that rendered the officials of an offending district liable to life imprisonment or execution.[53]

During the following year, 1935, Chiang Kai-shek's troops entered Guizhou in pursuit of the Communists on their Long March. For Chiang to bring the Southwest and its political cliques under control, he had to undermine their independent opium monopolies. Chiang therefore turned his military campaign in Guizhou into an opportunity to keep the drug from being shipped through Guangxi to the south, and instead diverted opium supplies to the Yangzi River where they merged with the flow via Hankou to Shanghai. Luo Zhonggong, a Guizhou native named commissioner of finance after the Nationalists entered the province, headed the opium monopoly; at the same time, Du Yuesheng and his opium combine gained monopoly exporting rights to carry Guizhou opium out of the province to Hankou and Shanghai.[54]

Chiang's diversion of Guizhou opium forced the Guangxi clique to turn to Yunnan for alternative supplies. The Nanjing government retaliated by building a highway from Yunnan to the as yet uncompleted Hankou-Guangzhou railway. But even after the highway was inaugurated in the autumn of 1935, the Yunnan opium caravans continued to move through Guangxi because transit taxes were much lower in that province. Nevertheless, the Guangxi authorities felt the economic pinch, while Chiang's own coffers were undoubtedly enhanced by the special monopoly arrangements that he had worked out with Du Yuesheng and the Shanghai narcotics interests.[55]

In Shanghai considerable competition emerged over control of the local opium suppression campaign. In the early stages of the 1934 New Life Movement, T. V. Soong decided to form a kind of tax police to bring the Shanghai narcotics market under the public control of the national government's newly declared opium monopoly. Naming himself director of opium suppression in Shanghai, Soong recruited a uniformed squad of several hundred crack police to do his bidding. This challenged directly the Green Gang's private control of the drug market as semi-legal tax farmers. The underworld quickly retaliated. As T. V. Soong waited to catch a train in the Shanghai railroad station, shots were fired. One of Soong's secretaries fell to the ground dead. Soong himself threw aside his white panama hat, an easy target, and hid in the crowd behind a steel girder.[56] Not long after this, Soong's opium police force was disbanded, and Chiang Kai-shek's chief secretary, Yang Yongtai, negotiated a new agreement with Du Yuesheng to reopen the South Market morphine factories. Thereafter Du's chemists monopolized the final refinement process of all crude drugs sent downriver from Chongqing, Yizhang, and Hankou.[57]

These private deals notwithstanding, the opium suppression campaign was pursued publicly with zeal in Greater Shanghai, beginning with the compulsory registration of addicts in November 1934. Known addicts who failed to present themselves were fined Ch. $50–300, and in November-December nearly sixteen thousand people registered and were sent by public health officials to one of three hospitals especially equipped to receive them.[58] After being fingerprinted, they were disintoxicated and then released with a certificate that they had given up opium (*jieyan zhizhao*). They were supposed to return in six months' time to be checked again and reissued a second certificate of clean health.[59]

In the early months of 1935, however, registration flagged due to lack of persistent investigation, control, and motivation. Once again, it was a matter of trying to mobilize public action bureaucratically from the top down, and through threatened sanctions rather than by rewards or ideological means. (Very few addicts came forward to register in the foreign concessions, where the Chinese police had no sway.) On June 26, 1935, the municipal government received a directive from Chiang Kai-shek ordering that it pursue registration with fresh vigor. Chief Cai Jingjun assigned responsibility for suppressing "the opium evil" to the Fourth Department, a new division specially charged with narcotics problems under the command of Dai Lizhen.[60] Registration teams were assembled, given a monthly budget, and put to work between September 13–30 conducting investigations of their district and compiling lists of addicts. The addicts were then informed that they had until the end of the month to register voluntarily, and that thereafter they would face sanctions, starting with fines and ending with prison sentences.[61]

There was no question about the government's sincere and serious intentions during the 1934–36 opium suppression campaign. By 1937 more than a thousand *jieyan yiyuan* or *jieyan shi* (detoxification hospitals or centers) had been constructed throughout China, and one Shanghai clinic claimed that over 7,000 cured patients had been discharged. Nationwide over 4 million opium smokers were registered. In Jiangsu 20,000 persons were prosecuted under the opium suppression laws, and after the deadline of January 2, 1937, over 2,000 narcotics offenders were executed.[62] Between July 1935 and September 1936, 43,020 opium addicts were registered.[63] Since by now there was a total of four opium treatment centers in Shanghai with 550 beds, and detoxification took about two weeks, only about 40 percent of the addicts, or 16,500 patients, could be treated.[64] And since many addicts went unreported or moved to the International Settlement or French Concession rather than register, the opium problem persisted.[65]

In April 1936 Chiang's Military Affairs Commission (MAC) made yet another effort to accelerate the effort to suppress opium in Shanghai. Sending a special adviser, Ma Liang, to work with Chief Cai Jingjun, the MAC endorsed a plan to have the Public Security Bureau lead a campaign to report offenders (*jianju*). In other words, the opium suppression campaign turned decisively toward a police-inspired program of denunciation. It was left to PSB personnel to work out the details of this campaign, which they divided into three phases: propaganda and investigation, propaganda and arrests, investigation and verification. To propagandize, the PSB used posters, handbills, radio broadcasts, movie clips, newspaper announcements, lecture teams, and personnel posted to "mass education offices" (*minzhong jiaoyu guan*) to inform the people about the campaign. For investigation, all local police posts were instructed to investigate households. For investigation and verification, special police teams were sent out to each precinct and neighborhood post to see if progress really was being made. Also, opium shops were visited and customers were told to register themselves, letters were sent to the households of the purchasers of opium, and so forth. Finally, house-to-house searches were made, and addicts were required to produce proof that they had registered themselves. Between May 10 and September 10, 1936, 24,144 addicts were registered. Of these, about 5,600 were sent to detoxification clinics.[66]

On October 28, 1936, the Garrison Command called a meeting of all Shanghai opium suppression units. The authorities had found that the most common users of opium were workers and vagrants. Household registration simply was not going to reach many of the latter, and uniformed police teams should therefore be sent out to give lectures, issue warnings, and do whatever they could to get addicts to turn themselves into the drug clinics. At the same time more effort must be devoted to the arresting of drug salesman—many of whom were Japanese and Korean *rōnin* selling drugs brought into Shanghai from Tianjin.[67]

Japan's Role in the Drug Trade

Tianjin was the center of the "special trade" in narcotics that sprang up in the Japanese-controlled areas of North China after 1935 when enormous quantities of Persian opium and refined drugs were imported from Japan and Manchukuo.[68] The production, manufacture, and sale of narcotic drugs to the Chinese by now formed a gigantic national industry for Japan and the puppet state of Manchukuo, where the drug output grew from 2,498 kilograms in 1911 to 35,930 kilograms in 1926.[69] After 1933, under the protection of the Japanese army, Manchukuo drug traffickers spread rapidly across the Great Wall and down into North China, where Tianjin would become the largest distributing center for opium in East Asia.[70] The Japanese opium traffic was concealed from the world until the U.S. exposed it before the Advisory Opium Commission at Geneva in 1934, accusing the Japanese of operating the world's largest single venture in illicit drugs through the Manchukuo Opium Monopoly, which garnered profits of nearly Ch. $10 million between June 1933 and June 1934.[71]

The "special trade" in narcotics was secretly sponsored by the Japanese military, whose Kwantung Army soldiers were told in official handbooks:

> The use of narcotics is unworthy of a superior race like the Japanese. Only inferior races, races that are decadent like the Chinese, Europeans, and the East Indians, are addicted to the use of narcotics. This is why they are destined to become our servants and eventually disappear.[72]

Requests to Japanese consular officials to help suppress the drug trade in the North were useless because the diplomats were utterly helpless before their military officers, who were not to be deterred from "crippling China's finances by smuggling, and drugging the virile population of China."[73]

The extent of the Japanese-protected trade in 1937 was staggering. According to a survey conducted by the Chinese Anti-Opium Association in the Japanese Concession of Tianjin, there were 248 foreign firms dealing in morphine and heroin, and 137 opium shops and smoking dens, plus additional shops and dens on the streets just outside the concession boundary.[74] Dr. Wu Liande (Wu Lien-teh) made a ten-day swing through the Tianjin area in February 1937 and reported that traffickers daily carried the drugs in from the refineries in the North and then peddled the narcotics at cheap prices and with sales pitches that brought more and more school-age boys and girls into addiction.[75]

Chiang Kai-shek's government tried to compete with the Japanese dope dealers by establishing an Opium Suppression Committee in Tianjin late in 1935. Plans were to have the local monopoly authorities open fifty sales agencies outside the foreign concessions, backed up by a Beiping-Tianjin Opium Suppression Inspectorate that was inaugurated on February 18, 1936.[76] In the meantime, however, "the smuggling activities of the Japanese rōnin [had already] spread to Shanghai," and soon they were openly brawling with Chinese customs inspectors. Nevertheless, until the Japanese actually occupied the city, Shanghai's complex native network of opium suppression and sales agencies kept at bay the various Japanese "special organs" (*tokumu kikan*) and their *yakuza* clients from Japan, Taiwan, and Korea.[77]

The key to dominance of the narcotics traffic was still official Chinese government support. In Shanghai this support was secured by a holding company called the Special Goods Association (SGA), which was originally formed by all the large narcotics manufacturers and retailers in the city. The SGA levied its own tax of 10 cents a tael (1.3 ounces) on all opium from Hankou sold in the city, and with this fund it handled production, purchase, transportation, distribution, and sale of all narcotics in Shanghai. The fund was also used for bribes. The practice for the past several years had been to give the commissioner of public security a monthly payoff of $250,000 to distribute as he saw fit among his police officers. Upon becoming chief of police, Cai Jingjun demanded an additional $100,000 per month. When the opium merchants refused, General Cai closed down their dens for three days. On May 5, 1935, Du Yuesheng held a dinner in honor of General Cai to negotiate on behalf of the mer-

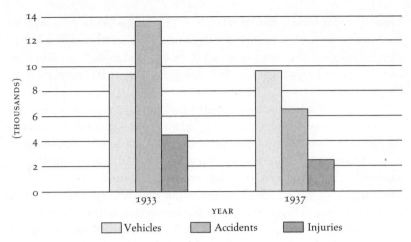

FIGURE 10. Traffic accident rates, 1933 and 1937. Source: *SMC*, 1937 (P61A), 80–84.

·chants; a compromise was reached: the monthly payment would thereafter be $300,000. The next day, the opium divans were reopened.[78] The bribery fund of the SGA also facilitated the appointments of association representatives to leading positions on all opium suppression bodies. That was one factor among others that enabled Du Yuesheng, as chairman of the Chinese Ratepayers Association, to become the leading member of the standing committee of the Shanghai Opium Suppression Committee.[79]

The trouble was, however, that the situation in Shanghai was growing increasingly unstable as competition between the Chinese and the Japanese in the drug traffic increased. On January 1, 1937, new laws were announced by Chiang Kai-shek to punish users of refined opium derivatives. According to the Shanghai Municipal Police, this was a sally in the war between Japan and China to control the drug traffic.[80]

Moreover, drugs and espionage were becoming more intimately connected than ever. As the Japanese expanded their influence in the North, the linkage between their special services units and narcotics became increasingly evident, and once the Japanese launched their invasion of Central China after the Marco Polo Bridge Incident in July 1937, they began to take over drug networks in the South—either by co-opting Du Yuesheng's men or by trying to introduce their own agents into the traffic.[81]

Well-meaning proponents of drug legalization like Dr. Wu Liande could argue quite cogently about the need for a government-controlled monopoly that would enable public health authorities to use the system of registration and detoxification clinics (*jieyan shi*) to cure addicts of their habit. Political "realists" like the Generalissimo's brother-in-law T. V. Soong could emphasize the importance to the state of appropriating vast private revenues that otherwise fell into gangsters' hands. And important military and police advisers such as Chief Cai Jingjun could underscore the urgency of depriving provincial warlords and Japanese "special organs" of such lucrative resources. But the fact remained that Chiang Kai-shek and his supporters fooled no one when they claimed that by seeking to monopolize the sale of opium they were really "killing two birds with one stone" (*yi ju liang de*): covering military costs on the one hand while curing drug addicts on the other.[82] The state's *jieyan shi* (detoxification clinics) were no more than opium shops, progressive journalist Zou Taofen scornfully wrote; and Zou reminded Chiang Kai-shek that Sun Yat-sen had said that there was to be "absolutely no compromise" in the war against opium. Had not Sun said that selling opium was "tantamount to selling out the country" (*maiguo xingwei*)?[83]

These were harsh words of denunciation that were bound to cast even the best accomplishments of the Shanghai police forces in doubt.[84] That is to say, even though the police were bringing greater measures of surface "order" (*zhixu*) to Shanghai's swarming streets (see Figure 10), at a deeper level the traffic in drugs undermined all of the Public Security Bureau's efforts to live up to the bright hopes of 1927 when Mayor Huang Fu and General Chiang Kai-shek had so fervently promised to rid the city of crime and corruption.[85]

Conclusion
Resolutions

On the corner a decapitated Sikh policeman lay with his arms
outstretched as though against oncoming traffic. Yellow,
slowly lifting, high explosive fumes exposed the terrible scene
in Nanking Road. Flames from blazing cars were incinerating
the bodies of their riddled occupants. In grotesque heaps where
they had been huddling in doorways and annexes of the
Cathay and Palace hotels were heaps of refugees whose blue
coolie clothes were turning red. Heads, arms, legs lay far from
mangled trunks. For the full long stretch of both buildings,
pavements and roadway were littered with bodies.

  Rhodes Farmer, *Shanghai Harvest: A Diary of Three Years*
        in the China War

On July 7, 1937, Japanese and Chinese armed forces clashed at Lugouqiao
(Marco Polo Bridge) just west of Beiping—an incident that precipitated
China's War of Resistance and eventually the Japanese attack on Ameri-
ca's fleet at Pearl Harbor. Chiang Kai-shek's response to this new aggres-
sion was very different from his reactions to earlier provocations by the
Japanese. On July 17, 1937, he addressed his fellow Chinese:

> China is a weak country, and if, unfortunately, we should reach
> the limit of our endurance, then there remains only one thing to
> do, namely, to throw the last ounce of our national energy into a
> struggle for the independent existence of our nation. To seek peace
> once war has begun would be to invite the subjugation of our na-
> tion and the annihilation of our race. . . . Should we hesitate and
> vainly hope for temporary safety, we shall perish forever. If we
> allow one more inch of our territory to be lost, then we would be
> committing an unpardonable offense against our race.[1]

As commander-in-chief, Chiang could count on about 250,000 German-
trained regulars of the central armies, and the 200,000 men of the Guangxi provincial standing army. By the time the Generalissimo made the
speech just quoted, the Imperial Japanese Army had concentrated 100,000
regular troops in the Tianjin area, supported by a few squadrons of bombers, light tanks, and motor transport.[2] More Japanese reinforcements were
already on their way.[3]

Chiang Kai-shek was willing to have the war spread from North China to East China for two reasons. First, his own forces heavily outnumbered Japanese forces in the Shanghai region, and the Generalissimo well remembered what a difficult time the Japanese had experienced against lesser odds in 1932, trying to fight the Nineteenth Route Army through the streets of Zhabei. Second, Japanese aggression so very close to Shanghai's investments might invite the intervention of the powers, though Western governments clearly wanted to avoid involvement in the war. Consequently, Chiang Kai-shek ordered his Shanghai regional commanders to send "Peace Preservation Troops" into the Zhabei demilitarized zone.[4]

The Japanese promptly protested this move to the local authorities, but Chiang's men ignored the warnings and went on to refortify Wusong, which guarded the entrance to the Huangpu River. They also constructed a boom of junks above the French Bund, and sank ten steamers below Jiangyin in order to block Yangzi River communications with Nanjing and Wuhan.[5] By the time Japanese warships landed several thousand troop reinforcements at Yangtzepoo (Yangzipu) just downriver from Shanghai, the Japanese Consulate in Hankou had already begun evacuating Japanese civilians out of what was now certain to become a war zone.[6]

Meanwhile, within Shanghai the motley alliance of officials, policemen, and gangsters who dominated the drug traffic began to organize for underground warfare as well. Du Yuesheng typically took the lead in organizing anti-Japanese resistance by means of the Shanghai Citizen's Emergency Committee, which had been formed during the hostilities in 1932. Clearly seeking "a patriot's halo," Du flamboyantly volunteered to scuttle some of the vessels from his own Ta-Ta Steamship Company to impede Japanese warships in the lower Yangzi, and he publicly offered his bulletproof sedan to one of the Chinese generals defending Shanghai.[7] At the same time, he made covert arrangements with Chiang Kai-shek's secret police chief, Dai Li, to prepare an underground resistance movement against the Japanese during what was certain to be a hard-fought battle for Shanghai.[8]

Dai Li had turned his attention to Shanghai immediately following the Marco Polo Bridge Incident. His most important agent in Shanghai at this point was Wang Zhaohuai, Detective Brigade Commander of the Garrison Command and a member of Du Yuesheng's Hengshe.[9] The resources of the Shanghai Station until then had mostly been devoted to actions against the Communist Party, and very little intelligence was being gathered among the Japanese. Shen Zui, who was then the group head (zuzhang) of the Hongkou (Hongkew) operation of Juntong, only had one primary agent, the owner of a pawnshop on Dongyouheng Road. The rest of his informants in "Little Tokyo" were all double agents who worked for Japanese intelligence officers as collaborators. Juntong could adduce Japanese intentions from the kinds of tasks they assigned to their Chinese agents, so that the Chinese at least had some sense of the direction of Japanese military ambitions. But it was all maddeningly vague—like the report from one agent that his Japanese case officer, when drunk a few days after the Marco Polo Bridge Incident, had said: "It's only going to take a few days time before Shanghai is going to be ours. Then your work is going to really get busy all of a sudden."[10]

On August 9 the most serious casus belli transpired. Early that evening Sublieutenant Ohyama Isao and seaman Saito Yozo of the Japanese Naval Landing Party tried to drive by car to the Chinese military airport at Hongqiao, beyond the Western perimeter.[11] When they ignored the order to stop, members of the Peace Preservation Corps fired upon them. Both Japanese were killed, along with one of the Chinese sentries.[12] The following day Japanese marines took up battle positions in Hongkou from Suzhou Creek northwards and east into Zhabei. On August 11 the Japanese Third Fleet steamed up the Huangpu, and the flagship *Idzumo* set its anchors directly in front of the International Settlement.[13] Moored behind it were twenty-six other Japanese warships, while several thousand marine reinforcements waited on transports anchored farther down the river. The Japanese demanded that all Chinese troops withdraw thirty miles outside Shanghai, but on August 12 the crack Eighty-seventh and Eighty-eighth Divisions arrived from Nanjing and took up positions in Jiangwan and Zhabei, bringing total Chinese troop strength at Shanghai to about 45,000 men.[14] The Japanese Naval Landing Party consisted at that time of about 3,500 marines. That same day, both sides began to put barbed wire around their zones and to build up emplacements for machine guns.[15]

On August 13, 1937, residents of the International Settlement, which had been under martial law for five days, were especially tense.[16] As squalls swept across the city, most thoroughfares leading into Avenue Edward VII and Avenue Foch were barricaded, causing traffic jams that lasted as long as twenty minutes. Rains pelted down upon the closed roof gardens of the department stores and amusement centers, and that night most slept fitfully, some awakening to the sound of gunfire exchanged between Japanese and Chinese outposts along the Zhabei-Hongkou boundary.[17]

The gunfire continued on the morning of August 14, when it was learned that the Chinese had presented the Japanese with an ultimatum demanding their withdrawal by 4:00 P.M. that same day. It seemed an ordinary if somewhat stormy Saturday morning at first in the International Settlement; but more gunfire could be heard from Zhabei, and as refugees began to stream out of Hongkou into the Settlement, the squalls turned into a real storm, with gale force winds whistling down Nanking Road.[18]

Around noon five Chinese Northrop bombers flew low over the Settlement and dropped some small bombs on a godown along the waterfront. The bombs were evidently intended for the *Idzumo*. As the Japanese flagship turned its anti-aircraft guns toward the planes, one of the aircraft dropped a two-thousand-pound bomb short of its target.[19] The bomb, armed with a graze fuse, arced down Nanking Road, landing at the intersection with the Bund in the confined space between the two towering Cathay and Palace hotels where refugees huddled in the doorways out of the wind. The explosion was devastating.

> It seemed as if a giant mower had pushed through the crowd of refugees, chewing them to bits. Here was a headless man; there a baby's foot, wearing its little red-silk shoe embroidered with fierce dragons. Bodies were piled in heaps by the capricious force of the explosions. Women still clutched their precious bundles. One body, that of a young boy, was flattened high against a wall, to which it clung with ghastly adhesion.[20]

More than seven hundred died instantly, and as many more lay maimed and mutilated in the street.[21]

Not far away in the French Concession, at the junction of Avenue Edward VII and Yu-ya-ching Road, thousands of curious people standing outside the New World Amusement Center (where rice was being distributed to a crowd of refugees) and a movie theater converted to a shelter, saw another Chinese bomber wing fly overhead toward the *Idzumo*. One of the aircraft was hit by a Japanese fighter, and its wounded pilot turned back toward Hongqiao Aerodrome. As the plane lost altitude the pilot tried to jettison his two shrapnel bombs over the racetrack, but the missiles fell short by three hundred yards, striking the center of the intersection.

> The first bomb, exploding as it struck the asphalt street, apparently had detonated the second a few feet above the street level, causing its load of death-dealing explosives to spray across the crowded plaza. Dozens of motor cars and their occupants were riddled with shrapnel or incinerated by their exploding gasoline tanks, while hundreds of pedestrians were dropped in their tracks for a block in all directions. The worst carnage was among the crowd of refugees

massed in front of the New World Amusement Center, where the food was being dispensed. Mangled bodies of men, women and children, with most of their clothing burned away, were heaped against the building to a height of five feet.[22]

All told more than three thousand people were killed or injured.[23]

"Bloody Saturday"—August 14, 1937—marked the beginning of Shanghai's second military ordeal with Japan. In the beginning, the Nationalist troops commanded by Generals Zhang Fakui (Pudong sector), Chen Cheng (Zhabei-Wusong sector), and Yang Hu (Nanshi) had an overwhelming numerical advantage over the 3,500 Japanese marines dug in behind sandbagged breastworks along a three-mile front from the business districts of Zhabei to the factory slums of Yangzipu.[24] Only the fire from the Japanese warships saved the marines from annihilation during the ten days that followed. The Chinese, meantime, clung to their own positions on the boundary of Shanghai, securing their right flank and forcing a curtailment of the use of fire power. Though they usually remained quiescent during the day, their "murderous skill in hand-to-hand night fighting" took a heavy toll on the Japanese marines.[25] "No quarter was given and no dead were buried. Fly-blown corpses lay in the August sun until the smells of death and burning were wafted over Soochow [Suzhou] Creek into the Western areas."[26]

As Chinese refugees continued to stream out of Zhabei, however, the Nationalist commanders realized how little they knew of the enemy's intentions and troop movements now that marine reinforcements were landing along the Hongkou waterfront and redeploying inland. Dai Li, as head of military intelligence, attempted to infiltrate radio-equipped teams of agents into the occupied zone north of Suzhou Creek, but it was too easy for the Japanese to spot spies moving against the human tide in the other direction.[27] Juntong agent Shen Zui did manage to assemble a team of eight people, including his brother, which set up a single cell in Hongkou. But they were spotted by Japanese counterintelligence within a few days and had to scatter.[28]

On August 23, the Japanese expeditionary force under General Matsui, numbering thirty thousand men, landed near Wusong. Another force landed at Hangzhou Bay, and shallow draft motor scows, holding thirty to fifty men and a field gun transported from Japan on a landing ship with stern doors, were now seen along the China coast. This led to the first realization that Japan had pioneered the technique of combined sea-land operations. The Japanese were prepared now to go on the offensive in Shanghai.[29]

Despite Japan's superiority in military equipment and training, the defenders of Shanghai hoped for an army/partisan victory in the bloody block-by-block battle for Zhabei. Their vision was of a kind of *levée en masse* in which the Thirty-second, Eighty-seventh, and Eighty-eighth Divisions would fight alongside or be supplied by urban partisans recruited as militiamen or mobilized through the Green Gang and its vast networks of clients and members.[30]

At first, these gangs—already resisting the Japanese military squads' attempts to seize their opium stocks—fought as disorganized units that scattered whenever they encountered regular Japanese forces, and that botched an attempt to sink the Japanese flagship *Idzumo* at anchor in the Huangpu River.[31] But they soon took on a more formal paramilitary cast, helping the Thirty-second Division fight the Japanese by supplying motor vehicles, gasoline, electrical equipment, wireless radios, and even military uniforms.[32] In the last two weeks of August and the early part of September, some of these secret society elements came together with army cadres outside of Shanghai to form a Special Action Corps (Biedongdui).[33]

According to intelligence reports gathered by the Shanghai Municipal Police, Chiang Kai-shek's Military Affairs Commission decided at the beginning of September to organize an Emergency Period Service Group (Feichang shiqi fuwutuan) to deal with traitors and spies.[34] Shanghai already had a Peace Preservation Corps, but its purpose had been mainly to serve as the surrogate police force for the Chinese municipality after the Japanese withdrew in July 1932.[35] In order to fight the Japanese now, both before and behind enemy lines, Chiang decided to create an urban guerrilla force. The Military Affairs Commission accordingly set aside $500,000 for this group, which was put under the orders of General Wang Jingjiu, commander of the Eighty-seventh Division.[36]

The Citizens' Militia

General Wang's deputy commanders of the Emergency Period Service Group were Police Chief Cai Jingjun and Du Yuesheng, who immediately tried to turn the new organization to his own use.

> On receiving their appointments and instructions, General Wang Jingjiu and General Cai Jingjun found it inconvenient in their present positions and the work they entailed to actively participate, so left the matter of organizing this new unit in the hands of Mr. Du Yuesheng, deputy commander. In carrying out the organizing of this unit, Mr. Du saw a chance to use his own followers as heads of sections and appointed Mr. Lu Jingshi, Chief Judge of the Military

Court at Longhua, and Mr. Zhu Xuefan, [Chairman of the Shanghai General Labor Union,] to those positions.[37]

However, when Du Yuesheng submitted the names of his lieutenants to the Military Affairs Commission, they were rejected, greatly annoying him and insulting Lu Jingshi and Zhu Xuefan.[38]

In the face of this denial, General Cai stepped in and established a headquarters for the special group within the just-renamed Shanghai Police Bureau with the help of the Loyal and Patriotic Association (Zhongyihui), a group described by SMP informants as being "composed of Whampoa cadets" and led by Pu Fengming.[39] He and General Cai subsequently set up two squads or regiments (*tuan*): the Defense and Protection Squad (Fanghutuan) and the Special Services Squad (Tewutuan).[40]

The Defense and Protection Squad performed different functions north and south of Suzhou Creek. In the northern parts of the city, and especially in Hongkou, they formed a "Shanghai Snipers Corps," which was composed mainly of "loafers" and unemployed workers given Mauser rifles or pistols to snipe at the Japanese behind enemy lines.[41] According to Rhodes Farmer, who was taken on a hasty and nerve-wracking tour of Hongkou, these "Chinese snipers had put [the] whole district into a prickly heat of apprehension."[42] South of the creek, in Nanshi, the Fanghutuan consisted mainly of residents conscripted to dig bomb shelters. The principal tenant in every house in South Market was supposed to supply one member of the household daily for work with the squad, which was commanded by one of General Cai's lieutenants, Shen Xinfu, out of an office in the Wu'an Primary School at Luxiangyuan Road. By September more than three hundred persons were serving as conscripts and fifty-seven dugouts had been finished.[43]

The Special Services Squad had its headquarters in a private school which was part of the Shaoxing guildhall off of Liyuan Road in Nanshi.[44] It was commanded by General Cai's former CID superintendent, Liu Huai. He had two deputies, Shanghai Police Bureau Inspector Chen Bannong and a former bus conductor named Zhang Guoquan.[45] Regular members of the Special Services Squad were recruited mainly from among the ranks of unemployed workers. They were promised a wage of $9 a month, plus room and board on the premises of the school, which was built to house one thousand people. By late September 1937, about four hundred men had enlisted.[46]

The Special Services Squad also had an investigation section, which consisted of thirty members under a man named Yang Fulin. These men were billeted in the Jingqin Primary School on Xilin Road outside the West Gate. One of them, a primary school principal named Fu Duoma, reported that he had been assigned by Liu Huai to report on the activities of Japanese plainclothesmen in the International Settlement. He had also been instructed to investigate Chinese "traitors," and if sufficient evidence could be found, to get the Chinese police to arrest the collaborators and remand them to the custody of the Special Services Squad headquarters for further questioning.[47]

Dai Li undoubtedly had his men among the two groups serving under General Cai, and especially within the investigation section of the Special Services Squad. But the secret police chief concentrated most of his own attention on Du Yuesheng's networks of disciples among the labor unions, in mercantile circles, and within the underworld. It was apparently Dai Li who brought the insulted racketeer and his Green Gang followers back into the orbit of the Military Affairs Commission in late September and early October by persuading Chiang Kai-shek to establish a Jiangsu and Zhejiang Operations Committee (Junshi weiyuanhui Su-Zhe xingdong weiyuanhui) in order to transform "gangland" (banghui) members (some of whom were members of the Hengshe) into paramilitary cadres.[48]

Chiang Kai-shek himself chaired the Su-Zhe Operations Committee, and its members included Du Yuesheng, Huang Jinrong, Wang Xiaolai, Yu Xiaqing, Zhang Xiaolin, Yang Hu, Mei Guangpei, Xiang Songpo, and Lu Jingshi. Dai Li, the secretary-general (shujizhang), set up offices off of Shanzhong Road in the French Concession. The committee's activities were divided by departments (chu) for planning (canmou), political indoctrination (zhengxun), intelligence (qingbao), training (xunlian), and general affairs (zongwu); and the department chiefs were Juntong officers such as Chen Xudong, Wang Zuhua, Xie Ligong, and Yu Lexing.[49]

Training cadres and enrolling militiamen were the main tasks at hand. Special classes opened in Songjiang and Qingpu to train people to join and lead action teams (zhidui). Then, in early October, Dai Li used the authority of the committee to organize a General Command Headquarters for the Special Action Army (Biedongjun zongzhihui bu). The headquarters of what would become known as the Songhu Chief Special Action Corps (Songhu biedong zongdui) was located at 1 Shenjiazhai near Fenglinqiao opposite Route Ghisi in South Market. Although nominally directed by Du Yuesheng, the organization's real chief—according to one of the corps' members—was Dai Li, "who is known to be [the] leader of the Blue Shirt Society."[50] Du Yuesheng's "foreign affairs" assistant, the old Green Gang warlord from Shandong, Liu Zhilu, served as titular deputy-head of the Special Action Corps. But the key department personnel were all Dai Li's men: Chen Xudong as chief of staff, Fang Chao as staff executive, Zhou Weilong in charge of indoctrination, Zhou Jiali and later Tan Liangfu as chief managers, Zhou Jiwen responsible for general affairs, and Yu Lexing looking after technical matters. Yu was also responsible, along with Xie Ligong, for the Songjiang and Qingpu training camps.[51] All officers from district brigade commanders on up served either as agents of Dai Li's Juntong or as "backbone cadres" from the Hengshe.[52]

The rank and file of these eight thousand militiamen, drawn from various social sectors of the *xiao shimin* (petty urbanites), included retail clerks (*dianyuan*) from the Shanghai Shopkeepers Association, local ruffians (*dipi* and *liumang*) from the gangs, routed Guomindang soldiers, laborers thrown out of work by the closing of the factories and shops during the Japanese attack, and organized labor union members.[53] A Shanghai "merchants militia" (*shangtuan*) had been formed as early as February 1937, when the Chinese Chamber of Commerce had taken out advertisements in the Shanghai press offering free courses in civic training to shop assistants. One of the young men who answered the ad was twenty-one-year-old Tao Minzhou from Shaoxing. He was put through a four-month course (March–June) in Zhabei. Tao returned to his civilian job in a dyeing shop after the course but when hostilities broke out in August 1937 he joined the Peace Preservation Corps in Nanshi, and in early September this corps was reorganized as the Fifth Section of the Shanghai Special Action Corps under Colonel Tao Yishan, who had been named by Nanjing head of all the Shanghai civic training centers and whose headquarters was in the Wusong-Shanghai Garrison Command.[54]

Tao Minzhou subsequently acquired from Colonel Tao a Mauser pistol, ten rounds of ammunition, and four hand grenades. Quartered in an unnumbered house across from the Sun Sing (Shenxin) Cotton Mill, his assignment was to examine pedestrian and vehicular traffic at the Branan Road barrier to make sure that no "traitors" entered Chinese territory. Tao Minzhou's official brevet consisted of two cloth badges. One identified him as "Number 06595" of the "Shanghai Special Service Corps," and enjoined him to "obey instructions, maintain strict discipline; be loyal to your duties; resist to the bitter end." Another identified its bearer as being attached to the Special Service Corps of the "Jiangsu and Zhejiang Movement Committee." On October 24, 1937, Tao Minzhou and a comrade tried to search a truck and were impeded by SMP Constable F. P. S. Smith. When they pulled out their Mauser pistols, Smith grabbed Tao, who was arrested. The other man escaped. Eventually Tao Minzhou was handed over to the Shanghai Garrison Command.[55]

Colonel Tao Yishan's merchant and worker unit formed one of several groups provided with khaki uniforms and armed with old Mauser rifles.[56] Barracked at the East Asia Athletic School on Luban Road in Nanshi, Section Two helped the police preserve law and order in that area.[57] However, according to the testimony of one Yun Huifang, a member of the Special Action Corps (SAC) well-known to the International Settlement police "for his terrorist activities in 1932," the purpose of his section of the corps (armed with Mauser pistols) was to locate "traitors" (hanjian), whom they supposedly turned over to the nearest Chinese police bureau.[58]

Section Three was assigned to Zhu Xuefan, the chairman of the Shanghai General Labor Union whose nomination had originally been turned down by the Military Affairs Commission. It was intended to maintain labor control.[59] Other working-class units included branch teams of postal workers and seamen under Lu Jingshi, and a longshoremen's brigade.[60]

Many of the recruits were simply unemployed youths. Lin Defu, an eighteen-year-old hawker from Ningbo, was arrested near Race Course Road by the International Settlement police for trying to recruit "plainclothes boy scouts." Under interrogation, Lin said that he himself had been brought into the SAC by a thirty-year-old newspaper vendor named Li who had harangued a group of young males on Jiujiang Road into enlisting in the militia. Moved by his appeal to their patriotism, or just plain curious about the opportunities he seemed to offer, Lin and about forty other young men had followed the vendor to the Special Action Corps depot at the Shaoxing guildhall. Once there they were told that if they were willing to receive military training they would get $9 a day plus two meals and a place to sleep. If they refused they could return home. About six hundred men remained, "young and strong fellows" all between eighteen and thirty-six years of age.[61]

But the physical youth and strength of these "petty urbanites," even when heightened by patriotic zeal, hardly constituted weapons enough as the Battle of Shanghai worsened. Tens of thousands of regular troops fought back and forth across the lines around Zhabei Railroad Station, exchanging machine gun and mortar fire, grenades and artillery strikes. During the sixty-six days in which control of the station was contested, and while Zhabei was practically destroyed by bombs, Japanese casualties were estimated at twenty thousand; the Chinese lost many times more.[62] To many observers of this devastating mêlée—"thousands of tons of steel, from the air, from artillery, and from naval cannon, rained down on Chapei [Zhabei], which military experts said received the heaviest concentration of fire ever laid on one piece of earth"[63]—the Special Action Corps formed nothing more than a "motley rabble" (wuhe zhi zhong), and the "rising in mass" had very little military effectiveness against the Japanese, who by November 8, 1937, had 200,000 men in the field.[64] Du Yuesheng's SAC lieutenants, Lu Jingshi and Shui Xiangyun, resplendently adorned in bright uniforms, ostensibly defended the zone from the south bank of Suzhou Creek along Fanwangdu and Caojiadu across to Rihuigang. But once the Japanese marines launched an attack across that line, the Special Action Corps broke and fled.[65]

Most Special Action Corps units subsequently made a dash for the Anhui-Jiangsu border area, and especially for Tunxi and Shexian counties, where they either fell in with warlords like the former Hunanese bandit Chen Shihu and became guerrillas (*youjidui*) who "wandered but never attacked" (*you er bu ji*), or else later became organized into units of the Loyal and Patriotic Army (Zhongyi jiuguo jun) that was eventually trained and armed by American soldiers under the nominal direction of the Office of Strategic Services (OSS).[66] The last batch of Special Action Corps withdrew from Shanghai on February 1, 1938, issuing a farewell letter to the Chinese press which stated that they were leaving the concessions "for the safety of the residents of the foreign settlements."[67] By then Dai Li had escaped from Shanghai to Changsha via Hong Kong, and the Su-Zhe Operations Committee was completely dissolved.[68]

As the Japanese troops fought their way into the Chinese portions of Shanghai, the most prominent leaders of the resistance left the city. In November 1937, Mayor Yu Hongjun, T. V. Soong, Qian Xinzhi, and Wang Xiaolai all secretly went to Hong Kong.[69] On November 23, Shanghai Police Bureau Chief Cai Jingjun also left for Hong Kong.[70] Shortly afterward, Du Yuesheng joined them there as well.[71]

All that remained for the Nationalists, as they traded ground and men for time during the Japanese offensive up the Yangzi to Nanjing and Wuhan, was to settle accounts in Shanghai. Hundreds of collaborators were assassinated in the following months; among the most prominent victims could be counted the leading Chinese detectives and gangsters who had dominated the comprador police system that the Guomindang initially combatted and ultimately countenanced. The first to go was Shanghai Municipal Police Superintendent Tan Shaoliang, no longer so pivotal a triple agent now that the Japanese had taken over Greater Shanghai. Superintendent Tan was assassinated by a team of Chinese secret service agents in May 1938 just as he was leaving the very hotel where his treachery had begun six years before.[72] Not long afterward, Green Gang leader Zhang Xiaolin, who planned to take over Du Yuesheng's narcotics network with the help of the Japanese, was killed by Dai Li's men.[73] Finally, on August 18, 1938, Lu Liankui, Chief of the Chinese detective squad of the SMP and by then an "asset" of the Japanese special services, was executed by three gunmen as he sat in his car in front of the Central Hotel on Canton Road.[74]

Lu Liankui's death particularly shocked the members of Shanghai's Anglo-American community, who had come to think of him as "the best Chinese police official in the annals of Shanghai police history."[75] Chief Detective Lu had been one of the most flamboyant policemen in the city, and his funeral was appropriately garish. The mile-long mourning procession—the most lavish in twenty-five years—took an hour to pass by. Lu Liankui's corpse, in a $3,000 *nanmu* casket, had a $10,000 pearl in its mouth and a $4,000 jade bracelet on one arm. The hearse carrying his remains was followed by sixteen Chinese and foreign plainclothesmen who kept their gunhands on their revolvers "for every inch of the eight mile course." The parade of more than one hundred cars and trucks— followed by Chinese bands, Daoist priests, Buddhist monks and nuns, a convertible carrying the chief detective's cap, and a procession of officials including Commissioner Bourne and Special Japanese Deputy Commissioner Akagi—was witnessed by more than a million Shanghainese, lined five and six deep on the sidewalks as the cortège passed by.[76]

The public's avid fascination with the grandest private parade since Du Yuesheng's celebration in 1931 was understandable, given the isolation within the foreign concessions' boundaries of "island Shanghai," surrounded by a sea of Japanese occupation forces. Shanghai remained, after all, a place where one always looked eagerly up, wanting to make that next rung, envying the gaudy and ostentatious, willing to twist the law to make a score. Chief Detective Lu, with his Green Gang connections and his rough Huzhou origins, stood as a beat cop who made it good, looking the other way when he had to, and doing what was necessary to get by.[77]

The End of an Era

Was it after all so remarkable that the funeral of a corrupt policeman could toll the end of a decade of Nationalist rule in Shanghai? Chiang Kai-shek had inaugurated the decade by saying, "If the Shanghai Special Municipality cannot be regulated, then China's military, economic and communications [systems] will be in a hopeless tangle."[78] Was this not a prophecy come true? When Mayor Huang Fu took office in 1927, he had declared that the Guomindang's successful policing of Shanghai would "cause the foreigners to lose their excuses for monopolizing power."[79] Was this not a promise proved false? The Chinese would indeed recover their sovereignty over the foreign settlements of Shanghai, but only with indifferent ambiguity when their Japanese overlords handed the city over to Wang Jingwei's puppet government on January 9, 1943.[80]

In retrospect, the Nationalists could hardly have chosen a more difficult and hostile environment for their experiment in municipal police reform. Shanghai's extraterritoriality encouraged criminal enclaves that in turn forced policemen and gang members into the same clandestine brotherhoods. The port's position as an entrepôt in the international drug traffic generated colossal illicit revenues that corrupted many senior police officials and vitiated the Nationalists' revolutionary puritanism. The city's centrality to the Chinese Communist Party's labor movement focused the Public Security Bureau's attention on "Reds" so exclusively that their other tasks, including the recovery of police sovereignty and the prevention of nonpolitical crimes, were compromised. And Shanghai's exposure to amphibian invaders from the Imperial Japanese Navy twice wreaked havoc on municipal political institutions in general and on Nationalist police practices in particular, compelling the security forces to place militarization above regular civilian law enforcement.

Time and again the Guomindang authorities tried to cope with Shanghai's social intricacies by bringing in outsiders, and especially northerners. Indeed, the just-renamed Shanghai Police Bureau had once more been engaged in that process just as the War of Resistance erupted in 1937. Time and again, outsiders had either to rely upon internal allies, or to become insiders themselves by adopting Shanghai's shifting and expedient cultural mores—a cultural style that in its own intentionally corrupted way reflected the dynamic, infectious commingling of Chinese and foreign cultures.

Entirely unanticipated developments lay ahead for the city during the next twelve years: the spread of crime through the "badlands" west of the city after 1937, the devastating round of political assassinations during the early 1940s, the locking down of the city's control system into rigid mutual responsibility units during World War II, the food shortages and bombings of the war itself, the brief euphoria of deliverance from the Japanese followed by the extended dismay over Nationalist carpetbaggers, the further spread of prostitution to meet the needs of American GIs stationed in the city after VJ Day, the Shanghai police riots of 1947, and the student protest movements of 1948.[81] Yet many of the same problems that had faced the Nationalists in 1927 also confronted the Communists on May 25, 1949, when "the red flag appeared over buildings and flew outside stores which twenty-two years earlier had quite as enthusiastically flown the Kuomintang flag."[82]

By then the Shanghai police had been infiltrated by Communist Party cadres.[83] They formed a tiny handful of underground agents among the more than fourteen thousand members of the police force, but they played a critical role in preparing to hand the city's police stations over to the *jieguan zhuanyuan* (special personnel to take control) of the People's Liberation Army (PLA).[84] The latter cadres, prepared to the point of knowing exactly which office and bureau they would occupy, moved swiftly after the Nationalists' acting chief of police surrendered the Fuzhou Road headquarters to the PLA vanguard of security personnel at 10:00 on the morning of May 25.[85] Within five days, in an "orderly and peaceful" (*zhixu jing'an*) way, the Communist cadres had begun the process of "dismantling the house and then constructing it over again" (*chai wu chong jian*): that is, destroying the police force as an entity, while reemploying individual policemen after they had been investigated and reeducated.[86]

On June 7, 1949, Mayor Chen Yi ordered members of the Policemen's Representative Assembly (Yuanjing daibiao dahui) to attend a meeting in the Tianshanwutai Theater, formerly owned by the Subei Green Gang leader Gu Zhuxuan. The new mayor told the police representatives that their responsibility under the revolutionary régime was to protect the people's government and to conduct their work in good conscience. Anyone who sincerely requested to "serve the people" would be given work by the people's government, which would also reeducate them. As for the nature of the new régime, well, they should judge that for themselves.

> It's not enough for us to talk about how good the Communist Party is and how bad the Guomindang is. . . . You have seen the Japanese invade Shanghai and the Guomindang recover Shanghai, and now you've also seen the conditions of Shanghai after the Communist Party took over. So you can realize that there is quite a big difference. The moment the big Guomindang officials [responsible for] recovering Shanghai stepped off the airplane, they all got busy at carpetbagging (*wuzi dengke*).[87] But our responsible comrades shared comforts and hardships (*tonggan gongku*) with everyone else. I myself don't even have a single dollar bill in my pocket.[88]

Chen Yi concluded by warning that those who failed to change their past attitudes of exploitation, who planned to use the people's government for their own ends, or who lurked in ambush against the Communist Party would inevitably be punished. Those with merit would be rewarded. Study conscientiously, he said; reflect upon yourselves, serve the people, strive for merit.[89]

We do not know how many former Nationalist policemen managed to negotiate the transition to Communist rule.[90] Many continued to "eat white rice, attend white plays [i.e., never pay for theater tickets], oppress the masses, and carry out interrogations with torture." The majority of those who listened to Chen Yi's speech "wavered" (*paihuai*) and had a "wait and see" (*guanwang*) attitude.[91] But if only because of the vastly increased ability of the Public Security Bureau to penetrate society (buttressed by the power gained through lane and block Residence Committees, the Census Police, the Civil Administration Department, the Health Department, the Democratic Women's Federation, and so forth), a considerable number of Shanghai Police Bureau officers must have found appealing the promise of working for the Communists.[92]

Those who agreed to stay on had to go through the by-now highly refined regimens of thought control supervised by "study committees" (*xuexi weiyuanhui*), but the survivors of this process of self-criticism probably found gratification in the Public Security Bureau's success in clearing peddlers off the streets, restoring traffic controls, ending currency speculation, drastically reducing robbery rates, resettling demobilized Nationalist troops, terminating opium addiction, and stamping out prostitution.[93] All of these goals had been promised by the Nationalists, and accomplished in the end by the Communists, whose political legitimacy correspondingly expanded.

Dreadful tolls were paid for this successful passage, however, as many Shanghai policemen discovered to their personal rue when the first mass campaigns began in 1950, continued in 1953, and intensified after 1957.[94] Other costs emerged as well for such intrusively effective control mechanisms—human costs that are still being paid.[95] But all of that we have already glimpsed dimly in the purposeful growth of autocratic power from the late Qing's "New Laws" through the Nanjing decade's failed second revolution to the spectacular disorder of the dictatorship of the proletariat. It is what Michel Foucault has called the "carceral city": not the "country of tortures" but the network of forces—"walls, space, institution, rules, discourse"—that at their very center conspire to fabricate disciplinary human beings.[96] What we need to behold distinctly now is how such introverted networks spread and took hold in twentieth-century China, and how in their interstices the individual managed to survive. But that is quite another police story, terrifying yet redeeming, still to be told.

TABLES

Table 1. Occupations in the Chinese Part of Shanghai in January 1932

Occupation	Number	Percentage
Household service	384,872	21.3
Workers (*gong*)	366,814	20.3
Unemployed	319,587	17.7
Commerce	186,560	10.3
Peasants	172,141	9.5
Laborers (*laogong*)	113,482	6.3
Educators (*xue*)	84,930	4.7
Miscellaneous professions	69,822	3.9
Servants (*yonggong*)	61,562	3.4
Communications work	23,902	1.3
Students (*xuetu*)	7,599	0.4
Officers and military	5,132	0.3
Police	5,036	0.3
Government (*zheng*)	4,887	0.3
Doctors	1,696	0.1
Engineers	248	[a]
Party (*dang*)	242	[a]
Lawyers	187	[a]
Reporters	76	[a]
Accountants	47	[a]
Total	1,808,822	100.0

[a]Percentage is less than 0.1.
Source: *SSG*, vol. 5, table after 220.

Table 2. Budgeted Expenses of the Shanghai
Public Security Bureau, 1927–1937

Year	Expenses (yuan)
1927–28	974,059
1928–29	994,104
1929–30	1,629,062
1930–31	1,974,918
1931–32	2,181,421
1932–33	3,096,606
1933–34	3,435,076
1934–35	3,656,252
1935–36	3,234,600
1936–37	3,463,670

Source: Henriot, "Le gouvernement municipal de Shanghai," 198; SSG, vol. 4, 72–73.

Table 3. Cases Prepared for Preliminary Court Hearings by the
Shanghai Public Security Bureau, 1929–1930 and 1931–1932

Type of Crime	1929–30	1931–32	(% of change)
Disorderly conduct	123	224	82
Public disturbances	34	35	3
Social disturbances	39	174	346
Illegal flight	3	4	33
Concealing felons	5	4	−20
False witness and libel	73	23	−69
Danger to public	110	98	−11
Counterfeiting	56	66	18
Forgery	17	16	−6
Indecent behavior	34	138	306
Harm to marriage and family	357	560	57
Opium-related crimes	1,678	2,630	57
Gambling	363	773	113
Homicide	50	75	50
Battery	325	786	142
Abandonment	—	4	—
Attacks on personal freedom (*ziyou*)	—	204	—
Slander	33	7	−79
Theft	680	1,598	135
Robbery	402	548	36
Kidnapping	—	62	—
Squatting (illegal occupation of land)	25	72	188
Swindling	168	298	77
Extortion	11	27	146
Receiving stolen goods	38	68	79
Property damage	8	15	88
Crimes related to military affairs	—	18	—
Other	81	—	—
Total	4,713	8,527	81

Note: The police year ran from July 1 to June 30.
Source for the 1929–30 data: *SSG*, vol. 3, table after 108. Source for the 1931–32 data:
SSG, vol. 5, table after 220.

Table 4. Cases Prepared for Preliminary Court Hearings by
the Shanghai Public Security Bureau, 1931–1932

Type of Crime	Females	Males
Opium-related crimes	363	2,267
Theft	76	1,522
Battery	87	699
Gambling	66	707
Harm to marriage and family	192	368
Robbery	27	521
Swindling	25	273
Disorderly conduct	3	221
Attacks on personal freedom (*ziyou*)	56	147
Social disturbances	4	170
Indecent behavior	26	112
Danger to public	7	91
Homicide	7	68
Squatting	1	71
Receiving stolen goods	5	63
Counterfeiting	4	62
Kidnapping	5	57
Public disturbances	3	32
Extortion	1	26
False witness and libel	2	21
Crimes related to military affairs	0	18
Forgery	0	16
Property damage	2	13
Slander	0	7
Illegal flight	0	4
Concealing felons	1	3
Abandonment	1	3
Total	964	7,562

Source: *SSG*, vol. 5, table after 220.

Table 5. Fingerprint Records for Cases Docketed by the Shanghai
Public Security Bureau, January 1930

Type of Crime	Females	Males
Narcotics	167	821
Larceny[a]	31	839
Political	23	338
Gambling	42	314
Theft[b]	38	310
Seduction and rape	123	158
Battery	29	218
Swindling	7	149
Banditry	20	107
Robbery	6	79
Forgery	6	63
Receiving stolen goods	2	49
Violating police regulations	3	45
Smuggling military weapons and ammunition	7	37
Extortion	2	21
Arson	1	5
Smuggling liquor	0	5
Private printing of documents	0	3
Total	507	3,561

[a]Statutory offenses by which property is obtained by tricks, fraud, embezzlement,
and breach of trust.
[b]The felonious physical taking and removing of personal property.
Source: *SSG*, vol. 3, table after 108.

Table 6. Offices of the Zhabei Branch of the Public Security Bureau after Japanese Evacuation on May 16, 1932

Office	Address	Commander	Number of Staff
Hdqrs. Police Training Depot	Kungwu Rd.	Huang Ming	1200
4th District Station	319 Changan Rd.	Wu Zhaolin	100
4th District, 1st Substation	Mongolia Rd.	Sheng Zezhu	50
4th District, 2d Substation	Maiyuan Rd.	Han Tiexian	50
Detective Dept. Police Training Depot	Kungwu Rd.	Lu Ying	20
Reserve Unit Office	1036 Sing Ming Rd.[a]	Huang Ming	370
Public Utility Bureau	66 Minli Rd.	Jiang Shicheng	150

[a]Temporary quarters in Kung Sing Theater, Mongolia Road.
Source: French intelligence report, in SMP, D-3648, 19 May 1932.

Table 7. Change in the Registered Population of the Special
Municipality of Shanghai after the January 1932 Incident

Type of Dwelling	July–Dec. 1931	Jan.–June 1932	Percentage Drop
Residence	323,520[a]	172,766	47
	1,420,274[b]	777,441	45
Store	38,159	25,227	34
	234,618	165,089	30
Shed	30,563	14,504	53
	129,682	62,546	52
Public place	3,114	1,756	44
	81,258	54,759	33
Totals	395,396	214,253	46
	1,865,832	1,059,835	43

[a]Households.
[b]Persons.
Source: *SSG,* vol. 5, table after 220.

Table 8. Registered Businesses in the Special Municipality of Shanghai before and after the January 1932 Incident

Business[a]	July 1931	July 1932
Jewelry shops	288	186
Banks	12	10
Native banks	30	24
Pawnshops (*diandang*)	52	34
Pawnshops (*yapu*)	52	27
Hotels	136	69
Brokerages (Stock Exchange)	1	1
Insurance	2	1
Communications offices	360	300
Food stores	3,468	2,358
Newspaper offices	2	1
Foreign goods stores	891	575
Antique stores	91	76
Theaters	16	5
Movie houses	12	5
Recreation halls	21	4
Gardens	36	25
Swimming pools	9	1
Storytelling halls	38	29
Clubs	14	6
Total	5,531	3,737

[a]The order of listing of stores, banks, and so on, follows the original ranking.
Source: *SSG*, vol. 5, table after 220.

APPENDIXES

Shanghai Public Security Bureau Regulations for Eradicating "Huahui" Lotteries 1927–1928

A number of regulations were stipulated for eradicating private lotteries like *huahui* ("flower club") and *hangchuanzi* ("passenger ships"):

First, strict orders will go out to each precinct, station, and squad to send policemen randomly to places where these games are known to be played. Once the information has been secretly gathered, preparations will be made for arrests. Officers are to make sure that the arrests are conducted by regular inspectors so that the regular policemen will not be able to take advantage of the search to cause misfortune.

Second, residents will be urged to report gambling operations to the authorities. One-half of the moneys seized in the ensuing raid will go to these informers; the other half will be used to reward the participating officers and policemen.

Third, if possible, precincts and stations should report large gambling operations to headquarters in advance of raids. But in cases of urgency, then the arrests could be made and the report sent along at the same time.

Fourth, all gamblers arrested, along with the evidence seized, will be sent to central headquarters.

Fifth, efforts should be made to close down major gambling casinos in the foreign parts of Shanghai as well.

Sixth, special commendations will be given to policemen who help shut down major gambling operations. Accumulating a certain number of these will result in promotion.

Seventh, any policemen caught protecting a gambler in exchange for a bribe will be dismissed and prosecuted.

Eighth, if there is indisputable proof of a major gambling enterprise being operated in a precinct for a considerable period of time, then the officers and men of that precinct will all be punished.

Ninth, if a policeman plants evidence or falsely incriminates others, the injured party will be compensated and the policeman will be dismissed and handed over to the court for punishment.

Tenth, if a precinct station raids a large gambling operation without reporting to headquarters, and if the felons escape or if evidence is destroyed, then there will be an immediate investigation.

Eleventh, if police privates seize gambling funds they will be punished.

Twelfth, these regulations will be obeyed from the moment they are promulgated.

Source: *SSG, jishi,* 53–54.

Shanghai Municipality Peace Preservation Corps in December 1932

First Regiment. Headquartered in the Police Training Depot in Zhabei under Chen Zhuomin.

> *First Battalion.* Five hundred infantrymen armed with rifles and machine guns, also stationed in Zhabei. This unit had a motorcycle corps.

> *Six Companies.* One hundred twenty-four men each, barracked in Zhabei. Three of these companies were armed with automatic weapons. The other three were either armed with rifles or were unarmed. Some had motorcycle units. One was housed in a benevolent association, one in a temple, three in police depots, and one elsewhere.

Second Regiment. Headquartered in the Shaoxing guildhall in Nanshi (South Circuit or South Market). Forty-two men armed with automatic weapons.

> *Thirteen Companies.* One hundred twenty-four men each. Five of these companies had machine guns. Eight were housed in benevolent guilds, four in temples, and two elsewhere.

Source: SMP, D-3648, 30 Dec. 1932.

The Shanghai "Silver Orgy" and the Effect of the Great Depression on Shanghai's Police

China was at first insulated from the world economic depression that started in 1929 because of the continuing decline of silver prices in the world market. Since China used silver as money, the depreciation of silver prices meant the devaluation of her foreign exchange, which promoted exports and encouraged capital inflow. As silver prices slowly fell in world markets, commodity prices slowly rose in China and the country enjoyed a mild prosperity.[1]

At that time Shanghai held the largest concentration of silver on earth: about 400 million ounces. After 1931, silver prices began to rise on the London and New York money markets because of currency devaluations by Great Britain, Japan, and the United States. To boost existing treasury reserves, the U.S. government passed the Silver Purchase Act in June 1934, buying silver in the open markets of the world until its silver holdings reached a certain proportion of its gold reserves. Altogether, the U.S. anticipated buying 1.3 billion ounces of silver. A marked rise in the value of the Chinese silver yuan followed.

Finance Minister T. V. Soong, meanwhile, abolished the tael, which was a weight in silver, and issued a new national silver dollar corresponding roughly to the Chinese dollars already in use.[2] The currency was coined in the Shanghai mint and transported to the Central Bank of China in red armored cars topped with machine guns.[3]

The new Shanghai dollar was quoted below its parity in silver in terms of pounds or U.S. dollars. That is, in London, a Shanghai dollar was worth Ch. $1.10 in terms of its silver value, so that a profit of 10 percent could be realized if Shanghai silver dollars were sold abroad. Over the protests of Nanjing, the Shanghai bankers began loading their ships with silver and sending the currency to London.[4]

This appreciation in the value of silver encouraged the outflow of silver and made imported goods cheaper. Silver poured into Shanghai from the hinterland at the rate of hundreds of millions of dollars a year. From Shanghai it was shipped out of China so that between June 1934 and November 1935 over Ch. $230 million left the country. Hauser described the "silver orgy" colorfully but accurately:

> It was a curious situation, if you to stop to think of it. For more than twenty years Shanghai had drained China of her silver. The landowners and the smalltown bankers and the gentry and the loan sharks and the warlords had sent their silver to the Settlement because the Settlement was the safest place in China. And the Taipans, who were guarding the safety of the Settlement, had been guarding China's silver. It was like a trust, almost. And now the silver began to disappear. Millions of hard silver dollars disappeared every day. And million dollar profits were realized. In the markets of the world the price for silver was still climbing. Americans bought silver, bought it at rising prices, and the Bund banks sold it. The Bund banks sold and Taipans and Griffins forgot all about cotton goods and machinery and silk and tea and coal and hides and thought about silver. The silver price was rising. The Shanghai gentlemen bought silver, bought it as fast as they could, bought it on margin, invested all they had, sold it in London. The silver price was rising. Shanghai went crazy over silver.[5]

As the price of silver went up, commodity prices in China went down, and this depressing effect soon spread throughout the entire economy.[6] During the four years 1932–35, wholesale prices fell by about a quarter and the total value of foreign trade decreased by more than a half, which was 40 percent in real terms. In 1934 about one-third of the factories and 40 percent of the stores were closed down; 1.2 million workers were out of jobs.[7] A grave economic crisis gripped China.[8]

After about one-quarter of China's silver stocks had been shipped out of the country, the Nanjing Ministry of Finance imposed a customs duty, effective October 15, 1934, of 10 percent on exports of silver. Since there was an additional equalization charge to offset any differences between the theoretical parity of London silver and the official exchange rate of the Central Bank of China, this new duty amounted to an official embargo of silver exports. For a while silver continued to be smuggled out of China, then the flow diminished and finally stopped. However, during that process the value of the Chinese dollar declined by 20 percent and inflation ensued.[9]

To cope with the currency crisis T. V. Soong was made governor of the privately-owned Bank of China, taking over control from Zhang Jia'ao. Neville Chamberlain, Conservative chancellor of the Exchequer, sent his government's chief economic adviser, Sir Frederick Leith-Ross, to Shanghai to confer with Soong and the major bankers, including the directors of the Hong Kong and Shanghai Bank (Huifeng yinhang). Shortly after Leith-Ross arrived, in November 1935, China abandoned the silver standard and suspended the circulation of silver. All silver stocks were ordered to be turned over to the government, and the issuance of legal tender was confined to the government's Central Bank of China and to the Nanjing-dominated Bank of Agriculture, Bank of Communications, and Bank of China. This fiscal coup de main by Soong and H. H. Kong concentrated immense financial powers in the hands of the Nationalist régime's Central Bank of China, and ended the monetary reign of the Ningbo bankers over the two private Chinese financial giants of Shanghai: the Bank of China and the Communications Bank.[10]

During the difficult winter of 1936-37 when the world was sunk in economic depression, resources were limited for both the International Settlement police and for the Public Security Bureau. The Shanghai Municipal Police had been living for years off the Ch. $81 million reserve fund generated by the sale of the electric power plant in 1929. In order to avoid another annual deficit, the council had tried to raise land taxes in 1936 from 14 to 16 percent, but the Japanese ratepayers had strenuously objected.[11]

Since the International Settlement's net indebtedness—secured by the Ch. $67 million of land and buildings owned by the SMC—was already $39,692,284 in June 1936, the council had no choice but to dip into its electricity plant reserves for another Ch. $2 million to balance the budget. The same was true for the 1937 budget, which would eat up another $3,250,000 of the rapidly diminishing reserve fund.[12] In late November 1936, therefore, the SMC adopted special measures to economize, including a police pay cut of 8 percent and the reduction of various police allowances.[13]

The Public Security Bureau was less strapped, even though its 1936–37 budget was cut by 5 percent to Ch. $3,463,670.[14] At the same time, however, its resource needs were much higher than the SMP's, both in terms of territory covered and population governed (see Figure 7). The per capita cost of policing the Chinese municipality of Shanghai was, with the single exception of Weihaiwei, the highest in the nation (see Figure 8).

REFERENCE MATTER

Abbreviations

BIA   Bureau of Investigation Archives

CA   *Chinese Affairs: Weekly Survey of Important Events*

CC   *China Critic*

CD   *China Daily*

CWR   *China Weekly Review*

DZ   *Dongfang zazhi*

MG   Council for the Foreign Settlement of Shanghai, *Municipal Gazette*

NCD   *North China Daily News*

NCH   *North China Herald*

NTN   Number Two National Archives

RDS   For 1910–1929: U.S. Department of State, *Records of the Department of State Relating to Internal Affairs of China, 1910–29. 839.00. Political Affairs.* For 1930–1939: U.S. Department of State, Records of the Department of State Relating to the Internal Affairs of China, 1930–1939. Microfilm.

SAM   Shanghai Archives Microfilms*

SB   *Shenbao*

SMA   Shanghai Municipal Archives

SMC   *Shanghai Municipal Council Report*

SMP   Shanghai Municipal Police (International Settlement) Files

SSG   *Shanghai shi gonganju yewu baogao*

SSN   Shanghai shi nianjian weiyuanhui, *Shanghai shi nianjian*

STS   *Shanghai tebie shi gonganju yewu jiyao, Minguo shiliu nian ba yue zhi shiqi nian qi yue*

SYZ   Shanghai tongshe, comp., *Shanghai yanjiu ziliao*

*These are the microfilms of selected police documents that the Berkeley Center for Chinese Studies acquired from the Shanghai Municipal Archives in 1989.

Notes

CHAPTER 1. LAW AND ORDER

1. Xin Zhonghua zazhi she, eds., *Shanghai de jianglai*, 3.
2. Ibid., 4–5.
3. Ibid., 4.
4. *CWR*, 11 May 1927, 226.
5. See, for example, *MG*, 28 Oct. 1927, 355.
6. *MG*, 16 Sept. 1927, 318–19.
7. *STS, jishi*, 31, 36, 48.
8. Both the Shanghai Municipal Police of the International Settlement and later the Public Security Bureau of the Special Municipality kept elaborate statistical records of crimes committed. The latter especially devoted considerable manpower to this effort, almost as though pie charts and lavishly illustrated graphs were a way of subduing crime and imposing order upon a city that was constantly threatening to get out of control.
9. *CWR*, 27 Oct. 1928, 278.
10. Finch, "Gun-Running," 112. Crime waves seemed related to temporary military demobilization, which drove out-of-work soldiers into Shanghai to live off of the citizenry. "A positive fact has been established: while there is war around Shanghai there are few robberies, because the people who commit them are drafted into the army. As soon as fighting ceases and 'peace' is declared, then the influx of criminals starts. After that an abnormal crime wave sets in and takes some time before it disappears."
11. See, for example, the Shanghai Municipal Police's role as strikebreakers in the February 9 strike at the Nagai Wata Kaisha cotton mills, detailed in the SMP, D-6010, 10 Feb. 1925; and D-6023, 11 Feb. 1925. See also, for the role of the SMP (Shanghai Municipal Police) "Intelligence Office," ibid., D-6065, 6 July 1925; and D-6027, 18 Feb. 1925; and Wasserstrom, "The First Chinese Red Scare," 32–51.
12. *MG*, 18 Oct. 1927, 355. In 1924 the SMP director of criminal intelligence was ordered to present a plan to prosecute publishers of extremist literature, to continue paying rewards to informants, to deny residence rights to persons publicly advocating Bolshevism, and to create an organization interested in preventing

the spread of Bolshevism and anti-foreignism in China. SMP, D-5942, 29 Nov. 1924.

13. Chen Weimin, "Zhonggong chengli chuqi Shanghai gongren yundong shuping," 11. The identification of crime waves with "Reds" was not peculiar to Shanghai. As used in the English-language press, and especially by American editors in Shanghai, the term "crime wave" was part of a post–World War I journalistic lexicon. The first "crime waves" were reported by newspapers in many parts of the United States in the spring of 1919. Nathan Douthit, "Police Professionalism," 319–21.

14. Increased social disorder was accompanied by increasing litigiousness. Huey, "Law and Social Attitudes," 313–14. The 1931 civil code also made it markedly easier for women to sue for divorce, as works in progress by Kathryn Bernhardt and Susan Glosser confirm.

15. By the late 1920s Shanghai was the fifth largest seaport in the world, ranking below New York, London, Rotterdam, and Hamburg. Pal, *Shanghai Saga*, 9.

16. *SSG*, vol. 3, 76.

17. "The Chinese police, in pursuing robbers, have to stop on the border of the Settlement. When the permission from the authorities of the Settlement to arrest these outlaws is obtained, they have already escaped to the French Concession. Cooperation is impossible." C. Y. W. Meng, "A Tale of Two Cities," 420.

18. These figures do not include the Shanghai military garrison of 4,083 people. Xu Gongsu and Qiu Jinzhang, "Shanghai gonggong zujie zhidu," 12. See also Hershatter, "Prostitution in Shanghai," 13; and Hershatter, "The Hierarchy of Shanghai Prostitution," 464–65.

19. The Shanghai Power Company, which was bought by American interests for US $32 million in 1929, ran one of the largest electric plants in the world. Hauser, *Shanghai: City for Sale*, 236.

20. Green, ed., *Shanghai of Today*, 9. Between 1900 and 1935 the Chinese population of the International Settlement grew from 345,000 to 1,120,000 in 8.94 square miles. Chinese houses, however, increased during that same period only from 52,000 to 82,000. There were then 200 persons per acre, but since that overall figure comprised the foreign population, the density in the Chinese industrial districts was much greater. CC, 17.2 (4 Aug. 1937), p. 34.

21. *All About Shanghai*, 76; and Finch, *Shanghai and Beyond*, 5.

22. Pan Ling, *In Search of Old Shanghai*, 39.

23. Finch, *Shanghai and Beyond*, 13. See also Hauser, *Shanghai: City for Sale*, 34.

24. Finch, *Shanghai and Beyond*, 34. During the summer of 1925 the streets were deserted from 10:00 P.M. to 4:00 A.M. with squads of men patrolling the brightly lit thoroughfares throughout the night. Booker, *News Is My Job*, 102.

25. Xu Zhucheng, *Du Yuesheng zhengzhuan*, 23.

26. The first films reached China in August 1896 when they were presented as part of a teahouse variety show in Shanghai. The first public film show as such was in 1902 in the capital, where the Fengtai photo shop in Liulichang began recording Beijing opera scenes on movie film in 1905. The Fengtai photo shop owners moved to Shanghai in 1909. Clark, *Chinese Cinema*, 6–7.

27. The first movie shown there was *The Dragon Nest* (*Long chao*). SYZ, *xuji*, 541.

28. By 1935 there were forty-eight movie companies in Shanghai. Of the seventy-two motion pictures made, fifty-two were made by the three big studios: Lianhua yingye gongsi, Mingxing gongsi, and Tianyi gongsi. *SSN* (1936), 55–57.

29. *SYZ, xuji*, 532–41; Tu Shipin, ed., *Shanghai shi daguan*, part 3, 40.

30. McCormick, *Audacious Angles on China*, 98.

31. Hauser, *Shanghai: City for Sale*, 262. This is more than slightly exaggerated, especially when it comes to the thespian sophistication of the educated Chinese community. See Levenson, *Revolution and Cosmopolitanism*; and Yeh, *The Alienated Academy*, ch. 2.

32. Lu Xun also wrote a celebrated essay about Ruan Lingyu entitled: "Gossip Is a Fearful Thing." *CD*, 26 Mar. 1968, 5; Clark, *Chinese Cinema*, 13.

33. Clark, *Chinese Cinema*, 9.

34. Spence, *The Gate of Heavenly Peace*, 184.

35. Ch'ien Chung-shu, *Fortress Besieged*, 59.

36. Mao Tun, "Comedy," 248–49.

37. See, in this regard, Lin Yutang's only slightly ambivalent "Hymn to Shanghai," in Lin Yutang, *With Love and Irony*, 63–66.

38. Xu Huifang and Liu Qingyu, "Shanghai nüxing fan de shehui fenxi." *Dalu zazhi* 1.4:87; and C. Y. W. Meng, "The 'Hwa Hui' Gambling Evil," *CWR*, 334.

39. Sun Guoqun, "Lun jiu Shanghai changji zhidu de fazhan he tedian," 3.

40. Booker, *News Is My Job*, 25–26. Earlier, around 1906 when there was an attempt to deport American prostitutes from the International Settlement, the term "American girl" was synonymous with Western women of the night. President Theodore Roosevelt ordered the 1906 drive against these mainly San Francisco prostitutes ("famed for their beauty, culture, and charm"), 27–28.

41. *CWR*, 14 June 1930, 57. The teahouses had small compartments with curtains in each room.

42. von Sternberg, *Fun in a Chinese Laundry*, 82–83.

43. *CWR*, 14 June 1930, 57. The Great World was within the International Settlement. The *CWR* commented sarcastically: "The visitors are of course Chinese and the situation affects the foreign community so little that our city fathers can well afford to overlook it."

44. Xu Huifang and Liu Qingyu, "Shanghai nüxing fan de shehui fenxi," 86–87; Sheng Ke, *Qing Hong bang zhi heimu*, 18.

45. Yen, "Crime in Relation to Social Change," 156–58.

46. Even the sociologists agreed upon the structural importance of extraterritoriality in accounting for illegal activities. Xu Huifang and Liu Qingyu, "Shanghai nüxing fan de shehui fenxi," 86.

47. Many foreigners agreed. "When the city of Shanghai is all placed under one unified police control, then only will crime begin to diminish." *CWR*, 17 Jan. 1931, 243.

48. There was a sensational disclosure in January 1929 that one of the Criminal Investigation Department (CID) interpreters in the Shanghai Municipal Police was the leader of a gang of kidnappers. *CC*, 10 Jan. 1929, 22; *CWR*, 12 Jan. 1929, 273; Fontenoy, *The Secret Shanghai*, 71.

49. Han, "French Colonial Policy in China," 240. According to a survey conducted during November 1936–January 1937 by a group of women's organiza-

tions, 51 brothels were registered by the police in a single red-light district. *CC,* 4 April 1937, 8. For details see Pan Ling, *Old Shanghai,* 58–59.

50. Han, "French Colonial Policy in China," 239.

51. On January 19, 1928, the Shanghai Public Security Bureau announced that the foreign concessions would thereafter be referred to as "special zones." *DZ,* 25 Mar. 1928, 129.

52. The SMP had been established in 1854 after the Small Sword Society uprising. Land Regulation 11 permitted the organization of a "watch or police force." "History of Police Force Is Traced by Speaker," 27 Feb. 1937, in SMP. Microfilms from the U.S. National Archives. D-2961, 28/2/37; "The Shanghai Municipal Police," part 1, 24 Dec. 1909, 747. See also Chief Yuan Liang's speech of Jan. 13, 1930. *SSG,* vol. 3, 151.

53. Han, "French Colonial Policy in China," 239.

54. *STS, zuzhi,* 1. See also Orchard, "Shanghai."

55. *STS, jishi,* 48; Shen Yi, "Shanghai shi gongwuju shi nian."

56. Reformers hereafter connected systematic police organization with "modernization" (*xiandaihua*) at least through the early 1940s. See, e.g., He Qideng, "Dangqian zhi jingzheng jigou wenti," 18.

57. "The main duty of the police is to preserve law and order" (*baochi gonggong anning*). Fang Guoxi, "Jingcha xingzheng yu difang zizhi," 10.

CHAPTER 2. FROM CONSTABULARY TO POLICE

1. The city was patrolled by a county lieutenant (*xianwei*) and an inspector (*xunjian*). Li, "The Development of the Chinese Police," 49; *SYZ,* 89.

2. This was a perfectly functional response to the extraordinary disorder of the times. "Public police replace private police when the capacity of groups within society to undertake effective enforcement action is no longer sufficient to cope with insecurity." Bayley, *Patterns of Policing,* 34.

3. *SYZ,* 89. The first *zongxun* was Mu Shuzhai. See also Zhu Yisheng, "Shanghai jingcha yange shi," 4, and Li, "The Development of the Chinese Police," 62–64.

4. Under the command of Chief Patrol Officer Zhu Huan, it virtually eliminated banditry in the Pudong area during the later years of the nineteenth century. Zhu Yisheng, "Shanghai jingcha yange shi," 5–6. The term "police" refers to "people authorized by a group to regulate interpersonal regulations within the group through the application of physical force." Bayley, *Patterns of Policing,* 209.

5. In the Qing *baojia* system, every ten households set up a *paitou* (placardhead), every ten *pai* (placards) a *jiatou* (tithing head), and every ten *jia* (tithes) a *baozhang* (ward head). At the end of each month the *baozhang* was supposed to submit a bond to the authorities, guaranteeing that all the male members of his group were behaving properly. Hsiao, *Rural China,* 44–45.

6. A force of night watchmen was provided for the International Settlement in the Land Regulations of 1845, but an actual police force was not organized until 1854. Johnstone, Jr., *The Shanghai Problem,* 74. The first Chinese to write about the concession police—Ge Yuanxu in the *Hu you zaji* (1876)—described its use of

detectives and patrolmen. Wang Jiajian, *Qing mo min chu wo guo jingcha zhidu xiandaihua de licheng,* 19–20; Li, "The Development of the Chinese Police," 63–65.

7. By 1927, the Chinese municipality had 172 kilometers of roads, the International Settlement had 171 kilometers, and the French Concession had 92 kilometers. Henriot, "Le gouvernement municipal de Shanghai," 230.

8. *SYZ,* 92; *Shanghai zujie wenti,* 63.

9. Henriot, *Shanghai 1927–1937,* 18. During the reform movement of 1898, the governor of Hunan established a Bureau of Defense (Baoweiju) in Changsha. Modeled on the constabulary of Shanghai's International Settlement, it was strongly supported by the city's merchants, particularly after crimes rapidly declined in frequency. Yee, "Police in Modern China," 9.

10. For *gong,* see Ch'eng I-fan, "*Kung* as an Ethos." For the connection between guilds, professional associations (*fatuan*), and gentry self-rule, see Rowe, *Hankow;* Rowe, "The Public Sphere in Modern China," 309–29; and Strand, *Rickshaw Beijing,* 98–99.

11. In 1898 the bureau was renamed the South Market Road Works and Reconstruction Bureau (Nanshi malu gongcheng shanhou ju). *SYZ,* 89. See also Henriot, *Shanghai 1927–1937,* 22–24.

12. *SYZ,* 89–90; Henriot, "Le gouvernement municipal de Shanghai," 11–12.

13. Also, when the English, American, and French governments got the Qing government to agree to extend the foreign concessions from 1,500 acres to 5,584 acres, the Yangshupu police station was demolished. Wang Jiajian, *Qing mo min chu wo guo jingcha zhidu xiandaihua de licheng,* 63.

14. Ibid., 34.

15. *SYZ,* 104; Bays, *China Enters the Twentieth Century,* 77; Gao, "Police Administration in Canton," 337–39.

16. MacKinnon, "A Late Qing-GMD-PRC Connection," 5.

17. Li, "The Development of the Chinese Police," 75.

18. Lao She's constable ridiculed the police training given before 1911. The teachers were either old men who were mostly opium addicts or "young boys who kept going on about foreign rubbish—about the Japanese police, about French police law, and all that. Anyone would have thought we were a bunch of bloody foreigners." "This Life of Mine," 114.

19. MacKinnon, "Police Reform in Late Ch'ing Chihli," 82–99.

20. Details of the Beijing police reforms are given in *Jingcha faling* [Police laws], 2.

21. Ames, *Police and Community in Japan,* 9–10; Yee, "Police in Modern China," 1. The English word "police"—which was first used to denote a body of men in 1758—was borrowed from the French. Palmer, *Police and Protest in England and Ireland,* 69.

22. Oura Kanetake, "The Police of Japan," 281–95.

23. Strand, *Rickshaw Beijing,* 67; Shen Zui, *Juntong neimu,* 3. Kawashima argued that, "There is no country that does not have a police system. It stands as the complement of military strength. One is the preparation . . . to protect national interests and rights. The other is an instrument for internal control to restrain the people in order to extend national laws and national orders. These are the two greatest forces of the country and cannot be done without for even one day." Li, "The Development of the Chinese Police," 33.

24. Zhu Yisheng, "Shanghai jingcha yange shi," 3; Chen Yaofu, "Qingmo Shanghai shezhi xunjing de jingguo," 104.

25. The River Police were also formed at this time with subscriptions from commercial houses and merchants in South Market. The River Police mounted patrols along the Chinese Bund, protecting commerce and shipping. Other local government bureaus subsequently sprang up elsewhere in the Chinese sections of Shanghai, to cope with dike repairs as well as construction and maintenance of roads, establishment of schools, distribution of medical relief and vaccines to the poor, and management of a police bureau to patrol the area. *SSN* (1936), 1–13; Henriot, "Le gouvernement municipal de Shanghai," 15.

26. *SYZ,* 90; Henriot, "Le gouvernement municipal de Shanghai," 12.

27. Wang Jiajian, *Qing mo min chu wo guo jingcha zhidu xiandaihua de li-cheng,* 63–64.

28. Chen Yaofu, "Qingmo Shanghai shezhi xunjing de jingguo," 104–6.

29. *SYZ,* 91.

30. The term *kōban* was used in early Meiji for dormitory-like buildings in Tokyo where policemen lived and patrolled. The police box system was actually suggested to the Japanese Home Ministry by Heinrich Friedrich Wilhelm Höhn of the Berlin Metropolitan Police. Li, "The Development of the Chinese Police," 29–30; Yee, "Police in Modern China," 11–18; Ames, *Police and Community in Japan,* 24; Bayley, *Forces of Order,* 13–32.

31. *Fenju* (branch bureaus) were opened in the eastern part of the old city at the Ouwang Temple, in the southern sector at the Palace of the Water Immortals (Shuixiangong), near the west gate at the Guandi Temple (and later moved to the Yugongci), and in the northern quarter at the Chenxiang Pavilion (Chenxiangge).

32. Zhu Yisheng, "Shanghai jingcha yange shi," 3, 6–7; *SYZ,* 91.

33. Chang Zhaoru, "Guomindang tongzhi shiqi de jingcha zhidu," 337–38.

34. Nationalist police centralizers later emphasized the importance of not rely-ing upon local elites for the financing of police, which "must not be allowed to carry the slightest feudal flavor" by being confused with local gentry-supported militia. Calling for national budgeting of police expenses, one expert stressed that "if you want to create a modern country, and yet wish to avoid the cost of police and their equipment by using militiamen (*zhuangbing*) at no public expense, then I am afraid this will be most unlikely." He Qideng, "Dangqian zhi jingzheng jigou wenti," 22.

35. Yu Xiuhao (Frank Yee), *Jingcha shouce,* 1. At the time of publication, Yu was chief of the Changchun police force.

36. Strand, *Rickshaw Beijing,* 65. But note that state building is not always associated with the creation of a modern police system. The linkage is strong in the case of France and Italy, for example; weak in the case of Germany; invisible in the case of Great Britain. Bayley, "The Police and Political Development in Europe," 355–56.

37. Yee, "Police in Modern China," 38–39.

38. Rankin, *Elite Activism and Political Transformation in China,* 27, 136–69.

39. Li, "The Development of the Chinese Police," 3; Gao, "Police Administra-tion in Canton," 691.

40. Elvin, "The Gentry Democracy in Shanghai." Elvin, "The Administration of Shanghai," 239–62.

41. Gamewell, *The Gateway to China*, 32. By 1927 the Volunteer Corps consisted of 1,400 men and 80 officers, including the commanding officer and adjutant who were second officers of the British Army. Gwynn, *Imperial Policing*, 187. The Chinese Merchant Corps also stemmed from a Chinese Merchants Calisthenics Association (Huashang ticao hui) founded in 1905 by the banker Yu Xiaqing (1863–1945), who was from Zhenhai. Yu became a comprador and started several important shipping companies supported by Ningbo merchants in Shanghai. In 1908 he and others founded the Ningbo Bank (Siming yinhang). When the Shanghai Stock and Commodity Exchange (Shanghai wupin jiaoyisuo) was founded in 1921, Yu developed close ties with Guomindang figures and the exchange covered the debts of Chiang Kai-shek when the latter left for Guangdong. Tsao Jr-lien, "On the Nature of the Chinese Capitalists," 2–6; Coble, Jr., *The Shanghai Capitalists*, 22–25.

42. Wang Jiajian, *Qing mo min chu wo guo jingcha zhidu xiandaihua de licheng*, 64.

43. *SYZ*, 90; Zhu Yisheng, "Shanghai jingcha yange shi," 8.

44. Zhu Yisheng, "Shanghai jingcha yange shi," 7. An additional two thousand policemen were to be recruited, and the police budget was increased to 255,000 taels, of which more than 120,000 came from military and customs allocations. The police reinforcements included cavalry patrols, fire protection brigades, a detective squad, and a river patrol force. Wang Jiajian, *Qing mo min chu wo guo jingcha zhidu xiandaihua de licheng*, 64.

45. When the viceroy ordered that what had been a magistrate's responsibility be elevated to a circuit intendant's concern, he justified it on larger national grounds: "Peace and order in the Hu area involve the situation in general. We must concentrate on this with all of our energy so that we can protect our sovereign rights (*zhuquan*)." *SYZ*, 91.

46. The South Market General Works Bureau also had a fire department (*jiuhuo lianhehui*). All four stations were connected with a merchant militia (*shangtuan*) that had been set up in 1906 by Li Zhongjue and that by 1911 consisted of three thousand men. For an astute account of the ambiguous relationship between this militia and Chen Qimei, see Elvin, "The Revolution of 1911 in Shanghai," 119–61.

47. Members of the local elite took over at least partial control (and a share of the financing) of the county police outside the city—police that had originally been organized by the district magistrate. Zhu Yisheng, "Shanghai jingcha yange shi," 3, 8–11; Henriot, "Le gouvernement municipal de Shanghai," 19, 22–23; Henriot, *Shanghai 1927–1937*, 26–27.

48. Henriot, "Le gouvernement municipal de Shanghai," 15–16.

49. Wang Jiajian, *Qing mo min chu wo guo jingcha zhidu xiandaihua de licheng*, 131; Zhu Yisheng, "Shanghai jingcha yange shi," 8–11.

50. Yuan announced in February that local self-governing institutions were going to be abolished. Although he did compromise the following December by promulgating regulations for *difang zizhi* (local self-government), in Shanghai the municipal government (*shizhengting*) became the general office of public works, patrols, and city taxes. Li, "The Development of the Chinese Police," 24.

51. *SYZ*, 91.

52. There was also a merchants' river patrol, organized by some of the *gongsuo*

with twenty-four patrolmen (*xunding*) and two inspectors (*jicha*) to supervise cargo and prevent pilferage. The river patrol came into conflict with the River Police Brigade. STS, *jishi*, 40.

53. With the exception of one district change, this organizational structure was retained intact, mainly under the command of Police Prefect Xu Guoliang, for the next thirteen years. STS, *zuzhi*, 1, and *jishi*, 30–31; Zhu Yisheng, "Shanghai jing-cha yange shi," 4. After Wusong became a separate port, the sixth district was changed into the Wusong Port Police Bureau (Wusong shangbu jingchaju).

54. SYZ, 91, 104.

55. For the military spit-and-polish of the Beijing gendarmes (*baoandui*) who were trained in German drill by Lt. General John Wilhelm Norman Munthe, see Military attaché China, report no. 5127, 6, in U.S. Department of War, Military Intelligence Reports, China 1911–1941. It was common practice for Shanghai police commanders to send deputies into Hebei and Shandong to recruit officers and men on the grounds that "police work in this city is vexatious and troubling. There is the most extreme hardship and toil. Northerners have strong and healthy physiques, so they can endure all this." During the Jiangsu-Zhejiang war of 1924–25, an entire contingent of 504 Beijing policemen was transferred down to Shang-hai and remained there once the war was over. SYZ, 105.

56. Zhuang Tiandiao, "Tanjing zhi heimu yi," vol. 1, 1. Chinese patrolmen working for the foreign police were often called "foreign dogs" or "foreign slaves." Bourne, "The Shanghai Municipal Police," 30.

57. Detective squads in general were held in low esteem in China at this time. Of the Canton detective force it was said: "they are unfortunately a group of swindlers, rascals, and villains. They are absolutely lacking in scientific training. The reason for recruiting the force from such a class is based on the principle of 'using a thief to catch a thief.' " Gao, "Police Administration in Canton," 876.

58. Zhuang Tiandiao, "Tanjing zhi heimu yi," vol. 1, 2–3.

59. Lee, *The Underworld of the East*, 265.

60. Hauser, *Shanghai: City for Sale*, 167.

CHAPTER 3. FOUL ELEMENTS

1. Martin, "'The Pact with the Devil,'" 2.

2. Martin, "Warlords and Gangsters," 5; Wang Yangqing and Xu Yinghu, "Shanghai Qing Hong bang gaishu," 63–65.

3. Rowe, "The Qingbang and Collaboration," 493–94.

4. Honig, "Women Cotton Mill Workers," 118; Honig, *Sisters and Strangers*, 120–31; STS, *jishi*, 62. For Shanghai beggars, see Gamewell, *The Gateway to China*, 55; CWR, 30 May 1925, 360.

5. Informers were also frequently murdered and dismembered. Pal, *Shanghai Saga*, 71–72.

6. Organized crime regulates illegal but persistent transactions in informal economies. Smart, "The Informal Regulation of Illegal Economic Activities," 1. Or, in Carmine ("the Snake") Persico's words: "Why [pay the mafia a 'tax' on criminal proceeds]? Because *we* let you do it. We're the government," in Abadin-sky, *The Criminal Elite*, 64. "They're like the police department for wise guys." Ibid., 56.

7. Zhuang Tiandiao, "Tanjing zhi heimu yi," vol. 1, p. 2. See also Martin, "Tu Yueh-sheng and Labour Control in Shanghai," 106. Organized crime in turn provided liaison to the government while protecting its own clients from government interference. This function, Robert Merton would remind us, was quite similar to the role played by political parties vis-à-vis legitimate business. Merton, *Social Theory and Social Structure*, 134.

8. Zhang Jungu, *Du Yuesheng zhuan*, 59–63; Rowe, "The Qingbang and Collaboration," 492. The Green Gang probably descended from one of the branches of the Patriarch Luo sect (Luozujiao) of the late Ming. Ma Xisha and Cheng Xiao, "Cong Luo jiao dao Qingbang," 12–13; Hu Zhusheng, "Qingbang shi chutan," 103–5; Martin, "The Green Gang and 'Party Purification,'" 4; Sheng Ke, *Qing Hong bang zhi heimu*, 2–3.

9. Hu Zhusheng, "Qingbang shi chutan," 107; Rowe, "The Qingbang and Collaboration," 493; Xu Zhucheng, *Du Yuesheng zhengzhuan*, 13.

10. The Qingbang did not reject natal family relationships: "To honor the demands of natural kin relationships, fathers and sons were not permitted to take the same teacher and thereby become brothers." Kelley, "Sect and Society," 139, 153.

11. Wang Yangqing and Xu Yinghu, "Shanghai Qing Hong bang gaishu," 63; Martin, "The Green Gang and 'Party Purification,'" 51–52; Xue Gengxin, "Jindai Shanghai de liumang," 160.

12. Wang Yangqing and Xu Yinghu, "Shanghai Qing Hong bang gaishu," 63. But see also, for evidence of anti-Qing activities, Hu Zhusheng, "Qingbang shi chutan," 106–7. For a present-day version of this saying, accompanied by a naturalistic explanation, see Chin, *Chinese Subculture and Criminality*, 21.

13. Hu Zhusheng, "Qingbang shi chutan," 109.

14. The first accounts of Green Gang activity in the Shanghai vicinity are contained in the Qingpu county gazetteer for 1889. The gang was locally called the "bare eggs" (*guangdan*). Shao Yong, "Ershi shiji chuqi Qingbang zai Shanghai jiaoxian de huodong," 163–64.

15. Hu Zhusheng, "Qingbang shi chutan," 109.

16. Ibid., 64.

17. Ibid., 117. At the time, Chen Qimei explained that because the Qingbang and Hongbang "played no small part in the revolution and they have advanced from dark secrecy into the open, we are using the name 'Joint Progress.'" Su Zhiliang, "Shanghai banghui shi gaishu," 4. The original Gongjinhui was founded in 1907 by the Hubei contingent in the Tongmenghui, and fell under the leadership of Jiao Dafeng. Fung, "The Kong-chin-hui," 194.

18. Su Zhiliang, "Shanghai banghui shi gaishu," 5. Yuan Shikai's two sons, Yuan Kewen and Yuan Keding, were said to be members of the Green Gang, but this was probably only an honorific membership as they never took disciples themselves. Xu Zhucheng, *Du Yuesheng zhengzhuan*, 13–14.

19. By the 1920s the Shanghai Green Gang was well differentiated from other Green Gang groups in rural areas of northern Jiangsu, Hebei, and Shandong. Martin, "The Green Gang and 'Party Purification,'" 4–5.

20. Estimates of membership ranged from 20,000 to 100,000. Probably the smaller figure is the more accurate one. Isaacs, ed., *Five Years of Kuomintang Reaction*, 93.

21. Chang, *The Rise of the Chinese Communist Party*, vol. 1, 173.

22. Chang, *The Rise of the Chinese Communist Party*, 172–73. Romanization changed to pinyin. For the Green Gang's domination of Shanghai's docks and wharves, see Sheng Ke, *Qing Hong bang zhi heimu*, 21.

23. "Li Lisan tongzhi dui eryue bagong he wusa yundong de huiyi (fangwen jilu)," vol. 1, 144.

24. Chang, *The Rise of the Chinese Communist Party*, 174.

25. For instance, BAT union leaders Chen Peide and Gu Ruofeng were the disciples of Du Yuesheng and Huang Jinrong. After T. V. Soong arranged an agreement between the Guomindang and BAT to end the 1928 strike, Chen and Gu turned in Communist union leader Li Chenggui to the authorities. Four other Communist labor organizers were arrested by the Public Security Bureau shortly afterward, leaving the union in gangster hands. Perry, "Shanghai on Strike," 42–45.

26. Martin, "The Green Gang and 'Party Purification,'" 7. See also Wang Yangqing and Xu Yinghu, "Shanghai Qing Hong bang gaishu," 63.

27. Martin, "Warlords and Gangsters," 5; Martin, "'The Pact with the Devil,'" 5; Pan Ling, *Old Shanghai*, 36. "The majority of the Chinese detectives in the French police are members of the Green pang of Doo Yueh Seng [Du Yuesheng], and some belong to the Red pang." SMP, 8 July 1933. See also Yen, "Crime in Relation to Social Change in China," 268. Detectives who were members were said to receive more income from the gangs than from their actual salaries. *CWR*, 22 Mar. 1930, 124. See also Pal, *Shanghai Saga*, 19.

28. Feetham, *Report of the Hon. Richard Feetham, C.M.G., to the Shanghai Municipal Council*, vol. 2, 159. See also Martin, "'The Pact with the Devil,'" 7–8.

29. Pan Ling describes the post of Chinese detective as being "an odd office that combined the comprador, contractor and police investigator, and whose bearers, to use the Shanghainese term for them, might be called 'contract detectives.'" Pan Ling, *Old Shanghai*, 23.

30. The two leading members of the "Gentry-Councillor Clique" were Lu Baihong and Zhu Zhiyao, who belonged to families that had originally converted to Catholicism in the seventeenth century. Martin, "'The Pact with the Devil,'" 10.

31. Ibid., 1–2.

32. There is a fascinating file on the murder of an informant by his fellow criminals in SMP, 6 July 1929.

33. This was true as well of customs officers, who paid their stool pigeons out of pocket but who received 10 percent of the contraband sold at public auction. Pal, *Shanghai Saga*, 60, 71–72.

34. Zhuang Tiandiao, "Tan jing zhi heimu yi," in Qian Shengke, ed., *Shanghai heimu huibian*, 1929, vol. 1, 1–2.

35. Qi Zaiyu, *Shanghai shi renzhi*, 165. See also Coble, Jr., *The Shanghai Capitalists*, 37.

36. Zhu Zijia (Jin Qiongbai), *Huangpu jiang de zhuo lang*, 72–74; Xu Zhucheng, *Du Yuesheng zhengzhuan*, 20–21. Another fictional analogue was *Water Margin*, the late Ming vernacular novel about the bandits of Liangshanbo. "Indeed the peculiar legal and administrative situation in Shanghai resulting from the existence of three autonomous administrations enabled the Green Gang to transpose to an urban environment the rural bandits' classic strategy of establishing

their 'lairs' in the no man's land between two or more county or prefectural jurisdictions: in the fullness of time the French Concession became a veritable urban
Liang-shan-po." Martin, "The Green Gang and 'Party Purification,'" 4.

37. Xu Zhucheng, *Du Yuesheng zhengzhuan*, 14; Xue Gengxin, "Jindai Shanghai de liumang," 162; Fu Xiangyuan, *Qingbang da heng*, 16. At the height of his
power, Huang Jinrong was described as having hundreds of representatives of
Chinese and foreign organizations pay calls upon him, as well as having thousands
of retainers waiting outside of his doorway hoping for his protection. Qi Zaiyu,
Shanghai shi renzhi, 165.

38. Ding had a peasant background before becoming a boatman. Cheng, who
had studied for three years in a *sishu*, had worked as an apprentice in a Zhenjiang
grain store. His enormous gripping strength was said to have come from hauling
grain sacks. The former was related to, and the latter a sworn blood brother of,
Xue Gengxin. See Xue Gengxin, "Jindai Shanghai de liumang," 162.

39. Wang Yangqing and Xu Yinghu, "Shanghai Qing Hong bang gaishu," 64.

40. For the organization of the French police, see Xue Gengshen, "Wo yu jiu
Shanghai Fa zujie," 149–51.

41. At the time, there were thirteen Chinese plainclothes detectives and
thirteen European inspectors on the French police force. Pan Ling, *Old Shanghai*, 25.

42. Ding Shunhua later resigned from the force to open up a hotel near Huang
Jinrong's teahouse at the Dongxin Bridge. Huang Jinrong subsequently introduced him to Lin Kanghou, who helped him get an appointment in 1943 as a
detective on the railway line to Hangzhou. Xue Gengxin, "Jindai Shanghai de
liumang," 162. The "dense web of runners" who "nosed out suspects" for their
detective-bosses were called "Three-Times Bare Fellows, seeing that they had neither office nor salaries nor rations." Pan Ling, *Old Shanghai*, 24. The British
termed them "seconds," as in Superintendent Aiers's comment: "Superintendent
Yao has a number of seconds and I am afraid some of them are of rather shady
character." SMP, D-4009, 14 Sept. 1932.

43. Zhang Jungu, *Du Yuesheng zhuan*, vol. 1, 47–52; Xue Gengxin, "Jindai
Shanghai de liumang," 161–62. There were several cases the French detectives
could not crack, and they had to agree to give Huang a permit to open a theater
in the French Concession (the proceeds of which were to pay for his runners) in
order to get him back. Pan Ling, *Old Shanghai*, 25.

44. "Two successive heads of the Sûreté, Messrs. Traissac and Sidaine, Huang's
nominal superiors, lost their positions in 1924 and 1925, respectively, for turning
a blind eye to the involvement of Chinese detectives in the gambling and narcotics
operations in the Concession." Martin, "'The Pact with the Devil,'" 9.

45. Huang's popular Shanghai nickname was "the Great Wall of peace and
order in the French Concession." Ibid., 8–9.

46. Marshall, "Opium and the Politics of Gangsterism in Nationalist China,"
33; Coble, Jr., *The Shanghai Capitalists*, 37.

47. Wang Yangqing and Xu Yinghu, "Shanghai Qing Hong bang gaishu," 63.

48. Pan Ling, *Old Shanghai*, 25–26. Huang also carried on a version of the
"Moll Cutpurse" system practiced by seventeenth- and eighteenth-century private detectives or "thief takers" in England. In effect, Huang gave the rightful
owners of stolen goods an opportunity to buy them back through his own media-

tion with the felons. Emsley, *Crime and Society in England,* 62–64; Tobias, *Urban Crime in Victorian England,* 29; and Weisser, *Crime and Punishment,* 124.

49. Yang Wei, *Du Yuesheng waizhuan,* 38. Xu Zhucheng, *Du Yuesheng zhengzhuan,* 21–23. Control of gambling is almost always crucial to a racketeer's system of authority. Also, one of the ways policemen reduce the tension between outer demands for law enforcement and their own connection with racketeers is by striking out against competition that threatens the racketeer and leads to violence, thereby increasing the pressure on the police officer. Whyte, *Street Corner Society,* 139–40.

50. Wang Yangqing and Xu Yinghu, "Shanghai Qing Hong bang gaishu," 64.

51. Xue Gengxin, "Jindai Shanghai de liumang," 165; Wang Yangqing and Xu Yinghu, "Shanghai Qing Hong bang gaishu," 64; Tan Shaoliang's report, "Citizen's Maintenance Association," in SMP, D-3445, 8 Apr. 1932, 4–5; *CWR,* 24 June 1933, 147.

52. Zhang Jungu, *Du Yuesheng zhuan,* 52–53.

53. Martin, "'The Pact with the Devil,'" 9.

54. Wang Yangqing and Xu Yinghu, "Shanghai Qing Hong bang gaishu," 64; Xu Zhucheng, *Du Yuesheng zhengzhuan,* 14–15. Wei Tingrong, who was also the commander of the Shanghai Chinese Merchant Volunteers (Huaren shangtuan), and Huang Jinrong were rivals for the hand of Lü Meiyu, the actress. When she left Huang to marry Wei, the racketeer dared not attack Wei directly because the bride's father, Zhu Baosan, was such an important municipal figure. Fearing vengeance, however, Wei Tingrong tried to get Huang out of the way by denouncing him to the French Ministry of Foreign Affairs. Xue Gengxin, "Jindai Shanghai de liumang," 162–63.

55. For example, the Green Gang boss in Hongkou, Sun Jiefu, placed many of his henchmen in the local warlord police ranks. Martin, "The Green Gang and 'Party Purification,'" 7, 51.

56. Du Yuesheng, for instance, furthered his career considerably in 1921 or 1922 when he opened up a jewelry shop on Rue du Consulat. The store, which he called the Meizhenhua ji and which was managed by one of his followers, "was used for meetings between Du and junior officers of the Chinese police and smuggling prevention squads." According to police intelligence reports, the opening of the store plus the establishment of an opium smuggling concern "raised Du's prestige to a great extent, with the result that loafers in various districts and detectives of various police stations applied to be followers of Du." "Memorandum on Mr. Tu Yueh-sung, Alias Tu Yuin." Special Branch Secret Memorandum, in SMP, D-9319, 1 Sept. 1939, 2–3. The jewelry store manager's name was Li Yingsheng.

57. Gurr, *Rogues, Rebels, and Reformers.* See also Robinson, "The Mayor and the Police," 282. There is an enthralling portrait of a Calcutta *goonda* (hired killer) in the unpublished manuscript by Basu and Freeman, "Mallabir: Life History of a Calcutta Gangster."

58. *STS, jishi,* 49. "Magnify the difficulties of enforcement of prohibition of alcohol in the United States by many times, and one may then appreciate the immensity of this particular obstacle to good government in China." U.S. Department of War, Military Intelligence Reports, China, 1911–1941, U.S. Military Attaché, "Comment on Current Events (November 1–15, 1928)," 7.

59. By the mid-1840s opium was openly sold at Wusong (Woosung), the outer port twelve miles down the Huangpu River. Hao, "Commercial Revolution in Modern China," 130.

60. Ibid., 131–32.

61. Most of the opium was imported by Jardine's, Dent's, Lindsay's, and Sassoon's. In the 1860s the Shanghai office of Jardine's was headed by its various partners including William Keswick and F. B. Johnson. Ibid., 136.

62. Ibid., 58–60.

63. Finch, *Shanghai and Beyond*, 278; Marshall, "Opium and the Politics of Gangsterism," 19; Spence, "Opium Smoking in Ch'ing China," 153–54.

64. Lee, *The Underworld of the East*, 246. The quotation is taken from descriptions of the city ca. 1906. See also Hauser, *Shanghai: City for Sale*, 73.

65. Lee, *The Underworld of the East*, 247.

66. Martin, "Warlords and Gangsters," 2. Chaozhou men also formed tough Cantonese gangs within the Shanghai Hongbang (Red Gang), which was, however, dominated by middle Yangzi boatmen under the Shaanxi leader, Xu Langxi. Wang Yangqing and Xu Yinghu, "Shanghai Qing Hong bang gaishu," 65; Xue Gengxin, "Jindai Shanghai de liumang," 161.

67. The United States authorities were interested in curbing opium because of their acquisition of the Philippines, which had 25,000 Chinese opium smokers. Parssinen and Meyer, "International Narcotics Trafficking," 8–9.

68. Martin, "Warlords and Gangsters," 3; Hauser, *Shanghai: City for Sale*, 73; Finch, *Shanghai and Beyond*, 278–79.

69. The managing committee was composed of representatives from the leading houses mentioned earlier. Hauser, *Shanghai: City for Sale*, 118–19.

70. Together, the Opium Merchants Combine and the Swatow clique requested the Municipal Council in January 1916 to close down the small retail shops dealing in smuggled opium. Martin, "Warlords and Gangsters," 3–5.

71. Ibid.

72. See, for the classification of different kinds of opium: "Shanghai's Varied 'Taste' in Opium," *CWR*, 24 May 1930, 493–94.

73. This was far out of line with world prices. In 1914 a chest of Indian opium sold for 6,800 taels wholesale, 10,000 taels retail in Shanghai, and 50,000 taels retail in remoter places. Shipped to a non-China market, the same chest was worth the equivalent of only 500 taels. Martin, "Warlords and Gangsters," 4.

74. Ibid.

75. Ibid., 2, 6–7. Domestic opium was shipped from Sichuan and Yunnan via the Yangzi, or by rail to Haiphong and thence by steamer to Shanghai. Overseas opium came via Bushire in the Persian Gulf or from Constantinople. Most hijacking took place between the French Concession and the Chinese city along the Boulevard des Deux Républiques where the opium warehouses were located. Pan Ling, *Old Shanghai*, 29.

76. Lu Yongxiang was described as looking like a prosperous silk merchant. Finch, *Shanghai and Beyond*, 20–21.

77. Martin, "Warlords and Gangsters," 7–8.

78. In May 1922 the Zhili faction headed by Wu Peifu defeated Zhang Zuolin's forces in the first Zhili-Fengtian War. Li Yuanhong was placed in the presidency, and in May 1923 Sun Chuanfang was sent to take over Fujian. The Zhili faction

thus controlled most of the provinces of China while facing three main antagonists: Sun Yat-sen in the South, Zhang Zuolin in the Northeast, and Lu Yongxiang in Shanghai and Zhejiang. Yomano, "Reintegration in China under the Warlords," 25.

79. The first director was a Suzhou native named Wu Yingzhi, who was one of Lu Yongxiang's advisers. He was succeeded by the magistrate of the military court of the Longhua garrison. Report by Deputy Inspector Givens in SMP, D-5374, 2 May 1924.

80. Martin, "Warlords and Gangsters," 11.

81. Ibid., 16.

82. *CWR*, 1 May 1926, 217–20.

83. The Ezra brothers' front for their opium dealing was the Dahloong Tea Company. Marshall, "Opium and the Politics of Gangsterism," 29.

84. Ezra himself never recovered the opium, because his claim of Spanish nationality was denied by the Mixed Court, which meant that he reverted to the citizenship of his parents, who were Turkish. Since Turkey, along with Austria, Germany, and the other central European powers whom China fought in World War I, had forfeited its treaty privileges, Mr. Ezra did not enjoy extraterritoriality.

85. Documents seized in the Ezra raid included an agreement to transport opium to the Shanghai arsenal, which was under the direct control of the Nationalist defense commissioner. The contracts stipulated that the Chinese navy, army, and police would protect the narcotics shipped by the syndicate. *CWR*, 7 Mar. 1925, 1, and 28 Mar. 1925, 93–94; Wu Lien-teh, "Opium Problem Reaches Acute State," 2.

86. Pal, *Shanghai Saga*, 36–40.

87. There were said to be about five million addicts in the Yangzi valley alone. Martin, "Warlords and Gangsters," 2–3. See also *CWR*, 20 July 1929, 323; and Sues, *Shark Fins and Millet*, 7.

88. In 1921 the military governor of Gansu announced to a public gathering of officials, gentry, and merchants that he was going to encourage planting opium poppies all over the province in order to stop financial panic and pay his troops. Marshall, "Opium and the Politics of Gangsterism," 20.

89. Ibid., 26.

90. Ibid.; Pal, *Shanghai Saga*, 29, 41.

91. Yomano, "Reintegration in China under the Warlords," 25.

92. Shanghai shehui kexue yuan, zhengzhi falü yanjiusuo, shehui wenti zu, comp., *Da liumang Du Yuesheng*, 12–13.

93. Xu Zhucheng, *Du Yuesheng zhengzhuan*, 16.

94. Adams II, "China: The Historical Setting," 379. Heroin was invented in 1898 by Bayer, a German pharmaceutical company. Block and Chambliss, *Organizing Crime*, 31.

CHAPTER 4. POLICING THE NEW CIVIC ORDER

1. Eisenstadt, *Tradition, Change, and Modernity*, 18.

2. Burchell, Gordon, and Miller, eds., *The Foucault Effect*, 102.

3. Bayley, *Patterns of Policing*, 47.

4. *SB*, 7 July 1927, 14; *CWR*, 9 July 1927, 140; *NCH*, 9 July 1927, 47; *DZ*, 10

Sept. 1927, 116. The foundation of the municipal government was delayed because Huang Fu—former prime minister, minister of foreign affairs, and minister of education—twice refused the post of mayor. He finally heeded Chiang Kai-shek's request to take on the assignment in order to balance the influence of Bai Chongxi and reassure the foreign powers in Shanghai. Henriot, "Le gouvernement municipal de Shanghai," 33.

5. *NCH*, 9 July 1927, 58. Huang Fu always refused to enter the Guomindang to avoid being confused with the mass of opportunists who filled the Nationalist Party ranks after 1927. Henriot, "Le gouvernement municipal de Shanghai," 429.

6. *SB*, 8 July 1927, 13. The parallel phrases read: "The revolution has yet to be accomplished," and "Comrades must continue to exert themselves." *DZ*, 10 July 1927, frontispiece.

7. *SB*, 8 July 1927, 13. These were all revolutionary cronies of Huang Fu. Henriot, "Le gouvernement municipal de Shanghai," 429–30.

8. *SB*, 8 July 1927, 13.

9. Boorman et al., eds., *Biographical Dictionary of Republican China*, vol. 2, 259.

10. Ibid., 188.

11. The heart of the plan of "taking back the concessions to run for ourselves" (*qu zujie er dai zhi*) was to "coordinate two major elements—the first being the opening of a harbor at Wusong, the second being the moving of Shanghai's main railway station to the north—and link the railroad and commercial port together" so that the foreign concessions were completely bypassed economically. Shen Yi, "Shanghai shi gongwuju shi nian," 17. Sun's *Jianguo fanglüe* proposed building a "Great Eastern Port" on Hangzhou Bay, and dredging a canal through Pudong parallel to the Huangpu River (which would then be filled in) in order to give Chinese Shanghai a deep-water port under its own control. But many people in Shanghai thought the "Great Eastern Port" should be Shanghai proper. Sun Yat-sen, *The International Development of China*, 30–39; Henriot, "Le gouvernement municipal de Shanghai," 239–40.

12. *SB*, 8 July 1927, 13.

13. Ibid. The English-language version of Chiang's comments sounded this theme even more emphatically: "We must establish in Shanghai a real municipal government, a municipal government which can compare favorably with if not be better than the foreign settlements so that when the time arrives we will be prepared to [take] the settlements back. Foreigners then cannot object to their return on the old ground that we are unprepared to administer affairs." *NCH*, 9 July 1927, 58. See also Zheng Zu'an, "Guomindang zhengfu 'da Shanghai jihua' shimo," 209.

14. *NCH*, 9 July 1927, 58.

15. Ibid., 48.

16. Shen Yi, "Shanghai shi gongwuju shi nian," 11.

17. Contemporaries believed that Shanghai had more prostitutes, dope addicts, and common criminals per capita than any other city in the world. Lee, *The Underworld of the East*, 238; Hauser, *Shanghai: City for Sale*, 268–269.

18. *CWR*, 17 Sept. 1927, 78. The Chinese authorities asked the consular body of the Municipal Council to close down the brothels established on streets along the Settlement borders. *CWR*, 20 Aug. 1927, 316.

19. *SB*, 8 July 1927, 13. See also *STS*, *jishi*, 52–53; Shen Yi, "Shanghai shi gongwuju shi nian," part 1, 17. This was not the Nationalists' theme alone. In founding "Greater Shanghai" two years earlier, the warlord Sun Chuanfang had remarked that "only by proving that they could administer a town as well as the foreigners would the Chinese be able to prove their right to recover the administration of the foreign settlements." Green, ed., *Shanghai of Today*, 10. The contrast also worked in the opposite direction, providing foreigners with "a continuing reassurance that the Chinese were unfit to manage their own affairs and that foreign privilege must continue." Clifford, "The Western Powers and the 'Shanghai Question,'" 6. See also Bruce, "The Foreign Settlement at Shanghai," 132–33.

20. *NCH*, 9 July 1927, 48.

21. Coleman, "Municipal Authority and Popular Participation," 4–5.

22. *NCH*, 9 July 1927, 48. Canton developed an excellent Public Safety Bureau, by 1930 one of the very best in China. Gao, "Police Administration in Canton," 349; Snow, "How 5,200 Policemen Keep Order in Canton," *CWR*, 29 Nov. 1930, 468. A police-box system had been initiated as early as 1918. Li Xixian, "Wei Bangping ren Guangdong shenghui jingcha tingzhang," 109–10.

23. After the Nationalist government had been formed in Nanjing, the GMD party branch in Shanghai had drawn up proposals for an administrative assembly elected by the populace and presided over by the mayor. Huang Fu, however, had produced a revised set of regulations, which eliminated the assembly, reunited Shanghai and rural Baoshan District into a single administrative (and partly rural) entity, and created an assembly of counselors (*canshi hui*) completely appointed by the mayor, whose own powers were close to those of a French prefect. Henriot, "Le gouvernement municipal de Shanghai," 35, 38–40.

24. Henriot, *Shanghai 1927–1937*, 50–51. See, for the Guomindang and Chiang Kai-shek's centralizing tendencies at this time, Yamada, "The Foundations and Limits of State Power," 197.

25. *NCH*, 9 July 1927, 14.

26. Wilson, *Varieties of Police Behavior*, 67, 16.

27. "In a modern national political system the police are actually the lowest level public official; the police constitute the base level organization for preserving peace in society. The maintenance of peace and social order entirely depends upon the police." Xuan Tiewu, "Renshi jingcha," 15. Xuan was chief of the Shanghai police in 1946.

28. The chief of the Songhu Police Prefecture (Songhu jingcha ting), Shen Yulin, announced on July 3 plans to change his organization into a Public Security Bureau just as soon as the municipal government was founded on July 7. *NCH*, 4 July 1927, 15.

29. *STS*, *jishi*, 24.

30. *STS*, *xuyan*, 1. See also the various measures suggested by the Foreign Affairs Division of the PSB to recover police rights of roads, residences, factories, and so on, in *SSG*, vol. 3, 84–87.

31. *STS*, *zuzhi*, 2; *SSN*, F-58. See, for the founding of the special municipality, Orchard, "Shanghai." The creation of Public Security Bureaus was eventually authorized under the "county organization law" (*xian zuzhi fa*), which was passed by the standing committee of the Central Executive Committee of the Guomindang. Wei, *Counterrevolution in China*, 192.

32. The PSB also disbanded the merchants' river patrol and took full responsibility for security along the Huangpu. *STS, jishi,* 40. The Hu River police launch had been confiscated by the military during the hostilities in 1927, when it was sunk at Zhenjiang. Later the vessel was repaired with public funds and returned to the River Police.

33. Ibid., 31. See also Westley, *Violence and the Police,* 155–58, 189.

34. *STS, zuzhi,* 2, and *jishi,* 24.

35. The police units of the South Market Guild (Nanshi gongsuo) and the Zhabei Roadworks and Patrol Contribution Office (Gongxun juan ju) were amalgamated with the new Nationalist police in August 1927. *STS, jishi,* 5.

36. *STS, xuyan,* 1.

37. See, for Secretary Liu's lectures, ibid., *jishi,* 34.

38. *STS, jishi,* 31.

39. Approximately Ch. $2,402 were provided during the first year for building repairs, divided among the various precincts. *STS, jishi,* 40–42.

40. *SSG,* vol. 3, 66.

41. As of 1929 all SMP Chinese policemen were armed with a .380 Colt automatic. Bourne, "The Shanghai Municipal Police," 35–36.

42. Finch, "Gun-Running," 112. Although China ostensibly ranked only fifteenth worldwide as a market for British-manufactured arms, the equipment needs of over 1,300 warlords who fought more than 140 provincial and interprovincial wars between 1912 and 1928 were met by hosts of small arms smugglers and weapons salesmen representing weapons manufacturers in the United States, France, Czechoslovakia, Norway, Denmark, Italy, and Germany. Despite the Arms Embargo Agreement of 1919, these dealers annually imported thousands of tons of weapons into China, where considerable amounts of guns and ammunition—especially after the partial demobilization of some warlord armies in the wake of the Northern Expedition—found their way into the hands of Shanghai gangsters. Ibid. For the extent of this trade, see Chan, *Arming the Chinese,* 45–53.

43. *STS, jishi,* 39.

44. "Police officers of the Shanghai Public Safety Bureau commenced on August 14 to collect one month's rent directly from Chinese tenants of houses outside the Settlement and French Concession. The programme of the Nationalist Government is to collect two months' rent from each tenant, the money to be used for military purposes." *MG,* 16 Sept. 1927, 320. The municipal rate on the assessed rental of houses in the International Settlement was increased from 14 percent to 16 percent on 23 June 1927. *MG,* 25 June 1927.

45. *STS, jishi,* 38–39; *SSG,* vol. 3, 66, and vol. 4, 69.

46. On this point, see Wei, *Shanghai: Crucible of Modern China,* 100.

47. The school backgrounds of higher-ranking officers in the Shanghai PSB in 1932 included the Beijing School of Law and Administration, the Jiangsu Police Training Institute, the Baoding Police Training Institute, the Central Military Academy's Military Police School, the Beiyang Police Academy, and so forth. *SSG,* vol. 5, 257–94.

48. The SMP also preferred recruits from Shandong, Hunan, and Hubei because of their superior physiques and conduct. "The Shanghai Municipal Police," *The North China Herald and South China and China Gazette,* part 2, 31 Dec.

1909, 801. Chinese police specialists believed that the London police deliberately recruited farmers for their simplicity and amiability. Tung, "Improved Police Administration in the Capital," *CWR*, 14 Dec. 1929, 66, 89.

49. Henriot, "Le gouvernement municipal de Shanghai," 167–168.

50. *SSG*, vol. 4, table after 156.

51. *SSG*, vol. 3, 63. For other examples of regional specialization in the work force, see Honig, *Creating Chinese Ethnicity*, 40–44.

52. In Canton they favored country boys for jobs as patrolmen, believing recruits from the agricultural districts outside of the city to be more patient than urbanites and better able to endure hardship. Gao, "Police Administration in Canton," 679.

53. Shanghai police personnel manuals repeatedly emphasized the importance of selecting people of the highest moral caliber and physical strength to preserve public order. *SSG*, vol. 3, 59. The British who ran the International Settlement police also preferred northerners because they were thought to be more courageous, loyal, self-reliant, even-tempered, and trustworthy than the natives of Jiangnan. Bourne, "The Shanghai Municipal Police," 30.

54. The SMP's Chinese branch, which in 1928 consisted of 2,380 men (including seventeen inspectors and subinspectors), initially engaged inspectors directly from Beijing. By 1921, however, these posts were filled from the ranks of the International Settlement's own force. Ibid., 30, 32–33.

55. The rivalry between northerners and southerners thus fitted into a familiar rivalry between patrolmen and detectives, characteristic of almost all police forces. Westley, *Violence and the Police*, 43.

56. To northern militarists, Shanghai—the South itself—was a corrupting force as such. Marshal Sun Chuanfang (who was from Shandong) once told Qi Xieyuan that it was unwise for an army to remain too long in Jiangsu and Zhejiang, lest the luxurious life there turn them soft. Sokolsky, "What Stops Progress in Nanking?" 14, 18.

57. *CA*, 30 June 1932, 48. "The work of a policeman attracts the Chinese and there is never any lack of recruits." Gamewell, *The Gateway to China*, 30.

58. Although individual police officers frequently praised the northern municipal police forces, the police-box system was not explicitly linked to the Baoding-Tianjin model in the PSB documents that I have read.

59. *STS, jishi*, 42. For the location of each of the precinct stations, see the organizational chart in *STS, zuzhi*.

60. Henriot, "Le gouvernement municipal de Shanghai," 170, 375; *STS, jishi*, 56; *SSG*, vol. 4, *huiyi*, 9.

61. Since there were an additional Ch. $7,000 provided by the Shanghai Municipal Guild and the Hubei Roadworks and Patrol Contribution Office (Hubei gong xun juanju), this was actually higher altogether than the monthly share of Ch. $60,000 allotted to the new Public Security Bureau after its formation in July 1927.

62. In December 1927 the quota of policemen was increased by 527 owing to the increase in banditry and disorder since the "military uprising" (*junxing*). *STS, jishi*, 30. In 1928, the PSB's monthly budget was Ch. $83,182. By the following year, that monthly figure had gone up to Ch. $115,342 on paper, though the annual expenditures for 1929 only totaled Ch. $1,275,582. Between 1928 and

1935, 2,100 additional policemen were hired, along with 3,000 members of the Peace Preservation Corps after 1932. Henriot, "Le gouvernement municipal de Shanghai," 164–65.

63. *STS, jishi*, 38; *SSG*, vol. 3, 72–74.

64. *SB*, 8 July 1927, 13.

65. *STS, jishi*, 25–26. "Special municipalities" were cities with more than one million inhabitants. Henriot, "Le gouvernement municipal de Shanghai," 45.

66. Studying the careers of two thousand municipal bureaucrats during the decade 1927–37, Henriot finds only three cases of lateral transfer from one bureau to another. Henriot, "Le gouvernement municipal de Shanghai," 165.

67. Ibid., 147, 174–5, 178.

68. The first chief of police, Chen Chuan, resigned along with General Yang Hu and Mayor Huang Fu on August 13, 1927, when Chiang Kai-shek announced his retirement after returning from the front. At that point Bai Chongxi, leader of the Guangxi clique (which was less sympathetic to the Shanghai burghers' hope for municipal representation), became head of the Wusong garrison. The new mayor, Zhang Boquan, held office for approximately eighteen months before being injured in an automobile accident. Shen Yulin, a fellow townsman of Chen Guofu and Chen Lifu, succeeded as the next PSB chief, bringing in a large proportion of policemen from his native Zhejiang. And he was followed in turn, on September 25, by Dai Shifu, who brought in fifty-one assistants from his native province of Jiangxi. Colonel Dai was in turn suspended by Chiang Kai-shek (who returned to power on January 7, 1928); and when Dai left the post of chief of police, 36 percent of the central staff—sixty-six persons altogether—departed with him. By the time the new director, Huang Zhenxing, took office on December 4, 1928, another twenty-one persons had left, so that 47 percent of the central staff of the PSB had turned over within eighteen months of the bureau's formation. Huang Zhenxing, who was one of Shanghai garrison commander Xiong Shihui's close followers, served as police chief until May 1929, when Yuan Liang took over the directorship. Henriot, "Le gouvernement municipal de Shanghai," 80, 175–6, 433, 452, 459; Shen Yi, "Shanghai shi gongwuju shi nian," 14, 17; *MG*, 16 Sept. 1927, 319; Cavendish, "The 'New China' of the Kuomintang," 160; Coble, Jr., *The Shanghai Capitalists*, 42–44.

69. Wilson, *Varieties of Police Behavior*.

70. *SSG*, vol. 3, 131–32.

71. The collection of curricula vitae of all police officers in the First Detachment of the PSB Central Brigade (Dadui) in 1929 provides further data on the high educational levels, especially in military and police training schools, of middle and higher-ranking officers. SAM, No. Diwei 1 2660 DEPT 895.24, file 15.

72. *SSG*, vol. 3, 64; *STS, jishi*, 34.

73. There were three classes per year, graduating at the end of March, July, and November. In the tenth class, graduating on July 29, 1930, there were 140 cadets. *SSG*, vol. 4, 4, 67–68.

74. *STS, jishi*, 26–27; *SYZ*, 106.

75. Policewomen were assigned to precinct stations but often went far afield to search women suspects. *SSG*, vol. 4, 116–17. Most female criminals (29.2 percent of the jailed population) were convicted of drug violations, followed closely by women judged guilty of abduction and kidnapping [i.e., procurement in the West-

ern sense] (28.6 percent). Many of the latter were widows over fifty years of age. Yen, "Crime in Relation to Social Change in China," 302–3.

76. The other sixty students were appointed sergeants when vacancies occurred. *SSG*, vol. 4, 68–69. There were also promotions within ranks. Between July 1929 and June 1930, 130 *xunzhang* and 1,197 *xunjing* were promoted. Fifty-nine were demoted and 592 were dismissed. *SSG*, vol. 3.

77. Oura Kanetake, "The Police of Japan," vol. 1, 292–93. For the introduction of *Türnen*, see Wakeman, Jr., *History and Will*, 163–65, 203–4.

78. In 1909 a *jingwu tiyuhui* (police physical education society) was formed in Shanghai; Zhang Zhijiang advocated the renewal of *guoshu* in 1928 and a central martial arts office was set up in Nanjing. *SYZ*, 448.

79. *STS, jishi*, 35.

80. For the bureaucratic importance of a certain degree of social insulation, see Strauss, "Bureaucratic Reconstitution and Institution-Building," 296.

81. Class photograph in frontispieces to *STS*.

82. Photograph of 1928 Shanghai PSB headquarters group among frontispieces in *STS*.

83. *SSG*, vol. 4, *huiyi*, 7.

84. For a list of general rules stipulating the responsibilities of each precinct captain, reporting procedures, and so forth, see *STS, zhangze*, 1–6.

85. *STS, jishi*, 55–63. "Mass movements" (*minzhong yundong*) were political movements outside the Nationalist Party, which preferred "popular organizations" (*minzhong tuanti*) it could control. Cavendish, "The 'New China,'" 141. See also Eastman, "New Insights," 8–9.

86. For a complete breakdown of the sections, see *Shizheng gaikuang*, 43–44.

87. Organizational chart after the *zuzhi* section in *STS*.

88. Ibid.

89. *STS, jishi*, 42.

90. *SSG*, vol. 4, *huiyi*, 4–5; "Xunling," NTN, 12(5)/715, 2 Nov. 1934, *Jingcha yuekan*, 24–25.

91. Wilson, *Varieties of Police Behavior*, 31.

92. *SSG*, vol. 3, 60; *STS, jishi*, 16.

93. *SSN*, 73; *STS, jishi*, 24.

94. *SSG*, vol. 4, 69–70, plus table; *STS, jishi*, 32–33.

95. *SSG*, vol. 3, 65.

96. The PSB was afloat in paperwork. Between July 1929 and June 1930 headquarters received 35,092 documents in exchange for 34,151 sent out. Ibid., front tables.

97. *STS, jishi*, 33.

98. Yu Xiuhao, *Jingcha shouce*, 18–22.

99. The Japanese police scholar Takahashi Yusai was cited for this opinion. Ibid., 18. But he himself was simply reflecting the ideas of his mentor, August Vollmer, who had endorsed the publication of Takahashi's book. (See Takahashi, *The Patrol System*.)

100. Policemen were often referred to as "tramps" and "stinky feet." Lao She, "This Life of Mine," 113. See also Strand, *Rickshaw Beijing*, 71.

101. The numerous injunctions to police precincts to help neighboring precincts in the event of danger to public order (see, e.g., *STS, jishi*, 50) suggest that

there was a formalistic adherence to precinct boundaries in law enforcement. One is reminded of the problems of county, prefecture, and province jurisdictional boundary restraints under the old imperial administration.

102. Yu Xiuhao, *Jingcha shouce*, 37–38.

103. Ibid., 23.

104. Ibid., 27–28. Bank messengers were frequently robbed in Shanghai. See *CWR*, 9 Oct. 1926, 163.

105. The Chinese terms for local police units—*fenzhusuo* and *paichusuo*—were drawn from the Japanese neologisms. Organizational chart after the *zuzhi* section in *STS*.

106. *SSG*, vol. 3, tables after 56; *SSG*, vol. 4, 24.

107. *SSG*, vol. 4, 28. *STS*, *jishi*, 8.

108. Yu Xiuhao, *Jingcha shouce*, 23. Solicitude was expressed for beat patrolmen in inclement weather, and provisions were made for food and shoe allowances, special canteens and rain gear, and so forth. *SSG*, vol. 4, *huiyi*, 9, and 63–64.

109. The bank robbery conducted with "high-powered motorcars" was the quintessential crime of modern times, especially in the United States after the stock market crash of 1929. Vollmer and Parker, *Crime and the State Police*, 24; Douthit, "Police Professionalism," 329.

110. Yu Xiuhao, *Jingcha shouce*, 30–32.

111. In 1928 the Shanghai PSB took credit for clearing up streets around the concession, recovering police authority over Hongkou, enacting regulations for a census, and building police boxes. *STS*, *jishi*, 24.

112. Ibid., 37.

113. Ibid., 42.

114. Yu Xiuhao, *Jingcha shouce*, 24; *STS*, *jishi*, 24.

115. Chiang, "Achievements of the Ministry of the Interior," 60.

116. In its July 1927 report, the Shanghai Municipal Police reported that forty-nine Chinese were executed for robbery. There are many other examples in ensuing monthly reports. Among those killed was the "paymaster of the Communists in Shanghai." *MG*, 10 Aug. 1927, 288–89.

117. The police were ordered to cooperate fully with military units garrisoned in their jurisdiction. Patrols were maintained from dusk till dawn, and any persons found on the streets at night were supposed to be stopped and interrogated, especially during the "winter defense" (*dongfang*) from December to February when vehicles were randomly searched, patrol routines were changed from night to night, and special attention was paid to potentially troublesome groups like "shed people." *STS*, *jishi*, 50; *SSG*, vol. 4, 28–29, 79–80.

118. The Songhu Garrison Command received a secret report that the Communists' Shanghai Action Committee (Shanghai xingdong weiyuanhui) was plotting to carry out an insurrection on November 8, 9, and 10. All policemen were readied, but the rebellion did not occur. *STS*, *jishi*, 51.

119. Although Sun Yat-sen initially promoted people's rights, in his later years he increasingly emphasized the primacy of the state over the individual. This statist principle, which denied civil rights to anyone who opposed the National Revolution or the Three Principles of the People, continued to be enunciated throughout the Republican period and was embodied in the 1946 constitution

drafted by liberal jurist Wu Jingxiong. Greiff, "The Principle of Human Rights in Nationalist China."

120. During 1930, 1,549 persons were arrested under those laws; of these, 572 were in Shanghai. During 1931, 345 were arrested in Shanghai out of a total of 964. Gourlay, "'Yellow' Unionism in Shanghai," 111. This new "emergency" legislation did, needless to say, create certain conflicts with the new criminal code (Zhonghua minguo xingfa, Sept. 1, 1928), which was based upon the Japanese criminal code. Macauley, "The Chinese Criminal Code of 1935," 52–56. See also Liang, "The New Criminal Code, *CWR*, Sept. 8, 1928, 62; S. Y. Wang, "The Revised Criminal Code," 37–38.

121. On May 30, 1925, students demonstrating outside the Louza Police Station on Nanking Road were fired upon by Sikh and Chinese constables commanded by Inspector Everson of the SMP. Eleven were killed and twenty were wounded. Clifford, *Shanghai, 1925*, 15–17.

122. *MG*, 22 July 1927, 250–51.

CHAPTER 5. ASSERTING SOVEREIGNTY THROUGH POLICING

1. *CWR*, 5 Nov. 1929, 48.

2. *CWR*, 5 Nov. 1927, 226.

3. "Shanghai at the Crossroads," *NCH*, 2 July 1927, 6.

4. In this 1927 case, the newspaper was the *China Courier*. *CWR*, 15 Sept. 1928, 72.

5. Coble, Jr., *The Shanghai Capitalists*, 32–35. Commissioner Barrett also blamed the "political element" in the Guomindang for Shanghai's crime. The *China Weekly Review*, in many respects unique in its oppositional stance to the Settlement government, chose to emphasize the commissioner's anti-Communist rhetoric.

6. The greatest wave of White Russian immigrants came to Shanghai in December 1923 aboard twenty-six or twenty-seven battered ships of the old régime, commanded by two Tsarist admirals, that had left Vladivostok when the Bolsheviks arrived. *CWR*, 15 June 1929, 102; Hauser, *Shanghai: City for Sale*, 266; Booker, *News Is My Job*, 161.

7. *CWR*, 15 Oct. 1927, 174–75.

8. *CWR*, 5 Nov. 1927, 226.

9. The *China Weekly Review* thus looked to international intervention rather than to Chinese Nationalist solutions. In October 1927, the Japanese Residents Association, after several members of a Japanese naval patrol were detained by the SMP on September 24, had called for "drastic reform in all departments of the police department, all of which for many years have been drifting into corruption." *CWR*, 8 Oct. 1927, 146. The *Review* cautiously applauded the Japanese demand for reorganization of a local municipal government that pretended to be international in character, but really was 95 percent British. *CWR*, 15 Oct. 1927.

10. For details on the recruitment of these agents, see the report on Special Branch Section One in SMP, D-8, n.d.

11. The police department also employed a staff of translators who made daily translations of articles appearing in the local Chinese press, supplying these trans-

lations to the local foreign press with similar instructions regarding secrecy. *CWR*, 25 Aug. 1928, 412–13.

12. Sun Chuanfang's collapse shattered the false sense of security along with the wishful thinking that had transformed Sun into a defender of the Western establishment in Shanghai. Residents of the Settlement immediately went to the other extreme, becoming victims of a "fear complex." *CWR*, 25 Aug. 1928, 412.

13. The Special Branch had six sections: S.1—general inquiries and supervision, Russian inquiries, Japanese inquiries, Jewish affairs, foreign inquiries; S.2—Chinese liaison; S.3—film censorship and plays; S.4—Indian affairs; S.5—newspapers and translations; and S.6—boardinghouses, license applications, and shipping. SMP, D-8/25, 31 Oct. 1939.

14. SMP, D-667, 28 Nov. 1929.

15. *CWR*, 29 Dec. 1928, 187–88.

16. SMP, D-707, 29 Nov. 1929.

17. *CWR*, 29 Dec. 1928, 188.

18. Ibid., 189.

19. It was also claimed that some of the volunteers had served under Grigori Semenov, who headed the Baikal Cossacks and who fled to Japan after his attempt to instigate an uprising against the Bolsheviks in Vladivostok failed. For Semenov see Oakes, *White Man's Folly*, 257–58.

20. *CWR*, 12 Nov. 1927, 261. Until 1930, when clandestine activities were transferred to the agency of the Soviet merchant marine, the Soviet Consulate housed the Russian intelligence services, who tried to use "turned" White Russians to infiltrate the SMP. Vice-Director Gourbatiouk of the Chinese Eastern Railway ran a very active GRU "net" of Eastern European agents out of his residence. Faligot and Kauffer, *Kang Sheng*, 77–78. Max Bauer, German adviser to Chiang Kai-shek, may also have been trying to place some of his men in the CID. SMP, D-80, 5 Mar. 1929.

21. There had been a demonstration that morning at 11:00 when White Russians tore down the consulate's anniversary flags.

22. Oakes, *White Man's Folly*, 259–60. The Shanghai Municipal Police riot squad, called the Reserve Unit, consisted of 130 Chinese, 24 Sikhs, 12 Japanese, and 24 Europeans. Forty were ready to respond within two minutes from their armory headquarters. Extremely well trained in riot control, they used lights and sirens on their armored van to disorient rioters. "How Riots are Dealt With," 67–68.

23. *CWR*, 19 Nov. 1927, 291.

24. In an average month of police work, these uniformed Russian police volunteers in the pay of the Municipal Council searched 20,000 persons, 6,000 motorcars, 17,000 rickshaws (this sum actually represents the total number of rickshaws in the International Settlement [8,000 licensed] and French Concession [9,000 without licenses]), 1,500 motor buses, 2,000 trams, and 2,200 carriages. *CWR*, 15 Sept. 1928, 72; McCormick, *Audacious Angles*, 54; *CWR*, 23 Mar. 1929. The figures are given by the *Shanghai Sunday Times* in an undated clipping in SMP, D-8, n.d.

25. *CWR*, 15 Sept. 1928, 73.

26. Memorandum from the Shanghai Special Municipality government to the Public Security Bureau, SMA, 1-5-526, 11.

27. STS, jishi, 5.

28. SSN, H-4; Xu Gongsu and Qiu Jinzhang, "Shanghai gonggong zujie zhidu," 18. The roads to the north of the International Settlement encompassed 1,700 mu of land; to the west, 45,840 mu. Zheng Zu'an, "Guomindang zhengfu 'da Shanghai jihua' shimo," 210. See also Silliman, "Sino-Foreign Conflict," 5–6.

29. Carney, Foreign Devils Had Light Eyes, 18; Green, ed., Shanghai of Today, 11; Pan Ling, In Search of Old Shanghai, 46. For Landstadt or "country town," see Weber, The Growth of Cities in the Nineteenth Century, 14–16. See also Goldfield, "The Urban South."

30. "Some of the handsomest residences on Bubbling Well Road are owned by wealthy Chinese. Pleasant afternoons and evenings, automobiles by the score flash up and down this wide, smoothly paved road and onto the delightful suburbs beyond, many of them crowded to overflowing with merry-making Chinese, women as well as men." Gamewell, The Gateway to China, 46–47. Bubbling Well Road, or Jing'an (the name of a shrine that is now a plastics factory) Road, was the western extension of Nanking Road. Pan Ling, In Search of Old Shanghai, 54.

31. "The Council has claimed authority to function as police officers on property abutting upon municipal roads, and on property the chief entrance of which is from a municipal road." Enclosure in Dispatch 6275 from Shanghai (Consul General Cunningham) to Legation, 26 Nov. 1929, in RDS, vol. 69. See also Silliman, "Sino-Foreign Conflict," 8–9.

32. In July 1904 the Shanghai circuit intendant was impelled to recognize the Shanghai Municipal Council's right to purchase land to build access roads to areas like Baoshan, where the Chinese had allowed foreigners to construct factories. There followed naturally the matters of supplying water outside the Settlement, sanitary regulations, and police protection. Green, ed., Shanghai of Today, 11; Pal, Shanghai Saga, 11. The SMC built its first police station on an extra-settlement road in 1884 during the Sino-French War. Silliman, "Sino-Foreign Conflict," 6.

33. "It is believed that when forced to do so, [the Chinese officials] will admit that Land Regulation Number 6 gives full authority for the construction of roads outside the Settlement." Bylaw 9 supposedly added the right of policing those roads. Enclosure in Dispatch 6275 from Shanghai (Consul General Cunningham) to Legation, 26 Nov. 1929, in RDS, vol. 69. This constituted what might be called a "rental constitution." White III, "Non-governmentalism," 22–23.

34. Quoted in Dispatch 6275 from Shanghai (Consul General Cunningham) to Legation, 26 Nov. 1929, in RDS, vol. 69.

35. A piece of land along the Bund or on lower Nanking Road cost more than a similar plot in the heart of London or New York. Although there was wild speculation in the 1910–19 period, especially by American adventurers and con men driven out of the Philippines by Governor Taft, the main increase occurred between 1929 and 1936, when Sir Victor Sassoon's land speculation drove up prices. Powell, My Twenty-five Years in China, 15–17; Hauser, Shanghai: City for Sale, 273.

36. Enclosure in Dispatch 6275 from Shanghai (Consul General Cunningham) to Legation, 26 Nov. 1929, in RDS, vol. 69. Put another way, the total municipal control of the foreign settlers of Shanghai, including the external roads, amounted to 191 square miles over the 320 square miles of Chinese-ruled Shanghai. MacPherson, "Designing China's Urban Future."

37. After the May Thirtieth incident of 1925, the Chinese authorities presented a set of demands to the SMC. One stated: "The Shanghai Municipal Council shall not construct roads beyond the Settlement boundaries. The roads already constructed shall be turned over unconditionally to the Chinese government." The SMC temporarily suspended new road construction while ignoring the second part of the demand. Quoted in Silliman, "Sino-Foreign Conflict," 11. Clashes occurred between SMP patrols and Chinese prefectural police as early as 1907–8. Chen Junde, "Shanghai xiren jiuliu quyu (sucheng gonggong zujie) jiewai malu kuozhang lüeshi," 44. See also Davidson-Houston, *Yellow Creek*, 115.

38. As late as October 23, 1924, the SMC commissioner of public works was preparing plans to extend six more roads six miles beyond the boundary of the Settlement. SMA, 1-5-601, 3.

39. Letter from Hsu Yuan, Bureau of Foreign Affairs, Shanghai, to Consul General Cunningham, 25 June 1926, in SMA, 1-5-601.

40. Dispatch 4860, 16 Aug. 1926, in SMA, 1-5-601.

41. Lockwood, Jr., "The International Settlement at Shanghai," 1038.

42. SMA, 1-5-601, 13.

43. On September 11, 1927, the Special Municipal Government launched a public struggle against the SMP for establishing a "patrol bureau" (*bufang*) on the extra-settlement Hongqiao Road. *DZ*, 13 Sept. 1927, 129. Earlier, on August 10, 1927, the Jiangsu Bureau of Foreign Affairs office in Shanghai sent a memorandum to the SMC commissioner of public works, demanding compensation to a Chinese citizen over whose land an SMC road had been built. SMA, 1-5-601, 64.

44. *STS, jishi*, 35.

45. *SB*, 31 Oct. 1927, 9.

46. The SMC issued plans on June 17, 1929, for road widenings and to extend Scott Road. These plans were not formally conveyed to Commissioner of Public Works (Special Municipality) Shen Yi until January 17, 1930. SMA, 1-5-601, 46.

47. SMA, 1-5-526, 1–5. The Secretariat of the Special Municipality promptly ordered the head of its Local Land Bureau to devise a solution. Letter dated 20 Mar. 1928, in ibid., 6–7.

48. SMA, 1-5-526, 14.

49. Ibid., 21–22. "Road sovereignty" is also described in a Foreign Affairs Bureau memorandum of May 9, 1929, as being a matter of "national sovereignty" (*guojia zhuquan*). Ibid., 29.

50. Ibid., 33.

51. SMA, 1-5-601, 44.

52. Ibid., 27. The budget increase was authorized sometime between March 18 and May 29, 1929.

53. A November 14, 1929, letter from the PSB, via the Jiangsu commissioner of foreign affairs, to the senior consul, protested repairs by the SMC on 4,800 feet of Hongqiao Road and noted that 5,000 feet of Hongqiao Road had already been converted to macadam. Enclosure in dispatch 6275 from Shanghai (Consul General Cunningham) to Legation, 26 Nov. 1929, in *RDS*, vol. 69.

54. Silliman, "Sino-Foreign Conflict," 15–17.

55. SMA, 1-5-601, 48.

56. Ibid., 47.

57. *STS, jishi*, 36; *SB*, 6 Apr. 1928, 4.

58. *STS, jishi*, 5, 26, 45. In the 1920s, half of all China's automobiles were on Shanghai's streets. Clifford, "The Western Powers and the 'Shanghai Question,' " 6.

59. The movie director Stephen Spielberg managed to capture that peculiarly defensive quality of the glassed-in motorcar in the crowd scene on the bridge over Suzhou Creek in *Empire of the Sun*.

60. McCormick, *Audacious Angles*, 30–31.

61. This was hardly Shanghai's problem alone. It was a product of the invention itself and taken by many to be an alarming sign of the perils of modernity. Hickey, *Our Police Guardians*, 79. See also Cumming, "The Police Services of the Empire," 543–44.

62. *STS, jishi*, 44.

63. For examples of foreigners being killed by buses or causing accidents, see *SB*, 6 Apr. 1929, 16, and 26 June 1929, 15.

64. Meng, "A Tale of Two Cities," 420.

65. *STS, jishi*, 44.

66. International Settlement driver's licenses were only good on their own extra-boundary roads, like the three-mile drive to the Hongqiao Airport. If you drove off the road onto Chinese territory, the fine might be as much as $250. Carney, *Foreign Devils Had Light Eyes*, 91–94. All sorts of vehicles were licensed, from carts to automobiles. *SB*, 29 July 1929, 14; Dec. 1930, 16.

67. *STS, jishi*, 44–45.

68. Referring to reports from the Shanghai Consulate, the American legation reported that "Local Chinese police charged with enforcing traffic regulations are doing so with the apparent desire to cause the maximum humiliation and annoyance to foreigners concerned." Dispatch to the Secretary of State from Peking Legation, 24 Aug. 1928, in *RDS*, vol. 69.

69. The French and International Settlement authorities literally tried to fence themselves in during 1927 and 1929, building large iron gates with concrete posts at the intersections of all streets leading into the Chinese city to protect against "possible attacks by Chinese mobs or soldiers." *CWR*, 22 June 1929, 178.

70. *CWR*, 30 Mar. 1929, 176.

71. This too was viewed by foreign diplomats as part of a concerted Guomindang flouting of reasonable principles of justice. See the reports from Jenkins in the Canton Consulate (8 Sept. 1928) and the Shanghai Consul General (15 Sept. 1928) in *RDS*, vol. 70.

72. Hoh, "The Shanghai Provisional Court," 162. The rules of 1902 regarding the mixed courts in the Shanghai concessions were designed to benefit the foreign plaintiff or complainant. Contrary to the general principle of civil or criminal procedure that the residence of the defendant in civil cases or the place where the crime was committed in criminal cases should be the main criterion of the jurisdiction of the court, the 1902 rules made the nationality of the foreign plaintiff or complainant the sole criterion. *CA*, nos. 142–43, pp. 437–38.

73. Hoh, "The Shanghai Provisional Court," 163–64.

74. Ibid., 163–65. The same was true of the mixed court system in the French Concession. *CA*, nos. 74–75, pp. 4–5. See also Lockwood, Jr., "The International Settlement at Shanghai," 1031.

75. According to a U.S. government report, "following serious communistic

activities," tenants in both the International Settlement and the Chinese-controlled parts of Shanghai agitated for a 50 percent reduction in rent. This was successfully opposed by landlords at first: a proclamation from the SMC protected those within the Settlement, and a declaration from Chiang Kai-shek sheltered those without. The tenants continued their campaign, however, and the Shanghai municipal government eventually imposed a rent-tax equal to two months' rent per annum. "A Brief History of Rent Reduction Agitation," enclosure in Dispatch 6275 from Shanghai (Consul General Cunningham) to Legation, 26 Nov. 1929, in *RDS*, vol. 69.

76. In Shanghai the tenant traditionally paid the tax on the house and the landlord on the land. Gamewell, *The Gateway to China*, 74.

77. Coble, Jr., *The Shanghai Capitalists*, 40.

78. *SSG*, vol. 4, 83–85.

79. Ibid., 11–12.

80. *SB*, 4 Jan. 1930, 8; 12 Jan. 1930, 8; 13 Jan. 1930, 8; 17 Jan. 1930, 8; 18 Jan. 1930, 7; 20 Jan. 1930, 9; 21 Jan. 1930, 7, 13.

81. *CA*, nos. 70–71, pp. 19–21.

82. *CA*, nos. 142–43, p. 436. The old mixed court of the French Concession was replaced in 1931 similarly. Both agreements were renewed for three years in February 1933. Lockwood, Jr., "The International Settlement at Shanghai," 1938.

83. However, the court police had to be "recommended" by the SMC. *CA*, nos. 66–67.

84. The Nationalist government unilaterally abrogated extraterritoriality on December 26, 1929. Macauley, "The Chinese Criminal Code of 1935," 50.

85. Botjer, *A Short History of Nationalist China*, 99. The Western powers also ignored articles 3, 4, 5, and 9 of the 1935 Criminal Code toward the same end. Macauley, "The Chinese Criminal Code of 1935," 61.

86. *STS, jishi*, 45.

87. Zhang Qun was born in 1889 in Huayang (Sichuan), and he was educated at Baoding Military Academy and the Shikan gakko before participating in the Revolution of 1911 in Shanghai under the command of Huang Fu. Zhang returned from three years' exile in 1916. For his career see Henriot, "Le gouvernement municipal de Shanghai," 477.

88. Communists regarded him then as a virulent anti-Communist who had tortured many of their comrades before execution. Zeng Kuoqing, "He Mei xieding qian Fuxingshe zai Huabei de huodong," 138–39.

89. *SSG*, vol. 3, *tongsu*, 1. After his tour of duty as PSB chief, Colonel Yuan Liang became mayor of Beiping. *Who's Who in China*, supplement to the 5th ed., 136; Henriot, "Le gouvernement municipal de Shanghai," 475; Shen Yi, "Shanghai shi gongwuju shi nian."

90. Although they are frequently cited below and in the appendixes, Chinese police statistics for criminal offenses are only as useful as most published criminal statistics elsewhere in the world. Discussions of this issue are included in Nye, "Crime in Modern Societies," 492; Rudé, *Criminal and Victim*, 25–28.

91. *SYZ*, 106. Universal fingerprinting based upon the Berkeley model was vigorously advocated by Frank Yee, who became an adviser to the Shanghai PSB after he returned from study in America. Yu Xiuhao, "Meiguo Baikeli shi jingcha pubian zhiwen dengji yundong chenggong," 145–47.

92. "Reactionaries" and "counterrevolutionaries" were taken by the Guomindang to be Communists, members of "third parties," and others who opposed the Three Principles of the People of Sun Yat-sen. George E. Sokolsky, "Third Party Congress and Its Work," 1.

93. *SSG*, vol. 3, 150–51. Yuan Liang's census pre-dated the national government's order to each locale to take a census. *CA*, nos. 108–9, 6.

94. As of 1909, SMP policemen were required to study Shanghai dialect for an hour a day, with time off from regular duty, during the first three years of their service. Language examinations were held every six months, and bonuses were awarded to those who passed various levels of proficiency. *The North China Herald and South China and China Gazette*, 31 Dec. 1909, 784.

95. The International Settlement's foreign-administered police force provided constant reminders that the PSB needed to acquire the latest telecommunications equipment and to employ the most modern forensic methods.

96. *SSG*, vol. 3, 153.

97. *CWR*, 19 Dec. 1928, 194. The SMP had a four-month training course for its Chinese recruits. About two hundred men passed through the training depot annually. Bourne, "The Shanghai Municipal Police," 33.

98. In spite of his own education, Yuan Liang made light of Japanese police training. He argued that Japan's national police academy had lapsed and later instruction was really just a matter of lectures and not of real police training. *SSG*, vol. 3, 152.

99. Minister of Interior official Feng Yukun was also a fervent admirer of modern American law enforcement who favored standardized fingerprinting, modus operandi filing, and centralized police training. Vollmer, letter from Feng Yukun dated 2 Aug. 1932.

100. The German advisory mission that Max Bauer recruited in the summer of 1928 numbered twenty-six men. Four of these were civilian police advisers. Kirby, *Germany and Republican China*, 55.

101. At that time, the two most frequently cited books for the study of police administration around the world were Fosdick, *European Police Systems* and *American Police Systems*. See Cumming, "A Select Book List," 389.

102. Vollmer's recruitment of college graduates was, interestingly enough, inspired by Confucius. Parker, *The Berkeley Police Story*, 24.

103. *CWR*, 23 Feb. 1929, 542.

104. *SSG*, vol. 3, 154–55. See also Carte and Carte, *Police Reform*, 1–3, 33. American Marxists credit Vollmer with sponsoring the Progressives' main strategies for turning police into an instrument of "social engineering" in the U.S.: centralization, professionalization, use of technology (Vollmer once referred to the patrol car as "a swift angel of death"), specialized preventive functions, and increased contact with potentially troublesome groups. Platt et al., *The Iron Fist and the Velvet Glove*, 35–39.

105. On July 1, 1930, the Shanghai Special Municipality Public Security Bureau changed its name to the Shanghai Municipality Public Security Bureau. *SSG*, vol. 4, 1.

106. Fingerprinting was first used in the late 1890s by Sir Edward Henry, the inspector-general of the Bengal police. When Henry became commissioner of London police in 1903 he introduced fingerprinting there, and soon it became a practice all over the world, illustrating the way control mechanisms were perfected

in colonies and then fed back into the imperial metropolis. Gaustad, "Colonial Police in Africa and India," 6.

107. In an effort to prevent local police forces from imposing fines on their own, the Ministry of Interior had on April 8, 1928, forbidden Public Security Bureaus from raising funds. *CA*, nos. 66–67, pp. 11–12.

108. *SSG*, vol. 3, 121–31.

109. *MG*, 17 Feb. 1928, 57.

110. The same was true for the French Concession. On April 23, 1935, a group of PSB men returning from a parade drill in the South Market was halted by a French policeman and his Annamese assistants. Like the Sikhs (the *hongtou asan* or "turbaned number threes" who were known for savagely beating hapless Chinese coolies), the Annamese (or Tonkinese) were hated for serving as collaborators with the foreigner; their presence may have helped provoke the Chinese policemen. Whatever the cause, the result was a fracas in which the French officer was dragged over a bridge into Chinese territory and was badly beaten by the PSB officers. Consular intervention at the highest level helped prevent a major international incident. SMP, D-6677, 26 Apr. 1935. For Annamese and Sikh relations with the Shanghainese, see *SYZ*, 101–2; *CWR*, 4 Mar. 1933, 16; *CC*, 6 Aug. 1931; Ch'ien, *Fortress Besieged*, 132–33.

111. They were not allowed to carry arms, of course. SMP, D-137, 26 Mar. 1929. On this particular occasion the cadets traveled in two motor lorries. In June the previous year, the SMP arrested as many as 150 uniformed Chinese cadets on their way through the International Settlement to a review at the Chinese public recreation ground by Generals He Yingqin and Qian Dajun. This greatly intensified anti-foreignism in the city. *CWR*, 16 June 1928, 79.

112. *SSG*, vol. 4, *huiyi*, 8.

113. See the Wang Yansong affair described in Chapter 10.

114. Promises to editor Chen to cease and desist were later ignored by Special Branch chief Robertson. SMP, D-505, 12 Sept. 1929, 1–2.

115. *SSG*, vol. 4, *huiyi*, 8.

116. Gun control seemed out of the question to the Chinese police as long as the French and English concessions "interlocked like dogs' teeth" and offered a place to conceal weapons for criminals who later used the firearms to commit crimes in the Chinese parts of the city. *SSG*, vol. 5, 67.

117. *SB*, 10 Dec. 1930, 14.

118. CID translation, dated January 28, 1931, of a report that appeared in *Zhongguo shibao* and other local newspapers. SMP, D-199, 28 Jan. 1931.

119. Ibid. See also the discussion in *SSN*, H-4.

120. Note, however, that at the Sixth Congress of the Guomindang held in Shanghai during April 1930, the PSB was accused of repressing the people and holding the power of the party in contempt. The Congress demanded Yuan Liang's resignation as police chief and that the PSB submit to the partial control of the party. Henriot, "Le gouvernement municipal de Shanghai," 71.

CHAPTER 6. CRIME AND SOCIAL CONTROL

1. *SSG*, vol. 5, 79.

2. Meng, "A Tale of Two Cities," 420.

3. *CWR*, 29 Sept. 1928, 137.

4. Weisser, *Crime and Punishment,* 15. There are two different academic interpretations of the origins of criminal law. One (see Nettler, *Explaining Crime*) is that crime consists of acts that offend collective sentiments; law codifies and enforces moral consensus. The other, Neo-Marxist definition (see Chambliss, *Functional and Conflict Theories of Crime*) is that crime is an act that threatens the interests and offends the sensibilities of social elites. Gurr, *Rogues, Rebels, and Reformers,* 13.

5. Yen, "Crime in Relation to Social Change in China," 302.

6. See, in this regard, Weisser, *Crime and Punishment,* 124.

7. *STS, jishi,* 16.

8. Two of the most frequent kinds of crime were robberies where two or three burglars would ransack a house, and holdups on the street or highway. The latter usually involved a weapon. Because toy pistols were sometimes used, the Chinese police prohibited manufacturers from making replicas of guns. Ibid., 51.

9. *SSG,* vol. 3, table after 108, and vol. 5, table after 220.

10. Similar societies were established in Mukden, Dairen, and Tianjin. *CC,* 4 Jan. 1937, 13.

11. Ibid., 12. For the "body price" of concubines who were bought out of prostitution, see Hershatter, "The Subaltern Talks Back," 16.

12. Sung Nyoh-san, the comprador of the Ewo Cotton Mills, was kidnapped by Wang Tianxiang and Cheng Dexiang in 1926. Both men were found guilty by Judge Wen Yingxing—later police chief of Shanghai—and shot on the Shanghai drill grounds at the order of Marshal Sun Chuanfang. *CWR,* 18 Sept. 1926, 81.

13. Fontenoy, *The Secret Shanghai,* 69.

14. Han, "Kidnapping in Shanghai," 148. In 1927 a group of wealthy Chinese presented the SMP with $41,000 as a special "crime suppression fund" to offer an inducement to the police to break up gangs of kidnappers. *CWR,* 28 Jan. 1928, 210; 17 Jan. 1931, 242–43; *MG,* 20 Jan. 1928, 19.

15. Han, "Kidnapping in Shanghai," 248.

16. There were 321 cases of armed robbery reported to the PSB during the same year. Of the latter, 106 were solved and the culprits arrested. *SSG,* vol. 5, 211. There were eleven kidnapping cases reported to the PSB in 1929, and eight in 1930. Woodhead, ed., *The China Yearbook 1933,* 672. For the increase in unreported kidnappings, see *CC,* 10 Jan. 1929, 27, and 28 Mar. 1929, 246.

17. For the pressure on Shanghai financiers and the threat of kidnapping see Coble, Jr., *The Shanghai Capitalists,* 60–65. Zhang Jia'ao (Chang Kia-ngau), head of the Bank of China and brother of Zhang Junmai (see below), left Shanghai at this time for a ten months' visit to eighteen countries, probably to avoid being kidnapped. Jeans, "The Trials of a Third-Force Intellectual," 26.

18. *SB,* 24 Mar. 1929, 15.

19. The gang's leader, Wang Erjin, was sentenced to three years in jail. *SB,* 9 Apr. 1929, 15.

20. *SB,* 2 Apr. 1929, 15. Hu was released by his kidnappers two weeks later, presumably after a ransom had been paid. *SB,* 16 Apr. 1929, 15.

21. *CC,* 11 Apr. 1929, 286.

22. *SB,* 5 Apr. 1929, 15.

23. *SB,* 8 Apr. 1929, 15.

24. *SB*, 15 Apr. 1929, 15. Li "escaped" from his kidnappers on April 14 and received treatment for nervous shock. *SB*, 16 Apr. 1929, 15.

25. *SB*, 9 Apr. 1929, 15.

26. *CC*, 13 Apr. 1929, 267; 16 May 1929, 386. For Zhu's prominence, see Xue Gengxin, "Jindai Shanghai de liumang," 162–63.

27. The insurance executive, Ye Daming, was shot on May 31, 1929, and the two boys were kidnapped on June 19. *SB*, 1 June 1929, 15, and 20 June 1929, 15.

28. Zhang Junmai believed that he had been seized by special agents of the Garrison Command. One of his brothers, Zhang Jiaju, was certain the abductors were ordinary gangsters. Jeans, "The Trials of a Third-Force Intellectual," 23–25.

29. *SSG*, vol. 3, 115–16; *SSG*, vol. 4, *huiyi*, 2; *SSG*, vol. 5, 5; *SB*, 17 Aug. 1930, 15. They were not so successful in the case of the kidnapping of the playboy son of Zhou Xiangyun, the real estate magnate, who was seized at a roadblock by armed men while he was on his way to his horseback riding lesson at Jiangwan racetrack. *SB*, 19 Oct. 1930, 15.

30. *SB*, 25 Apr. 1929, 15.

31. *CWR*, 3 Jan. 1931, 175–76. During the last week of December 1930, the SMP recorded 232 arrests, including 36 suspects in recent kidnapping enterprises. Ibid., 174.

32. "Whenever a wealthy Chinese resident of the Settlement is kidnapped his relatives are always flooded with offers from various quarters to assist in his release—always for a consideration. These offers often come from interesting sources, something suggesting that the dividing line between armed kidnappers and certain official organs within the foreign settlements is not entirely distinct." *CWR*, 17 Jan. 1931, 243.

33. *CWR*, 12 Sept. 1931, 70.

34. *CWR*, 11 Apr. 1931, 193.

35. Quoted in *CWR*, 3 Jan. 1931, 174.

36. *CWR*, 28 Mar. 1931, 138. The French police were faulted for stationing as many policemen as possible on busy thoroughfares while neglecting the "silent outlying streets" where "ruffians" terrorized pedestrians, especially during winter nights. *CWR*, 7 Feb. 1931, 356.

37. *CWR*, 17 Jan. 1931, 243. See also the account of Yuan Shunwu's kidnapping in *SB*, 25 Oct. 1930, 15, and 30 Oct. 1930, 11. Of course, there were far fewer kidnappings to deal with in the Special Municipality: only 8–9 percent as many as in the International Settlement. CID translation of a report that appeared in *Zhongguo shibao* and other local newspapers, SMP, D-199, 28 Jan. 1931. The new regulations stipulated the death sentence for kidnappers; confiscation of property used as a safe house; prison sentences for relatives of the victims who negotiated with the kidnappers without telling the police; and so on. British Foreign Office Records, FO 671-500, 6703-30-46.

38. Wilson, *Varieties of Police Behavior*, 67.

39. *SSG*, vol. 3, 1–18.

40. *SSG*, vol. 5, 54. See also *STS*, *jishi*, 49.

41. The national government's Act Concerning the Settlement of Labor Disputes of June 1928 called for the formation of conciliation committees. These turned out to be a bureaucratic fiction. Gourlay, "'Yellow' Unionism in Shanghai," 109.

42. *STS, jishi*, 46–47.

43. Ibid., 19, 47. For an example of mediation, see the China Merchants Trolleycar Company (Huashang dianche gongsi) dispute of September 9, 1927. Ibid., 6. See also Strand, *Rickshaw Beijing*, 77–78.

44. Honig, "Women Cotton Mill Workers," 116; Honig, *Sisters and Strangers*, 240–41.

45. In May 1931 the PSB tried to register stevedores (*jianyunfu*) and posted regulations stipulating that a foreman had to be an experienced worker over twenty-five years old—thereby preventing young hoods from exploiting the workers. The regulations also had a right-to-work clause, forbidding foremen to interfere if a party wanted to hire stevedores directly. *SSG*, vol. 4, 92–95.

46. See, for example, the account of Detective Inspector Prince's role in the East Hanbury Road cotton mill dispute on June 1, 1927, in *NCH*, 2 July 1927, 30.

47. Isaacs, ed., *Five Years of Kuomintang Reaction*, 67. Note Gurr, Grabosky, and Hula's suggestion that "Collective disorder is more threatening to elites than is crime, and this discrepancy has been sufficient to render elites more willing to invest additional resources in standby forces that can be used for crowd control than in manpower for crime control per se." Gurr et al., *The Politics of Crime and Conflict*, 714. Bayley's post–World War II data from three countries nonetheless show that increases in police strength could not be attributed to an upsurge of rioting. Bayley, *Patterns of Policing*, 90. See also Gurr, *Rogues, Rebels, and Reformers*, 15–16.

48. After 1911 most local governments made health administration a police function. The first city to establish a health department was Canton in 1920, followed by Shanghai in 1926. *Chinese Medical Journal* 12:117–19.

49. The bureau had a strong history of its own, and was not directly under the municipal government. Henriot, "Le gouvernement municipal de Shanghai," 285.

50. *STS, jishi*, 42, 63.

51. The Chinese Benevolent Cemetery Association (a merchant philanthropy group) also hired men in motor trucks to pick up the bodies of dead beggars and abandoned children. Finch, *Shanghai and Beyond*, 12.

52. Hauser, *Shanghai: City for Sale*, 136.

53. Of these corpses, thirty-four thousand were the bodies of infants, many probably killed by parents. Isaacs, ed., *Five Years of Kuomintang Reaction*, 63.

54. *SSG*, vol. 4, *huiyi*, 3, 5–6. During 1930–31, the Shanghai police issued regulations on public swimming pools, which had to pay Ch. $20 for their license. No mixed bathing was allowed. No one under twelve without a responsible person, no one with skin disease, mental illness, paralysis of the limbs, or who appeared to be drunk, would be allowed to swim. Bathers had to shower before entering the pool, and women and children with long hair had to wear caps. *SSG*, vol. 4, *huiyi*, 80–81. For the "white scourge" of tuberculosis, which was said to be very common among poor Eurasians, see Gamewell, *The Gateway to China*, 41.

55. Responsibility for cleaning the streets was handed over to the PSB on December 16, 1930. *SB*, 17 Dec. 1930, 15. See also *SSG*, vol. 4, *huiyi*, 28, 98. Chief Yuan urged local precincts to find ways to get others to clean the streets and not to use their own men. *SSG*, vol. 4, *huiyi*, 4.

56. The symbolic linkage of modern police professionalism and medicine also

extended to recruitment. Crucial to the notion of a modern police force was the process of having recruits be examined by a physician, their bodies ultimately being in the control of the organization. Vollmer and Parker, *Crime and the State Police*, 103.

57. *SSG*, vol. 3, 107.

58. "Judicial police" (*sifa jingcha*) were distinguished from ordinary "detectives" (*zhenji renyuan*). Hui Hong, *Xingshi jingcha xue*, 6.

59. *SSG*, vol. 3, 147–48.

60. The motive was partly political. The September minutes of the second general affairs conference (*yewu huiyi*) at the Shanghai PSB headquarters identified as the most important reason for keeping the household registers up to date the prevention of "reds" and "reactionaries" from hiding among the people. *SSG*, vol. 4, *huiyi*, 14.

61. *SSG*, vol. 3, 103–4.

62. *STS, jishi*, 26. In June the PSB received permission to carry out an experimental household investigation, and 162 policemen were designated as investigators and given four weeks of training in census-taking. At the same time, a propaganda campaign was waged to educate the public neither to conceal nor refuse to divulge information. Ibid., 43–44.

63. *CC*, 10 Jan. 1929, 28.

64. Chief Yuan Liang had his men prepare a special simplified form for this census-taking. The form was also designed to keep track of transients, including merchants. *SB*, 23 Aug. 1930, 16.

65. British Foreign Office Records, FO 671-500, 7020-30-51.

66. *SSG*, vol. 5, 211. The Yangzi floods were among the most catastrophic in all of Chinese history, affecting 25 million people. *SB*, 30 Aug. 1931, 13, and weekly pictorial supplement of 23 Aug. 1931, 3; Finch, *Shanghai and Beyond*, 219–20.

67. According to the July 1930 census taken by the Public Security Bureau, there were 185,684 households (*zhenghu*) in the Chinese section of the city. With subtenants these households totaled 355,000 people. British Foreign Office Records, FO 671-500, 7020-30-51.

68. These are actually aggregate figures. During that same period police records showed that 13,196 males and 10,728 females were born, and 10,275 males and 9,369 females died. During 1930 proper 84,260 *hu* and 297,072 *kou* moved into Shanghai; 55,410 *hu* and 192,910 *kou* were reported to have left the city. *SSG*, vol. 4, table after 102.

69. In July 1931 the police placed special emphasis upon registering households in South Market. *SSG*, vol. 5, 56.

70. There had been a fresh effort in July 1931 "to get statistics that are detailed and accurate." The police particularly emphasized investigating rental arrangements in order "to prevent bad elements from hiding their traces in our city." Ibid., 55.

71. The Shanghai police also registered violent and accidental deaths apart from the household registration. During the police year 1931–32 there were 216 such deaths. Ibid., table after 220.

72. It is clear from the minutes of their meetings that the various PSB division

chiefs were constantly being exhorted by the chief to bring their household registers up to date in order to keep track of transients. See, for example, ibid., vol. 4,
huiyi, 6.

73. Ibid., vol. 5, 211. In Qing times there was a terminological vagueness about
the distinction between *liumin* (refugees who are worthy of relief) and *youmin*
(indigent homeless despised for lax morals). Perdue, "Vagrancy and Famine Relief," 6.

74. *SSG,* vol. 5, 71.

75. Gamewell, *The Gateway to China,* 55.

76. Hauser, *Shanghai: City for Sale,* 240–41.

77. Martin, "The Green Gang and 'Party Purification,'" 3, 48. For the tendency
of "loafers" to form associations, see Xu Ke, *Qing bai lei chao,* vol. 7, *bai 84,*
12–17.

78. Henriot, "Le gouvernement municipal de Shanghai," 308, 422. The death
rate of Chinese in the International Settlement was 15.41 per 1,000 as compared
to 14.27 per 1,000 for foreign residents. Fifty percent of the bodies picked up in
the streets were victims of tuberculosis. Hauser, *Shanghai: City for Sale,* 248.

79. Cited in Isaacs, ed., *Five Years of Kuomintang Reaction,* 62.

80. Henriot, "Le gouvernement municipal de Shanghai," 312–13; Wu Te-chen
[Wu Tiecheng], "Greater Shanghai Places Emphasis on Social Reconstruction,
Welfare," 49.

81. Honig, "Women Cotton Mill Workers," 83; Honig, *Sisters and Strangers,*
23–26.

82. *SSG,* vol. 3, 168.

83. Since rustic travelers entering the city were easy prey for *liumang* who
posed as porters, the Shanghai police required anyone who wanted to transport
luggage in the city by land or by tender to have a permit with his photograph on
the front. *SSG,* vol. 4, 82.

84. Jiang Shaozhen, "Du Yuesheng," in Li Xin and Sun Sibai, eds., *Minguo
renwu zhuan,* vol. 1, 316; Xu Zhucheng, *Du Yuesheng zhengzhuan,* 54–55. *Liumang* were said to be virtually fearless of all but the gang chiefs. Zhu Zijia (Jin
Qiongbai), *Huangpu jiang de zhuo lang,* 81.

85. *SSG,* vol. 4, 3.

86. Ibid., 167–68.

87. *SSG,* vol. 3, 170–75.

88. Actual felons who fled to Shanghai from neighboring towns like Wuxi
were arrested and returned to the local authorities for punishment. *STS, jishi,* 20.

89. Ibid., 62.

90. *SB,* 6 Nov. 1930, 16. The principle of corrective education in prison had
been enunciated as early as October 1907 in a memorial to the throne by Shen
Jiaben, who was revising the Qing code. Macauley, "The Chinese Criminal Code
of 1935," 39.

91. *SSG,* vol. 5, 72. The Shanghai police, together with the GMD Bureau of
Social Affairs, also opened up a reception center for refugees from the Yangzi
River floods on September 10, 1931. Ibid., 9.

92. In this respect, see Hoh, "Existing Conditions in Chekiang First Prison,"
289.

93. O'Brien, *The Promise of Punishment,* 20–21.

94. Gamewell, *The Gateway to China*, 24–25.

95. "Crime is society's disease. Criminals are society's sick people. Prisons are society's hospitals. With respect to sick people who have already committed crimes, naturally we ought to exert every effort to cure the disease in order to prevent the criminal from recidivism once he leaves the prison." Xu Huifang and Liu Qingyu, "Shanghai nüxing fan de shehui fenxi," 91. For prisoners as "convalescents" (even in Dai Li's terrifying secret prison system), see Rissov, *Le Dragon enchaîné*, 189–90.

96. *SSG*, vol. 4, 107.

97. *STS, jishi*, 27–28.

98. *CWR*, 8 Nov. 1930, 364. This decision may have had something to do with the discussions about prisons at the conference on the Shanghai Provisional Court in January 1930. The powers were unwilling to hand over the prisoners in the concessions before the final settlement of the extraterritoriality issue, there being some concern over the state of Chinese prisons. *CA*, nos. 66–67, 7.

99. Foucault, *Discipline and Punish*, 205. The Beijing Municipal Prison, which I visited on June 15, 1985, bears a distinct architectural resemblance to the Panopticon. I do not know if this was intentionally so designed.

100. The Confucian notion of moral transformation was also different, in the case of penal organization, from Western evangelical practices of prison discipline that stressed separation and solitary confinement, which would break down the prisoner's wayward will and prepare him for the chaplain's comfort and eventual salvation. Henriques, "The Rise and Decline of the Separate System of Prison Discipline," 78–79.

101. The auditorium in the Shanghai No. 1 Special District Court Women's Prison (Shanghai di yi tequ fayuan nü jian), located in the International Settlement on North Zhejiang Road, was called a *jiao hui shi* (instructional room). Xu Huifang and Liu Qingyu, "Shanghai nüxing fan de shehui fenxi," 88–89.

102. For "polyvalent" disciplinary inversion, see Foucault, *Discipline and Punish*, 210–11.

103. STS, *jishi*, 27.

104. Xu Huifang and Liu Qingyu, "Shanghai nüxing fan de shehui fenxi," 91.

105. Yu Xiuhao, *Jingcha shouce*, 14. The instructions to policemen to be teachers and nurturers came from Chiang Kai-shek's speeches.

106. Ibid., 12–13.

107. Ibid., 10. A policeman's action has to be based upon the law (*faling*). Otherwise he wantonly destroys popular rights and loses the public's trust—"which is why our country's police were so much of a failure in the past." Ibid., 14.

108. *SSG*, vol. 5, 58. For a postwar collection of police administrative laws, see *Jing zheng faling*. See also Strand, *Rickshaw Beijing*, 70–71.

109. In the concessions, and especially after the special district courts were established, Chinese courts had the authority to adjudicate cases arising under this law. Covering sheet to *Law of Penalties for Breaches of Police Regulations Promulgated by the Nationalist Government on July 21, 1928*, in SMP, D-6810, 25 Feb. 1935.

110. Ibid., 4.

111. Ibid., 3.

112. Ibid., 8.

113. Ibid., 10–11.

114. *STS, jishi,* 50. There was roughly the same volume of adjudicated or police-rule cases during the police year 1930–31: 4,844 altogether. *SSG,* vol. 4, 105.

115. Bryan's comments on Article 26 of the *Law of Penalties for Breaches of Police Regulations,* 6. Bryan, an attorney and the author of *An Outline of Chinese Civil Law,* was appointed police prosecutor to the Shanghai Municipal Council in May 1928. He was one of the few Americans to hold a position of prominence in the Shanghai municipal government. *CWR,* 9 June 1928, 45.

116. Judgments were often harsh, on the grounds that "This bureau has the responsibility of maintaining order (*zhixu*) and preserving the peace (*zhi'an*). People who break police regulations should be arrested and punished; it will not do to be lenient and release them." *SSG,* vol. 3, 107.

117. *SSN,* F-58–59.

118. *SSG,* vol. 4, 76.

119. Wilson, *Varieties of Police Behavior,* 49.

120. During July 1931–June 1932, for example, there were 32,620 cases of "breaking police rules." *SSG,* vol. 5, table after 220. Note, by the way, that Chinese detectives in the SMP also saw themselves as upholding moral standards by arresting social deviants. For a fascinating discussion of this particular form of policing, see Ye Xiaoqing, "Popular Culture in Shanghai," 23.

121. "Customs (*fengsu*) are much more decadent and corrupt here than in other places . . . and [the people] naturally have to be told from time to time to reform in the hope that over time they will gradually improve." *SSG,* vol. 3, 80.

122. *STS, jishi,* 19–20, 22. Films showing physiological dissections were banned; restaurants were prohibited from featuring naked dancing; cigarette rolling factories were kept from using gambling instrument designs on their packages; men were told not to let their hair grow long. Ibid., 46. Some of this puritanism emanated from the government in Nanjing, where the Special Municipality "expressly prohibited the wearing of indecorous clothes by women" in order "to preserve Chinese culture." Meng, "A Tale of Two Cities," 420.

123. *SSG,* vol. 4, table after 102. For dancehall girls, see ibid., 92, 95–96.

124. Ibid., *huiyi,* 5. For an example of that confusion, see Madame Chiang Kai-shek, "Madame Chiang Kai-shek Traces Ideals and Growth," 18. For the potential conflict between regular law enforcement and vice control, see Smith, *Policing Victorian London,* 205–206; Westley, *Violence and the Police,* 143; and Carte and Carte, *Police Reform in the United States,* 15–16.

125. *SSG,* vol. 3, 82–83.

126. Ibid., 80–82.

CHAPTER 7. VICE

1. Letter from the Director-General of the Shanghai Municipal Council to the Commissioner of Police, cited in *CC,* 30 Oct. 1930, 1035. In 1935 the Shanghai Municipal Police estimated that slot machines alone in the International Settlement took in approximately $1 million per annum. *CC,* 27 June 1935, 294.

2. *CWR,* 13 July 1929, 286, and 3 Aug. 1930, 44. According to the 1931 *World*

Almanac, 686, the gross receipts at Monte Carlo for the fiscal year April 1, 1930–March 31, 1931, were US $5,250,000, which was about 28 percent of Shanghai's annual gross gambling receipts.

3. *CWR,* 6 Dec. 1930, 5; 3 Jan. 1931, 174; 7 Feb. 1931, 356; 19 Sept. 1931, 83; Han, "Gambling Dens a Menace to Chinese at Shanghai," 248.

4. *CC,* 30 Oct. 1930, 1035; *CWR,* 6 Dec. 1930, 5, and 19 Sept. 1931, 83.

5. After the January 28 incident, Chiang Kai-shek established a special lottery to finance the purchase of airplanes. Later, administered by the National State Lottery Association under the Ministry of Finance, it was also used to raise money to construct highways, which were mainly for military use. Five hundred thousand tickets were offered for sale every two months at $10 each, with half ($2,500,000) the funds being paid back out in prizes. One could win $500,000 on a single $10 ticket, which was divided into ten shares at $1 each. *All About Shanghai,* 79; Xu Zhucheng, *Du Yuesheng zhengzhuan,* 55.

6. Xu Zhucheng, *Du Yuesheng zhengzhuan,* 29. According to the present-day manager of the prudishly refurbished Great World, there used to be a special place on the roof for those gamblers who wanted to commit suicide. Browning, "Mirrors Reflect Racy Past," 25a.

7. *CWR,* 28 Feb. 1931, 464; Pal, *Shanghai Saga,* 19–20.

8. "Some time ago a mosquito paper [that is, a tabloid] carried the news that every day there is someone committing suicide in the French Concession. The investigation made by the paper alleged that the sole cause is the gambling evil." Han, "French Colonial Policy in China," 240.

9. See the particularly poignant case of You Jiaxiang described in *SB,* 19 Oct. 1930, 15.

10. *CWR,* 1 June 1929, 49; Han, "French Colonial Policy in China," 239.

11. Han, "Gambling Dens a Menace to Chinese at Shanghai," 302. Chinese style gambling houses opened at 1:00 P.M. and closed at 3:00 A.M.

12. *CWR,* 8 Mar. 1930, 44.

13. Another gambling resort in the French Concession sent cars to the jetty to pick up tourists just off their cruise ship. *CWR,* 18 July 1931, 245. Du Yuesheng had negotiated with Captain Fiori and Verdier, the chief administrative officer of the French Concession, in 1927 for rights to run five large casinos. He also had numerous gambling dives in the Baoxingli area for working-class customers. Martin, "'The Pact with the Devil,'" 21.

14. Xu Zhucheng, *Du Yuesheng zhengzhuan,* 29. The gambling house was protected by several hundred of Du's "casino guards" (*baotaijiao*). Xue Gengxin, "Jindai Shanghai de liumang," 163.

15. "The place was fitted up mechanically for a quick change. The table on which the gambling was being done was suspended from the ceiling by four wires running through the ceiling into the room above: apparently a private apartment. The table had no legs and the underside of it exactly matched the ceiling, fitting into a recess so that, when drawn up quickly by mechanical means with all evidence of the game, it couldn't be distinguished from the surrounding ceiling." Lee, *The Underworld of the East,* 239.

16. Coates, *China Races,* 21–44, 113–30, 231–35.

17. Gamewell, *The Gateway to China,* 46.

18. Hauser, *Shanghai: City for Sale,* 94.

19. *CC*, 27 June 1935, 294.

20. *CWR*, 13 July 1929, 286.

21. Ibid.

22. In January 1928 Chiang Kai-shek's agents tried to persuade the two Chinese race courses each to loan Ch. $500,000 to the government. When that attempt failed, T. V. Soong demanded that revenue stamps be placed on admission and sweepstakes tickets. Coble, Jr., *The Shanghai Capitalists*, 45.

23. On January 19, 1928, the brother of the chairman of the board of directors of the Far Eastern Recreation Club was kidnapped in the French Concession and held for ransom. Ibid.

24. *CWR*, 13 July 1929, 286; Henriot, "Le gouvernement municipal de Shanghai," 191.

25. During this period jailai frontons were built as well in Shanghai. For a description of jailai betting, see Mao Xiaocen, "Jiu Shanghai de da duku—huili qiuchang," 128–48.

26. *CWR*, 15 June 1929, 103.

27. *CWR*, 1 June 1929, 5; 20 July 1929, 356; and 22 Mar. 1930, 124.

28. If you did not have a free ticket, you could buy one for ten cents from the many urchins lining the streets leading to the greyhound race courses. Meng, "A Tale of Two Cities," 420.

29. *CWR*, 6 Dec. 1930, 5. "The low salary clerk is much in evidence, and young girls still in their teens struggle at the pari-mutuel with all sorts and conditions of men to buy their ticket on the dog they fancy.... Men and women push each other to get a ticket before the ringing announces the closing of the pari-mutuel for that particular race." Ibid., 4.

30. Meng, "A Tale of Two Cities," 420.

31. *CWR*, 1 June 1929, 5, and 13 July 1929, 286.

32. *CWR*, 3 Jan. 1931, 175.

33. *CWR*, 21 Apr. 1928, 217.

34. Meng, "The 'Hwa Hui' Gambling Evil," 334.

35. *Shanghai shenmi zhinan*, 87; Wu Yu et al., *Minguo hei shehui*, 98–100.

36. Meng, "The 'Hwa Hui' Gambling Evil," 334.

37. For the origins and development of huahui in the Qing period, see Xu Ke, *Qing bai lei chao*, vol. 6, bai 76, 47.

38. *STS, jishi*, 52.

39. Meng, "The 'Hwa Hui' Gambling Evil," 334.

40. Ibid. See also Xu Zhucheng, *Du Yuesheng zhengzhuan*, 29.

41. *STS, jishi*, 53.

42. Ibid., 53. See, for examples of SMP suppression of gambling during 1927–29, *CWR*, 10 Sept. 1927, 52, and 10 Aug. 1929, 465.

43. *STS, jishi*, 53.

44. Carney, *Foreign Devils Had Light Eyes*, 20.

45. *CWR*, 8 Mar. 1930

46. *CWR*, 13 July 1929, 284.

47. *CWR*, 15 June 1929, 95.

48. The SMC threatened to close the municipal roads leading to the race club entrance if the proprietors refused to comply. *CWR*, 1 June 1929, 5.

49. Ibid., 5–6.

50. CC, 25 July 1929, 585.

51. CWR, 15 June 1929, 95–96; 13 July 1929, 285; 20 July 1929, 356; 8 Mar. 1930, 44.

52. CWR, 13 July 1929, 285.

53. The Luna Park enterprise had to open up a dog breeding farm on 18 *mu* of land after the Chinese authorities forbade the import of greyhounds from England or Australia into China. CWR, 10 Jan. 1931, 212.

54. CWR, 22 Feb. 1930, 414.

55. Pal, *Shanghai Saga*, 16; CWR, 19 July 1930. SMC Chairman Fessenden wrote them on January 9, 1931. CWR, 17 Jan. 1931, 245–46.

56. CWR, 18 Mar. 1933, 106.

57. Han, "French Colonial Policy in China," 239.

58. CWR, 22 Mar. 1930, 124. Since most important business houses and industrial enterprises were in the International Settlement, it was suggested at the time that the French Concession tolerated so many vice establishments because they were such a crucial source of municipal revenue. Han, "French Colonial Policy in China," 240.

59. CWR, 25 Oct. 1930, 272.

60. CC, 27 June 1935, 294.

61. CWR, 26 Sept. 1931, 123–24.

62. Han, "French Colonial Policy in China," 239. Many wrote of the foreigners' indifference to suffering. "Sooner or later the foreigner becomes oblivious. . . . He becomes accustomed to seeing men filling the role of pack animals. . . . His sense of social outrage is atrophied and he is able to look upon suffering and misery utterly unmoved. . . . He must choose between indifference—and the lunatic asylum." Houghton, "The Shanghai Mind," 539.

63. CWR, 11 July 1931, 203–4.

64. CWR, 26 Sept. 1931, 123–24.

65. See Martin, "'The Pact with the Devil,'" 32.

66. STS, *jishi*, 53.

67. CWR, 26 Jan. 1935, 258.

68. Liu Zhaorong, "Huang Chujiu ban Da shijie," 77–80. See also Bergère, *L'age d'or de la bourgeoisie chinoise*.

69. Scott, *Actors Are Madmen*, 75–76.

70. Ke Zhaojin, "'Great World.'" Avenue Edward VII is today's Yan'an Road.

71. Those "haha" distorting mirrors are still in The Great World. Browning, "Mirrors Reflect Racy Past," 25a.

72. Carney, *Foreign Devils Had Light Eyes*, 19; Chan, "The Organizational Structure of the Traditional Chinese Firm," 230.

73. Scott, *Actors Are Madmen*, 76.

74. Ibid., 76–77.

75. Ibid., 78.

76. Ke Zhaojin, "'Great World,'" 250; Browning, "Mirrors Reflect Racy Past," 25a.

77. Ke Zhaojin, "'Great World,'" 5.

78. In 1966 the Great World was labeled bourgeois and closed down. For many years it was a warehouse for export goods used by the Shanghai Trade Corporation. In 1973 the Youth Palace on Jiangxi Road moved back in, but later the Shang-

hainese clamored for the restoration of the Great World. In 1979 many of the "good" amusements were restored, and in January 1987 it was renamed the Great World Entertainment Center. It currently receives about ten thousand visitors a day. Ibid.; Browning, "Mirrors Reflect Racy Past," 25a; Shi Zhikang, "Palace's Colourful Activities," 5.

79. Groth, "Forbidden Housing," passim.

80. Ba Ren, "Xishi," 290–91. The story was written in 1940 but is published here for the first time.

81. McCormick, *Audacious Angles on China*, 43; Powell, *My Twenty-five Years in China*, 7.

82. The French Concession police licensed dancing schools; the SMP did not. *CC*, 1 Apr. 1937, 9.

83. Finch, *Shanghai and Beyond*, 304–5.

84. One of the earliest nightclubs was a Chinese farmhouse across from Bubbling Well and appropriately called St. George's Farm. It was owned by a German or Greek named Fredericks. Carney, *Foreign Devils Had Light Eyes*, 54.

85. "In social life the foreigner finds himself strangely free from the restraints that surround him at home." Houghton, "The Shanghai Mind," 538–40. Zhu Zijia, *Huangpu jiang de zhuo lang*, 119.

86. Hauser, *Shanghai: City for Sale*, 261.

87. Carney, *Foreign Devils Had Light Eyes*, 55. "A considerable part of the Russian colony in Shanghai, perhaps one-third of the whole, lives on the earnings of women who work in the local bars and dance halls. About a thousand Russian women are employed in these places down to ordinary sailor resorts. Their legitimate incomes range from $50 to $150 monthly." *CWR*, 22 Dec. 1928, 163.

88. Wren, "Once-Wicked Shanghai," 4.

89. Finch, *Shanghai and Beyond*, 304.

90. Hauser, *Shanghai: City for Sale*, 261.

91. Pal, *Shanghai Saga*, 76.

92. Booker, *News Is My Job*, 164.

93. "At first Chinese girls could be seen in the role of dancing partners in bars only, but gradually they appeared in dancing halls and also cafés. Less than ten years ago, Chinese dancing partners were a rarity in Shanghai." Yen, "Crime in Relation to Social Change in China," 103.

94. Ibid.

95. *CC*, 1 Apr. 1937, 9. There were 700 to 800 sing-song girls in 1937 as well.

96. There were seven Chinese massage houses and twenty-eight Chinese masseuses registered with the French police. There were also three foreign establishments, but the number of masseuses was unknown. *CC*, 1 Apr. 1937, 8.

97. Ibid. See also Hauser, *Shanghai: City for Sale*, 269.

98. Yen, "Crime in Relation to Social Change in China," 102.

99. Hershatter, "The Hierarchy of Shanghai Prostitution," 494, 465; Hershatter, "Prostitution in Shanghai," 13–14.

100. Xia Lin'gen and Ding Ning, "Jianguo yilai Shanghai shi yanjiu shuping," 80.

101. Sun Guoqun, "Lun jiu Shanghai changji zhidu de fazhan he tedian," 3–4. See also Hershatter, "The Hierarchy of Shanghai Prostitution," 466.

102. Sun Guoqun, "Lun jiu Shanghai changji zhidu de fazhan he tedian," 4.

103. See especially John Colton's popular American play *The Shanghai Gesture.*

104. The Louza (Laozha) Police Station was located just off of Nanjing Road on Jiujiang Road. Pan Ling, *In Search of Old Shanghai,* 60–61.

105. *CWR,* 5 Jan. 1929, 226.

106. Ibid.

107. Hauser, *Shanghai: City for Sale,* 269. The pimps for some of the white prostitutes in Shanghai were French adventurers who had typically worked as panderers in Montmartre, the Rue de Récoletté in Marseilles, and overseas in Buenos Aires or Valparaiso. See the semi-fictive account in Champly, *The Road to Shanghai,* 217. In 1936 there were 34 registered and about 270 clandestine European prostitutes in the French Concession. *CC,* 1 Apr. 1937, 7.

108. Xu Huifang and Liu Qingyu, "Shanghai nüxing fan de shehui fenxi," 75.

109. *CWR,* 5 Jan. 1929, 226.

110. In the early 1920s there was a kind of grand tour for prostitutes across the Pacific, passing through Honolulu, Hong Kong, Manila, Singapore, and Java. Finch, *Shanghai and Beyond,* 45.

111. Excepting, of course, the Japanese. "Little Tokyo" in Hongkou had three branches of well-known Japanese geisha houses. Because of the large numbers of wealthy Japanese businessmen who came to Shanghai, the major Tokyo houses regularly dispatched groups of leading geishas to their Hongkou branches. Pal, *Shanghai Saga,* 77.

112. Finch, *Shanghai and Beyond,* 37–41.

113. Ibid., 48.

114. "The appearance of white women in such disgraceful capacity as that of prostitutes among the natives of the lowest class, affects very deeply the prestige of the Western nations in the Orient." Report of the International Committee . . . to Investigate Prostitution, quoted in Pal, *Shanghai Saga,* 20–21. For an egregiously racist account of "white women, real women, horribly done up and undressed . . . drinking, dancing and offering themselves at the behest of a clientèle exclusively Yellow," see Champly, *The Road to Shanghai,* 194.

115. Booker, *News Is My Job,* 164.

116. Ibid.

117. Hershatter, "The Hierarchy of Shanghai Prostitution," 473.

118. But according to a night guide to Shanghai, probably published around 1930, they also took Chinese clients, especially if the customer could speak English. *Shanghai shenmi zhinan,* 42–43.

119. These "salt water sisters" (*xianshui mei*) had come under special Admiralty regulations in 1877 to be medically examined in a lock hospital for venereal disease. They thereafter used their hospital registration cards with photo identification as advertisements for their services until prostitution was officially forbidden in the Settlement in 1920. Hershatter, "The Hierarchy of Shanghai Prostitution," 472–73; Davidson-Houston, *Yellow Creek,* 96; MacPherson, *A Wilderness of Marshes,* 219–35.

120. The hierarchy, which is discussed briefly below, is drawn almost entirely from Hershatter's excellent studies "The Hierarchy of Shanghai Prostitution" and "The Class Structure of Shanghai Prostitution, 1920–1949." The range of fees reflected this hierarchy. In 1936 higher-class prostitutes earned $10–15 a night;

middle-class ones were paid from $3 to $10. At the lowest level, prostitutes received thirty to forty cents per visit. *CC*, 1 Apr. 1937, 8.

121. Hershatter, "Prostitution in Shanghai," 4–5; Yen, "Crime in Relation to Social Change in China," 83–84; Sun Guoqun, "Lun jiu Shanghai changji zhidu de fazhan he tedian," 2–3.

122. "Long threes" referred to a domino with two groups of three dots each. *Changsan* prostitutes used to charge three yuan for drinking with guests, and three more to spend the night; hence, the name. Hershatter, "Prostitution in Shanghai," 6.

123. *SYZ*, 564–66.

124. Zhang Jungu, *Du Yuesheng zhuan*, 44; Hershatter, "Prostitution in Shanghai," 6.

125. Gamewell, *The Gateway to China*, 46–48.

126. Hershatter, "Prostitution in Shanghai," 6–7; Fontenoy, *The Secret Shanghai*, 50.

127. Hershatter, "Prostitution in Shanghai," 8. But note this description of Foochow Road in the 1930s: "As I walked along I saw at the entrance of numerous courts leading into the streets groups of young Chinese girls with highly painted faces and costumes splendid standing chatting among themselves, meanwhile eyeing the passers-by out of the corners of their eyes. Most of them appeared to be girls from twelve to eighteen years of age, the latter age being considered quite matronly for girls of this profession. When a likely customer approached they stood with a demure expression and downcast eyes." Lee, *The Underworld of the East*, 237.

128. Hershatter, "Prostitution in Shanghai," 7.

129. Booker, *News Is My Job*, 27; Lee, *The Underworld of the East*, 238; Hauser, *Shanghai: City for Sale*, 262.

130. Sun Guoqun, "Lun jiu Shanghai changji zhidu de fazhan he tedian," 7; Hershatter, "Prostitution in Shanghai," 9.

131. Many came from Hangzhou and Suzhou, where they were bought cheaply at a tender age. In districts beset by flood or famine, they could be had for a couple of dollars apiece. Hauser, *Shanghai: City for Sale*, 268. *CC*, 1 Apr. 1939, 7.

132. Xu Huifang and Liu Qingyu, "Shanghai nüxing fan de shehui fenxi," 79–84. One of the less reliable first-person accounts of the vices of Shanghai describes houses of sodomy in both the International Settlement and the French Concession. Pressure from the English clergy closed down the former and led to the expansion of the latter. Fontenoy, *The Secret Shanghai*, 33–35.

133. *CWR*, 26 Apr. 1930, 334.

134. *CC*, 1 Apr. 1937, 11.

135. Hershatter, "Prostitution in Shanghai," 18–19, 26.

136. Yet contemporary observers were also quick to note the danger of frequenting unlicensed prostitutes who did not undergo medical inspections regularly. *CWR*, 14 June 1930, 57.

137. Hershatter, "Prostitution in Shanghai," 35–37.

138. Ibid., 37–38.

139. During the years just before the 1911 Revolution, Chen Qimei and other Tongmenghui conspirators also used bordellos as meeting places safe from the

surveillance of the Qing government. Sun Guoqun, "Lun jiu Shanghai changji zhidu de fazhan he tedian," 7.

140. Hershatter, "Prostitution in Shanghai," 39–40; Finch, *Shanghai and Beyond*, 46–47.

141. Finch, *Shanghai and Beyond*, 11. See also *CWR*, 5 Jan. 1929, 226; Yen, "Crime in Relation to Social Change in China," 103. *CC*, 1 Apr. 1937, 7.

142. Finch, *Shanghai and Beyond*, 39–42. Quote, 42.

143. *CC*, 1 Apr. 1937, 7.

144. *CWR*, 20 Aug. 1927, 316.

145. Sun Guoqun, "Lun jiu Shanghai changji zhidu de fazhan he tedian," 4; *CC*, 1 Apr. 1937, 8.

146. *CC*, 1 Apr. 1937, 9. The Chinese delegation included Xiong Shili, representing the World Red Swastika Society of China. Hershatter, "Prostitution in Shanghai," 42–43.

147. Sun Guoqun, "Lun jiu Shanghai changji zhidu de fazhan he tedian," 4. "Shanghai has often been called the Paris of the Orient. This is only half true. Shanghai has all the vices of Paris and more but boasts of none of its cultural influences." *CWR*, 14 June 1930.

CHAPTER 8. NARCOTICS

1. Quoted in Pal, *Shanghai Saga*, 41–42.

2. In the early twentieth century, morphine and heroin were not manufactured in China. The entire world's supply was produced by a few European, American, and Japanese pharmaceutical firms. The expansion of Chinese demand had a dramatic impact on these firms. For instance, the British manufacturer T. Whiffen and Sons increased morphine sales from 77,000 pounds in 1909 to 469,000 pounds in 1916. Parssinen and Meyer, "International Narcotics Trafficking," 8. "Red pills" were potent combinations of morphine, strychnine, and other drugs to be smoked. Marshall, "Opium and the Politics of Gangsterism," 28.

3. Xu Zhucheng, *Du Yuesheng zhengzhuan*, 21.

4. Zhang Jungu, *Du Yuesheng zhuan*, 25–40; Pal, *Shanghai Saga*, 72; Scott, *Actors Are Madmen*, 60–61; Wan Molin, *Hushang wangshi*, vol. 4, 696–98; Xue Gengxin, "Jindai Shanghai de liumang," 164.

5. His original name was Yuesheng. Later he changed his name (*ming*) to Yong, and took Yuesheng as his *hao* (honorific or public name). Jiang Shaozhen, "Du Yuesheng." In Li Xin and Sun Sibai, eds., *Minguo renwu zhuan*, 314. The "legend" of Du Yuesheng is so powerful among young people in the PRC that publishers have been sentenced to jail for printing biographies of the man. For a recent example of such a book, see Shao Shi, *Du Yuesheng chuanqi*.

6. Jiang Shaozhen, "Du Yuesheng," 314; Pan Ling, *Old Shanghai*, 7–15.

7. Shanghai *liumang* were hired as bouncers ("punters" or *chengtou*) in local brothels. Zhu Zijia (Jin Qiongbai), *Huangpu jiang de zhuo lang*, 82.

8. According to Pan Ling, Du was introduced to the Green Gang at the age of twenty by the gambler for whom he worked as a runner. *Old Shanghai*, 16.

9. Ibid.

10. Shanghai shehui kexue yuan, comp., *Da liumang Du Yuesheng*, 6. Pan Ling, *Old Shanghai*, 26–27.

11. Mrs. Huang, in return for Du's recovery of one of her opium shipments, persuaded her husband to give Du Yuesheng a cut in the protection of the Gong-xingji, one of the three biggest casinos in the French Concession. Pan Ling, *Old Shanghai*, 30–32.

12. For a list of the major members of this drug gang, see Shanghai shehui kexue yuan, comp., *Da liumang Du Yuesheng*, 8–9.

13. Jiang Shaozhen, "Du Yuesheng," 314; Martin, "'The Pact with the Devil,'" 11–12. The importation of drugs had an inherent tendency toward centralization because of the limits on access to the market and the capital necessary to operate. This was quite different from prostitution where there was virtually no economy of scale. Smart, "The Informal Regulation of Illegal Economic Activities," 16.

14. *San wei yi ti* (three positions, one body) represented this tripartite division. Xu Zhucheng, *Du Yuesheng zhengzhuan*, 25.

15. The "four lords" then were Hou Fangyu, Fang Yizhi, Mao Xiang, and Chen Zhenhui. Wakeman, Jr., *The Great Enterprise*, vol. 1, 359.

16. There were also the "four great lords" (*si da gongzi*): Zhang Xueliang, Lu Xiaojia, Sun Ke (Sun Yat-sen's son), and Duan Hongye (Duan Qirui's son). Xu Zhucheng, *Du Yuesheng zhengzhuan*, 23.

17. Chen Dingshan, *Chun Shen jiu wen*, 6.

18. Xu Guoliang, a leading member of the opium syndicate, was allegedly killed by Lu Yongxiang and He Fenglin, but many contemporary observers—including George Sokolsky—believe that he was murdered because he failed to consider gangster interests. Martin, "Warlords and Gangsters," 10.

19. Chen Dingshan, *Chun Shen jiu wen*, 6–7.

20. Xu Zhucheng, *Du Yuesheng zhengzhuan*, 23; Fu Xiangyuan, *Qingbang da heng*, 43.

21. Xu Zhucheng, *Du Yuesheng zhengzhuan*, 24.

22. After the 1911 Revolution each of the provincial warlords had his own military police units. Zhuo Jian'an, "Gu Zhenglun yu Guomindang xianbing," 227.

23. Xu Zhucheng, *Du Yuesheng zhengzhuan*, 24.

24. Zhang Xiaolin, who was originally a textile worker from Hangzhou, had excellent political contacts. By being able to "reach heaven" (*tong tian*) he could provide the other Green Gang leaders with access to national leaders like Li Yuan-hong and warlords such as Lu Yongxiang. Zhang Jungu, *Du Yuesheng zhuan*, 139–49; Pan Ling, *Old Shanghai*, 36.

25. For the important connection between outside reputation and a gang lead-er's group standing, see Whyte, *Street Corner Society*, 258–60. Whyte also points out that in urban criminal gangs leadership does not change because of the bottom members rising up but because of a shift in relations between men at the top of that structure. Ibid., 261.

26. Xu Zhucheng, *Du Yuesheng zhengzhuan*, 25.

27. In a single month five different military leaders claimed control of the city. Finch, *Shanghai and Beyond*, 24–25.

28. Yomano, "Reintegration in China under the Warlords," 25–26; Henriot, "Le gouvernement municipal de Shanghai," 25–26.

29. Zhang Jungu, *Du Yuesheng zhuan*, 131; Fu Xiangyuan, *Qingbang da heng*, 59.

30. Many sources claim that French Consul General E. Hagglar (Naggiar) was a full partner in the Big Company. Xu Zhucheng, *Du Yuesheng zhengzhuan*, 27; Martin, "The Green Gang and 'Party Purification,'" 151. For articles on the implication of the French police's involvement with the Big Company, see *NCH*, 26 Feb. and 5 Mar. 1927.

31. These negotiations, held over a three-month period, are carefully analyzed in Martin, "'The Pact with the Devil,'" 12–13.

32. Memorandum from Douglas Jenkins, Consul General at Shanghai, to the Secretary of State, Washington, 16 Mar. 1931, State Department Decimal File 893, #114 Narcotics/208, 1–2.

33. At this same time Du purchased Portuguese citizenship and made the French Concession his own personal headquarters. In 1925 he and Zhang Xiaolin together built a three-storied western-style residence divided into two screened-off areas on a large two-*mu* lot on Rue Wagner in the French Concession. Each of Du's three wives had her own floor in the house, and when Du later took a Beijing opera singer as his fourth wife she had to move into a separate residence at Rue Lafayette. The first wife, whom he married in 1915, was unfertile and they had to adopt a boy. The two concubines, both from Suzhou and fifteen years old at the time, were originally given to Du by friends; they bore him six sons. His fourth wife gave birth to a girl. Wan Molin, *Hushang wangshi*, vol. 1, 7; Pan Ling, *Old Shanghai*, 34–35; Martin, "'Pact with the Devil,'" 5. Four wives notwithstanding, Du Yuesheng made frequent visits to brothels. Sun Guoqun, "Lun jiu Shanghai changji zhidu de fazhan he tedian," 7.

34. If a den was caught underreporting the number of pipes rented out, then it had to pay a fine of $50 per pipe.

35. The Green Gang employed "gangster lawyers" (*qiangdao lüshi*) like Jin Yu who knew every detective in town. Zhu Zijia (Jin Qiongbai), *Huangpu jiang de zhuo lang*, 84.

36. "Memorandum on Mr. Tu Yueh-sung, alias Tu Yuin." Special Branch secret memorandum in SMP, D-9319, 1 Sept. 1939, 3. It was said that "mediation in kidnapping cases proved very lucrative for Du and his Frenchtown gang. They were believed to receive fifty percent of the ransom paid in all cases." Ibid. Romanizations have been changed to pinyin.

37. There are suggestions in the memoir literature that the Gentry-Councillor Clique, and especially Wei Tingrong, may have engineered Huang's resignation from the detective squad. Martin, "'The Pact with the Devil,'" 17. As a philanthropist, Huang took a special interest in charity for prisoners, often gifting inmates at Caohejing Prison and the Jiangsu Provincial Prison with articles of apparel. *SB*, 8 Dec. 1930, 12.

38. Marshall, "Opium and the Politics of Gangsterism," 33. It would be interesting to do a careful comparison of this Chinese model of confederated leadership with American organized crime groups, like the five "families" (Gambino, Bonanno, Colombo, Genovese, and Lucchese) in New York City in the 1970s. For the latter, see Raab, "John Gotti: Running the Mole," 70.

39. Du always left them a fairly good profit of their own. He "cut the skin but not the flesh." Xu Zhucheng, *Du Yuesheng zhengzhuan*, 27.

40. Martin, "The Green Gang and 'Party Purification,'" 6, 50.

41. It was said that the SMP constables (*xunbu*) also turned the other way when they recognized the Swatow merchants' trucks traveling to one of the large underground warehouses. Xu Zhucheng, *Du Yuesheng zhengzhuan*, 27.

42. Ibid.

43. Martin, "The Green Gang and 'Party Purification,'" 5–6, 50. See also *CWR*, 30 Oct. 1926, 249.

44. Sues, *Shark Fins and Millet*, 67. Du Yuesheng also became chairman of the French Concession's Chinese General Chamber of Commerce and supervisor of the French Concession's Chinese Ratepayers Association. Martin, "The Green Gang and 'Party Purification,'" 7.

45. See the discussions—which cover Huang Jinrong's meetings with Chiang Kai-shek at Jiujiang in November 1926, and in Shanghai in the spring when Huang presented himself as head of the Federation of Commercial and Industrial Bodies—in Martin's excellent and authoritative study "The Green Gang and 'Party Purification,'" 13; and in Marshall, "Opium and the Politics of Gangster-ism," 31. For the unexpectedness of Chiang's coup, see Zhu Zijia (Jin Qiongbai), *Huangpu jiang de zhuo lang*, 47. This is also conveyed in Pan Ling, *Old Shanghai*, 54–56.

46. Henriot, "Le gouvernement municipal de Shanghai," 27. Initially, the Green Gang's narcotics monopoly was threatened by Sun's soldiers, but arrange-ments were eventually worked out to pay off the warlord. Zhang Jungu, *Du Yue-sheng zhuan*, 153–55.

47. On February 20, 1927, Du Yuesheng intervened personally to keep Chinese merchants from joining the general strike in the French Concession. In return, on February 26 Consul General P. E. Naggiar requested 300 rifles and 10,000 car-tridges and increased that by early March to 600 rifles plus 150 revolvers and 1,000 steel helmets. These were the weapons used on April 12. Martin, "'The Pact with the Devil,'" 18.

48. Martin, "The Green Gang and 'Party Purification,'" 11.

49. Ibid., 53. Moreover, Green Gang bosses had a little earlier provided safe passage through Shanghai to Whampoa Academy recruits en route to Canton. Tsao Jr-lien, "On the Nature of the Chinese Capitalists," 48.

50. On the side of the CCP, Wang Shouhua (alias He Songling) initiated a policy of conciliation toward the Green Gang and tried to get their support for the general strike and uprising of February 24, 1927. After the strike began, however, the CCP resumed its policy of systematically assassinating "contract foremen" (*baogong*), who were usually Green Gang members. Wang did report to Zhou Enlai on March 19 that "Du Yuesheng has asked us to help him. . . . He requests that we not raise the opium issue. Meanwhile, he hopes to reorganize all the Green and Red gangs in Shanghai under our command." On April 9, however, Du Yuesheng invited Wang Shouhua to his new house on Rue Wagner, luring the Communist labor leader out of his heavily guarded Shanghai General Labor Union's headquarters in the Huzhou guildhall. According to the most sensational account, no sooner was Wang in the building than two Green Gang killers tried unsuccessfully to garrote him. Du Yuesheng suddenly appeared at the head of the stairs. "Not here, not in my house," he cried. Rui Qingrong, Du's chief bodyguard and enforcer, led Wang at pistol point outside to a car. His corpse was found

several days later: he had been buried alive. Faligot and Kauffer, *Kang Sheng*. But see also Zhu Zijia (Jin Qiongbai), *Huangpu jiang de zhuo lang*, 50–51; and Pan Ling, *Old Shanghai*, 49–51. The quotation is from Perry, "Shanghai on Strike," 36. Note, however, that other sources maintain that Zhang Xiaolin supervised the abduction and murder. Martin, "The Green Gang and 'Party Purification,'" 19–22, 56, 64–65.

51. In Hongkou, for example, Sun Jiefu, who was the local Green Gang boss and who controlled the police force, sent two hundred to one thousand of his own gang members to help the police try to recapture police stations occupied by the workers' pickets. Du Yuesheng had to intervene personally to persuade Sun to call off his Green Gang followers. Zhang Xiaolin, who was initially opposed to an alliance with the GMD, supposedly changed his mind when the opium guarantees were made. Martin, "The Green Gang and 'Party Purification,'" 14–17, 26, 55.

52. Once outside Shanghai, Chiang and his bodyguard made their way gingerly into the French Concession, waiting for fifteen minutes at the boundary until a flustered constable was able to get back-up from French police officers who welcomed the future Generalissimo through iron gates into that portion of the city. Mi Xi, "Wo zai Jiang Jieshi shenbian de shihou," 23–24.

53. Between April 1 and 4, this group advanced Chiang Ch. $3 million to help him launch his coup. Coble, Jr., *The Shanghai Capitalists*, 29–31; Bush, *The Politics of Cotton Textiles*, 19–20.

54. Anonymous. *Chongdang "Si yi er" da tusha de kuaizishou*, 2–3; Pal, *Shanghai Saga*, 19; Finch, *Shanghai and Beyond*, 185.

55. Martin, "The Green Gang and 'Party Purification,'" 33; Martin, "'The Pact with the Devil,'" 18.

56. Martin, "Tu Yueh-sheng and Labour Control," 104; Chesneaux, *The Chinese Labor Movement*, 363–64.

57. Ch'en Li-fu, "The Board of Organization," 54.

58. The special seamen's party branch covered an area from Shanghai to North China, Manchuria, and on to Vladivostok. In the South it stretched all the way to Guangdong, and it went inland to Hankou. Members were seamen working on coastal vessels, and dock workers. Ibid., 57. Chiang had sent Yang Hu in January 1927 to Jiujiang, Anqing, Wuhu, and Nanjing to contact Green Gang groups and prepare to carry out the "Nanchang Policy" of extirpating CCP influence in local GMD branches. Martin, "The Green Gang and 'Party Purification,'" 22–23. During the "purification" in Shanghai, Yang Hu was escorted to and from Northern Expedition Army headquarters by French Concession Police Chinese detectives provided as bodyguards by Huang Jinrong. Lu Chupeng, "Yang Hu yishi liang ze," 71.

59. *MG*, vol. 20, 187; Fontenoy, *The Secret Shanghai*, 129; Finch, *Shanghai and Beyond*, 158. For Yang Hu's relationship to Du Yuesheng, Zhang Xiaolin, and Huang Jinrong, see SMP, D-351, p. 40a. For Yang Hu's role in the shooting of Chen Duxiu's son Chen Yannian, see *SB*, 5 July 1927, 1.

60. *DZ*, 24.17, p. 116.

61. The full title was Beifa donglujun zhengzhibu Shanghai shi qingdang weiyuanhui (Committee to Purify the Party of Shanghai Municipality of the Political Section of the Eastern Route Army of the Northern Expedition). The Eastern Route Army was Bai Chongxi's front headquarters. Martin, "Tu Yueh-sheng and

Labour Control," 102–3. Chen Qun, who also served as Du's private secretary, later became professor of religion at Ji'nan University. Isaacs, ed., *Five Years of Kuomintang Reaction*, 95.

62. Martin, "Tu Yueh-sheng and Labour Control," 104.

63. The Pan-Pacific Trade Union Secretariat estimated that in 1927, 231,700 persons lost their lives in China at the hands of the Right. Isaacs, ed., *Five Years of Kuomintang Reaction*, 7, 95.

64. Gourlay, "'Yellow' Unionism in Shanghai," 106–7.

65. *CWR*, 2 July 1927, 116.

66. On a typical banking day in 1930 about £13 million was issued in notes by the different banks in Shanghai, which at the same time held over £16 million in silver reserves. Bruce, "The Foreign Settlement at Shanghai," 131.

67. Coble, Jr., *The Shanghai Capitalists*, 12, 32–36.

68. Xue Gengxin, "Jindai Shanghai de liumang," 164.

69. Xu Zhucheng, *Du Yuesheng zhengzhuan*, 49–54.

70. Coble, Jr., *The Shanghai Capitalists*, 39.

71. Members of the Preparatory Committee included Shang Mujiang, a Green Gang boss from Hangzhou close to Zhang Xiaolin, and Cheng Zhusun, also suspected of being a Green Gang member. Martin, "'The Pact with the Devil,'" 21.

72. Ibid., 21–22.

73. The actual kidnapper was a Suzhou policeman named Zhao Weixian. Wei was kidnapped on July 24, 1929, as he was accompanying his children to their school in a chauffeured limousine. *SB*, 24 Aug. 1931, 15, and 25 Aug. 1931, 15.

74. Gourlay, "'Yellow' Unionism in Shanghai," 123.

75. See George Sokolsky's articles denouncing the Green Gang labor bosses and the Shanghai "Tammany" in the *NCH*, 13 Aug. and 29 Aug. 1927.

76. In May 1928 the Guomindang central headquarters tried to end the military-party rivalry by forming a "Shanghai Labor Unions Reorganization Committee" with representatives from both sides. This grand coalition failed, and in October 1928 Party Center finally put all matters related to union organization under the Shanghai *dangbu*. This was regarded as a big victory for the "CC" clique. Chan, "Organized Labor in China," 9–10.

77. Honig, "Women Cotton Mill Workers," 160.

78. By this time Huang Jinrong had become a formally sworn member of the Green Gang.

79. Martin, "Tu Yueh-sheng and Labour Control," 106. Zhang and Du had long been close friends. Earlier, when applying for a pistol permit (which was denied), Zhang gave Du's address as his own. SMP, D-117, 4 Apr. 1924; D-5374, 9 Apr. 1924.

80. Perry, "Shanghai on Strike," 43.

81. Ianni with Reuss-Ianni, *A Family Business*, 32. But note the rumor, which none of the police files substantiate, that Du Yuesheng had Soong Mayling (Song Meiling or Madame Chiang) kidnapped and then returned in the winter of 1927. "Du deplored the fact that the Generalissimo had found no time to arrange for suitable protection for himself and Madame—a very dangerous omission in a big city like Shanghai." Sues, *Shark Fins and Millet*, 70.

82. Ch'en Li-fu, "The Board of Organization," 53.

83. See, for example, Seagrave, *The Soong Dynasty.*

84. "Did more Party members join the Green Gang and vice versa after the purge? Yes, there was more mixing. In general, did gang members who joined the KMT achieve high Party positions? They were just ordinary members. Usually these men did not achieve their position through gang membership. There was usually some other factor." Ch'en Li-fu, "The Board of Organization," 40.

85. Marshall, "Opium and the Politics of Gangsterism," 32. Huang Jinrong also received legion of honor medals of the second class for his special services in maintaining public order in the French Concession. Qi Zaiyu, *Shanghai shi renzhi,* 165. For an impressive list of Du's official titles, see *SSN,* X-25.

86. The *Dagong bao* story is cited in Isaacs, ed., *Five Years of Kuomintang Reaction,* 96. See also Martin, "'The Pact with the Devil,'" 29.

87. Despite these later arrangements linking narcotics with right-wing terrorism, Du Yuesheng and Chiang Kai-shek's interests were far from identical. Martin, "Tu Yueh-sheng and Labour Control," 107–8. As time went by, GMD members working in the labor movement "found it convenient to join the gang" and Wu Kaixian became very friendly with Du Yuesheng, who also called upon Chen Lifu whenever he visited Shanghai. Ch'en Li-fu, "The Board of Organization," 40.

88. Sokolsky, "China in Search of a Government," 18. The execution of Chen Duxiu's son caused a considerable stir in July 1927. *DZ,* 24.17, p. 116; *SB,* 5 July 1927, 13.

89. Su Zhiliang, "Shanghai banghui shi gaishu," 6–7. The Joint Progress Association was consequently disbanded by the government.

90. Approximately five thousand people were killed by the "purification" squads between April and September 1927, in Shanghai alone. Martin, "The Green Gang and 'Party Purification,'" 44–45.

91. Ibid.

92. Other Du Yuesheng disciples included Liu Yunfang in the Fourth Section and Yao Guangnai, head of the West Gate branch of the PSB. "Memorandum on Mr. Tu Yueh-sung, Alias Tu Yuin." Special Branch Secret Memorandum, in SMP, D-9319, 1 Sept. 1939, 10.

93. "Heroin, despite its forbidden status, stands as a stark metaphor for many more legitimate products that have become indispensable to our society. First of all, the opium poppy is a crop which distorts the economies of those poor countries where it is grown. It requires ingenuity in the harvesting, refining, and processing (the production of morphine and its acetylation); it calls for great daring and risk-taking and enterprise in its transport and distribution. It creates vast wealth for those who trade in it. But above all—and this is where it really lights up the dark heart of capitalist marketing, and betrays the closely guarded secret of the 'magic of the markets'—it creates its own demand." Seabrook, "The Heroin Trade," 8. See also Trocki, *Opium and Empire,* 237.

94. Overcultivation of opium in Shaanxi province between 1928 and 1933 took as many as 6 million lives in four provinces. Perhaps a third of the entire population of Shaanxi was wiped out. Farmers were forced to pay an opium cultivation tax whether they produced poppies or not. Buckley, "China's Failure to Suppress Opium Traffic," 80; Marshall, "Opium and the Politics of Gangsterism," 24.

95. Fontenoy, *The Secret Shanghai*, 165. Moreover, the corruption was "complex, highly organized, and clandestine." Sherman, *Scandal and Reform*, 116.

96. According to U.S. Treasury agent M. R. Nicholson, Du Yuesheng paid the Nationalists $400,000 per month for permission to operate his morphine and heroin factories. Parssinen and Meyer, "International Narcotics Trafficking," 37–38.

97. Woodhead, "The Truth About Opium in China," 56.

98. *MG*, 16 Sept. 1927, 320.

99. Ibid.

100. Lee, "Opium Suppression in China," 69. Sun Yat-sen's Canton régime had licensed opium dens and brothels. Marshall, "Opium and the Politics of Gangsterism," 20. However, Sun had decisively rejected advice that the opium problem could be resolved by legalization and government monopoly. He had even suggested that addicts who resisted cure "are not to be [recognized] as citizens of the republic." Cited in Chang and Gordon, *All Under Heaven*.

101. Chiang's Australian adviser, William H. Donald, claimed that when he had advocated ruthless suppression, arguing that Chiang had the armies and machine guns to mow down every "damned son of a bitch" who continued to poison the nation with opium, the Generalissimo had published a six-year plan for the drug's eradication. Yet later, after Donald fell ill and spent almost a year in the hospital, the whole opium policy changed because Chiang had been persuaded to add an opium monopoly "for better control" and to reduce production gradually. Sues, *Shark Fins and Millet*, 57.

102. Adams II, "China: The Historical Setting," 381.

103. Lee, "Opium Suppression in China," 68.

104. There were over 334 opium seizure cases in the 1927–28 police year. *STS*, *jishi*, 49.

105. Lee, "Opium Suppression in China," 70. An Opium Suppression Act was passed on September 10, 1928, prohibiting traffic in opium, morphia, cocaine, heroin, and their derivatives. *CWR*, 1 Dec. 1928, 8; Adams II, "China: The Historical Setting," 381.

106. Some sources report that the tip came from General Xiong Shihui.

107. "Editorial," *NCH*, 5 Jan. 1929; *CWR*, 12 Jan. 1928, 8; Henriot, "Le gouvernement municipal de Shanghai," 348; Lary, *Region and Nation*, 138; Buckley, "China's Failure to Suppress Opium Traffic," 78–79.

108. *MG*, 21 Dec. 1928, 36.

109. Lary, *Region and Nation*, 138.

110. Henriot, "Le gouvernement municipal de Shanghai," 66. For gun-running in general, see Chan, *Arming the Chinese*, 67–108. For Shanghai in particular, see Finch, *Shanghai and Beyond*, 71–72; Oakes, *White Man's Folly*, 59; and Pal, *Shanghai Saga*, 79–80.

111. *CC*, 20 Dec. 1928, 584.

112. Henriot, "Le gouvernement municipal de Shanghai," 66. Pan himself was a part-owner of *Shang bao* (*Shanghai Tribune*) along with Chen Bulei, Chiang Kai-shek's private secretary. Ibid., 431–32.

113. Gourlay. "'Yellow' Unionism in Shanghai," 112–13.

114. Colonel Fu was identified as chief of the intelligence corps of the Long-hua military headquarters. *CWR*, 8 Dec. 1928, 52.

115. Henriot, "Le gouvernement municipal de Shanghai," 459. The chairman of the Judicial Yuan, Dr. Wang Zhonghui, insisted that the State Council would instruct the Jiangning district court to conduct a trial of the detectives of the Intelligence Corps of the Shanghai and Wusong Military Police Headquarters on charges of conniving to smuggle opium. This trial never seems to have taken place. *CWR*, 29 Dec. 1928, 194.

116. *SB*, 2 Dec. 1928, 13; 5 Dec. 1928, 14.

117. Once senior police gave in to temptation and accepted bribes, new police-men likely followed suit, corruption being a form of membership in the force. For this phenomenon elsewhere, see Baker, *Cops*, 33–35; and Meyer, Jr., "Defi-nitional and Etiological Issues in Police Corruption," 55.

118. Military attaché's comments on current events, 1–15 Dec. 1928, and "Report on Trip to Shanghai and Nanking," 25 Jan. 1929, 14, in U.S. Military Intelligence Reports, China 1911–1941.

119. *SSG*, vol. 3, 150.

120. Many foreigners liked to believe that Chiang had a criminal background himself, and that the Shanghai police department had several warrants for his arrest. "Every newcomer to Shanghai is informed of this story—to the effect that General Chiang Kai-shek was involved in criminal activities when he was a youth in Shanghai. . . . The story is constantly whispered about Shanghai with a knowing wink." There were no such warrants. *CWR*, 5 Nov. 1929, 448.

121. Finch, *Shanghai and Beyond*, 287.

122. *SSG*, vol. 3, 107.

123. Marshall, "Opium and the Politics of Gangsterism," 20.

124. Merrill, *Japan and the Opium Menace*, 25–27.

CHAPTER 9. REDS

1. Mao Tun, "Comedy," 253.

2. *CWR*, 19 Jan. 1929, 347.

3. *STS, jishi*, 8.

4. Ibid., *jishi*, 40–41. The committee included members from the military as well as from the police, and its inspectors (*duchayuan*) found and listed about nineteen thousand items per year that were considered suspect and undesirable. *SSG*, vol. 4, 120.

5. Ibid., 2.

6. *SSG*, vol. 3, 115, and vol. 4, 5.

7. Xu Enzeng had earlier, in 1928, set up the first GMD wireless broadcasting network in Jiangsu. The network was under the higher direction of Chen Lifu, who had turned the Zhejiang Telegraph Bureau (Dianbao ju), which he headed, into a clandestine recruiting organization. The radio network was thus also an intelligence gathering unit under the direction of the GMD's Dangwu diaocha ke (Investigation Section for Party Affairs), and from its training school graduated a number of future Zhongtong agents as well as the famed Communist mole, Qian Zhuangfei. In 1930, following the instructions of Chiang Kai-shek, Xu established

a commercial branch of the wireless company in Shanghai and turned its management over to the Ministry of Communications. Xu Enzeng, "Wo he Gongdang douzheng de huiyi," BIA, doc. no. 6002; Mu Xin, *Chen Geng tongzhi zai Shanghai,* 34.

8. *SSG,* vol. 5, 211.

9. Quoted in Isaacs, ed., *Five Years of Kuomintang Reaction,* 12.

10. For the press law, passed on January 9, 1931, see ibid., 77.

11. *CA,* nos. 114–15, 32–34.

12. *SSG,* vol. 4, 119, and vol. 5, 8–51.

13. Henriot, "Le gouvernement municipal de Shanghai," 107.

14. "May Day is not just the day on which we celebrate the labor festival; it is a day of struggle, a day of bloody battles!" *Partisan,* cited in Hunter, "The Chinese League of Left-Wing Writers," 125.

15. SMP, D-2880, 11 Nov. 1931.

16. See, for an example of this concern about "reds" and "red elements," *SSG,* vol. 4, 119.

17. Chief Yuan Liang consistently related law and order to the end of extraterritoriality, arguing that, as long as the international concessions offered refuge to criminals, the Shanghai PSB could not prevent felonies from being committed. Translation of article from *China Times,* 28 Jan. 1931, in SMP, D-1949.

18. See, for example, the daily intelligence report in *SMP,* D-4003, 19 Sept. 1932.

19. Letter dated 7 Mar. 1932 from the chief of the PSB to Captain Martin, Commissioner of Police, in SMP, D-3312, 8 Mar. 1932.

20. For example, the British consul general on May 8, 1930, sent to the Special Branch a transmission from the Straits Settlement CID containing an intercept from Shanghai "Central" to the Singapore Communist Party. The message mentioned a certain Chiu Yung Bookstore at 176 Chengdu Road in Shanghai. The SMP not only commenced an intensive surveillance of the bookstore; it also passed on information about the intercept to the Shanghai special district court, which issued a warrant for all persons to be found on the premises. SMP, D-7873, 18 June 1930.

21. Zeng Kuoqing, "He Mei xieding qian Fuxingshe zai Huabei de huodong," 142–43; Shen Zui, *Juntong neimu,* 43, 52, 74, 117. But see, for an instance of claimed abuse by SMP questioners, the account by Yih Hai-sheng of his water and cigarette torture in *CC,* 18 June 1936, 270.

22. See, for example, the surveillance of the Ming Dan Middle School, in SMP, D-3922, 8 Oct. 1932.

23. In June 1935, Superintendent Tan was formally given a share of the responsibility "for the loyalty and general good behavior of the Chinese staff of the Special Branch." SMP, D-8/5, 3 June 1935.

24. Di Weimin, "Shanghai zujie liang jianguan yuci neimu," part one, 13.

25. Pal, *Shanghai Saga,* 19.

26. Shanghai patrolmen carried wooden clubs that had a flowery decoration on the handle.

27. Lu Liankui lacked discrimination. One major group of gangsters in the 1920s and 1930s came from Shengxian, near Shaoxing. Shengxian also produced legitimate actors and opera performers colloquially known as *diduban.* (See *Tour-*

ing Metropolitan Shanghai, 66–67.) Though innocent of wrongdoing, the latter were often related by lineage or neighborhood to the former. Whenever Lu Liankui arrested a Shengxian gangster he also dragged in all of the crook's *diduban* acquaintances, who just as often as not ended up disfigured or dead. Di Weimin, "Shanghai zujie liang jianguan yuci neimu," part two, 30; Wan Molin, *Hushang wangshi,* vol. 1, 45.

28. Di Weimin, "Shanghai zujie liang jianguan yuci neimu," part three, 15.

29. Journalists estimated that about 1,500 Communists were arrested in the International Settlement between 1931 and 1937. Finch, *Shanghai and Beyond,* 187.

30. *SSG,* vol. 4, 119.

31. *SSG,* vol. 3, 77, and vol. 5, 16.

32. Costs for public security in Shanghai came to constitute more than 30 percent of the total municipal budget. Salaries made up the bulk of police expenses. Henriot, "Le gouvernement municipal de Shanghai," 201.

33. These signs were especially troubling if they showed up elsewhere in the British Empire. For example, considerable effort was devoted to investigating the author Zheng Zhenduo in May 1932 because his name had turned up as a result of a police raid on the offices of the local Communist committee in Perak, Malaya, and then was forwarded to the SMP by "H.M.S." via the British Consulate General. SMP, D-3564, 26 Mar. 1932 and 16 May 1932.

34. *SB,* 2 Mar. 1929.

35. Mu Xin, *Chen Geng tongzhi zai Shanghai,* 53–60; Chen Senwen, "Zhong Gong zaoqi tewu gongzuo zhi yanjiu," 112–13.

36. Concession Française de Changhai, doc. no. 237/S, 53–56. This document (a copy of which is deposited in the Center for Chinese Studies Library at Berkeley) was given to me by Dr. Richard Kagan, who originally obtained it in Paris. It is a mimeographed report for French police and counterespionage agents, signed by Director of Police Services L. Fabre and endorsed by the chief of the Political Service, R. Sarly. This particular copy is numbered #17.

37. Boorman et al., eds., *Biographical Dictionary of Republican China,* vol. 2, 307.

38. Xu Enzeng, "Wo he Gongdang douzheng de huiyi," 21a; Zhongyang diaocha tongjiju, compilers, "Zhonggong tewubu buzhang Gu Shunzhang zhi zishou ji qi yu zhonggong zhi daji," BIA, 3; Chang, *The Rise of the Chinese Communist Party,* vol. 2, 174; Faligot and Kauffer, *Kang Sheng,* 56; Di Weimin, "Shanghai zujie liang jianguan yuci neimu," part two, 30; Isaacs, *The Tragedy of the Chinese Revolution,* 176. Note that Gu has also been identified as Zhou Enlai's "only Communist superior in Shanghai," although he is usually described as being Zhou's special assistant. Schaller, "Changing American Strategic and Political Views," 85.

39. Xu Enzeng, "Wo he Gongdang douzheng de huiyi," 19.

40. Li Tianmin, *Zhou Enlai pingzhuan,* 110; Zhongyang diaocha tongjiju, compilers, "Zhonggong tewubu buzhang Gu Shunzhang zhi zishou ji qi yu zhonggong zhi daji," BIA, 21. For an example of Gu's tradecraft (*tewu jishu*), see Zhang Guotao's description of his trip to the Ou-Yu-Wan Soviet area from Shanghai in the winter of 1930–31. At that time Gu "was actually in charge of the communications network between the Central Committee of the Chinese Communist Party

and the soviets at various places." Chang, *The Rise of the Chinese Communist Party*, vol. 2, 174–75. Zhang Guotao had just that winter come to the attention of the SMP Special Branch as the agent sent by Moscow to reorganize the Central Committee of the CCP. They knew nothing of him before then, despite his work in the labor movement. SMP, D-516/7, 28 Jan. 1931.

41. Xu Enzeng, "Wo he Gongdang douzheng de huiyi," 21a.

42. Ibid., 21b; Di Weimin, "Shanghai zujie liang jianguan yuci neimu," 30.

43. One recalls Trotsky's comment: "We do not enter the kingdom of socialism with white gloves on a polished floor." Quoted in Monas, "The Political Police," 182.

44. Xu Enzeng, "Wo he Gongdang douzheng de huiyi," 7a. The penetration of mass organizations was not conducted by the red special service units. Ibid., 8b.

45. Central Committee Directive No. 69, cited in Li Tianmin, *Zhou Enlai pingzhuan*, 104–5. The usual date given for the formation of the Central Committee's Special Services Committee (Tewu weiyuanhui or Tewei) under the supervision of Zhou Enlai, Xiang Zhongfa, and Gu Shunzhang, is 1929. Mu Xin, *Chen Geng tongzhi zai Shanghai*, 34.

46. In 1930 a branch of the Special Bureau was organized at the Central Bureau of the Organization of the Soviet districts. After this latter bureau was transformed into the Provisional Central Soviet Government of China, the branch was reorganized as the Central Office of the GPU. Concession Française de Changhai, doc. no. 237/S, 51–52.

47. Xu Enzeng, "Wo he Gongdang douzheng de huiyi," 7b–8a.

48. In June 1930, the amount of goods and currency sent by the Red Army amounted to just over Ch. $50,000. The Soviets sent 700 ounces of gold from western Fujian that same month; and a little more than 2,000 ounces of gold was remitted from southwestern Jiangxi at the end of the year. Ibid., 16a.

49. "Xiaomie Gongfei Hongdui an chi jingyan jianshu," BIA, 276/7435/59400, 1.

50. Xu Enzeng, "Wo he Gongdang douzheng de huiyi," 7b.

51. Ibid., 8a.

52. Mu Xin, *Chen Geng tongzhi zai Shanghai*, 34.

53. Ibid., 35.

54. Hu Di was from Anhui, as was Zhang Zhenhua, and they met at the Anhui guildhall while Hu Di was still a student at China University. After graduating, Hu Di moved in with Qian and Zhang. Ibid.

55. Ibid., 36.

56. Li Kenong had played an important role in organizing Communist cadres in the Anhui river port of Wuhu. The left wing had established a middle school there, the Minsheng zhongxue, which was the source of numerous party workers within the First United Front. Ibid., 36–37.

57. Apparently some local CCP regional party members opposed the idea of having Qian, Li, and Hu going to work for the enemy's intelligence apparatus, but Zhou Enlai simply brought the three of them under Party Center's authority and assigned them to work under Chen Geng. Ibid., 38.

58. Ibid., 38–39.

59. The cell was set up in 1930. It was exposed and several of its members (including Li Luoping and Wang Fan) were arrested in 1933. Liu Feng, "Zai wei

jingchaju li de douzheng" (*shang*), 175–77. See also Wan Ren, "Guomindang Shanghai jingchaju li de dixia gongzuo," 19–20.

60. On June 6, 1931, the French police arrested members of a Committee of Revolutionary Foreign Soldiers at Shanghai (Comité des soldats étrangers révolutionaires à Changhai), which included six Annamite Communists. Ibid., 30.

61. "This study was carried out with the help of the Political Intelligence Services (Services de Renseignements Politiques), and through the intermediary of informant agents recruited among members of the Chinese Communist Party and its auxiliary organizations. The internal struggle between these different groups on the one hand enormously facilitated—we have to say—the recruitment of these agents, the members of the 'cliques' of the opposition having often furnished precious information on the activity of their opponents." Concession Française de Changhai, doc. no. 237/S, 26–27.

62. *Shanghai Times*, 27 Feb. 1937; Gould, "The Unapproachable Police," 178. At this time there were said to be about three thousand Indians in Shanghai, including merchants, watchmen, and policemen. Most of these had come as SMP constables (some with dependents) and they had stayed on after completing their terms of enlistment. *CWR*, 6 July 1929, 233; 10 Jan. 1931, 212.

63. Gaustad, "Colonial Police in Africa and India," 12–13. One important medium of communication, during pre-Interpol days, was the *Criminal Police Times*, a police organ published in Germany in French, English, and German. See also the *North China Herald and South China and China Gazette*, 31 Dec. 1909, 781; Gwynn, *Imperial Policing*, 187; Cumming, "The Police Services of the Empire," 538–45; Woods, "Some Aspects of Training," 365; and Edwardes, *The Bombay City Police*, 72.

64. The first Hong Kong police force was organized in 1841, consisting of eleven Europeans recruited from seamen and troops and twenty-one locally recruited Chinese. In 1869 Scottish constables were brought in by the governor of Hong Kong because they were thought to be less prone to corruption. However, by 1897 it was found that almost all the Hong Kong police—European, Chinese, and Indian—were receiving money illegally from Chinese gambling syndicates. Lethbridge, *Hong Kong*, 193; Li, "The Development of the Chinese Police," 31. For an opposite view, see Andrew, *Diary of an Ex-Hong Kong Cop*, 59. By the late 1920s British recruits were also being enlisted in the United Kingdom through London agents of the SMC, who sent them on to Shanghai to pass through the police training depot. Bruce, "Shanghai: The International Settlement," 133.

65. Lethbridge, *Hong Kong*, 193; Andrew, *Diary of an Ex-Hong Kong Cop*, 2–20.

66. The chief detective inspector of the Criminal Investigation Department was directly responsible to the captain superintendent. No parallel for this existed in other police administrations because the police force was also at the disposal of any consular official who wished to exercise his power in a legitimate manner. Also, the CID was the "principal medium of communication between the municipal and French police," overseeing all detectives, native and foreign, on the SMP. *North China Herald and South China and China Gazette*, 31 Dec. 1909, 780. For the organization and work of the Special Branch, see the voluminous files in SMP, D-8. The covering note on the file is dated 11 Apr. 1942 and the organizational sheets cover the period from 1929 to 1941.

67. See the public letter entitled "The Persecution of Indian Nationalists in China (An Appeal to Fair-Minded People)," signed by the Raj Paltao Party, dated Nanjing, 3 June 1929, in *CWR*, 8 June 1929, 16. Information from India concerning suspected Communists or Indian nationalists came through C. M. H. Halland, the military intelligence officer in the Shanghai British Consulate General. Halland often shared his reports with American military intelligence. SMP, D-2313, 11 Sept. 1931.

68. *MG*, vol. 20, 216.

69. SMP, D-8/8, 11 Feb. 1936.

70. Section Four was set up "primarily for the collection of information of subversive political activity among British Indians." Ibid., 19 Dec. 1936.

71. SMP, D-8, 18 June 1929.

72. SMP, D-8/8, 11 Feb. 1936. Section Four kept copious records. By 1936, its files contained detailed biographies of 250 activists and 280 sympathizers; and briefer biographies of 3,500 other persons.

73. *CWR*, 17 Nov. 1928, 419, and 24 Nov. 1928, 460. For the organization of the Sikh branch and the working conditions of its constables, sergeants, and jemadars, see *North China Herald and South China and China Gazette*, 31 Dec. 1909, 801.

74. "Corsicans, there as everywhere, hold the principal posts. They are hard men, and mocking; with a distrust of journalists and contempt for the consular corps." Fontenoy, *The Secret Shanghai*, 120. For a scathing bestiary of the French Concession Police, see Ch'ien, *Fortress Besieged*, 132. The French police (Garde municipale [Fr.], Zhi'an bu [Ch.]), which answered directly to the consul general, was almost exclusively composed of French and Vietnamese who had served in the French army. *SSN* (1935), L-30; Martin, "'The Pact with the Devil,'" 6–7; *SYZ*, 96. The head of the political section, Lieutenant Roland Sarly, for instance, was a Parisian whose mother was Moroccan and who had seen action in Africa during World War I. Xue Gengshen, "Wo yu jiu Shanghai Fa zujie," 150–52.

75. Martin, "'The Pact with the Devil,'" 6.

76. Faligot and Kauffer, *Kang Sheng*, 96.

77. See, for example, the Special Branch's September 11, 1931 report to Major W. C. Powers, Headquarters, U.S. Marine Corps, in SMP, D-2313, 11 Sept. 1931. Intelligence officers in the British Consulate in Shanghai would request the SMP to put under surveillance suspected Communists whose names had been gotten from police raids on Communist organizations in Malaya. This was how the writer Zheng Zhenduo got on the SMP's suspects list. SMP, D-3564, 26 Apr. 1932. The French police shared their intelligence reports—including regular reports on the labor movement—with the SMP also. See, for example, SMP, D-8, 29 Jan. 1929.

78. The title "Intelligence Officer" was in use through the end of 1927, when the term was ostensibly dropped. SMP, CS-183, 7 Mar. 1931. For an application from a Communist Party member wanting to serve as a "secret detective" for $200 per month in 1932, see the correspondence in SMP, D-3381, 16 Mar. 1932.

79. SMP, CS-183, 7 Mar. 1931.

80. Ibid.

81. For the hazards of the calling, as well as an extremely revealing account of the network of connections, see the file on the Mao Guobao case in SMP, D-3427.

82. *CWR*, 29 Dec. 1928, 188–89.

83. *CWR,* 13 Oct. 1928, 205.

84. *CWR,* 5 Nov. 1929, 48.

85. *MG,* vol. 20 (1927), 216. There had been a major strike by Sikh policemen in 1907 when they learned that they were being paid 20 to 30 percent of what they could earn in the United States at that same time working as guards. *SYZ,* 100–101.

86. The SMP's intelligence section also kept tabs on an "Oriental Communists School" which had twenty pupils and operated under the cover of the "Women's Self-Protection School" (*Ziquan funü zhiye xuexiao*); it had been run by a Henanese named "Li Sian" since September 17, 1928, and supposedly received a subsidy of $458 per month from Soviet Russia to train Asian agents. Regular classes were only held four hours a week. SMP, D-123, 28 Mar. 1929.

87. Members of the Indian Youth League at 241 Paoshing Road, Zhabei, were under Chinese police protection. However, the SMP and SIS would send Chinese "rowdies" to pick fights with the young Indians, and then when they were arrested for disorderly and drunken conduct or carrying unlicensed weapons, get them extradited to the International Settlement where they were tried for sedition before the British Supreme Court. *CWR,* 10 Jan. 1931, 212.

88. *SSG,* vol. 4, *huiyi,* 28.

89. There was great concern about preservation of secrecy in the Shanghai police force in 1930 as the result of details about a number of Communist cases in the third *suo* of the fifth precinct becoming known to the public. Ibid., 30.

90. For the attack on the Jiangsu left wing, see the remarks in Fewsmith, "Response to Eastman," 19–27; and Geisert, "Probing KMT Rule," 28–39.

91. Xu Enzeng, "Wo he Gongdang douzheng de huiyi," 25b.

92. Poretsky, *Our Own People,* 53; Krivitsky, *In Stalin's Secret Service,* 51–53; Deakin and Storry, *The Case of Richard Sorge,* 63; Willoughby, *Shanghai Conspiracy,* 27–28; Johnson, *An Instance of Treason,* passim.

93. It was also decided, by Soviet intelligence if not the Comintern, that there would be a complete separation between Soviet intelligence agents and local Communist Party groups—especially after the Chinese expelled Borodin and Galen. This split was carried out partly at Richard Sorge's recommendation to the Fourth Bureau when he returned to Moscow in 1929 and just before he was sent to Shanghai to direct a China intelligence net. Willoughby, *Shanghai Conspiracy,* 29–30.

94. In Shanghai, for instance, Soviet intelligence used the Centrosojus Russian Tea Company as a front for espionage. Office of Strategic Services, U.S. Army, XL24029, 16 Oct. 1945.

95. The international clandestine apparatus of the Comintern, which was the group that controlled Richard Sorge when he came to Shanghai on January 10, 1930, was under the chief of intelligence of the Red Army, General Jan Karlovich Berzin. Faligot and Kauffer, *Kang Sheng,* 77.

96. Wright with Greengrass, *Spycatcher,* 287–88. See also Pincher, *Too Secret Too Long;* and MacKinnon and MacKinnon, *Agnes Smedley,* 367.

97. This was the amount received—about 125,000 francs (Gold $5,000) per month—during the year of July 1930–June 1931. In that same period the Shanghai branch of the Pan-Pacific Trade Union also spent nearly 125,000 francs per month. Together, therefore, the Comintern and Profintern were spending 17 mil-

lion francs (Gold $680,000) each year in the Far East. Concession Française de Changhai, doc. no. 237/S, 134–35.

98. It is clear that the French were able to trace these couriers from Shanghai to Dairen thanks to reports they were receiving from Japanese Intelligence sources. Ibid., 138–39, 142–44.

99. This was parallel to the Political Department under Gerhart Eisler, and it was responsible for Communist activities in Asia outside of the Red-occupied zones of China. The Pan-Pacific Trade Union Secretariat was the Far Eastern branch of the Profintern, the Comintern-controlled organization of International Red Trades Unions, which was originally headquartered in Vladivostok. Deakin and Storry, *The Case of Richard Sorge*, 86–87.

100. Poretsky, *Our Own People*, 62–63. See also Isaacs, ed., *Five Years of Kuomintang Reaction*, 21. Isaacs insisted that Ruegg's "honorable and rightful title" was Secretary of the Pan-Pacific Trade Union Secretariat. Isaacs, "I Break with the Chinese Stalinists," 76–78.

101. His noms de guerre included "Henry" (which was featured on a list of paid agents of the Far Eastern Bureau), "Coty" (which was used on the internal envelopes of the Comintern letters sent from Berlin), and "Wales" (which he used to sign his own letters to Berlin). Other aliases included W. Almas and Dr. H. C. Smith. The name "Hillyer Noulens" was attached to an authentic passport (# 102573, issued in Ottawa on June 10, 1931) loaned to him by a Canadian Communist of that name. Concession Française de Changhai, doc. no. 237/S, 141.

102. Ibid., 136–37. See also Finch, *Shanghai and Beyond*, 317. These funds mainly came from the Western European Bureau of the Comintern in Berlin. In 1931 the Far Eastern Bureau was spending between £120,000–150,000 a year, of which £95,000 was in China. Deakin and Storry, *The Case of Richard Sorge*, 87.

103. Concession Française de Changhai, doc. no. 237/S, 127.

104. Ducroux was born in 1904 at Belleville-sur-Saone, the son of Joseph and Claudine Sautier. A militant Communist since 1923, he came to China in 1926 as secretary to James H. Dolsen, a radical American journalist and author of *The Awakening of China*. (Dolsen was probably a Comintern agent named "Leon," who directed the Pan-Pacific Trade Union Secretariat from its opening in Shanghai until February 1931. Dolsen or "Leon" also helped lead the Philippine Communist Party's Congress in March 1931.) Concession Française de Changhai, doc. no. 237/S, 144–46.

105. Ibid., 128. Deakin and Storry write of one scrap of paper with the notation: "Hilanoul, Box 208." Deakin and Storry, *The Case of Richard Sorge*, 85.

106. Concession Française de Changhai, doc. no. 237/S, 128. There is a large collection of SMP documents on the Noulens case which were not microfilmed. These can be found in Box D, File 2510, in the Military Reference Division of the National Archives.

107. Standard book codes were used, with certain sentences serving as keys. The two books were discovered by cryptographers to be the *Holy Bible* and Sun Yat-sen's *Three Principles of the People*. Finch, *Shanghai and Beyond*, 318.

108. Concession Française de Changhai, doc. no. 237/S, 128, 137–42.

109. Madame Noulens had left Brussels on May 7, 1930, for Shanghai via Germany and the USSR. Her other known aliases at this point were Gertrude

Ruegg, M. Motte, and Frau Coty. Concession Française de Changhai, doc. no. 237/ S, 140–42.

110. Poretsky, *Our Own People*, 63; Pincher, *Too Secret Too Long*, 32.

111. Concession Française de Changhai, doc. no. 237/S, 128–29.

112. Ibid., 129–30.

113. Ibid., 130–31.

114. Poretsky, *Our Own People*, 64.

115. Concession Française de Changhai, doc. no. 237/S, 130–32; MacKinnon and MacKinnon, *Agnes Smedley*, 148–49.

116. But see Braun's version: "In 1930 the Comintern agent Noulens-Ruegg had been arrested and his office, full of important documents, sacked. Only by bribing the corrupt Chinese judge was it possible to avert his death sentence and execution." Braun, *A Comintern Agent in China*, 2.

117. Concession Française de Changhai, doc. no. 237/S, 132–33; Finch, *Shanghai and Beyond*, 317–19; Shen Zui, *Juntong neimu*, 68.

118. Concession Française de Changhai, doc. no. 237/S, 147.

119. Nguyen Ai Quoc was actually released in March 1933. Ibid., 147.

120. Ibid.

121. Boorman et al., eds., *Biographical Dictionary of Republican China*, vol. 2, 307; Thornton, *China, the Struggle for Power*, 50. Some people believe Gu defected to the Nationalists because his rival Kang Sheng was named head of the CCP Organization Department in January 1931. At that time Gu was moved out of the Central Committee and into the Political Bureau. Faligot and Kauffer, *Kang Sheng*, 87.

122. "Xiaomie Gongfei hongdui an chi jingyan jianshu," BIA 276/7435/59400, 4. Note, however, that Li Tianmin claims Gu Shunzhang was there to set up an intelligence net along the Yangzi River and to arrange for the transportation of loot from the interior provinces. According to one of Li's anonymous oral sources, Gu may also have been arranging for Secretary-General Xiang Zhongfa's travel to Jiangxi, where Mao Zedong hoped to welcome him so as to bring the head of the Politburo to Ruijin. Li Tianmin, *Zhou Enlai pingzhuan*, 104. Gu was one of the chief liaison officers between the rural Soviets and the urban cells of the CCP. Zhongguo Guomindang zhongyang zuzhi bu diaocha ke, eds., *Zhongguo gongchandang zhi toushi*, 316.

123. Zhongyang diaochu tongjiju. BIA, 276/7435a/19930, 3–5. Xu Enzeng later claimed that when Li Ming left his hotel he was spotted by one of Xu's agents who had formerly been a Communist serving under Gu Zhunzhang. Xu Enzeng, "Wo he Gongdang douzheng de huiyi," 19b. According to yet another version, seven CCP members were arrested in Wuhan in February 1931. One of them, You Chongxin, defected. He hoped to gain credit with his new employers by spotting other Communists, and so took to hanging out on the streets looking for familiar faces. He spotted Gu Shunzhang at an athletic field. Li Tianmin, *Zhou Enlai pingzhuan*, 104. Finally, it was said that a former Communist named Wang Zhuqiao recognized Gu when he was getting off of the Wuchang-Hankou ferry. Mu Xin, *Chen Geng tongzhi zai Shanghai*, 81.

124. Mu Xin, *Chen Geng tongzhi zai Shanghai*, 82–83.

125. The rule-of-thumb then simply was that whenever CCP members sur-

rendered, they had to demonstrate their sincerity by betraying a comrade, which resulted in a "blood debt" (*xuezhai*) that could never be wiped out. Xu noted that it was a measure of the success of the Nationalists' policy of encouraging defection that there were so many investigations on the mainland of China after 1951 of CCP members suspected of having incurred "blood debts" in the past. Xu Enzeng, "Wo he Gongdang douzheng de huiyi," 18a.

126. Ibid., 20a. Although our account relies heavily on Xu Enzeng's self-serving record of the Gu Shunzhang Affair, other Central Bureau of Information and Statistics materials corroborate the details. Xu's own self-vaunting has been taken with a grain of salt.

127. For Gu's age, see Wang Jianmin, *Zhongguo Gongchandang shi*, vol. 2, 149.

128. Xu Enzeng, "Wo he Gongdang douzheng de huiyi," 19b–20a.

129. Ibid., 20b; Zhongyang diaochu tongjiju comp., "Zhonggong tewubu buzhang Gu Shunzhang zhi zishou ji qi yu zhonggong zhi daji," BIA 6; "Xiaomie Gongfei Hongdui an chi jingyan jianshu," 4.

130. Qian made his way to Shanghai, from where he managed to contact Hu Di in Tianjin. Later Qian went to the Jiangxi Soviet headquarters in Ruijin. He died on the Long March in Guizhou in March 1935. Mu Xin, *Chen Geng tongzhi zai Shanghai*, 90.

131. One agent exchanged clothes with Gu Shunzhang, so that Gu's wife would trust him when he asked her to go with him back to Nanjing.

132. According to Li Tianmin, there was only one address, which was on Weihaiwei Road. Li Tianmin, *Zhou Enlai pingzhuan*, 105. But the BIA documents mention two places from which relatives were abducted by Zhou Enlai's agents: Weihaiwei Road and South Chengdu Road. Zhongyang zuzhi bu, tewuzu, diaocha ke, ed., "Zhou Enlai cansha Gu Shunzhang jiashu," BIA doc. D112(276/7435B/19933), 10, 1.

133. Xu Enzeng, "Wo he Gongdang douzheng de huiyi," 20b.

134. "The Fascist or 'Blue Shirt' Party in China." Special Branch Secret Memorandum, Nov. 23, 1934, in SMP, D-4685, 1–2.

135. Qian Jun, "Hongdui," 94.

136. Xu Enzeng, "Wo he Gongdang douzheng de huiyi," 21b.

137. Concession Française de Changhai, doc. no. 237/S, 30–31.

138. Xu Enzeng, "Wo he Gongdang douzheng de huiyi," 21b.

139. Zhongyang zuzhi bu, tewuzu, diaocha ke, ed., "Zhou Enlai cansha Gu Shunzhang jiashu," 10; "Xiaomie gongfei hongdui an chi jingyan jianshu," 1.

140. Li Tianmin, *Zhou Enlai pingzhuan*, 104.

141. Pan Hannian had to flee to the Jiangxi Soviet area in the fall of 1931. In Jiangxi he became head of the Central Committee's Propaganda Department and was publicly assigned to work in the Baoweiju (Security Bureaus) of both the Red Army and the civilian government. Li Zhaochun, "Shenfen fuza de Pan Hannian," 115.

142. Zhongyang zuzhi bu, tewuzu, diaocha ke, ed., "Zhou Enlai cansha Gu Shunzhang jiashu," 336–37. Note, however, that in another Nationalist secret service source, the chair of the committee is identified as Guang Hui'an, who was also said to be chief of Operations (Xingdong). "Xiaomie gongfei hongdui an chi jingyan jianshu," 2–3.

143. Shen Zui, *Juntong neimu*, 63–64. Faligot and Kauffer associate the term with the leadership of Kang Sheng, who took over this task from Guang Hui'an after a secret meeting on the Shanghai docks on January 7, 1933. Faligot and Kauffer, *Kang Sheng*, 105.

144. Concession Française de Changhai, doc. no. 237/S, 55–56.

145. According to former CCP leaders like Gong Chu: "The security men constituted an elite within the elite, their task being to watch the actions of higher officers. . . . They were so special and secretive that even high officers and army commanders knew nothing about their identities and activities." Chang, "The Rise of Wang Tung-hsing," 124.

146. Communists already in GMD hands, like Yun Daying (a major party theoretician and secretary of the district party committee in Shanghai) who had managed to conceal his identity and was serving a five-year jail sentence in Nanjing as an ordinary party member, were "blown" by Gu's defection and subsequently executed. Xu Feng and Zhang Yusheng, eds., *Minguo heiwang, neimu, miwen*, 39–42.

147. Zhongyang diaochu tongjiju, comp., "Zhonggong tewubu buzhang Gu Shunzhang zhi zishou," 20. As a result of the execution of the editors of *Red Flag*, for example, there were virtually no "red" publications appearing at all in Jiangsu by June 1931. Concession Française de Changhai, doc. no. 237/S, 30.

148. Isaacs, ed., *Five Years of Kuomintang Reaction*, 3.

149. Concession Française de Changhai, doc. no. 237/S, 31. As a countermeasure to demonstrations, the Nationalist authorities began to take prisoners out on "red days" and shoot them in front of curious crowds. In Hankou over a thousand men and women were executed from August 1930 to February 1931 "to teach the people a lesson." A year later, on May Day of 1932, Chiang Kai-shek had twenty-five Communists publicly shot to death in Nanjing as a warning to others not to demonstrate or protest. Isaacs, ed., *Five Years of Kuomintang Reaction*, 19.

150. Xiang (1888–1931) was originally a coolie from Hubei where he became active in union work before going to the Soviet Union. He was among the "Twenty-Eight Returned Bolsheviks." During the Sixth National Congress in Moscow in the summer of 1928 he was elected secretary-general to succeed Qu Qiubai. Boorman et al., eds., *Biographical Dictionary of Republican China*, vol. 2, 87–88.

151. Zhongyang zuzhi bu, tewuzu, diaocha ke, ed., "Zhou Enlai cansha Gu Shunzhang jiashu," 355. The term "Chinese Stalin" is from Concession Française de Changhai, doc. no. 237/S, 29.

152. Concession Française de Changhai, doc. no. 237/S, 29.

153. Ibid., 30.

154. Ibid., 29–30. After the discovery in the French Concession of the principal safe houses, clandestine printing plants, and storage places for "agitational literature," the Agitprop section of the Jiangsu CCP ceased further activity.

155. Ibid., 31–32.

156. The language is from Barton Ingraham, who in turn acknowledges his debt to Neil Smelser. Ingraham, *Political Crime in Europe*, 321.

157. Li Tianmin, *Zhou Enlai pingzhuan*. Xu, "The Tragedy within China's Communist Palace," 14.

158. See, for example, the SMP Special Branch and PSB raid on the morning

of May 1 of A93 Annam Road in an attempt to arrest Wang Yipo, who was suspected of being the "chairman of the Hunan Soviet Communists" on the basis of intelligence from Henan. The occupant, Li Shaoji, who denied being a Communist, was handed over to the Chinese with no objection from the SMC procurator. Case No. 5/27095 in SMP, D-2316, 8 May 1931.

159. Xu, "The Tragedy within China's Communist Palace," 13.

160. Faligot and Kauffer, *Kang Sheng*, 99–100.

161. Yeh, "Progressive Journalism."

162. These assassination cases are enumerated in "Xiaomie Gongfei Hongdui an chi jingyan jianshu."

163. Ibid., 6. The Shanghai office, which was also the chief's residence, was at No. 39, Street Three, Siwenli Village, Xinzha Road.

164. Xu Enzeng, "Wo he Gongdang douzheng de huiyi," 25b.

165. The Special Services Bureau was located at No. 219, Yipinxiang, Thibet Road. Zhongyang zuzhi bu, tewuzu, diaocha ke, ed., "Zhou Enlai cansha Gu Shunzhang jiashu," 10.

166. Xu Enzeng, "Wo he Gongdang douzheng de huiyi," 22; Zhongyang zuzhi bu, tewuzu, diaocha ke, ed., "Zhou Enlai cansha Gu Shunzhang jiashu," 2; Concession Française de Changhai, doc. no. 237/S, 53–54.

167. Zhongyang zuzhi bu, tewuzu, diaocha ke, ed., "Zhou Enlai cansha Gu Shunzhang jiashu," 2. Wang was said by foreigners to resemble a "consumptive Chinese tailor." Finch, *Shanghai and Beyond*, 321–23.

168. Xu Enzeng, "Wo he Gongdang douzheng de huiyi," 22b.

169. Ibid., 22b–23a; Zhongyang zuzhi bu, tewuzu, diaocha ke, ed., "Zhou Enlai cansha Gu Shunzhang jiashu," 3–4.

170. Zhongyang zuzhi bu, tewuzu, diaocha ke, ed., "Zhou Enlai cansha Gu Shunzhang jiashu," 4. See also Li Tianmin, *Zhou Enlai pingzhuan*, 106–7.

171. Xu Enzeng, "Wo he Gongdang douzheng de huiyi," 23a.

172. Zhongyang zuzhi bu, tewuzu, diaocha ke, ed., "Zhou Enlai cansha Gu Shunzhang jiashu," 5.

173. Xu Enzeng, "Wo he Gongdang douzheng de huiyi," 23a–23b.

174. Zhongyang zuzhi bu, tewuzu, diaocha ke, ed., "Zhou Enlai cansha Gu Shunzhang jiashu," 7.

175. The Nationalist agents discovered in this and other Communist burials of executed victims in Shanghai a consistent pattern. The executioners would typically dig a hole fifteen or twenty feet deep, virtually down to the water table. Corpses would be buried in a chamber in the bottom, then covered with four to five feet of earth plus a layer of cement, and that in turn covered by six to seven feet of earth. Most workers excavating these graves stopped after they broke through the concrete and discovered yet more earth. Because of the watery soil, the corpses almost always could not be identified. Xu Enzeng, "Wo he Gongdang douzheng de huiyi," 25a; Zhongyang zuzhi bu, tewuzu, diaocha ke, ed., "Zhou Enlai cansha Gu Shunzhang jiashu," 10.

176. Xu Enzeng, "Wo he Gongdang douzheng de huiyi," 24a. See also Zhongyang zuzhi bu, tewuzu, diaocha ke, ed., "Zhou Enlai cansha Gu Shunzhang jiashu," 8–9.

177. Li Tianmin, *Zhou Enlai pingzhuan*, 107.

178. Xu Enzeng, "Wo he Gongdang douzheng de huiyi," 24b.

179. Zhongyang zuzhi bu, tewuzu, diaocha ke, ed., "Zhou Enlai cansha Gu Shunzhang jiashu," 10.

180. Xu Enzeng, "Wo he Gongdang douzheng de huiyi," 25b. The affair also increased the determination of turncoats to stick with the Guomindang once they had defected. See also Di Weimin, "Shanghai zujie liang jianguan yuci neimu," part two, 12 Jan. 1985, 30.

181. Zhongyang zuzhi bu, tewuzu, diaocha ke, ed., "Zhou Enlai cansha Gu Shunzhang jiashu," 10.

182. Xu Enzeng, "Wo he Gongdang douzheng de huiyi," 24b–25a. One of the reasons for Detective Superintendent Tan Shaoliang's long survival—even after the discovery by the Guomindang secret service that he was a Japanese spy—was because he served as the major liaison in the political section of the SMP to implement this November 1931 agreement between the Nationalists' SSB and the International Settlement police. Di Weimin, "Shanghai zujie liang jianguan yuci neimu," part two, January 12, 1985, 30.

183. Gould, "The Unapproachable Police," 178.

184. *CWR*, 13 Aug. 1927, 288, and 28 Mar. 1936, 111.

185. Faligot and Kauffer, *Kang Sheng*, 57, 74, 77. Hergé's cartoon-story was first published in Brussels in 1934. The story was set in 1931. Hergé, *The Adventures of Tintin*, frontispiece. For Givens (called "Dawson" in the comic strip), see especially 36.

186. *CWR*, 28 Mar. 1936, 111.

187. Isaacs, ed., *Five Years of Kuomintang Reaction*, 112. This was not the first such award. In 1934, Major F. W. Gerrard, commissioner of police; Major K. M. Bourne, deputy commissioner; T. Robertson, superintendent; and G. W. Gilbert, assistant commissioner of police were decorated by the Chinese government in appreciation for their services in the suppression of Communists in Shanghai. *CWR*, 22 Sept. 1934, 140.

188. *SSG*, vol. 4, *huiyi*, 30.

189. Shen Zui, *Juntong neimu*, 117.

CHAPTER 10. MAKING CHOICES

1. By the end of 1930 the total size of the PSB was 5,033 men and women, of which 4,286 were actual police (*jingshi*). *SSG*, vol. 4, table after 56. There is a complete register of the names, salaries, arms, and uniforms of the Fourth Detachment of the PSB central Police Brigade (Dadui) for 1929 in SAM, No. Diwei 1 2660 DEPT 895.24, file 14.

2. "In 1928 Beijing became Beiping and was given the status of special municipality along with a mayor and a reorganized municipal government, but the municipal government was really a marginally expanded version of the previous pattern of militarists' agent (now mayor instead of or as well as garrison commander) in temporary control of the police (now *gonganju*) and seven understaffed and weakly financed bureaus." Strand, "Feuds, Fights, and Factions," 413.

3. At its largest the Beiping police numbered twelve thousand. In 1930, after reductions, it still consisted of seven thousand officers and men.

4. *SSG*, vol. 3, 149–50. Police capacity is probably related to the amount of territory covered, rather than population. Bayley, *Patterns of Policing*.

5. The population of Shanghai at this time was about 3.5 million, of which 1.7 million were under Chinese jurisdiction. For the financial burden, which amounted to about 30 percent of the municipal budget, see Henriot, "Le gouvernement municipal de Shanghai," 163, 179, and 201.

6. Ibid., 389–90.

7. For the pressure on the PSB in 1927–28 to set up a rational budgeting system, see *STS, jishi,* 39. See also Chang, "On Chinese Municipal Government," 268.

8. Henriot, "Le gouvernement municipal de Shanghai," 180.

9. In July 1927 the Nationalists proposed to collect two months' rent from Chinese living in the concessions for government military expenses. At the same time the Guomindang supported opposition to the proposed 2 percent increase in the International Settlement's municipal rates. British editorialists grimly predicted that within a year the GMD in Shanghai would be "auctioning administrative offices to expectant officials and the trade of the port will be conducted by armed merchantmen lying outside Woosung with smugglers and pirates." *NCH,* 2 July 1927, 6. By July 1930, incidentally, there were more than one hundred pirate vessels manned by two thousand sailors lying off Wusong in the mouth of the Yangzi, preying on unarmed vessels. *CWR,* 12 July 1930, 226.

10. "A Brief History of Rent Reduction Agitation . . . " Enclosure in Dispatch 6275 from Shanghai (Consul General Cunningham) to Legation, 26 Nov. 1929, in 893.102S/205, *RDS,* vol. 69, 1–3.

11. Initially, the Jiangsu provincial authorities agreed to pay police salaries for one year while the municipal government promised to remit local land and real estate taxes to the province. Neither side lived up to the agreement. Henriot, "Le gouvernement municipal de Shanghai," 42–43. After the abolition of the likin tariff in 1931, the provincial government of Jiangsu adopted a business tax (*yingye shui*), but merchant organizations resisted paying it until 1935. Geisert, "Toward a Pluralist Model of KMT Rule," 4–5.

12. Henriot, "Le gouvernement municipal de Shanghai," 180–81.

13. *SSG,* vol. 3, 107.

14. *SSG,* vol. 4, 76.

15. In March 1927 monthly costs were about Ch. $39,000. After the Nationalists reorganized the police and added personnel, monthly costs climbed to Ch. $60,000. Henriot, "Le gouvernement municipal de Shanghai," 390.

16. By January 1929, monthly credits were Ch. $80,000; by May 1929, they had climbed to Ch. $83,000. Ibid., 390.

17. *STS, jishi,* 39. In 1928 the salary of a Chinese police sergeant was $328; of a Chinese teacher, $1,120; of a municipal hospital nurse, $1,680; of a foreign police sergeant, $3,500; of a foreign school teacher, $5,000. *CWR,* 23 Dec. 1928.

18. *SSG,* vol. 3, 121–23, and vol. 4, 75.

19. *SSG,* vol. 4, 74.

20. Take, for example, the gunfight on March 18, 1929, when several bystanders were wounded by stray bullets during a shootout between SMP police and robbers in one of the most crowded sections of the city. "In any other country the policemen responsible would be held for manslaughter." *CWR,* 23 Mar. 1929, 132; and see also 13 Apr. 1935, 225.

21. *CWR,* 23 Mar. 1929, 132.

22. However, before the days of double-action automatics, the chamber was empty. The men were taught to load as they drew. *Oriental Affairs* 5.2, 68. "All the police in Shanghai . . . go about armed and shoot without hesitation as occasion arises." Buchler, "The Police in China," 255.

23. *STS, jishi*, 55; Bruce, "Shanghai: The International Settlement," 133.

24. Bourne, "The Shanghai Municipal Police," 31.

25. "Tanjing zhi heimu yu," in Qian Shengke, ed., *Shanghai heimu huibian*, vol. 1, 1. There are lists of sixty-six PSB policemen killed in the line of duty in *STS*, front matter; *SSG*, vol. 3, tables after 60, vol. 4, tables after 66, and vol. 5, tables after 220. During roughly that same period, the SMP's Chinese uniform branch lost eight men to robbers; seventeen others were also wounded. Bourne, "The Shanghai Municipal Police," 32. See also Pal, *Shanghai Saga*, 13; Carney, *Foreign Devils Had Light Eyes*, 16.

26. *SSG*, vol. 4, 52, table after 66.

27. *SSG*, vol. 3, 153–54.

28. SMP, D-57.

29. SMP, D-57, 20 Feb. 1929.

30. The three major local leaders were Pan Gongzhan, Wu Kaixian, and Wang Yansong, graduates respectively of St. John's, Shanghai Law School (Shanghai fasheng daxue), and Shanghai College of Commerce. Henriot, "Le gouvernement municipal de Shanghai," 61–62; Henriot, *Shanghai 1927–1937*, 56. Officers of the SMP were still extremely hostile to the local party branch at this time. When Colonel Yuan Liang tried to get the SMP to issue Wu Kaixian a pistol license for the International Settlement, he was rudely rebuffed on the grounds that Wu was "no better than other members of the Koumingtang [sic], whose policy is always aggressive and hostile to the Settlement authorities." SMP, D-1194, 25 Apr. 1930.

31. SMP, D-57, 23 Feb. 1929.

32. SMP, D-702, 27 Nov. 1929. In his letter to the SMP, dated November 26, Judge Hsu cited a missive from the GMD Central Executive Committee attacking the "Reactionary Party" of the Reorganizationists for usurping the name of the Guomindang, and said that military and political organs throughout the country were ordered strictly and secretly to prohibit the "Reactionary Party's" printed propaganda and to punish their rumormongers.

33. SMP, D-623, 2 Nov. 1929.

34. Ibid.

35. SMP, D-702, 28 Nov. 1929.

36. See Wasserstrom, *Student Protests in Twentieth-Century China*, passim.

37. SMP, D-825, 31 Dec. 1929.

38. Revolutionaries in turn tried to disguise their mailings in spurious printed envelopes or addressed envelopes in writing of various hands to evade discovery by postal censors expert at scanning the contents of envelopes. SMP, D-1791/6, 4 May 1934.

39. Isaacs, ed., *Five Years of Kuomintang Reaction*, 73–75.

40. CID office notes dated 27 Apr. 1930, signed by Robertson. SMP, D-1216, 30 Apr. 1930; Isaacs, ed., *Five Years of Kuomintang Reaction*, 10–11. Brigadier General E. B. MacNaughten, chairman of the council; Mr. Stirling Fessenden, director general of the council; and Colonel H. B. Orpen Palmer, commander of the Shanghai Volunteer Corps also attended the conference.

41. At 1066 Wetmore Road, the police seized 1,500 Communist pamphlets, 300 copies of "a communistic mosquito newspaper" (*Shanghai bao*), and a letter from the tramway employees club. At 228 Avenue Road "a large quantity of communistic literature" and a small printing press were seized, and one man was arrested; and at 102 Burkill Road one man was arrested, and a large basket containing "communistic pamphlets" in Chinese and English was confiscated. SMP, D-1210, 29 Apr. 1930.

42. Ibid.

43. The president was Wu Fufu, and the vice president was Lu Yunsheng. The company manager was a Mr. Taylor. Ibid., 19 Aug. 1930.

44. Of the twelve, nine were given four months' imprisonment and three were sentenced to two years in jail. The extradition hearing was held on May 30, 1930. Mr. Wang was charged by the Chinese with political offenses, returned to the Settlement authorities for arraignment on November 7, 1930, and, upon a second application, was handed over to representatives of the Wusong and Shanghai military authorities a second time. His subsequent fate is unknown. Ibid., 19 Aug. 1931.

45. The same was true in the other direction, as well. Even before the Guomindang took power, the Chinese authorities (in this case, the Sun Chuanfang government) had not always honored extradition requests by the SMP, as in the case of Sun Lianghui, the leading "agitator" in the February 1925 strike at the Nagai Wata Kaisha cotton mill. SMP, D-6023, 31 Mar. 1925.

46. CWR, 17 Sept. 1927, 78, and 29 Oct. 1927, 78.

47. Isaacs, ed., *Five Years of Kuomintang Reaction*, 10.

48. Chinese prosecutors could not arrest Chinese living in the Settlement. They had to ask the SMP to make the arrest. However, the SMC would normally not extradite a Chinese subject unless a preliminary hearing were held at which the SMC was represented. Hauser, *Shanghai: City for Sale*, 247.

49. The two primary suspects were Wang Zhongling and Yang Yinxian. SMP, D-7873, 17 June 1930.

50. SSG, vol. 3, 8–51, 119; Hunter, "The Chinese League of Left-Wing Writers," 111.

51. Isaacs, ed., *Five Years of Kuomintang Reaction*, 75–76.

52. In 1929 the PSB suppressed 1,876 publications (484 at the order of the central government; 1,392 at their own instigation). Of the latter, 564 were classified as "reactionary" (*fandong*), 793 as Communist, 24 as "reorganizationist" (*gaizupai*), 9 as "nationalistic" (*guojia zhuyi*), and 2 as anarchistic. SSG, vol. 3, table after 76.

53. SSG, vol. 4, 120. During the period July 1930–June 1931 the Shanghai Chinese police prohibited 442 "reactionary," 2,320 Communist, 3 anarchist, 23 "reorganizationist," and 8 "nationalistic" publications. Ibid., table after 82.

54. Ibid., 77–78.

55. *Geming gongren* (*Revolutionary Worker*), *Chise haiyuan* (*Red Seaman*, published by the propaganda committee of the National Seamen's Federation), *Pinglun zhoubao* (*Pinglun Weekly*, a supplement to the *Haiguang* circulated through schools and bookstores), *Zhongguo Suwei'ai huabao* (*China and Soviet Pictorial*), *Hong qi* (*Red Flag*), *Haiguang* (*Sea Light*), *Dongfang* (*Orient*), and *Da feng* (*Big Wind*). SMP, D-1639, 8 Oct. 1930.

56. SMP, D-1639, 8 Dec. 1930, 15 Dec. 1930.

57. *SB*, 9 Dec. 1930, 11.

58. SMP, D-7873, 14 Apr. 1927 and afterward. See also Isaacs, ed., *Five Years of Kuomintang Reaction*, 76.

59. The police file on these bookstore raids is voluminous, consisting of over 124 pages of materials detailing the arrests of bookstore owners and investigations of their backgrounds. SMP, D-1939.

60. SMP, D-2033, 2 Mar. 1931.

61. The Central Propaganda Bureau report read in part: "Therefore, apart from writing to the State Council for issuance of necessary instructions to the military and police authorities in Shanghai and to the Shanghai Special District Court to seal up the said bookstore, and apart from instructing various Guomindang headquarters, propaganda department[s], and the postal matters censors to suppress and to seize such reactionary literatures, we have to instruct that the military and police authorities at Shanghai and the Shanghai Special District Court be approached with a view to having the said bookstore sealed." SMP, D-2048, 18 Feb. 1931.

62. SMP, D-2048, 18 Feb. 1931.

63. SMP, D-1939, 62–67, 71.

64. They also coincided with increasingly repressive policies against radical Taiwanese activists throughout the Japanese Empire as well. Fix, "Alternative Activism," 6.

65. SMP, D-516, 15 Jan. 1931.

66. Rumor was that the police were tipped off by a rival faction within the Chinese Communist Party, backed by the "returned Bolsheviks." I have been unable to verify this rumor in the Shanghai Municipal Police files released to date by the U.S. Central Intelligence Agency.

67. Eighteen years later the victorious Communists exhumed the martyrs' bodies. Autopsies of the remains showed that some had been buried alive and that one of the executed women was pregnant. Their remains were transferred to the Shanghai Martyrs Memorial Cemetery. Hunter, "The Chinese League of Left-Wing Writers," 145–47; Spence, *The Gate of Heavenly Peace*, 192–94.

68. "Tracking Down Reds in Shanghai," in SMP, D-1939. The court session was held on February 3.

69. Report from Detective Sergeant Moore, 27 Apr. 1932. Special Branch members, accompanied by a PSB officer, had tried to arrest two suspected Communists at the Jiuhua silk shop. The two shop assistants were not on the premises and the Shanghai Special District Court warrant was returned for cancellation. SMP, D-3578, 28 Apr. 1932.

70. Torture was certainly also practiced by the French Concession Police, whose interrogators deliberately dislocated and broke their victims' jaws, sliced off fingers, and used electric voltage generators to try to extort confessions—much to the amusement of White Russian detectives who lounged about to "see the fun." Isaacs, ed., *Five Years of Kuomintang Reaction*, 15–16.

71. In December 1932, twenty-seven foreigners formally charged that prisoners in the Amoy Road jail of the International Settlement were beaten by officers and petty officers with wooden sticks and tortured with seven different methods. *CWR*, 24 Dec. 1932, 151–52, and 19 Sept. 1929, 257–58.

72. The secretariat of the Guomindang headquarters in Nanjing urged the Chinese Ministry of Foreign Affairs to make representations to the foreign consular body in Shanghai protesting the routine use of torture by the Settlement police. *CWR*, 7 May 1930, 180.

73. Isaacs, ed., *Five Years of Kuomintang Reaction*, 38. I have altered the translation slightly, changing "organ" to "command." Conditions in the regular Jiangsu Second Prison were comparatively comfortable. Xu Huifang and Liu Qingyu, "Shanghai nüxing fan de shehui fenxi," 72, 80–81. On October 15, 1930, PSB Chief Yuan Liang ordered each of the police stations under his command to clean up their holding cells and jails for reasons of public health. *SB*, 16 Oct. 1930, 16.

74. Enclosure in SMP, D-2302, 29 Apr. 1931.

75. Ibid.

76. Letter translated in ibid., D-2303, 1 May 1931.

77. Ibid.

78. Ibid., D-7333, 6 June 1936.

79. *Shanghai Times*, 31 May 1931, cited in Isaacs, ed., *Five Years of Kuomintang Reaction*, 11.

80. During the 1930–31 police year there were 110 instances of forming associations (*jieshe*) and 320 instances of public assemblies (*jihui*). *SSG*, vol. 4, 80.

81. By August 1931, the PSB calendars were routinely listing the sending of agents to the SMP to pick up groups of "communist bandits." *SSG*, vol. 5, 6.

82. Dispatch No. 6950 to the SMP commissioner of police from President Yang Shaoshun, transmitting Letter No. 679 from the Jiangsu provincial government, in SMP, D-2459, 5 June 1931. The dispatch contained the names of twenty-five men, aged twenty-five to forty, all mainly from Jiangyin and identified as "leader of the 14th red army," "captain of the first branch, Jiangyin," "communist, committee of the Jiangyin government," and so forth. Descriptions ("tall, heavy build, student style") were also provided. The French Concession Police also executed search warrants issued by the Jiangsu High Court. SMP, D-3922, 10 Aug. 1932.

83. In July 1931 a total of seventy-two "reactionary" items, including fifty Communist publications, were seized. *SSG*, vol. 5, 52–53.

84. During the 1931–32 police year, the PSB proscribed 969 "reactionary," Communist, and "nationalistic" works. Ibid., table after 220.

85. SMP, D-2665, 31 Aug. 1931, 5 Sept. 1931. In addition to Vladimir Ilyich Lenin's *Materialism and Empirio-Criticism; Critical Comments on a Reactionary Philosophy* (New York, 1927), titles included: René Fulop-Miller, *Lenin and Gandhi* (Zürich, 1927); Karl Kautsy, *Die Agrarfrage: eine Übersicht über die Tendenzen der modernen Landwirtschaft und die Agrarpolitik de Sozialdemokratie* (Stuttgart, 1902); Leonard Woolf, *Imperialism and Civilization* (London, 1928); S. Stepniak [S. M. Kravchinskii], *Underground Russia: Revolutionary Profiles and Sketches from Life* (London, 1883); and Leon Trotsky, *Mein Leben, Versuch einer Autobiographie* (Berlin, 1930).

86. SMP, D-3922, 18 Oct. 1932.

87. *SSG*, vol. 4, 77–78.

88. *SSN*, F-58–59. During the Shanghai police year of 1930–31 there were 8 kidnapping cases recorded with 27 arrested, and 280 robberies with 173 robbers seized. There were also 1,411 cases involving drugs and 474 cases of gambling. *SSG*, vol. 4, 106.

89. *SSG*, vol. 4, 1–22, passim.

90. A standard report form was drawn up by the "duties" (*qinwu*) office. Its entries included route, time of the investigation, which local station was involved, circumstances of the crime, number of prisoners, and so forth. A copy of this form is given in *STS, jishi,* 58–59.

91. During the police year 1930–31 most of the criminals arraigned for preliminary legal action were from Jiangsu (2,950 males and 350 females), Zhejiang (2,115/206), Anhui (609/408), Fujian (530/116), Shandong (460/63), Guangdong (216/51), and Henan (140/29). The rest of China's provinces each accounted for less than 100 males or females each. *SSG*, vol. 5, table after 220.

92. For 1931–32, 38 percent of the criminals were between twenty-one and thirty, 30 percent were between thirty-one and forty, 18 percent were between forty-one and fifty, and 14 percent were either younger than twenty-one or older than fifty. Ibid.

93. Ibid.

94. Ibid. Purse-snatching seems to have increased dramatically. *CC,* 10 Jan. 1929, 22.

95. *CWR,* 29 Dec. 1928, 189.

96. At the same time, the central leadership of the Guomindang ordered the Ministry of the Interior to take over direct administration of the Capital Police Department in Nanjing. Coleman, "Municipal Authority and Popular Participation," 5.

97. Xiong had been appointed acting Garrison Commander in January 1928, but he resigned to participate in the Northern Punitive Expedition. He was reappointed Garrison Commander in 1929 and served until 1931, when he became chairman of the Jiangxi provincial government. *Who's Who in China,* 5th ed., 91.

98. The Federation of Street Unions of the International Settlement, organized in 1920 by small businessmen who could not get membership in the Chamber of Commerce, was the most radical of Shanghai's business groups. Coble, Jr., *The Shanghai Capitalists,* 22.

99. Henriot, "Le gouvernement municipal de Shanghai," 82–83.

100. SMP, D-521, 13 Sept. 1929, 16 Sept. 1929, 23 Sept. 1929.

101. The head of the British CID noted in one marginal comment about the case, "this arrest is said to be the real cause of the Kuomintang attack on Yuan Liang. It would be a good thing for local administration if Yuan wins, but the strength of Kuomintang influence in Nanking is against it." Ibid., 23 Sept. 1929.

102. Chen Xizeng was thirty-three years old in 1929. He came from Wuxing (Jiaxing, Zhejiang) and was Chen Qimei's nephew. After graduating from military academy, he served as a special officer at Whampoa, and then become secretary to the general headquarters of the National Revolutionary Army and chief of the Department of Political Affairs in the rear line general headquarters as well as superintendent of telegraphic administration in Guangdong. (The telegraph administration had an intelligence-gathering function as well.) Later he was head (*zhuren*) of Chiang Kai-shek's aides-de-camp (*shicong shi*). In 1931 he was also a member of the executive committee of the Guomindang. Xu Zhucheng, *Du Yuesheng zhengzhuan,* 49; Henriot, "Le gouvernement municipal de Shanghai," 434, 446; *SSG*, vol. 4, *tongxun,* 1.

103. SMP, D-521, 15 Oct. 1929.

104. Henriot, "Le gouvernement municipal de Shanghai," 83.

105. Zhang Qun was both Chiang Kai-shek's intimate friend and military academy classmate, and Yu Xiaqing's crony. Yu helped Zhang Qun meet his liabilities when he went bankrupt, and then—together with Green Gang boss Huang Jinrong—gave him financial assistance when he left for Guangdong in 1919 to become a counselor to Dr. Sun Yat-sen. CID biography of Chiang Kai-shek in SMP, D-529, 25 Sept. 1929.

106. In general, Zhang Qun was much more willing to deal with representatives of the local bourgeoisie than his predecessors, who had confirmed, with the publication of the Municipal Law of 1928, the demise of the burghers' municipal council. Henriot, "Le gouvernement municipal de Shanghai," 80–81.

107. The local notables were Yu Xiaqing, Wang Xiaolai, Ye Huijin, Wang Binyan, and Yao Mulian. Wang Yansong represented the GMD, and in addition to Yuan Liang, the municipal government was represented by Li Yingshi and Sun Baorong.

108. Henriot, "Le gouvernement municipal de Shanghai," 83–84.

109. Four months later, on May 20, 1930, the national government changed all "special municipalities" (tebie shi) to ordinary shi that were brought directly under the Executive Yuan. SSN, F-6. Henriot, "Le gouvernement municipal de Shanghai," 46, 52–54.

110. CWR, 7 Mar. 1931, 500.

111. Henriot, "Le gouvernement municipal de Shanghai," 84.

112. SSG, vol. 4, 1. Yuan Liang took a month's leave at the end of December 1930 but returned on January 10 to supervise the "winter defense." On February 2, 1931, he asked to resign and in turn on February 3 received orders to proceed to Japan to study police administration. He had been chief of police for nearly twenty months. Yuan actually continued in office until February 6, and Chen took over on February 11. SB, 31 Dec. 1930, 14; 11 Jan. 1931, 18; 4 Feb. 1931, 13; 7 Feb. 1931, 13. Chen brought in a significant number of new personnel after he was formally sworn in on March 2, 1931. There were 206 new members of headquarters personnel nominated between July 1929 and June 1931. Henriot, "Le gouvernement municipal de Shanghai," 175–76.

113. Xu Zhucheng, Du Yuesheng zhengzhuan, 49.

114. "They arrived quietly, on Japanese ships. They brought their graceful wives and their well-kept, well-washed, well-combed children. They settled down in the northern part of the settlement, where they had their Japanese stores, their Japanese restaurants, and their Japanese schools. They hardly ever went south of Soochow Creek, where the foreigners lived and worked, unless it was for business reasons." Carney, Foreign Devils Had Light Eyes, 126–27.

115. Honig, "Women Cotton Mill Workers," 21.

116. In 1931 British commercial investments in Shanghai were estimated to be worth £130 million. Davidson-Houston, Yellow Creek, 192.

117. Hauser, Shanghai: City for Sale, 191–93.

118. Honig, "Women Cotton Mill Workers," 22.

119. SSG, vol. 5, 202.

120. SMP supervisors were dubious about the impartiality of the force's Japanese detectives when it came to dealing with the rōnin. See the marginal comments at the foot of the report by D. C. Imamura on the Japanese Red Jacket Protection Corps in SMP, D-3969, 18 Oct. 1932.

121. The word yakuza is synonymous with gambling and takes its meaning

from the worst possible hand (the worst score is twenty, a sum of eight [*ya*], nine [*ku*], and three [*za*]) in the Japanese card game Hanafuda. However, a *yakuza* is not just a *bakuto* (gambler); he is a member of a gang with which he has a fictive parent-child (*oyabun-kobun*) or brother-brother (*kyōdai-bun*) sworn relationship. Ames, *Police and Community in Japan*, 108. See also Myer et al., "The Gangs of Asia," 9.

122. *CWR*, 27 Mar. 1926, 102. Muraji was succeeded that same year as chief by T. Ukizawa.

123. Ames, *Police and Community in Japan*, 122.

124. Watanabe Report: "Recent Movements of the Japanese Naval Landing Party," in SMP, D-3969, 12 Sept. 1932, 1. Korean gangsters dominated the Japanese-sponsored drug traffic in North China; Taiwanese gangsters did the same for the South. Parssinen and Meyer, "International Narcotics Trafficking," 44. At present, up to 70 percent of the gangsters in Western Japan are of *burakumin* (*eta*, or "outcasts") status; ethnic Koreans and Chinese also join gangs in lesser numbers. Ames, *Police and Community in Japan*, 112–13.

125. Watanabe Report: "Recent Movements of the Japanese Naval Landing Party," 1–2; Second Watanabe Report: "Alleged Organizations of 'Red Jacket Corps' and 'Japanese Police Corps,'" in SMP, D-3969, 18 Oct. 1932, 1.

126. *SSG*, vol. 5, 12, 14, 62. On October 23, 1931, the Japanese fired on and wounded Chinese police.

127. SMP, D-2588/8, 23 July 1931.

128. Ibid.

129. SMP, D-2588, 7 July 1931, and 20 July 1931. There was a provisional government of Korea in Shanghai, headquartered at 1 Puqingli, Rue Brenier de Montmorand. Ibid., 22 July 1931. For the anti-Japanese activities of Korean nationalists, including assassinations in April 1932, see *SSN*, H-11–12.

130. SMP, D-2588/6, 6 Aug. 1931.

131. SMP, D-2588/9, 14 Aug. 1931, and D-2588/12, 20 Aug. 1931. For Shanghai merchants' support of the anti-Japanese boycott, see the interviews with Yu Xiaqing in *The Shanghai Evening Post and Mercury*, 27 July 1931, 4, and 28 July 1931, 14.

132. The local Guomindang branch instantly tried to gain control of this newly formed youth league by forming a Resist-Japan Society (Kang-Ri hui) run by party leaders and members of the Chinese Chamber of Commerce. Wasserstrom, "Student Protest in Shanghai," ch. 5, p. 19.

133. Ibid., 20.

134. Ibid., 22; Shimada Toshihiko, "The Extension of Hostilities," 305. The enormity of the Manchurian Incident and the humiliation that it entailed is hard to realize. Japan conquered one-fifth of China's territories, which included half of the country's railways, four-fifths of its iron production, and a tenth of its customs revenue. Kirby, *Germany and Republican China*, 86.

135. Shimada Toshihiko, "The Extension of Hostilities," 305–6.

136. Henriot, "Le gouvernement municipal de Shanghai," 96–97. According to intelligence reports, the Chinese Communist Party planned to foment trouble over that question on October 10, but once again the deployment of undercover police and the seizure of "reactionary" items helped keep the peace. *SSG*, vol. 5, 65.

137. *SSG*, vol. 5, 71, 236. The elevation of Shanghai police concerns from a

municipal to a national level accompanied the nationalization, as it were, of the city's Chinese government. After 1930 the mayor of the special municipality was named and appointed by the president of the Executive Yuan in Nanjing. He was nominally the chief of all municipal services and his fiats did not have to pass through the municipal council. The only check on his power was a vote of censure, which was practically impossible to obtain, and which in any case had to be submitted to the Executive Yuan for ultimate arbitration. Henriot, "Le gouvernement municipal de Shanghai," 47–48.

138. November 7 brought yet another major "red party" (*chi dang*) occasion, and the police again sent out special undercover agents to watch strategic locations, including telephone bureaus and transportation centers. Ibid., 16. On November 13 the PSB received a report from the Guomindang on student political activities. Ibid., 60.

139. Henriot, "Le gouvernement municipal de Shanghai," 100–103.

140. French police daily intelligence report, 9 Nov. 1931, in SMP, D-2880, 11 Nov. 1931.

141. *The China Press*, 9 Dec. 1931, 2.

142. Wasserstrom and Liu Xinyong, "Student Life and Student Protest," 5; Henriot, *Shanghai 1927–1937*, 93–95.

143. "Student Demonstrations," NCH, 16 Dec. 1931, 4; SSG, vol. 5, 238; Shen Yi, "Shanghai shi gongwuju shi nian," part 1, 18.

144. "Student Demonstrations," NCH, 16 Dec. 1931, 4, and see also NCH, 13 Jan. 1931, 48; Wang Min et al., eds., *Shanghai xuesheng yundong da shi ji*, 140. The General and Madame Chiang secretly flew to Ningbo and then drove on to Fenghua by automobile. CWR, 26 Dec. 1931, 107–8.

145. Chiang continued to control central financial and military power. He formally reassumed office on March 18, 1932, while Wang Jingwei became premier. By October Wang felt constrained to take a "leave of absence" in Europe. Kirby, *Germany and Republican China*, 88–89.

146. Shimada Toshihiko, "The Extension of Hostilities," 308. Xiong was nominally replaced by a Cantonese officer, Dai Ji. Henriot, "Le gouvernement municipal de Shanghai," 105.

147. Finch, *Shanghai and Beyond*, 240–41. The Nineteenth Route Army had been formed in 1930 out of the Sixtieth and Sixty-first Divisions during the campaign against Feng Yuxiang and Yan Xishan. The commander of the army then was Jiang Guangnai, with Cai serving as field commander. Cai began as commander-in-chief when the Nineteenth Route Army was transferred to Fujian late in 1932. Boorman et al., eds., *Biographical Dictionary of Republican China*, vol. 3, 291.

148. CWR, 12 Jan. 1932, 201.

149. CWR, 26 Dec. 1931, 107–8, 16 Jan. 1932, 201. Wang Jingwei's Reorganizationists met in the Great World Amusement Center. Isaacs, ed., *Five Years of Kuomintang Reaction*, 101.

150. CWR, 16 Jan. 1932, 201.

151. Finch, *Shanghai and Beyond*, 242–43.

152. Wu Tiecheng was the third commissioner of police in Canton. Gao, "Police Administration in Canton," 672.

153. Henriot, "Le gouvernement municipal de Shanghai," 111.

154. Shen Yi, "Shanghai shi gongwuju shi nian," part 1, 18.

155. *SSG*, vol. 5, 257; Henriot, "Le gouvernement municipal de Shanghai," 464. The Military Police Training Institute (Xianbing jiaoliansuo) was formally established by Gu Zhenglun in 1929, who was nominally the first director. However, Gu put the management of the school in Wen's hands because of the latter's earlier experience training police for the Beiyang government. Zhuo Jian'an, "Gu Zhenglun yu Guomindang xianbing," 229.

156. See the frontispiece photographs in *SSG*, vol. 5.

157. Henriot, "Le gouvernement municipal de Shanghai," 176, 177, 376.

158. *SB*, 7 Jan. 1931, 18; and 4 Sept. 1932, 17.

159. Wenxin-Xinwen bu, ed., *Shanghai de fenghuo*, 1.

160. Shimada Toshihiko, "The Extension of Hostilities," 306–7.

161. *NCH*, 13 Jan. 1932, 48.

162. The meeting was convened by the Support Committee of the December 17 Tragedy in Nanjing and by the National Salvation Association of Shanghai Masses to Resist Japan, meeting with representatives from the China Public School (Wusong) and the Western District Laborers Federation (445 Branan Road). SMP, D-3088, 14 Jan. 1932.

163. *SB*, 11 Jan. 1932, in Shanghai shehui kexue yuan, comp., *Jiuyiba-yierba, Shanghai junmin kang-Ri yundong shiliao*, 83.

164. SMP, D-3088, 13 Jan. 1932. *CWR*, 26 Jan. 1938, 348. Actual police reserves were called Police Specials, and their commander for many years was Charles A. Stewart, an American citizen connected with the local tobacco industry. *CWR*, 5 Mar. 1932, 30.

165. Henriot, "Le gouvernement municipal de Shanghai," 361.

166. He Li, *Kang-Ri zhanzheng shi*, 4.

167. Shimada Toshihiko, "The Extension of Hostilities," 307–8; Zhonghua minguo waijiao wenti yanjiuhui, comp., *Ri jun qinfan Shanghai yu jingong Huabei*, 5–6.

168. *SSG*, vol. 5, 78.

169. Ibid., 117; Shimada Toshihiko, "The Extension of Hostilities," 308; Hauser, *Shanghai: City for Sale*, 202–3. The Japanese claimed that on January 28, Chinese armed plainclothesmen (*bianyidui*) and regular troops attacked Japanese bluejackets. *The Shanghai Incident*, 3–5.

170. Hauser, *Shanghai: City for Sale*, 290–1. A year before, the Japanese marines had hired a Chinese construction company to begin building the steel reinforced cement structure. The Japanese did not even ask for a building permit, somewhat to the relief of the municipal Bureau of Works. However, afterward the Chinese contractor had his building license lifted. Du Yuesheng asked Mayor Wu to renew the license, and, after some embarrassment, Wu Tiecheng agreed to let the man resume business under a new company name. Shen Yi, "Shanghai shi gongwuju shi nian," part 2, 26.

171. Henriot, "Le gouvernement municipal de Shanghai," 115.

172. Zhonghua minguo waijiao wenti yanjiuhui, comp., *Ri jun qinfan Shanghai yu jingong Huabei*, 20.

173. Henriot, *Shanghai 1927–1937*, 97.

174. Ibid., 116–17.

175. Zhonghua minguo waijiao wenti yanjiuhui, comp., *Ri jun qinfan Shanghai yu jingong Huabei*, 23.

176. The Defense Committee was founded in 1850. It was composed of the

military commanders of the various foreign powers in Shanghai. The committee had met on December 18, 1931, and assigned Japan a new defense zone which extended into Chinese territory about 640 meters west of North Sichuan Road. The Chinese were not informed of this assignment, which was an inexcusable political blunder on the part of the British. Shimada Toshihiko, "The Extension of Hostilities," 309.

177. The Japanese normally had six thousand soldiers and three thousand civil reservists based in Shanghai, but were shorthanded because of the war in Manchuria.

178. Shimada Toshihiko, "The Extension of Hostilities," 308–10.

179. Davidson-Houston, *Yellow Creek*, 141. The soldiers were joined by a "dare to die squad" (*gansidui*) led by Anhui secret society chief Wang Yaqiao. Cai Shaoqing, *Zhongguo mimi shehui*, 337.

180. Finch, *Shanghai and Beyond*, 242–43; Hauser, *Shanghai: City for Sale*, 204.

181. The Japanese admiral's justification read: "The Imperial Navy, feeling extreme anxiety about the situation in Zhabei where Japanese nationals reside in such great numbers, have [sic] decided to send out troops to this section for the enforcement of law and order." Hauser, *Shanghai: City for Sale*, 203–4.

182. Zhonghua minguo waijiao wenti yanjiuhui, comp., *Ri jun qinfan Shanghai yu jingong Huabei*, 24–26.

183. Ch'i, *Nationalist China at War*, 46.

184. Finch, *Shanghai and Beyond*, 244.

185. Shimada Toshihiko, "The Extension of Hostilities," 310.

186. An American press correspondent, cited in Communist International, comp., *Hell over Shanghai*, 5.

187. The Commercial Press's collection of 268,000 Chinese-language and 80,000 Western-language rare books was entirely destroyed. Henriot, "Le gouvernement municipal de Shanghai," 368.

188. Ibid., 118.

189. Woodhead, ed., *The China Yearbook 1933*, 672. The Chinese municipal government set up refugee camps in the hinterland and negotiated an accord with the river and railway transport companies so that transportation was either free or at a reduced rate. A total of 137,000 persons were sent back to their families or to sites far from the battle zone; of these, 17,605 refugees were given free transportation. The Bureau of Social Affairs also set up offices to lend up to Ch. $20 per person to the indigent. Ibid., 671; Henriot, "Le gouvernement municipal de Shanghai," 122–23, 131–32. Mayor Wu sent in special missions to rescue more than 75,000 from the inferno. Ibid., 121.

190. Zhonghua minguo waijiao wenti yanjiuhui, comp., *Ri jun qinfan Shanghai yu jingong Huabei*, 28.

191. For the interservice rivalry between the Japanese navy and army that kept reinforcements from being sent sooner, see Shimada Toshihiko, "The Extension of Hostilities," 310–11.

192. Hauser, *Shanghai: City for Sale*, 207–8.

193. All members of the municipal administration received a monthly stipend of Ch. $50 for daily living costs during the duration of the hostilities.

194. Shen Yi, "Shanghai shi gongwuju shi nian," part 2, 25.

195. Kaufman, "The Film 'Street Angel,'" 2.

196. The Association for Provisional Assistance for the Refugees in the War Zones of Shanghai (Shanghai zhanqu nanmin linshi jiuji hui), which was established by the higher elite of Shanghai under the leadership of major officials like Yu Hongjun and Pan Gongzhan, collected more than Ch. $236,000 for the relief of more than thirty refugee camps. Henriot, "Le gouvernement municipal de Shanghai," 119, 364; Henriot, *Shanghai 1927–1937*, 110–11.

197. In January 1929, thirty-six stores agreed to donate 5 percent of their total daily income for a week to famine relief organized by the Shanghai General Chamber of Commerce. Shanghai rickshaw boys donated over Ch. $100 from their salaries as well. By the end of the year as many as twenty thousand refugees depended upon "pagoda donations" to survive. Tsao, "The 1928–1930 Famine and the Urban Conscience," 20–23.

198. Over twenty million people were affected. That summer the Han, Yellow, and Yangzi Rivers all flooded, inundating over seventy thousand square miles. Candlin, *The Breach in the Wall*, 269.

199. Only four hundred people died in those two months in the centers, and nearly ninety thousand received medical care. Isaacs, ed., *Five Years of Kuomintang Reaction*, 101.

200. Henriot, "Le gouvernement municipal de Shanghai," 121–23, 310–31.

201. Hauser, *Shanghai: City for Sale*, 209.

202. The Japanese admiralty blamed the spread of vigilantism upon the PSB, which it accused of abandoning its posts in Zhabei. Henriot, "Le gouvernement municipal de Shanghai," 361–62.

203. The Green and Red Gang leaders also set up a Shanghai Citizens' Emergency Committee to provide war relief. Du Yuesheng himself provided ammunition to the Nineteenth Route Army, plus money for tanks. After Shi Liangcai was assassinated by Dai Li's men, Du became head of the Shanghai Civic Federation. Boorman et al., eds., *Biographical Dictionary of Republican China*, vol. 3, 329; Marshall, "Opium and the Politics of Gangsterism," 33.

204. A. T. Steele witnessed the same cruelty by these men—shopkeepers, clerks, and gardeners—who were military reservists. Armed with axe handles, heavy canes, and often revolvers, they were used at the rear of the Japanese forces like a form of military police to direct traffic, guard barricades, search houses, and round up "suspicious" characters. To the Chinese, the *rōnin*'s special armbands "came to symbolize the most primitive in the Japanese character." Steele, *Shanghai and Manchuria*, 8.

205. Hauser, *Shanghai: City for Sale*, 208.

206. Private dwellings abandoned by their owners had to be protected against ransackers and pillagers. *SSG*, vol. 5, 84–85.

207. Ibid., 54. On February 23, for example, the police arrested a *hanjian* (traitor) named Tang Yongshan, who was a Japanese spy. He was sentenced according to martial law and given a public execution by the police. See the photographs on 214 of *SSG*, vol. 5.

208. Ibid., 82.

209. On March 12, 1932, Zheng Zeqiu, the commander of the Eighth Middle Brigade of the Peace Preservation Corps, led a group of PSB men along with SMP officers in a raid on rooms 29 and 34 of the Great Eastern Hotel (Dadong lüshe)

on Nanking Road. They arrested nine men. Another major leader of the plot, an officer named Jiang Mingjie, was seized later and executed at the order of the Nanjing Military Tribunal. Ibid., 213. For a complete account of the arrests and a collection of clippings about this curious plot, see SMP, D-3369, and especially the "Golder Plot Report" dated 20 Apr. 1932.

210. The Yipinxiang served as a Landsmannschaft or provincial guesthouse for Sichuanese in Shanghai. It was presided over by two old Sichuanese gentlemen, Xie Wuliang and Zeng Tongyi. Zhou Xunyu, who represented the Sichuanese warlords in Shanghai, set up his office there. Zhou was also secretly working for Dai Li. Shen Zui, *Juntong neimu*, 46–47.

211. Di Weimin, "Shanghai zujie liang jianguan yuci neimu."

212. Ibid.

213. Ibid.

214. Ibid.

215. More than Ch. $12 million of contributions flooded in, the majority coming from Cantonese communities overseas. Henriot, "Le gouvernement municipal de Shanghai," 362.

216. Shimada Toshihiko, "The Extension of Hostilities," 312–13.

217. Ibid., 313.

218. Ibid., 313–14.

219. Ibid., 367; Finch, *Shanghai and Beyond*, 246; Boyle, *China and Japan at War*, 28–29.

220. Zhonghua minguo waijiao wenti yanjiuhui, comp., *Ri jun qinfan Shanghai yu jingong Huabei*, 48.

221. Steele, *Shanghai and Manchuria*, 8–9.

CHAPTER 11. THE IMPACT OF THE JAPANESE
ON MUNICIPAL POLICING

1. Hauser, *Shanghai: City for Sale*, 214. Estimates vary, but there were probably 4,200 dead and 9,800 wounded among the Chinese troops. Over 6,000 civilians were killed and more than 10,000 were missing in Zhabei, Jiangwan, and Wusong. Henriot, "Le gouvernement municipal de Shanghai," 363; White III, "Nongovernmentalism," 45.

2. Hauser, *Shanghai: City for Sale*, 214–15. In this fire, incidentally, the novelist Ba Jin lost the original manuscript of his novel *New Life*. Ba Jin, *Autumn in Spring and Other Stories*, 141. The League resolution was passed on March 4.

3. Japan was represented by General Ueda. China was represented by Guo Taiqi, the University of Pennsylvania graduate who served as political vice minister of foreign affairs and who had just been named minister to the Court of St. James. Guo was branded an appeaser by student "patriots," who threw copper coins in his face and nearly blinded him with a tea bowl. The truce had to be signed on May 5 in the hospital room where he lay recovering from the beating. Boorman et al., eds., *Biographical Dictionary of Republican China*, vol. 2, 279; Finch, *Shanghai and Beyond*, 250–51; Shimada Toshihiko, "The Extension of Hostilities," 316–17.

4. Lockwood, Jr., "The International Settlement at Shanghai," 1043; Shimada Toshihiko, "The Extension of Hostilities," 317.

5. Admiral Nomura, General Ueda, Consul General Murai, and Minister Shigemitsu were all wounded.

6. Shimada Toshihiko, "The Extension of Hostilities," 317–18.

7. Steele, *Shanghai and Manchuria,* 12.

8. "Still, the Japanese army was not satisfied. And as soon as another opportunity presented itself, in 1937, it would pour in a much larger contingent of forces to recapture Shanghai." Shimada Toshihiko, "The Extension of Hostilities," 319.

9. Hauser, *Shanghai: City for Sale,* 213.

10. Boyle, *China and Japan at War,* 29. During the "Shanghai Incident of January 28, the Communists intensified their activities in the counties of northern Jiangxi and also tried to capture Ganzhou in the southern part of the province." Wei, *Counterrevolution in China,* 47. The Nationalist régime regarded the 1932 Shanghai campaign as a victory of sorts, and concluded from it that "city fighting was preferable to field operations because it would neutralize the Japanese superiority in firepower, mobility, and logistics." This was one reason why Chiang Kai-shek chose to commit his elite troops to the Shanghai campaign in August 1937, thereby losing 300,000 men. Ch'i, *Nationalist China at War,* 46.

11. If you took the Settlement boundary running north from Suzhou Creek and extended a dotted line up to the railway, then the area north of the railway remained in Japanese hands, as did the area east of that dotted line up to North Station. Just slightly south of Markham Road yards another line extended all the way to the railway, and the area within this boundary was also to be evacuated. The rest remained in Japanese hands. Map in SMP, D-3648, 18 May 1932.

12. Twenty thousand of the original ninety thousand troops had already been transferred to the Northeast to "pacify" Manchuria. Henriot, "Le gouvernement municipal de Shanghai," 367.

13. Translated in French intelligence report in SMP, D-3445, 19 Apr. 1932.

14. Henriot, "Le gouvernement municipal de Shanghai," 125.

15. Confidential report by Superintendent Tan Shaoliang, SMP, D-3445, 19 Apr. 1932. The quote is from an article translated from *Xin wan bao,* dated 27 Apr. 1932, in ibid., D-3445, 27 Apr. 1932.

16. Article translated from *Xin wan bao* on 5 Apr. 1932, in SMP, D-3445, 5 Apr. 1932. See also Tan Shaoliang's April 5 report in the same file. Despite his covert service for the Japanese, Tan remained one of the most reliable political intelligence analysts for the CID.

17. Tan Shaoliang's report, "Citizen's Maintenance Association," in SMP, D-3445, 8 Apr. 1932, 1–2. See also French intelligence report, "Association for the Maintenance of the Situation," dated 7 Apr. 1932, in SMP, D-3445, 19 Apr. 1932; Honig, "The Politics of Prejudice," 267; Honig, "Creating Ethnicity," 26; Honig, "Migrant Culture in Shanghai," 10.

18. Tan Shaoliang's report, "Citizen's Maintenance Association," 4; Article translated from *Xin wan bao* on 5 Apr. 1932, in SMP, D-3445, 5 Apr. 1932.

19. Tan Shaoliang's report, "Citizen's Maintenance Association," 2.

20. SMP, D-3445, 7 Apr. 1932; French intelligence report, "Association for the Maintenance of the Situation."

21. Tan Shaoliang's report, "Citizen's Maintenance Association," 3.

22. Ibid.

23. French intelligence report, "Association for the Maintenance of the Situation." See also Honig, "The Politics of Prejudice," 267.

24. Tan Shaoliang's report, "Citizen's Maintenance Association," 2–3. See also SMP intelligence report dated 5 Apr. 1932, in SMP, D-3445, 6 Apr. 1932; Honig, "Creating Ethnicity," 26.

25. Tan Shaoliang's report, "Citizen's Maintenance Association," 4; SMP, D-3445, 7 Apr. 1932.

26. Quoted in the report by D. S. Golder to Special Branch, SMP, D-3445, 7 Apr. 1932.

27. The Japanese were not giving monetary assistance for the detectives' and constables' promised monthly salaries ($35 to $40 and $18 per month respectively). In fact, the constables were being paid the same wages as the street cleaners (fifty cents a day) and the investigators or detectives received no pay at all. D. S. Golder to Special Branch, SMP, D-3445, 7 Apr. 1932; French intelligence report, "Association for the Maintenance of the Situation." Golder's informant was "Nyien Tung Yuen," who is identified as the chief of the social affairs department of the puppet organ. This may refer to a man called "Jausen Sen" who was a compositor for the *Shanghai Times* and who later became an interpreter for the Chinese lawyer Jin Liren, one of Huang Jinrong's followers. Tan Shaoliang's report, "Citizen's Maintenance Association," 3–4.

28. Tan Shaoliang's report, "Citizen's Maintenance Association," 4–5.

29. Ibid., 5.

30. Honig, "The Politics of Prejudice," 267; Honig, "Creating Ethnicity," 26.

31. D. S. Golder to Special Branch, SMP, D-3445, 7 Apr. 1932.

32. The soup kitchen had formerly been run by the Zhabei Benevolent Institutions Association. Tan Shaoliang's report, "Citizen's Maintenance Association," 1.

33. Translation of an announcement in *Xin wan bao*, 7 Apr. 1932, in SMP, D-3445, 7 Apr. 1932.

34. Tan Shaoliang's report, "Citizen's Maintenance Association," 1.

35. SMP, D-3445, 11 Apr. 1932.

36. Gu placed an ad in *Xin wan bao* announcing that a report in the *Shanghai Evening Post and Mercury* that he was connected with the Maintenance Association was untrue. Attachment to SMP, D-3445, 7 Apr. 1932.

37. This was possibly Cheng Achang.

38. The detective is identified as the "ex-CDSI of the SMP." Secret agent's report dated 5 May 1932, in ibid., D-3445, 27 May 1932. See also Henriot, "Le gouvernement municipal de Shanghai," 125–26.

39. Report dated 2 May 1932, probably by Detective Inspector Thurgood. SMP, D-3445, 27 May 1932. A secret police agent reported on May 5 that five opium smoking dens had been moved from the French Concession to Zhabei. For their names and details of their operations, see the report in ibid.

40. Marshall, "Opium and the Politics of Gangsterism," 33.

41. "The bribing was carried out in a tactful manner by Tu [Du Yuesheng] himself, and consequently the Chinese and senior foreign members of the staff of the French police and French Consulate were anxious to ingratiate themselves with him with the result that his influence in the French Concession increased

greatly." "Memorandum on Mr. Tu Yue-sung, alias Tu Yuin," Special Branch Secret Memorandum, in SMP, D-9319, 1939, 4–5.

42. Adams II, "China: The Historical Setting," 381.

43. "Memorandum on Mr. Tu Yue-sung, alias Tu Yuin," Special Branch Secret Memorandum, in SMP, D-9319, 1939, 5.

44. Martin, "'The Pact with the Devil,'" 24–25, 27–28. "It is claimed that the vice ring in the French Concession has become so powerful as to practically constitute a supergovernment which actually controls the area." *CWR*, 18 July 1931, 246.

45. Pan Ling, *Old Shanghai*, 3–4; Isaacs, ed., *Five Years of Kuomintang Reaction*, 97.

46. The home authorities had sent the new ambassador, Auguste Wilden, to investigate the situation in Shanghai in mid-1930. His conclusion was that Koechlin and Fiori were too closely involved with the gangsters to be able to clean up the situation themselves. Martin, "'The Pact with the Devil,'" 28.

47. Also, Jacques Reclu, a leftist, came to Shanghai to teach French in the "Paris of the Orient" and was horrified by the corruption he saw in the police force. One of his cousins was a senator, and he wrote a detailed report to him about the corruption of the Corsican police in the French Concession. Faligot and Kauffer, *Kang Sheng*, 95–96.

48. The journal was published by Destrées, a French lawyer of radical tendencies who finally left Shanghai after September 15. *CWR*, 21 Nov. 1931, 465.

49. *CWR*, 19 Sept. 1931, 84.

50. There is evidence that the garbage collectors' strike in July 1931 was incited by Du Yuesheng to intimidate French officials who were threatening to close his casinos. Martin, "'The Pact with the Devil,'" 29–30. There was suspicion in September 1931 that the "moral wave" afflicting the French police force was due to a fear that the Chinese delegation to the Institute of Pacific Relations was planning a sensational exposure of the conditions in the French Concession in order to back up Chinese demands that the foreign concessions be rendered over. *CWR*, 26 Sept. 1931, 124.

51. Martin, "'The Pact with the Devil,'" 30–31.

52. When the Japanese invaded the French Concession after Pearl Harbor, Louis Fabre shot himself in the head, demoralized because he had not left earlier with Robert Jobes and twenty-four other policemen to join the Free French in London. Faligot and Kauffer, *Kang Sheng*, 102.

53. Rumor had it that Du Yuesheng was sending a Chinese delegation to Paris to bribe the home government. In mid-April 1932, Zheng Yuxiu (Soumay Tcheng) and Madame H. H. Kong went to Paris to lobby. Madame Wellington Koo also lobbied Ambassador Wilden in Beiping. Ibid.; Martin, "'The Pact with the Devil,'" 32.

54. Ibid.; Faligot and Kauffer, *Kang Sheng*, 101–2.

55. Champly, *The Road to Shanghai*, 182–83.

56. Meyrier is cited ("morts pour France au service de notre concession") in Martin, "'The Pact with the Devil,'" 32.

57. Ibid., 32–33. Detailed records of "punitions" were kept for each patrolman. I was able to examine these personnel records briefly in September 1988 during a

rare, and possibly one-time-only, visit to the inner storerooms of the Shanghai Municipal Archives.

58. "Memorandum on Mr. Tu Yueh-sung, Alias Tu Yuin," Special Branch Secret Memorandum, in SMP, D-9319, 1939.

59. The Xinji Company, operated by the notorious Yaoguiji morphine dealership from an office on Boulevard de Montigny, had factories at Rue Porte de l'Ouest, Rue Hennequn, and the corner of Route des Soeurs and Rue Lafayette. Its receiving and distributing depot was in the Oriental Press Building on Avenue Edward VII. Memorandum from Jenkins, Consul General, to the Secretary of State, Washington, 16 Mar. 1931, State Department Decimal File 893, #114 Narcotics/208, 1.

60. In 1931 Dr. Wu Lien-teh, China's representative at the Hague opium conferences in 1912 and 1918 and former chief of the National Quarantine Service, argued that a government-controlled monopoly—that is, legalization and the registration of addicts—was the only feasible way to wipe out opium abuse, as the Japanese had proved on Taiwan. His position, which he had held since at least 1920, was supported by T. V. Soong, who was attracted by the immense revenue potential of officially marketing opiates, and a monopoly was actually established in 1931 but then quickly abandoned because of attacks in the press. Lee, "Opium Suppression in China," 18–19, 66–67; Marshall, "Opium and the Politics of Gangsterism," 20–21.

61. Marshall, "Opium and the Politics of Gangsterism," 33–34; Martin, "'The Pact with the Devil,'" 32.

62. "Memorandum on Mr. Tu Yueh-sung, Alias Tu Yuin," Special Branch Secret Memorandum, in SMP, D-9319, 1939, 5–6.

63. Isaacs, ed., Five Years of Kuomintang Reaction, 96; Martin, "'The Pact with the Devil,'" 29.

64. Report from Superintendent Tan Shaoliang dated 15 Apr. 1932, in SMP, D-3445, 19 Apr. 1932.

65. Fan Huichun was originally an opium smuggler. Ibid.

66. Article translated from Xin wan bao, in SMP, D-3445, 27 Apr. 1932.

67. Newspapers reported on April 18 that the old association had been dissolved and that a new administration of the "puppet government" had been formed at 66 Minli Road. Dispatch from the Eastern Times, clipped in SMP, D-3445, 19 Apr. 1932. See also Henriot, "Le gouvernement municipal de Shanghai," 126, 366.

68. Article translated from Xin wan bao, in SMP, D-3445, 27 Apr. 1932; report by Detective Sergeant Golder in ibid., 29 Apr. 1932.

69. The association was also known as the "Shanghai Northern District Refugees Rehabilitation Committee" to the SMP.

70. Report by Detective Sergeant Golder in SMP, D-3445, 29 Apr. 1932.

71. Report by Detective Sergeant Golder, based upon information gathered by "Agent Number 6," in ibid., 2 May 1932.

72. As we shall see, however, all of this was a thinly orchestrated rehearsal for what happened after 1937.

73. SMP, D-3445, 27 May 1932.

74. SMP, D-4003, 17 Sept. 1932, and D-3969, 12 Sept. 1932.

75. Report by Superintendent Tan Shaoliang in SMP, D-3433, 1 Apr. 1932. Dr. Muck was expected to come to Shanghai to discuss police reorganization mea-

sures with General Wen Yingxing. He is identified as a Nazi in D-4724, 7 May 1933 and 10 Apr. 1933.

76. Report by Superintendent Tan Shaoliang in SMP, D-3433, 1 Apr. 1932.

77. See the photographs of Major General Lu Lu, commissioner in charge of the new Zhabei police, arriving in Beiping with his wife, in the *Shanghai Times*, Sunday edition, 29 May 1932. Copies in SMP, D-3648, 30 May 1932.

78. French police intelligence report dated 16 May 1932 in SMP, D-3648, 18 May 1932. The station at 118 Linping Road was known as the Third Section, Fifth District police station. Inspector Wu commanded one hundred uniformed police and six detectives. Ibid., 12 June 1932. Lu Lu's deputy was Zhang Wenjie; his chief training officer, Ma Hongru; and the two corps commanders, Liu Wanjun and Yan Yong. French police intelligence report dated 16 May 1932, in ibid., 18 May 1932.

79. Tan Shaoliang's report in SMP, D-3589, 2 May 1932.

80. Henriot, "Le gouvernement municipal de Shanghai," 125.

81. Ibid., 367.

82. The small pocket east of the area would continue to be under Japanese jurisdiction as would the railway line, including the station and the area to the north of it. French intelligence report in SMP, D-3648, 18 May 1932. "The Japanese defense sector after 1932 became a quasi-legal enclave within a quasi-legal enclave." Fire stations were established, businesses were licensed—all by the Japanese. "Municipal Council authorities had no control in the Japanese sector. This new administration was run by Japan's local naval commander, not by Tokyo." White III, "Non-governmentalism," 46.

83. Foreign Affairs Secretary Hong Qi delivered the letter in person. Translated in SMP, D-3648, 18 May 1932.

84. The Beiping policemen were organized into two corps each composed of two groups of 112 each. Three of the groups were armed with rifles, the fourth with pistols. French police intelligence report dated 16 May 1932, in ibid.

85. The SMP officers estimated that about 900 Chinese policemen crossed the Settlement. Other sources only stipulate 750 men. Ibid.

86. See the account of the *hukou* investigation in *SSG*, vol. 5, 92.

87. French intelligence report in SMP, D-3648, 19 May 1932.

88. Letters from Wen Yingxing to Gerrard, translated in ibid., 19 May 1932 and 17 June 1932; Henriot, "Le gouvernement municipal de Shanghai," 129. Jiangwan was taken back on May 18, Zhenru on May 22, and Wusong on May 24.

89. Henriot, "Le gouvernement municipal de Shanghai," 128.

90. Ibid., 368. In June 1932 there were 158,593 main (*zheng*) households, 143,045 dependent (*fu*) households, and 1,486,267 individuals (854,068 males, 632,199 females), plus 9,967 foreigners, registered with the Chinese police. *SSG*, vol. 5, table after 220.

91. "Most of the Chinese-owned factories in the industrial area along both banks of Suzhou Creek had been destroyed. The sale of industrial power by the Shanghai Power Company dropped in 1932 from 506,000,000 kilowatt hours to 452,000,000 kwh." Orchard, "Shanghai," 27. Partly because of the boycott, which triggered a price war between Japanese and Chinese textile firms, and partly because of the Yangzi floods, Chinese cloth and garment mills were badly hit by the

disasters of these years. Twelve of the thirty-one Chinese mills in Shanghai by mid-1933 had ceased operations. Honig, "Women Cotton Mill Workers," 23–24.

92. Hauser, *Shanghai: City for Sale*, 214–15.

93. The municipal government estimated that the Chinese city had suffered a total damage of 1.5 billion yuan (Gold $370 million). Henriot, "Le gouvernement municipal de Shanghai," 128. See also Wang, "The Growth and Decline of Native Banks in Shanghai," 131.

94. Lu Xun, "Inscription for the Stupa of the Three Fidelities," in "Selected Classical Poems," 149. I have changed the tense of the verb.

95. The municipal government had to order the PSB to take measures to prevent a vast slum from arising. Henriot, "Le gouvernement municipal de Shanghai," 131.

96. According to the PSB, the total population of Shanghai in June 1932 was 2,938,909. This included 36,471 foreigners and 971,397 Chinese in the International Settlement, and 12,922 foreigners and 421,885 Chinese in the French Concession. *SSG*, vol. 5, table after 220.

97. Henriot, *Shanghai 1927–1937*, 115–16.

98. Hauser, *Shanghai: City for Sale*, 220.

99. The Bureau of Finance had all of its buildings in Zhabei destroyed and its dossiers completely scattered. It was not even operational until July 1932. Henriot, "Le gouvernement municipal de Shanghai," 132. It was estimated that the aggregated losses inflicted by the Japanese bombardment in Zhabei alone were $132,488,751. The losses for Wusong equaled $16,743,096. Woodhead, ed., *The China Yearbook 1933*, 671.

100. Ordinarily, the revenue of the municipal government consisted of 40 percent from the tax on habitations (*fang juan*), 30 percent from the tax on racetracks (*masai juan*), and 30 percent from taxes on boats, vehicles, docks, and so forth. There was initially very little that the government could tax in the combat zones right after the May withdrawal. Henriot, "Le gouvernement municipal de Shanghai," 363.

101. Ibid., 135–37, 197, 201.

102. Ibid., 370.

103. Ibid., 200. The additional burden on the municipal budget came to Ch. $1.5 million per year.

104. *CA*, 30 June 1932, 48–49.

105. Ibid., 47–48.

106. Ibid., 48.

107. Henriot, "Le gouvernement municipal de Shanghai," 383.

108. The first battalion was composed of members of the reserve unit of the PSB; the second battalion was the Beiping policemen; and the third battalion was still being organized under Jiang Shengtao. SMP, D-3648, 27 July 1932.

109. The national government was hesitating before announcing this formal incorporation of regular military troops for fear of opposition from the foreign powers.

110. This was hardly an unfamiliar assignment for Wu Tiecheng. In 1926 he had commanded the Guards Army (Jingwei jun), which was the forerunner of the military police, in the General Headquarters of Chiang Kai-shek.

111. SMP, D-3648, 27 July 1932 and 30 Dec. 1932.

112. Henriot, "Le gouvernement municipal de Shanghai," 138.

113. *SSG*, vol. 5, 211. One hundred fifty-eight Communists in seventy-two different cases were arrested during that police year.

114. Ibid., 3.

115. Chiang Kai-shek organized military police in June 1926 in Canton out of the Police Guards Units (Jingwei lian) of the Whampoa Academy, and attached them to He Yingqin's First Army. This unit was merged with an additional Military Police Traffic Corps in 1931, when Chiang Kai-shek ordered Gu Zhenglun to establish a Military Police Headquarters (Xianbing silingbu) in Nanjing and named him commander. During Gu's tenure, which lasted until 1940, the military police increased to nineteen *tuan* (regiments) and two *ying* (battalions), and a military police academy was established. Zhuo Jian'an, "Gu Zhenglun yu Guomindang xianbing," 225, 228.

116. Wu Xingya was director for three years, until 1935. Since Pan Gongzhan, who was director in 1927–31 and 1936–37, was also identified with the Chen brothers, the bureau appeared to contemporaries to be a "CC" clique stronghold. Chan, "Organized Labor in China," 10. Wu Xingya was also thought to be the head of General Chiang Kai-shek's Shanghai intelligence service. French police report, "Activities of the Blue Shirts," dated 3 Aug. 1933. In SMP, D-4685, 26 Aug. 1933.

117. Henriot, "Le gouvernement municipal de Shanghai," 74–75, 138, 327.

118. The council was organized in eight groups (*zu*) which studied projects by sector. The public security *zu* had two council members: Du Yuesheng and Wang Xiaolai. Ibid., 351.

119. Ibid., 90, 100, 139. Needless to say, Shanghai's Chinese police force was not yet nationally centralized. In nationally centralized police structures a single center routinely exerts operational direction over subunits throughout an entire country such as in France, Italy, Ireland, or the Soviet Union. The very opposite of that formation can be found in highly decentralized systems such as the United States', where no one really knows how many police forces exist throughout the country. Bayley, *Patterns of Policing,* 55–63; Yu Shuping, "Jingcha jianzhi wenti," 17.

120. See, in this regard, Coleman's argument that "The more the central government interfered in city affairs to achieve its own objectives, the more it undermined municipal authority and ultimately its own interests." Coleman, "Municipal Authority and Popular Participation," 5.

CHAPTER 12. A SECOND CHANCE

1. Henriot, "Le gouvernement municipal de Shanghai," 112.

2. Bergère, Castelino, Henriot, and Pui-yin Ho, "Essai de prosopographie," 908–9.

3. See Shen Yi, "Shanghai shi gongwuju shi nian," passim.

4. MacPherson, "Designing China's Urban Future," 48.

5. Wu Tiecheng, "Greater Shanghai," cited in Henriot, "Le gouvernement municipal de Shanghai," frontispiece.

6. Qian Hongtao wrote: "Shanghai is a cosmetic heaven. From the front, full-faced, there are tall foreign buildings and busy streets. From the back, on the other

side of that face, there are crimes of all kinds and the tragedy of starvation." Xin Zhonghua zazhi she, eds., *Shanghai de jianglai*, 6.

7. "Shanghai is nothing if not a city of contrasts." Gamewell, *The Gateway to China*, 53–54.

8. Xin Zhonghua zazhi she, eds., *Shanghai de jianglai*, 1.

9. Ibid., 5–6.

10. Ibid., 2.

11. The irony is self-evident, given Shanghai's housing crisis. In 1937 the Shanghai Municipal Council's special housing committee announced that "as a whole Shanghai industrial workers cannot live on what they earn." It reported that "probably no industrial family is adequately housed." *CC*, 4 Aug. 1937, 35. "Housing proved harder to find than a job," Hung-chien discovers in *Fortress Besieged*, set in the fall of 1939. "Shanghai seemed to expect every newcomer to bring his own house with him the way a snail carries its shell." Ch'ien, *Fortress Besieged*, 327.

12. Xin Zhonghua zazhi she, eds., *Shanghai de jianglai*, 2–3.

13. After the May Thirtieth Incident in 1925, when SMP police shot down student demonstrators, the imagery of blood stained the consciousness of intellectuals. "I think to myself the blood has already penetrated the earth for good. . . . This piece of earth is blood's earth, it is the blood of our companions. . . . Irrigated by blood the flowers of blood bloom here." Ye Shengtao, "Wuyue sanshiyi zhi jiyu zhong," 215. See also Clifford, *Shanghai, 1925*, 16–17.

14. Xin Zhonghua zazhi she, eds., *Shanghai de jianglai*, 9–10. Zhu You also predicted the demise of imperialism, but at great loss of life. Shanghai, with its huge profits, would not be handed over by the imperialists. Indeed, they would prefer to see the city destroyed than to turn it over to the Chinese people. The blood that would be spilled, he feared, would be worse than that sacrificed in Zhabei during the January 28 incident. Ibid., 8–9.

15. Ibid., 10–11.

16. Ibid., 11.

17. On December 1, 1935, Doo Zung-foo, SMP police chauffeur constable number 3067, reported that two British police officers, Sergeant Ernest William Peters (the later author of *Shanghai Policeman*) and Probationary Sergeant Alfred William Judd, had thrown a sick forty-eight-year-old Chinese beggar named Mau Ah-piao or Moh Teh-piau headfirst into Hongkou Creek. The beggar was pulled from the creek but he died in St. Luke's Hospital from additional pneumonia contracted during the immersion. The two officers were tried for murder and acquitted by a jury of twelve British nationals on February 11, 1936. *CC*, 20 Feb. 1936, 172, 175–77.

18. Xin Zhonghua zazhi she, eds., *Shanghai de jianglai*, 5.

19. Henriot, "Le gouvernement municipal de Shanghai," 85. The new council consisted of nineteen members: seven bankers, including Du Yuesheng; six financiers and businessmen, including Yu Xiaqing and Wang Xiaolai (who were extremely close to Chiang Kai-shek); three university administrators and educators; one publisher, the soon-to-be assassinated Shi Liangcai; and one representative each for labor and the party. Ibid., 86.

20. Ibid., 85.

21. MacPherson, "Designing China's Urban Future," 48. The population fig-

ures are for 1936, when an additional 1,393,282 Chinese lived in the International Settlement and French Concession.

22. *Oriental Affairs* 7.5 (January 1937), 239–40.

23. SMA, 1-5-526, 49.

24. Ibid., 65. As of about 1931 the foreign utility companies began to negotiate with the Chinese municipality directly. In January 1935, the Western District Power Company, a subsidiary of the Shanghai Power Company, signed a franchise to provide service to the extra-settlement roads area. Silliman, "Sino-Foreign Conflict," 18, 24–25.

25. Document dated 13 Oct. 1932, SMA, 1-5-528, 1–2.

26. Letter from National Wuhan University to the Special Municipality, dated 11 Oct. 1932, in ibid., 6.

27. Letter from Tianjin Municipality to the Shanghai Special Municipality, dated 27 Mar. 1933, in ibid., 16–17.

28. The Japanese *rōnin* organized armed street patrols of Hongkou in August 1932 after a collaborator's store was bombed. These patrols by the so-called Red Jacket Corps were completely illegal, and they were disavowed by the Japanese authorities. Watanabe Report: "Recent Movements of the Japanese Naval Landing Party," in SMP, D-3969, 12 Sept. 1932, 1.

29. Silliman, "Sino-Foreign Conflict," 28–36; Lockwood, Jr., "The International Settlement at Shanghai," 1043.

30. SMA, 1-5-529, 3–15. After July 1933, the Japanese began demanding more representation in the SMP, including appointment of one Japanese deputy commissioner and of two additional Japanese assistant commissioners. *CWR*, 15 July 1933, 275.

31. Silliman, "Sino-Foreign Conflict," 39–40.

32. Ibid., 13–14, 19, 53.

33. *SMC*, 85; *CWR*, 28 Nov. 1936, 437.

34. *CWR*, 28 Nov. 1936, 437, and 12 Dec. 1936, 68.

35. Henriot, "Le gouvernement municipal de Shanghai," 198. The cost of finishing up the magnificent new civic center at Jiangwan had been considerable. *CWR*, 19 Sept. 1936, 75.

36. Letter dated January 19, 1935, Shanghai Police Files, cited in Willoughby, *Shanghai Conspiracy*, 13.

37. The three police forces readily united in September-October 1933 to expel Lord Marley and other leaders of the World League Against War, which tried to hold a congress in Shanghai. Concession Française de Changhai, doc. no. 237/S, 41–42.

38. Zhou served until shortly before May 5, 1932, when Chen Shaoyu replaced him, and Zhou pulled back for "still obscure reasons" to become "head of the Chinese GPU." Ibid., 36.

39. Ibid., 33.

40. This was carried out after September 1931 by a Japanese Communist Party cell organized by students at the Tōa Dōbun Academy. The cell was broken up by Japanese consular authorities in March 1933. Ibid., 35–36.

41. Ibid., 36.

42. Ibid., 52–53.

43. For a good example of an anti-Communist SMP-PSB joint operation at this

time, see the Zai Zau San case in SMP, D-4131, 10 Oct. 1932. For an example of a less effective SMP-FCP operation, see D. S. Moore's report in ibid., D-4003, 20 Sept. 1932. The Communist Youth League was especially hard hit. See ibid., D-3388, 18 Mar. 1932, 24 Mar. 1932, 26 Mar. 1932, 29 Mar. 1932, 24 June 1932. In this case, the suspected Communists, who were arrested between March 17–22, were Zhang Guangzhen (a nineteen-year-old Hunanese student said to be a major figure in the Left-Wing Cultural Association of China—Zhongguo zuoyi wenhua lianmeng), Zhang Zongshun, Ji Chushu, and Zhang Yunqing.

44. Respectively on October 15 and November 18, 1932, and on April 7, 1933. The Agitprop committee had replaced the revolutionary foreign soldiers group broken nearly two years earlier.

45. In September 1932 the French Concession Police also arrested two leading members of the Indochinese Communist Party. Concession Française de Changhai, doc. no. 237/S, 37–39.

46. Ibid., 40–41; Nym Wales and Kim San, *Song of Ariran*, 265–66; Thomas, *Labor and the Chinese Revolution*, 41–42.

47. In mid-May 1932 a secret order was delivered to all Chinese newspapers from the propaganda department of the Central Executive Committee of the GMD, ordering that no reports of the execution of Communists be published because of the bad publicity abroad. Isaacs, ed., *Five Years of Kuomintang Reaction*, 20–21.

48. Concession Française de Changhai, doc. no. 237/S, 39–40.

49. Li Tianmin, *Zhou Enlai pingzhuan*, 107.

50. Concession Française de Changhai, doc. no. 237/S, 55. Wang Yonghuan was originally named Jian Yizhang. A native of Rugao (Jiangsu), he had graduated from middle school in Nanjing. After defecting to the Guomindang, he was given the rank of judicial magistrate in the military court of Chiang Kai-shek's Wuhan headquarters. *CWR*, 2 Sept. 1933, 29.

51. Yang Xingfo was assassinated by Dai Li's Military Intelligence agents on June 18, 1933. The hit squad was led by Zhao Lijun, chief of the operations group, who took with him Li Ada, Guo Decheng, and Shi Yunfei. The assassins—who had sworn to each other not to let themselves be captured alive—hid themselves in the freight doorway of the international publications division of the Academia Sinica on Yaerpei Road. As Yang Xingfo's car pulled up in front of the door, the killers stepped forward and opened fire. Yang was hit ten times. Zhang Weihan, "Dai Li yu 'Juntong ju,'" 132; Shen Zui, "Wo suo zhidao de Dai Li," 9.

52. *CWR*, 24 June 1933, 147.

53. Ibid.

54. Ibid., 2 Sept. 1933, 29; Concession Française de Changhai, doc. no. 237/S, 55.

55. Concession Française de Changhai, doc. no. 237/S, 55; Faligot and Kauffer, *Kang Sheng*, 106, 109.

56. Three men and a woman were seized, along with six pistols and ammunition. One of the three men was identified as the assassin from the hospital. Dai Li wanted to interrogate the Communist agents himself, but the French police insisted that they had the right to a preliminary investigation because the suspects had been arrested in the concession proper. After Dai Li acceded, the French interrogators learned that these were key members of the *dagou tuan* ("dog-killers

squad") that had been executing Communist defectors throughout Shanghai. Since their victims were agents working for the Nationalists, the prisoners were turned over to Dai Li's men in the Garrison Command. Eventually the members of the assassination squad were remanded to Nanjing, sentenced to death, and executed. Shen Zui, *Juntong neimu,* 64.

57. *NCD,* 29 Aug. 1933.

58. Henriot, "Le gouvernement municipal de Shanghai," 437–38, 463.

59. In March 1932, for instance, the PSB and SMP forestalled a radical demonstration near the Kawamura Memorial Tower on Robison Road by the Chinese Women's Anti-Japanese and National Salvation League. Two men and nine women "of the student type" were arrested. SMP, D-3314, 8 Mar. 1932. See also SMP, D-3312, 8 Mar. 1932. This was also known as the Shanghai Women's Anti-Imperialist League, housed in the Guanghua Primary School, 1266 Robison Road. Five of the eleven arrested were sentenced to prison for possession of Communist literature. "Since that time, this society is reported to have been inactive." SMP, D-3922, 10 Aug. 1932. For a long list of incidents and offenses regarding the anti-Japanese boycott, see SMP, D-3753.

60. SMP, D-3922, 10 Aug. 1932.

61. SMP, D-4003, 17 Sept. 1932.

62. French daily intelligence report, in ibid., 19 Sept. 1932.

63. The arrested included five workers from Jiangyin, Suzhou, and Changzhou; one unemployed worker from Sichuan; a Red Cross employee from Xiyang; a carpenter from Ningbo; a weavers' foreman from Sichuan; and an unemployed person from Yizhen. Their average age was twenty-five years old. Ibid.

64. Ibid.

65. For boycotts, see the lengthy files in SMP, D-3753.

CHAPTER 13. THE NEW LIFE AND NATIONAL
SALVATION MOVEMENTS

1. The extent of the National Salvation Movement can be gauged by the way in which satirist Ming San described a Shanghai of the future utterly devoted to "national salvation" (*jiuguo*): "Important people will meet every day in their villas to discuss a national salvation plan; newspaper offices will every day issue a special salvation edition; radio stations will broadcast every day a national salvation announcement; every institute of higher learning will also add a national salvation course and teach national salvation studies." In Xin Zhonghua zazhi she, eds., *Shanghai de jianglai,* 3.

2. Sun, "The Shanghai Intellectual Community," 18–19.

3. NTN, 12(5)/718, 29 Feb. 1936, *Jingcha yuekan,* 14.

4. *CWR,* 2 Mar. 1935, 12; Henriot, "Le gouvernement municipal de Shanghai," 438, 443. A picture of Cai in military uniform appears in NTN, 12(5)/716, 30 Mar. 1935, *Jingcha yuekan.*

5. Wu Tiecheng's speech to the eighteenth graduating class of the Police Academy, 11 Mar. 1935. NTN, 12(5)/716, 30 Mar. 1935, *Jingcha yuekan,* 3.

6. Note the similarity to the "revivalist" language of the Blueshirts examined below.

7. Wu Tiecheng's speech to the eighteenth graduating class of the Police Academy, 11 Mar. 1935, 3.

8. Even so proud a Cantonese as Wu Tiecheng maintained the tradition of recruiting northerners for police service in Shanghai.

9. *SSN* (1936), F-72.

10. A PSB officer was sent to the SMP to be trained in November 1934, and a Ballistics Section was established at the PSB in May 1935 after his training was over. Ibid., F-73.

11. Ibid., F-72. This was on January 1, 1935.

12. Ibid. Mayor Wu felt that the PSB should bear more of a direct responsibility for firefighting. Ibid., F-77.

13. Xunling, NTN, 12(5)/715, 2 Nov. 1934, *Jingcha yuekan*, 35–36. The term "police box" is in English in the original document.

14. Ibid., 36.

15. *SSN*, F-71. In September 1934 the *qu* and *suo* were renamed *fenju* and *jingcha suo* respectively. *SSN*, F-76.

16. The American influence continued to be strong. For example, the police gazette published a complete translation of Chandler's *Policeman's Manual* and advised using Vollmer's police survey questionnaires in criminological research. NTN, 12(5)/715, 2 Nov. 1934, *Jingcha yuekan*, 3–6; and 12(5)/719, 31 Mar. 1936, *Jingcha yuekan*, 11–18.

17. Cai increased the capacity of the Detective Brigade to solve important criminal cases by raising the salaries of these sorely underpaid detectives, by redistributing their case loads so as to relieve the overworked, and by elevating their "ethical and technical" levels of knowledge through special training courses especially designed for detective inspectors. *SSN* (1936), F-76. Cai also arranged for a special four-month course to train policewomen. Ibid., F-77.

18. An article in the same police gazette that carried Chief Cai's instructions on education described this "dread and abhorrence." "Jingcha yu renmin," NTN, 12(5)/718, 29 Feb. 1936, *Jingcha yuekan*, 39.

19. At the time of retirement they would have their photographs taken and put on file so that they could not apply again under an assumed name.

20. Each of these categories was covered in detail in the 1937 printed compilation, "Jingcha changshi huibian" to be found with cover calligraphy by Chief Cai in SAM No. Diwei 1 2660 DEPT 895.24, file 21. See also NTN, 12(5)/718, 19 Feb. 1936, *Jingcha yuekan*, 17. There was a widely shared belief in 1936 that this was a "year of crisis" (*weiji zhi nian*) and that the police should prepare for air raid defense, counterespionage, liaison with military units, keeping tabs on people with radios, and so forth. Yang Zheng'an, "Zhan shi jingcha de renwu," ibid., 12(5)/717, 31 Jan. 1936, *Jingcha yuekan*, 5–10.

21. Cai Jingjun, "The Police Must Absolutely Be Honest and Strive to Make Progress." Speech at the Shanghai Police Academy. NTN, 12(5)/718, 29 Feb. 1936, *Jingcha yuekan*, 9.

22. Cai Jingjun's inauguration speech, 1 Mar. 1935, NTN, 12(5)/716, 30 Mar. 1935, *Jingcha yuekan*, 5.

23. NTN, 12(5)/717, 31 Jan. 1936, *Jingcha yuekan*, 15. The other three tasks were to extend the prohibition of opium, to conduct household registration, and to train fresh police. Ibid., 12. General Cai frequently expressed anger at the

way in which precinct offices lightly treated his orders to suppress opium and carry out the New Life Movement. See NTN, 12(5)/718, 29 Feb. 1936, *Jingcha yuekan*, 19.

24. Cai Jingjun subsumed both police education and popular transformation under the rubric of "training" (*xunlian*). Talk at the 17 Feb. 1936, Sun Yat-sen Memorial Meeting, NTN, 12(5)/718, 29 Feb. 1936, *Jingcha yuekan*, 15.

25. Xiong Shihui and members of the Rehabilitation Planning Commission drew up a proposal for the movement on the evening of February 15. After it was endorsed by Yang Yongtai, Chiang supported the movement at a meeting of the commission in Nanchang; and on February 19, at a mass rally of more than one hundred thousand people representing 142 organizations, Chiang Kai-shek gave a speech launching the effort. Wei, *Counterrevolution in China*, 76–78.

26. Xunling, NTN, 12(5)/715, 2 Nov. 1934, *Jingcha yuekan*, 31, 37; 12(5)/715, 31 Jan. 1936, *Jingcha yuekan*, 28.

27. The local Guomindang and other political organizations were supposed to enforce certain rules of cleanliness. SB, 11 Apr. 1934, translated in SMP, D-5729, 12 Apr. 1934. The Chamber of Commerce meeting "failed to materialize" because only fifteen representatives showed up after 240 notifications were mailed out to the various trade associations. SMP, D-5729, 12 Apr. 1934.

28. SMP, D-5729, 12 Apr. 1934.

29. SMP, D-5729/1, 17 Apr. 1934.

30. Ibid.

31. For the design and building of the center, see Zheng Zu'an, "Guomindang zhengfu 'da Shanghai jihua' shimo," 212.

32. A New Life Movement Acceleration Committee of social and educational units was formed. SMP, D-5729, 19 Apr. 1934.

33. Ibid., and D-5729/3, 23 Apr. 1934.

34. Henriot, "Le gouvernement municipal de Shanghai," 250–51.

35. Ibid., 323.

36. SMP, D-5729, 3 Apr. 1934; 1 May 1934.

37. *SSN* (1936), B-104.

38. Ibid. The New Life Movement was also part of a long-standing endeavor by the authorities to provide positive alternatives to the "negative" culture of radicalism. In 1930, for instance, the government had proposed to open in Shanghai a Nationalist bookshop where "the tastes of youth shall be ignored and youth be given what is good for them." Isaacs, ed., *Five Years of Kuomintang Reaction*, 76.

39. SMP, D-5729, 9 May 1934; 10 May 1934.

40. SMP, 14 May 1934.

41. Xinyun zonghui huikan, NTN, 3/681, August–December 1934, copies 1–13.

42. *SSN*, B-104–5.

43. Gan Guoxun, "Guanyu suowei 'Fuxingshe' de zhenqing shikuang," 38. The locus classicus of "lixing" is the *Zhong yong*: "The Master said: 'To be fond of learning is to be near to knowledge. To practice with vigor (*lixing*) is to be near to magnanimity (*ren*). To possess the feeling of shame is to be near to energy (*yong*).'" *The Doctrine of the Mean*, ch. 20, part 10, in Legge, *The Chinese Classics*, vol. 1, 407.

44. Gan Guoxun, "Guanyu suowei 'Fuxingshe' de zhenqing shikuang," 38.

45. Ibid., 81.

46. Burton, "Chiang's Secret Blood Brothers," 310.

47. "Shortly after the movement was launched by the Generalissimo, a group of Whampoa Fascists ('Blue Shirts') tried to use the movement for subversive political purposes, and it was they, not the Generalissimo, who endowed the movement with such trappings as the restrictions on smoking, dancing, dress, bobbed hair, etc." In that respect, G. W. Shepherd, the American-educated missionary from New Zealand, was seen as "rescuing the Movement from Fascist domination." "Political Implications of 'The New Life Movement' in China." Nanking dispatch no. 473, 21 May 1937, in *RDS*, 19 June 1937.

48. The Japanese were well aware of the intimate connections between the Blueshirts and the Green Gang. Yamamoto Sanehiko, *Shina*, 144–45. I am grateful to Professor Joshua Fogel for this reference.

49. Deng Yuanzhong, *Sanminzhuyi lixingshe shi*, 111.

50. The meeting was held on January 7, 1934.

51. *Osaka Mainichi and the Tokyo Nichi Nichi Supplement: The China Emergency*, 20 Oct. 1937, 29.

52. Xiao Zuolin, "Fuxingshe shulüe," 39.

53. Ibid., 42–43.

54. Ibid., 38.

55. *Zhongguo wenxue* was originally published in Nanjing as *Liulu*. It was edited by Zhao Jingshan. Ibid., 39–40.

56. The special issue (*zhuanhao*) was the eighth issue of the second fascicle of the monthly, published in 1934.

57. Xiao Zuolin, "Fuxingshe shulüe," 41–42.

58. See, for example, the stress on "vigorous effort" in order to cure the Chinese people's "illness" in Zeng Xianhua, "Zemyang zan neng fuxing Zhonghua minzu," NTN, 12(5)/716, 30 Mar. 1935, *Jingcha yuekan*, 30. See also pages 18–29 of the gazette for some sense of the effort devoted by the Ministry of Interior and the police to the New Life Movement.

59. Xiao Zuolin, "Fuxingshe shulüe," 56; *Beiping chenbao*, date unknown, translated in Special Branch Report, 29 June 1933, in SMP, No. D-4685, 2; "The Fascist or 'Blueshirt' Party in China." Special Branch Secret Memorandum, 23 Nov. 1934, in SMP, D-4685, 3. "The Blue Shirt Society began to exercise control of and gain a foothold in the local educational circles, the press, and other public organizations by installing instructors in schools and universities, editors and associate editors in newspaper offices, and secretaries in public bodies." "Memorandum on the Blue Shirt Society." Special Branch Secret Memorandum, 9 Dec. 1940, in SMP, D-4685, 7.

60. *Beiping chenbao*, 2.

61. Wang Xingming, who was a native of Zhejiang, formerly had been Professor of Journalism at the China Public School, Wusong. He Bingsong had been Professor of History at Guanghua University and Great China University. Wu Yugan, formerly Professor of Political Science at Ji'nan University, had served as an adviser to the Shanghai City Government Council. Sun Hanbing, in addition to being a dean, was chief editor of the Liming Bookstore at 254 Fuzhou Road. Huang Wenshan, from Jiangsu, was formerly Professor of Social Sciences at

Guanghua University. Fan Zhongyun, a native of Jiangsu, was formerly a dean of the China Public School. Sa Mengwu had earlier been Professor of Political Science at Fudan University. "Memorandum on the Blue Shirt Society," Special Branch Secret Memorandum, 9 Dec. 1940, in SMP, D-4685, 2–4.

62. According to a Shanghai police report, "In 1933 the Blue Shirt Society organized a student association known as the Cultural Promotion Society with the object of affording more direct control over the students and at the same time concealing its own connection with the student movement." SMP, No. D-4685, 27 Jan. 1936.

63. The director of Ji'nan University, Zheng Hongnian, was said to have joined the "Fascist Party" in the beginning of 1933. Extract from French Police Daily Intelligence Report, 12 Aug. 1933. In SMP, No. D-4685, 26 Aug. 1933.

64. Xiao Zuolin, "Fuxingshe shulüe," 56. Police intelligence reports associated the influence of the "fascisti" on campus with the dismissal of faculty of liberal persuasion by the Ministry of Education during the 1933 "partification" (*danghua*) movement at universities such as Ji'nan—where they claimed that more than one-fourth of the professors lost their jobs. "The Fascist or 'Blueshirt' Party in China," Special Branch Secret Memorandum, 23 Nov. 1934, in SMP, D-4685, 3.

65. Xiao Zuolin, "Fuxingshe shulüe," 56.

66. During the initiation ceremonies, which were held before a sword and dagger to represent the "blood and iron" of the brigade, groups of cadets from the Central Air Force Academy and the Jiangsu Police Training School lined up in military uniform to form an honor guard. The thousands of spectators who looked on as the new brigade members swore an oath of allegiance in front of the naked weapons appeared to be deeply moved by the order and solemnity of the occasion. Ibid., 40–41.

67. Ibid., 42. At a joint meeting of various precincts and stations of the Shanghai PSB, held on the afternoon of June 29, 1934, at the Zhonghua Road Public Safety Bureau in Nanshi, a PSB branch office of the New Life Movement Acceleration Association was formed. SMP, D-5729, 30 July 1934.

68. The founder of Lianhua was Luo Mingyou. The other major film company was Mingxing (founded in 1922), whose *Ge nü hong mudan* (*Sing-Song Girl Red Peony*) was China's first talkie, filmed in 1931. Mingxing was dominated by the Film Group, whose leader Xia Yan headed the studio's main script team. Clark, *Chinese Cinema*, 10–11.

69. Ibid., 11–12.

70. Kaufman, "The Film 'Street Angel,'" 2–3; Hunter, "The Chinese League of Left-Wing Writers," 262.

71. Kaufman, "The Film 'Street Angel,'" 3–4.

72. *SMC*, 95.

73. Kaufman, "The Film 'Street Angel,'" 1.

74. In 1934 the following newspaper circulation was reported: *Shenbao*, 150,000 (40% in Shanghai, 60% outside the city); *Xinwen bao*, 150,000 (40%, 60%); *Shibao*, 94,000 (47%, 53%); and *Shishi xinbao*, 90,000 (60%, 40%). The rest of the newspapers published in Shanghai had circulations under 50,000, and closer to 10,000 or 20,000. SSN, V-7.

75. In 1934 there were 212 magazines being published in Shanghai: 29 general,

5 women's, 3 youth, 12 children's, 3 publishing, 6 international, 3 law, 1 police, 1 sociological, 7 educational, 1 aeronautical, 10 economics, 5 communications, 17 industrial, 6 natural science, 6 engineering and architecture, 8 telecommunications, 1 chemical industry, 2 agricultural, 21 medical, 18 painting, 1 drama, 10 movie, 4 photographic, 2 music, 1 history, and 29 literary. *SSN* (1935), T-17.

76. Ibid., F-67.

77. Hunter, "The Chinese League of Left-Wing Writers," 265–66, 273.

78. On October 30, 1933, the Guomindang Ministry of Education issued a secret order concerning the threat that proletarian art and literature posed to the country. Instructions were given to launch an attack on what Chiang Kai-shek called "the green shoots of chaos" (*luan meng*). Ibid., 263–64.

79. Typically, a Jiangsu court judge would issue a search warrant at the request of the PSB, which would then be handed over to the SMP, "To search for and seize certain reactionary publications," followed by a title, "on the above mentioned premises." SMP, D-7855, 6 Apr. 1937.

80. SMP, D-6864, 25 July 1935.

81. For example, on May 3, 1936, the anniversary of the Ji'nan Incident, the Shanghai authorities on the one hand flew their flags at half mast; and, on the other, they took special precautions against "reactionary" [i.e., Communist] elements. *Zhongyang ribao*, 4 May 1936.

82. SMP, D-7855, 6 Apr. 1937.

83. Yet, after the Communists appealed to the Nationalists on August 25, 1936, to end civil war and begin resistance, the central government endorsed a strongly patriotic manifesto issued by sixty-six leading Beiping intellectuals, and Chiang Kai-shek began to use the term "national salvation." Rosinger, *China's Wartime Politics*, 19.

84. *CWR*, 19 June 1937, 81.

85. These demonstrations often emerged quite spontaneously. On July 9, 1937, seven Chinese shop assistants and apprentices were arrested in the Bund gardens during a band concert for chanting "national salvation songs, which was picked up by the other inmates of the garden and was carried on spasmodically by the Chinese populace there. . . . The songs were not being sung by any one group of persons in the garden, but as soon as one person finished, it was carried on by another who was in the vicinity, and so it was passed on." SMP, D-7999, 13 July 1937.

86. *Central China Daily News*, translated in SMP, D-7333, 4 May 1936.

87. *Central China Daily News*, 16 Apr. 1936, enclosed in SMP, D-7333, 26 Apr. 1936.

88. SMP, D-7333, 1 June 1936.

89. Farmer, *Shanghai Harvest*, 12.

90. SMP, D-7675A, 29 Dec. 1936.

91. Ibid.

92. This was the estimate of the *Shanghai Times*, 29 Dec. 1936, in ibid. The police estimated the crowd at thirty thousand, mainly students.

93. Ibid. There were similar meetings held in Pudong, Jiangwan, and Wusong with four thousand, five thousand, and three thousand persons respectively. They, too, were followed by processions.

94. However, this was not the same civic ideal of an urban moral order that

prevailed, say, among Progressive reformers in the United States earlier in the century. See the analysis of the St. Louis Pageant and Masque of 1914 in Boyer, *Urban Masses,* 256–60.

95. Note the utter absence of collective demonstrations in Hankou before the mid-1890s as described in Rowe, *Hankow: Conflict and Community,* 207. See also Mann, *Local Merchants,* 70–93; and Elvin, "Market Towns and Waterways," 441–73.

96. "The tenor of Nanking's approach to the problems of reconstruction was etatist and bureaucratic; it was focused on the activities of the state and paid little attention to the wider political potentialities of the party and the movements, or to the public opinion which had proved so valuable between 1919 and 1927." Cavendish, "The 'New China' of the Kuomintang," 172.

CHAPTER 14. NATIONALIZING THE POLICE AND MAKING CRIMINALITY RESPECTABLE

1. Yee, "Police in Modern China," 30.
2. Coleman, "Municipal Authority and Popular Participation," 5.
3. Yee, "Police in Modern China," 33–34.
4. Zhang Weihan, "Dai Li yu 'Juntong ju,'" 86.
5. Vollmer, Correspondence from Frank Yee, 25 July 1934, and 13 Nov. 1934.
6. Ibid., 25 May 1934, and 2 Jan. 1935. There is an eighteen-page printed pamphlet by Yee (Yu Xiuhao) entitled *Meiguo jingcha zhidu* in the Bancroft Library at Berkeley. The handwritten inscription in English to Vollmer reads: "My dear chief, this is one of the series of pamphlet materials I prepared in a great hurry for the training of the chiefs of police in Losan this summer. Best regards to Mrs. and the V-men. Frank. June 23, 1935."
7. Ibid., 10 Sept. 1934.
8. Chiang is quoted by Yu Xiuhao as having said: "To establish a country, you first have to establish the police." Yu Xiuhao, *Jingcha shouce,* 1. See also Chiang's speech quoted in Yee, "Police in Modern China," 38–39. For Nationalist state building, see Perry, "Collective Violence in China," 430.
9. Yee, "Police in Modern China," 36.
10. He Qideng, "Dangqian zhi jingzheng jigou wenti," 18.
11. *Dai Yunong xiansheng nianpu,* 31–32. The *baojia* system was ordered implemented nationally in 1932. In addition to maintaining population records within each one-hundred-family unit, the system was also supposed to sustain a *bao* troop commander to organize a self-defense unit and maintain law and order. Bunge and Shinn, eds., *China: A Country Study,* 441.
12. Vollmer, Correspondence from Frank Yee, 6 Aug. 1936; *Dai Yunong xiansheng nianpu,* 32.
13. Vollmer, Correspondence from Feng Yukon, 7 Nov. 1936. See also the report by Superintendent Tan Shaoliang, SMP, D-7675A, 4 Feb. 1937.
14. Yee, "Police in Modern China," 41–42. In rural areas too poor and remote to afford regular police, law enforcement duties would be assigned to the former *baojia* mutual responsibility units. Vollmer, Correspondence from Frank Yee, 14 May 1937. Six weeks earlier Yee wrote: "Plans have already drown [*sic*] up to transform all the peace-preserving units in the various parts of the country into

police, and the central police academy is hurriedly making preparation to give them the necessary supplementary police training in a large scale for a period of three years." Ibid., 24 Mar. 1937.

15. According to the 1936 administrative reforms the provincial governor was expected to appoint special administrative supervisors to direct the work of magistrates and extend the purview of the province into police matters. Chiang, "Achievements of the Ministry of the Interior," 60.

16. This raised questions about the relation between these new local police stations and the office of the district magistrate. Was the police station to be entirely separate, or was it to be merged with the magistrate's office under a special police assistant (*jingzuo*)? In October 1939 the Committee for National Defense ruled that the two would remain separate, but that ultimate authority would reside within the police assistant's office. In other words, the district magistrate supposedly retained ultimate police authority within his jurisdiction. He Qideng, "Dangqian zhi jingzheng jigou wenti," 19.

17. Ibid., 18–19.

18. These leading police officials were Wang Gupan (Nanjing Police chief), Li Guojun (Nanjing chief inspector), Zhao Longwen (Zhejiang Police Academy president), Li Shizhen (Nanjing Police Officer Training School president), Li Songfeng (director of Police Administration, Ministry of Interior), and Dai Li (head of Chiang's Special Services).

19. *Dai Yunong xiansheng nianpu*, 32–33; CWR, 3 July 1937, 180.

20. SSN, F-59.

21. Prisoners were to be held thereafter in the North Station police office and picked up three times a day by police cars and taken to headquarters. Ibid., F-72. The construction of the new central police headquarters had commenced in 1933. It was finished at a cost of Ch. $120,000 by May 5, 1935, which was the day Chief Cai started moving in. SSN (1937), F-76.

22. For "critical events," see Wilson, *Varieties of Police Behavior*, 79.

23. These were one-month training courses. SSN (1937), F-76–77.

24. NTN, 12(5)/718, 29 Feb. 1936, *Jingcha yuekan*, 9–21. On June 1, 1937, teleprinter communication was established between the French Concession Police and the SMP. SMC, 79.

25. The work began at the behest of the Nanjing government, which showed Shanghai planners how to camouflage pillboxes in this way; but the moneys came from municipal funds, which set a limit to the number of revetments that could be built. This meant that there was a fairly large distance between each of the bunkers. Shen Yi, "Shanghai shi gongwuju shi nian," part 3, 83.

26. Shanghai jingzheng shebei jihua ji yusuan. NTN, 12/5683, 16 Jan. 1937. See also NTN, 12(6)/5693/1937, Neizhengbu: Benbu shi jing Shanghai jingzheng. The Ministry of the Interior approved the request on May 22, 1937.

27. *Ten Years of Nationalist China*, 42–43.

28. Dai Li tried many times to recruit Lu Ying into Juntong in order to gain control of the headquarters detective brigade (*zhenji zongdui*), but Lu was always unwilling to join. Shen Zui, *Juntong neimu*, 49. (Properly speaking, Dai Li's Special Services group at this time was not yet formally entitled "Juntong," but I shall use that form in order to simplify identification of the military secret police.)

29. Chen Zhiqiang had been a Shanghai *liumang* before joining the third class at Huangpu. Shen Zui, *Juntong neimu*, 37–38.

30. Ibid., 45. The Shanghai Station was then under the command of Yu Lexing. When Yu took over the Shanghai Station in the fall of 1932 it was expanded and a special operations group was added: the East China District Operations Group (Huadong qu xingdong zu). This special action group, which first consisted of nearly twenty thugs and gangsters who were experienced robbers and murderers, was led by Zhao Lijun, whose penchant for torture and murder later led to his own demise. The assassination work that Zhao conducted was directly under the supervision of the Nanjing General Affairs Office, which also controlled personnel and budget matters of the operations group. Kidnapping and secret arrests in the area, however, were commanded by the East China Region director independently of Nanjing. Ibid., 38, 147; Zhang Weihan, "Dai Li yu 'Juntong ju,'" 132.

31. Shen Zui, *Juntong neimu*, 46.

32. Ibid., 48–49; Shen Zui, "Wo suo zhidao de Dai Li," 10.

33. Shen Zui, *Juntong neimu*, 49.

34. Ibid., 43.

35. Ibid. Shanghai natives called the Baiyunguan "Maoshandian." Ibid., 71.

36. Weng Guanghui was a native of Zhejiang who had graduated from the Third Class of Whampoa to become an intelligence agent in the navy while he captained a warship during the Northern Expedition. Ibid., 37–38.

37. In 1932 the French Concession Police raided an underground Communist safe house in Shanghai, seizing a CCP report on Red Army units in Jiangxi. Chief Detective Fan Guangzhen passed a copy on to Juntong Shanghai Station Chief Weng Guanghui, who decided to score an intelligence coup by conveying the information directly to Chiang Kai-shek himself on a Chinese warship he commandeered to sail to Jiujiang. When Dai Li got wind of this he flew from Nanjing to Jiujiang with a contingent of special agents, and seized Weng Guanghui. Miraculously, Weng Guanghui managed to escape death, although he was temporarily removed from his position. Shen Zui, "Wo suo zhidao de Dai Li," 15–16.

38. Shen Zui, *Juntong neimu*, 51–52.

39. Ibid. Wang Zhaohuai, who continued as brigade commander until the Japanese drove the Nationalists out of Shanghai, was a member of the Hengshe and a disciple of Du Yuesheng, Xu Zhucheng, *Du Yuesheng zhengzhuan*, 99.

40. Shen Zui, *Juntong neimu*, 117.

41. Ibid., 43, 52, 74.

42. Ibid., 43. Qin Chengzhi became regional secretary for Juntong.

43. The head of the Suzhou section of the railroad police, Han Shangying, gained responsibility for coordinating the transport of prisoners, most of them torture victims, from the Shanghai regional office of Juntong. Ibid., 43–44, 52.

44. Wang Xinheng compiled two important Juntong training manuals with materials he translated from Russian. Zhongyang diaocha tongji ju, comp., "You guan Gu Shunzhang deng po an jingguo." BIA, 276/7435/59400, 4.

45. Shen Zui, *Juntong neimu*, 44. Wang Xinheng remained head of the Shanghai regional office until the very eve of the war with Japan, when he was succeeded by Zhou Weilong.

46. Shen Zui, "Wo suo zhidao de Dai Li," 8.

47. Gu also had no opportunity to commit homicide. Chen Lifu suggested that this made him more and more unstable. Chen Lifu, interview by author, Taipei, 15 Sept. 1988.

48. In a psychological profile of Gu, Zhongtong analysts decided that as a former Communist trained by the GPU, Gu was unable also to accept the Nationalist secret services' notion of "anonymous heroes" (*wuming yingxiong*) who fought selflessly. Zhongyang diaochu tongji ju, comp., "Zhonggong tewubu buzhang Gu Shunzhang zhi zishou ji qi yu zhonggong zhi daji," BIA, 276/7435a/19930, 22. For the concept of "anonymous heroes," see Yeh, "Dai Li and the Liu Geqing Affair," 559.

49. This knowledge was written up as a book, *Tegong lilun he jishu* (*The Theory and Technique of Special Operations*), which was used as a training text by the Nationalist secret services. Zhongyang diaocha tongji ju, comp., "You guan Gu Shunzhang deng po an jingguo," BIA, 276/7435/59400, 4.

50. Zhang Weihan, "Dai Li yu 'Juntong ju,'" 87–88. This is also hinted at it in Chen Weiru, "Wode tewu shengya," 188.

51. Chen Lifu, interview by author, Taibei, 15 Sept. 1988.

52. Zhongyang diaochu tongji ju, comp., "Zhonggong tewubu buzhang Gu Shunzhang zhi zishou ji qi yu zhonggong zhi daji," 22. Note, however, that some sources give 1935 as the year of this dénouement: Chen Weiru, "Wode tewu shengya," 188; Wang Jianmin, *Zhongguo Gongchandang shi*, vol. 2, 149.

53. Zhongyang diaochu tongji ju, comp., "Zhonggong tewubu buzhang Gu Shunzhang zhi zishou ji qi yu zhonggong zhi daji," 23; Xu Enzeng, "Wo he Gongdang douzheng de huiyi," BIA, doc. no. 6002, 21b.

54. Zhongyang diaochu tongji ju, comp., "Zhonggong tewubu buzhang Gu Shunzhang zhi zishou ji qi yu zhonggong zhi daji," 23–24; Xu Enzeng, "Wo he Gongdang douzheng de huiyi," 21b–22a. The Communists claimed credit for Gu's death, attributing it to the long reach of Zhou Enlai. The latter would have seen no need to disavow the charge, since it served his purpose to appear such an omnipotent avenger. The Nationalists, on the other hand, had no wish to alarm other defectors or would-be-defectors at the time by setting the record straight. It is a different matter now, which is no doubt one reason why the author was permitted to view documents long buried in the Bureau of Investigation Archives.

55. Henriot makes the important point that the big bankers who became members of the Chinese Municipal Council in 1932 were turning into quasi-bureaucrats. The 1935 reform of the banking system completed that transformation. Henriot, "Le gouvernement municipal de Shanghai," 87.

56. In April 1932 Chiang Kai-shek honored all three of the Green Gang leaders by inviting Du Yuesheng, Huang Jinrong, and Zhang Xiaolin to attend the National Anti-Communist Emergency Conference in Luoyang. Marshall, "Opium and the Politics of Gangsterism," 32.

57. The four characters *wen xing zhong xin* (literature, conduct, loyalty, truthfulness) were a direct allusion to *Analects* 7.24: "There were four things which the master taught—literature, conduct, loyalty, and truthfulness." These "four teachings" (*sijiao*) inspired the name of the mansion itself, as the following encomium to Huang Jinrong shows: "In 1931, the master (*xiansheng*) completed the construction of the Mansion of the Four Teachings (Sijiao ting) at Caohejing. . . . Adjoining is the Huang garden, where springs flow between [the trees] by layers

and layers of stones. . . . This is a place of scenic beauty, reflecting the delight and joy of the master, where his disciples (*dizi*) can hasten forward to receive the benefit of his instruction." Quoted in Qi Zaiyu, *Shanghai shi renzhi,* 165. The Huang mansion is now a public park.

58. Ibid., 87–88.

59. Jiang Shaozhen, "Du Yuesheng," in Li Xin and Sun Sibai, eds., *Minguo renwu zhuan,* vol. 1, 316. "Hengshe" is also sometimes translated as "Perseverance Society." See also Pan Ling, *Old Shanghai,* 76.

60. Su Zhiliang, "Shanghai banghui shi gaishu," 7.

61. Wang Yangqing and Xu Yinghu, "Shanghai Qing Hong bang gaishu," 64.

62. The Renshe membership included, for example, such notables as Han Fuju, Jiang Dingwen, Zhu Shaoliang, Chen Guangfu, and Qian Xinzhi. Su Zhiliang, "Shanghai banghui shi gaishu," 7.

63. Xu Zhucheng, *Du Yuesheng zhengzhuan,* 99.

64. Huang Jinrong's Rongshe, for example, was by the late 1940s to be particularly closely associated with the detective force of the Nationalist police. Wang Yangqing and Xu Yinghu, "Shanghai Qing Hong bang gaishu," 64.

65. SMP, S-1 Special Branch 7870, 11 May 1937.

66. Enclosure in ibid.

67. Jiang Shaozhen, "Du Yuesheng," 316; Zhang Weihan, "Dai Li yu 'Juntong ju,'" 92, 132; Shen Zui, "Wo suo zhidao de Dai Li," 9; MacKinnon and MacKinnon, *Agnes Smedley,* 368.

68. *Xiao gongbao,* 12 Aug. 1933, in SMP, D-4685, 14 Aug. 1933.

69. Zhao Yongxing may be an alias of Zhao Lijun. The street location of each corps was given as well. Ibid.

70. Ibid.

71. Zhang Weihan, "Dai Li yu 'Juntong ju,'" 133.

72. Zhu, who had founded the Zhejiang Police Academy and nominally headed Central Statistics in the 1930s, masterminded the government's "partification" (*danghua*) of education. His repression of student rioters at Central University (Zhongyang daxue) prompted attacks by Shi Liangcai's *Shenbao,* which characterized these moves as reactionary components of a larger strategy designed to suppress Chiang's internal opponents while he bought time from the Japanese by refusing to mount a united opposition against the external aggressors. These charges, made by the chief editor of *Shenbao,* Li Liewen, in his column "Free Talk" (Ziyou tan), infuriated Chiang and his supporters. When Wu Xingya, head of the Guomindang Social Affairs Bureau and a leader of the right-wing youth movement, demanded that Li Liewen be dismissed, Shi Liangcai refused. Yeh, *The Alienated Academy,* 173–76. See also Wenxin xinwen bu, ed., *Shanghai de fenghuo,* 2.

73. Shi once told Chiang that he controlled several hundred thousand readers while the Generalissimo had an army of several hundred thousand men. "If you and I cooperated what could we not do!" According to Martin, Shi's murder "revealed the limits to the accommodation that the Nanjing Government was prepared to make with the bourgeoisie." Martin, "The Green Gang and the Guomindang Polity," 43.

74. Zhang Weihan, "Dai Li yu 'Juntong ju,'" 133.

75. Ibid.; Jing Shenghong, *Minguo ansha yao'an,* 225.

76. Zhang Weihan, "Dai Li yu 'Juntong ju,'" 134; Shen Zui, "Wo suo zhidao de Dai Li," 9.

77. Coble, "Superpatriots and Secret Agents," 16.

78. Henriot, "Le gouvernement municipal de Shanghai," 90–91.

79. Zhao also represented China at the meeting of the International Police Commission. His followers hoped that he would take over the National Police Academy after he returned to China. Vollmer, Correspondence from Frank Yee, 14 May 1937.

80. Zhang Weihan, "Dai Li yu 'Juntong ju,'" 134.

81. Madancy, "Propaganda Versus Practice," 16.

82. But see Tilly's wry observations on Arthur Stinchcombe's cynically agreeable comment that legitimacy does not depend so much on the assent of the governed as on the recognition by other power-holders of the authority of the person who is wielding power. Tilly, "Warmaking and Statemaking," 171.

83. Ma Yinchu, quoted in Zou Taofen, *Xiao yanlun,* 6.

CHAPTER 15. CRIMINALIZING THE GOVERNMENT

1. Parssinen and Meyer, "International Narcotics Trafficking," 52.

2. Ibid., 19–21.

3. Ibid., 28–29, 53.

4. Eli Liopoulos was from a prominent Piraeus trading family. His main connection in China was with John Voyatzis, a Greek narcotics dealer in the French concession of Tianjin. Liopoulos, who operated out of Paris, was expelled from France in 1931. Ibid., 21–22, 26.

5. Cited in ibid., 28.

6. *CWR,* 8 July 1933, 225, and 24 July 1937, 264. For Chinese connections to the Luciano syndicate, see Marshall, "Opium and the Politics of Gangsterism," 28–30. See also Parssinen and Meyer, "International Narcotics Trafficking," 37.

7. *CA,* 30 June 1932, 3–4, 46–47.

8. Ibid., 107.

9. SMP, D-4009, 14 Sept. 1932, 3.

10. "It would appear that the police action of late has to some extent forced [the "Old Company"] to forsake road transport in favor of river transport. . . . the Kiangsu (Jiangsu) River Police who also operate on the river are not trustworthy and receive monthly fees from the [opium] combines or through Doo Yeu Sung [Du Yuesheng]." Ibid., 3–4.

11. T. V. Soong's reappointment as Minister of Finance may have marked a partial reconciliation between him and Du Yuesheng. During that "campaign," Soong was supported by the Shanghai labor unions, the Chinese Ratepayers Association, and the Shanghai Citizens' Federation, which Du controlled. Marshall, "Opium and the Politics of Gangsterism," 46.

12. Tien, *Government and Politics in Kuomintang China,* 24.

13. Marshall, "Opium and the Politics of Gangsterism," 21. In 1932 the Hankou tax bureau collected over $16 million on opium shipments.

14. Ibid., 21–22.

15. Merrill, *Japan and the Opium Menace,* 33.

16. Ibid.; Marshall, "Opium and the Politics of Gangsterism," 21.

17. Ma Yinchu, quoted in Zou Taofen, *Xiao yanlun,* 6.

18. Marshall, "Opium and the Politics of Gangsterism," 33–34; "Memorandum on Mr. Tu Yueh-sung, Alias Tu Yuin," Special Branch Secret Memorandum, 1939, in SMP, D-9319; Martin, "'The Pact with the Devil,'" 29, 32; Isaacs, ed., *Five Years of Kuomintang Reaction,* 96.

19. "Memorandum on Mr. Tu Yueh-sung, Alias Tu Yuin," Special Branch Secret Memorandum, in SMP, D-9319, 1 Sept. 1939, 5. Under the terms of this agreement, opium from Sichuan, Guizhou, and Yunnan was shipped down the Yangzi under government protection. When the opium reached Hankou it was picked up by Green Gang representatives who distributed it to Shanghai and other places. Marshall, "Opium and the Politics of Gangsterism," 234.

20. SMP, D-5645, 25 Nov. 1933.

21. In 1933 Nanjing forces seized several hundred tons of Persian opium from the Nineteenth Route Army. Most of this was given to Du Yuesheng, who converted it to heroin. Marshall, "Opium and the Politics of Gangsterism," 33; Madancy, "Propaganda Versus Practice," 15.

22. "Memorandum on Mr. Tu Yueh-sung, Alias Tu Yuin," Special Branch Secret Memorandum, in SMP, D-9319, 1 Sept. 1939, 6.

23. SMP, D-5645, 30 Nov. 1933.

24. Ibid., 25 Nov. 1933.

25. Ibid.

26. "Memorandum on Mr. Tu Yueh-sung, Alias Tu Yuin," Special Branch Secret Memorandum, in SMP, D-9319, 1 Sept. 1939, 6.

27. SMP, D-5645, 30 Nov. 1933. Shen Zui accuses Dai Li of later having had a hand in the death of Wen Jian'gang. Shen Zui, "Wo suo zhidao de Dai Li," 19.

28. Estimates of the value of the drug ranged from this figure to $600,000. SMP, D-5645, 30 Nov. 1933.

29. SMP, 23 Nov. 1933.

30. Ibid., 30 Nov. 1933. See also Marshall, "Opium and the Politics of Gangsterism," 34.

31. SMP, D-5645, 25 Nov. 1933.

32. "Memorandum on Mr. Tu Yueh-sung, Alias Tu Yuin," Special Branch Secret Memorandum, in SMP, D-9319, 1 Sept. 1939, 7.

33. SMP, D-5645, 29 Nov. 1933, 4 Dec. 1933, 11 Dec. 1933, and 14 Dec. 1933. Xu Jinyuan took over as chief of staff and Gan Hailai became general adjutant on December 12, 1933.

34. Ibid., 28 Nov. 1933.

35. These included Yang Yongtai (Chiang's secretary), Wu Xingya (head of the Bureau of Social Affairs), and Zhu Jiahua (minister of communications). Ibid., 10 Dec. 1933, 17 Dec. 1933.

36. Ibid., 23 Nov. 1933.

37. Ibid., 30 Nov. 1933.

38. In his instructions to his secret agents Dai Li emphasized the importance of getting to know and manipulate that stratum of officials who served as the staff of important leaders. These were the military advisers (*junshi*) appointed confidential secretaries and chiefs-of-staff of the army generals who ran China. Dai Li believed that if you had these men in your grasp, then everything else

would follow: "The ether penetrates from top to bottom, and once you penetrate one you penetrate ten thousand" (*shangxia tong qi, yi tong wan tong*).

39. Zhang Weihan, "Dai Li yu 'Juntong ju,'" 92–93; Shen Zui, "Wo suo zhidao de Dai Li," 16; Wen Qiang, "Dai Li qi ren," 188.

40. SMP, D-5645, 29 Nov. 1933.

41. Ibid., 1 Dec. 1933, 6 Dec. 1933, 11 Dec. 1933.

42. Ibid., 30 Nov. 1933, 4 Dec. 1933, 11 Dec. 1933.

43. Ibid., 28 Nov. 1933.

44. Private conversation with Dr. Ch'en Yung-fa (Academia Sinica), who is publishing an article on this topic.

45. Guan Gong had been accused of negligence before the Central Committee of the Guomindang by the Zhonghua Seamen's Special Guomindang branch in November 1934 for interference in labor union activities. SMP, D-5645, 12 Dec. 1934.

46. Ibid., 4 Dec. 1934.

47. Ibid., 17 Dec. 1934.

48. Merrill, *Japan and the Opium Menace*, 27–28.

49. Lee, "Opium Suppression in China," 73–74.

50. Registration became mandatory in 1935, when the new criminal code rendered punishments against addicts and traffickers more severe. Wang, "The Revised Criminal Code," 38.

51. In practice, many smokers hesitated to register for fear of public humiliation, punishment (if former addicts began smoking again they were to be summarily executed), and tax assessments. *SSN*, F-76; Adams II, "China: The Historical Setting," 382; Madancy, "Propaganda Versus Practice," 10–12. Enforcement of the code in 1936 led to the execution before firing squads of nearly one thousand dealers and hopeless addicts in Central and North China. CC, 4 Jan. 1937, 12.

52. Marshall, "Opium and the Politics of Gangsterism," 22.

53. CA 6.9, 15 Oct. 1934, 210; Madancy, "Propaganda Versus Practice," 12–13.

54. Marshall, "Opium and and the Politics of Gangsterism," 22, 34.

55. Ibid., 26–27.

56. Ibid., 33; Sues, *Shark Fins and Millet*, 70.

57. Marshall, "Opium and the Politics of Gangsterism," 34.

58. A detoxification clinic was opened in 1934 at Longhua to take care of addicts arrested by the armed forces, and in January and May 1935, two additional clinics were opened in Zhabei and Nanshi. *SSN*, B-79; Henriot, "Le gouvernement municipal de Shanghai," 291.

59. SSN, F-72–76.

60. SMP, D-7138, 12 Dec. 1935.

61. SSN, F-72–74.

62. Merrill, *Japan and the Opium Menace*, 32. After an order was issued in April 1936 to all military and civilian personnel to stop smoking opium, several dozen Shanghai PSB officers and patrolmen were put under investigation. Only two officers, however, were actually sent to the Garrison Command to be punished. SSN (1937), F-78.

63. Eighty percent of those who registered were workers or unemployed vagrants. They were often too drugged to eat, and after kicking the habit their appe-

tite returned and they needed relief and welfare. Former smokers were sent to work in factories in Nantong, Tongshan, and other counties. Ibid., F-81–82.

64. Ibid., F-79–80. The actual number of addicts sent to opium treatment centers between July 1935 and December 31, 1936, totaled 17,600 people. Most volunteered for treatment. Ibid., F-80.

65. Ibid., F-81. Because of extraterritoriality, the Chinese police had great difficulty looking after drug commissaries, hospitals, and medical schools in the concessions during the 1934–36 drug suppression campaign. Over 90 percent of the drug companies, for example, were in the concessions. Ibid., F-78.

66. Of the twenty-four thousand, about three thousand were ordinary householders and twenty-one thousand were urban poor. Ibid., F-78.

67. Ibid., F-79. There was thus a Shanghai-Tianjin "corridor" in drugs as well as in regular items of trade. See Leung, "The Shanghai-Tientsin Corridor," 209–18.

68. "1933 nian Hankou Ri zujie guanyu yapian ji qita dupin zhi baogao," NTN, 12/370/1933, 2a. See also CWR, 26 June 1937, 114; and Madancy, "Propaganda Versus Practice," 20–21.

69. Lee, "Opium Suppression in China," 55.

70. Ynlow, "Japan's 'Special Trade,'" 143.

71. Lee, "Opium Suppression in China," 53–54. The traffic was described to the U.S. government by Treasury agent Nicholson, who noted in 1934 that "the Japanese Army in North China is now engaged openly in the illicit traffic. Opium and heroin moves in cartloads from Jehol [Rehe] under the protection of Japanese armed guards." Cited in Parssinen and Meyer, "International Narcotics Trafficking," 47.

72. Kwantung Army handbook, cited in Madancy, "Propaganda Versus Practice," 19. For the Japanese military's connection with the drug traffic, see CC, 11 Feb. 1937, 124.

73. CC, 11 Feb. 1937, 123.

74. CWR, 26 June 1937, 114. See also Marshall, "Opium and the Politics of Gangsterism," 24.

75. "Every passenger traveling on the Mukden-Peiping train, if he wishes, is free to carry a [package] of drugs. Japanese protection has made these people immune from the search of the customs and Chinese police officials." CC, 11 Feb. 1937, 123.

76. Marshall, "Opium and the Politics of Gangsterism," 22.

77. CWR, 1 Apr. 1937, 3.

78. This account is based on Narcotics Bureau reports cited in Marshall, "Opium and the Politics of Gangsterism," 34.

79. Merrill, *Japan and the Opium Menace*, 34–36; Marshall, "Opium and the Politics of Gangsterism," 34.

80. Marshall, "Opium and the Politics of Gangsterism," 24–25.

81. One of the most important figures in the secret world of opium and espionage in which Du Yuesheng operated was Ye Jinghe, a.k.a. Paul Yip, head of the Fujian drug monopoly. Although supposedly executed by the Nationalists for his narcotics dealings with the Japanese, he was actually pardoned secretly in the fall of 1937 after Du Yuesheng handed over enormous sums to the Nationalist mili-

tary. Ye served as an important link to the Japanese and the Taiwanese *rōnin* engaged in the Fuzhou-Amoy traffic. Ye's brother, Ye Chien-shoon, worked for the Japanese secret service in Hong Kong. Marshall, "Opium and the Politics of Gangsterism," 39.

82. Chiang Kai-shek and Du Yuesheng's efforts to extend the registration of addicts and monopoly sale of opium into the International Settlement were correctly seen as a revenue-gathering device that would make it impossible for the SMP to control traffickers. *CWR*, 22 July 1937, 77; Merrill, *Japan and the Opium Menace*, 35.

83. Zou Taofen, *Xiao yanlun*, 294–95.

84. According to the Shanghai Municipal Police report for 1937, the number of crime cases was 915 less than in 1936. The percentage of convictions of persons sent to trial was an astonishingly high rate of 88.63 percent. The value of property stolen increased 24.62 percent over the previous year, but 46 percent of this was white-collar crime. Serious offenses against persons and property were both down. In 1937 there were twenty-two "true cases" of murder and five of armed abduction in the International Settlement. Altogether, there were 2,647 serious offenses against property, including 464 armed robberies. *SMC*, 85. Until historians have access to the court records now in the Shanghai Municipal Archives, it will be impossible to distinguish between larceny for acquisition and larceny for survival in these crimes against property. Palmer, *Police and Protest*, 78–81.

85. It was commonly believed that the foreign concessions police were more zealous about catching some hapless motorist in a minor traffic infringement than in suppressing real crime. *CWR*, 28 Nov. 1936, 437.

CONCLUSION: RESOLUTIONS

1. Cited in Farmer, *Shanghai Harvest*, 15.

2. "It must be borne in mind that the Japanese did not have a prepared blueprint for the subjugation of China." Li, *The Japanese Army in North China*, 41.

3. Farmer, *Shanghai Harvest*, 14–15.

4. Davidson-Houston, *Yellow Creek*, 145; White III, "Non-governmentalism," 46–47.

5. Davidson-Houston, *Yellow Creek*, 145.

6. Farmer, *Shanghai Harvest*, 37.

7. Boorman, *Biographical Dictionary of Republican China*, vol. 3, 329; Marshall, "Opium and the Politics of Gangsterism," 38; Scott, *Actors Are Madmen*, 61.

8. Xu Zhucheng, *Du Yuesheng zhengzhuan*, 95.

9. Ibid., 99.

10. Shen Zui, "Wo suo zhidao de Dai Li," 20.

11. He Li, *Kang-Ri zhanzheng shi*, 63.

12. Ibid., 37–38; Davidson-Houston, *Yellow Creek*, 146.

13. Borg, *The United States and the Far Eastern Crisis*, 301–2.

14. The two model divisions, trained by German advisers commanded by General Von Falkenhausen, numbered about twenty-five thousand men. Davidson-Houston, *Yellow Creek*, 146.

15. Farmer, *Shanghai Harvest*, 38.

16. Over seventeen thousand soldiers and policemen—including the armed forces of the powers, the Shanghai Volunteers Corps, the SMP and the Police Reserves—protected the Settlement.

17. Farmer, *Shanghai Harvest*, 38; *CWR*, 13 Aug. 1937, 340.

18. Farmer, *Shanghai Harvest*, 38–39.

19. Finch saw two "dark cylinders" fall, one hitting the Palace Hotel and the other the Cathay across the street. Finch, *Shanghai and Beyond*, 254.

20. Ibid., 255–56.

21. The official death toll for the Nanking Road tragedy was 729 dead, 865 wounded. Ibid., 256; and Farmer, *Shanghai Harvest*, 48.

22. Powell, *My Twenty-five Years in China*, 301.

23. One set of statistics claimed that the total casualties in both incidents amounted to 1,226 dead and 1,578 wounded. Another source stated that 1,740 people were killed and 1,873 wounded. Twenty-six of the victims were foreigners. *SMC*, 77; Davidson-Houston, *Yellow Creek*, 146–47.

24. Police Chief Cai Jingjun was assigned to help General Yang Hu with the defense of Nanshi. *CWR*, 25 Dec. 1937, 89.

25. "The young Chinese regulars knew all the requirements for street fighting. British officers standing beside me gave them full marks for their slickness, efficiency, and air of tremendous determination that gave the lie to their bobtail appearance." Ibid., 50.

26. Davidson-Houston, *Yellow Creek*, 150.

27. Shen Zui, "Wo suo zhidao de Dai Li," 20–21.

28. Shen Zui and his radio man, Qiu Shenghu, made good their own escape by concealing their transmitter in Qiu's one-year-old's baby carriage, but they were so shaken by the close call that Shen Zui refused to go back into enemy territory and for some time not a single Juntong agent existed in the Hongkou area. Shen Zui, *Juntong neimu*, 82.

29. Davidson-Houston, *Yellow Creek*, 151–54.

30. Cai Shaoqing, *Zhongguo mimi shehui*, 336–37.

31. Shen Zui, "Wo suo zhidao de Dai Li," 22–23; *CWR*, 25 Dec. 1937, 88–89.

32. Cai Shaoqing, *Zhongguo mimi shehui*, 338.

33. Xu Zhucheng, *Du Yuesheng zhengzhuan*, 95.

34. This was also known as the Wartime Service Group. *SMC*, 93.

35. SMP, D-3648, 27 July 1932.

36. His headquarters at Jiangyin had already been training cadets for intelligence work in a *junguan xunlianban* (officers training unit) that was also a "preliminary training" (*rumen xunlian*) course for the Special Services Department. SMP, D-8039A, 10 Sept. 1937. For the connection of the officers training unit with the SSD, see Xu Zhucheng, *Du Yuesheng zhengzhuan*, 100.

37. "Emergency Period Service Group Report," in SMP, D-8039a, 23 Sept. 1937, 1. I have put the names in pinyin romanization instead of using the original spelling of the intelligence report, e.g., Ong Chin-chiu, Loh Ching-dz, and so forth.

38. Ibid., 1–2.

39. On January 1, 1937, the PSB adopted a more professional and less political public image by renaming itself the Shanghai Police Bureau (Shanghai shi jing-chaju). Shortly afterward, the SPB announced plans to expand its membership of

5,073 men and women and improve the ratio of police to population by recruiting a fresh batch of cadets from outside of the city. Recruiters were actually in the process of selecting an additional three thousand police force candidates from Hebei, Shandong, and Hunan when war erupted. *SSN*, F-76; *Zhongyang ribao*, 17 Dec. 1936, translated in SMP, D-7479, 17 Dec. 1936.

40. Ibid., 2; SMP, D-8039A, 10 Sept. 1937. On September 13, Feng Yukun (Vollmer's former student, now chief of Police Administration in the Ministry of the Interior and one of Dai Li's men) came to Shanghai to present General Cai with a $10,000 reward for the police force's valor in fighting at the front and maintaining order in the rear. SMP, D-8088, 17 Sept. 1937.

41. Ibid., D-8039A, 10 Sept. 1937.

42. Farmer, *Shanghai Harvest*, 57. The Japanese described them to Farmer as "plainclothesmen, rooftop guerrillas, very dangerous."

43. "Emergency Period Service Group Report," in SMP, D-8039a, 23 Sept. 1937, 3–4.

44. On September 11, 1937, the SMP received information from the French police that the headquarters of the SSS was at 545 Hwa Ngoh Fang on Jiujiang Road. This was the address of the Dagong News Agency, closely connected with the Shanghai General Labor Union, headed by Zhu Xuefan. SMP, D-8039a, 12 Sept. 1937.

45. Zhang Guoquan, who had worked for the China General Omnibus Company, lived in the Great West Gate area of South Market with a police inspector identified as Chen Bailong, and who probably was the same person as the Chen Bannong mentioned in the text. Zhang was arrested by the SMP on August 25, 1937, on a charge of agitation. He was later handed over to the Chinese authorities, who released him. "Emergency Period Service Group Report," in SMP, D-8039a, 23 Sept. 1937, 2–3; SMP, D-8039A, 28 Sept. 1937.

46. "Emergency Period Service Group Report," in SMP, D-8039a, 23 Sept. 1937, 3–4.

47. Fu Duoma, twenty-seven years old and a native of Dinghai, joined the Special Action Corps on August 20, 1937. After hostilities broke out on August 13, he moved into the closed-down Xinguang Primary School (of which he was the former principal) at Changxingli in Zhabei. Fu was arrested by the SMP on September 16, 1937. SMP, D-8039A, 10 Sept. 1937.

48. Wan Molin, *Hushang wangshi*, vol. 1, 27; Xu Zhucheng, *Du Yuesheng zhengzhuan*, 99; Shen Zui, "Wo suo zhidao de Dai Li," 21; Jiang Shaozhen, "Du Yuesheng," 316.

49. Shen Zui, "Wo suo zhidao de Dai Li," 21–22.

50. "Special Service Corps Arrest," report by Detective Sergeant Pitt, 25 Oct. 1937, in SMP, D-8039a, 3.

51. Zhang Weihan, "Dai Li yu 'Juntong ju,'" 100–101.

52. Xu Zhucheng, *Du Yuesheng zhengzhuan*, 99–100; "Shanghai Special Service Corps Arrest," in SMP, D-8039a, 2.

53. Zhang Weihan, "Dai Li yu 'Juntong ju,'" 100–101.

54. "Shanghai Special Service Corps Arrest," in SMP, D-8039a, 1; Zhang Weihan, "Dai Li yu 'Juntong ju,'" 101; Shen Zui, "Wo suo zhidao de Dai Li," 21–22.

55. "Shanghai Special Service Corps Arrest," in SMP, D-8039a, 3–4; SMP, D-8039K, 25 Oct. 1937.

56. SMP, D-8039A, 10 Sept. 1937.

57. This detachment was divided into two sections with six subsections each containing twenty members. Five of Section Two's six subsections operated in Nanshi, and one in Zhabei. The latter was stationed at Changleli under the command of Wang Yingming, an officer of the Eighty-seventh Division. SMP, D-8039A, 10 Sept. 1937.

58. Ibid.

59. "Shanghai Special Service Corps Arrest," in SMP, D-8039a, 2.

60. Shen Zui, "Wo suo zhidao de Dai Li," 21–22.

61. SMP, D-8039A, 28 Sept. 1937.

62. "The slaughter had been tremendous and the creeks were filled with rotting corpses. In the fields stray dogs grew fat." Davidson-Houston, *Yellow Creek*, 154. See also White III, "Non-governmentalism," 48. Altogether, there were 40,000 Japanese and 250,000 to 300,000 Chinese casualties during the entire Battle of Shanghai. Eastman, "Facets of an Ambivalent Relationship," 293.

63. Snow, *The Battle for Asia*, 50.

64. Zhang Weihan, "Dai Li yu 'Juntong ju,'" 103.

65. Xu Zhucheng, *Du Yuesheng zhengzhuan*, 100–101.

66. Shen Zui, "Wo suo zhidao de Dai Li," 22–23; Miles, *A Different Kind of War*, passim.

67. *Da mei wanbao*, 1 Feb. 1938, translated in SMP, D-8039A, 4 Feb. 1938. The newspaper commented that, "The death of most of the Chinese traitors may have been the work of the corps."

68. Zhang Weihan, "Dai Li yu 'Juntong ju,'" 101.

69. Xu Zhucheng, *Du Yuesheng zhengzhuan*, 95.

70. Rumors placed General Cai in Shanghai again in December, but he was actually in Hankou, receiving Chiang Kai-shek's congratulations for having fought so well. French police report, 2157/S, 13 Jan. 1938, enclosed in SMP, D-8194, 18 Jan. 1938.

71. Zhang Weihan, "Dai Li yu 'Juntong ju,'" 147.

72. This was, of course, the Yipinxiang lüshe. Di Weimin, "Shanghai zujie liang jianguan yuci neimu," part two, 30.

73. Xue Gengxin, "Jindai Shanghai de liumang," 55; Wan Molin, *Hushang wangshi*, vol. 1, 21.

74. At the time, it was believed that Lu was killed by Japanese agents. However, the Nationalist secret service knew that Lu reported almost daily to the Japanese Naval Landing Party, and it is most probable that Dai Li's Juntong or loosely affiliated "Blueshirts" were the actual assassins. Di Weimin, "Shanghai zujie liang jianguan yuci neimu," part three; CWR, 20 Aug. 1938, 404, and 27 Aug. 1938, 432; RDS, 893.00PR/149, August 1938, 18.

75. *CWR*, 27 Aug. 1938, 432.

76. Ibid.

77. Di Weiming, "Shanghai zujie liang jianguan yuci neimu," part two, 30.

78. *SB*, 8 July 1927, 13.

79. *NCH*, 9 July 1927, 48.

80. The Japanese did this in part to mobilize Chinese support after the Nazis had been defeated at Stalingrad and the Allies were advancing in the Solomon Islands and in North Africa. White III, "Non-governmentalism," 50.

81. All of this has become the lore of numerous recent studies published in

China, e.g., Xu Feng and Zhang Yusheng, eds., *Minguo heiwang, neimu, miwen* (see especially 146 ff.).

82. Finch, *Shanghai and Beyond,* 339. See also Barber, *The Fall of Shanghai,* 159.

83. Liu Feng, "Zai wei jingchaju li de douzheng," 178.

84. Shanghai shi gonganju gongan shi ziliao zhengji yanjiu lingdao xiaozu bangongshi, comp., "Cuihui jiu jingcha jigou, baowei renmin zhengquan," 109. Counting firemen and civilian employees, the total roster of the Shanghai police numbered over twenty thousand. Lu Dagong, "Shanghai jingzheng daquan hui dao renmin shouli," 67–68.

85. Ibid., 69–70.

86. Shanghai shi gonganju gongan shi ziliao zhengji yanjiu lingdao xiaozu bangongshi, comp., "Cuihui jiu jingcha jigou, baowei renmin zhengquan," 109. The PLA's emphasis on maintaining social order (*weichi shehui zhixu*) was rhetorically identical to the Nationalists' concern in 1927. See, for example, the May 29, 1949, directive addressed to the Peace Preservation Brigade in Shanghai shi dang'anguan, ed., *Shanghai jiefang,* 128.

87. Literally, "five things [that you get after you] pass the examinations": *jinzi* (gold), *chezi* (limousine), *nüzi* (women), *chuzi* (chef), *fangzi* (mansion).

88. Shanghai shi gonganju gongan shi ziliao zhengji yanjiu lingdao xiaozu bangongshi, comp., "Cuihui jiu jingcha jigou, baowei renmin zhengquan," 110.

89. Ibid.

90. Chen Yi himself claimed that over 95 percent of former Guomindang personnel stayed at their posts after the Communists took the city. Gardner, "The *Wu-fan* Campaign in Shanghai," 493. According to an official Communist source, 90 percent of the police accepted the new provisional regulations of the Communists' Public Security Bureau. Some counterrevolutionaries managed to get through the investigation and had to be dealt with later. About 1,500 policemen "changed vocation" and "engaged in productive work." *Shanghai jiefang yinian, 1949–1950,* 15.

91. Shanghai shi gonganju gongan shi ziliao zhengji yanjiu lingdao xiaozu bangongshi, comp., "Cuihui jiu jingcha jigou, baowei renmin zhengquan," 110.

92. Hershatter, "Regulating Sex in Shanghai," 39–41; Barber, *The Fall of Shanghai,* 220; Chen Jianhua, "Wuxing zhi gang," 26–29. The new régime's increased level of state control was reflected in the greater "currency" of compliance, participation, and legitimation available to state leaders in Shanghai after 1949. For these three indicators, see Migdahl, *Strong Societies and Weak States,* 32–33.

93. Shanghai shi gonganju gongan shi ziliao zhengji yanjiu lingdao xiaozu bangongshi, comp., "Cuihui jiu jingcha jigou, baowei renmin zhengquan," 111–17.

94. White III, *Policies of Chaos,* 87–103.

95. Cheng, *Life and Death in Shanghai,* passim.

96. Foucault, *Discipline and Punish,* 308.

APPENDIX 3

1. Wang, "The Growth and Decline of Native Banks in Shanghai," 131–32; Hauser, *Shanghai: City for Sale,* 225–27.

2. Strauss, "Bureaucratic Reconstitution and Institution-Building," 230.

3. Hauser, *Shanghai: City for Sale*, 222–24, 230.

4. Ibid., 227; Ynlow, "Japan's 'Special Trade,'" 143.

5. Hauser, *Shanghai: City for Sale*, 228–29.

6. The existence of this "depression" is challenged in a working paper by Loren Brandt and Thomas Sargent titled "Notes on China and Silver during the Great Depression."

7. In 1930 there were 107 Chinese-owned silk filatures in Shanghai. By 1935 that number had dropped to 30. Honig, "Women Cotton Mill Workers," 25.

8. Honig, *Sisters and Strangers*, 56–57; Hauser, *Shanghai: City for Sale*, 231; Wang, "The Growth and Decline of Native Banks in Shanghai," 132. At the end of 1935, China's national debt totaled Ch. $1,799,536,000. This indebtedness absorbed nearly 70 percent of total yearly revenue, of which 52 percent came from customs receipts. Ynlow, "Japan's 'Special Trade,'" 140.

9. Hauser, *Shanghai: City for Sale*, 231–33.

10. Ibid., 232–34; Davidson-Houston, *Yellow Creek*, 144.

11. SMC, 85; CWR, 28 Nov. 1936, 437.

12. CWR, 28 Nov. 1936, 437.

13. Two weeks later, on December 7, 1936, Police Commissioner Gerrard held a meeting at Fuzhou Road with two representatives from each of the SMP's stations to explain the cuts and mollify his men. CWR, 12 Dec. 1936, 68.

14. Henriot, "Le gouvernement municipal de Shanghai," 198. The costs of finishing up the magnificent new civic center at Jiangwan had been considerable. CWR, 19 Sept. 1936, 75.

Bibliography

Abadinsky, Howard. *The Criminal Elite: Professional and Organized Crime.* Westport, Conn.: Greenwood Press, 1983.

Adams, Leonard P., II. "China: The Historical Setting of Asia's Profitable Plague." In *The Politics of Heroin in Southeast Asia,* by Alfred W. McCoy, Cathleen B. Read, and Leonard P. Adams II, 363–83. New York: Harper and Row, 1972.

Alford, William P. "Of Arsenic and Old Laws: Looking Anew at Criminal Justice in Late Imperial China." *California Law Review* 72: 1180–1256.

All About Shanghai: A Standard Guidebook. Hong Kong: Oxford University Press, 1983.

Ames, Walter L. *Police and Community in Japan.* Berkeley, Los Angeles, London: University of California Press, 1981.

Amnesty International. *Report on Torture.* New York: Farrar, Straus, and Giroux, 1975.

Anderson, Benedict R. O'G. "Old State, New Society: Indonesia's New Order in Comparative Historical Perspective." *Journal of Asian Studies* 42.3 (May 1983): 477–96.

Andrew, Kenneth W. *Diary of an Ex-Hong Kong Cop.* Saint Ives, Cornwall, 1977.

Argus. "Motives Behind the Reorganization of the Puppet Government." *China Weekly Review,* 6 Sept. 1941, 11, 28.

Auxion de Ruffe, R. d'. *La bataille de Shanghai.* Paris: Editions Berger-Levrault, 1938.

Ba Jin. *Autumn in Spring and Other Stories.* Beijing: Panda Books, 1981.

Ba Ren. "Xishi" [Happy event]. In *Shanghai "gudao" wenxue zuopin xuan* [A collection of literary writings from Shanghai as an "isolated island"], edited by Shanghai shehui kexueyuan, wenxue yanjiusuo, vol. 1: 280–305. Shanghai: Shanghai shehui kexueyuan, 1986.

Bailey, Victor. "Introduction." In *Policing and Punishment in Nineteenth Century Britain,* edited by Victor Bailey, 11–24. New Brunswick, N.J.: Rutgers University Press, 1981.

Baker, Mark. *Cops: Their Lives in Their Own Words.* New York: Simon and Schuster, 1985.

Ballard, J. G. *Empire of the Sun*. London: Victor Gollancz, 1984.

Bamford, James. *The Puzzle Palace: A Report on America's Most Secret Agency*. New York: Penguin Books, 1983.

Banister, Judith. "Mortality, Fertility and Contraceptive Use in Shanghai." *China Quarterly* 70: 255–95.

Barber, Noel. *The Fall of Shanghai*. New York: Coward, McCann, and Geoghegan, 1971.

Barnett, A. Doak. *Communist China: The Early Years, 1949–55*. New York: Frederick A. Praeger, 1964.

Basu, Dilip K., and James M. Freeman. "Mallabir: Life History of a Calcutta Gangster." Unpublished ms.

Bates, M. S. "The Narcotics Situation in Nanking and Other Occupied Areas." *Amerasia* 3.11 (January 1940): 525–27.

Bayley, David H. *Forces of Order: Police Behavior in Japan and the United States*. Berkeley: University of California Press, 1976.

———. *Patterns of Policing: A Comparative International Analysis*. New Brunswick, N.J.: Rutgers University Press, 1985.

———. "The Police and Political Development in Europe." In *The Formation of National States in Western Europe*, edited by Charles Tilly, 328–79. Princeton: Princeton University Press, 1975.

Bays, Daniel H. *China Enters the Twentieth Century: Chang Chih-tung and the Issues of the New Age, 1895–1909*. Ann Arbor: University of Michigan Press, 1978.

Becker, Gary S. "Crime and Punishment: An Economic Approach." *Journal of Political Economy* 76 (1968): 169–217.

Beijing shi gonganju. *Da shiji* [Major chronicle]. Beijing: Gonganbu, 1986.

Bell, Lynda S. "Cocoon Merchants in Wuxi County: Local Autonomy vs. State Control." Paper prepared for the Center for Chinese Studies Regional Conference, University of California, Berkeley, 1982.

Bergère, Marie-Claire. *L'age d'or de la bourgeoisie chinoise, 1911–1935*. Paris: Flammarion, 1986.

Bergère, Marie-Claire, Noël Castelino, Christian Henriot, Pui-yin Ho. "Essai de prosopographie des élites Shanghaïennes à l'époque républicaine, 1911–1949." *Annales ESC*, no. 4 (July-August 1985): 901–29.

Block, Alan A., and William J. Chambliss. *Organizing Crime*. New York: Elsevier, 1981.

Boissevain, Jeremy. "Preface." In *Network Analysis: Studies in Human Interaction*, edited by Jeremy Boissevain and J. Clyde Mitchell, vii–xiii. The Hague, Paris: Mouton, 1973.

Booker, Edna Lee. *News Is My Job: A Correspondent in War-Torn China*. New York: Macmillan, 1940.

Boorman, Howard L. et al., eds. *Biographical Dictionary of Republican China*. 5 vols. New York: Columbia University Press, 1967–71, 1979.

Borg, Dorothy. *The United States and the Far Eastern Crisis of 1933–1938: From the Manchurian Incident through the Initial Stage of the Undeclared Sino-Japanese War*. Cambridge, Mass.: Harvard University Press, 1964.

Botjer, George F. *A Short History of Nationalist China, 1919–1949*. New York: G. P. Putnam Sons, 1979.

Bourne, K. M. "The Shanghai Municipal Police: Chinese Uniform Branch." *Police Journal* 2.1 (January 1929): 26–36.

Boyer, Paul S. *Urban Masses and Moral Order in America, 1820–1920.* Cambridge, Mass.: Harvard University Press, 1978.

Boyle, John Hunter. *China and Japan at War, 1937–1945: The Politics of Collaboration.* Stanford: Stanford University Press, 1972.

Branch, Taylor, and Eugene M. Propper. *Labyrinth.* Harmondsworth, England: Penguin Books, 1982.

Brandt, Hans. "Shedding a Tear at Memories of Shanghai." *San Francisco Chronicle*, 12 Jan. 1983.

Braun, Otto. *A Comintern Agent in China, 1932–1939.* Stanford: Stanford University Press, 1982.

British Foreign Office Records. London: Her Majesty's Public Record Office.

Bronner, Milton. "Sassoon's Greatest Boosters of Shanghai Seriously Affected by Japanese War." *China Weekly Review*, 29 Jan. 1938, 237–38.

Brooks, Barbara. "Spies and Adventurers: Kawashima Yoshiko." Paper presented at the Center for Chinese Studies Regional Seminar, Berkeley, 21 Mar. 1987.

Browning, Michael. "Chiang Kai-shek: China's Turnabout." *Miami Herald*, 11 May 1986, 60.

———. "Mirrors Reflect Racy Past of Chinese Den of Iniquity." *Miami Herald*, 22 Mar. 1987, 25a.

Bruce, C. D. "The Foreign Settlement at Shanghai and Its Future Security: From the Report of the Hon. Mr. Justice Feetham, C.M.G." *Police Journal* 5.1 (January 1932): 130–44.

———. "The Restoration of Law and Order in China." *Police Journal* 3.1 (January 1930): 127–38.

———. "Shanghai: The International Settlement and Its Municipal Police Force." *Police Journal* 1.1 (1928): 128–38.

Buchler, Walter. "The Police in China." *Justice of the Peace and Local Government Review*, 14 Apr. 1928: 254–55.

Buckley, Frank. "China's Failure to Suppress Opium Traffic." *Current History and Forum* 35 (October 1931): 77–80.

Bunge, Frederica M., and Rinn-Sup Shinn, eds. *China: A Country Study.* Washington, D.C.: U.S. Government, Department of the Army, 1981.

Bunker, Gerald E. *The Peace Conspiracy: Wang Ching-wei and the China War, 1937–1941.* Cambridge, Mass.: Harvard University Press, 1972.

Burchell, Graham, Colin Gordon, and Peter Miller, eds., *The Foucault Effect: Studies in Governmentality, with Two Lectures by, and an Interview with, Michel Foucault.* Chicago: University of Chicago Press, 1991.

Burton, Wilbur. "Chiang's Secret Blood Brothers." *Asia* (May 1936): 308–10.

Bush, Richard C. *The Politics of Cotton Textiles in Kuomintang China, 1927–1937.* New York and London: Garland Publishing, 1982.

Butcher, John G. *The British in Malaya, 1880–1941: The Social History of a European Community in Colonial South-East Asia.* Kuala Lumpur: Oxford University Press, 1979.

Cadart, Claude, and Cheng Yingxiang. *Mémoires de Peng Shuzhi: L'Envol du communisme en Chine.* Paris: Gallimard, 1983.

Cai Shaoqing. *Zhongguo mimi shehui* [Chinese secret societies]. Hangzhou: Zhejiang renmin chubanshe, 1989.

Caldwell, Oliver J. *A Secret War: Americans in China, 1944–1945.* Carbondale
and Edwardsville: Southern Illinois University Press, 1984.

Candlin, Enid Saunders. *The Breach in the Wall: A Memoir of the Old China.*
New York: Paragon House Publishers, 1987.

Carney, Sanders. *Foreign Devils Had Light Eyes: A Memoir of Shanghai, 1933–
1939.* Ontario: Dorset Publishing, 1980.

Carr, E. H. *The Bolshevik Revolution, 1917–1923.* 3 vols. London: Penguin Books,
1966.

Carte, Gene E., and Elaine H. Carte. *Police Reform in the United States: The
Era of August Vollmer, 1905–1932.* Berkeley: University of California Press,
1975.

Cavendish, Patrick. "The 'New China' of the Kuomintang." In *Modern China's
Search for a Political Form,* edited by Jack Gray, 138–86. London: Oxford University Press, 1969.

Center for Research on Criminal Justice, eds. *The Iron Fist and the Velvet Glove:
An Analysis of the U.S. Police.* Berkeley: The Center for Research on Criminal
Justice, 1977.

Ch'en Li-fu. "The Board of Organization, 1932–1935." In materials relating to the
oral history of Mr. Ch'en Li-fu, done with Miss Julie Lien-ying Hao as part
of the Chinese Oral History Project of the East Asian Institute of Columbia
University between December 1958 and July 2, 1968.

Ch'eng I-fan. "*Kung* as an Ethos in Late Nineteenth-Century China: The Case of
Wang Hsien-ch'ien (1842-1918)." In *Reform in Nineteenth Century China,*
edited by Paul A. Cohen and John E. Schrecker. Cambridge, Mass.: East Asian
Research Center, Harvard University, 1976.

Ch'i, Hsi-hseng. *The Chinese Warlord System: 1916–1928.* Washington: American University Center for Research in Social Systems, 1969.

———. *Nationalist China at War: Military Defeats and Political Collapse, 1937–
1945.* Ann Arbor: University of Michigan Press, 1982.

———. *Warlord Politics in China, 1916–1928.* Stanford: Stanford University
Press.

Ch'ien, Chung-shu. *Fortress Besieged.* Translated by Jeanne Kelly and Nathan K.
Mao. Bloomington and London: Indiana University Press, 1979.

Chambliss, William J. *Functional and Conflict Theories of Crime.* New York: MSS
Modular Publications, 1974.

Champly, Henry. *The Road to Shanghai: White Slave Traffic in Asia.* Translated
by Warre B. Wells. London: John Long, 1933.

Chan, Anthony B. *Arming the Chinese: The Western Armaments Trade in Warlord China, 1920–1928.* Vancouver: University of British Columbia Press,
1982.

Chan, Ming K. "Organized Labor in China under the Nanking Regime, 1927–37:
Some Preliminary Observations of the Shanghai Labor Scene." 1983. N.p.

Chan, Wellington K. K. "The Organizational Structure of the Traditional Chinese
Firm and its Modern Reform." *Business History Review* 56.2 (Summer 1982):
218–35.

Chang, C. W. "Wang Fang." *Inside China Mainland,* June 1987, 30.

———. "Yen Ming-fu." *Inside China Mainland,* May 1987, 31.

Chang, Fu-yun. "The Reformation of the Chinese Customs: A Memoir." Unpublished typescript, ca. 1970.

Chang, Kuo-t'ao. *The Rise of the Chinese Communist Party, 1921–1927.* 2 vols. Lawrence: University Press of Kansas, 1971.

Chang, Maria Hsia. *The Chinese Blue Shirt Society: Fascism and Developmental Nationalism.* Berkeley: Institute of East Asian Studies, University of California, 1985.

———. "'Fascism' and Modern China." *China Quarterly* 79: 553–67.

Chang, Parris H. "The Rise of Wang Tung-hsing, Head of China's Security Apparatus." *China Quarterly* 73 (March 1978): 122–37.

Chang, Ray. "On Chinese Municipal Government." *Chinese Administrator* 24.3 (1935): 265–75.

Chang, Sidney, and Leonard H. D. Gordon. *All Under Heaven . . . Sun Yat-sen and His Revolutionary Thought.* Stanford: Hoover Institution Press, 1991.

Chang, T'ien Fu. "The Campaign against Illiteracy in Shanghai." *China Weekly Review,* 8 June 1935.

Chang Zhaoru. "Guomindang tongzhi shiqi de jingcha zhidu" [The police system during the period of Guomindang rule]. In *Zhongguo jingcha zhidu jianlun* [Brief essays on the Chinese police system], edited by Zhongguo shehui kexue yuan, faxue yanjiusuo, 337–57. Beijing: Qunzhong chubanshe, 1985.

Chen, Pin-ho. "The Militia of Kwangsi." *China Critic* 18.3 (15 July 1937): 58–60.

Chen, Yung-fa. *Making Revolution: The Communist Movement in Eastern and Central China, 1937–1945.* Berkeley, Los Angeles, London: University of California Press, 1986.

Chen Bin. "Chenji sanshiwu nian de 'Zhongguo Fuermosi'" [China's Sherlock Holmes after 35 Years of Silence]. *Jingbao* 1985.5 (May 10): 70.

Chen Dingshan. *Chun Shen jiu wen* [Old news of the Shen (River) in spring]. Taibei: Chenguang yuekan she, n.d.

———. *Chun Shen jiu wen, xu ji* [Old news of the Shen (River) in spring, continued collection]. Taibei: Chenguang yuekan she, n.d.

Chen Gongshu. *Kangzhan houqi fanjian huodong* [Counterespionage activities during the later phase of the War of Resistance]. Taibei: Zhuanji wenxue chubanshe, 1986.

———. *Lanyi she neimu* [The inside story of the Blue Shirt Society]. Shanghai: Guomin xinwen tushu yinshua gongsi, 1942.

———. *Yingxiong wuming: Beiguo chujian* [Anonymous heroes: Weeding out traitors in North China]. Taibei: Zhuanji wenxue chubanshe, 1981.

Chen Guofu. "Shiwu nian zhi shiqi nian jian congshi dangwu gongzuo de huiyi" [Recollections of party affairs during 1926 to 1928]. In *Beifa shiqi de zhengzhi shiliao: yijiuerqi nian de Zhongguo* [Historical documents concerning politics during the period of the Northern Expedition: China in 1927], edited by Jiang Yongjing. Taibei: Zhengzhong shuju, 1981.

Chen Jianhua. "Wuxing zhi gang" [Invisible nets]. *Guangchang* [Square] 3 (October 1990): 26–29.

Chen Junde. "Shanghai xiren jiuliu quyu (sucheng gonggong zujie) jiewai malu kuozhang lüeshi" [An outline history of the expansion of the extra-settlement roads in Shanghai's foreign settlement (commonly known as the international concession)]. *Dongfang zazhi* 28.8 (25 April 1931): 43–47.

Chen Senwen. "Zhong Gong zaoqi tewu gongsuo zhi yanjiu" [Research on the early secret service work of the Chinese Communists]. M.A. thesis, Guoli zhengzhi daxue, Taipei, 1978.

Chen Weimin. "Zhonggong chengli chuqi Shanghai gongren yundong shuping" [On labor movements in Shanghai during the early period after the foundation of the Chinese Communist Party]. Paper presented at the International Symposium on Modern Shanghai, Shanghai Academy of Social Sciences, 7–14 Sept. 1988.

Chen Weiru. "Wode tewu shengya" [My career as a spy]. In *Tegong zongbu— Zhongtong* [Secret service headquarters—Central Statistics], edited by Zhang Wen, 142–88. Hong Kong: Zhongyuan chubanshe, 1988.

Chen Xiuhe. "Kang zhan shengli hou Guomindang jun ru Yue shou xiang jilüe" [Brief account of the Guomindang army entering and accepting the surrender of Vietnam after the victory in the War of Resistance]. In *Wenshi ziliao xuanji* [Selections of historical materials], edited by Chinese People's Political Consultative Conference National Committee, Wenshi ziliao yanjiu weiyuanhui, fascicle 7: 14–29. Beijing: Zhonghua shuju, July 1960.

Chen Xiuliang. "Dang ren hun—ji Pan Hannian (xia)" [The soul of a party man— remembering Pan Hannian (part two)]. *Shanghai tan* [Sands of Shanghai] 1989, no. 1: 12–15.

Chen Yaofu. "Qingmo Shanghai shezhi xunjing de jingguo" [The process of setting up police patrolmen in late Qing Shanghai]. In *Wenshi ziliao xuanji (Shanghai)* [Selections of historical materials (Shanghai)], compiled by Chinese People's Political Consultative Conference, Shanghai weiyuanhui, Wenshi ziliao gongzuo weiyuanhui, fascicle 13: 104–6. Shanghai: Zhonghua shuju, 1962.

Chen Yunwen. *Zhongguo de jingcha* [Police in China]. Shanghai: Commercial Press, 1935.

Cheng, Nien. *Life and Death in Shanghai.* New York: Grove Press, 1987.

Cheng Yiming. *Cheng Yiming huiyilu* [Memoirs of Cheng Yiming]. Beijing: Qunzhong chubanshe, 1979.

Chesneaux, Jean. *The Chinese Labor Movement, 1919–1927.* Translated by H. M. Wright. Stanford: Stanford University Press, 1968.

Chi, Hsi-hseng. *The Chinese Warlord System: 1916–1928.* Washington: American University Center for Research in Social Systems, 1969.

Chiang, Tso-pin. "Achievements of the Ministry of the Interior." *Ten Years of Nationalist China: The China Press Weekly Supplement* 3.16 (18 April 1937): 60.

Chiang Kai-shek, Madame. "Madame Chiang Kai-shek Traces Ideals and Growth during Past Two Years of New Life Movement; Success Achieved." *China Press Double Tenth Supplement.* Shanghai, 1935: 17–19.

Chin, Ko-lin. *Chinese Subculture and Criminality: Nontraditional Crime Groups in America.* Westport, Conn.: Greenwood Press, 1990.

The China Press Weekly Supplement: Ten Years of Nationalist China. Shanghai, 1937.

Chinese Affairs: A Weekly Survey of Important Events Relating to China. Shanghai: International Relations Committee, 1930.

Chinese Student (Chicago, 1936).

Chong, Key Ray. "Cheng Kuan-ying (1841–1920): A Source of Sun Yat-sen's

Nationalist Ideology?" *Journal of Asian Studies* 28.2 (February 1969): 247–67.

Chongdang "Si yi er" da tusha de kuaizishou: dengshang Jiang jia wangchao de zhengzhi tai (1927 nian, ji 40 sui) [Playing the role of an executioner in the great slaughter of April 12: Climbing upon the political platform of the Jiang Dynasty (1927, 40 Years Old)]. N.p., n.d. [A portion of a draft biography of Du Yuesheng prepared by members of the Institute of Modern History in the Shanghai Academy of Social Sciences and given to me by Emily Honig.]

Clark, Paul. "Changsha in the 1930 Red Army Occupation." *Modern China* 7.4 (October 1981): 413–44.

———. *Chinese Cinema: Culture and Politics Since 1949.* Cambridge, England: Cambridge University Press, 1987.

Clifford, Nicholas R. *Shanghai 1925: Urban Nationalism and the Defense of Foreign Privilege.* Michigan Papers on Chinese Studies, No. 37. Ann Arbor: Center for Chinese Studies, University of Michigan, 1979.

———. "The Western Powers and the 'Shanghai Question' in the National Revolution of the 1920s." Paper presented at the International Symposium on Modern Shanghai, Shanghai Academy of Social Sciences, 7–14 Sept. 1988.

Coates, Austin. *China Races.* Hong Kong and New York: Oxford University Press, 1983.

Coble, Parks M., Jr. *The Shanghai Capitalists and the Nationalist Government, 1927–1937.* Cambridge, Mass.: Council on East Asian Studies, Harvard University, 1980.

———. "Superpatriots and Secret Agents: The Blue Shirts and Japanese Secret Services in North China." Paper presented at the Center for Chinese Studies Regional Seminar, Berkeley, 21 Mar. 1987.

Cochran, Sherman, and Andrew C. K. Hsieh, with Janis Cochran. *One Day in China: May 21, 1936.* New Haven and London: Yale University Press, 1983.

Coleman, Maryruth. "Municipal Authority and Popular Participation in Republican Nanjing." Paper presented at the annual meeting of the Association of Asian Studies, San Francisco, 27 Mar. 1983.

Communist International, comp. *Hell over Shanghai.* London: Modern Books, 1932.

Concession Française de Changhai, Direction des Services de Police, Service Politique. Document No. 237/S. *Étude—Le mouvement communiste en Chine, 1920–1933.* Shanghai, 15 Dec. 1933.

Council for the Foreign Settlement of Shanghai. *The Municipal Gazette, Being the Official Organ of the Executive Council of the Foreign Settlement of Shanghai,* vol. 20, 1927.

Crichton, Tom. "Unsung Heroes of China's Ordeal of Japanese Invasion." *Free China Review,* December 1986: 56–60.

Crotty, William J., ed. *Assassinations and the Political Order.* New York: Harper and Row, 1971.

Cumming, John. "The Police Services of the Empire." *United Empire* 21 (October 1930): 538–45.

———. "A Select Booklist for Students of Police Administration." *Police Journal* 4.3 (July 1931): 386–397.

Cyr, Paul. "We Blew the Yellow River Bridge." *Saturday Evening Post,* 23 Mar. 1943.

Dai Li. *Zhengzhi zhentan* [Political detective work]. N.p., n.d.

Dai Yunong xiansheng nianpu [Chronological Biography of Dai Yunong]. Taibei: Guofang bu qingbao ju, 1966.

Davidson-Houston, J. V. *Yellow Creek: The Story of Shanghai.* Philadelphia: Defour Editions, 1964.

De Felice, Renzo. *Il fascismo e l'Oriente: Arabi, ebrei e indiani nella politica di Mussolini.* Bologna: il Mulino, 1988.

Deakin, Frederick W., and G. R. Storry. *The Case of Richard Sorge.* London: Chattow and Windus, 1966.

Deng Baoguang. "Wo suo zhidao de Dai Li he Juntong" [The Dai Li and Military Statistics Bureau that I knew]. *Shanghai wenshi ziliao xuanji* 55: 150–63. Shanghai: Shanghai renmin chubanshe, 1986.

Deng Wenyi. *Congjun baoguo ji* [A record of joining the military and repaying the country]. Taibei: Zhongzheng shuju, 1979.

Deng Youping. "Jianxi 'Zhong-Mei hezuosuo jizhongying'" [A brief analysis of the Sino-American Cooperative Organization's concentration camps]. *Meiguo yanjiu* 1988.3: 26–39.

Deng Yuanzhong. *Sanminzhuyi lixingshe shi* [A history of the Sanminzhuyi lixingshe]. Taibei: Sixian chubanshe, 1984.

Detwiler, Donald S., and Charles Burdick, eds. *War in Asia and the Pacific, 1937–1949.* 15 vols. New York: Garland, 1980.

Di Weimin. "Shanghai zujie liang jianguan yuci neimu." [The inside story of two Shanghai International Settlement policemen who were assassinated]. *Shijie ribao,* part one, 11 Jan. 1985; part two, 12 Jan. 1985; part three, 13 Jan. 1985.

Dirlik, Arif, and Edward S. Krebs. "Socialism and Anarchism in Early Republican China." *Modern China* 7.2 (April 1981): 117–52.

Dobbins, Charles G. "China's Mystery Man." *Collier's* 16 (February 1946): 19, 65–67, 69.

Douthit, Nathan. "Police Professionalism and the War Against Crime in the United States, 1920s–30s." In *Police Forces in History,* edited by George L. Mosse, 317–33. Beverly Hills: Sage Publications, 1975.

Downton, Eric. *Wars Without End.* Toronto: Stoddart Publishing, 1987.

Dray-Novey, Alison Jean. "Policing Imperial Peking: The Ch'ing Gendarmerie, 1650–1850." Ph.D. diss., Harvard University, 1981.

Durdin, Tillman. "U.S. 'Cloak and Dagger' Exploits and Secret Blows in China Bared." *New York Times,* 14 Sept. 1945, 1, 5.

Eastman, Lloyd E. "Facets of an Ambivalent Relationship: Smuggling, Puppets, and Atrocities during the War, 1937–1945." In *The Chinese and the Japanese: Essays in Political and Cultural Interactions,* edited by Akira Iriye, 275–303. Princeton: Princeton University Press, 1980.

———. "Fascism and Modern China: A Rejoinder." *China Quarterly* 80 (December 1979): 838–42.

———. "New Insights into the Nature of the Nationalist Regime." *Republican China* 9.2 (February 1984): 8–18.

———. *Seeds of Destruction: Nationalist China in War and Revolution, 1937–1949.* Stanford: Stanford University Press, 1984.

———. "Who Lost China? Chiang Kai-shek Testifies." *China Quarterly* 88 (December 1981): 658–68.

Edwardes, S. M. *The Bombay City Police: A Historical Sketch, 1672–1916.* London, Bombay, Calcutta, Madras: Oxford University Press, 1923.

Eisenstadt, S. N. *Tradition, Change, and Modernity.* New York: John Wiley and Sons, 1973.

Elkins, W. F. "Fascism in China: The Blue Shirts Society, 1932–37." *Science and Society* 33.4 (1969): 426–33.

Elvin, Mark. "The Administration of Shanghai." In *The Chinese City between Two Worlds,* edited by Mark Elvin and G. William Skinner, 239–62. Stanford: Stanford University Press, 1974.

———. "The Gentry Democracy in Shanghai, 1905–1914." Ph.D. diss., Cambridge University, 1967.

———. "Market Towns and Waterways: The County of Shanghai from 1480–1910." In *The City in Late Imperial China,* edited by G. William Skinner, 441–73. Stanford: Stanford University Press, 1977.

———. "The Revolution of 1911 in Shanghai." *Papers on Far Eastern History* 29 (March 1984): 119–61.

Emsley, Clive. *Crime and Society in England, 1750–1900.* London: Longman, 1987.

Epstein, Israel. *The Unfinished Revolution in China.* Boston: Little, Brown & Co., 1947.

Espinal, Rosario. "Labor, Politics, and Industrialization in the Dominican Republic." Kellogg Institute for International Studies, University of Notre Dame, 1987.

Fairbank, John K. "His Man in Canton." *New York Review of Books,* 28 May 1981.

———. "Review: A Different Kind of War." *Pacific Affairs* 41.2 (summer 1968): 275–76.

Faligot, Roger, and Remi Kauffer. *Kang Sheng et les services secrets chinois (1927–1987).* Paris: Robert Laffont, 1987.

Fang, Fu-an. "Almost Everybody Has His Secret Society in China." *China Weekly Review* 53 (14 June 1930): 60.

Farmer, Rhodes. *Shanghai Harvest: A Diary of Three Years in the China War.* London: Museum Press, 1945.

Feetham, Richard. *Report of the Hon. Richard Feetham, C.M.G., to the Shanghai Municipal Council.* 2 vols. Shanghai: North China Daily News and Herald, 1931.

Fei, Hsiao-tung. *Peasant Life in China: A Field Study of Country Life in the Yangtze Valley.* London: Routledge and Kegan Paul, 1939.

Fei Yunwen. *Dai Li de yi sheng* [The life story of Dai Li]. Taibei: Zhongwai tushu chubanshe, 1980.

Fetter, Frank Whitson. "China and the Flow of Silver." *The Geographical Review* 26.1 (Jan. 1936): 32–47.

Fewsmith, Joseph. "From Guild to Interest Group: The Transformation from Private to Public." Unpublished paper, 1980.

———. *Party, State, and Local Elites in Republican China: Merchant Organizations and Politics in Shanghai, 1890–1930.* Honolulu: University of Hawaii Press, 1985.

————. "Response to Eastman." *Republican China* 9.2 (February 1984): 19–27.

Finch, Percival. "Gun-Running an Organized Business in Shanghai." *China Weekly Review* 37 (3 July 1926): 112.

————. *Shanghai and Beyond.* New York: Charles Scribner's Sons, 1953.

Fitzgerald, John. "Guomindang Political Work in the Armed Forces during the Guangdong Provincial Campaigns, 1925–26." *Papers on Far Eastern History* 32 (September 1985): 71–98.

Fix, Douglas L. "Alternative Activism: Elite Maneuvering in Taiwan in the 1930s." Paper presented at the annual meeting of the Association of Asian Studies, Washington, D.C., 17–19 Mar. 1989.

Fogel, Joshua A. "Liberals, Marxists, and Collaborators: The Research Department of the South Manchurian Railway Company." Paper presented at the Center for Chinese Studies Regional Seminar, Berkeley, 21 Mar. 1987.

Follett, Ken. "The Oldest Boy of British Intelligence." *New York Times Book Review*, 27 Dec. 1987, 5–6.

Fontenoy, Jean. *The Secret Shanghai.* New York: Grey-Hill Press, 1939.

Ford, Franklin L. *Political Murder: From Tyrannicide to Terrorism.* Cambridge, Mass.: Harvard University Press, 1985.

Foucault, Michel. *Discipline and Punish: The Birth of the Prison.* Translated by Allen Sheridan. New York: Pantheon Books, 1977.

Fu, Poshek. "Intellectual Resistance in Shanghai: Wang Tongzhao and a Concept of Resistance Enlightenment, 1937–1939." Paper presented at the annual meeting of the Association for Asian Studies, San Francisco, 24 Mar. 1988.

————. "Passivity, Resistance, and Collaboration: Intellectual Choices in Occupied Shanghai, 1937–1945." Ph.d. diss., Stanford University, 1989.

Fu Xiangyuan. *Qingbang da heng.* [Green Gang bigshots]. Hong Kong: Zhongyuan chubanshe, 1987.

Fung, Edmund S. K. "The Kong-chin-hui: A Late Ch'ing Revolutionary Society." *Journal of Oriental Studies* 11.2 (July 1983): 193–206.

Gamewell, Mary Ninde. *The Gateway to China: Pictures of Shanghai.* New York: Fleming H. Revell Co., 1916.

Gan Guoxun. "Guanyu suowei 'Fuxingshe' de zhenqing shikuang" [The true conditions and actual circumstances of the so-called Fuxingshe]. *Zhuanji wenxue: shang,* 35.3 (September 1979): 32–38; *zhong,* 35.4 (October 1979): 68–73; *xia,* 35.5 (November 1979): 81–86.

Gao, Hwei-shung. "Police Administration in Canton." Parts one, two, and three. *The Chinese Social and Political Science Review* 10.2 (April 1926): 332–54; 10.3 (July 1926): 669–98; 10.4 (October 1926): 872–90.

Gardner, John. "The *Wu-fan* Campaign in Shanghai: A Study in the Consolidation of Urban Control." In *Chinese Communist Politics in Action*, edited by A. Doak Barnett, 477–533. Seattle: University of Washington Press, 1969.

Gaustad, Blaine. "Colonial Police in Africa and India." Seminar paper, University of California, Berkeley, 1983.

Gee, Kennson. "Effect of Freezing on Interior Remittances." *China Weekly Review,* 23 Aug. 1941, 369.

Geisert, Bradley. "Probing KMT Rule: Reflections on Eastman's 'New Insights.'" *Republican China* 9.2 (February 1984): 28–39.

————. "Toward a Pluralist Model of KMT Rule." *Chinese Republican Studies Newsletter* 7.2 (February 1982): 1–10.

Gillin, Donald G. *Warlord: Yen Hsi-shan in Shansi Province, 1911–1949.* Princeton: Princeton University Press, 1967.

Gillin, Donald G., with Charles Etter. "Staying On: Japanese Soldiers and Civilians in China, 1945–1949." *Journal of Asian Studies* 42.3 (May 1983): 497–518.

Gittings, John. *The Role of the Chinese Army.* London: Oxford University Press, 1967.

Goldfield, David R. "The Urban South: A Regional Framework." *American Historical Review* 86.5 (December 1981): 1009–34.

Goldman, Merle. *Literary Dissent in Communist China.* New York: Atheneum, 1971.

Goleman, Daniel. "The Torturer's Mind: A Complex View Emerges." *International Herald Tribune,* 18–19 May 1985, 16.

Goodfellow, Millard Preston. Papers. Hoover Archives, Stanford, California. 4 boxes.

Gould, Randall. "The Unapproachable Police." *China Critic,* 23 May 1935.

Gourlay, Walter E. "'Yellow' Unionism in Shanghai: A Study of Kuomintang Technique in Labor Control, 1927–1937." *Papers on China,* vol. 7: 103–35. Cambridge, Mass.: Harvard University Committee on International and Regional Studies, 1953.

Graham, Gerald S. *The China Station: War and Diplomacy, 1830–1860.* Oxford: Clarendon Press, 1978.

Green, O. M., ed. *Shanghai of Today: A Souvenir Album of Thirty-Eight Vandyke Prints of the "Model Settlement."* Shanghai: Kelly and Walsh, 1927.

Gregor, A. James, and Maria Hsia Chang. "*Nazionalfacismo* and the Revolutionary Nationalism of Sun Yat-sen." *Journal of Asian Studies* 39.1 (November 1979): 21–37.

Greiff, Thomas E. "The Principle of Human Rights in Nationalist China: John C. H. Wu and the Ideological Origins of the 1946 Constitution." *China Quarterly* 103 (September 1985): 441–61.

Groth, Paul Erling. "Forbidden Housing: The Evolution and Exclusion of Hotels, Boarding Houses, Rooming Houses, and Lodging Houses in American Cities, 1880–1930." Ph.D. diss., University of California, Berkeley, 1983.

Gu Sheng, ed. *Dai Li jiangjun yu kang-Ri zhanzheng* [General Dai Li and the War of Resistance against Japan]. Taibei: Huaxin chuban youxian gongsi, 1975.

Guofang bu qingbao ju [Intelligence Office of the Ministry of National Defense], ed. *Dai Yunong xiansheng quanji* [Complete works of Mr. Dai Yunong]. 2 vols. Taibei, 1979.

———. *Zhong-Mei hezuo suo zhi* [History of the Sino-American Cooperative Organization]. Taibei, 1970.

Gurr, Ted Robert. *Rogues, Rebels, and Reformers: A Political History of Urban Crime and Conflct.* Beverly Hills: Sage Publications, 1976.

Gurr, Ted Robert, Peter N. Grabosky, and Richard C. Hula. *The Politics of Crime and Conflict: A Comparative History of Four Cities.* Beverly Hills: Sage Publications, 1977.

Gwynn, Charles W. *Imperial Policing.* London: Macmillan and Co., 1934.

Haishang mingren zhuan bianji bu, eds. *Haishang mingren zhuan* [Biographies of national public figures]. N.p., n.d.

Han, Meng-kuang. "French Colonial Policy in China as Reflected in the Shanghai French Concession." *China Weekly Review*, 23 Jan. 1932, 239–40.

———. "Gambling Dens a Menace to Chinese at Shanghai." *China Weekly Review*, 25 July 1931, 302–3.

———. "Kidnapping in Shanghai." *China Weekly Review*, 17 Jan. 1931, 248.

Hao, Yen-p'ing. "Commercial Revolution in Modern China: The Rise of Sino-Western Commercial Capitalism." Unpublished ms.

Haritos-Fatouros, Mika. "The Official Torturer: A Learning Model for Obedience to the Authority of Violence." Paper to be published in *Journal of Applied Psychology*.

Harootunian, Harry D. "The Function of China in Tokugawa Thought." In *The Chinese and the Japanese: Essays in Political and Cultural Interactions*, edited by Akira Iriye, 9–36. Princeton: Princeton University Press, 1980.

Hauser, Ernest O. *Shanghai: City for Sale*. New York: Harcourt, Brace and Co., 1940.

Hayes, James. *The Hong Kong Region, 1850–1911: Institutions and Leadership in Town and Countryside*. Hamden: Archon Books, 1977.

He Li. *Kang-Ri zhanzheng shi* [History of War to Resist Japan]. Shanghai renmin chubanshe, 1985.

He Qideng. "Dangqian zhi jingzheng jigou wenti" [Problems concerning present-day structures of police administration]. *Lixing yuekan* 2.5 (30 Aug. 1940): 18–23.

He Wenlong. *Zhongguo tewu neimu* [Chinese intelligence services behind the screen]. Hong Kong: Fengyu shuwu, 1947.

Henriot, Christian. "Le gouvernement municipal de Shanghai, 1927–1937." Thèse pour le doctorat de 3ème cycle présenté à l'Université de la Sorbonne Nouvelle (Paris III), June 1983.

———. "Municipal Power and Local Elites." *Republican China* 11.2 (April 1986): 1–21.

———. *Shanghai 1927–1937: Élites locales et modernisation dans la Chine nationaliste*. Paris: Edition l'école des hautes études en sciences sociales, 1991.

Henriques, U. R. Q. "The Rise and Decline of the Separate System of Prison Discipline." *Past and Present* 54 (February 1972): 61–93.

Hergé. *The Blue Lotus*. Tournai: Casterman, 1985.

Hershatter, Gail. "The Class Structure of Shanghai Prostitution, 1920–1949." Paper presented at the annual meeting of the American Historical Association, San Francisco, 28 Dec. 1989.

———. "The Hierarchy of Shanghai Prostitution, 1870–1949." *Modern China* 15.4 (October 1989): 463–98.

———. "Prostitution in Shanghai, 1919–1949." Paper presented at the International Symposium on Modern Shanghai, Shanghai Academy of Social Sciences, 7–14 Sept. 1988.

———. "Regulating Sex in Shanghai: The Reform of Prostitution in 1920 and 1951." In *Shanghai Sojourners*, edited by Frederic Wakeman, Jr. and Wen-hsin Yeh. Berkeley: Institute of East Asian Studies, 1992, 145–85.

———. "The Subaltern Talks Back: Prostitution, Reform, and Gendered Power in Republican China." Paper prepared for a conference entitled "After 'Orientalism': East Asia in Global Cultural Criticism," University of California, Berkeley, 24–25 Apr. 1992.

Hickey, John J. *Our Police Guardians: History of the Police Department of the City of New York.* New York: N.p., 1925.

Historical Research Institute, Chinese Academy of Sciences, and History Department, Beijing University, comp. *Zhongguo shixue lunwen suoyin* [Index of articles on Chinese history]. Beijing kexue chubanshe, 1957, vol. 1.

Hoh Chieh-shiang. "The Shanghai Provisional Court. Its Past, Present and Future." *China Weekly Review*, 10 Oct. 1928, 162–65, 193.

Hoh Chih-hsiang. "Existing Conditions in Chekiang First Prison." *China Weekly Review*, 26 July 1930, 289.

Hong Zuoyao. "Du Yuesheng yu Zhang Xiaolin dajinlaile" [Du Yuesheng and Zhang Xiaolin break their way in]. In *Wenshi ziliao xuanji (Shanghai)* [Selections of historical materials (Shanghai)] compiled by Chinese People's Political Consultative Conference, Shanghai weiyuanhui, Wenshi ziliao gongzuo weiyuanhui, fascicle 14: 40–43. Shanghai: Zhonghua shuju, 1962.

Honig, Emily. *Creating Chinese Ethnicity: Subei People in Shanghai, 1850–1980.* New Haven: Yale University Press, 1992.

——. "Creating Ethnicity: Subei People in Shanghai." Unpublished paper, 1988.

——. "Migrant Culture in Shanghai: In Search of a Subei Identity." N.p., n.d.

——. "The Politics of Prejudice: Subei People in Republican-Era Shanghai." *Modern China* 15.3 (July 1989): 243–74.

——. *Sisters and Strangers: Women in Shanghai Cotton Mills, 1919–1949.* Stanford: Stanford University Press, 1986.

——. "Women Cotton Mill Workers in Shanghai, 1919–1949." Ph.D. diss., Stanford University, 1982.

Houghton, West. "The Shanghai Mind." *China Critic*, 4 June 1931.

Houn, Franklin W. *To Change a Nation: Propaganda and Indoctrination in Communist China.* East Lansing: Michigan State University, 1961.

"How Riots are Dealt with in the Settlement." *Oriental Affairs* 5.2 (February 1936): 67–71.

Hsiao, Kung-chuan. *Rural China: Imperial Control in the Nineteenth Century.* Seattle: University of Washington Press, 1960.

Hsiao, Tso-liang. *Power Relations within the Chinese Communist Movement, 1930–1934: A Study of Documents.* Seattle: University of Washington Press, 1961.

Hsieh, Tu-pi. "The Work of the Ministry of the Interior during the Political Tutelage Period." *China Weekly Review* 46 (10 Oct. 1928): 14.

Hu, Dennis T. "A Linguistic-Literary Approach to Ch'ien Chung-shu's Novel *Wei-ch'eng.*" *Journal of Asian Studies* 37.3 (May 1978): 427–43.

Hu Menghua. "CC waiwei zuzhi Chengshe shimo" [The whole story of the CC front organization in the Sincerity Club]. In *Wenshi ziliao xuanji* [Selections of historical materials], edited by Chinese People's Political Consultative Conference National Committee, Wenshi ziliao yanjiu weiyuanhui, fascicle 14: 147–65. Beijing: Zhonghua shuju, February 1961.

Hu Zhusheng. "Qingbang shi chutan." [A preliminary exploration of the Green Gang]. *Lishi xue jikan* 1979.3: 102–20.

Huang, Shu-min. *The Spiral Road: Change in a Chinese Village through the Eyes of a Communist Party Leader.* Boulder, Colo.: Westview Press, 1989.

Huang Jiqing et al. *Zhongguo faxisi tewu zhen xiang* [The true facts about the Chinese Fascist intelligence services]. N.p.: Xinhua shudian, 1949.

Huang Kangyong. "Wo suo zhidao de Dai Li" [The Dai Li that I knew]. In Wenshi ziliao yanjiu weiyuanhui, eds., *Zhejiang wenshi ziliao xuanji*, no. 23: 152–70. *Neibu* publication. Zhejiang: Renmin chubanshe, 1982.

Huang Qihan. "Gui Xi ji qi fandong de zhengzhi zuzhi" [The Guangxi clique and its reactionary political organizations]. In *Wenshi ziliao xuanji* [Selections of historical materials], edited by Chinese People's Political Consultative Conference National Committee, Wenshi ziliao yanjiu weiyuanhui, fascicle 7: 119–29. Beijing: Zhonghua shuju, July 1960.

Huang Yong. "Huangpu xuesheng de zhengzhi zuzhi ji qi yanbian" [Whampoa students' political organizations and their evolution]. In *Wenshi ziliao xuanji* [Selections of historical materials], edited by Chinese People's Political Consultative Conference National Committee, Wenshi ziliao yanjiu weiyuanhui, fascicle 11: 1–20. Beijing: Zhonghua shuju, November 1960.

Huey, Herbert. "Law and Social Attitudes in 1920s Shanghai." *Hong Kong Law Journal* 14.3 (1984): 306–22.

Hui Hong. *Xingshi jingcha xue* [Criminal police studies]. Shanghai: Commercial Press, 1936.

Hummel, Arthur W. *Eminent Chinese of the Ch'ing Period (1644–1912).* 2 vols. Washington, D.C.: Government Printing Office, 1943.

Hunter, Neale. "The Chinese League of Left-Wing Writers, Shanghai, 1930–1936." Ph.D. diss., Australian National University, August 1973.

Ianni, Francis A. J., with Elizabeth Reuss-Ianni. *A Family Business: Kinship and Social Control in Organized Crime.* New York: Russell Sage Foundation, 1972.

Ingraham, Barton L. *Political Crime in Europe: A Comparative Study of France, Germany, and England.* Berkeley: University of California Press, 1979.

Institute of Pacific Relations, comp. *Agrarian China: Selected Source Materials from Chinese Authors.* Chicago: University of Chicago Press, 1938.

Isaacs, Harold R. "I Break with the Chinese Stalinists." *The New International* 1.3 (September-October 1934): 76–78.

———. *The Tragedy of the Chinese Revolution.* Second revised edition. New York: Atheneum, 1966.

———, ed. *Five Years of Kuomintang Reaction.* Reprinted from the special May 1932 edition of *China Forum.* Shanghai: China Forum Publishing Company, May 1932.

Israel, John. *Student Nationalism in China, 1927–1937.* Stanford: Stanford University Press, 1966.

Jansen, Marius B. *Japan and China: From War to Peace, 1894–1972.* Chicago: Rand McNally, 1975.

Jeans, Roger B. "The Trials of a Third-Force Intellectual: Zhang Junmai (Carson Chang) during the Early Nanjing Decade, 1927–1931." In *Roads Not Taken: The Struggle of Opposition Parties in Twentieth-Century China*, edited by Roger B. Jeans, 37–60. Boulder, San Francisco, and Oxford: Westview Press, 1992.

Jia Yijun, ed. *Zhonghua minguo mingren zhuan* [Eminent men of the Chinese Republic]. 2 vols. Beiping: Wenhua xueshe, 1932–33.

Jiang Fangzhen and Liu Bangji. *Sunzi qianshuo* [A simplified elucidation of the *Sunzi*]. Shanghai: Dazhong shuju, 1930.

Jiang Shaozhen. "Du Yuesheng." In *Minguo renwu zhuan* [Biographies of Republican personages], edited by Li Xin and Sun Sibai, vol. 1: 314–19. Beijing Zhonghua shuju, 1978.

Jiang zongtong xunye huaji bian zuan weiyuanhui, eds., *Jiang zongtong xunye huaji* [A collection of the contributions of President Jiang]. Tabei: Xingzheng yuan xinwenju, 1969.

Jing Shenghong. *Minguo ansha yao'an* [Important assassination cases during the Republic]. Jiangsu: Jiangsu guji chubanshe, 1989.

Jing zheng faling [Police administrative law]. Shanghai: Shanghai canyi hui mishuchu, ca. 1947.

Jingcha faling [Police laws]. N.p., n.d. (ca. 1944, published evidently by the Wang Jingwei Ministry of Interior).

Johnson, Chalmers. *An Instance of Treason: Ozaki Hotsumi and the Sorge Spy Ring*. Stanford: Stanford University Press, 1964.

Johnson, Nelson Trusler. "Blueshirts Organization." Report from Nanking Legation to Secretary of State, 8 May 1937. In *Records of the Department of State Relating to the Internal Affairs of China, 1930–1939*, no. 00/14121 (10 June 1937).

Johnston, Michael. "The Political Consequences of Corruption: A Reassessment." *Comparative Politics* 18.4 (July 1986): 459–77.

Johnstone, William Crane, Jr. *The Shanghai Problem*. Westport, Conn.: Hyperion Press, 1973. Reprint of 1937 edition.

Jonas, George. *Vengeance*. New York: Bantam Books, 1984.

Jordan, Donald A. *The Northern Expedition: China's National Revolution of 1926–1928*. Honolulu: University of Hawaii Press, 1976.

Kangzhan huace [War of Resistance album]. N.p., n.d.

Kaufman, Peter. "The Film 'Street Angel': A Study in Camouflaged Dissent." History seminar paper, University of California at Berkeley, 1982.

Ke Zhaojin. "'Great World' a Must for Amusement Seekers." *China Daily*, 27 Apr. 1985, 5.

Keller, Suzanne. *The Urban Neighborhood: A Sociological Perspective*. New York: Random House, 1968.

Kelley, David E. "Sect and Society: The Evolution of the Luo Sect among Qing Dynasty Grain Tribute Boatmen, 1700–1850." Ph.D. diss., Harvard University, 1986.

Kirby, William C. *Germany and Republican China*. Stanford: Stanford University Press, 1984.

Krebs, Edward S. "Assassination in the Republican Revolutionary Movement." *Ch'ing-shih wen-t'i* 4.6 (December 1981): 45–80.

Krivitsky, Walter G. *In Stalin's Secret Service*. Frederick, Md.: University Publications of America, 1985.

Kuo, Thomas C. *Ch'en Tu-hsiu (1879–1942) and the Chinese Communist Revolution*. South Orange, N.J.: Seton Hall University Press, 1975.

Lamson, H. D. "The Effect of Industrialization upon Village Livelihood: A Study of Fifty Families in Four Villages near the University of Shanghai." *Chinese Economic Journal* 9.4: 1025–82.

———. "The Geographical Distribution of Leaders in China: An Analysis of the Fourth Edition of 'Who's Who in China.'" *China Critic*, 16 Feb. 1933, 176–81.

———. "Influences Which Have Produced Leadership in China—An Analysis of Who's Who in China." *China Weekly Review* 56 (7 Mar. 1931): 490–94.

Landis, Richard B. "Training and Indoctrination at the Whampoa Academy." In *China in the 1920s: Nationalism and Revolution*, edited by F. Gilbert Chan and Thomas H. Etzhold, 73–93. New York: Franklin Watts, 1976.

Lao She. "This Life of Mine." *Chinese Literature*, spring 1985: 94–156.

Lary, Diana. *Region and Nation: The Kwangsi Clique in Chinese Politics, 1925–1937*. Cambridge, England: Cambridge University Press, 1974.

———. "Violence, Fear, and Insecurity: The Mood of Republican China." *Republican China* 10.2 (April 1985): 55–63.

LeCarré, John. *The Little Drummer Girl*. New York: Bantam Books, 1984.

Lee, James S. *The Underworld of the East, Being Eighteen Years' Actual Experiences of the Underworlds, Drug Haunts and Jungles of India, China, and the Malay Archipelago*. London: Sampson Low, Marston & Co., Ltd., preface dated 1935.

Lee, Yip Tin. "Opium Suppression in China." M.A. thesis, Stanford University, 1942.

Legge, James. *The Chinese Classics with a Translation, Critical and Exegetical Notes, Prologomena, and Copious Indexes*. 7 vols. Taibei: Wenxing shudian, 1966.

Lestz, Michael Elliot. "The Meaning of Revival: The Kuomintang 'New Right' and Party Building in Republican China, 1925–1936." Ph.D. diss., Yale University, 1982.

Lethbridge, Henry. *Hong Kong: Stability and Change—a Collection of Essays*. Oxford: Oxford University Press, 1978.

Leung, Yuen-sang. "Regional Rivalry in Mid-Nineteenth-Century Shanghai: Cantonese vs. Ningpo Men." *Ch'ing-shih wen-t'i* 4.8 (December 1982): 29–50.

———. "The Shanghai Taotai: The Linkage Man in a Changing Society, 1843–1890." Ph.D. diss., University of California, Santa Barbara, 1980.

———. "The Shanghai-Tientsin Corridor: A Case-Study of Intraprovincial Relations in Late Nineteenth-Century China." In *Proceedings of the First International Symposium on Asian Studies*, vol. 1: 209–18. Hong Kong, 1979.

Levenson, Joseph R. *Revolution and Cosmopolitanism: The Western Stage and the Chinese Stages*. Berkeley: University of California Press, 1971.

Leyton, Edwin T. *"And I Was There": Pearl Harbor and Midway—Breaking the Secrets*. New York: William Morrow, 1985.

Li, Lincoln. *The Japanese Army in North China, 1937–1941: Problems of Political and Economic Control*. London: Oxford University Press, 1975.

Li, Victor H. "The Development of the Chinese Police during the Late Ch'ing and Early Republican Years." Paper prepared for Professor Jerome Cohen's Seminar on Contemporary Chinese Law, Harvard Law School, May 1965.

"Li Lisan tongzhi dui eryue bagong he wusa yundong de huiyi (fangwen jilu)" [Comrade Li Lisan's reminiscences of the February strike and the May 30th movement (record of an interview)]. In *Wusa yundong shiliao* [Historical materials on the May 30th movement]. Vol. 1, 142–48. Shanghai: Shanghai Academy of Social Sciences, 1981.

Li Tianmin. *Zhou Enlai pingzhuan* [A critical biography of Zhou Enlai]. Hong Kong: Youlian yanjiusuo, 1975.

Li Xixian. "Wei Bangping ren Guangdong shenghui jingcha tingzhang jian Guangdong quan sheng jingwu chuzhang shi de jingcha (yijiuyiqi—yijiuershi)" [The police when Wei Bangping was chief of the Guangdong provincial capital police department and chief of the Guangdong provincial police affairs department (1917–1920)]. In *Guangzhou wenshi ziliao* [Historical materials on Guangzhou], compiled by Chinese People's Political Consultative Conference, Guangdong sheng, Guangzhou shi weiyuanhui, fascicle 11: 105–10. Guangzhou, 1964.

Li Zhaochun. "Shenfen fuza de Pan Hannian" [The complicated identities of Pan Hannian]. *Gongdang wenti yanjiu* 9.3: 114–18.

Liang, Yeung-li. "The New Criminal Code." *China Weekly Review*, 8 Sept. 1928: 61.

Liang Dingming, *Kang zhan huace* [Paintings of the War of Resistance against Japan]. N.p., n.d.

Liang you [Youthful companion]. Shanghai weekly pictorial.

Liangxiong. *Dai Li zhuan* [A biography of Dai Li]. Taibei: Dunhuang shuju (Caves), 1979.

Lin, Yutang. *With Love and Irony*. New York: John Day, 1940.

Lin Xie. "Guomin yijian shu" [Writings on the concept of the citizen]. In *Xinhai geming qian shi nian jian shi lun xuanji* [Anthology of writings from the decade prior to the 1911 Revolution], edited by Zhang Nan and Wang Renzhi, vol. 2: 892–921. Beijing: Xinhua shudian, 1960.

Linz, Juan J. "An Authoritarian Regime: Spain." In *Mass Politics: Studies in Political Sociology*, edited by Erik Allardt and Stein Rokkan, 251–83. New York: Free Press, 1970.

Liu, Hsing Hwa. "Min Tuan of Kwangsi." *China Critic* 17.8 (20 May 1937): 178–80.

Liu, Kwang-ching. "Credit Facilities in China's Early Industrialization: The Background and Implications of Hsu Jun's Bankruptcy in 1883." In *Conference on Modern Chinese Economic History*, 543–53. Taibei: Institute of Economics, Academia Sinica, 1977.

Liu Feng. "Zai wei jingchaju li de douzheng" [The struggle in the collaborationist police force]. In *Wenshi ziliao xuanji Shanghai jiefang sanshi zhounian zhuanji* [Selections of historical materials special collection for the thirtieth anniversary of the liberation of Shanghai], compiled by Chinese People's Political Consultative Conference, Shanghai weiyuanhui, Wenshi ziliao gongzuo weiyuanhui, *shang*, 175–94. Shanghai: Shanghai renmin chubanshe, 1979.

Liu Gong. "Wo suo zhidao de Zhongtong" [The Central Committee Statistics Bureau that I knew]. *Wenshi ziliao xuanji*, no. 36, 59–117. Beijing: Wenshi ziliao chubanshe, December 1962.

Liu Peichu. *Fusheng lüeying ji* [Chapters from a floating life]. Taibei: Zhengzhong shuju, 1968.

Liu Shiji. "Ming-Qing shidai Jiangnan shizhen zhi shuliang fenxi" [Numerical

Analysis of the Towns of Jiangnan during the Ming and Qing Periods]. *Si yu yan* 16.2 (July 1978): 128–49.

Liu Zhaorong. "Huang Chujiu ban Da Shijie" [Huang Chujiu runs the Great World]. In *Shanghai zhanggu* [Shanghai anecdotes], edited by Cao Geng, 77–80. Shanghai: Shanghai wenhua chubanshe, 1982.

Lo, Kuang-pin and Yi-en Yang. *Red Crag.* Beijing: Foreign Languages Press, 1978.

Lockwood, William W., Jr. "The International Settlement at Shanghai, 1924–34." *American Political Science Review* 28.6 (December 1934): 1030–46.

Loh, Robert, and Humphrey Evans. *Escape from Red China.* New York: Coward-McCann, 1962.

Loo, H. M. "The Mania of Gambling." *China Critic* 18.4 (22 July 1937): 82–83.

Lu, Yen-ying. "Can China Become Fascist?" *China Critic,* 14 June 1934: 560–64.

Lu Chongpeng. "Yang Hu yishi liang zi" [Two sets of anecdotes about Yang Hu]. *Zhuanji wenxue* 11.6 (October 1967): 70–73.

Lu Dagong. "Shanghai jingzheng daquan hui dao renmin shouli" [The authority of police administration in Shanghai returns to the hands of the people]. In *Wenshi ziliao xuanji* [Selections of historical materials], compiled by Chinese People's Political Consultative Conference, Shanghai weiyuanhui, Wenshi ziliao gongzuo weiyuanhui, fascicle 37, 61–73. Shanghai: Shanghai renmin chubanshe, 1981.

Lu Xun. "Selected Classical Poems." Translated by J. E. Kowallis. *Renditions* 26 (autumn 1986): 132–50.

Lubot, Eugene. *Liberalism in an Illiberal Age: New Culture Liberals in Republican China, 1919–1937.* Westport, Conn.: Greenwood Press, 1982.

Luo Guangbin. *Hong yan* [Red cliffs]. Beijing: Zhongguo qingnian chubanshe, 1977.

Lutz, Jessie G. "Occupied China and Student Activism in the Christian Colleges." Paper presented at the commemoration of the fiftieth anniversary of the "July 7 Incident," City College of New York, July 1987.

Ma Xisha and Cheng Xiao. "Cong Luo jiao dao Qingbang" [From the Luo sect to the Green Gang]. *Nankai shixue* [Nankai historical studies] 1984.1: 1–28.

Macauley, Melissa. "The Chinese Criminal Code of 1935 in the Transformation of Chinese Criminal Law." M.A. thesis, Georgetown University, 1984.

MacKinnon, Janice R., and Stephen R. MacKinnon. *Agnes Smedley: The Life and Times of an American Radical.* Berkeley: University of California Press, 1988.

MacKinnon, Stephen R. "A Late Qing-GMD-PRC Connection: Police as an Arm of the Modern Chinese State." *Selected Papers in Asian Studies,* new series, paper no. 14 (1983).

———. "Police Reform in Late Ch'ing Chihli." *Ch'ing-shih wen-t'i* 3.4 (December 1975): 82–99.

MacKinnon, Stephen R., and Oris Friesen. *China Reporting: An Oral History of American Journalism in the 1930s and 1940s.* Berkeley: University of California Press, 1987.

MacPherson, Kerrie L. "Designing China's Urban Future: The Greater Shanghai Plan, 1927–1937." *Planning Perspectives* 5 (1990): 39–62.

———. *A Wilderness of Marshes: The Origins of Public Health in Shanghai, 1843–1893.* Hong Kong and New York: Oxford University Press, 1987.

Madancy, Joyce Ann. "Propaganda Versus Practice: Official Involvement in the Opium Trade in China, 1927–1945." M.A. thesis, Cornell University, 1983.

Mann, Susan. *Local Merchants and the Chinese Bureaucracy, 1750–1950*. Stanford: Stanford University Press, 1987.

Mao Dun [Shen Yanbing]. *Fushi* [Corrosion]. Chengdu: Sichuan renmin chubanshe, 1981.

———. "The Road I Travelled." *Chinese Literature*, July 1981, 9–39.

Mao Tun [Shen Yanbing]. "Comedy." In *Straw Sandals: Chinese Short Stories, 1918–1933*, edited by Harold Isaacs. Cambridge, Mass.: MIT Press, 1974.

———. *Midnight*. Beijing: Foreign Languages Press, 1979.

Mao Xiaocen. "Jiu Shanghai de da duku—huili qiuchang" [A big gambling den of old Shanghai—the Jaialai fronton]. In *Wenshi ziliao xuanji (Shanghai)* [Selections of historical materials (Shanghai)], compiled by Chinese People's Political Consultative Conference, Shanghai weiyuanhui, Wenshi ziliao gongzuo weiyuanhui, fascicle 15: 128–48. Shanghai: Zhonghua shuju, 1963.

Mao Xiaotian and Wang Mengyun. "Wang Wei 'tegong zongbu' qishiliu hao de jianli" [The creation of no. 76 "special mission headquarters" of Wang the Usurper]. In *Wang Jingwei guomin zhengfu chengli* [The founding of Wang Jingwei's nationalist government], edited by Huang Meizhen and Zhang Yun. Shanghai: Renmin chubanshe, 1984.

Marsh, Susan H. "Chou Fo-hai: The Making of a Collaborator." In *The Chinese and the Japanese: Essays in Political and Cultural Interactions*, edited by Akira Iriye, 304–27. Princeton: Princeton University Press, 1980.

Marshall, Jonathan. "Opium and the Politics of Gangsterism in Nationalist China, 1927–1945." *Bulletin of the Committee of Concerned Asian Scholars* 8.3 (July-September 1977): 19–48.

Martin, Brian G. "The Green Gang and the Guomindang Polity in Shanghai 1927–1937." Paper presented to the biennial conference of the Association of Asian Studies of Australia, Griffith University, Queensland, July 1990.

———. "The Green Gang and 'Party Purification' in Shanghai: Green Gang-Kuomintang Relations, 1926–1927." Symposium on the Nanking Decade, 1928–1937: Man, Government and Society. Taibei, 15–17 Aug. 1983.

———. "'The Pact with the Devil': The Relationship Between the Green Gang and the French Concession Authorities, 1925–1935." In *Shanghai Sojourners*, edited by Frederic Wakeman, Jr. and Wen-hsin Yeh, 266–304. Berkeley: Institute of East Asian Studies, 1992.

———. "Tu Yueh-sheng and Labour Control in Shanghai: The Case of the French Tramways Union, 1928–32." *Papers on Far Eastern History* 32 (September 1985): 99–137.

———. "Warlords and Gangsters: The Opium Traffic in Shanghai and the Creation of the Three Prosperities Company, 1913–1926." Paper presented at the sixth national conference of the Asian Studies Association of Australia, Sydney, 11–16 May 1986.

Matossian, Mary. "Ideologies of Delayed Industrialization: Some Tensions and Ambiguities." In *Political Change in Underdeveloped Countries: Nationalism and Communism*, edited by John H. Kautsky, 252–64. New York: Wiley and Sons, 1962.

Maze, Frederic W. "Japanese Smuggling in North China." *China Quarterly,* 15 Oct. 1937, 597–607.

McAlary, Mike. *Buddy Boys: When Good Cops Turn Bad.* New York: Charter Books, 1989.

McCormack, Gavan. *Chang Tso-lin in Northeast China, 1911–1928: China, Japan and the Manchurian Idea.* Stanford: Stanford University Press, 1977.

McCormick, Elsie. *Audacious Angles on China.* New York: D. Appleton and Company, 1923.

Meng, C. Y. W. "The 'Hwa Hui' Gambling Evil." *China Weekly Review* 47 (19 Jan. 1929): 334.

———. "A Tale of Two Cities." *China Weekly Review,* 27 July 1929, 420.

Meng Zhen. "Zhongtong diandi (zhiyi)" [A bit about Central Statistics (part 1)]. *Jiushi niandai yuekan* [Nineties monthly], June 1986, 89–91.

———. "Zhongtong diandi" [A bit about Central Statistics (part 2)]. *Jiushi niandai yuekan* [Nineties monthly], July 1986, 87–89.

Merrill, Frederick T. *Japan and the Opium Menace.* New York: Institute of Pacific Relations and the Foreign Policy Association, 1942.

Merton, Robert K. *Social Theory and Social Structure.* New York: Free Press, 1968.

Meyer, John C., Jr. "Definitional and Etiological Issues in Police Corruption: Assessment and Synthesis of Competing Perspectives." *Journal of Police Science and Administration* 4.1 (March 1976): 46–55.

Mi Xi. "Wo zai Jiang Jieshi shenbian de shihou" [While I Was at Chiang Kai-shek's Side]. In *Zhejiang wenshi ziliao xuanji* [Selections of historical documents on Zhejiang], compiled by Wenshi ziliao yanjiu weiyuanhui, fascicle 23: 1–41. *Neibu* publication. Zhejiang: Renmin chubanshe, 1982.

Migdahl, Joel S. *Strong Societies and Weak States: State-Society Relations and State Capabilities in the Third World.* Princeton: Princeton University Press, 1988.

Miles, Milton E. *A Different Kind of War: The Little-Known Story of the Combined Guerrilla Forces Created in China by the U.S. Navy and the Chinese during World War II.* Garden City, N.Y.: Doubleday and Company, 1967.

———. Papers. Hoover Archives, Stanford, California.

Mitchell, J. Clyde. "Networks, Norms and Institutions." In *Network Analysis: Studies in Human Interaction,* edited by Jeremy Boissevain and J. Clyde Mitchell, 15–35. The Hague, Paris: Mouton, 1973.

Molotsky, Irvin. "OSS Lives Again at Spies Reunion." *New York Times,* 21 Sept. 1986, 37.

Monas, Sidney. "The Political Police: The Dream of a Beautiful Autocracy." In *The Transformation of Russian Society: Aspects of Social Change Since 1861,* edited by Cyril E. Black, 164–90. Cambridge, Mass.: Harvard University Press, 1960.

Morley, James William, ed. *The China Quagmire: Japan's Expansion on the Asian Continent, 1933–1941.* New York: Columbia University Press, 1983.

Mu Xin. *Chen Geng tongzhi zai Shanghai* [Comrade Chen Geng at Shanghai]. Beijing: Wenshi ziliao chubanshe, 1980.

Murphy, Charles J. V. "Shanghai: Reopened under New Management." *Fortune*, February 1946, 141–48, 206–23.

Murray, Dian. "Mid-Ch'ing Piracy: An Analysis of Organizational Attributes." *Ch'ing-shih wen-t'i* 4.8 (December 1982): 1–28.

Myer, Michael et al. "The Gangs of Asia." *Newsweek*, 1 Apr. 1985, 8–12.

Nettler, Gwynn. *Explaining Crime.* New York: McGraw-Hill, 1974.

Niu Xianming. "Kangzhan shiqi Zhongguo qingbao zhan suyi" [Recollections on Chinese intelligence warfare during the War of Resistance]. *Zhuanji wenxue* 27.6 (December 1975): 7–10.

Number Two National Archives.

Nye, Robert A. "Crime in Modern Societies: Some Research Strategies for Historians." *Journal of Social History* 11.4 (1978): 491–507.

Nym Wales and Kim San. *Song of Ariran: A Korean Communist in the Chinese Revolution.* San Francisco: Ramparts Press, 1972.

Oakes, Vanya. *White Man's Folly.* Boston: Houghton Mifflin, 1943.

O'Brien, Patricia. *The Promise of Punishment: Prisons in Nineteenth Century France.* Princeton: Princeton University Press, 1982.

Office of Strategic Services Archives, War Department. U.S. National Archives, Military Reference Division.

Office of Strategic Services, U.S. Army. U.S. National Archives, Military Reference Division.

Orchard, John E. "Shanghai." *Geographical Review* 26.1 (January 1936): 1–31.

Osaka Mainichi and the Tokyo Nichi Nichi Supplement: The China Emergency, 20 Oct. 1937.

Oura Kanetake. "The Police of Japan." In *Fifty Years of New Japan,* compiled by Okuma Shigenobu, vol. 1: 281–95. New York: E. P. Dutton, 1909.

Pal, John. *Shanghai Saga.* London: Jarrolds, 1963.

Palmer, Stanley H. *Police and Protest in England and Ireland, 1780–1850.* Cambridge, England: Cambridge University Press, 1988.

Pan Ling. *In Search of Old Shanghai.* Hong Kong: Joint Publishing Company, 1982.

———. *Old Shanghai: Gangsters in Paradise.* Hong Kong: Heinemann Asia, 1984.

Papp, E. "General Chiang Kai-shek." CID office notes in Shanghai Municipal Police (International Settlement) Files, D-529, 25 Sept. 1929. Microfilms from the U.S. National Archives.

Parker, Alfred E. *The Berkeley Police Story.* Springfield, Ill.: Charles C. Thomas, 1972.

———. *Crime Fighter: August Vollmer.* New York: Macmillan Co., 1961.

Parssinen, Terry M., and Kathryn B. Meyer. "International Narcotics Trafficking in the Early Twentieth Century: Development of an Illicit Industry." Unpublished paper.

Perdue, Peter. "*Liumin* and Famine Relief in Eighteenth-Century China." Unpublished ms.

Perkins, Dwight. "Government as an Obstacle to Industrialization: The Case of Nineteenth-Century China." *Journal of Economic History* 27.4 (December 1967): 478–92.

Perry, Elizabeth J. "Collective Violence in China, 1880–1980." *Theory and Society* 13 (1984): 427–54.

———. "Shanghai on Strike: Work and Politics in the Making of a Chinese Proletariat." Paper presented at the International Symposium on Modern Shanghai, Shanghai Academy of Social Sciences, 7–14 Sept. 1988.

———. "Tax Revolt in Late Qing China: The Small Swords of Shanghai and Liu Depei of Shandong." *Late Imperial China* 6.1 (June 1985): 83–112.

Peters, Edward. *Torture*. New York: Basil Blackwell, 1985.

Pickowicz, Paul G. *Marxist Literary Thought in China: The Influence of Ch'ü Ch'iu-pai*. Berkeley, Los Angeles, London: University of California Press, 1981.

Pileggi, Nicholas. *Wise Guy: Life in a Mafia Family*. New York: Pocketbooks, 1985.

Pincher, Chapman. *Too Secret Too Long: The Great Betrayal of Britain's Crucial Secrets and the Coverup*. London: Sidgwick and Jackson, 1984.

Plate, Thomas, and Andrea Darvi. *Secret Police: The Inside Story of a Network of Terror*. Garden City, N.Y.: Doubleday, 1981.

Poretsky, Elisabeth K. *Our Own People: A Memoir of "Ignace Reiss" and His Friends*. London: Oxford University Press, 1969.

Powell, John B. *My Twenty-five Years in China*. New York: Macmillan Co., 1945.

Price, Don C. "Sung Chiao-jen's Political Strategy in 1912." Paper delivered at the Conference on the Chinese Republic and Its History, Institute of Modern History, Academia Sinica, Taipei, August 1983.

Qi Jingwu. "Fuxingshe Henan fenshe de pianduan huiyi" [Fragments of reminiscences about the Fuxingshe branch in Henan]. In *Henan wenshi ziliao* [Historical materials on Henan], compiled by Chinese People's Political Consultative Conference, Henan sheng weiyuanhui, Wenshi ziliao yanjiu weiyuanhui, fascicle 5, 107–14. Henan: Henan renmin chubanshe, 1981.

Qi Zaiyu. *Shanghai shi renzhi* [Current biographical gazetteer of Shanghai]. Shanghai: Zhanwang chubanshe, 1947.

Qian Jun. "Hongdui" [Red brigade]. *Gongdang wenti yanjiu* 8.7: 94–104.

Qian Shengke, ed. *Shanghai heimu huibian* [A classified compendium from behind Shanghai's black screen]. 4 vols. Shanghai: Haishang zhentan yanjiu hui, 1929.

Qiao Jiacai. *Dai Li jiangjun he tade tongzhi: kang-Ri qingbao zhan di yi, er ji* [General Dai Li and his comrades: Intelligence war in the War of Resistance, sets one and two]. Taibei: Zhongwai tushu chubanshe, 1981.

———. "Dai Li xiansheng de renqingwei," parts 1, 2, and 3. *Zhongwai zazhi*, vol. 13, nos. 1, 3, 4.

———. *Haoran ji* [Record of magnanimity]. 4 vols. Taibei: Zhongwai tushu chubanshe, 1981.

Qiu Yuping. "Wo suo zhidao de Zhongyi jiuguo jun" [What I know about the Loyal and Patriotic Army]. In *Wenshi ziliao xuanji* [Selections of historical materials], compiled by China People's Political Consultative Conference, Shanghai shi weiyuanhui, Wenshi ziliao gongzuo weiyuanhui, fascicle 39: 124–32. Shanghai: Shanghai renmin chubanshe, 1982.

Qu Yunzhang. "Guomindang Junweihui xibei qingnian laodong ying de zhen-xiang" [The true facts of the Northwestern Youth Labor Camp of the Military Committee, Nationalist Party]. *Wenshi ziliao xuanji*, no. 36: 118–38. Beijing: Wenshi ziliao chubanshe, December 1962.

Qunzhong chubanshe, eds. *Jiang bang tewu zuixing lu* [A record of the crimes of the Jiang gang's special services]. Beijing: Qunzhong chubanshe, 1979.

Raab, Selwyn. "John Gotti: Running the Mole." *New York Times Magazine*, 2 Apr. 1989, 30–33, 42, 70–71, 80–82, 92.

Rankin, Mary Backus. *Elite Activism and Political Transformation in China: Zhejiang Province, 1865–1911*. Stanford: Stanford University Press, 1986.

Rawski, Evelyn S. "Education and Mobility in Republican China." Paper presented at the Regional Seminar in Chinese Studies, Center for Chinese Studies, 11–12 Apr. 1986.

Rissov, Constantin. *Le dragon enchaîné: De Chiang Kai-shek à Mao Ze Dong—Trente-cinq ans d'intimité avec la Chine*. Paris: Robert Laffont, 1985.

Robinson, Cyril D. "The Mayor and the Police—the Political Role of the Police in Society." In *Police Forces in History*, edited by George L. Mosse, 217–315. Beverly Hills: Sage Publications, 1975.

Romanus, Charles F., and Riley Sunderland. *United States Army in World War II: China-Burma-India Theater*. Vol. 3, *Time Runs Out in CBI*. Washington, D.C.: Office of the Chief of Military History, Department of the Army, 1959.

Rosen, Christine Meisner. "Great Fires and the Problems and Processes of City Growth." Ph.D. diss., Harvard University, 1980.

Rosinger, Laurence K. *China's Wartime Politics, 1937–1944*. Princeton: Princeton University Press, 1944.

Rowe, William. *Hankow: Commerce and Society in a Chinese City, 1796–1889*. Stanford: Stanford University Press, 1984.

———. *Hankow: Conflict and Community in a Chinese City, 1796–1895*. Stanford: Stanford University Press, 1989.

———. "The Public Sphere in Modern China." *Modern China* 16.3 (July 1990): 309–29.

———. "The Qingbang and Collaboration under the Japanese, 1939–1945: Materials in the Wuhan Municipal Archives." *Modern China* 8.4 (October 1982): 491–99.

———. "Urban Control in Late Imperial China: The *Pao-chia* System in Hankow." In *Perspectives on a Changing China: Essays in Honor of C. Martin Wilbur on the Occasion of His Retirement*, edited by Joshua A. Fogel and William T. Rowe, 89–112. Boulder, Colo.: Westview Press, 1979.

Rudé, George. *Criminal and Victim: Crime and Society in Early Nineteenth-Century England*. Oxford: Clarendon Press, 1985.

Schaller, Michael. "Changing American Strategic and Political Views of China, Japan and Southeast Asia, 1945–1953." International Conference on the United States and the Asia-Pacific Region in the Twentieth Century. Chinese Academy of Social Sciences, Beijing, 23 May 1991.

———. *The U.S. Crusade in China, 1938–1945*. New York: Columbia University Press, 1979.

Schoppa, R. Keith. *Chinese Elites and Political Change: Zhejiang Province in the Early Twentieth Century*. Cambridge, Mass.: Harvard University Press, 1982.

Schwarcz, Vera. "The Chinese Enlightenment: The May Fourth Movement and the Intellectuals' Legacy." Unpublished ms.

Schwartz, Benjamin I. "The Primacy of the Political Order in East Asian Societies: Some Preliminary Generalizations." In *Foundations and Limits of State Power in China*, edited by S. R. Schram, 187–202. Hong Kong: Chinese University Press, 1987.

Scott, A. C. *Actors Are Madmen: Notebook of a Theatregoer in China*. Madison: University of Wisconsin Press, 1982.

Seabrook, Jeremy. "The Heroin Trade: Paradigm of Mrs. Thatcher's Capitalism." *The Guardian*, 21 May 1983, 8.

Seagrave, Sterling. *The Soong Dynasty*. New York: Harper and Row, 1985.

Seybolt, Peter J. "Terror and Conformity: Counterespionage, Campaigns, Rectification, and Mass Movements, 1942–1943." *Modern China* 21.1 (January 1986): 39–73.

The Shanghai Incident. Shanghai: The Press Union, 1932.

Shanghai jiefang yinian, 1949–1950. [A year of Shanghai's liberation]. Shanghai: Jiefang ribao she, 1950.

Shanghai Municipal Council. *Report for the Year 1937 and Budget for the Year 1938*. Shanghai: North China Daily News and Herald, 1938.

———. *Annual Report, 1939*. Shanghai: North China Herald, 1940.

Shanghai Municipal Police (International Settlement) Files. Microfilms from the U.S. National Archives.

Shanghai shehui kexue yuan, comp. *Jiuyiba-yierba, Shanghai junmin kang-Ri yundong shiliao* [Historical materials on the Shanghai army and people's anti-Japanese movement from September 18 to January 28]. Shanghai: Shanghai shehui kexue yuan, 1986.

Shanghai shehui kexue yuan, zhengzhi falü yanjiusuo, shehui wenti zu, comp. *Da liumang Du Yuesheng* [Big gangster Du Yuesheng]. Beijing: Qunzhong chubanshe, 1965.

Shanghai shehui kexue yuan jingji yanjiusuo, eds. *Rong jia qiye shiliao* [Historical materials on the Rong Family Enterprise], vol. 1, 1896–1937. Shanghai: Shanghai renmin chubanshe, 1980.

Shanghai shenmi zhinan. [Guide to Shanghai's mysteries]. N.p., n.d.

Shanghai shi dang'anguan, ed. *Shanghai jiefang* [The liberation of Shanghai]. Shanghai: Dang'an chubanshe, 1989.

Shanghai shi gonganju gongan shi ziliao zhengji yanjiu lingdao xiaozu bangongshi, comp. "Cuihui jiu jingcha jigou, baowei renmin zhengquan" [Smashing the old police organs, protecting the people's sovereignty]. In *Shanghai wenshi ziliao xuanji*, vol. 46 (1984): 104–18.

Shanghai shi gonganju yewu baogao [Shanghai Municipality Public Security Bureau report of affairs], vol. 3 (July 1929–June 1930).

Shanghai shi gonganju yewu baogao [Shanghai Municipality Public Security Bureau report of affairs], vol. 4 (July 1930–June 1931); vol. 5 (July 1931–June 1932).

Shanghai shi nianjian weiyuanhui, comp. *Shanghai shi nianjian* [Annual mirror of Greater Shanghai], vol. 1 (1935); vol. 2 (1936). Shanghai: Shanghai shi tong-zhi guan, 1935.

Shanghai shi tongzhi guan nianjian weiyuanhui, comp. *Shanghai shi nianjian* [Annual mirror of Greater Shanghai]. Shanghai: Zhonghua shuju, 1937.

Shanghai shiren zhi [Who's who in Shanghai]. Shanghai: Zhanwang chubanshe, 1947.

Shanghai tebie shi gonganju yewu jiyao, Minguo shiliu nian ba yue zhi shiqi nian qi yue [Summary of the affairs of the Shanghai Special Municipality Public Security Bureau from August 1927 to July 1928]. Shanghai: Shanghai Municipal Public Security Bureau, 1928.

Shanghai tongshe, comp. *Shanghai yanjiu ziliao* [Research materials on Shanghai]. Shanghai: Zhonghua shuju, 1936.

———, comp. *Shanghai yanjiu ziliao, xuji* [Research materials on Shanghai, continued]. Shanghai, n.d.

Shanghai tushuguan, comp. *Shanghai difang ziliao; xiwen zhuzhe mulu* [Local materials on Shanghai: Western-language authors catalog]. Shanghai: Shanghai tushuguan, 1963.

Shanghai xin mao [The new appearance of Shanghai]. Shanghai: Shanghai renmin meishu chubanshe, 1965.

Shanghai zhanshi huakan [Shanghai war pictorials], no. 1, 25 Feb. 1932.

Shanghai zujie wenti [The Shanghai concessions problem]. Taibei: Zhengzhong shuju, 1981.

Shao Ping, Zhang Yuanyou, and Li Ying. "Guomindang 'Zhongtong' zai Chengdu de fandong xinwen huodong" [The reactionary journalistic activities of the Guomindang's "Central Statistics (Bureau)" in Chengdu]. In *Sichuan wenshi ziliao xuanji* [Selections of historical documents on Sichuan], compiled by Chinese People's Political Consultative Conference, Sichuan weiyuanhui, Wenshi ziliao yanjiu weiyuanhui, fascicle 24, 64–72. Chengdu: Sichuan renmin chubanshe, 1981.

Shao Shi. *Du Yuesheng chuanqi.* [The legend of Du Yuesheng]. Beijing: Tuanjie chubanshe, 1988.

Shao Yong. "Ershi shiji chuqi Qingbang zai Shanghai jiaoxian de huodong" [Activities of the Green Gang in counties bordering Shanghai during the early part of the twentieth century]. In *Shanghai yanjiu luncong* [Papers on Shanghai studies], fascicle 5, 163–66. Shanghai: Shanghai shehui kexueyuan chubanshe, 1990.

Shen Yi. "Shanghai shi gongwuju shi nian" [Ten years in the Shanghai Municipal Bureau of Works]. *Zhuanji wenxue*, part 1: vol. 70, no. 2 (August 1970): 11–18; part 2: vol. 70, no. 3 (September 1970): 25–30; part 3: vol. 70, no. 4 (October 1970): 81–85.

Shen Zhongyu. "'Si yi er' shibian zai Huangpu xuexiao" [The April Twelfth Incident at the Huangpu Academy]. In *Guangzhou wenshi ziliao* [Historical materials on Guangzhou], compiled by Zhengxie Guangdong sheng Guangzhou shi weiyuanhui, Wenshi ziliao yanjiu weiyuanhui, fascicle 6, 77–79. Guangzhou, 1962.

Shen Zui. *Dalu shenghuo sanshi nian* [Thirty years of life on the mainland]. 2 vols. Hong Kong: Jingbao wenhua qiye youxian gongsi, 1983.

———. "Jiang Jieshi zhunbei ansha Li Zongren de yinmo" [Chiang Kai-shek's secret plot to assassinate Li Zongren]. *Wenshi ziliao xuanji,* no. 32: 118–21. Beijing: Wenshi ziliao chubanshe, December 1962.

———. *Juntong neimu* [The inside story of the Military Statistics (Bureau)]. Beijing: Wenshi ziliao chubanshe, 1984.

———. *A KMT War Criminal in New China.* Translated by Liang Xintu and Sun Binghe. Beijing: Foreign Languages Press, 1986.

———. "Wo suo zhidao de Dai Li" [The Dai Li I knew]. In Shen Zui and Wen Qiang, *Dai Li qi ren* [Dai Li the man], 1–176. Beijing: Wenshi ziliao chubanshe, 1980.

———. "Zhongmei tezhong jishu hezuo suo neimu" [Inside story of the Sino-American Cooperation Office]. *Wenshi ziliao xuanji,* no. 32: 213–61. Beijing: Wenshi ziliao chubanshe, December 1962.

Sheng Ke. *Qing Hong bang zhi heimu* [Behind the black curtain of the Green and Red gangs]. Shijiazhuang: Hebei renmin chubanshe, 1990.

Sherman, Lawrence W. *Scandal and Reform: Controlling Police Corruption.* Berkeley: University of California Press, 1978.

Shi Zhikang. "Palace's Colourful Activities." *China Daily,* 10 Feb. 1984.

Shimada Toshihiko. "The Extension of Hostilities, 1931–1932." Translated by Akira Iriye. In *Japan Erupts: The London Naval Conference and the Manchurian Incident, 1928–1932,* edited by James William Morley, 241–335. New York: Columbia University Press, 1984.

Shizheng gaikuang [Survey of the municipal government]. Shanghai: Printing Office of the Secretariat of the Shanghai Special Municipality, 1928.

Shu Jiheng. "Guomindang Juntong ju zai Tianjin de tewu huodong gaikuang" [A sketch of the Guomindang's MSB in Tianjin]. *Tianjin wenshi ziliao xuanji,* no. 26: 169–76.

Sih, Paul T. K., ed. *The Strenuous Decade: China's Nation-Building Efforts, 1927–1937.* New York: St. John's University Press, 1970.

Silliman, Adam Borut. "Sino-Foreign Conflict and the Extra-Settlement Roads of Shanghai." Senior essay in History, Yale University, 1989.

Sima Qian. *Shi ji* [Records of the historian]. 6 vols. Hong Kong: Zhonghua shuju, 1969.

Simon, Herbert A. "Notes on the Observation and Measurement of Political Power." *Journal of Politics* 15 (November 1953): 500–516.

Smart, Alan. "The Informal Regulation of Illegal Economic Activities: Comparisons Between the Squatter Property Market and Organized Crime." Paper to be published in *International Journal of the Sociology of Law.*

———. "Invisible Real Estate: Investigations into the Squatter Property Market." *International Journal of Urban and Regional Research* 10.1 (1986): 29–45.

Smith, Phillip Thurmond. *Policing Victorian London: Political Policing, Public Order, and the London Metropolitan Police.* Westport, Conn.: Greenwood Press, 1985.

Snow, Edgar. *The Battle for Asia.* Cleveland: The World Publishing Company, 1942.

———. "How 5,200 Policemen Keep Order in Canton." *China Weekly Review,* 29 Nov. 1930.

Snyder, David. "Theoretical and Methodological Problems in the Analysis of Governmental Coercion and Collective Violence." *Journal of Political and Military Sociology* 1976, no. 4 (fall): 277–93.

Sokolsky, George E. "China in Search of a Government." *North China Daily News,* 30 Nov. 1928.

———. "Third Party Congress and Its Work." *North China Daily News,* 10 Apr. 1929.

———. "What Stops Progress in Nanking?" *North China Daily News,* 16 Nov. 1928.

Songhu yu Ri xuezhan da huabao [Illustrated review of the bloody conflict with Japan in Shanghai]. Shanghai: Wenhua meishu tushu gongsi yinyang, n.d.

Spence, Jonathan D. *The Gate of Heavenly Peace: The Chinese and Their Revolution, 1895–1980.* New York: Viking, 1981.

———. "Opium Smoking in Ch'ing China." In Frederic Wakeman, Jr. and Carolyn Grant, eds., *Conflict and Control in Late Imperial China,* 143–73. Berkeley: University of California Press, 1975.

Spunt, Georges. *A Place in Time.* New York: G. P. Putnam's Sons, 1968.

Staub, Ervin. "Social Evil: Perpetrators and Bystanders of Cruelty." Paper presented at the meetings of the International Society of Political Psychology, Washington, D.C., 1982.

Steele, A. T. *Shanghai and Manchuria, 1932: Recollections of a War Correspondent.* Tempe: Center for Asian Studies, Arizona State University, 1977.

Sterling, Abigail. "The Whangpoo Conservancy Board, 1912–1927." Seminar paper, University of California, Berkeley, 1978.

Strand, David G. "Feuds, Fights, and Factions: Group Politics in 1920s Beijing." *Modern China* 11.4 (October 1985): 411–35.

———. *Rickshaw Beijing: City People and Politics in the 1920s.* Berkeley: University of California Press, 1989.

Stratton, Roy. "Navy Guerrilla." *United States Naval Institute Proceedings,* 83–87. July 1963.

Strauss, Julia Candace. "Bureaucratic Reconstruction and Institution-Building in the Post-Imperial Chinese State: The Dynamics of Personnel Policy, 1912–1945." Ph.D. diss., University of California, Berkeley, 1991.

Stross, Randy. "Marketing and Modernization in Republican China's Countryside: The Puzzling Case of Western Jiangsu." *Republican China* 9.2 (February 1984): 1–7.

Su Shouzu. "Zongcai jingxun tixi" [Planning a system of police training]. In *Shanghai jingcha* [Shanghai police], edited by Zhu Yisheng, 27–35. Shanghai: Shanghai shi jingcha mishushi, 1946.

Su Zhiliang. "Shanghai banghui shi gaishu" [A summary of the history of secret societies in Shanghai]. Paper presented at the International Symposium on Modern Shanghai, Shanghai Academy of Social Sciences, 7–14 Sept. 1988.

Sues, Ilona Ralf. *Shark Fins and Millet.* Garden City, N.Y.: Garden City Publishing Co., 1944.

Sun, Lung-kee. "The Shanghai Intellectual Community, 1927–1937: A Research Note." *Chinese Republican Studies Newsletter* 8.1 (October 1982): 17–19.

Sun Guoqun. "Lun jiu Shanghai changji zhidu de fazhan he tedian" [On the development and characteristics of the prostitute system in old Shanghai]. Paper presented at the International Symposium on Modern Shanghai, Shanghai Academy of Social Sciences, 7–14 Sept. 1988.

Sun Yat-sen. *The International Development of China*. New York: G. P. Putnam's Sons, 1922.

Sun Yufeng. "Du Yuesheng de liumang shouduan" [Du Yuesheng's gangster methods]. In *Wenshi ziliao xuanji (Shanghai)* [Selections of historical materials (Shanghai)], compiled by Chinese People's Political Consultative Conference, Shanghai weiyuanhui, Wenshi ziliao gongzuo weiyuanhui, fascicle 14, 43–46. Shanghai: Zhonghua shuju, 1962.

Takahashi, Yusai. *The Patrol System*. Berkeley, 1938.

Tang Tao. "Zhong-Mei hezuosuo di liu tezhong jishu xunlian ban neimu" [The inside story of the sixth special training unit of SACO]. In *Fujian wenshi ziliao xuanji* [Selections of historical documents on Fujian], compiled by Chinese People's Political Consultative Conference, Fujian weiyuanhui, Wenshi ziliao bianji shi, fascicle 4, 148–63. Fuzhou: Fujian renmin chubanshe, 1980.

Tang Zhenchang. "Zai Tianjin choubei huiji shang de fayan" [Speech at the Tianjin Preparatory Meeting]. *Zhongguo difang shizhi tongxun* [Communication on Chinese Local Histories] 1.1 (10 January 1981): 14–17.

Ten Years of Nationalist China: The China Press Weekly Supplement 3.16 (18 Apr. 1937).

Teng Ssu-yü. *Protest and Crime in China: A Bibliography of Secret Associations, Popular Uprisings, Peasant Rebellions*. New York: Garland Publications, 1981.

Thaxton, Ralph. "State Making and State Terror: The Formation of the Treasury Police and the Origins of Collective Protest in Rural North China before the Revolution of October 1, 1949." Paper prepared for the Conference on State-Organized Terror, Michigan State University, East Lansing, 2–5 Nov. 1988.

Thoden Van Velze, H. U. E. "Coalitions and Network Analysis." In *Network Analysis: Studies in Human Interaction*, edited by Jeremy Boissevain and J. Clyde Mitchell, 219–50. The Hague, Paris: Mouton, 1973.

Thomas, S. Bernard. *Labor and the Chinese Revolution: Class Strategies and Contradictions of Chinese Communism, 1928–1948*. Ann Arbor: Center for Chinese Studies, University of Michigan, 1983.

Thomasson, Robert de. "Prise de vues à Shanghai." *Les oeuvres libres*, no. 210 (December 1938): 277–347.

Thornton, Richard C. *China, the Struggle for Power, 1917–1972*. Bloomington: Indiana University Press, 1973.

Tian Shengji. "Meidi zhijie zhihui de 'Zhong-Mei hezuo suo'" [The American imperialists' directly commanded "Sino-American Cooperative Organization"]. In *Sichuan wenshi ziliao xuanji* [Selections of historical documents on Sichuan], compiled by Chinese People's Political Consultative Conference, Sichuan weiyuanhui, Wenshi ziliao yanjiu weiyuanhui, fascicle 17, 82–88. Chengdu, 1965.

Tiedemann, R. G. "The Persistence of Banditry: Incidents in Border Districts of the North China Plain." *Modern China* 8.4 (October 1982): 395–433.

Tien, Hung-mao. *Government and Politics in Kuomintang China, 1927–1937*. Stanford: Stanford University Press, 1972.

Tien, Wei-wu. *The Sian Incident: A Pivotal Point in Modern Chinese History*. Ann Arbor: University of Michigan Press, 1976.

Tilly, Charles. "Warmaking and Statemaking as Organized Crime." In *Bringing the State Back In*, edited by Peter B. Evans, Dietrich Rueschemeyer, Theda Skocpol, 169–91. Cambridge, England, and N.Y.: Cambridge University Press, 1985.

Tobias, J. J. *Urban Crime in Victorian England*. New York: Schocken Books, 1972.

Tong, Te-kong, and Li Tsung-jen. *The Memoirs of Li Tsung-jen*. Boulder, Colo.: Westview Press, 1979.

Torture in Greece: The First Torturers' Trial, 1975. New York: Amnesty International Publications, 1977.

Touring Metropolitan Shanghai. Shanghai: Shanghai Cultural Publishing House, 1984.

Tretiak, Daniel. "Political Assassinations in China, 1600–1968." In *Assassination and Political Violence: A Report to the National Commission on the Causes and Prevention of Violence*, edited by James F. Kirkham, Sheldon G. Levy, and William J. Crotty, 635–71. New York: Praeger Publishers, 1970.

Trocki, Carl A. *Opium and Empire: Chinese Society in Colonial Singapore, 1800–1910*. Ithaca, N.Y.: Cornell University Press, 1990.

Tsai, Jung-fang. "The Predicament of the Comprador Ideologists: He Qi (Ho Kai, 1859–1914) and Hu Liuyuan (1847–1916)." *Modern China* 7.2 (April 1981): 191–225.

Tsao, Jr-lien. "The 1928–1930 Famine and the Urban Conscience." Seminar paper, University of California, Berkeley, 1987.

———. "On the Nature of the Chinese Capitalists during the Republican Period." Seminar paper, University of California, Berkeley, 1984.

Tsou, Tang. "Twentieth-Century Chinese Politics and Western Political Science." *Political Science* 20.2 (spring 1987): 327–33.

Tu Shipin, ed. *Shanghai shi daguan* [Overview of Shanghai city]. Shanghai: Zhongguo tushu zazhi gongsi, 1948.

Tuchman, Barbara W. *Stilwell and the American Experience in China, 1911–1945*. New York: Macmillan Co., 1970.

Tung, David Foo-hsu. "Improved Police Administration in the Capital." *China Weekly Review*, 14 Dec. 1929.

U.S. Department of State. Confidential Central Files. China, Internal Affairs, 1940–1944. Microfilm.

———. *Foreign Relations of the United States. Diplomatic Papers, 1939*. Vol. 4, The Far East, the Near East, and Africa. Washington, D.C.: Government Printing Office, 1955.

———. *Foreign Relations of the United States. Diplomatic Papers, 1940*. Vol. 4, The Far East. Washington, D.C.: Government Printing Office, 1955.

———. *Foreign Relations of the United States. Diplomatic Papers, 1942, China*. Washington, D.C.: Government Printing Office, 1956.

———. *Foreign Relations of the United States. Diplomatic Papers, 1943, China*. Washington, D.C.: Government Printing Office, 1957.

———. *Records of the Department of State Relating to Internal Affairs of China, 1910–1929*. 893.00 Political Affairs, vols. 69, 70. Washington, D.C.: National Archives, 1960.

———. *Records of the Department of State Relating to Internal Affairs of China,*

1910–1929. 893.10. Political Order, Safety, Health, and Works; Charities and Philanthropic Organizations. Washington, D.C.: National Archives, 1960.

———. *Records of the Department of State Relating to the Internal Affairs of China, 1930–1939.* Government Documents Library, microfilm 31217.

———. *Records of the Department of State Relating to Political Relations between China and Other States, 1910–1929.* 34 reels. Washington, D.C.: National Archives, 1960.

U.S. Department of War. Military Intelligence Reports, China, 1911–1941.

———. Military Intelligence Reports, China, 1900–1949. Microfiche ed.

U.S. Senate Committee on the Judiciary. Subcommittee to Investigate the Administration of the Internal Security Act and Other Internal Security Laws. *The Amerasia Papers: A Clue to the Catastrophe of China.* 2 vols. Washington, D.C.: Committee Print, 1970.

Ungar, Sanford J. *F.B.I.* Boston: Little, Brown & Co., 1976.

Van Slyke, Lyman P. *Enemies and Friends: The United Front in Chinese Communist History.* Stanford: Stanford University Press, 1967.

Vollmer, August. Correspondence and Papers. University of California, Berkeley, Bancroft Library.

Vollmer, August, and Alfred E. Parker. *Crime, Crooks, and Cops.* New York: Funk and Wagnalls, 1937.

———. *Crime and the State Police.* Berkeley: University of California Press, 1935.

Von Sternberg, Joseph. *Fun in a Chinese Laundry.* New York: Collier, 1965.

Wakeman, Carolyn, and Yue Daiyun. "Women in Recent Chinese Fiction—a Review Article." *Journal of Asian Studies* 42 (August 1983): 879–88.

Wakeman, Frederic, Jr. "The Evolution of Local Control in Late Imperial China." In *Conflict and Control in Late Imperial China,* edited by Frederic Wakeman, Jr. and Carolyn Grant, 1–25. Berkeley: University of California Press, 1975.

———. *The Great Enterprise: The Manchu Reconstruction of Imperial Order in Seventeenth-Century China.* Berkeley and Los Angeles: University of California Press, 1985.

———. *History and Will: Philosophical Perspectives of the Thought of Mao Tsetung.* Berkeley: University of California Press, 1973.

Waldron, Arthur. "War and Nationalism in China: The Zhili-Fengtian War of 1924 and its Aftermath." Unpublished ms.

Walker, C. Lester. "China's Master Spy." *Harper's* (August 1946): 162–69.

Walker, Richard A. "A Theory of Suburbanization: Capitalism and the Construction of Urban Spaces in the U.S." In *Urbanization and Urban Planning in Capitalist Society,* edited by Michael Dear and Allen Scott, 383–429. London: Methuen, 1981.

———. "The Transformation of Urban Structure in the Nineteenth Century and the Beginnings of Suburbanization." In *Urbanization and Conflict in Market Societies,* edited by Kevin Cox, 165–213. Chicago: Maaroufa Press, 1978.

Waltner, Ann Beth. "The Adoption of Children in Ming and Early Ch'ing China." Ph.D. diss., University of California, Berkeley, 1981.

Wan Molin. *Hushang wangshi* [Shanghai bygones]. 4 vols. Taibei: Zhongwai tushu chubanshe, 1973.

Wan Ren. "Guomindang Shanghai jingchaju li de dixia gongzuo" [Underground work in the police force of Guomindang Shanghai]. In *Shanghai wenshi ziliao xuanji* [Selections of historical materials on Shanghai], compiled by Chinese People's Political Consultative Conference, Shanghai weiyuanhui, Wenshi ziliao gongzuo weiyuanhui, fascicle 44, 19–25. Shanghai: Shanghai renmin chubanshe, 1983.

Wang, Betty. "The War of Resistance: 1937–1945." *Free China Review* 37.7 (July 1987): 2–8.

Wang, S. Y. "The Revised Criminal Code." *China Critic*, 11 Apr. 1935, 37–39.

Wang, Yeh-chien. "Evolution of the Chinese Monetary System, 1644–1850." In *Conference on Modern Chinese Economic History*, 469–96. Taibei: Institute of Economics, Academia Sinica, 1977.

———. "The Growth and Decline of Native Banks in Shanghai." *Academia Economic Papers* 6.1 (March 1978): 111–42.

Wang Anzhi. "Juntong ju 'cefan' hanjian Zhou Fohai de jingguo" [Sequence of events concerning Zhou Fohai's defection upon the instigation of the Military Statistics Bureau]. *Wenshi ziliao xuanji*, no. 64: 193–201. Beijing: Zhonghua shuju, 1979.

Wang Bin et al., comp. *Jiangshan xianzhi* [Jiangshan district gazetteer]. 3 vols. 1873 ed. Taibei: Chengwen chubanshe, 1970.

Wang Ching-wei. *A la mémoire de M. Tsen-Tson-Ming*. Hanoi, 6 Apr. 1939. Pamphlet in U.S. Department of State, *Records of the Department of State Relating to the Internal Affairs of China, 1930–1939*, 893.00/14394.

Wang Fangnan. "Wo zai Juntong shisi nian de qinli he jianwen" [What I experienced and learned during my fourteen years in the Military Statistics Bureau]. In *Wenshi ziliao xuanji* [Selections of historical materials], compiled by Chinese People's Political Consultative Conference Editorial Committee, fascicle 107 (*zong*), 140–66. Beijing: Zhongguo wenshi chubanshe, 1987.

Wang Heng. "Guangxi zhi mintuan ji qi yiyi" [The Militia of Guangxi and its significance]. *Guowen zhoubao*, part 1: 11.16 (23 Apr. 1934); part 2: 11.17 (30 Apr. 1934).

Wang Jiajian. *Qing mo min chu wo guo jingcha zhidu xiandaihua de licheng.* (Yijiulingyi—yijiuerba) [The process of modernization of our country's police system at the end of the Qing and the beginning of the republic (1901–1928)]. Taibei: Taiwan Commercial Press, 1984.

Wang Jianmin. *Zhongguo Gongchandang shi* [History of the Chinese Communist Party]. Vol. 2, *Jiangxi shiqi* [The Jiangxi period]. Taibei: Hanjing wenhua shiye youxian gongsi, 1988.

Wang Min et al., eds. *Shanghai xuesheng yundong da shi ji* [Record of major events of the Shanghai student movement]. Shanghai: Xuelin, 1981.

Wang Yangqing and Xu Yinghu. "Shanghai Qing Hong bang gaishu" [A general account of Shanghai's Qing and Hong Gangs]. *Shehui kexue* 1982.5: 63–65.

Wasserstein, Bernard. "Secrets of Old Shanghai." *Times Literary Supplement* 1–7 Apr. 1988.

Wasserstrom, Jeffrey. "The First Chinese Red Scare? 'Fanchi' Propaganda and 'Pro-Red' Responses during the Northern Expedition," *Republican China* 11, no. 1 (1985): 32–51.

———. "Student Protest in Shanghai." Ph.D. diss., University of California, Berkeley, May 1989.

———. *Student Protest in Twentieth-Century China: The View from Shanghai.* Stanford: Stanford University Press, 1991.

Wasserstrom, Jeffrey, and Liu Xinyong. "Student Life and Student Protest: Shanghai, 1919–1949." Unpublished paper.

Watson, James L. "Chinese Kinship Reconsidered: Anthropological Perspectives on Historical Research." *China Quarterly* 92 (December 1982).

Wei, Betty Peh-t'i. *Shanghai: Crucible of Modern China.* Hong Kong: Oxford University Press, 1987.

Wei, William. *Counterrevolution in China: The Nationalists in Jiangxi during the Soviet Period.* Ann Arbor: University of Michigan Press, 1985.

Wei Daming. "Pingshu Dai Yunong xiansheng de shigong" [Critical discussion of the acts and achievements of Mr. Dai Yunong]. *Zhuanji wenxue: shang* 38.2 (February 1981): 40–45; *zhong* 38.3 (March 1981): 47–54; *xia* 38.4 (April 1981): 94–100.

Weisser, Michael R. *Crime and Punishment in Early Modern Europe.* Hassocks, Sussex: The Harvester Press, 1979.

Wen Qiang. "Dai Li qi ren" [Dai Li the man]. In Shen Zui and Wen Qiang, *Dai Li qi ren,* 177–258. Beijing: Wenshi ziliao chubanshe, 1980.

———. "Sun Dianying toudi jingguo" [Sequence of events leading toward Sun Dianying's surrender to the enemy]. *Wenshi ziliao xuanji,* no. 64: 114–66. Beijing: Zhonghua shuju, 1979.

———. "'Zhongyuan wang' Tang Enbo" [Tang Enbo, "Prince of the Central Plain"]. *Wenshi ziliao xuanji,* no. 32: 179–212. Beijing: Wenshi ziliao chubanshe, December 1962.

Wenxin xinwen bu, ed. *Shanghai de fenghuo* [The Beacon of Shanghai]. Shanghai: Wenyi xinwen she, 1932.

Westley, William A. *Violence and the Police: A Sociological Study of Law, Custom and Morality.* Cambridge, Mass., and London: The MIT Press, 1970.

White, Lynn T., III. "Bourgeois Radicalism in Shanghai." In *Class and Social Stratification in Post-Revolution China,* edited by James L. Watson, 142–74. Cambridge, England: Cambridge University Press, 1984.

———. "Deviance, Modernization, Rations, and Household Registers in Urban China." In *Deviance and Social Control in Chinese Society,* edited by Amy Auerbacher Wilson, Sidney Leonard Greenblatt, Richard Whittingham Wilson, 151–72. New York: Praeger Publishers, 1977.

———. "Low Power; Small Enterprises in Shanghai, 1949–1967." *China Quarterly* 73 (March 1978): 45–76.

———. "Non-governmentalism in the Historical Development of Modern Shanghai." In *Urban Development in Modern China,* edited by Laurence J. C. Ma and Edward W. Hanten, 19–57. Boulder, Colo.: Westview Press, 1981.

———. *Policies of Chaos: The Organizational Causes of Violence in China's Cultural Revolution.* Princeton: Princeton University Press, 1989.

White, Theodore H., and Annalee Jacoby. *Thunder Out of China.* New York: William Sloane Associates, 1946.

Who's Who in China. 5th ed. Shanghai: The China Weekly Review, 1936.

Who's Who in China. Supplement to the 5th ed. Shanghai: The China Weekly Review, 1940.

Who's Who in China. 6th ed. Shanghai: The China Weekly Review, 1950.

Who's Who in China: Biographies of Chinese Leaders. 4th, 5th eds. Shanghai: The China Weekly Review, 1931, 1936.

Whyte, William Foote. *Street Corner Society: The Social Structure of an Italian Slum.* Chicago: University of Chicago Press, 1943.

Wieger, Léon. *Chine moderne.* Vol. 5. 2d ed. Sienhsien, 1934.

Wilbur, C. Martin. "The Nationalist Revolution: From Canton to Nanking, 1923–1928." In *The Cambridge History of China.* Vol. 12. *Republican China, 1912–1949,* part 1, edited by John K. Fairbank, 527–720. Cambridge, England: Cambridge University Press, 1983.

Wilbur, C. Martin, and Julie Lien-ying Hao, eds. *Missionaries of Revolution: Soviet Advisors and Nationalist China, 1920–1927.* Cambridge, Mass.: Harvard University Press, 1989.

Willoughby, Charles A. *Shanghai Conspiracy: The Sorge Spy Ring.* New York: E. P. Dutton, 1952.

Wilson, Dick. *Zhou Enlai: A Biography.* New York: Viking, 1984.

Wilson, James O. *Varieties of Police Behavior: The Management of Law and Order in Eight Communities.* New York: Atheneum, 1986.

Wong, Charles C. S. "Extrality and the Narcotic Peril in China." *China Critic* 18.3 (15 July 1937): 56–57.

Wong, Homer S. "Fascism and China." *China Critic,* 7 Feb. 1935, 135–39.

Woodhead, H. G. W. "The Truth About Opium in China, Being a Report of a Complete Series of Articles Appearing Daily in the Shanghai Evening Post and Mercury in March, 1931." Shanghai: Shanghai Evening Post and Mercury, 1931.

———, ed. *The China Yearbook.* Tientsin and Shanghai: North-China Daily News and Herald, 1912–1939.

Woods, Arthur. "Some Aspects of Training for Police Service." *Police Journal* 2 (1929): 355–66.

Wou, Odoric Y. K. "Student Activisim in Henan: The December Nine Movement and Communist Power." Paper presented to the Chinese History Society Conference on the 50th anniversary of the Marco Polo Bridge Incident, New York, July 1987.

Wren, Christopher S. "Once-Wicked Shanghai Is a Puritan Port of Call." *New York Times,* 5 Nov. 1982.

Wright, Arnold, ed. *Twentieth-Century Impressions of Hong Kong, Shanghai, and Other Treaty Ports of China: Their History, People, Commerce, Industries and Resources.* London: Lloyd's Greater Britain Publishing Company, 1908.

Wright, Peter, with Paul Greengrass. *Spycatcher.* New York: Dell, 1987.

Wright, Tim. "Sino-Japanese Business in China: The Luda Company, 1921–1937." *Journal of Asian Studies* 39.4 (August 1980): 711–27.

Wu, Harry. "'Lao Gai—The Chinese Gulag': The Labor Camp System in the P.R.C." *China Forum* 1.2 (February 1991): 1–6.

Wu Jimin. "Changqi bei kan zuo hanjian de nü gemingjia (xia)" [A woman revolutionary long made out to be a traitor (part two)]. *Shanghai tan* 1989.7: 40–44.

Wu Lien-teh. "Opium Problem Reaches Acute State: A Case for International Cooperation and Control." Reprinted from *The Chinese Nation* 1.33 (28 Jan. 1931).

Wu Te-chen [Wu Tiecheng]. "Greater Shanghai Places Emphasis on Social Reconstruction, Welfare; Good Start Now Well on Way to Success." *China Press Double Tenth Supplement*, 1935: 49, 59.

Wu Tien-wei. "Chiang Kai-shek's March Twentieth Coup d'État of 1926." *Journal of Asian Studies* 27.3 (May 1968): 585–602.

Wu Yu et al. *Minguo hei shehui* [The Republican underworld]. Jiangsu: Jiangsu guji chubanshe, 1988.

Wusa yundong shiliao. [Historical materials on the May 30th movement], vol. 1. Shanghai: Shanghai Academy of Social Sciences, 1981.

Xia Lin'gen and Ding Ning. "Jianguo yilai Shanghai shi yanjiu shuping" [A review of research on the history of Shanghai since the founding of the country]. *Xueshu yuekan* [Academic monthly] 1982.5: 77–80.

Xiao Zuolin. "Fuxingshe shulüe" [A brief account of the Revival Society]. In *Wenshi ziliao xuanji* [Selections of historical materials], edited by Chinese People's Political Consultative Conference National Committee, Wenshi ziliao yanjiu weiyuanhui, fascicle 11, 21–71. Beijing: Zhonghua shuju, November 1960.

"Xiaomie Gongfei Hongdui an chi jingyan jianshu" [A concise account of the experience of the case of the elimination of the Communist bandits Red Brigade]. Bureau of Investigation Archives, Hsin-tien (Xindian), doc. 276/7435/59400.

Xie Fengnian. "Guixi tewu zuzhi 'Guangxi sheng zhengfu zhuxi bangongshi' gaikuang" [The general circumstances of the Guixi special services organization: The "chairman's office of the Guangxi provincial government"]. In *Guangxi wenshi ziliao*, no. 12, 208–40. Guangxi: Chinese People's Political Consultative Conference, Guangxi Zhuangzu zizhiqu weiyuanhui, Wenshi ziliao weiyuanhui, March 1982.

Xin Zhonghua zazhi she, eds. *Shanghai de jianglai* [The Future of Shanghai]. Shanghai: Zhonghua shuju, 1934.

Xiong Zhuoyun. "Fandong tongzhi shiqi de Chengdu jingcha" [The Chengdu police during the period of reactionary rule]. In *Sichuan wenshi ziliao xuanji* [Selections of historical documents on Sichuan], compiled by Chinese People's Political Consultative Conference, Sichuan weiyuanhui, Wenshi ziliao yanjiu weiyuanhui, fascicle 17, 108–29. Chengdu, 1965.

Xu, Guomin. "The Tragedy within China's Communist Palace: The Wu Hao Incident and Relations between Chairman Mao and Premier Zhou." M.A. thesis, San Jose State University, 1983.

Xu Chi et al. *Shanghai zhongsheng xiang* [Forms of lives in Shanghai]. Shanghai: Xin Zhongguo bao she, 1941.

Xu Enzeng. "Wo he Gongdang douzheng de huiyi" [Recollection of my struggles with the Communist Party]. In Bureau of Investigation Archives, Hsin-tien (Xindian), doc. 6002.

Xu Feng and Zhang Yusheng, eds. *Minguo heiwang, neimu, miwen* [Black networks, inside stories, and secret tales of the Republican period]. Hubei: Hubei renmin chubanshe, 1989.

Xu Gongsu and Qiu Jinzhang. "Shanghai gonggong zujie zhidu" [The System of the Shanghai International Settlement]. In *Shanghai shi ziliao congkan: Shanghai gonggong zujie shigao* [Collection of Shanghai historical materials: Draft history of the Shanghai International Settlement]: 1–297. Shanghai: Shanghai renmin chubanshe, 1980.

Xu Huifang and Liu Qingyu. "Shanghai nüxing fan de shehui fenxi" [A social analysis of female crime in Shanghai]. *Dalu zazhi* 1.4 (October 1932): 71–92.

Xu Ke. *Qing bai lei chao*. [Classified notes on Qing romances]. 7 vols. Shanghai: Commercial Press, 1917.

Xu Zhaoming. "Hanjian Zhou Fohai goujie Juntong jiqi xiachang" [Chinese traitor Zhou Fohai's unsavory alliance with the Military Statistics Bureau and his final outcome]. *Wenshi ziliao xuanji*, no. 64: 202–16. Beijing: Zhonghua shuju, 1979.

Xu Zhucheng. *Du Yuesheng zhengzhuan* [A straightforward biography of Du Yuesheng]. Hangzhou: Zhejiang sheng xinhua shudian, 1982.

Xu Zongyao. "Zuzhi Juntong Beiping zhan heping qiyi de qianqian houhou" [Before and after the Juntong's organization of the suppression of Beiping Station peaceful uprising]. In *Wenshi ziliao xuanji*, no. 68, 126–51. Beijing: Zhonghua shuju, 1980.

Xuan Tiewu. "Fakanci" [Foreword]. In *Shanghai jingcha* [Shanghai police], edited by Zhu Yisheng, opening issue: 1–2. Shanghai: Shanghai shi jingchaju mishushi, 1946.

———. "Renshi jingcha" [Know the police]. In *Shanghai jingcha* [Shanghai police], edited by Zhu Yisheng, opening issue: 15–16. Shanghai: Shanghai shi jingchaju mishushi, 1946.

Xue Gengshen. "Wo yu jiu Shanghai Fa zujie" [I and old Shanghai's French Concession]. In *Wenshi ziliao xuanji* [Selections of historical materials], compiled by Chinese People's Political Consultative Conference, Shanghai Municipal Committee, Wenshi ziliao gongzuo weiyuanhui, fascicle 28, 149–69. Shanghai: Shanghai renmin chubanshe, 1979.

Xue Gengxin. "Jindai Shanghai de liumang." [Modern Shanghai's ruffians]. In *Wenshi ziliao xuanji* [A compilation of historical materials] 1980.3: 160–78. Shanghai: Shanghai renmin chubanshe, 1980.

Yamada, Tatsuo. "The Foundations and Limits of State Power in Guomindang Ideology—Government, Party, and People." In *Foundations and Limits of State Power in China*, edited by S. R. Schram, 187–202. Hong Kong: Chinese University Press, 1987.

Yamamoto Sanehiko. *Shina* [China]. Tokyo: Kaizosha, 1936.

Yang Fan. "Yang Fan zai jingtao hailong zhong (xia)" [Yang Fan in the midst of terrifying waves and perilous billows (part 2)]. *Shanghai tan* [Sands of Shanghai] 1989.5: 30–35.

Yang Jialuo. *Minguo mingren tujian* [Illustrated biographies of famous men of the Republic]. 2 vols. Nanjing: Zhongguo cidian guan, 1937.

Yang Jiezeng and He Wannan. *Shanghai changji gaizao shihua*. [A history of the reform of Shanghai prostitutes]. Shanghai: Shanghai sanlian shudian, 1988.

Yang Shouqing. *Zhongguo chuban jie jianshi* [A simple history of Chinese publishing circles]. Shanghai: Yongxiang yinshuguan, 1946.

Yang Wei. *Du Yuesheng waizhuan* [An outer biography of Du Yuesheng]. Taizhong: Jinyang chubanshe, 1967.

Yardley, Herbert O. *The Chinese Black Chamber: An Adventure in Espionage*. Boston: Houghton Mifflin Company, 1983.

Ye Shengtao, "Wuyue sanshiyi zhi jiyu zhong" [In the midst of the May 31 downpour]. *Xiaoshuo yuebao* 16.7:5 (July 1925). Translated in Vera Schwarcz,

"The Chinese Enlightenment: The May Fourth Movement and the Intellectuals' Legacy."

Ye Xiaoqing. "Popular Culture in Shanghai in the Late Nineteenth Century." Paper presented at the Berkeley Seminar on Chinese Popular Culture. Berkeley, 4 Sept. 1990.

Yee, Frank Ki Chun. "Police in Modern China." Ph.D. diss., University of California, Berkeley, 1942.

Yeh, Wen-hsin. *The Alienated Academy: Culture and Politics in Republican China, 1919–1935.* Cambridge, Mass.: Council on East Asian Studies, Harvard University Press, 1990.

———. "Culture and Education in Republican China: The Intellectual Profile of the University Man." Paper presented at the Pacific Coast Branch, American Historical Association, San Francisco, 1982.

———. "Dai Li and the Liu Geqing Affair: Heroism in the Chinese Secret Service during the War of Resistance." *Journal of Asian Studies* 48.3 (August 1989): 545–62.

———. "Progressive Journalism and Shanghai's Petty Urbanites: Zou Taofen and the *Shanghai Weekly, 1926–1945.*" In *Shanghai Sojourners.* Berkeley: Institute of East Asian Studies, 1992, pp. 186–238.

Yen, Ching-yueh. "Crime in Relation to Social Change in China." *American Journal of Sociology* 40.3 (1934–35): 298–308.

Yi nuli fazhan shengchan lai qingzhu Shanghai jiefang zhounian [Actively expand production to celebrate the anniversary of the liberation of Shanghai]. Shanghai: Huadong gongye bu lingdao ge dianqi gongye gongchang, 1950.

Ynlow, Burke. "Japan's 'Special Trade' in North China, 1933–37." *Far Eastern Quarterly* 6.2 (February 1947): 139–67.

Yomano, Shelly. "Reintegration in China under the Warlords, 1916–1927." *Republican China* 12.2 (April 1987): 22–27.

Yu, Wentao. "Late Film Star Still Shines." *China Daily,* 26 March 1968.

Yu Dafu. "Intoxicating Spring Nights." In *Masterpieces of Modern Chinese Fiction, 1919–1949,* edited by Lu Xun et al., 140–53. Beijing: Foreign Languages Press, 1983.

Yu Shuping. "Jingcha jianzhi wenti" [Questions about the organizational system of the police]. In *Shanghai jingcha* [Shanghai police], edited by Zhu Yisheng, 17–20. Shanghai: Shanghai shi jingcha mishushi, 1946.

Yu Xiangqin. "Shanghai lunxian qijian sinian dixia gongzuo zhuiji" [Ruminations on four years of underground work when Shanghai was sunk in surrender]. *Zhuanji wenxue* 33.2: 43–47; 33.3: 84–88; 33.4: 100–104.

Yu Xiuhao. *Jingcha shouce* [Police handbook]. Shanghai: Shanghai jingsheng shuju, 1948.

———. "Meiguo Baikeli shi jingcha pubian zhiwen dengji yundong chenggong" [The success of the American Berkeley municipal police universal fingerprint registration movement]. *Jingsheng zhoukan* [Voice of the police weekly] 27 (May 1937): 145–47.

Yuan, Lizhuang and Li Nianpei. "When Shanghai Was Liberated." *China Daily,* 12 February 1927.

Yun Yiqun. *Sanshi nian jianwen zaji* [Miscellaneous jottings on thirty years of what was seen and heard]. Zhenjiang: Jinling shuhuashe, 1983.

Zeng Kuoqing. "He Mei xieding qian Fuxingshe zai Huabei de huodong" [The activities of the Fuxingshe in North China before the He Mei Agreement]. In *Wenshi ziliao xuanji* [Selections of historical materials], edited by Chinese People's Political Consultative Conference National Committee, Wenshi ziliao yanjiu weiyuanhui, fascicle 14, 131–46. Beijing: Zhonghua shuju, February 1961.

Zhang Jungu. "Dai Li de gushi" [The story of Dai Li]. *Zhuanji wenxue* 14.1: 8–19.

———. *Du Yuesheng zhuan* [The biography of Du Yuesheng]. Vol. 1. Zhuanji wenxue congkan, no. 9. Taibei, 1967.

Zhang Shizhao. "Shu Qi jiang yu" [Writing on the Qi River case]. In *Wenshi ziliao xuanji* [Selections of historical materials], edited by Chinese People's Political Consultative Conference National Committee, Wenshi ziliao yanjiu weiyuanhui, fascicle 7, 64–65. Beijing: Zhonghua shuju, July 1960.

Zhang Weihan. "Dai Li yu 'Juntong ju'" [Dai Li and the Military Statistics Bureau]. In *Zhejiang wenshi ziliao xuanji* [Selections of historical documents on Zhejiang], edited by Wenshi ziliao yanjiu weiyuanhui, fascicle 23, 79–151. *Neibu* publication. Zhejiang: Renmin chubanshe, 1982.

Zhang Wen. "Zhongtong ershi nian" [Twenty years with Central Statistics]. In *Zhongtong meimu* [Behind the curtain at Central Statistics], edited by Chinese People's Political Consultative Conference, Jiangsu Provincial Committee, Wenshi Ziliao yanjiu weiyuanhui, 1–115. Jiangsu: Jiangsu guji chubanshe, 1987.

Zhang Xin. "Hu Zongnan qi ren" [Hu Zongnan the man]. In *Zhejiang wenshi ziliao xuanji*, edited by Wenshi ziliao yanjiu weiyuanhui, no. 23, 171–83. *Neibu* publication. Zhejiang: Renmin chubanshe, 1982.

Zhang Yanfo. "Kangzhan qianhou Juntong tewu zai xibei de huodong" [Military Statistics Bureau activities in the Northwest before and after the War of Resistance]. *Wenshi ziliao xuanji*, no. 64: 78–113. Beijing: Zhonghua shuju, 1979.

Zhang Zetao. "Shanghai shi dang'an guan" [The Shanghai municipal archives]. *Lishi dang'an* 4 (1981).

Zhanshi huabao [War illustrated], no. 2. Shanghai: Liangyou tushu zazhi chuwai, November 1937.

Zheng Tingji. "Huangpu wu qi 'qing dang' de huiyi" [Recollections of "purifying the party" in the 5th class at Whampoa]. In *Wenshi ziliao xuanji* [Selections of historical materials], edited by Chinese People's Political Consultative Conference National Committee, Wenshi ziliao yanjiu weiyuanhui, fascicle 9, 123–24. Beijing: Zhonghua shuju, September 1960.

Zheng Zu'an. "Guomindang Shanghai tebie shi shizheng yanjiu" [A study of the municipal administration of the Guomindang's Greater Shanghai]. Paper presented at the International Symposium on Modern Shanghai, Shanghai Academy of Social Sciences, 7–14 Sept. 1988.

———. "Guomindang zhengfu 'da Shanghai jihua' shimo" [The Guomindang government's "plan for a greater Shanghai" from beginning to end]. In *Shanghai shi yanjiu* [Research in the history of Shanghai], compiled by Wang Pengcheng et al., 208–28. Shanghai: Xuelin chubanshe, 1984.

Zhong Heming. *Riben qin Hua zhi jiandie shi* [History of espionage during the Japanese aggression against China]. Hankou: Huazhong tushu gongsi, 1938.

Zhong Xiangbai. "Wo suo zhidao de Zhong-Mei tezhong jishu xunlian disan ban—Linru xunlianban" [What I know about the third Sino-American special technical training unit—the Linru training unit]. In *Henan wenshi ziliao* [Historical materials on Henan], compiled by Chinese People's Political Consultative Conference, Henan sheng weiyuanhui, Wenshi ziliao yanjiu weiyuanhui, fascicle 5, 125–33. Henan: Henan renmin chubanshe, 1981.

Zhonggong Shanghai shi wei dangshi ziliao zhengji weiyuanhui, eds. *Shanghai renmin geming shi huace* [The Shanghai people's revolutionary history pictorial]. Shanghai: Shanghai renmin chubanshe, 1989.

Zhongguo Guomindang zhongyang weiyuanhui, dang shi weiyuanhui, comp. *Zhonghua minguo zhongyao shiliao chubian—dui-Ri kangzhan shiqi* [Preliminary collection of important historical materials on the Chinese Republic—the period of the war against Japan]. 4 vols. *Zhonggong huodong zhenxiang* [The truth of Chinese Communist activities], part 5. Taibei, n.d.

———, eds. *Xian zongtong Jiang gong sixiang yanlun zongji* [Complete collection of the ideas, speeches, and writings of the late president Chiang Kai-shek]. Taibei, 1984.

Zhongguo guomindang zhongyang zuzhi bu diaocha ke, eds. *Zhongguo gongchandang zhi toushi* [An x-ray view of the Chinese Communist Party]. Taibei: Wenxing shudian, 1962.

Zhonghua minguo shi hua bian zuan xiaozu, eds. *Zhonghua minguo shi hua* [Republican China historical pictorial]. Jindai Zhongguo chubanshe, 1978.

Zhonghua minguo waijiao wenti yanjiuhui, comp. *Ri jun qinfan Shanghai yu jinggong Huabei* [The Japanese army's encroachment upon Shanghai and its assault on North China]. Taibei: Zhonghua minguo waijiao wenti yanjiuhui, 1965.

Zhonghua tuhua zazhi [The China pictorial]. Shanghai: Dongfang tuhua chubanshe.

Zhongtongju [Central Statistics Office], eds. "Zhonggong zai Jiangsu zhi zuzhi yu huodong" [The organization and activities of the Chinese Communist Party in Jiangsu]. Bureau of Investigation Archives 270.21/815/7302-C.1.

Zhongyang diaocha tongji ju [Central Bureau of Investigation and Statistics], comp. "You guan Gu Shunzhang deng po an jingguo" [The whole process of solving the case concerning Gu Shunzhang and others]. Bureau of Investigation Archives, 276/7435/59400.

———. "Zhonggong tewubu buzhang Gu Shunzhang zhi zishou ji qi yu zhonggong zhi daji" [The surrender of the director of the department of special services of the Chinese Communist Party, Gu Shunzhang, and his attack upon the Chinese Communist (party)]. Bureau of Investigation Archives, 276/7435a/19930.

Zhongyang zuzhi bu, tewuzu, diaocha ke, ed. "Zhou Enlai cansha Gu Shunzhang jiashu ji yiji fenzi sanshi yu ren maicang Shanghai zujie quyu zhi faxian" [Zhou Enlai's slaughter of Gu Shunzhang's dependents and the discovery of more than thirty deviate elements buried in the Shanghai Concession region]. Bureau of Investigation Archives, D112(276/7435B/19933).

Zhou Zhendong. "Dai Li tewu 'Yu san ke,' 'Rong zu,' ji 'Xi Kang zu' zai junshi fangmian de huodong (1935 nian–1936 nian)" [The military aspects of the activities of Dai Li's special services "Yu san ke," "Rong zu," and "Xi Kang zu" (1935–36)]. In *Sichuan wenshi ziliao xuanji* [Selections of historical documents on Sichuan], compiled by Chinese People's Political Consultative Conference, Sichuan weiyuanhui, Wenshi ziliao yanjiu weiyuanhui, fascicle 22, 280–88. Chengdu, 1980.

Zhu Shikang. "Guanyu Guomindang guanliao ziben de jianwen" [Information about Guomindang bureaucratic capital]. In *Wenshi ziliao xuanji* [Selections of historical materials], edited by Chinese People's Political Consultative Conference National Committee, Wenshi ziliao yanjiu weiyuanhui, fascicle 11, 72–88. Beijing: Zhonghua shuju, November 1960.

Zhu Yisheng. "Shanghai jingcha yange shi" [History of the evolution of the Shanghai police]. In *Shanghai jingcha* [Shanghai police], edited by Zhu Yisheng, opening issue: 3–13. Shanghai: Shanghai shi jingchaju mishushi, 1946.

Zhu Yisheng, ed. *Shanghai jingcha* [Shanghai police], opening issue. Shanghai: Shanghai shi jingchaju mishushi, 1946.

Zhu Zijia. [Jin Qiongbai]. *Huangpu jiang de zhuo lang* [Muddy waves of the Huangpu River]. Hong Kong: Wuxingji shubao she, 1964.

Zhuang Tiandiao, "Tanjing zhi heimu yi." In *Shanghai Heimu huibian* [A Classified compendium from behind Shanghai's black screen], edited by Qian Shengke. Vol. 1. Shanghai: Haishang zhentan yanjiuhui, 1929.

Zhuo Jian'an. "Gu Zhenglun yu Guomindang xianbing" [Gu Zhenglun and the Guomindang Military Police]. *Guiyang wenshi ziliao xuanji* 5 (1982): 225–54.

Zou Taofen. *Xiao yanlun* [Humble opinions]. Shanghai: Shenghuo shudian, 1937.

Glossary-Index

Compositor: Maple-Vail Book Mfg. Group
Text: 10/13 Aldus
Display: Aldus
Printer: Maple-Vail Book Mfg. Group
Binder: Maple-Vail Book Mfg. Group